LYLE

OFFICIAL
ANTIQUES
REVIEW 2002

LYLE
OFFICIAL
ANTIQUES
REVIEW 2002

A PERIGEE BOOK

A Perigee Book
Published by The Berkley Publishing Group
A division of Penguin Putnam Inc.
375 Hudson Street
New York, New York 10014

First Edition: December 2001

Published simultaneously in Canada.

The Penguin Putnam Inc. World Wide Web site address is
http://www.penguinputnam.com

Printed in the United States of America

10 9 8 7 6 5 4 3 2 1

INTRODUCTION

This year over 100,000 Antique Dealers and Collectors will make full and profitable use of their Lyle Antiques Price Guide. They know that only in this one volume will they find the widest possible variety of goods – illustrated, described and given a current market value to assist them to BUY RIGHT AND SELL RIGHT throughout the year of issue.

They know, too, that by building a collection of these immensely valuable volumes year by year, they will equip themselves with an unparalleled reference library of facts, figures and illustrations which, properly used, cannot fail to help them keep one step ahead of the market.

In its thirty-two years of publication, Lyle has gone from strength to strength and has become without doubt the pre-eminent book of reference for the antique trade throughout the world. Each of its fact filled pages is packed with precisely the kind of profitable information the professional Dealer needs – including descriptions, illustrations and values of thousands and thousands of individual items carefully selected to give a representative picture of the current market in antiques and collectibles – and remember all values are prices actually paid, based on accurate sales records in the twelve months prior to publication from the best established and most highly respected auction houses and retail outlets in Europe and America.

This is THE book for the Professional Antiques Dealer. 'The Lyle Book' - we've even heard it called 'The Dealer's Bible'.

Compiled and published afresh each year, the Lyle Antiques Price Guide is the most comprehensive up-to-date antiques price guide available. THIS COULD BE YOUR WISEST INVESTMENT OF THE YEAR!

Anthony Curtis

The publishers wish to express their sincere thanks to the following for their involvement and assistance in the production of this volume.

ANTHONY CURTIS (Editor)

EELIN McIVOR (Sub Editor)

ANNETTE CURTIS (Editorial)

CATRIONA DAY (Art Production)

ANGIE DEMARCO (Art Production)

NICKY FAIRBURN (Art Production)

KAYLEIGH PURVES (Art Production)

PHILIP SPRINGTHORPE (Photography)

CONTENTS

ANTIQUES REVIEW

ACKNOWLEDGEMENTS

AB Stockholms Auktionsverk, Box 16256, 103 25 Stockholm, Sweden
Abbotts Auction Rooms, The Auction Rooms, Campsea Ash, Woodbridge, Suffolk
James Adam, 26, St Stephens Green, Dublin 2
Afonwen Antiques, Arts & Crafts Centre, Afonwen, nr Caerwys, Mold, Flintshire CH7 5UB
Henry Aldridge & Son, Devizes Auction Rooms, Wine Street, Devizes SN10 1AP
Amersham Auction Rooms, 125 Station Road, Amersham, Bucks. HP7 OAH
Jean Claude Anaf, Lyon Brotteaux, 13 bis place Jules Ferry, 69456, Lyon, France
Anderson & Garland, Marlborough House, Marlborough Crescent, Newcastle upon Tyne NE1 4EE
Antiques on High, 85 High Street, Oxford
The Antiques Warehouse, Badshot Farm, St. Georges Road, Runfold, Farnham, Surrey GU9 9HR
Atlantic Antiques, Chenil House, 181–183 Kings Road, London SW3 5ED
The Auction Galleries, Mount Rd., Tweedmouth, Berwick on Tweed
Auction Team Köln, Postfach 50 11 19, D-50971 Köln, Germany
Auktionshaus Arnold, Bleichstr. 42, 6000 Frankfurt a/M, Germany
Baddow Antiques Centre, Church Street, Great Baddow, Chelmsford
Barkham Antiques Centre, Barkham Street, Barkham, nr Wokingham, Berkshire RG40 4PJ
Barmouth Court Antiques Centre, Barmouth Road, off Abbeydale Road, Sheffield S7 2DH
Bearne's, St Edmunds Court, Okehampton Street, Exeter EX4 1DU
Berkshire Antiques Centre, Unit 2 Kennet Holme Farm Buildings, Bath Road, Midgham, Reading,
Biddle & Webb, Ladywood Middleway, Birmingham B16 0PP
Black Horse Agencies Ambrose, 149 High Street, Loughton, Essex 1G10 4LZ
Black Horse Agencies, Locke & England, 18 Guy Street, Leamington Spa
Boardman Fine Art Auctioneers, Station Road Corner, Haverhill, Suffolk CB9 0EY
Bonhams & Brooks, Montpelier Street, Knightsbridge, London SW7 1HH
Bonhams & Brooks Chelsea, 65–69 Lots Road, London SW10 0RN
Bonhams & Brooks West Country, Dowell Street, Honiton, Devon
Bosleys, The White House, Marlow, Bucks SL7 1AH
Andrew Bottomley, The Coach House, Huddersfield Rd, Holmfirth, West Yorks.
Michael J. Bowman, 6 Haccombe House, Near Netherton, Newton Abbot, Devon
Brightwells, The Antiques & Fine Art Saleroom, Ryelands Road, Leominster HR6 8NZ
Bristol Auction Rooms, St John Place, Apsley Road, Clifton, Bristol BS8 2ST
British Antique Replicas, School Close, Queen Elizabeth Avenue, Burgess Hill, Sussex
Douglas Bryan, The Old Bakery, St. David's Bridge, Cranbrook, Kent TN17 3HN
Butterfield & Butterfield, 220 San Bruno Avenue , San Francisco CA 94103, USA
Butterfield & Butterfield, 7601 Sunset Boulevard, Los Angeles CA 90046, USA
Canterbury Auction Galleries, 40 Station Road West, Canterbury CT2 8AN
Central Motor Auctions, Barfield House, Britannia Road, Morley, Leeds, LS27 0HN
H.C. Chapman & Son, The Auction Mart, North Street, Scarborough.
Chapman Moore & Mugford, 8 High Street, Shaftesbury SP7 8JB
Chappells & The Antiques Centre, King Street, Bakewell, Derbyshire
Cheffins Grain & Comins, 2 Clifton Road, Cambridge
Chipping Norton Antiques Centre, Ivy House, 1 Market Square, Chipping Norton, OX7 5NH
Christie's (International) SA, 8 place de la Taconnerie, 1204 Genève, Switzerland
Christie's France, 9 avenue Matignon, 75008 Paris
Christie's Monaco, S.A.M, Park Palace 98000 Monte Carlo, Monaco
Christie's Scotland, 164–166 Bath Street, Glasgow G2 4TG
Christie's South Kensington Ltd., 85 Old Brompton Road, London SW7 3LD
Christie's, 8 King Street, London SW1Y 6QT
Christie's East, 219 East 67th Street, New York, NY 10021, USA
Christie's, Cornelis Schuytstraat 57, 1071 JG Amsterdam, Netherlands
Christie's SA Roma, 114 Piazza Navona, 00186 Rome, Italy
Christie's Swire, 2804–6 Alexandra House, 16–20 Chater Road, Hong Kong
Christie's Australia Pty Ltd., 1 Darling Street, South Yarra, Victoria 3141, Australia
Clarke & Gammon, The Guildford Auction Rooms, Bedford Road, Guildford, GU1 4SE
Cleethorpes Collectables, 34 Alexandra Road, Cleethorpes, DN35 8LF
Bryan Clisby, Andwells Antiques, Hartley Wintney, North Hants.
The Clock House, 75 Pound Street, Carshalton, Surrey SM5 3PG
Clola Antiques Centre, Shannas School, Clola, by Mintlaw, Nr Peterhead, Aberdeenshire
Collectors Corner, PO Box 8, Congleton, Cheshire CW12 4GD
Collins Antiques, Wheathampstead, St Albans AL4 8AP
Cooper Hirst Auctions, The Granary Saleroom, Victoria Road, Chelmsford, Essex CM2 6LH
Coppelia Antiques, Holford Lodge, Plumley, Cheshire.
The Cotswold Auction Co., Chapel Walk Saleroom, Chapel Walk, Cheltenham GL50 3DS
The Crested China Co., Station House, Driffield, E. Yorks YO25 7PY
Cundalls, The Cattle Market, 17 Market Square, Malton, N. Yorks.
The Curiosity Shop, 127 Old Street, Ludlow, Shropshire
Dandelion Clock Antiques Centre, Lewes Road, Forest Row, East Sussex
Clifford Dann, 20/21 High Street, Lewes, Sussex
Dargate Auction Galleries, 5607 Baum Blvd., Pittsburgh PA 15206
Julian Dawson, Lewes Auction Rooms, 56 High Street, Lewes BN7 1XE
Dee & Atkinson & Harrison, The Exchange Saleroom, Driffield, Nth Humberside YO25 7LJ
Diamond Mills & Co., 117 Hamilton Road, Felixstowe, Suffolk
David Dockree Fine Art, Landmark House, 1st Floor, Station Road, Cheadle Hulme SK8 7BS
Dorking Desk Shop, 41 West Street, Dorking, Surrey
William Doyle Galleries, 175 East 87th Street, New York, NY 10128, USA

Douglas Ross, Charter House, 42 Avebury Boulevard, Central Milton Keynes MK9 2HS
Dreweatt Neate, Donnington Priory, Newbury, Berks.
Dreweatt Neate, Holloways, 49 Parsons Street, Banbury
Hy. Duke & Son, 40 South Street, Dorchester, Dorset
Du Mouchelles Art Galleries Co., 409 E. Jefferson Avenue, Detroit, Michigan 48226, USA
Sala de Artes y Subastas Durán, Serrano 12, 28001 Madrid, Spain
Ben Eggleston Antiques, The Dovecote, Long Marton, Appleby, Cumbria
Eldred's, Box 796, E. Dennis, MA 02641, USA
R H Ellis & Sons, 44/46 High Street, Worthing, BN11 1LL
Ewbanks, Burnt Common Auction Rooms, London Road, Send, Woking GU23 7LN
Fellows & Son, Augusta House, 19 Augusta Street, Hockley, Birmingham
Fidler Taylor & Co., Crown Square, Matlock, Derbyshire DE4 3AT
Finan & Co., The Square, Mere, Wiltshire BA12 6DJ
Finarte, 20121 Milano, Piazzetta Bossi 4, Italy
Peter Francis,19 King Street, Carmarthen, Dyfed
Fraser Pinney's, 8290 Devonshire, Montreal, Quebec, Canada H4P 2PZ
Freeman Fine Arts, 1808 Chestnut Street, Philadelphia PA19103, USA
Galerie Koller, Rämistr. 8, CH 8024 Zürich, Switzerland
Galerie Moderne, 3 rue du Parnasse, 1040 Bruxelles, Belgium
GB Antiques Centre, Lancaster Leisure Park, Wynesdale Rd, Lancaster LA1 3LA
Geering & Colyer (Black Horse Agencies) Highgate, Hawkhurst, Kent
Gloucester Antiques Centre, 1 Severn Road, Gloucester GL1 2LE
The Goss and Crested China Co., 62 Murray Road, Horndean, Hants PO8 9JL
The Grandfather Clock Shop, Little House, Sheep Street, Stow on the Wold 9L54 1AA
Graves Son & Pilcher, Hove Auction Rooms, Hove Street, Hove, East Sussex
Greenslade Hunt, Magdalene House, Church Square, Taunton, Somerset, TA1 1SB
Hampton's Fine Art, 93 High Street, Godalming, Surrey
Hanseatisches Auktionshaus für Historica, Neuer Wall 57, 2000 Hamburg 36, Germany
William Hardie Ltd., 141 West Regent Street, Glasgow G2 2SG
Andrew Hartley Fine Arts, Victoria Hall, Little Lane, Ilkley
Hastings Antiques Centre, 59–61 Norman Road, St Leonards on Sea, East Sussex
Hauswedell & Nolte, D-2000 Hamburg 13, Pöseldorfer Weg 1, Germany
Halifax Antiques Centre, Queens Road/Gibbet Street, Halifax HX1 4LR
Heanor Antiques Centre, 1-3 Ilkeston Road, Heanor, Derbyshire
Hobbs Parker, New Ashford Market, Monument Way, Orbital Park, Ashford TN24 0HB
Honiton Antiques Centre, Abingdon House, 136 High Street, Honiton, EX14 8JP
Paul Hopwell Antiques, 30 High Street, West Haddon, Northants NN6 7AP
Hotel de Ventes Horta, 390 Chaussée de Waterloo (Ma Campagne), 1060 Bruxelles, Belgium
Jackson's, 2229 Lincoln Street, Cedar Falls, Iowa 50613, USA.
Jacobs & Hunt, Lavant Street, Petersfield, Hants. GU33 3EF
P Herholdt Jensens Auktioner, Rundforbivej 188, 2850 Nerum, Denmark
Kennedy & Wolfenden, 218 Lisburn Road, Belfast BT9 6GD
G A Key, Aylsham Saleroom, Palmers Lane, Aylsham, Norfolk, NR11 6EH
George Kidner, The Old School, The Square, Pennington, Lymington, Hants SO41 8GN
Kingston Antiques Centre, 29-31 London Road, Kingston, Surrey
Kunsthaus am Museum, Drususgasse 1–5, 5000 Köln 1, Germany
Kunsthaus Lempertz, Neumarkt 3, 5000 Köln 1, Germany
Lambert & Foster (County Group), The Auction Sales Room, 102 High Street, Tenterden, Kent
W.H. Lane & Son, 64 Morrab Road, Penzance, Cornwall, TR18 8AB
Langlois Ltd., Westaway Rooms, Don Street, St Helier, Channel Islands
Lawrence Butler Fine Art Salerooms, Marine Walk, Hythe, Kent, CT21 5AJ
Lawrence Fine Art, South Street, Crewkerne, Somerset TA18 8AB
Lawrence's Fine Art Auctioneers, Norfolk House, 80 High Street, Bletchingley, Surrey
David Lay, The Penzance Auction House, Alverton, Penzance, Cornwall TA18 4KE
Lloyd International Auctions, 118 Putney Bridge Road, London SW15 2NQ
Longmynd Antiques, Crossways, Church Stretton, Shropshire SY6 6NX
Brian Loomes, Calf Haugh Farm, Pateley Bridge, North Yorkshire
Lots Road Chelsea Auction Galleries, 71 Lots Road, Chelsea, London SW10 0RN
R K Lucas & Son, Tithe Exchange, 9 Victoria Place, Haverfordwest, SA61 2JX
Duncan McAlpine, Stateside Comics plc, 125 East Barnet Road, London EN4 8RF
McCartneys, Portcullis Salerooms, Ludlow, Shropshire
Mainstreet Trading, Main Street, St. Boswells TD6 0AT
John Mann, Bruntshielbog, Canonbie, Dumfries DG14 0RY
Christopher Matthews, 23 Mount Street, Harrogate HG2 8DG
John Maxwell, 133a Woodford Road, Wilmslow, Cheshire
May & Son, 18 Bridge Street, Andover, Hants
Morphets, 4–6 Albert Street, Harrogate, North Yorks HG1 1JL
Neales, The Nottingham Saleroom, 192 Mansfield Road, Nottingham NG1 3HU
D M Nesbit & Co, 7 Clarendon Road, Southsea, Hants PO5 2ED
Newark Antiques Centre, Regent House, Lombard House, Newark, Notts.
John Nicholson, Longfield, Midhurst Road, Fernhurst GU27 3HA
Occleshaw Antiques Centre, The Old Major Cinema, 11 Mansfield Road, Edwinstowe, Notts. NG21 9NL
The Old Brigade, 10a Harborough Rd, Kingsthorpe, Northampton NN1 7AZ
The Old Cinema, 157 Tower Bridge Rd, London SE1 3LW
Old English Pine, 100/102 Sandgate High Street, Folkestone

Old Mill Antiques Centre, Mill Street, Low Town, Bridgnorth, Shropshire
Onslow's, The Depot, 2 Michael Road, London, SW6 2AD
Outhwaite & Litherland, Kingsley Galleries, Fontenoy Street, Liverpool, Merseyside L3 2BE
Oxford Street Antiques Centre, 16-26 Oxford Street, Leicester LE1 5XU
Pendle Antiques Centre, Union Mill, Watt Street, Sabden, Lancashire, BB7 9ED
Pendulum of Mayfair, 51 Maddox Street, London W1
Phillips Manchester, Trinity House, 114 Northenden Road, Sale, Manchester M33 3HD
Phillips Son & Neale SA, 10 rue des Chaudronniers, 1204 Genève, Switzerland
Phillips West Two, 10 Salem Road, London W2 4BL
Phillips, 11 Bayle Parade, Folkestone, Kent CT20 1SQ
Phillips, 49 London Road, Sevenoaks, Kent TN13 1UU
Phillips, 65 George Street, Edinburgh EH2 2JL
Phillips, Blenstock House, 7 Blenheim Street, New Bond Street, London W1Y 0AS
Phillips Marylebone, Hayes Place, Lisson Grove, London NW1 6UA
Phillips, New House, 150 Christleton Road, Chester CH3 5TD
Andrew Pickford, 42 St Andrew Street, Hertford SG14 1JA
Pieces of Time, 26 South Molton Lane, London W1Y 2LP
Pooley & Rogers, Regent Auction Rooms, Abbey Street, Penzance
Preston Antiques Centre, Horrocks' Yard, off Newhall Lane, Preston, Lancashire PR15NQ
The Quay Centre, Topsham Quay, nr Exeter, Devon, EX3 0JA
Harry Ray & Co, Lloyds Bank Chambers, Welshpool, Montgomery SY21 7RR
Peter M Raw, Thornfield, Hurdle Way, Compton Down, Winchester, Hants SC21 2AN
Remmey Galleries, 30 Maple Street, Summit, NJ 07901
Rennie's, 1 Agincourt Street, Monmouth
Riddetts, 26 Richmond Hill, Bournemouth
Ritchie's, 429 Richmond Street East, Toronto, Canada M5A 1R1
Derek Roberts Antiques, 24–25 Shipbourne Road, Tonbridge, Kent TN10 3DN
Romsey Auction Rooms, 56 The Hundred, Romsey, Hants S051 8BX
Simon & Penny Rumble, Causeway End Farmhouse, Chittering, Cambs.
Schrager Auction Galleries, 2915 N Sherman Boulevard, PO Box 10390, Milwaukee WI 53210, USA
Scottish Antique & Arts Centre, Abernyte, Perthshire
Scottish Antique & Arts Centre, Doune, Stirlingshire
Selkirk's, 4166 Olive Street, St Louis, Missouri 63108, USA
Sidmouth Antiques Centre, All Saints Road, Sidmouth, Devon EX10 8ES
Skinner Inc., Bolton Gallery, Route 117, Bolton MA, USA
Allan Smith, Amity Cottage, 162 Beechcroft Rd. Upper Stratton, Swindon, Wilts.
Soccer Nostalgia, Albion Chambers, Birchington, Kent CT7 9DN
Sotheby's, 34–35 New Bond Street, London W1A 2AA
Sotheby's, 1334 York Avenue, New York NY 10021
Sotheby's, 112 George Street, Edinburgh EH2 2LH
Sotheby's, Summers Place, Billingshurst, West Sussex RH14 9AD
Sotheby's, Monaco, BP 45, 98001 Monte Carlo
David South, Kings House, 15 High Street, Pateley Bridge HG3 5AP
Southgate Auction Rooms, 55 High Street, Southgate, London N14 6LD
Don Spencer Antiques, 36a Market Place, Warwick CV34 4SH
Spink & Son Ltd., 5–7 King Street, St James's, London SW1Y 6QS
Michael Stainer Ltd., St Andrews Auction Rooms, Wolverton Rd, Boscombe, Bournemouth BH7 6HT
Michael Stanton, 7 Rowood Drive, Solihull, West Midlands B92 9LT
Station Mill Antiques Centre, Station Road, Chipping Norton, Oxon
Street Jewellery, 5 Runnymede Road, Ponteland, Northumbria NE20 9HE
Stride & Son, Southdown House, St John's Street, Chichester, Sussex
G E Sworder & Son, 14 Cambridge Road, Stansted Mountfitchet, Essex CM24 8BZ
Taviner's of Bristol, Prewett Street, Redcliffe, Bristol BS1 6PB
Tennants, Harmby Road, Leyburn, Yorkshire
Thomson Roddick & Laurie, 24 Lowther Street, Carlisle
Thomson Roddick & Laurie, 60 Whitesands, Dumfries
Thimbleby & Shorland, 31 Gt Knollys Street, Reading RG1 7HU
Tool Shop Auctions, 78 High Street, Needham Market, Suffolk IP6 8AW
Venator & Hanstein, Cäcilienstr. 48, 5000 Köln 1, Germany
T Vennett Smith, 11 Nottingham Road, Gotham, Nottingham NG11 0HE
Garth Vincent, The Old Manor House, Allington, nr. Grantham, Lincs. NG32 2DH
Wallis & Wallis, West Street Auction Galleries, West Street, Lewes, E. Sussex BN7 2NJ
Walter's, 1 Mint Lane, Lincoln LN1 1UD
Anthony Welling, Broadway Barn, High Street, Ripley, Surrey GU23 6AQ
Wells Cundall Nationwide Anglia, Staffordshire House, 27 Flowergate, Whitby YO21 3AX
West Street Antiques, 63 West Street, Dorking, Surrey
Whitworths, 32–34 Wood Street, Huddersfield HD1 1DX
A J Williams, 607 Sixth Avenue, Central Business Park, Hengrove, Bristol BS14 9BZ
Peter Wilson, Victoria Gallery, Market Street, Nantwich, Cheshire CW5 5DG
Wintertons Ltd., Lichfield Auction Centre, Fradley Park, Lichfield, Staffs WS13 8NF
Woltons, 6 Whiting Street, Bury St Edmunds, Suffolk IP33 1PB
Woodbridge Gallery, 3 Market Hill, Suffolk IP12 4LX
Woolley & Wallis, The Castle Auction Mart, Salisbury, Wilts SP1 3SU
Worthing Auction Galleries, 31 Chatsworth Road, Worthing, W. Sussex BN11 1LY
Robert Young Antiques, 68 Battersea Bridge Road, London SW11

ANTIQUES
REVIEW
2002

The Lyle Antiques Price Guide is compiled and published with completely fresh information annually, enabling you to begin each new year with an up-to-date knowledge of the current trends, together with the verified values of antiques of all descriptions.

We have endeavored to obtain a balance between the more expensive collector's items and those which, although not in their true sense antiques, are handled daily by the antiques trade.

The illustrations and prices in the following sections have been arranged to make it easy for the reader to assess the period and value of all items with speed.

You will find illustrations for almost every category of antique and curio, together with a corresponding price collated during the last twelve months, from the auction rooms and retail outlets of the major trading countries.

When dealing with the more popular trade pieces, in some instances, a calculation of an average price has been estimated from the varying accounts researched.

As regards prices, when 'one of a pair' is given in the description the price quoted is for a pair and so that we can make maximum use of the available space it is generally considered that one illustration is sufficient.

It will be noted that in some descriptions taken directly from sales catalogs originating from many different countries, terms such as bureau, secretary and davenport are used in a broader sense than is customary, but in all cases the term used is self explanatory.

An Austria Liliput miniature step drum calculator by Math. Bäuerle under licence from Herzstark, Vienna, 1904.
(Auction Team Köln) $1,412

A Double Brunsviga Model D 13 R-2 calculating machine for special functions such as land registry, circa 1960.
(Auction Team Köln) $248

A Kuli four-function latch drive adding machine with double 10 keyboard, 1909.
(Auction Team Köln) $4,235

A demonstration model of The Millionaire, with glazed sides giving a view of the mechanism, 1893.
(Auction Team Köln)
$6,777

A Peerless Baby German miniature cylinder calculator by Math. Bäuerle, with lever entry, 9-place entry and 12-place result, 1904.
(Auction Team Köln) $1,242

An Art Nouveau Omega manual adding machine with 9 slide rows and reckoning table mechanisms in the lid, by Justin Bamberger, Munich, 1904.
(Auction Team Köln) $3,671

A Brunsviga Model MIII four-function spoke-wheel calculator with 9,8 and 13 place reckoning, circa 1920.
(Auction Team Köln)   £225

The only known example of a German Sirius calculating machine, with five vertical countwheels and direct result display, 1912.
(Auction Team Köln) $3,219

An unusual Haman Selecta electric Universal adding machine with 2 full keyboards and two insertion mechanisms, 1934.
(Auction Team Köln) $395

A Badenia Model 1 desk-form spoke wheel calculating machine by Math. Bäuerle, St. Georgen, Black Forest, 9-row full keyboard with 8-place insertion, circa 1905.
(Auction Team Köln) $620

Tate's Patent Arithmometer, a four-function cylinder calculator by C & E Layton, London, with brass plate, in brass-mounted mahogany case, 1907.
(Auction Team Köln) $5,648

The Procento, a very rare Hungarian brass step drum adding machine with 7-place insertion and double 13 place result, circa 1912.
(Auction Team Köln) $2,710

A Universal cylinder calculator, a Swiss logarithm drum calculator by Daemen-Schmid, Zürich, on wooden plinth.
(Auction Team Köln) $282

An Austria Model 5 brass step drum machine with 9 place entry and 18 place result, circa 1920.
(Auction Team Köln) $1,355

A Curta Type 1 four-function miniature calculator by Curt Herzstark, Vienna/Liechtenstein, with metal box, 1948.
(Auction Team Köln) $621

An electric TIM Model 1 four-function miniature cylinder calculator with full keyboard and rare 'outboard motor', circa 1930.
(Auction Team Köln) $1,581

An Aderes brown bakelite pocket calculator, in the style of an Adix, rare post war export model with 9 keys and result lever, circa 1953.
(Auction Team Köln) $124

An unusual Kuli latch four-function adding machine with two-row keyboard, 12 place result, 1909.
(Auction Team Köln) $1,355

A very rare Gräber's Arithmometer four function cylinder adding machine by Josef Gräber, Vienna, 1902.(Auction Team Köln)
$18.074

A Time Is Money four function arithmometer with slide entry, by Ludwig Spitz & Co., Berlin, in rare mahogany box with adjustable desk back, 1907.
(Auction Team Köln) $6,212

A three place Adix adding machine with latch drive and 9 keys by Pallweber & Bordt, Mannheim, in original velvet case.
(Auction Team Köln) $791

An Original Odhner Arithmos Type 5 spoke wheel calculator with wing nut entry clear, with 9-place entry and conversion, 1922.
(Auction Team Köln) $451

The Dactyle, an early model of the French spoke wheel adding machine with positive and negative figures, circa 1910.
(Auction Team Köln) $254

A Dux chain 7-place adding machine by Forum Schmidt, Copenhagen, with chromed casing.
(Auction Team Köln) $339

A cast, painted and gilded zinc trade sign, American, late 19th-early 20th century, molded in the form of a pocket watch, the circular dial face painted on both sides, 13½in. high.
(Christie's) $3,760

A painted trade sign, American, late 19th / early 20th century, with white-painted ground on one side centering black and gray shadow-painted letters, 18½ x 41¾in.
(Christie's) $11,750

A glass and tinned sheet metal trade sign lantern cover, American, late 19th century, three sides with Ice Cream painted in black with white-paint on interior, 28in. high.
(Christie's) $2,350

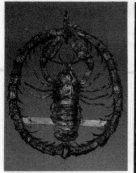

A French repoussé copper and wrought-iron fishmonger's sign, 19th century, modelled with a lobster within a seaweed wreath, 25in. high.
(Christie's) $12,173

A molded and gilded copper and iron pawnbroker's sign, American, 19th century, comprising three gilded copper balls hanging from three forged-iron arms projecting from a bracket hanger, 42 x 28in.
(Christie's) $4,935

Painted molded metal livery trade sign, probably France, late 19th century, the full-bodied horse's head with a faux patina painted surface, 20in. high x14in. wide.
(Skinner) $460

A painted sheet metal trade sign, signed *Booth & Co.*, probably American, late 19th century, rectangular with rounded corners and repeating C-scrolls and centering two black-painted boots, 18½ x 22in.
(Christie's) $2,585

An unusual painted composition trade sign in the shape of a hand, American, late 19th century, the full form of a hand with red and black painted cuff suspended from ring hangers, 34in. long.
(Sotheby's) $4,887

A gilded sheet metal and wrought-iron apothecary trade sign, American, 19th century, in the form of a mortar and pestle, gilded, with iron brackets for hanging, 40in. high. (Christie's) $3,055

A carved and painted cobbler's trade sign, American, late 19th century, the solid white-painted boot form with arched foot and delineated heel surmounted by a wrought iron eyelet, 19in. high. (Christie's) $4,465

Painted wood trade sign, American, 20th century, rectangular, the gray-painted ground with black edging and shadowed black letters advertising Meat Market, 43in. long. (Christie's) $4,465

A painted metal chemist's shop sign, late 19th or early 20th century, in the form of a pestle and mortar, with ruby bull's eye shades to the sides, on a scrolling iron bracket, 32in. high. (Christie's) $878

Vintage cast metal public house sign, the center decorated with scene of St George spearing the Dragon, inscribed *Fine Ales, Wines and Spirits*, 50in. wide. (G.A. Key) $236

Double-sided painted wooden trade sign, America, late 19th century, *Depot For Lucas Enamels Paints Lucas Varnish* on one side, three graduated stacked barrels, 49in. high. (Skinner) $2,645

A painted cast-iron butcher shop trade sign, American, early 20th century, cast in the half round in two parts: the bull's figure finial with articulated horns, mouth and tail, 24in. wide. (Christie's) $940

A cast, painted and gilded zinc and copper trade sign, American, probably 19th century, molded in the form of a pocketwatch, the central circular dial face painted on both sides, 30¾in. high. (Christie's) $4,935

A sculpted stone and wrought iron bound brewer's or inn sign, possibly 19th century, modelled as a hop, within a supporting frame with suspension chain, 12½in. high. (Christie's) $835

Cast zinc boot trade sign, America, 19th century, wrought iron angled bracket from which hangs a boot form, painted golden brown, impressed *570*, 22½in. high. (Skinner) $1,380

Italian carved alabaster bust of a young woman, circa 1800, after A. Cipniani, 22½in. high. (Skinner) $345

A pair of Italian alabaster models of the temples of Vespasian and Castor and Pollux, after the Antique, late 19th century, inscribed *Templvm Vespasiani* on plinth, 23½in. and 22¾in. high. (Bonhams) $3,925

An Italian alabaster bust entitled 'Rebecca', circa 1885, wearing a woven head-dress with a 'coin' head-band, each disk engraved with a letter spelling the name Rebecca, 21½in. high. (Christie's) $4,836

Italian, early 20th century, a bust of a lady wearing a lace bonnet, indistinctly signed, cream alabaster, 27½in. (Sotheby's) $14,800

An alabaster group of Cupid and Psyche, after Canova, Cupid leaning over Psyche holding her in his arms, raised upon a naturalistic base, 28¼in. high. (Bonhams) $1,694

An alabaster bust of Narcissus, after the antique, late 19th century, with his head inclined to dexter, raised upon a green marble circular socle, bust 22¼in. high. (Bonhams) $1,540

An Italian sculpted alabaster figure of a lady, late 19th or early 20th century, the figure shown partially draped with African head-dress and seated on a recumbent lion, 34in. high. (Christie's) $19,199

Alabaster center bowl on figural bronze base, late 19th/early 20th century, the bowl with everted rim, base formed as three crouching nude male figures, with a green marble base, bowl diameter 18¼in. (Skinner) $2,415

An Italian sculpted alabaster group, late 19th or early 20th century, modelled with a lady resting against a fountain with masks and dolphins, 68in. high. (Christie's) $17,371

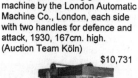

A Bajazzo pinball machine by Jentzsch & Meerz, Leipzig, brass mounted wooden case, post 1904, 63cm. high.
(Auction Team Köln) $2,372

The Knockout boxing game machine by the London Automatic Machine Co., London, each side with two handles for defence and attack, 1930, 167cm. high.
(Auction Team Köln) $10,731

A Treff mechanical three barrel machine with start button, wooden case with cast front, German, 1955, 72.5cm. high.
(Auction Team Köln) $367

A Roulomint Super roulette machine by Löwenautomat, Brunswick, with buttons for choosing colors and numbers, in working order, 1958.
(Auction Team Köln) $158

A British punchball machine with jackpot by Philip Shefras, London, wooden case with heavy cast metal base, bag hits platform and registers strength of the blow, 1930, 82in. high. (Auction Team Köln) $4,236

A Rotondo Junior gaming machine by OJ. Hoffmann, Hellenthal, electric 3-cylinder machine with two start buttons, wooden casing, 1961, 67.5cm. high.
(Auction Team Köln) $102

A Totomat shove ha'penny machine, (probably one of the last mechanical shove ha'penny machines), with two keys, by Günther Wolff, Berlin, 1950.
(Auction Team Köln) $1,073

An Imo Looping early electro-mechanical pinball machine with three lamps and an electric bell, by Jentzsch & Meerz, Leipzig, circa 1930, 78cm. high.
(Auction Team Köln) $1,976

A Derby Luxus 3 barrel amusement machine by T.H. Bergmann, Hamburg, wooden case with molded glass front, 1962, 72.5cm. high.
(Auction Team Köln) $423

A Sumerian stone head of a lion with gaping jaws revealing bared teeth, the eyes recessed and mane drilled, 3rd Millennium B.C., 4in. (Bonhams) $2,156

A sea-encrusted fragmentary pottery amphora with twin strap handles and flared rim, with an intricate coral branch emanating from the rim interior, Graeco-Roman, 1st century B.C./A.D., 14¼in. (Bonhams) $2,772

An Etruscan hollow terracotta left foot, ankle and heel missing, with a thick sole, long toes and naturalistically modelled toenails, circa 5th-4th century B.C., 9¾in. (Bonhams) $924

An Egyptian hollow gold head of Osiris wearing the atef crown surmounted by a sun disk, with frontal uraeus, Late Period, after 600 B.C., 3¾in. (Bonhams) $13,090

A Syrian black stone head of a female, her hair drawn back in thick locks and fastened in a bun at the base of her neck, with deeply drilled corners of the eyes, from the Hauran, Southern Syria, circa 1st Century B.C./A.D., 7¾in. (Bonhams) $672

A large damaged parthian green glazed amphora, with molded wreath decoration below the lip, the handles molded with plaited design and a central row of disks, circa 1st century A.D., 13in. (Bonhams) $728

An Etruscan bronze torch holder or sacrificial meat hook with seven curved prongs emanating from a central ring, circa 450-400 B.C., 11½in. (Bonhams) $1,020

A red jasper head of Pazuzu, the demon god, with finely modelled details, prominent eyes, snarling teeth with the tip of the tongue protruding, circa 800-500 B.C., 1¾in. (Bonhams) $16,940

A Roman fragmentary marble left hand, holding a tied scroll or cornucopia with the remains of carved decoration at one end, 1st-2nd Century A.D., 7in. (Bonhams) $1,120

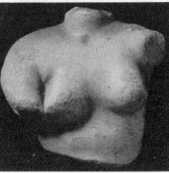

A Haniwa figure of a dog, Kofun Period (7th century), of low-fired reddish-clay pottery shaped into an abstract figure of a dog, old restoration, 16in. high.
(Christie's) $10,359

An Egyptian bead mummy mask strung on the original thread with pairs of glazed composition spacer beads, with a cream glazed bead face, Late Period - Ptolemaic., 6in.
(Bonhams) $515

A Jomon vessel, late to final Jomon Period (BC 200-300), of low-fired reddish-clay pottery of soshoku-hashu-tsuki fukabachi type, old restoration, 17¾in. high.
(Christie's) $5,000

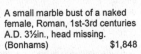

A large Roman olive green glass jug, with applied glass handle combed into eight vertical ribs, decorated around the body with three pairs of fine wheel-cut lines, 2nd-3rd century A.D., 7¾in.
(Bonhams) $2,772

A small marble bust of a naked female, Roman, 1st-3rd centuries A.D. 3½in., head missing.
(Bonhams) $1,848

A Lucanian round-bodied red-figure pelike decorated on side A: with a standing male figure wearing a himation and leaning on his staff with his legs crossed, Greek South Italy, circa 480 B.C., 13¼in.
(Bonhams) $4,620

A Roman marble bust of a female, head missing, wearing a chiton, with a knot or clasp between the breasts, 9½in. high.
(Bonhams) $847

A Haniwa figure of a man, Kofun Period (late 3rd-6th century), of low-fired clay shaped into the figure of a man, restoration, 20½in. high.
(Christie's) $13,394

An Italic bronze shield, of circular convex form, the central raised knop and concentric bands of repoussé decoration with stippled outline, circa 8th-7th century B.C., 11½in. (Bonhams) $3,080

A Mesopotamian terracotta zoomorphic vessel with ovoid body set on four stumpy legs, a short, cylindrical, ridged spout at the front, 3rd-2nd Millennium B.C., 6½in. (Bonhams) $2,464

A Coptic textile fragment showing a horse and rider, woven in two shades of brown wool, the central motif set within a roundel with vine boughs, circa 6th century A.D., 11½ x 11in. (Bonhams) $3,388

A Romano-Egyptian polychrome painted stucco funerary head of a youth with cropped hair colored black, a leafy wreath around his head, circa 2nd century A.D., approximately 8in.
(Bonhams) $23,100

An Egyptian limestone relief, carved with the bust of a male figure with exaggerated skull above a bunch of alternate lotus flowers, el-Amarna, New Kingdom, circa 1379-1362 B.C., 8 x 5¾in.
(Bonhams) $9,240

A large terracotta fragmentary head of stag, horns missing, the eye with pupil incised, pierced nostrils, Syria, 2nd-1st Millennium B.C., 6¾in. (Bonhams) $847

A Greek marble head of a female, her gaze cast down to her right wi idealised, contemplative expression, her wavy hair centrally parted and drawn back into thick, neat strands, circa 4th century B.C 13in. (Bonhams) $9,24

A Jordanian early Bronze Age terracotta votive idol of a stylized female of flattened form with accentuated hips, pinched-out buttocks and conical breasts, circa 3200-2900 B.C., 13cm.
(Bonhams) $8,470

An Apulian mis-fired red-figure bell krater decorated with added white to show on both sides the profile head of a lady of fashion, Greek South Italy, circa 330-300 B.C., 27cm. (Bonhams) $735

A large Villanoven pottery urn with carinated ribbed body, 16½in., together with a lid in the form of a up-turned bowl with narrow base, 10½in., 8th-7th century B.C.
(Bonhams) $659

An Assyrian stone fragment carved in low relief with a seated lion, its tail held aloft and curled at the tip, circa 9th-7th centuries B.C., 9 x 6.7cm. (Bonhams) $431

An Egyptian wooden canopic jar stopper, in the form of one of the Four Sons of Horus, the human-headed Imsety, Late Period, after 500 B.C., 4¼in. (Bonhams) $2,002

A marble bearded male head, with close cropped hair, furrowed brow and naturalistically rendered features, 3rd century A.D., 4¼in. (Bonhams) $3,850

A Hellenistic hollow terracotta lower right leg molded to show an elaborate sandal bound around the instep and lower ankle, Western Greek, late 4th century B.C., 9¼in. (Bonhams) $616

A large oval terracotta mold in the form of a male face, possibly a king, with deeply recessed almond-shaped eyes, curly beard and moustache, possibly Assyrian or Phoenician, 9¾ x 7½in. (Bonhams) $1,911

An Egyptian polychrome painted cartonnage mummy mask of a female, her face painted yellow, with central frontal uraeus, Late Period, after 500 B.C., 17in. high. (Bonhams) $4,312

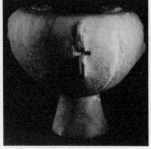

An Etruscan red-figure stamnos decorated in added white, to show on Side A; a large swan bearing a semi-draped youth wearing sandals and a wreath in his hair, circa 4th century B.C., 14³/₈in. high. (Bonhams) $3,234

A large Cycladic marble kandila, the marble streaked with gray with hemispherical body and four vertical pierced lug handles, early Bronze Age I, circa 3000-2800 B.C., 8in.(Bonhams) $4,620

An Egyptian Ramesside limestone relief fragment, carved with two standing facing figures, one a falcon-headed god, the other a Ramesside pharaoh, 19th Dynasty, 1293-1185 B.C., 15 x 12¾in. (Bonhams) $3,850

A very rare English funeral helmet, with high comb, visor with vision slits and bevor with ventilation holes, attached to a substantial and probably much earlier gorget. (Andrew Bottomley) $3,234

An Indian mail shirt, probably 17th century, of riveted and plain steel rings, thigh length, open up the front and partly up the back, the former with padded collar extending down the front, faced in green velvet, 86cm. long. (Bonhams) $840

A red-lacquered Tachi Do Gusoku armor, mid-Edo Period (late 18th century), including a sixty–two plate suji-bachi, black-lacquered with tehen-kanamono, maedate of copper kuwagata. (Christie's) $17,875

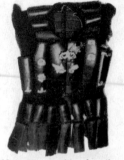

French Cuirassier's First Empire cuirass, rare Napoleonic War period example, breastplate of heavy polished steel, the left side with the Arsenal stamp *Wohlers*. (Bosleys) $544

A Moro armour cuirass from the Philippines, made from plates of black kabau horn joined by thick brass butted rings. Front plates applied with silver coloured metal foliate devices. (Wallis & Wallis) $360

A French Cuirassier's heavy breastplate, inside edge of skirt etched *Manufre Rle de Chatellerault Juin 1839-3T2L No 1272*. Turned brass studded borders, medial ridge. (Wallis & Wallis) $515

A fine Myochin School Uchidashi Tosei Gusoku armor, Edo Period (18th/19th century), the kabuto with russet-iron twelve-plate oboshi-hoshibachi with repoussé dragons applied to four of the plates. (Christie's) $64,296

A good French Cuirassier's breastplate dated *1845,* inside of lower edge etched *Manufre Rle de Chatellerault Aout 1845 3T 2L No 1020.* Raised medial ridge, turned over edges. (Wallis & Wallis) $432

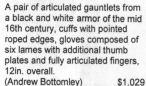

A Turkish breast-plate, late
15th/early 16th century, comprising
a circular central plate with three
smaller shaped plates, attached to
it by riveted iron rings, the main
plate with flat central boss bordered
by radiating flutes, 41cm. wide.
(Bonhams) $588

A pair of articulated gauntlets from
a black and white armor of the mid
16th century, cuffs with pointed
roped edges, gloves composed of
six lames with additional thumb
plates and fully articulated fingers,
12in. overall.
(Andrew Bottomley) $1,029

A 19th century breast and
backplate and morion, the sheet
metal helmet with plate brass
decoration, the armor with jointed
shoulder and arm plates.
(Stockholms AV) $1,017

A replica Prussian Garde du Corps
cuirass, to mark the bicentenary of
Frederick the Great, brass with
leather lining and ring collar.
(Stockholms AV) $2,284

A rare British Life or Horse Guards
Cavalry trooper's back and breast
plate, steel, but with blackened
finish for use at a state funeral.
(Andrew Bottomley) $1,000

A very rare, 17th century English
pikeman's breast plate and tassets,
of pinched waist form, with
pronounced central ridge, with
rolled edges.
(Andrew Bottomley) $2,720

A composite pikeman's armor,
partly first half of the 17th century,
of blackened steel, comprising
reproduction two-piece wide-
trimmed pot, cuirass with breast-
plate, back-plate, and large hinged
tassets. (Bonhams) $3,640

A Japanese Tosei-Gusoku (Do
only), banded plate Do with lower
part close laced in dark blue (kebiki
style). Made without Kusazuri
(apron defences). Early 19th
century.(Wallis & Wallis) $462

A good 19th century Indian ax from Chota Nagpur, broad moustache shaped blade 8in., swollen faceted socket, chiselled and red filled with 2 fish, scales, roped and geometric ornament. On its steel mounted wooden haft. (Wallis & Wallis) $206

An interesting European bronze battle ax head, with crescent shaped blade, circular socket and hooked rear fluke, 7in. overall. (Andrew Bottomley) $515

A 19th century Indian Muslim all steel ax, 21¼ overall, crescent head 6¼ chiselled with cartouche of Arabic above confronting elephants and foliage, reverse with dancing girl, flowers and foliage, steel haft. (Wallis & Wallis) $216

A very rare 18th century Danish naval boarding ax, head with large crescent shaped blade and rear square section pick blade. The wooden shaft with turned round ball butt, 31in. overall. (Andrew Bottomley) $1,838

A small Indo Persian all steel parade ax, with tapered square section spike, crescent shaped blade and rounded shaft with bulbous finial to base. 23in. overall. (Andrew Bottomley) $373

A 19th century fireman's ax, 25in., head 8in. with crescent edge 4½in., stamped WE, long side straps riveted to its painted wooden haft, red ribbed grip, copper plate stamped Fire 1807 Exon 3. (Wallis & Wallis) $154

erial German Ersatz conversion bayonet, a scarce Great War period example, triangular blade fitted into an
steel Ersatz pattern hilt with simulated ribbed grip and three-quarter muzzle ring. The blade is stamped with
ermanic letter. Blade length 18in. (Bosleys)
$647

German Third Reich Police dress bayonet by Alexander Coppel Solingen. Hilt with stylized eagle pommel,
: leaf decorated quillon and stag horn grips with police badge, nickel plated blade. Blade 13in.
drew Bottomley)
$412

azi police Officer's dress bayonet, plated blade 13in. by Alex Coppel. Two piece staghorn grips, regulation
e metal mounts, crosspiece with stamped *L Mg.118*. In its brown leather scabbard with white metal mounts
leather frog. (Wallis & Wallis)
$406

poleonic period 2nd pattern Baker bayonet, with a flat straight single edged 577mm. blade, the lower 16cm.
ble edged. The hilt with knuckle guard and ribbed grip. Retaining working spring action.
sleys)
$308

nch 1866 Pattern adapted Chassepot sabre bayonet, Yataghan shaped blade, with the date *1872,* the brass
with swept forward quillon, the hilt adapted and fitted with a steel knuckle guard, complete with steel
bbard. (Bosleys)
$156

7th century plug bayonet, 15½in., broad tapered shallow diamond section double edged blade 9in. Brass
sspiece with swollen finials. Turned fruitwood grip with brass ferrule and pommel.
allis & Wallis)
$700

azi army Officer's dress bayonet, plated blade 8in. etched *Zur Erinnerung an Meine Dienstzeit* in panel with
le and helmet, 2 piece composition grips, in its black painted sheath with patent leather frog and white fabric
ss knot. (Wallis & Wallis)
$218

tish 1871 Pattern Elcho sword bayonet, saw back bayonet for the Martini Henry rifle. This example with a
mber of Ordnance stamps and date stamp indication August 1884. (Bosleys)
$847

27

A fine cased American Colt .450 (Eley Short) single-action Army six-shot center-fire revolver, No. 25410 for 1877, with 14cm. blued sighted barrel, 28cm. (Bonhams) $10,205

A very fine pair of German 40 bore percussion duelling pistols, by Rieger in Munchen, 1847, 14½in. overall, blued octagonal barrels 9in. with single gold line at muzzles, 4 gold lines at breeches, single set triggers; walnut halfstocks with carved monster head fore ends, checkered panels and carved bands to butts. (Wallis & Wallis) $2,800

A 5 shot 54 bore Tranter 1856 double action percussion revolver, 12in. overall, barrel 6in. engraved on top strap B Cogswell, 224 Strand London, London proved; checkered walnut butt. (Wallis & Wallis) $3,360

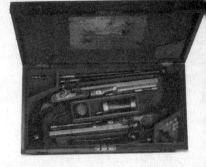

A good pair of 44 bore flintlock duelling pistols, b Thos Parsons, Salisbury, circa 1820, 15½in. overa heavy octagonal twist barrels 10in. with make poinçon and single platinum line at breeches; steppe locks with rainproof pans and rollers on frizzen walnut halfstocks, in a relined fitted mahogany cas (Wallis & Wallis) $5,85

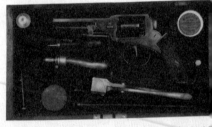

A cased 120-bore Webley Patent five-shot doub action percussion revolver by Webley & Son, Londo No. 3619, circa 1860-80, with blued octagonal sighte barrel, blued cylinder numbered from 1 to 5, ramm with sprung sidecatch, blued border engraved b and trigger-guard, and checkered walnut grip 22.5cm. (Bonhams) $1,05

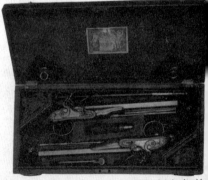

A fine pair of 16 bore flintlock duelling pistols, by H Mortimer & Co, London, circa 1810, 15½in. overa octagonal twist barrels 10in., gold touch holes; fl stepped locks with safety bolts, swan neck cocks a rollers on frizzen springs, walnut halfstocks with ho fore end caps. (Wallis & Wallis) $9,94

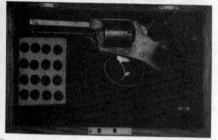

An unusual cased Tranter Patent .320 five-shot double-action revolver for The Ulster Bank, Belturbet, retailed by W. Richards, Old Hall St., Liverpool, circa 1870, with blued octagonal sighted barrel, border engraved blued frame, trigger-guard and butt-cap, 21.5cm. (Bonhams) $700

A very good pair of 28 bore percussion duelling pistols by John Manton, converted from flintlock, number 2653, 13½in. overall, browned octagonal twist barrels 8¾in., single gold line at breeches; stepped locks with safety bolts, nicely figured walnut fullstocks. (Wallis & Wallis) $4,900

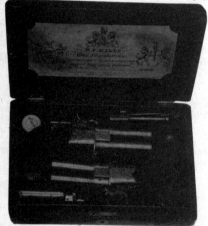

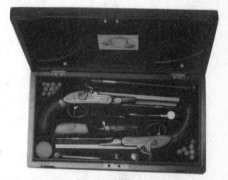

A very fine pair of 34 bore double barrelled over and under turnover percussion boxlock overcoat pocket pistols, by Mills, High Holborn, London circa 1840, 7½in. overall, turn off barrels 2½in. with London proofs at breeches; scroll engraved frames, top safety catches; hidden triggers.
(Wallis & Wallis) $3,570

A fine cased pair of 36 bore percussion holster pistols by A Thomson, Edinburgh, 13½in. overall, heavy octagonal twist barrels 8½in. with front and rear sights, sparsely scroll engraved locks, walnut halfstocks with rounded checkered butts, horn fore end caps, purple velvet lined fitted mahogany case. (Wallis & Wallis) $6,006

A cased 54-bore Deane-Harding Patent second model five-shot double-action percussion revolver, retailed by Deane & Son, London Bridge, circa 1860-65, with blued octagonal sighted take-down barrel hinged at the top of the standing breech, blued cylinder and frame, patent rammer and safety-catch, 30.5cm. (Bonhams) $1,820

A very fine pair of officer's 16 bore percussion holster pistols by Westley Richards, 13½in. overall, browned octagonal twist barrels 8in.; flat locks with safety bolts, the plates and hammers with maker's name and foliate engraving; pale walnut fullstocks with rounded checkered butts; blued steel mounts; swivel ramrods. (Wallis & Wallis) $6,300

A German slurbow, circa 1720-1730, fruitwood stock fitted with foresigh and leaf backsight and carved with cherub mask, 20¾in. (Sotheby's) $3,150

A German stonebow (Schnepper), early 17th century, with steel bov and later cord strings, later steel bolt-channel, folding baluster back sight mounted on the built-in gaffle, 73cm. (Bonhams & Brooks) $65:

A Saxon steel crossbow with associated cranequin, the stock wit panels of foliate etching, circa 1600, 70.cm. long. (Stockholms AV) $5,82

An 18th century sporting crossbow, probably German, 27in., spa 21½in., fruitwood stock, set triggers, steel lock, sprung bolt holde mount for missing sight. Bone inlay along top of stock, foliate engrave above cheekpiece which has a star shaped bone and ebony inlay original wound cord. (Wallis & Wallis) $1,15!

A small crossbow, Spanish or English, late 16th/early 17th century, perhaps for a child, of recurved form struck twice with maker's mark, slender walnut tiller swelling at the gaffle pivot, 20¾in. (Sotheby's) $1,750

A Caucasian kindjal, 19th century, with broad double-edged blade cut with two etched fullers on each side and damascened in gold with panels containing foliage, and waisted dark horn hilt with nielloed silver mounts decorated with foliage, 45cm. (Bonhams) $420

A fine quality 19th century Japanese tanto, 11.5in. blade, cord bound hilt with arrow shaped menuki, brass engraved fuchi and kashira, brass tsuba, black lacquered scabbard with green flecks. (Bosleys) $441

A large late 19th century Moroccan dagger jambiya, 17in., curved blade 9in., large one piece bone grip, white metal ferrule and pommel chiselled with foliage. In its white metal sheath chiselled with flowers and foliage overall. (Wallis & Wallis) $130

A Japanese dagger Aikuchi, blade 28.2cm., mumei, gunome hamon, hira zukuri. Same tsuka, shakudo menuki as cherry blossom, iron tsuba, fuchi kashira with repeated designs and flowers. (Wallis & Wallis) $397

A large 19th century Wahabite Arab dagger jambiya, 18¾in. with twin shallow fullers. Two piece horn grips applied with silver decoration with granulation in relief. In its leather sheath with large silver chape en-suite with hilt. (Wallis & Wallis) $462

A Japanese dagger tanto, blade 35cm. signed *Yoshisaku*. Tape bound same tsuka, gilt floral menuki, copper fittings carved with dragons and clouds, carp on fuchi, foliate engraved copper tsuba. (Wallis & Wallis) $1,360

A 19th century Persian dagger jambiya, watered double edged blade 9in. with raised central rib, etched at forte with Islamic inscription. One piece walrus tusk hilt. In its silver mounted green velvet covered sheath. (Wallis & Wallis) $504

31

A Victorian dagger for the American market, shallow diamond sectio
blade 5¾in., faintly etched with foliage and *Americans*..... . Recurve
steel crosspiece silver hilt embossed with the British Union flowers an
Victorian crown pommel. (Wallis & Wallis) $23

A German left-handed dagger, circa 1600, the double edged blade wit
straight quillons, cross guard ring, 40cm. long.
(Stockholms AV) $3,770

A 19th century Turkish watered steel dagger, blade 8in. of finel
watered dark steel, chiselled at forte with gilt Islamic inscription and lion
Gold inlaid brown jade hilt of three sections, Islamic inscription
chiselled to gilt ferrule. In its velvet sheath. (Wallis & Wallis) $840

A rare and very fine Spanish left hand dagger, Toledo, dated *1883*. Ir
17th century style, and finely etched overall with scrolling foliage
surrounding circular cartouches depicting warriors in classical Romar
helmets. Blade 11½in. (Andrew Bottomley) $690

A Bulgarian Army Officer's dagger, the hilt with white grip, brass mount
including guard with s-shaped quillon. Nickel plated double edge blad
with single fuller. Blade 9in. (Andrew Bottomley) $19

An early 17th century dagger for the left hand, hilt with beehive styl
pommel, ribbed wire bound grip, down curved quillons and upswep
shell guard pierced with small decorative holes, blade 13in
(Andrew Bottomley) $1,397

A good German main gauche dagger circa 1580-1600, tapere
diamond section blade 11½in., swollen baluster pommel and quillo
terminals, broad thumb ring integral with quillon block.   Fishskir
covered grip with four steel ribs and shaped ferrules.
(Wallis & Wallis) $82

A silver mounted Malayan dagger bade bade, 10in. overall, slende
slightly curved blase 7½in., foliate carved horn hilt, silver ferrule an
engraved silver pommel cap. In its wooden sheath with foliate carve
horn top. (Wallis & Wallis) $145

A Nazi NSFK dagger, blade 7in. with SMF Solingen trade mark. Blue leather covered grip and sheath, plated mounts. (Wallis & Wallis) $693

A Third Reich 'Teno' hewer, with single-edged Eickhorn, Solingen blade widening towards the clipped-back point and cut with a fuller along the back-edge on each side, silvered hilt, in black painted steel scabbard with nickel-plated locket and chape, 40.2cm. (Bonhams) $980

A German Third Reich dress Hirschfanger of the Reichsbund Deutsche Jägerschaft (National Hunting Association), single edge blade 13in. by H & F Horster, Solingen, etched and polished with hunting scenes. Staghorn grip, silvered mounts. (Wallis & Wallis) $847

SA dagger by Anton Wingen JB of Solingen, blade etched *Alles für Deutschland*, brown wooden grip inlaid with silvered eagle and enamelled circular SA device. (Bosleys) $398

A Nazi Army Officer's dagger, regulation blade 10¼in. by Alcosa. Regulation plated mounts, white spiral plastic grip, in its plated sheath. (Wallis & Wallis) $319

A Third Reich SS dagger, with Jacobs & Co., Solingen double-edged blade etched *Meine Ehre Heist Treue* in gothic script on one side, hilt of Holbein type with ebonized grip (insignia replaced), and chrome-plated quillons and pommel, in original blackened scabbard with chrome-plated locket and chape, and complete with suspension clip, 36.8cm. (Bonhams) $707

German RAD Leader's dagger, 1937 model by Eickhorn of Solingen, blade bearing etched motto *Arbeit adelt*, white two piece celluloid grip. (Bosleys) $559

A Nazi naval Officer's dirk, bi-fullered regulation blade by Eickhorn w
trade mark, etched with fouled mounts, white spiral grip, in its bra
sheath. (Wallis & Wallis) $45

A Third Reich N.S.K.K. dirk, with double-edged blade dated *1941*
one side and etched *Alles fur Deutschland* in gothic script on the othe
hilt of Holbein type with wooden grip inlaid with eagle and swastik
37.5cm. (Bonhams) $1,33

Georgian Royal Navy dirk, good straight blade example, with half leng
blue and gilt decoration, this depicts a crowned GR cypher Britanni
trophy of war etc., hilt of a square ivorine grip with fire gilt cross gua
terminating with an acanthus leaf bud. (Bosleys) $470

A Georgian naval Officer's dirk, circa 1800, the 7in. tapered doub
edged blade of flattened diamond section etched blued and gilt w
military trophy and foliage; copper gilt crosspiece chiselled with ro
decoration; turned ivory hilt. (Wallis & Wallis) $44

A Georgian naval Officer's dirk, circa 1800, the 7in. tapered doub
edged blade of flattened diamond section etched overall with foliag
and stand of flags; gilt ferrule and foliate crosspiece; turned ivory hi
(Wallis & Wallis) $63

An unusual Japanese dirk made from a polearm head yari, 27.1cm
signed and dated *Fumei*, single mekugi ana, of ken shape swolle
towards tip. Lacquered hilt with 2 bands of sanded same, shaku
menuki as recumbent oxen, black lacquered say
(Wallis & Wallis) $77

Georgian Royal Navy Midshipman's dirk, with double edged 13in. spea
point blade, with etched decoration incorporating a fouled anchor, fi
gilt quillon of scrolling floral design, turned white bone gri
(Bosleys) $70

A Nazi naval Officer's dirk, blade by P D Luneschloss etched with nav
motifs. Regulation brass mounts, white composition grip, wire bound.
its brass sheath with twin hanging rings. (Wallis & Wallis) $33

A Third Reich Second Pattern Luftwaffe dirk, with Eickhorn of Solingen double-edged blade of flattened hexagonal section, quillons formed as an eagle and swastika, pommel cast with branches of oak framing a swastika, 42cm. (Bonhams) $235

A Russian naval Officer's dirk kortek, hollow ground cruciform blade 10½in., recurved brass crosspiece, slightly swollen rectangular section casein grip, brass pommel and spherical button. (Wallis & Wallis) $144

A GVIR naval Officer's dress dirk, straight single edged blade 18in. etched with crowned *GVIR* and fouled anchor amidst foliage. Brass mounts, lion's head pommel and crosspiece, wire bound sharkskin grip. (Wallis & Wallis) $676

Georgian Naval dirk, small example with curved blade, decorated with threequarter length etched floral motifs, "S" shape crossguard in the form of a sea serpent, ebony carved grip surmounted by a lion's head pommel. (Bosleys) $141

A Third Reich D.R.K. (German Red Cross) dirk, with single-edged rebated blade fullered along the saw-back on each side, nickel-plated quillon with eagle and swastika emblem within an oval on one side, nickel-plated oval pommel, 41.5cm. (Bonhams) $182

Late 19th century Imperial Russian Midshipman's dirk, with straight spear point cruciform blade, hilt with plain brass "S" shape quillon and square white bone handle, brass pommel decorated with ball top. (Bosleys) $283

A Third Reich Luftschutz (Air Raid Protection) dirk, with bright double-edged W.K.C., Solingen blade of flattened diamond section, plated short fluted quillons with stylized eagle and swastika on one side, plated cap-shaped pommel, 36.5cm. (Bonhams) $490

A Third Reich 1936 Model Army Officer's dirk, with double-edged blade of flattened hexagonal section, scrolled silvered quillons with eagle and swastika on one side, pommel cast with oak leaves, and spirally twist ivorine grip, 39.5cm. (Bonhams) $220

91st Argyllshire Highlanders Officer's dirk, clipped back 11in. blade double edged for the lower 4in., the upper
section with a wide fuller and retains faint etching of crowned VR cypher and other decoration, black bogwood
grip, decorated with silver studs. (Bosleys) $1,33

A Highland dress dirk circa 1900 straight bifullered single edge blade 12¾in. with scalloped back edge, Bask
weave carved bog oak grip with piqué work, in its leather sheath with companion knife and for
(Wallis & Wallis) $7

93rd Sutherland Highlanders Officer's dirk, 1838-70 pattern, plain clipped back 10in. blade double edged for th
lower 5in., the upper section with a narrow fuller, black bogwood grip of an interlaced design decorated w
silver studs and surmounted by a plain silver pommel ornamented with a foiled citrin
(Bosleys) $1,33

A good pre-1881 Scottish Officer's dirk of the 71st (Highland Light Infantry) Regt, blade 14in. with broad a
narrow fullers and scalloped back edge, etched overall with battle honours to Hindoostan, ebony hilt carved w
strapwork, in its patent leather covered sheath. (Wallis & Wallis) $10

Highland dirk, by Wm. Anderson and Sons Ltd., single edged clipped back spear pointed blade, the last 6½i
double edged. Bog oak grip carved with Celtic design terminating in a cut glass pommel, in its black leath
scabbard complete with knife and fork. (Bosleys) $96

91st Argyllshire Highlanders Victorian Officer's dirk, Marshall and Son, the clipped back 11in. blade is doub
edged for the lower 4in., black bogwood grip, matching side by side knife and fork. (Bosleys) $1,5.

Silver mounted Scottish dirk, Wm. Anderson and Son, single edged spear pointed blade, the last 6½in. doul
edged. Bog oak grip carved with Celtic design and terminating in a flat silver pomm
(Bosleys) $1,3

A rare 40-bore Swedish double barrelled flintlock sporting gun, by Elias Gronstedt, Stockholm, circa 1800, with three-stage sighted barrels, octagonal breeches becoming polygonal, grooved tang, signed rounded locks each with safety-catch, figured walnut half-stock, 82.3cm. barrels. (Bonhams) $1,540

A 10-bore flintlock wildfowling gun by Richard Bees, early 19th century, with long two-stage sighted barrel, octagonal breech, grooved engraved tang, signed engraved flat bevelled lock with roller, walnut half-stock, checkered grip, 137.2cm. barrel. (Bonhams) $840

A 14-bore flintlock sporting gun, the lock by Hewson, late 18th century, with refinished two-stage barrel with octagonal breech and silver fore-sight cast and chased as a bearded satyr's face, platinum-lined touch-hole, tang engraved with rocailles, signed flat bevelled lock, London proof marks, 102cm. barrel. (Bonhams) $812

An Irish brass-barrelled flintlock blunderbuss by John Rigby, Dublin, late 18th century, with heavy three-stage barrel belled and turned at the muzzle, and signed on the breech flat, foliate engraved tang, signed flat bevelled lock engraved with foliage, 44.5cm. barrel. (Bonhams) $3,780

A 14-bore flintlock sporting gun by John Manton, London, No. 3689 for 1801, converted from percussion, with rebrowned three-stage sighted barrel octagonal at the breech then polygonal over its entire length, breech signed in gold, gold-lines and vent, 84.7cm. barrel (Bonhams) $630

A rare brass-barrelled flintlock coaching blunderbuss, by Mewis & Co., late 18th/ early 19th century, with three-stage brass barrel belled at the muzzle and fitted with a spring bayonet above, signed border engraved lock, walnut full stock, 77cm. (Bonhams) $3,080

A Tower 16 bore Paget flintlock cavalry carbine, 31½in. overall, barrel 16in. with Tower proofs, stepped lock with safety bolt and raised pan, the lock stamped with crowned *GR* and *Tower*, fullstocked with regulation brass mounts, saddle bar and ring on left. (Wallis & Wallis) $2,160

37

A 16 bore East India Company flintlock light dragoon pistol, 15½in. barrel 9¼in., London private proofs, engraved with VEIC heart and *Manton 1802*. Fullstocked, regulation flat lock. Regulation brass mounts, stock with VEIC heart stamp. (Wallis & Wallis) $1,925

A Balkan 18 bore miquelet-lock pistol, 19th century, with iron barrel with various brass-lined marks at the breech, characteristic lock, engraved steel trigger-guard, silver full stock with curved butt and bulbous pommel cast and chased with designs of foliage in low relief, 53cm. (Bonhams) $560

An Officer's 16 bore flintlock holster pistol by D Egg, 14in. overall, flat topped round barrel 9in. with front and rear sights; flat stepped lock with swan neck cock, safety bolt which also locks the frizzen, and raised pan; walnut fullstock with rounded checkered butt. (Wallis & Wallis) $588

A 25-bore flintlock box-lock pistol, by John 2 Joiner, London, circa 1765, with long three-stage turn-off cannon barrel, sliding trigger-guard safety catch engraved with a flowerhead at the bow, and flat-sided figured walnut butt inlaid with silver wire scrollwork, 33cm. (Bonhams) $448

A 36 bore flintlock duelling pistol, by Prosser, Charing Cross, London, circa 1820, 13½in. overall, octagonal twist barrel 8in. with gold line, poinçon and touch hole; flat stepped lock with safety bolt, swan neck cock, rainproof pan and roller on frizzen spring; walnut fullstock with checkered saw handle butt. (Wallis & Wallis) $1,540

A rare George III Dublin Cavalry flintlock pistol, early 19th century, with 22.9cm. barrel stamped with indistinct maker's mark at the breech, border engraved flat bevelled lock, walnut full stock with raised apron around the tang, 38cm. (Bonhams) $1,727

A scarce double barrelled over and under 18 bore flintlock sidelock holster pistol, by I Barber, circa 1760, 17in. overall, barrels 10in. with London and maker's proofs; half rounded locks with external main springs acting on the base of the cocks, and L shaped frizzen springs walnut butt. (Wallis & Wallis) $3,360

A .65in. New Land Pattern flintlock holster pistol, 15½in., barrel 9in., Tower military proofs. Fullstocked, regulation lock struck with Crowned *GR* and Tower. Regulation brass mounts, trigger guard bow engraved *29*, swivel ramrod. Stock struck with inspector's and storekeeper's marks. (Wallis & Wallis) $847

A scarce late 17th century Dutch 24 bore naval flintlock holster pistol, by Abraham Stout, Rotterdam, 19½in. overall, 3 stage brass barrel 13in., with octagonal breech struck with the Rotterdam town mark; brass lockplate, pan and steel faced frizzen. (Wallis & Wallis) $2,800

A 20 bore flintlock holster pistol, by Hollis & Sheath, probably made for the Turkish market, 17in. overall, 11½in. barrel, flat lock with ring neck cock and roller on frizzen spring, the plate engraved; walnut fullstock with checkered butt. (Wallis & Wallis) $847

An 18th century Scottish snaphaunce pistol, signed *I. O. Shiels*, with finely engraved stock and barrel, 33cm. long. (Stockholms AV) $1,542

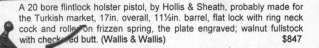

A scarce mid 19th century Turkish Miquelet flintlock blunderbuss pistol, the brass barrel with tapered muzzle and bearing inscription in calligraphy to the top flat of the octagonal breech section, barrel 8¼in. (Andrew Bottomley) $1,102

A good brass barrelled flintlock blunderbuss pistol, by J Parr, Liverpool, circa 1775, 13½in. overall, bell mouth barrel 8in. with octagonal breech bearing Tower private proofs, flat brass lock engraved, unbridled frizzen; nicely figured plain walnut stock. (Wallis & Wallis) $1,271

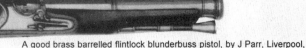

A flintlock blunderbuss-pistol, engraved *Webb & Riggs,* with two-stage brass barrel turned and belled at the muzzle and engraved *London* on the octagonal breech, engraved tang, signed brass lock with bevelled edge and engraved safety-catch, 36cm. (Bonhams) $1,470

39

German Artillery Officer's cap, of thick field gray material with red piping (Waffenfarbe) to welt of the crown and edges of the dark green band. (Bosleys) $294

Boer War Orange Free State Artitllery Pickelhaube. Polished black leather with rounded front peak and gilt metal fittings. (Bosleys) $1,194

Royal Renfrew Militia Victorian Officer's shako, dark blue body bearing a diced band, to the front, a silvered plate comprising eight pointed star. (Bosleys) $1,132

A Household Cavalry Veterinary Officer's cocked hat, ornamental gilt loop of special pattern, fore and aft tassels, in tin case with nameplate *Captain Lord Herbert*, and scarlet feather plume in tin case. (Wallis & Wallis) $441

A close-helmet, circa 1570, probably English, comprising one-piece skull rising to a prominent roped comb, pivoted prow-shaped upper-bevor and pointed visor, 29.5cm. high. (Bonhams & Brooks) $3,045

Royal Army Medical Corps Officer helmet, post 1902 example of the Officer's Home Service Pattern blu cloth helmet. Gilt Royal Arms helmet plate of the Royal Army Medical Corps to the front. (Bosleys) $44

Képi attributed to Capt. Dreyfus of the Dreyfus Affair, French Officer's black képi by Reynadd of Nancy bearing rank insignia for Lieutenant Colonel and Artillery pattern buttons supporting the gold braid chinstrap. (Bosleys) $1,470

Luftwaffe Paratrooper's helmet, early war example of the single decal "para" helmet. The blue gray painted finish retains Luftwaffe decal which is 99% present. (Bosleys) $2,310

East Surrey Regiment Staff Officer's cocked hat, worn by Colonel Hugh Wodehouse Pearse DSO, black beaver skin body, to the left side a black silk rosette with a loop of gold bullion lace. (Bosleys) $22

A scarce double decal M35 SS parade helmet, black with SS runes and swastika decals, original liner and chinstrap with RZM/SS stamp. (Wallis & Wallis) $1,117

9th (Queen's Royal Lancers) Officer's cap, post 1902 Officer's dress cap, dark blue crown, with scarlet piping to the welt of the crown. To the underside of the crown scarlet line quartering. (Bosleys) $191

A Nazi M34 fire police helmet with double decals, aluminium comb, leather liner and chin strap, black painted. (Wallis & Wallis) $122

th Royal Irish Lancers Officer's ance cap, Edward VII example by Hamburger & Rogers of London. The skull of black patent leather with the upper portion of scarlet melton cloth. (Bosleys) $6,300

1st (Hexham) Northumberland Fusiliers Vols Officer's gray cloth helmet, pre 1901 Home Service Pattern complete with lightly blackened silvered metal cross piece, spike and rose bosses. (Bosleys) $955

Life Guards Officer's helmet, post 1953 example. German silver skull ornamented with gilt laurel and oak leaf design, gilt and silver spike supporting the white horse hair plume. (Bosleys) $1,820

French steel helmet of the Garde epublicaine, brass peak binding, ed "shaving brush" plume in brass older, red hair falling back plume, d feather side plume in holder on ft. (Wallis & Wallis) $1,617

East Suffolk Militia early 19th century shako, of black patent leather with false tall front vaguely following the style of the Waterloo shako. (Bosleys) $1,270

Hertfordshire Rifle Volunteers 1878-80 OR's helmet, Home Service Pattern gray cloth helmet complete with blackened metal cross piece, spike and rose bosses. (Bosleys) $470

An Officer's shako of the Liverpool Rifle Volunteer Brigade, black patent leather peak, headband and top, silver lace top band. (Wallis & Wallis) $875

Royal Company of Archers cocked hat, worn by the bodyguard of Scotland. Black beaver skin body with black silk rose mounted with a gold buillion Order of the Thistle, with bullion tassels fore and aft. (Bosleys) $280

A fireman's brass helmet, helmet plate of crossed axes etc within ornamental escutcheon, comb with embossed dragon on each side. (Wallis & Wallis) $490

A French 3rd Empire fireman's 1833 pattern brass helmet of the Sapeurs Pompiers de Vron, ear to ear helmet plate with crowned eagle, and title, tall ornamental comb. (Wallis & Wallis) $322

An Imperial German Officer's black leather Pickelhaube of the 92nd Brunswick Infantry, with gilt front peak binding, top mount and spike, silver plated skull and crossbones badge with *Peninsula* scroll beneath. (Wallis & Wallis) $1,680

1844-55 Honourable Artillery Company Officer's shako, "Albert" pattern, the body of black beaver skin with black patent leather crown, eight pointed star, to the crown, a white worsted ball tuft. (Bosleys) $3,528

Queen's Own Worcestershire Yeomanry Trooper's helmet, worn by a Member of the Artillery Section. Skull, neck and front peak of boiled black enamelled leather, surmounted by a black hair plume. (Bosleys) $1,540

An Okitenugui kabuto, Momoyama Period (late 16th century), the russet-iron bowl of shallow form, the cap plate turning up in three places at the back and edged with soft metal fukurin. (Christie's) $12,502

An Officer's Albert pattern helmet of the North Somerset Yeomanry, white metal skull with gilt top mount, acanthus and oak wreath ornaments, leather backed chinchain and ear rosettes. (Wallis & Wallis) $1,205

Royal Air Force Officer's full dress busby, pre war example, the skull of black chromed leather, trimmed with seal dyed nutria, the plume of dyed ostrich feathers with gilt ring. (Bosleys) $659

An 1822 model Russian Dragoon's leather helmet, the helmet plate with the Imperial Arms, with brass chinguard.
(Stockholms AV) $1,199

A good French Officer's blue cloth shako, gilt plate of the Arms of Paris with motto scrolls, red white and blue roundel above plate and red feather plume.
(Wallis & Wallis) $770

An impressive French fireman's brass helmet of the Sapeurs Pompiers de St Leger, in the style of an early dragoon helmet, tall ornamental comb with black fur crest, red feather side plume in holder on left.
(Wallis & Wallis) $764

A Victorian Officer's lance cap of the 21st Lancers, as worn from 1897 to 1898 black patent leather skull with gilt lace bands, French gray cloth sides and tip with gilt cord cross lines.
(Wallis & Wallis) $6,160

Norwich Union Fire Officer's black leather helmet, brass front and back peak binding, ear to ear band, ear rosettes, Medusa head finial to comb and trophy of appliances badge with NUFO scroll below.
(Wallis & Wallis) $338

A good Officer's tall blue cloth shako of The Royal Dock Yard Battn, black patent leather peak and headband, white over red ball tuft in gilt socket.
(Wallis & Wallis) $1,120

A Kawarie Kabuto, Mid-Edo Period (18th century), the simple iron bowl extended and modelled in leather to represent a type of eboshi, the front with a bold demonic shishi molded in colored lacquers, the Hineno-jikoro of kiritsuke-kozane.
(Christie's) $25,560

A French Cuirassier Officer's 1871 pattern helmet, white metal skull with brass peak binding, ornamental comb with Medusa head finial, red "shaving brush" plume in socket and falling black hair plume.
(Wallis & Wallis) $1,453

Royal Scots Victorian Officer's helmet, pre 1901 example of an Officer's Home Service Pattern blue cloth helmet with gilt metal cross piece, spike and rose bosses. (Bosleys) $1,820

A late 16th century "Spanish" morion of good form, forged in one piece with high roped comb and border, upturned peaks to brim, brass rosettes around the base. (Wallis & Wallis) $2,002

Imperial German Prussian Reservist OR's felt Pickelhaube first pattern Ersatz issue, with gilt brass metal fittings. Complete with Prussian helmet plate. (Bosleys) $385

A good and desirable Victorian Officer's silver plated helmet of the Hampshire Carabiniers, gilt peak binding, gilt and silver plated star plate with black enamel backing to center rose, white hair plume with small gilt rosette. (Wallis & Wallis) $1,925

An important lance cap of the Duke of Cornwall's (Loyal Meneage) Yeomanry, circa 1816, believed to be the only remaining example, the skull of black leather, to the front a helmet plate of Sheffield plate, silver onto copper. (Bosleys) $12,012

An Imperial German trooper's helmet with parade eagle of the Garde du Corps, tombak skull with German silver binding to front and back peaks and studs to neck guard, leather backed detachable chinscales. (Wallis & Wallis) $4,200

South Salopian Yeomanry William IV Officer's helmet, "Roman pattern", polished metal edged with gilt metal turned edge, the skull is with gilt metal laurel leaf decoration. (Bosleys) $2,590

A French fireman's 1888 pattern brass helmet of the Sapeurs Pompiers Caen, white metal helmet plate surmounted by mural crown with laurel and oak sprays. (Wallis & Wallis) $182

A fine ERII trooper's helmet of the Royal Horse guards, plated skull with brass mounts, plated top spike and red hair plume with brass ball and plain rose leather lining. (Wallis & Wallis) $700

A Swiss combined percussion pistol and pocket-knife by Schneider, Genève, late 19th century, with octagonal barrel, hammer operated by the folding trigger also forming a corkscrew, large sprung folding knife-blade double-edged towards the point, 13cm. (Bonhams) $1,820

A scarce 2nd pattern Fairbairn Sykes personalized fighting knife, Parkerized grip with checkered design. Double edged spear point blade, fitted with straight oval cross guard. Contained in original dark brown leather scabbard with parkerized chape.
(Bosleys) $364

WW2 50/52 Middle East Commando knife, of the pattern adopted as a cap badge by 50/52 Middle East Commando. Brass parkerized knuckle duster grip with single edged six inch steel blade.
(Bosleys) $440

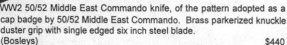

Late 19th century folding knife, Gebr Weyersberg of Solingen, single edge straight blade, two piece horn grip with folding cross guard, complete with original polished brown leather scabbard.
(Bosleys) $185

Late 18th century hunting knife, the blade double edged for the lower 3.5in., the back with a double stepped edge, hilt with a turned reeded grip and an upturned finger guard quillon to one side. Overall length 11.5in. (Bosleys) $235

Great War period Belgian training fighting knife, produced to train soldiers in the art of trench fighting. The hilt is identical to the fighting pattern, with one-piece wooden grip and oval disc shaped guard.
(Bosleys) $96

A rare US Army knife, with grooved wooden grip, bronze guard marked *US Springfield 734* and broad single edged trowel shaped blade. (Andrew Bottomley) $323

Imperial German Great War private purchase fighting knife, large example, double edged to the lower 2.5in. and with a fuller, hilt of stag's horn and fitted with a 'S' shape quillon. (Bosleys) $132

An Indian hunting knife, straight shallow diamond section blade 8in. stamped *Rodda & Co Calcutta, Mappin Brothers Sheffield* at forte. Thick white metal crosspiece, natural staghorn hilt, white metal pommel. (Wallis & Wallis) $338

A rare and unusual 19th century large knife, brass hilt with rounded pommel, decorated on one side with a stylized floral motif, guard with S-shaped quillons. Blade 12¼in. (Andrew Bottomley) $573

A rare massive mid 19th century Spanish navaja or folding knife, blade of steel with characteristic three ball decoration to the tail, stag horn grip scales, simple cruciform guard and characteristic spring catch locking mechanism, blade 15¼in. (Andrew Bottomley) $1,176

An Unwin & Rodgers Patent rim-fire knife-pistol, late 19th century, with octagonal sighted white-metal barrel, partly checkered dark horn side-plates, the butt with hinged trap cover for ammunition, 16.5cm. (Bonhams) $785

Great War French private purchase fighting knife, a scarce example of a commercially manufactured trench fighting knife, blade made from the 1871 Gras bayonet and fitted to an aluminum hilt with checkered cut decoration. (Bosleys) $162

A German Bowie type knife circa 1900, clipped back blade 8½in. stamped *Mann & Feb....n Solingen* at forte. Steel crosspiece with ball finials, 2 piece riveted staghorn grips. In its leather sheath. (Wallis & Wallis) $309

A good massive classical Bowie knife, hand forged blade 13¼in., flattened brass quillon with reversed terminals, the grip of solid finger grip shaped ivory with copper collar. (Wallis & Wallis) $3,850

A 19th century Indian Bowie knife, clipped back blade 9½in., stamped *Arnachellum Salem*. Steel crosspiece with swollen finials, natural staghorn hilt, steel pommel. In its leather sheath, cross hatched decoration overall with sprung retaining catch. (Wallis & Wallis) $441

A late Victorian Bowie type knife, broad single edged blade 7½in. stamped *..Ilotson & Co...lumbia Place Sheffield*. Thick white metal crosspiece, two piece staghorn grips. In its brown morocco leather covered sheath. (Wallis & Wallis) $576

A rare American Bowie knife, circa 1860, the pewter handle with black composition grips, inlaid with small mother of pearl circles and nickel silver escutcheon, straight edged blade, blade 7in. (Andrew Bottomley) $1,250

A 19th century folding Bowie knife, handle with lanyard ring, deer's foot grip and nickel silver bolsters decorated with stag's head. Folding guard and clipped point blade with thumb nail groove, blade 3½in. (Andrew Bottomley) $323

19th century Sheffield Bowie knife, by Ogden Brothers, Sheffield, double edged spear pointed blade with central raised rib, German silver mounts of embossed floral decoration. Two piece horn slab sided grips, overall length 11.75in. (Bosleys) $1,323

A 19th century Indian Bowie knife, broad straight single edged blade 8½in. with false edge. Steel crosspiece with swollen finials, two piece riveted natural staghorn grips of good colour. (Wallis & Wallis) $288

A good large brass-bound oak and leather cartridge magazine, by J. Purdey & Sons, for approximately 500 cartridges, red baize lined lid with maker's trade label.
(Bonhams) $1,884

An unusual miniature approximately 3.5mm (pin-fire) six-shot 'Le Petit Protecteur' ring revolver, with a full blued finish and foliate-scroll engraved brass ring ½in. chamber. In its velvet-lined presentation case with six pin-fire blanks.
(Christie's) $2,111

'Phoney War' 1940 caricature doll, as a British Tommy, wearing battledress uniform and tin hat to his head. The composition head retains a painted smiling face.
(Bosleys) $44

Even The Walls....Second World War propaganda poster, 76 x 51cm., 1939.
(Onslows) $293

H. Reuterdahl, All Together! Enlist In The Navy, lithograph in colors, 1917, backed on linen, 31 x 44½in.
(Christie's) $517

Abram Games, A.T.S. (the Alternative and Published Design to the Blonde Bombshell, poster, 76 x 51cm. (Onslows) $283

A fine Kynoch Ammunition cartridge display-mirror, the illustrations arranged around the central Kynoch trade-mark and comprising advertisements for proprietary cartridges, oak framed, 30¾in. x 26¾in. overall.
(Christie's) $1,625

Seven feather-and sawdust-filled glass ball-targets, of blue glass, with a meridian band and the following inscription N.B. Glass Works.Perth.
(Christie's) $700

A Kynoch cartridge case advertising display board, 16¾ x 15¾in., wooden frame, radial display of brass based paper cases including Kyblack, Bonax, Primax and Kardax; and .22 brass cases.
(Wallis & Wallis) $986

A scarce Georgian Officer's copper gorget of The Royal Marines, engraved 1801-16 Royal Arms over a shield with fouled anchor and laurel spray.
(Wallis & Wallis) $630

A scarce .177in. Haenel Model 26 air pistol, the top of the air chamber stamped *Haenel Mod 26 DRP/ Brit Pat No 277265/USA Pat No 1761993*, checkered brown plastic bakelite grips with Haenel logo, blued finish.
(Wallis & Wallis) $470

Sutherland Highlanders pipe banner, the tartan face embroidered with a thistle wreath in which rests a bullion crowned strap inscribed *Sutherland Highlanders*.
(Bosleys) $1,078

Join The Territorial Infantry "Yes Son, That's what I'd be doin, if I 'ad my time over again!" and Old Bill Ought to Know, TA Poster No 10, 73 x 49cm., 1938.
(Onslows) $628

Two rare Ligowsky Patent clay pigeons, by Georg Egestorff, with parts of the original newspaper packaging. (Bonhams) $252

Charles Wood, The Lifeline Is Firm Thanks to The Merchant Navy, Merchant Navy Comforts Service, double crown, with original envelope. (Onslows) $110

A fine Eley's Sporting Ammunition cartridge display-board, the cartridges arranged attractively around the central Eley Bros. Trademark, framed and glazed, 31in. x 25in. overall.
(Christie's) $2,708

Luftwaffe Navigator's wristwatch by Laco, black face with outer dial recording minutes, the inner dial hours. Fitted with a sweeping second hand.
(Bosleys) $565

A fine Kynoch cartridge-display board, the shot cartridges attractively arranged around the central G.E. Lodge print of a Peregrine falcon and grouse, and comprising approximately 140 cases, approximately 35in. x 40in. overall. (Christie's) $1,925

A US rifled percussion musket model 1861, 56in. overall, barrel 40in. with proof marks and *1863* at breech, walnut fullstock with maker's and inspector's stamps; steel mounts. (Wallis & Wallis) $847

A .44in. WCF Winchester Model 92 full tube magazine underlever carbine, 37½in. overall, round barrel 20in. stamped at breech *Model 92 Winchester 44 WCF* etc, Nitro proved, ladder rearsight, saddle ring on left, walnut stock. (Wallis & Wallis) $1,224

An unusual 6 shot 20 bore pin fire Belgian double action revolving sporting gun, 47½, octagonal smooth bore barrel 29½in. Liege proved. Sliding cartridge case ejector, side gate loading, elaborately scrolled trigger guard, plain steel buttcap, walnut stock. (Wallis & Wallis) $700

An 11mm Model 1866 Chassepot bolt action needle fire SS military rifle, 51½in. overall, barrel 32½in. numbered *H74816* and dated *1868* at breech, walnut fullstock, steel mounts with sling swivels and extending triangular section bayonet. (Wallis & Wallis) $378

A .54in. rimfire Spencer's Patent breech loading repeating carbine 39in. overall, barrel 22in. with hinged rearsight; walnut halfstock with steel mounts, short saddle bar and ring. (Wallis & Wallis) $1,425

A 15mm Prussian Jaeger military percussion rifle, 44in. overall, octagonal barrel 28½in. with deep 8 groove rifling; the half round lock of flintlock form with hinged nipple protector; walnut fullstock with cheek piece on butt. (Wallis & Wallis) $980

A .420in. (?) Winchester Model 1873 half tube magazine underlever sporting rifle, 43¼in. overall, octagonal barrel 24in. with London proofs for ".420", name and address on top flat, ratchet rearsight, walnut stock. (Wallis & Wallis) $735

A good German 16 bore sporting rifle, circa 1810, converted to percussion circa 1840, 44in. overall, heavy octagonal Persian barrel 28½in. with rounded breech and faceted muzzle, the breech decorated with silver inlay, double set triggers; walnut fullstock with cheek piece and sliding patch box cover. (Wallis & Wallis) $1,008

A German 8mm rimfire underlever hammerless Rook Rifle, 39¼in. overall, blued octagonal barrel 24½in. with matted top flat, double set triggers, walnut butt with cheekpiece and checkered pistol grip; sling swivels. (Wallis & Wallis) $432

A good .577in. Mark II Snider 3 band breech loading military rifle, 54in. overall, barrel 36½in. with Tower proofs, the lock marked with crowned *VR* and *1863 Enfield*; walnut fullstock with regulation brass mounts. (Wallis & Wallis) $805

A .577in. Snider 3 band Volunteer rifle, 55in. overall, barrel 36½in. with London proofs and stamped *LAC*, the tail of the lock plate stamped with crown over *VR*, nicely figured walnut fullstock, the butt stamped with London Armoury stamp. (Wallis & Wallis) $882

A .577/450in. Martini Henry Mark III military rifle, 49½in. overall, barrel 33¼in. with government proofs, walnut fullstock with bayonet lug on front barrel band, sling swivels. (Wallis & Wallis) $617

A scarce .451in. Whitworth P/63 hexagonal bore 3 band short military percussion rifle, 48½in. overall, barrel 33in. with Enfield and later London civilian proofs, the rearsight graduated for hexagonal or cylindrical bullets, walnut fullstock. (Wallis & Wallis) $2,520

A model 1854 Dreyse Needlefire military rifle, 49in., barrel 30in. numbered *457* on breech, two leaf rearsight to 800 metres. Regulation bolt action, brass mounts, steel sling swivels and extending triangular section bayonet. (Wallis & Wallis) $1,820

A Belgian 17mm. pinfire plated, brass barrelled blunderbuss, 20in., nickel plated ½in. octagonal flared barrel 9½in. Liege proved, with top sliding hammer safety catch. Foliate engraved plated back action lock and steel mounts, walnut stock. (Wallis & Wallis) $1,305

A 54-bore percussion sporting rifle by Jackson, London, mid-19th century, with twist octagonal leaf-sighted barrel rifled for a belted ball and signed on the top flat at the breech, scroll engraved breech with pierced platinum plug, 71.7cm. barrel. (Bonhams) $1,400

A good .300in. Westley Richards 'Sherwood' Matini action take down SS sporting rifle, 44in. overall, detachable barrel 27½in. with maker's name, patent dates and caliber, and fully adjustable rearsight; the frame with patent removable action, walnut halfstock with checkered for end and wrist. (Wallis & Wallis) $1,400

A 7.92mm Mauser Model 1896 bolt action cavalry carbine, 37½in. overall, barrel 18in., number 3926, by Ludw Loewe & Co, Berlin, short ladder rearsight, walnut fullstock. (Wallis & Wallis) $221

A good French 14 bore percussion target pistol, 15½in. overall, fine damascus octagonal barrel 10in. with deep rifling, and with front and rear sights, the lock engraved, walnut halfstock with carved fore end and fluted butt. (Wallis & Wallis) $691

A good 16 bore E.I.G. percussion lanyard pistol, 13½in. overall, blued barrel 8in., Tower military proved. Fullstocked. Regulation brass mounts, reblued swivel ramrod and lanyard ring, stock maker Isaac Hollis & Sons. (Wallis & Wallis) $770

An 18-bore percussion officer's pistol by Henry 2 Tatham, 37 Charing Cross, London, circa 1850, with rebrowned twist sighted barrel, scroll engraved breech with platinum line, scroll engraved back-action lock signed in full and fitted with a safety-catch, 35.5cm. (Bonhams) $308

A good double barrelled 16 bore percussion holster pistol, by G & J Deane, London Bridge, 13½in. overall, browned twist barrels 8in. with maker's name on rib and gold line at breech; back action locks engraved with scrollwork and maker's name; walnut fullstock with checkered butt. (Wallis & Wallis) $924

A 9mm Astra Para Model 600 semi-automatic pistol, No. 16118, blued overall and stamped *Unceta y Compania S.A. Guernica Espana*, grip-safety, checkered wooden grips, and much original finish, Spanish proof, 21cm. (Bonhams) $168

A scarce .753in. Tower 1842 pattern percussion Lancer pistol of the 16th Lancers, 15½in. overall, barrel 9in. with Tower proofs, and various inspector's marks at breech; the walnut fullstock with inspector's and government sale marks; regulation brass mounts. (Wallis & Wallis) $1,540

A .577in. Lancer's type Volunteer rifled percussion holster pistol, 16½in., blued barrel 10in. with London private proofmarks, standing rearsight. Fullstocked, color hardened lock, regulation brass mounts, swivel ramrod, steel lanyard loop to buttcap.(Wallis & Wallis) $732

A rare .22LR Remington 1891 target rolling block pistol, No. 46, circa 1892-98, with blued barrel and octagonal breech, the latter with blued back-sight of buckhorn type, case-hardened frame with patent dates on one side, 35.5cm. (Bonhams) $770

An Officer's 16 bore percussion holster pistol converted from flintlock with breech drum, by Prosser, Charing Cross, London, 14in. overall, flat topped round barrel 8¾in., plain stepped lock with safety bolt and engraved with maker's name; walnut stock with flattened checkered butt. (Wallis & Wallis) $280

A 28-bore percussion coastguard pistol, dated *1846*, with iron barrel, dated border engraved flat bevelled lock with tower and *VR* crowned, walnut full stock struck with inspector's marks and retailer's name *G. Ewart*, 29cm. (Bonhams) $336

Á 7.63 Mauser 'Broom Handle' semi-automatic pistol, circa 1966, blued overall and stamped *Waffenfabrik Mauser Oberndorf A Neckar*, blued adjustable back-sight calibrated from 50 to 1000, 30cm. (Bonhams) $2,520

A Spanish 15-bore percussion belt pistol signed for Jose Aranguren en Eibar, Ano 1858, with browned octagonal sighted barrel signed and dated in silver and inlaid with silver foliage, engraved breech and tang, foliate engraved back-action lock, walnut full stock, 26cm. (Bonhams) $336

A six-shot pin-fire pocket revolver of small bore, late 19th century, with blued octagonal sighted barrel, blued cylinder, blued frame with hinged loading gate, bright cartridge-extractor and folding trigger, checkered walnut grip, 19cm. (Bonhams) $112

A rare 54-bore Bentley Patent five-shot self-cocking percussion revolver, No. A664, circa 1855, with octagonal sighted barrel, cylinder, border engraved frame decorated with scrollwork, patent screw-rammer (hammer-safety incomplete), scroll engraved trigger-guard and butt, and checkered walnut grips (rust patinated overall), Birmingham proof marks, 31cm. (Bonhams) $588

A 5 shot 54 bore Tranter's patent double action percussion revolver, 12in. overall, barrel 6in. engraved on top flat *Jas Purdey, 314½ Oxford St, London;* London proved; scroll engraved frame, breech and rammer. (Wallis & Wallis) $840

An American Colt 1860 Model Army percussion revolver No. 54497 for 1862, with sighted barrel with New-York address, rebated cylinder with naval engagement scene, frame cut for a shoulder-stock, brass trigger-guard, rammer, walnut grips, 35cm. (Bonhams) $1,330

A 6 shot .44 Starr Arms Co SA Army percussion revolver, 13½in. overall, barrel 8in., number 26285 on frame and 27731 on cylinder, plain walnut butt. (Wallis & Wallis) $847

A 5 shot .32in. rimfire Smith & Wesson 3rd Model single action revolver, 7½in. overall, barrel 3½in., plain rosewood grips, the right frame engraved *From Lawrence Harrigan, Chief of Police, to L A Moffett, Dec 3rd.*
(Wallis & Wallis) $426

A 6 shot .36in. Whitney single action 2nd model Navy percussion revolver, 13in. overall, octagonal barrel 7¾in., faint traces of cylinder scene, bronze trigger guard, plain walnut grips. (Wallis & Wallis) $676

An unusual Belgian 6 shot 70 bore open frame ring trigger self-cocking percussion revolver, 13in. overall, octagonal barrel 7in. stamped on left side *David H..... Brevete*, and with hinged rammer; Liege proved and British view mark; scroll engraved frame; pale walnut one piece butt. (Wallis & Wallis) $595

A 6 shot .44 Starr Arms Co self-cocking Army percussion revolver, 11½in. overall, barrel 6in., number 22670; plain walnut butt. (Wallis & Wallis) $910

An American Colt 1849 model pocket percussion six-shot revolver, No. 201181 for 1862, with 10.2cm. octagonal sighted barrel with Hartford address, cylinder with roll engraved stagecoach hold-up scene, 22.5cm. (Bonhams) $672

A nickel-plated 120-bore five-shot self-cocking percussion revolver of Bentley type, late 19th century, with octagonal sighted barrel, top-strap engraved with foliage, foliate scroll engraved frame, trigger-guard and butt, Birmingham proof marks, 19in. (Bonhams) $266

A 6 shot 54 bore open frame bar hammer transitional percussion revolver, 12in. overall, octagonal barrel 5½in.-, B'ham proved; scroll engraved rounded frame, trigger guard and butt strap; checkered walnut grips. (Wallis & Wallis) $238

A good embossed copper gun size powder flask, 'overall', 8in overall, by Dixon charger for 3 to 4 drams. (Wallis & Wallis) $224

A good embossed copper pistol size powder flask, 'oak leaf', 5in. overall, by Hawksley, charger for ³/₈ to ⁵/₈ drams. (Wallis & Wallis) $420

A good embossed copper gun size powder flask, 'fluted', 8¼in. overall by Hawksley, charger for 2½ to 3½ drams. (Wallis & Wallis) $33

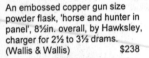

An embossed copper gun size powder flask, 'horse and hunter in panel', 8½in. overall, by Hawksley, charger for 2½ to 3½ drams. (Wallis & Wallis) $238

An early 19th century French horn powder flask, 7½in. overall; pear shaped body; brass top with plunger charger; 4 hanging rings. (Wallis & Wallis) $154

A good embossed copper pistol size powder flask, 'shell' , 5in. overall, with common top and tapered charger. (Wallis & Wallis) $182

A very fine mid 19th century German powder flask, carved from a section of stag horn. Depicting a pair of stags in a forest setting on one side, 6in. overall. (Andrew Bottomley) $1,838

An early 19th century French flattened horn powder flask, 12in. overall, the body decorated with ribbed designs, brass top with revolving charger and sight glass, plain brass base. (Wallis & Wallis) $308

A horn powder flask of the Percy Tenantry, Alnwick Castle, circa 1800, 12½in. overall; brass top with cup type charger, engraved I/41, the brass base engraved with the Percy Crest. (Wallis & Wallis) $462

An embossed copper powder flask, 8¼in. with three horse's heads within foliate frame, common brass top stamped G & J W Hawksley Sheffield. (Wallis & Wallis) $262

An embossed copper gun size powder flask 'panel', patent German silver top, with imitation hallmarks, by Dixon, charger for 2½ to 3½ drams, the center of the panel design engraved L. Mathias, Lamphey Court. (Wallis & Wallis) $434

An early 19th century French flattened horn powder flask, 10in. overall; brass top with revolving cut off and sight glass, the charger stamped Boche Bte a Paris; flat brass base. (Wallis & Wallis) $308

1st Royal Devon Yeomanry Cavalry Officer's sabretache, Victorian, black patent leather flap mounted with a gilt multi rayed star. (Bosleys) $864

2nd VB Somerset Light Infantry Officer's sabretache, mounted Officer's undress example of brown leather, flap bearing large ornate silvered strung bugle. (Bosleys) $204

Sherwood Rangers Victorian Officer's sabretache, dark green velvet face embroidered with bullion strung bugle surmounted by a large padded Crown with crimson velvet cap. (Bosleys) $1,256

Canadian Artillery Victorian Officer's sabretache, dark blue melton cloth ground richly embroidered with a gold bullion entwined VRI cypher, surmounted by a Guelphic style Crown. (Bosleys) $1,047

A good Victorian Officer's full dress embroidered crimson cloth sabretache, circa 1875 of The 11th (Prince Albert's Own) Hussars, embroidered Guelphic Crown, title, regimental badge and motto. (Wallis & Wallis) $1,295

North Somerset Yeomanry Victorian Officer's sabretache, dark blue melton cloth face embroidered with silver bullion VR Cypher surmounted by a padded Crown with crimson velvet cap. (Bosleys) $581

12th Royal Lancers Officer's undress sabretache, patent leather flap mounted with a gilt Regimental device of crossed lances pennons flying, surmounted by Prince of Wales plumes. (Bosleys) $1,099

A Victorian Officer's full dress embroidered sabretache of The Royal Artillery, gilt lace border, embroidered Royal Arms, laurel wreath and motto scrolls, solid gilt cannon. (Wallis & Wallis) $490

Victorian Yorkshire Hussars sabretache attributed to the Earl of Feversham, scarlet cloth face, edged with silver lace of regimental pattern, bearing large silver bullion Rose of the House of York. (Bosleys) $785

A General Officer's Victorian mameluke dress sword, blade 29½in. etched with crowned VR amidst foliage, by Hamburger Rogers & Co. Copper crosspiece chiselled with foliage in relief, two piece ivory grips with ornamental rivet heads. In its steel scabbard.
(Wallis & Wallis) $595

A good Officer's dress sword, circa 1835, of the Royal Horse Guards, plain, straight fullered blade, 39in. with hatchet tip, by *Prosser, Manufacturer to the King, London,* deeply struck proof mark at forte, ornamental brass hilt of special pattern with a rose on the back of the pommel, wirebound, fishskin covered grip.
(Wallis & Wallis) $2,940

A 1788 pattern Light Dragoon Officer's sword blade 33½in. etched *Light Dragoons* with Hussar mounted on prancing charger, trophy of arms. Regulation steel stirrup hilt, sharkskin covered ribbed grip. In its regulation steel scabbard. (Wallis & Wallis) $840

A Victorian Officer's 1854 pattern sword of the Coldstream Guards, very slightly curved fullered blade 32½in. by Wilkinson, etched with crowned VR cypher, regimental badge, 10 battle honours Lincelles to Sevastopol, owner's crest and motto. (Wallis & Wallis) $476

A very unusual Light Cavalry Officer's sword of 1796 pattern type, broad blade of T section, 32¾in., *AM*, false edge at tip. Steel stirrup hilt, silver wire bound fishskin covered grip, elongated pommel. In its steel scabbard. (Wallis & Wallis) $784

A hallmarked silver mounted smallsword, hollow ground triangular section blade 32½in. with traces of etched foliate devices. London hallmarks, guard, pommel and quillon block pierced with floral spray. (Wallis & Wallis) $1,050

An unusual mounted Rifle Officer's sword circa 1825, pipe back blade 31in. Steel triple bar guard with large pierced quillon, fishskin covered grip with three pairs of ornamental rivets. In steel scabbard. (Wallis & Wallis) $700

An Edward VII mark II drummer's sword, blade 13in., brass cruciform hilt with *ER VII*, cypher on quillon block, the pommel numbered 21, in its brass mounted leather scabbard. (Wallis & Wallis) $216

58

A Georgian Warrant Officer's sword circa 1825-32, blade 28in. etched with military trophies, flowers and foliage. Copper gilt stirrup hilt, fouled anchors in relief on langets, stepped pommel. Copper wire bound fishskin grip. (Wallis & Wallis) $446

A 1796 pattern type Cavalry Officer's sword, pipe back blade 32¾in. etched with traces of maker's name. Steel stirrup guard, swollen quillon finial, elongated steel pommel, wire bound sharkskin grip. (Wallis & Wallis) $302

A French Model 1882 Infantry Officer's presentation sword dated *1915*, slender double edged blade 33½in. with deep off set fullers, etched *A Monsieur Le Dr Waroux, Medecin Principal De lere Classe, Directeur. Calais le 15 Novbre 1915 – Le Personnel Medical Administratif De L'Ambulance Elisabeth.* (Wallis & Wallis) $455

A decorative Chinese double sword, straight double edged blades 28in. silver damascened overall. Brass crosspieces and pommels chiselled with dragons and etched with characters on flat reverse sides. Bone grips engraved with figures. In its black painted scabbards. (Wallis & Wallis) $456

A good mid 18th century Scottish three-quarter basket hilted backsword, bi-fullered single edged blade 36in. with false edge at tip. Basket well forged with rectangular openings, a row of 3 heart shapes at base, and 2 diamond shapes around bun shaped pommel with baluster button. (Wallis & Wallis) $1,680

A good Edward VII 1831 pattern General Officer's mameluke hilted sword, slightly curved, flat blade 33in. by Rogers & Co, retaining all original polish etched with crowned Edward VII cypher, cross sword and baton and palm wreaths within scrolled frosted panels, regulation gilt hilt. (Wallis & Wallis) $980

A good French russet gilt hilted smallsword, circa 1765, hollow ground triangular section blade 32in. etched with military trophies, and foliate devices. Iron hilt, pierced guard, quillon block, knucklebow and pommel with basket of flowers within geometric field, partly gilt. (Wallis & Wallis) $665

A French 1st Empire Infantry Officer's sword, slightly curved fullered single edged blade 28¾in. etched with military trophies and small foliate devices, blued and gilt for almost half length. Brass stirrup hilt, horn grip. (Wallis & Wallis) $720

1788 pattern Light Dragoon Officer's sword, single edged curved blade with fuller also retaining faint engraved decoration, hilt with single stirrup guard and shagreen grip. (Bosleys) $470

An unusual early S Indian broadsword, broad straight double edged blade 30in. with triple fullers and rounded tip. Good quality bronze hilt with swollen quillons and fluted pommel. (Wallis & Wallis) $631

A scarce 1788 pattern Light Dragoon Officer's sword, probably of the 12th Prince of Wales Light Dragoons, blade 34½in. etched crowned *GR* and Royal Arms, large Prince of Wales's feather device; and Woolley & Co. Regulation steel stirrup hilt, ribbed sharkskin covered grip. (Wallis & Wallis) $735

A good quality 19th century Chinese silver mounted sword, broad straight double edged blade 26¾in., silver crosspiece embossed and chased with a dragon in high relief. Copper grip inlaid on both sides with silver character, engraved silver ferrules. In its copper sheath (Wallis & Wallis) $1,078

A scarce Royal Horse Guards trooper's sword circa 1796, straight blade 35½in. with hatchet point, struck with government inspector's mark Regulations pierced steel hilt surrounded by triangular openings, knuckle-bow with twin supporting bars. In its steel scabbard faintly engraved *Woolley & Deakin Birmm*, with 2 hanging rings. (Wallis & Wallis) $1,890

A scarce 1814 pattern Household Cavalry Officer's sword, straight bi-fullered blade 34in. Regulation copper guard with crown bearing the lion upon further crown amidst foliage. Wire bound sharkskin grip, in its brass scabbard with sharkskin filled rectangular openings. (Wallis & Wallis) $3,500

A 15th Hussars Officer's levee sword circa 1870, blade 32in. etched with crowned *King's 15th Hussars*, Hawkes & Co London, Manufacturer to the Queen. Regulation brass mounts with traces of gilt, two piece ivory grips, partly checkered, partly foliate carved. In its copper gilt mounted scabbard. (Wallis & Wallis) $1,015

A good Victorian 1821 pattern Light Cavalry Officer's sword of the 15th (the King's) Hussars, slightly curved fullered blade 35in., by Henry Wilkinson, etched with Regimental badge, title and motto, crowned VR cypher, 8 battle honors *Emsdorf* to *Afghanistan 1878-80*. (Wallis & Wallis) $714

A composite rapier circa 1600, shallow diamond section blade 34½in. stamped both sides with crowned *G* at forte. Nicely formed guard with recurved quillons, and transverse 'S' shaped bar. Fluted steel wire bound grip. (Wallis & Wallis) $2,310

A massive 19th century Afghan "Khyber Sword", 47¼in., T section blade 42½in., engraved with floral and foliate decoration along back edge and overall. Two piece ribbed horn grips, brass gripstrap and ferrules. (Wallis & Wallis) $535

A Georgian infantry Grenadier Company Officer's saber, curved, fullered blade 29in., etched *Osborn's* and *Warranted* with crowned GR cypher,1801-16 Royal Arms, seated Britannia, trophy of arms and a small grenade. (Wallis & Wallis) $1,015

An impressive French polished steel and gilt hilted smallsword circa 1770, slender hollow ground triangular section blade 31in. etched *Liger Md fourbisseur rue Coquilliere a la justice Paris*, with military trophy, foliate and strapwork devices, the etching gilt. Steel hilt chiselled in low relief with trophies allegorical of war and the liberal arts against a granular gold foil ground. (Wallis & Wallis) $2,170

An unusual Persian shortsword Qama broad straight double edged blade 23¼in. of darkened steel, deep off set fullers, gold damascened on both sides with Islamic inscription dated *AH 1221* (=1806 AD). (Wallis & Wallis) $416

A scarce hallmarked silver hilted Scottish basket hilted broadsword, straight double edged bi-fullered blade 32½in. Basket hilt hallmarked for Edinburgh 1909, maker's mark *J.S.C.*, geometrically pierced overall and nicely engraved with Celtic ornaments and devices. (Wallis & Wallis) $2,240

A fine basket hilted broadsword circa 1740, English or Scottish, straight double edged blade 33½in. deeply struck in the short shallow fuller *Andria:Ferara* on both sides; chiselled with orb and running wolf maker's marks retaining some copper inlay. Finely wrought basket. (Wallis & Wallis) $2,849

A good 1796 Light Cavalry Officer's blued and gilt sword, broad blade 33in., etched blued and gilt with crowned GR cypher, Royal Arms (1801-16), trophies of arms, armed cavalryman on rearing charger, Union flowers and foliage for 19in., the rest polished. (Wallis & Wallis) $1,890

A fine Japanese ivory-mounted exhibition wakizashi, signed *Hokuka*, late 19th century, the efu-no-tachi-style scabbard, curved hilt and mokkogata tsuba deeply carved, and with two carved suspension loops (one detached), 106cm. long. (Bonhams & Brooks) $4,640

A sturdy Japanese katana, the blade unsigned, with blade honzukuri and shallow torii-zori, modern itomaki-no-tachi-style scabbard, hilt and gilt-metal fittings, purple itomaki, and a pair of late Edo Period bronze and gilt dragon menuki, 68cm. blade. (Bonhams & Brooks) $1,189

A Japanese katana, the blade unsigned, with blade honzukuri and shallow torii-zori, wide single grooves on omote, modern nashiji lacquered scabbard, oval iron tsuba, shakudo nanako and gold fuchi-kashira decorated with huts among pine in takabori, 66cm. blade. (Bonhams & Brooks) $696

An extremely fine mid 19th century daisho, comprising katana and wakisashi, each with matching hilts, furniture and scabbards, hilts with aquamarine blue braid bound shark skin covered grips, blades 27 and 19½in. (Andrew Bottomley) $21,315

A fine Nanbokucho Tachi blade attributed to Kinju, Nanbokucho Period, (14th Century), the blade, honzukuri, iorimune, toriizori with extended chugissaki, itame-masame with o-mokumehada and chikei and dense ji-nie, ko-midare hamon of nie with much sunagashi, hakikakke boshi, o-suriage nakago, Mino Province, 27½in., in its black ishimeji lacquer saya. (Christie's) $33,934

A good Japanese WWII army Officer's sword katana, blade 66.2cm., signed *Noshu Seki Ju Munetada* and dated *Showa*, with Seki arsenal stamp. Ko choji hamon, itame hada, fair polish. In shin gunto mounts, with khaki painted steel saya. (Wallis & Wallis) $870

A finely mounted katana, Mei: Norimitsu, Muromachi Period (15th century), the blade, honzukuri, iorimune, koshizori with chugissaki, itamehada with ji-nie, gunome hamon of nioi with sunagashi, hakikakke boshi,ubu nakago, 26½in., in its diagonally ribbed black lacquer saya with a set of matching shakudo han-dachi mounts. (Christie's) $9,556

A Japanese Itomaki-No-Tachi, the blade signed *Gyoen*, with blade honzukuri and torii-zori, Mito Mokkogata iron tsuba decorated with two puppies among flowers, and modern red lacquered scabbard and green itomaki koshirae with black lacquered 'fittings', 66.6cm. blade. (Bonhams & Brooks) $986

A Japanese katana, the blade unsigned, with blade honzukuri and torri-zorii, modern red lacquered saya, large
on mokkogata tsuba, iron fuchi decorated in iroe takazogan with three oni carrying off Shoki's hat, iron kashira
with two arrowheads in silver takazogan, and large gilt shakudo menuki each modelled as a fishing net and a
crescent moon, 68.6cm. blade. (Bonhams & Brooks)
$899

A Japanese Naval kaigunto, the tang with traces of signature, with regulation officer's pattern hilt, scabbard and
fittings, 70.1cm. blade. (Bonhams & Brooks)
$696

Japanese katana, the blade unsigned, 18th/19th century, with blade honzukuri and torii-zori, ubu nakago with
one mekugi-ana, gilt-iron aorigata tsuba, soft-metal fuchi-kashira and menuki, and modern ribbed black lacquer
scabbard, 61cm. blade. (Bonhams & Brooks)
$609

Japanese Eju-No-Tachi, 19th century, mounted in cloisonné enamel (shippo) and sentoku, the koshirae and
tuba decorated in colors on a black ground with prunus blossoms, 63cm. blade.
Bonhams)
$580

An unusual Japanese WWII army Officer's sword katana, blade 57.7cm. signed *Fumei* with identical inscription
both sides, and dated *Bunki 1501* on back edge of nakago, 2 mekugi ana. Bo hi gunome hamon. In shin
gunto mounts. (Wallis & Wallis)
$1,088

Japanese WWII army Officer's sword katana, blade 66cm. signed *Masayasu, Showa to*, Muji hada, gunome
hamon, fair polish, in shin gunto mounts with steel saya. (Wallis & Wallis)
$566

Japanese katana, the blade signed *Bizen Nagafune...chika*, 16th/17th century, with blade honzukuri and torii-
ri, wide groove on omote, ubu nakago with two mekugi-ana, mottled red and black lacquer saya with
ndachi-style copper-gilt nanako with fittings en suite to the hilt, bronze shishi-ni-botan menuki, and bronze
late mokkogata tsuba, 61.7cm. blade. (Bonhams & Brooks)
$1,230

Japanese katana, the blade unsigned, Edo Period, with blade honzukuri and shallow torii-zori, wild midare
mon (kizu), iron mokkogata tsuba decorated in takobori and iroe takazogan with the shochikubia, soft-metal
hi-kashira, and modern silk-covered saya fitted with an old iron kojiri, 60.4cm. blade.
onhams & Brooks)
$551

FASCINATING FACTS
JAPANESE SWORDS

The most valuable type of Japanese swords are traditional Samurai examples, which have been handed down in Japanese families through generations. The classic Samurai sword evolved with a slightly shorter blade between 24-36in., worn in its scabbard through the belt, with cutting edge facing upwards and is known as the katana. The wooden scabbards, often lacquered, are usually made of magnolia.

A katana would originally have been accompanied by a slightly smaller sword of similar shape called a wakizashi. This pairing is known as a daisho, literally meaning large and small.

In old Japan, a man entitled to wear a daisho would normally, on entering a host's home, leave his katana by the door as a mark of repect. Parting with the smaller wakizashi would be seen as an extra mark of trust.

Makers' signatures, where present, are engraved on the tangs of the blades, hidden inside the cloth bound handles. A wooden dowel holds the sharkskin covered handle onto the tang. Removing the handle from the metal tang to find the maker can be dangerous, however, and many an expert has cut himself at this stage.

(Michael Bowman)

An early Edo shinchu tsuba, Edo Period, (17th century), the mokkogata shinchu plate with a broad rim, inlaid with peonies, leaves and tendrils, 7.9cm.
(Christie's) $4,935

A fine large tsuba by Kobayashi Geiju signed *Unpu no ju Kobayashi Yashiro Geiju saku*, Edo Period (18th century), the iron plate carved with three shahihoko, the rim with traces of nunomezogan, 8.6cm.
(Christie's) $5,640

A sentoku tsuba by Shoami Kiyonari, signed, late 17th century, the rounded square sentoku plate pierced with mushrooms and sparsely decorated with pinecones in gilt, silver and shakudo, 7.7cm.
(Christie's) $10,575

A large iron mokko tsuba, signed, 8.2cm., of nicely forged etched mokume, raised rim, pierced with two dragon flies in negative silhouette.
(Wallis & Wallis) $406

An early umetada tsuba, Edo Period (early 17th century), the broad oval slightly dished sentoku plate with a fine ishime surface, inlaid in shakudo with fruit and leaves in the style of Myoju, 7.7cm.
(Christie's) $7,403

An early shoami tsuba, 17th century, the mokkogata sentoku plate chiselled with waves and inlaid in shakudo and gilt with pine trees, fishing boats and nets, gilt details, 8.2cm.
(Christie's) $3,340

A fine and important tsuba by Shaomi Denbei, signed, 17/18th century, the shibuichi plate chiselled with a combination of the Irinbo and tomoe within the rim, 7.9cm. (Christie's) $28,200

A sentoku tsuba by Sato Chinkyu, signed, Edo Period (circa 1700), the rounded square sentoku plate inlaid in copper and shakudo with a man poling a boat, 6.8cm. (Christie's) $12,690

A pierced and chiselled rounded iron tsuba, 7.2cm. with three flowering chrysanthemum blooms and leaves in relief, gold inlaid petals. (Wallis & Wallis) $152

A shakudo tsuba ascribed to hironaga, with signature *Ichijosai Hironaga* and a Kao, Edo Period (19th century), the broad oval plate decorated in iroe takazogan with the legend of the badger tea kettle, 7.6cm. (Christie's) $7,050

An iron tsuba by Yurakusai Sekibun, signed, 19th century, chiselled in shishiaibori with a cherry tree, the blossom inlaid in silver and gilt takazogan, gilt details, 6.67cm. (Christie's) $4,935

A large early Umetada School tsuba, unsigned, early 17th century, the sentoku plate formed as five overlapping plates with a fine ishime surface, with mon, pine needles and birds in silver and gilt, 7.9cm. (Christie's) $2,790

A tsuba ascribed to Otsuki Mitsuoki, signed, 19th century, irregular oval sentoku plate decorated in iroe takazogan with snow covered bamboo grass by a stream, 6.7cm. (Christie's) $12,338

A shakudo tsuba ascribed to Nagatsune, Edo Period (19th century), the oval shakudo nanako plate with New Year Festival decorations in relief, 6.1cm. (Christie's) $7,050

A shakudo tsuba with cloisonné inlay, 18/19th century, the oval shakudo plate inlaid with a mantis in gilt hirazogan and various insects inlaid in cloisonné enamel, 6.7cm. (Christie's) $5,640

A scarce Lieutenant's 1857 pattern full dress scarlet tunic of The 16th (Bedfordshire) Regt, yellow facings, gilt and crimson shoulder sash and tassels. (Wallis & Wallis) $616

Government of Bombay Officer's frock coat, turn of the century example of dark blue melton cloth. Across the chest, eight rows of black mohair lace. (Bosleys) $339

An Oberfeldwebel's parade tunic, of the 9th Transport Unit, with powder blue piping to the collar, cuffs and epaulettes. (Bosleys) $294

17th Lancers Officer's plastron tunic, of fine dark blue woollen cloth with white plastron to the front. White is repeated to the facings of the cuffs and collar, edged with gold regimental pattern flat lace. (Bosleys) $882

Petty Officer WRENS uniform and cap, comprising dark blue double breasted woollen jacket with gilt King's Crown naval buttons, complete with skirt and black velvet tricorn cap. (Bosleys) $280

The Edinburgh or Queen's Regiment of Light Infantry Militia Officer's tunic, 1856 pattern scarlet example with dark blue facings to collars and cuffs, each decorated with silver lace embroidery, single crimson loop shoulder cord. (Bosleys) $490

Royal Canadian Army Medical Corps WW2 battledress blouse, dated *April 1945* retaining original cloth insignia. To each sleeve embroidered RCAMC titles and 1st Canadian Corps badges. (Bosleys) $94

German WWII period Army combat tunic, M43 pattern, worn by a Private of a Cavalry Regiment (yellow). Green wool material, with pleats to the pocket. (Bosleys) $454

A Captain's full dress scarlet tunic of the Coldstream Guards, circa 1920, high square collar, blue facings, white piping, applied Garter Star, with Staff Officer's gilt and red aiguilette and tags. (Wallis & Wallis) $580

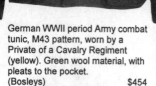

Major General's child's miniature uniform, worn by the son of Major General Dermott Dunlop CB, whilst General Officer Commanding Singapore. Khaki Drill jacket, with scarlet gorget patches and slip on Major General rank insignia to the shoulder strap. (Bosleys) $176

A scarce Officer's full dress scarlet tunic, circa 1859, of the 4th Madras Native Infantry, long and loose fitting, royal blue facings, gilt (faded) lace trim, good gilt scalloped edge buttons bearing elephant within circle *IV Regt Assaye*.(Wallis & Wallis) $206

17th Lancers Trooper's plastron tunic, of dark blue woollen cloth with white plastron to the front. White is repeated to the facings of the cuffs and collar. Yellow mohair epaulettes to the shoulders. (Bosleys) $353

Luftwaffe Flack NCO service tunic, worn by an Unteroffizier. The four pocket tunic has red (Anti Aircraft Artillery) collar patches mounted with one alloy double wing. Both the collar and shoulder boards are with silver lace edging. (Bosleys) $323

An Officer's uniform, circa 1925, of the Life Guards, comprising: full dress scarlet tunic, blue peaked cap, white leather pantaloons; overalls, khaki breeches. (Wallis & Wallis) $870

Victorian Royal Irish Regiment Officer's scarlet tunic, 1880 pattern full dress tunic, scarlet melton cloth with dark blue facings to the collar and cuffs. (Bosleys) $385

Royal Artillery WW1 Officer's cuff rank tunic, 1908 pattern, to each cuff, rank lace and insignia denoting Lieutenant Colonel. To the left breast, medal ribbons. (Bosleys) $470

91st Punjabi Rifles (Frontier Force) Officer's helmet and tunic. The foreign service style helmet is of the high crown pattern, Rifle pattern tunic of beige melton cloth with red facings to collar and cuffs. (Bosleys) $2,058

Royal Naval Division Officer's Great War tunic, khaki service dress tunic adopted by the Division during the Great War. To each cuff special pattern Naval rank lace indicating Commander, complete with bronzed Royal Navy buttons. (Bosleys) $864

Northumberland Fusiliers Militia Officer's scarlet 1880 pattern tunic. Brown facings to collar and cuffs, each edged with bullion lace. (Bosleys) $154

2nd or North Durham Militia Officer's coatee, scarlet melton cloth with white facings to the cuffs, collar and tails. (Bosleys) $882

Surrey Yeomanry Officer's full dress tunic, just prior to the Great War, dark blue material, with Lancer plastron front. (Bosleys) $308

Essex Imperial Yeomanry Officer's tunic, pre 1908 example of green melton cloth with scarlet facings to the cuff and collar, the collar edged with gold lace. (Bosleys) $210

19th century South Seas warrior's coconut jacket, a most unusual and rare example constructed of coconut fibers; cord loop fastening to front. Good condition for age. (Bosleys) $426

Late Victorian military pattern Officer's frock coat, dark blue melton cloth. Across the chest, four double rows of black worsted lace. (Bosleys) $338

Royal Buckinghamshire Hussars Trooper's uniform, pre Great War example of the Eton style tunic, dark blue material, with scarlet facings to the collar. (Bosleys) $529

Shropshire Militia pre 1855 Officer's coatee, scarlet melton cloth with green facings to the cuffs, collar, the tails, edged with white turn backs. (Bosleys) $588

Lincolnshire Militaria Victorian Officer's mess jacket, scarlet melton cloth jacket of stable pattern, with white facings to the collar and cuffs, bullion rank of Colonel with scarlet waist coat. (Bosleys)   £213

Trinity College Dublin Georgian Officer's coatee, worn by an Officer of the Infantry Corps, pattern introduced circa 1799. Scarlet cloth, with dark blue facings. (Bosleys) $1,617

Two "Flying Tiger" Chinese Air Force uniforms, American style Officer's tunic of light weight green material, bullion rank insignia denoting Colonel, with an American style cap, and other ORs Chinese uniform. (Bosleys) $1,848

Royal Household Postillion's state jacket, worn by the coachman of the Royal Household on state occasions, possibly Edwardian, scarlet melton cloth, royal blue facings. (Bosleys) $1,413

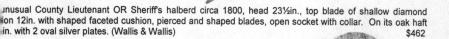

unusual County Lieutenant OR Sheriff's halberd circa 1800, head 23½in., top blade of shallow diamond
ion 12in. with shaped faceted cushion, pierced and shaped blades, open socket with collar. On its oak haft
in. with 2 oval silver plates. (Wallis & Wallis) $462

erman mace, 16th century, entirely of steel, the head with six rounded flanges, tubular haft with molding
ards the grip and a piercing for a thong, 53cm. (Bonhams & Brooks) $2,320

id 18th century French spontoon head, of the type carried by French officers and NCOs in America during
French and Indian wars of the 1750s, with broad central blade, two pairs of side flukes and long socket for
chment to shaft, 14in. overall. (Andrew Bottomley) $588

ictorian painted police truncheon, 16in., stamped *Field 233 Holborn*, nicely painted with crowned *VR* and
ce within cartouche; and another of turned wood with brass pommel. (Wallis & Wallis) $275

7th century halberd, head of traditional form with geometric piercings, etched with bust wearing a morion
'n oval cartouche upon a speckled ground, reverse with similar cartouche. Riveted straps, roped collar, on
riginal reeded oak haft. (Wallis & Wallis) $2,800

Benito Mussolini, signed postcard, with surname only, half-length in profile reading, image a little scuffed. (Vennett Smith) $246

Sherpa Tenzing, signed real photographic postcard, showing him half-length entitled *Mount Everest From Sandukphu*, with 25 snapshots of Darjeeling, Nepal, Everest. (Vennett Smith) $265

Rudolf Nureyev, signed 3.75 x to lower white border, head and shoulders.(Vennett Smith) $

Enrico Caruso, a fine signed and inscribed cabinet photo, showing him three quarter length in costume, London, 1908 (?), photo by Amie Dupont, as the Duke from Rigoletto.
(Vennett Smith) $1,000

William F. Cody/Buffalo Bill, a piece of paper signed and inscribed in black ink *Sincerely Yours, W.F. Cody "Buffalo Bill", 1904*, 2½ x 3¼in. (Christie's) $739

Erwin Rommel, signed postcard, with surname only, in characteris pencil, full-length standing, in profile, in large overcoat and cap alongside another Nazi, in the desert. (Vennett Smith) $1

Harry Houdini, signed and inscribed postcard, head and shoulders wearing coat and hat, dated *Cardiff 26th May 1914*.
(Vennett Smith) $2,646

D. Ben Gurion, a 22 x 18 color poster, showing him in front of Israeli flag, by Living Legends 1973, signed to white margin by both Ben Gurion and artist Herbert Davidson. (Vennett Smith) $370

Sarah Bernhardt, signed postca to lower white border, head and shoulders looking upwards. (Vennett Smith) $1

72

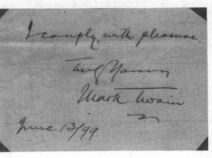

Enrico Caruso, signed postcard, head and shoulders, London, 1904, light staining to image. (Vennett Smith) **\$339**

Mark Twain, signed piece, 4 x 2.5, 13th June 1899, fold affecting text but not signature, stamp sticker to reverse. (Vennett Smith) **\$570**

Andy Warhol, signed 4 x 6 reproduction of one of his sketches of Mick Jagger, first name only. (Vennett Smith) **\$354**

Nasser Arafat, signed color 5 x 7, head and shoulders wearing familiar black and white headwear, State of Palestine presentation folder. (Vennett Smith) **\$135**

Salvador Dali, signed 9 x 8.5 magazine photo, half-length in flamboyant pose, signed to left white border. (Vennett Smith) **\$168**

William T. Sherman, signed piece, with four additional words in his hand and rank as Major General beneath signature, cut from the end of a letter, overmounted in blue beneath 5.5 x 6 reproduction photo. (Vennett Smith) **\$154**

Josephine Baker, signed postcard, head and shoulders looking back over one shoulder, photo by Baccarini & Porta of Milan. (Vennett Smith) **\$210**

Mikhail Gorbachev, a 12 x 32 German poster, advertising his memoirs, signed to top portion next to photo. (Vennett Smith) **\$139**

Lyndon B. Johnson., signed 8 x 10 color, with initials *LBJ* only, head and shoulders wearing suit. (Vennett Smith) **\$64**

Harry Houdini, signed 3.5 x 6, with surname only, in bold green ink, head and shoulders portrait wearing suit. (Vennett Smith) $1,330

Field Marshal B.L. Montgomery, signed 10 x 8, half-length in tank watching progress of Battle of El Alamein, signed *22nd May 1972*. (Vennett Smith) $246

Ed Murrow, signed 7 x 9 head an shoulders. (Vennett Smith) $15

Mikhail Gorbachev, signed color 9.5 x 12, to lower white border, head and shoulders wearing suit with red CCCP pin in lapel. (Vennett Smith) $200

Kennedy & De Valera, a good signed 10 x 12 by both John F. Kennedy and Eamon de Valera, to lower photographer's mount, full-length standing together in the doorway of an official residence. (Vennett Smith) $1,985

Agatha Christie, signed 5 x 7, he and shoulders with hands claspe Christie has gone over the signature twice as the first attemp with a different pen was not successful. (Vennett Smith) $33

Harry Houdini, autograph sentiment signed, on a 4 x 2in. piece of paper, no place or date, matted and framed with a miniature pair of handcuffs. (Christie's) $1,645

Michael Collins, signed 10 x 8, full-length walking with Armstrong and Aldrin, from rocket after countdown demonstration. (Vennett Smith) $354

Edward VIII, signed postcard, a Prince of Wales, head and shoulders wearing naval uniform and cap. (Vennett Smith) $32

Duke Ellington, signed 7.5 x 9.5, half-length with hands in pocket, photo by Bloom. (Vennett Smith) $246

Richard Strauss, signed postcard, three quarter length seated in chair. (Vennett Smith) $331

Margaret Thatcher, signed color 8 x 10, head and shoulders in silver ink. (Vennett Smith) $103

Amy Johnson, signed 6.5 x 8.5, with married signature Amy Mollison, head and shoulders wearing leather flying jacket, cap and goggles. (Vennett Smith) $147

Winston S. Churchill, a very fine signed 7.5 x 10, with a full signature to the lower photographer's mount and dated in his hand *1943*, photo by Walter Stoneman. (Vennett Smith) $2,790

Guy Gibson, a good signed and inscribed 4.5 x 6, half-length seated in RAF uniform, smiling towards the camera and holding a pipe in one hand, dated just four days before his death. (Vennett Smith) $2,800

Sarah Duchess of York, an excellent signed and inscribed 11.5 x 14.5 to lower mount, three quarter length seated, 1993. (Vennett Smith) $280

Cindy Crawford, signed 8 x 10, three quarter length topless in evening gown. (Vennett Smith) $71

W.F. Cody, signed card 3.25 x 1.5, in both forms, over-mounted in red beneath 5 x 6.5 photo as Buffalo Bill, framed and glazed. (Vennett Smith) $616

Louis Armstrong, signed and inscribed 8 x 10, head and shoulders singing into microphone, also signed *Satchmo*.
(Vennett Smith) $158

Arthur Conan Doyle, autograph note signed, in full *So sorry to miss you! Was staying at private house... I shan't be back in Manchester. Good Luck. Excuse travellers card.*
(Vennett Smith) $431

Mother Teresa, signed color 5 x 7.5, head and shoulders in blue and white robes wearing small crucifix, overmounted in burgundy, 8 x 10 overall.(Vennett Smith) $177

Eva Peron, small signed menu card, Maria E.d de Peron, also signed by Juan Duarte, the menu for the wedding of Carmen Franco Polo (only daughter of Franco) at Franco's Palace in Madrid, 15th June 1947.
(Vennett Smith) $1,386

Lillie Langtry, a full length sepia portrait of subject as Lady Ormond, taken by James Notman in Boston, 1886/7, signed in black ink *Lillie Langtry*, gilt and silk covered frame, 10¾ x 9½. (Christie's) $1,068

David Livingston, signed and inscribed hardback edition of Missionary Travels in South Africa, inscribed by Livingstone to the flyleaf *Mrs Dv. Bates, with kind salutations from David Livingstone, 28th Feb, 1858, Glasgow.*
(Vennett Smith) $1,109

Richard Strauss, signed sepia postcard, half length seated, to white margin.
(Vennett Smith) $370

David Lloyd George, a very large signed 14 x 18 photo, three quarter length seated in a formal pose, photo by Reginald Haines, of London, signed by Lloyd George to the lower photographer's mount.
(Vennett Smith) $420

Jesse Owens, signed card, 4 x 5.75, with laid down newspaper photo, half-length with medals and laurel. (Vennett Smith) $168

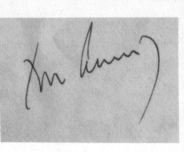

Andy Warhol, signed card, 4 x 6, Marilyn (1967), signed to lower white border.
(Vennett Smith) $439

John F. Kennedy, signed piece, cut from the end of a letter, probably signed as President.
(Vennett Smith) $462

Mussolini Benito, signed 7 x 9, surname only, 1934, half-length reading papers.
(Vennett Smith) $616

Margaret Thatcher, a good signed 9.5 x 11.5, to lower mount, three quarter length seated, framed and glazed, 11 x 13 overall.
(Vennett Smith) $123

Wallis Duchess of Windsor, signed 5 x 3.5 to lower white border, full-length standing alongside, but not signed by, Edward Duke of Windsor, apparently taken at RAF Nassau in the Bahamas.
(Vennett Smith) $223

Ronald Reagan, signed piece, 3.5 x 1.5, overmounted in white and black beneath 9.5 x 8.5, half-length in suit, framed and glazed.
(Vennett Smith) $142

Bram Stoker, autograph signed letter one and a half pages, to Barrington d' Alensida, 14th May 1892, referring to Mr. Irving and his requests.
(Vennett Smith) $354

Edward Duke of Windsor, and Wallis Windsor, signed crested card by both Edward and Wallis, such signed cards are now becoming scarce. (Vennett Smith) $364

Neil Armstrong, signed color 8 x 10, half-length wearing white spacesuit, with an image of the moon in the background.
(Vennett Smith) $644

Queen Victoria, hardback edition of The Early Years of HRH The Prince Consort, 1819-1841, by Lt. Gen. C. Grey (1867), signed and inscribed to *Mary Andrews from Victoria Osborne Jan. 1st. 1868.*
(Vennett Smith) $447

A Christmas card from Her Majesty The Queen and Prince Philip 1982, a color picture of The Queen, Prince Philip and Prince Andrew in an interior setting, 15.4 x 21.6cm.
(Bonhams) $118

H. Rider Haggard, autograph signed letter, one page, 28th May 1890, to Colin Hunter, stating that he cannot do as his correspondent asks as he has *retreated far from the madding crowd.*
(Vennett Smith) $294

Lord Alfred Tennyson, autograph signed letter, one page, 17th July 1865, thanking his correspondent for the Crusader and continuing *You are quite at liberty to dedicate your fourth volume of poems to me if you like it.*
(Vennett Smith) $162

An autographed photograph of Winston Churchill, 1955, seated, photograph 16 x 12.5cm. framed
(Bonhams) $1,960

A Christmas card from the Princess of Wales, 1994, *Manuela, love from, Diana.* in black ink, and a sepia toned photograph of The Princess and the two Princes, 15.3 x 20.2cm. (Bonhams) $1,250

Princess of Wales, a photograph of the Princess of Wales at the preview of Christie's 1997 sale of her dresses, dedicated and signed, *Dearest Audrey, Lots of love from Diana x,* 9½ x 12½in.
(Bonhams) $2,041

Martin Bormann, typed letter signed *Bormann,* one page, 7th Dec. 1941, to Dr. Krupp Von Bohlen and Halbach, in German, marked personal, on Bormann's personal stationery.
(Vennett Smith) $770

Mille Miglia XXIV, 1957; an original silk scarf awarded to competitors in the event; decorative color lithograph design. (Christie's) $973

F. Bourcart, "Cockatoo", an original mascot, designed as a decorative accessory for radiator ornament; nickelled bronze Art Deco style, and having blue glazed reflective eyes, French, circa 1920s. (Christie's) $469

Jaguar C-Type, an original bonnet from a production model of the famous sports road-racing machine; all aluminium construction, painted British Racing Green. (Christie's) $9,741

Minerva, Centurion's head, maker's mascot by P. de Soete for the 40CV Eight-cylinder models; chrome-plated bronze, Art Deco style, Belgian, circa 1930. (Christie's) $1,585

Castrol, a rare pre-war enamelled advertising garage thermometer, together with an enamel wall sign, French, circa 1920s. (Christie's) $467

Mille Miglia 1956, an original banner for this famous road-racing event, decorative stencil-printed motif on canvas, original pole mounting.(Christie's) $3,281

Alfa Romeo, a large garage advertising agent's sign, embossed relief design, lithographed on aluminum, Italian, circa 1940s, 32in. diameter. (Christie's) $2,670

A Rochester 10-gallon visible sight gas-pump fitted with American Gas illuminated globe, lacks hose, circa 1930s. (Christie's) $3,680

Maserati, scarce illuminated dealership garage sign, double-sided embossed motif design with electric illumination and original frame, Italian, circa 1960s. (Christie's) $2,336

Napier Railton, a pre war jig-saw puzzle depicting the outer-circuit Brooklands lap-record holder, decoratively framed and glazed. (Christie's) $144

Rolls-Royce; a decanter in the form of a Rolls-Royce radiator by "Ruddspeed"; chrome-plated with badge to front; English, circa 1960. (Christie's) $619

Scuderia Ferrari, the original works factory "clocking-in" time clock, made by Bürke, housed in black-painted steel casing with brass bezel to clock, Austrian, circa 1940s. (Christie's) $8,855

Klokien, Grossglockner Hillclimb, Auto Union, a very rare original poster; dramatic chromolithograph design for the 1938 event, depicting Hans Stuck on his winning Auto Union, 33 x 23in. (Christie's) $5,839

Misti (Ferdinand Mifliez), De Dion Bouton, an original poster for 2 and 4 seater 6hp & 8hp models; full color lithograph dated 1903 by Imprimerie J. Barreau, Paris, 37 x 50in. (Christie's) $5,313

Eifelrennen, Nürburgring 1939, the winner's sash from the laurel wreath for the event won by Hermann Lang in the W154 3-liter car; red silk with gold and silver braided tassels. (Christie's) $6,782

Speed Devil, a good pre-war mascot by Red Ashay, translucent glass, Art Deco style, mounted upon compendium base, circa 1930s. (Christie's) $1,501

Mercedes-Benz, a service sign in porcelain with white ring around circumference, 42in. diameter. (Christie's) $1,763

Gladiator, Automobiles & Cycles, original advertising poster depicting a four-seat tourer with bicycle to foreground, full color lithograph, linen backed, French circa 1905, unframed, 23 x 15in. (Christie's) $656

Michelin, portable garage tire compressor; featuring M. Bibendum astride the bomb-shaped appliance, electric 110 volt, French, circa 1930, 11in. long.
(Christie's) $534

Bosch, printed tinplate advertising sign for electrical equipment; decorative lithograph design by Bernhard Rosen, Italian, circa 1920s, 19 x 26in.
(Christie's) $3,003

Mercedes, a silver-plated spelter desk-piece in embossed relief design, depicting an SSK-style 2 seater racing car, stamped *H.B.* to base; German circa 1920s, 9in.
(Christie's) $2,302

Isotta-Fraschini, Spirit of Triumph, large pre-war mascot design by F. Bazin; silver-plated bronze Art Deco style, French, circa 1930.
(Christie's) $1,501

René Lalique, Tête de l'Aigle, a large eagle's head mascot in semi-opaque and polished glass; mounted on a nickel-plated, screw-thread radiator cap; 6in. high.
(Christie's) $851

Spirit of Ecstasy, a large silver-plated showroom display statuette, in the style of the Rolls-Royce emblem, silver plated, hollow-cast brass, 22in. high.
(Christie's) $2,889

Tripolis 1937-39, Hermann Lang's original cloth racing helmet, worn and used in achieving each of his three victories in succession in North Africa in three different cars.
(Christie's) $26,180

Gordon Bennett Races 1904, a rare printed commemorative souvenir of the races in Ireland for the "Irish Fortnight" commencing July 1st 1904, 13 x 13in.
(Christie's) $334

Ferrari Yearbook 1949, Victoires Affermazioni, a rare early factory publication detailing racing successes and well-illustrated by Klementaski with driver profiles and advertisements.
(Christie's) $900

A white metal medal by P. Wyon commemorating James Sadler's record speed flight, English, 1811, obverse: bust facing left *James Sadler. First English Aeronaut,* 51mm. (Bonhams) $369

A commemorative ceramic tea or coffee-pot stand, French, dated *1889,* titled *1889 Exposition Universelle* and printed in blue with the Eiffel Tower and two balloons within a 'bamboo' border, 23.5 x 23.5cm. (Bonhams) $339

A bronze medal by N.M. Gatteaux commemorating the first unmanned flight of a hydrogen balloon, French, 1783, obverse: two superimposed profiles after Houdon, 42mm. (Bonhams) $246

J Glaisher, C Flammarion, D de Fonville and G Tissandier, Travels In The Air, London: Richard Bentley, New Burlington Street, 1871, First Edition, 8vo., 398pp. (Bonhams) $231

A Treille and A Meyer, Solution D'Un Grand Problême La Navigation Aérienne Réalisable Par La Substitution Au Ballon Spherique Du Ballon En Couronne, Noyon (Oise); Mary-Dupuis, 1852, 14pp. (Bonhams) $308

A scarce 'Paris' porcelain veilleuse, French, dated *1850*, painted with Pilâtre de Rozier's first flight and the Charles & Robert Balloon, signed *J.Siguin 1850,* 23cm. high overall. (Bonhams) $2,464

A miniature of the first cross-channel flight, French, early 20th century, gouache on ivory after the print by L. Bonvalet showing Blanchard and Jeffries passing over farmers on the coast, 8.5cm. diameter. (Bonhams) $493

Rare creamware plate, French, second half 19th century, painted in colors with two figures in a brightly colored basket below the lower part of a spotted-yellow balloon decorated with a hirsute head, 23.3cm. diameter. (Bonhams) $277

A rare Lambeth Delft plate, English, circa 1785, painted in blue with Blanchard's balloon passing over houses, trees and fields, within a decorative border, 13.2cm. diameter.(Bonhams) $2,772

An important Philips & Co. Sunderland pearlware punchbowl, English, circa 1800-10, the inside: bat-printed with a cartoon titled The Ascent of the Aerial Ball, 41.3cm. diameter.(Bonhams) $2,772

A scarce pearlware jug, English, circa 1828, transfer printed in brown on both sides showing the Grahams' flight from White Conduit House, below a fruiting vine border, 22cm. high. (Bonhams) $1,001

A Lambeth Delft plate, English, circa 1784, painted in blue-green and manganese with Lunardi's balloon ascending over the fenced terrace of a house, 22.8cm. diameter. (Bonhams) $1,463

The Vauxhall Royal Balloon...First Ascent with 9 Persons Made From Vauxhall September 9th 1836, hand colored lithograph after Black published by F. Alvey, London Road (1836), 28 x 22cm. (Bonhams) $339

A Full And Correct Description Of This Extraordinary Machine, Aerial Ship, The Eagle, London: J. Thompson, 1835, 4pp, 8vo. With folding woodcut representation of the The First Aerial Ship The Eagle, 235 x 158mm.(Bonhams) $616

Stanley Spencer, Balloonist, signed postcard, head and shoulders in ballooning cap, published 1903, autograph signed note and address in his hand. (Vennett Smith) $132

A rare pearlware ewer with a polychrome ballooning medallion, English, mid 1820s, transfer decorated in blue with a central polychrome medallion of the ascent of Charles Green and Isaac Sparrow, 22.5cm. high. (Bonhams) $1,001

A Delft vase, Dutch, late 18th century, of baluster shape, decorated in blue with a hydrogen balloon with two figures in the gondola, vase 19cm. high. (Bonhams) $1,848

A large Lambeth Delft charger, English, circa 1784, painted in blue, green and manganese with Lunardi's balloon ascending over the fenced terrace of a house and garden, 35.3cm. diameter. (Bonhams) $3,080

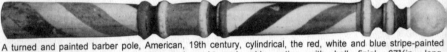

A turned and painted barber pole, American, 19th century, cylindrical, the red, blue and gold stripe-painted form with slant end and gold-painted acorn finial, 49in. long. (Christie's) $5,640

A turned and painted barber pole, American, 19th century, cylindrical, the red and white stripe-painted form with turned mid-section and red-painted spherical ends, 36in. long. (Christie's) $2,350

A turned and painted barber pole, American, 19th century, cylindrical, the red, white and blue stripe-painted form with similarly decorated ring and reel-turned mid section with ball finial, 67¾in. long. (Christie's) $1,410

A turned and painted barber pole, American, 19th century, cylindrical, the red and white stripe-painted form with squared integral base, ring-turned extremities and mid-section and red-painted ball finial, on a modern pyramidal base, 82in. long. (Christie's) $1,410

A turned and painted barber pole, American, 19th century, cylindrical, the blue and white stripe-painted form with red, gold and blue-painted turned mid-section and gold-painted sphere finial, 47in. long. (Christie's) $2,233

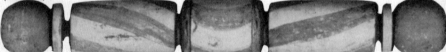

A turned and painted barber pole, American, 19th century, cylindrical, the red, white and blue wavy stripe-painted form with yellow-painted spherical ends and turned mid-section, 29½in. long. (Christie's) $3,055

A turned and painted barber pole, American, 19th century, cylindrical, the black and white-painted form with gold-painted acorn finial, 99½in. long. (Christie's) $1,880

A turned and painted barber pole, American, 19th century, the cylindrical form red, white, blue stripe-painted, with turned mid-section and gold-painted ball finial, on modern box base, 82in. long, excluding box. (Christie's) $4,465

A turned and painted barber pole, American, 19th century, cylindrical, the red and white stripe-painted form with gold and red-painted spherical ends, 36½in. long. (Christie's) $2,233

A turned and painted barber pole, American, 19th century, cylindrical, the red and white stripe-painted form, with red, white and blue-painted turned mid-section and gold-painted spherical finial, 47in. long. (Christie's) $4,465

An oak cased Fitzroy barometer, English, circa 1890, printed paper scale marked *Admiral Fitzroys Barometer*, 50in.(Bonhams & Brooks) $994

A burr walnut veneer stick barometer, Cary 7 Pallmall, London, circa 1900, 97cm. (Bonhams) $1,120

A small rosewood wheel barometer, C Tagliabue, London, circa 1830, 36in. (Bonhams) $1,680

An oak cased coastal stick barometer, Dolland, circa 1870, 42in. (Bonhams) $1,120

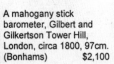

A mahogany stick barometer, Gilbert and Gilkertson Tower Hill, London, circa 1800, 97cm. (Bonhams) $2,100

A large rosewood and inlaid mother of pearl barometer with inset timepiece, Joseph Long, London, circa 1820, 51in. (Bonhams) $5,040

A mahogany bow front stick barometer, Bancks, London, circa 1820, 39½in. (Bonhams) $3,640

A mahogany cased wall barometer, Watkins & Smith, circa 1770, in a case with trunk above with a hinged panelled door and hygrometer inset, 39in. (Bonhams) $21,000

A mahogany and box strung wheel barometer, G Turconi, Liverpool, circa 1840, 97cm. (Bonhams & Brooks) $454

A mahogany wheel barometer, C Alietti, Oxford, circa 1820, 39in. (Bonhams & Brooks) $682

A 19th century stick barometer by James Barraclough, Thornton, Bradford, mahogany case with pierced gallery surmount, 38¾in. high. (Andrew Hartley) $840

A black lacquer wheel barometer, unsigned, second half 19th century, 10in. silvered dial, 42in. (Bonhams & Brooks) $497

A William IV banjo shape wheel barometer, dial inscribed *A Martinelli, 36 Charlotte Strt, Blackfriars Road*, 8in. diameter. (Woolley & Wallis) $832

A French ormolu wall clock and barometer en-suite, in the chinoiserie style, circa 1880, each with a drum-shaped case suspended from an elephant-head bracket with two chains, above twin-elephant head and flame finial, the twin-train movement striking on a bell, the aneroid barometer dial with French text and barometric scale of 73-79cm., 50½in. high. (Christie's) $23,920

English Regency mahogany banjo-style wheel barometer, early 19th century, the face signed *Pozzi & Co.*, 38⅜in. (Skinner) $1,610

Small native American splint basket, 19th century, old patina with black-painted fern designs, 4in. high. (Skinner) $345

Splint basket, New England, 19th century, of shallow round form with two curved loop handles, 7in. high. (Skinner) $210

Native American paint-decorated splint basket, 19th century, old surface with red and orange banding, 7½in. high. (Skinner) $1,000

Fine painted miniature basket, America, 19th century, the tapering cylindrical form with loop handles and old taupe paint, 5in. high. (Skinner) $1,150

Miniature painted basket, America, 19th century, melon-shaped basket with handle, black over green paint. (Skinner) $700

Miniature painted bushel basket, America, 19th century, old cream-white paint over red, 5¾in. diameter. (Skinner) $747

Miniature woven splint basket, America, late 19th/ early 20th century, ribbed basket with handle, 5½in. long. (Skinner) $173

Painted basket, America, probably late 19th century, the vertical shaped wooden slats joined by twisted wire banding, on wooden circular base, old painted surface, 18in. high. (Skinner) $862

Small orange painted basket, America, late 19th century, with fixed handle and twisted rim, 6in. high. (Skinner) $57

Eastern Woodland Indians paint decorated basket with cover, 19th century, alternating swabbed chrome yellow and natural splints with red and green, 20in. diameter. (Skinner) $700

Nantucket basket, early 19th century, with swing handle, 13¾in. diameter. (Skinner) $1,190

Forest green painted splint creel, America, early 19th century, with carved wooden wire-hinged top, 8½in. high. (Skinner) $920

A Macfarlane Lang & Co. 'Water Mill' biscuit tin, the rectangular mill building with operating water chute and wheel on one side, with entrance door on the other, 1930s, 18cm. high.(Christie's) $1,129

A Huntley and Palmer 'Good King Wenceslas' biscuit tin, book with red covers, open with illustration on left side and music on right side, 1913, 16cm. high. (Christie's) $950

A Crawford & Sons 'Barrel Organ' biscuit tin, the simulated wooden body with green pleated silk panels front and back and seated monkey with cap extended, 1912, 16cm. high. (Christie's) $1,382

A Macfarlane Lang & Co. 'Telephone' biscuit tin, simulated oak, with mouthpiece to front of lid and earpiece on hook to side, with bell above and segmental dial below, circa 1910, 22cm. high. (Christie's) $604

Huntley and Palmer hexagonal Eastern table, 16.5cm. high, 'Kashmir', with elephant's head on lid and other wild animals on panels around sides, 1904, and 'Syrian'. (Christie's) $368

A Huntley and Palmer 'Artist' biscuit tin, in form of artist's palette with hurdy-gurdy player on lid and Italian scenes around lid, 1900, 25cm. high. (Christie's) $259

Huntley and Palmer book biscuit tins, 'Literature', eight books in leather strap, 1901, 16cm. high. (Christie's) $184

Vintage Huntley & Palmer biscuit tin, modelled as a hearty goodfellow, 6in. $86

A Huntley and Palmer 'Easel' biscuit tin, 'Boy and Rabbit' and 'The Milkmaid' on easel, 1914, 21cm. high. (Christie's) $776

A Huntley and Palmer 'Palette (Universal)' biscuit tin, in form of artist's palette with scenes of contemporary transport on lid and around edge, 1900, 23.5cm. high. (Christie's) $483

A Macfarlane Lang & Co. 'Bird's Nest' biscuit tin, circular simulated nest, with clutch of six blue-gray speckled eggs, 1910, 14cm. diameter. (Christie's) $1,899

A Huntley and Palmer 'Cannon' on simulated wooden four-wheeled cradle, 1914, 12cm. high. (Christie's) $328

A MacFarlane Lang & Co 'Golf Bag' biscuit tin, simulated canvas, with leather straps and edgings, lady and gentleman golfers on each side and carrying handle to one side, 1913, 22cm. high. (Christie's) $658

Lefèvre-Utile 'Plates' biscuit tins, each comprising stack of seven plates, with top plate as lid, one with blue scrollwork decoration on cream ground and other after Quimper ware, 1905-1910, each 22cm. (Christie's) (Two) $950

A Macfarlane Lang & Co. 'Golf Bag' biscuit tin, simulated canvas, with leather straps and edgings, with heads of six golf clubs protruding from lid, lady and gentleman golfers on each side, 1913, 27cm. (Christie's) $3,800

A McVitie & Price 'bluebird' novelty biscuit tin, circa 1911, the Martin Brothers type bird with detachable head, 24cm. high. (Christie's) $980

Huntley and Palmer 'Dickens' biscuit tin, eight books in leather strap, 1911, 16cm. high. (Christie's) $536

A Huntley and Palmer 'Windmill', 1924, 23cm. high. (Christie's) $411

A Huntley and Palmer 'Windmill' 1924, 23cm. high. (Christie's) $1,640

A rare Co-Operative Wholesale Society Crumpsall Cream Crackers delivery van biscuit tin, circa 1920, finished in mainly cream and green with well detailed advertisements to the roof, 25cm. long. (Sotheby's) $3,150

Huntley and Palmer biscuit tin, 'water bottle', leather flask with ropework decoration and bugles on each side, 1915, 16cm. high. (Christie's) $147

A Lefèvre-Utile biscuit barrel, French, circa 1905, the brown lithographed tin finished to the sides with mice scurrying to look over the top of a wheat field, 16.5cm. high. (Sotheby's) $1,050

A Mackintosh 'rocking horse' biscuit tin, post war, the shaped tin with lid to one flank, to simulate a child's rocking horse, 14cm. long. (Sotheby's) $455

A Huntley and Palmer 'Camera' biscuit tin, with aperture, distance and shutter speed settings. 1913, 10cm. high.(Christie's) $950

A Gray, Dunn & Co. limousine biscuit tin, circa 1915, with lithographed uniformed driver, gentleman and lady looking out to one side, 16cm. long. (Sotheby's) $2,100

An unusual Carr & Co. Ltd., 'tambourine' biscuit tin, circa 1931, the circular tin lithographed with the Pied Piper of Hamelin, the young children skipping behind, 14cm. diameter. (Sotheby's) $1,050

A William Crawford & Sons biscuit tin, circa 1911, the well detailed wagon depicting caged lions, tigers, monkeys and leopards to the side, 12cm. high. (Sotheby's) $1,400

A good pair of female blackamoor figures, 20th century, each in standing pose offering a tray, dressed in turban and gilt polychrome decorated robes,181cm.
(Bristol) $7,350

A polychrome-decorated glazed faïence blackamoor stool, circa 1895, kneeling and supporting a cushion on his back, 20in. high.
(Christie's) $4,317

A pair of Venetian parcel-gilt polychrome-decorated blackamoors, in the Baroque style, circa 1865, each holding a candlestick to his shoulder, wearing oriental damask costumes, on a triform base, 69in. high.
(Christie's) $16,408

A pair of Venetian style blackamoor figures, each modelled as a Negro boy dressed in a gilt bordered brown jacket, breeches and crowned turban seated on a pedestal playing a pipe and with a monkey seated on one shoulder, 180cm. approximately.
(Bristol) $5,495

A pair of carved and gilt-wood painted dwarf blackamoor torchères, each holding a spirally gadrooned cornucopia, on simulated stone base, 129cm.
(Bristol) $4,082

A pair of Genoese parcel-gilt and polychrome-decorated blackamoors, circa 1885, each as a male figure, surmounted by a circular platform, holding a shell-shaped dish in one hand, on a naturalistic base, 80¼in. high.
(Christie's) $33,120

pair of Italian polychrome and iltwood blackamoor torchères, mid 0th century, modelled as a male nd female, the foliate carved ttings held aloft with arms raised, 5½in. high.
Christie's) $5,790

A pair of Venetian parcel-gilt and polychrome-decorated blackamoors, decorated by Testolini, circa 1880, each as a female figure wearing drapery, a coat of arms to the front.
(Christie's) $13,800

Two carved wood blackamoor torchères, painted in differing gilt and colors to the foliage decoration of the clothing, jewelled turbans, the faces with glass eyes, 6ft.½in. and 5ft.11¼in.
(Woolley & Wallis) $2,772

Frank Bruno's fight worn boxing trunks and robe, a pair of Title black fight worn boxing trunks with silver piping and *Frank Bruno* on the legs.
(Bonhams) $1,015

An Everlast glove signed by "Marvelous" Marvin Hagler and Sugar Ray Leonard.
(Bonhams) $1,160

Ali & Frazier, 20 x 16, signed in gold by both Muhammad Ali and Joe Frazier, showing them three quarter length from one of their fights.
(Vennett Smith) $277

An Evening News 'Clay v. Quarry – Full report & pictures' advertising bill, circa 1972, signed in ink and inscribed *To Paddy my main man in England....Peace'*, 29 x 20in.
(Bonhams) $160

Muhammad Ali, signed color 8 x 10, full length in action pose in boxing ring.
(Vennett Smith) $139

A black and white group portrait photograph of Jack Dempsey with George Perry and wife, signed in ink and inscribed *To our pal Trevor always the best*, and dated *'36*, 7 x 9in. (Bonhams) $145

The 'Sunshine' in my Life signed copy. My own story by Paddy Monaghan with foreword by Muhammad Ali, published 1993, signed in ink by Paddy Monaghan.
(Bonhams) $65

Muhammad Ali, signed color 16 x 20, Muhammad A.K.A. Cassius Clay, in silver ink, full-length standing over Sonny Liston in ring.
(Vennett Smith) $339

A black and white limited edition photographic print of Muhammad Ali and Elvis Presley, no.17/100, signed *Muhammad Ali '91* in black marker pen, 14 x 20in.
(Bonhams) $1,450

A black and white photographic print of Muhammad Ali and The Beatles, signed *Muhammad Ali aka Cassius Clay* in black marker pen, 15¾ x 20in. (Bonhams) $653

Muhammad Ali signed sparring gloves, fight-worn red leather, no. 4305, each signed *Muhammad Ali* in black marker pen and dated *2.18.89* (2). (Bonhams) $4,350

A black and white photographic print of Muhammad Ali in action, signed *From Muhammad Ali '93* in pencil, 15 x 11in. (Bonhams) $203

A black and white quarter length portrait of Gene Tunney signed in white ink *To Karl Pettit with every good wish Gene Tunney*, 9 x 7in. (Bonhams) $276

A pair of Everlast white and black satin boxing trunks signed by Muhammad Ali and Joe Frazier in black marker pen. (Bonhams) $1,378

A Muhammad Ali and Joe Frazier "Thrilla in Manilla" fight poster, inscribed *The Saga of Our Lifetime* and dated *Philippines 1975*, signed by Muhammad Ali in two places and Smokin' Joe Frazier, 22 x 14in. (Bonhams) $1,015

A black and white posed fight portrait of Randy Turpin signed in k *Best Wishes from Randy Turpin*, x 6in. (Bonhams) $348

A Wilson red leather boxing glove, no. 310, signed in ink *From Cassius Clay Next World Champion 1963*, with a certificate of authenticity. (Bonhams) $2,320

A black and white fight pose portrait photograph of Jack Dempsey signed in blue ink *To my friend George best regards Jack Dempsey*, 10 x 8in. (Bonhams) $290

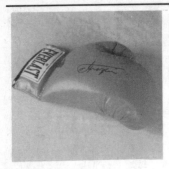

A red Everlast boxing glove signed *Joe Frazier* in black marker pen. (Bonhams) $653

An Everlast glove signed by "Iron" Mike Tyson, mounted in a framed display case.(Bonhams) $1,233

A red Bryan boxing glove signed *George Foreman* in black marker pen. (Bonhams) $551

A Lonsdale cotton tee-shirt, size XL, printed with a portrait of Muhammad Ali and inscribed, signed in red ink *Muhammad Ali*. (Bonhams) $261

A carved and painted figural group, American, 20th century, depicting the Dempsey-Firpoe fight, each figure with orange and yellow-painted trunks and gray and black-painted gloves and shoes, 12in. high. (Christie's) $4,113

A black and photographic print of Sugar Ray Robinson in fight action against Jake La Motta, signed in blue ink in two places, 7 x 9in. (Bonhams) $377

A fabric souvenir pennant inscribed World's Championship Fight at Madison Square Garden Center, March 8 1971, with fight portraits of Muhammad Ali and Joe Frazier, both portraits signed in black ink, 25in. long. (Bonhams) $1,087

Muhammad Ali & Joe Frazier, a red Everlast boxing glove, 12oz., signed by both, with certificate of authenticity. (Bonhams & Brooks) $369

An Odeon Theatre Vision fight bill, dated *22nd November 1965*, Cassius Clay v. Floyd Patterson, doodled upon in blue ink by Muhammad Ali with Cassius Clay scribbled over, 11 x 6in. (Bonhams) $37

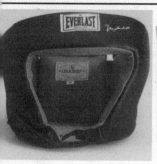

Muhammad Ali, a black Everlast Headguard, signed in silver *Muhammad Ali* with Certificate of authenticity.
(Bonhams & Brooks) $284

Muhammad Ali, a pair of white Everlast boxing boots, signed by Muhammad Ali, with certificate of authenticity.
(Bonhams & Brooks) $199

A pair of metal framed lightweight sunglasses and a photograph of Muhammad Ali and Paddy Monaghan the morning after the second Frazier fight.
(Bonhams) $841

sepia poster portrait of uhammad Ali in fight pose with csimile signature, signed by uhammad Ali in black marker pen d dated *6.6.92,* 38 x 27in.
onhams) $261

Sugar Ray Robinson, a marble effect plaque mounted with a black and white photograph of the boxer, signed *Best Wishes - Sugar Ray Robinson,* 13 x 10in.
(Bonhams & Brooks) $156

A black and white photographic print of Muhammad Ali standing over Sonny Liston, signed *Muhammad Ali* in silver marker pen, 16 x 20in. (Bonhams) $870

nnox Lewis, World Heavyweight ampion, a white Lonsdale boxing ve, signed on the fist in black, nox Lewis, mounted in a mirror ked perspex case.
nhams & Brooks) $220

A red Everlast boxing glove signed *Muhammad Ali 2000* in black marker pen, together with a certificate of authenticity.
(Bonhams) $1,232

Floyd Patterson, a Stars and Stripes U.S.A. white boxing glove, signed in full in black, with Certificate of authenticty.
(Bonhams & Brooks) $213

95

A 19th century bronze bust of a gentleman by Francis Derwent Wood, R.A. signed and dated 1919, dark brown patination, 28½in. high. (Andrew Hartley) $725

F Barbedienne, signed patinated bronze study of a classical maiden in a seated pose with her legs curled, clutching a seashell in one hand, the base signed, 9½in. high. (G.A. Key) $942

A bronze figure of the crouching Venus, after the Antique, brown patination, raised on circular bas with scrolled feet, 8½in. high. (Andrew Hartley) $

'Dagger Dancer', a cold-painted bronze figure of a dancer holding ivory daggers, cast and carved from a model by C.J.R. Colinet, signed, 49.5cm. high. (Christie's) $7,772

'Signal Man', a cold-painted bronze and ivory figure of a medieval archer, cast and carved from a model by P. Le Faguays, base signed Le Faguays, 65.1cm. (Christie's) $8,940

A Regency bronze and ormolu inkstand, in the manner of Thos Messenger, the hinged shell to enclosing three removable compartments, above a dolphin support, on a pink marble squar stepped base, 6in. high. (Christie's) $2,7

A bronze of a captive Negro slave, naked and roped to a tree stump, standing on a rectangular marble base, 8in. (Woolley & Wallis) $550

Auguste Seysses (French, born 1862), African elephant and rider, bronze with greenish black patina, stamped Susse Frères, 12¾in. high. (Skinner) $1,265

A bronze figure of the Young Mozart, depicted standing and holding a violin, signed P Dube brown patination, 25in. high. (Andrew Hartley) $2,9

Bronze figure of the revelling Bacchus, 20th century, the figure poised in dance, in grape leaf drapery and circlet, base signed M. Pritzsche, 28in. high. (Skinner) $1,495

Bronze figure of Dionysus, late 19th/20th century, the nude figure reclining against rocky outcrop with full wineskin, 9in. high. (Skinner) $748

An Art Deco patinated bronze figure, cast from a model by Lorence, in the style of Lorenzl, signed in the bronze, 26cm. high. (Christie's) $1,311

pair of Russian ormolu mounted malachite covered urns, mid 19th century, the handles of two figures of Pan with arms raised holding a laurel wreath with floral garland mounts, 62cm. high. (Christie's) $13,160

Demetre H. Chiparus, 'Almeria', 1920s, gilt, cold-painted bronze and ivory, modelled as a female dancer in a catsuit with wide sleeves and an open skirt balancing on tiptoe on her left leg, 44.7cm. (Sotheby's) $73,150

Austrian, early 20th century, a pair of busts of a North African man and woman, the man inscribed Giesecke and the woman inscribed Thiele, bronze-coated, with red and gold cold-paint, both 63cm. overall. (Sotheby's) $5,010

French bronze group of Pegasus and Aurora, 19th century, After Antoine Coysevox (1640-1720), the mythological classical maiden seated on the rearing winged horse, 9½in. high. (Christie's) $4,206

'The Bather', a silvered bronze cast from a model by Chiparus, signed on the base 45cm. high. (Christie's) $7,772

Pair of French gilt and patinated bronze-footed urns, late 19th century, each signed Barbédienne, depicting classical scenes, with masks and decorative motifs, 22in. high. (Skinner) $4,313

A silvered bronze figure, cast from a model by L. Fontinelle, of a fox, signed in the bronze, 31cm. wide. (Christie's) $2,239

An Italian bronze model of the Apollo Belvedere, third quarter 19 century, after the Antique, on a rectangular base, 15in. high. (Christie's) $2,6

Victorian Classical school, late 19th century, a bronze figure of a Youth playing cymbals, with tree-trunk support, 23in., on marble plinth. (Brightwells) $1,290

A pair of French bronze pointers, after the model by Henri Alfred Jacquemart (1824-1896), cast as two pointers both sitting on their haunches, on later painted faux malachite rectangular bases, 31½in. high. (Bonhams) $7,700

A 19th century bronze bust of Antinous depicted gazing downwards with fruiting vine in his hair, stamped *Vor. Paillard a Paris*, 8½in. high. (Andrew Hartley) $1,102

A 19th century Chinese bronze elephant with elaborately molded decoration with plinth base and attached candleholder, 7.5in. on wood base. (Brightwells) $75

Vincenzo Gemito, Italian, 1852-1929, Licco, a bust, bronze, rich mid-brown and dark brown patina, 18in. (Sotheby's) $9,867

François Pompon, 'Toy, Boston-Terrier', after 1931, black patinated bronze, on flat rectangular base, marked and impressed with found mark *Cire Perdue C. Valsuani*, 31cm. (Sotheby's) $20,00

A bronze model of a hunter, late 19th century, after John Willis Good (1845-79), mounted on a naturalistic base inscribed *J. Willis Good*, 18½in. wide.
(Christie's) $7,680

A bronze figure Il Spinario, after the Antique, raised on circular stone base, 12¾in. high.
(Andrew Hartley) $628

Jean-Leon Gérôme, French, 1824-1904, Napoleon entering Cairo signed: *J.L. Gerome* and inscribed *Siot.Decauville.Fondeur.Paris.*, gilt-bronze and ivory, 16 x 14¼in.
(Sotheby's) $22,770

Louis-Ernest Barrias, French, 1841-1945, a Contadina with a child, signed, inscribed and dated *Hommage amical à Madame Roger Ballu 1876*, bronze, dark brown patina, 37¾in.
(Sotheby's) $7,590

A pair of tiger-eye and gilt-bronze ewers by Ferdinand Barbedienne, French, circa 1870, after a model by Gouthière, with tapering cylindrical body, cast with a bacchic mask and a handle in the form of a maiden, each 41.5cm. high.
(Sotheby's) $16,032

A French bronze figure of a Gaulish warrior, late 19th century, from the workshops of F. Barbedienne, Paris, cast in the manner of the Capitoline Dying Gaul, his cloak, shield and sword beneath him on the ground, 28in. wide.
(Christie's) $3,948

An Italian bronze model of the standing Discobolus, late 19th century, after the Antique, on a rectangular base, 34.5cm. high.
(Christie's) $1,645

An Austrian bronze group of a tiger hunt, circa 1900, cast as a hunting party on an elephant being attacked by a tiger, on a shaped portor marble plinth, 10½in. high.
(Bonhams) $1,035

A Japanese bronze figure of a warrior, depicted standing in a fighting position and holding a stave, 12½in. high, Meiji period.
(Andrew Hartley) $2,030

A gilt patinated bronze bust, cast from a model by E.Villanis, signed in the bronze, impressed foundry mark, numbered *6772*, 14.5cm. high. (Christie's) $352

'Dancer with Thyrsus', a patinated and cold-painted bronze figure cast from a model by Le Faguays, incised signature to base, 53cm. high. (Christie's) $6,653

'Jockey', a patinated bronze and ivory figure inscribed in the bronze *Max Bearly* (?) and *P.E. Goureau*, 33.5cm. high. (Christie's) $1,487

A Charles I lead/bronze mortar, English, the waisted body cast with the date*1646*, flanked by the initials *W* and *T*, within a continuous central band of addorsed C scrolls, 9in. diameter. (Christie's) $1,180

A Belgian bronze bust of a bacchante, early 20th century, after a model by Jef. Lambeaux, with breasts exposed and grapes in her hair, signed to the reverse *JEF. LAMBEAUX*, 25½in. high. (Christie's) $822

A large French bronze figure of Hippomene, 19th century, after Franz Jacob Sauvage, shown with an arm raised about to throw down a golden apple in the path of the pursuing Atalanta, 51in. high. (Christie's) $19,000

Russian patinated bronze figure of "Cossack Plunder", circa 1874, by Eugene Lanceray (1848-86), blackish patina, 19in. high. (Skinner) $6,900

A pair of French bronze figures of dancing boys, late 19th century, the Neapolitan figures on circular bases inscribed *Delafontaine* and *Duret.F*, 17in. high.(Christie's) $3,496

A silvered bronze figure, cast from a model by J.D. Guirande, signed in the bronze, stamped foundry mark, impressed numerals *33*, 48cm. diameter.(Christie's) $2,235

A silvered and cold-painted bronze figure, cast from a model by D. Grisard, signed in the bronze, 44cm. diameter.
(Christie's) $1,788

A French bronze figure of a winged Cupid, early 20th century, after a model by Laurent Honoré Marqueste and stamped *1901*, 13in. high.(Christie's) $2,668

A gilt and patinated bronze vase, cast from a model by Louchet, signed in the bronze *Louchet Cisleur*, 8cm. high.
(Christie's) $314

Pair of bronzed trumpet vases applied with swan mounts and terminating in veined marble socles (1 socle damaged), 11½in.
(G.A. Key) $189

A gilded, silvered, and cold-painted bronze and ivory figure, cast and carved from a model by F.Preiss, modelled as a striding flute player, unsigned, 46cm. high.
(Christie's) $10,505

A Hagenauer sivered metal and stained wood figure group stamped marks (broken tail), 26cm. high.
(Christie's) $4,000

A pair of ormolu and bluejohn cassolettes, 19th century, each with urn-shaped body surmounted by reversible flaming-finial and nozzle, 9¼in. high.
(Christie's) $15,850

A bronze spouted ewer, Northern European, 15th century, of bellied form with loop handle, the slightly curving spout with strut support to the waisted neck, 9in. high.
(Christie's) $2,726

A pair of French bronze models of the Marly Horses, mid 19th century, after models by Charles Crozatier, the bases inscribed *CH.Crozatier*, 22½in. high.
(Christie's) $6,440

A Victorian red leather fire bucket, with the Royal Arms.
(Woolley & Wallis) $447

A 19th century Dutch mahogany jardinière of circular tapering form, with brass swing handle and brass liner, the sides as open trellis work, 23¼in. high.
(Andrew Hartley) $1,925

A George III mahogany plate bucket, brass bound, with one original side handle, 15in. diameter.
(Woolley & Wallis) $2,002

Painted leather fire bucket, America, early 19th century, inscribed *CITY OF BOSTON WARD NO.11 FIREMAN NO. 3 1826* in gilt on a black ground with black interior, 13¼in. high.
(Skinner) $1,495

Two George III brass bound mahogany buckets, circa 1800, a plate bucket with side recess and later liner, and a peat bucket with later liner, 18in. and 16¾in. high.
(Christie's) $6,400

A Neapolitan bronze twin handled bucket, last quarter 19th century, probably from the workshops of J. Chiurazzi and Fils, with three registers of stylized foliate motives and guilloche decoration cast in low relief, 34.4cm. diameter.
(Christie's) $3,948

A leather fire bucket, with the Royal Arms. Ex Walmer Castle, Deal.
(Woolley & Wallis) $495

Painted leather fire bucket, America, 19th century, inscribed *B-Stone*, in yellow on black ground with red band and interior, black handle, 14¾in.
(Skinner) $978

A 19th century leather fire bucket, of oval form, painted with the Royal Coat of Arms, 37cm. wide.
(Bonhams) $323

A fine enamel button, bordered in rose pink and with a central scene of cows grazing, 1½in., English, late 18th century.
(Christie's) $1,727

A jasperware button, with blue ground and white cameo of Neptune, Amphritrite, Triton and a dolphin, 1½in., late 18th/early 19th century. (Christie's) $656

A reverse painted glass button, 'en grisaille' with a galleon at sea, 1½in. late 18th century, probably French.(Christie's) $1,295

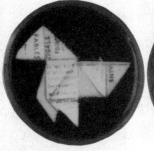

A black and white enamel conundrum button, depicting a folded sheet of paper revealing some of the opening words of La Cigale et le Fournis, 1¼in. French, late 18th century.
(Christie's) $735

An important 'Washington Inaugural' brass coat button, engraved *Long Live the President*, around the initials *GW*, and two others, 1½in., 1789.
(Christie's) $4,491

One of a set of four buttons, with blue stipple engravings, including a woman in classical dress decorating the tomb of Shakespeare, 1½in. probably 1780s, French.
(Christie's) (Four) $2,418

One of a set of three buttons, of glass reverse painted variously with a snail, an insect and a beetle, 1½in., French, circa 1775.
(Christie's) (Three) $5,527

One of a pair of topsy-turvy or inverted buttons, each printed with a man's head visible in different form when viewed from either side, 1½in., 18th century.
(Christie's) (Two) $1,382

A button, enamelled in shades of purple and gray, with a lady in classical dress kneeling at the Altar of Love holding a jug and bowl, 1½in., 18th century.
(Christie's) $1,036

A George III papier mâché oval tea caddy, early 19th century, the black ground heightened with trailing gilt foliage to the cover and lower body, 13cm. wide.
(Christie's) $1,562

A George III mahogany knife box, wormed. (Brightwells) $434

A Regency tortoiseshell veneered tea caddy, the molded bowed fron with star-burst decoration, the interior with ivory banding and subsidiary cover, 4¾in. wide.
(Christie's) $4,93

A George IV mahogany dressing case having cut brass inlay, the hinged lid revealing numerous silver lidded accessories, London 1821/22, drawer to base, 12½in.
(Brightwells) $1,160

A George III satinwood and rosewood crossbanded octagonal tea caddy, the cover and front panel with fan paterae flanked by Doric columns to the canted angles, 5½in. wide.
(Christie's) $1,562

A Victorian burr walnut cigar box of canted oblong form, with applied ivory and gilt metal mounts, 6¼in. wide. (Andrew Hartley) $55(

A Namikawa Studio cloisonné tea-caddy, Meiji Period (late 19th century), decorated in various thicknesses of wire and colored cloisonné enamels with butterflies and moths on a scroll ground, 2¾in. high. (Christie's) $3,929

A Black Forest carved wood decanter box, late 19th century, modelled in the form of a cottage, the roof surmounted by a prowling hunting dog, 17¼in. wide.
(Christie's) $2,926

A George III polished and bright-cut steel veneered tea caddy, faceted cover and ivory banding, with painted reserves of classical maidens to the cover, front and reverse, 11cm. wide.
(Christie's) $41,125

A Regency tortoiseshell tea caddy, circa 1820, the serpentine front with a hinged cover opens to reveal a fitted interior, set on bun feet, 19cm. wide. (Bonhams) $2,142

An octagonal rosewood tea caddy, mid 19th century, with trefoil shaped loop handle, the cover with boxwood inlaid cartouche, 5¾in. high. (Christie's) $822

A George III oval tea caddy, by Henry Clay, painted overall with bellflower and anthemion banding, a reserve to the front panel with a maiden and a bird, 4¾in. wide. (Christie's) $12,337

A George III tortoishell and ivory veneered tea caddy, of rectangular outline with canted angles and faceted cover, the interior with subsidiary cover, 4in. wide. (Christie's) $4,935

An early Victorian tortoiseshell veneered tea caddy, second quarter 19th century, the case with concave angles and ivory banding, the front panel inlaid with mother of pearl foliage, 6½in. wide. (Christie's) $3,657

A George III dark satinwood oval tea caddy, the cover inlaid with Prince of Wales feathers, the front panel with ribbon tied tulips and other foliage, 6in. wide. (Christie's) $2,303

A George III rolled paper navette shaped tea caddy, with gilt heightened decoration overall, the front panel with a circular reserve of a figure with cross, 7in. wide. (Christie's) $5,264

An antique oak standing spoon rack for 12, spoons in three tiers, fitted arched back and shaped apron, 13in. high, with six antique pewter spoons and five others. (Brightwells) $785

A George III or Regency octagonal tea caddy, possibly sycamore veneered, painted to the cover and front panels with flowers and foliage, 5¾in. wide. (Christie's) $2,467

A Regency tortoiseshell veneered tea caddy, second quarter 19th century, lion mask ring handles and claw feet, the interior with ivory banding and twin canisters, 11½in. wide. (Christie's) $6,580

A polychrome enamel box and cover, 18cm. high. (Christie's) $560

A William IV tortoiseshell veneered tea caddy, the bowed front and cover with mother of pearl and pique inlay, the interior with ivory banding and twin subsidiary covers, 8in. wide. (Christie's) $1,480

A 19th century tortoiseshell two-division tea caddy with two interior lidded compartments, shaped front with white metal line inlay, 6in. wide. (Brightwells) $2,187

A George III satinwood oval tea caddy, the cover and front panel inlaid with ribbon tied foliage, 12.4cm. wide. (Christie's) $739

A 19th century Italian ebony table casket, inset with porcelain plaques by Doccia depicting mythological figure scenes in low relief, 12¼in. wide. (Andrew Hartley) $3,625

A south German walnut casket, late 17th century, the sarcophagus shaped hinged lid enclosing a candlebox above a panelled body with carrying handles either side on later bun feet, 20¼in. wide. (Bonhams) $280

A George III tea caddy of sarcophagus shape with satinwood and oyster veneer having three interior cut-glass rectangular jars with white metal covers, 12¹/₅in. wide. (Brightwells) $6,580

A Tunbridgeware rosewood caddy of waisted oblong form, the domed lid depicting a stag, opening to reveal fitted interior with two compartments, 9in. wide. (Andrew Hartley) $1,193

An Anglo Indian ebony desk stand, 19th century, with porcupine quill veneer panels and ivory dot inlay to the frame, 16¼in. wide.
(Christie's) $1,463

A William IV coromandel travelling dressing case with brass corner mounts and stringing fitted with silver-gilt lidded cut-glass jars and bottles, London 1833, Maker: W.N, 12in.
(Brightwells) $2,793

A Directoire mahogany traveller's case, circa 1800, rectangular with shield escutcheons and angular loop handles, the morocco lined interior comprehensively fitted.
(Bonhams) $444

A George III apple-shaped fruitwood tea caddy, with stork to the cover, 4½in. high. overall.
(Christie's) $4,606

Late Regency brass inlaid rosewood tea caddy, 19th century, with foliate openwork inlay in the Boulle style, 12¼in. wide.
(Skinner) $920

A Regency tortoiseshell veneered and pewter-strung tea caddy, second quarter 19th century, of sarcophagus outline with curved sides, with silver-plated ball finial and on conforming feet, 6½in. wide.
(Christie's) $4,388

An 18th century Chinese blue and white tea caddy of rectangular form with willow pattern design, the hinged cover revealing three white metal canisters, 10in. wide.
(Brightwells) $3,080

An Export cabinet, Momoyama Period (late 16th century), decorated in gold hiramaki-e and inlaid with mother of pearl, with panels of chrysanthemums and fuyo to the sides, 14 x 10 x 10½in.
(Christie's) $5,358

An Italian ebony and marquetry tea caddy, Sorrento, mid 19th century, top and sides decorated with rustic figures within mosaic crossbandings, the compartmented interior with two olivewood covers, 8¼in. wide.
(Bonhams) $1,470

Decorative Victorian walnut inkstand, the back applied with a letter box with a sloping cover, fitted below for two bottles and pen tray and the frieze with a full width drawer, 12in. (G.A. Key) $276

A 19th century burr walnut tea caddy, with beaded edging and mother of pearl scrolling foliate inlay, hinged lid revealing two lift out containers and cut glass bowl, 13in. wide.
(Andrew Hartley) $628

Decorative 19th century mahogany decanter box, interior fitted with compartments and removable tray, the lid inlaid with an ebonized and ivorine strung cruciform motif, 13½in. (G.A. Key) $203

Red painted pine fitted storage box, possibly America, early 19th century, containing twelve blown olive amber gin bottles, 11 x 18 x 13½in. (Skinner) $1,725

George III fruitwood pear-shaped tea caddy, England, late 18th century, with stylized trefoil metal escutcheon, hinged lid with foil interior, stem off, but present, 5¾in. high. (Skinner) $3,220

A Napoleon III liqueur set in cabinet, of four engraved glass decanters with ball stoppers and fourteen glasses, held in gilt metal frame in ebonised mother of pearl and brass inlaid case with tulipwood banding, 32cm. wide.
(Bristol) $1,287

Regency period tortoiseshell and ivory tea caddy of canted rectangular form, the interior fitted with one compartment, 5in.. (G.A. Key) $1,233

A South German wrought iron strong box, 17th or early 18th century, bound with iron strapwork and twin scroll handles to the sides, the interior with pierced lockplate decorated with a figure amidst foliage, 23in. wide.
(Christie's) $3,108

A Victorian mother of pearl veneered tea caddy, of casket form with pilasters and bun feet, engraved and inlaid with flowers two lidded compartments inside, 17.4cm. (Bristol) $1,540

Oak three bottle tantulus, applied with formerly silver plated mounts and fitted for three bottles, 13in. (G.A. Key) $377

An early 19th century fruitwood tea caddy, pear shaped with hinged top, 6in. high. (Andrew Hartley) $4,082

A 19th century fitted burr walnut cased set of polished steel cockfighting spurs and bandages. (Brightwells) $770

Painted wooden wall box, America, 19th century, pierced round hanger above two open slant fronted compartments, shaped sides, painted brown, 24in. high. (Skinner) $2,070

Pair of Federal mahogany inlaid knife boxes, England, early 19th century, serpentine front with silver fittings, slant lid top with shell inlay, 15 x 8½ x 11in. (Skinner) $3,738

English George III fruitwood pear-shaped tea caddy, late 18th century, with metal oval escutcheon and upright stem, hinged lid, traces of foil to interior, 6¾in. high. (Skinner) $3,105

Victorian walnut vanity box, inset with brass name plate, similar escutcheon, the interior with silver plated fittings and also containing three hallmarked silver handled manicure items, 12in. (G.A. Key) $377

A 19th century Chinese lacquered games box, the detachable lid with black center panel depicting a river scene on gilded simulated fish skin ground, the interior with five boxes, 11½in. wide. (Andrew Hartley) $738

A 19th century camphor wood and lacquer "Valuables Port", fitted with three interlocking tiers surmounted by a fitted lid, set on a rectangular base with crossbar and handle, 74cm. wide. (Bonhams) $493

CAMERAS

Kombi camera 28160, Alfred C. Kemper, Chicago; rollfilm, anodized metal body, in maker's box. (Christie's) $695

Duplex Super 120 no. 1637, ISO, Italy; 120-rollfilm, with a pair of Iriar f/3.5 35mm. lenses nos. 1999 and 1847, in maker's ever ready case. (Christie's) $361

Horseman 970 camera no. 411725, Tokyo Kogaku, Japan; 120-rollfilm, with two rollfilm holders, in leather cases, a Horseman P.W f/5.6 6.5cm., lens. (Christie's) $758

Sonnet tropical camera, Contessa, Stuttgart; 6.5 x 9cm., teak body, brown leather bellows, with a Carl Zeiss Jena Triotar f/6.3 12cm. lens in a Compound shutter. (Christie's) $431

No. 2 Beau Brownie rollfilm, Art Deco styled rose-colored face-plate with a Doublet lens and rotary shutter. (Christie's) $578

Cartridge Kodak No. 3 camera, Eastman Kodak Co., Rochester, N.Y.; rollfilm, leather-covered exterior, mahogany interior, red leather bellows, with a Bausch & Lomb Rapid Rectilinear lens. (Christie's) $103

Triple Imperial Extension field camera, Thornton-Pickard Mfg. Co. Ltd., Altrincham; half-plate, brass and mahogany, with a brass bound Busch lens and double darkslides. (Christie's) $458

Aerial camera no. 183, Thornton-Pickard Mfg. Co., Altrincham; 5 x 4in., mahogany body, inset brass binding, rear focal-plane shutter. (Christie's) $2,528

TOP TIP

Early wooden and brass cameras are highly decorative and fascinating in their early technology, but 20th century models also have a devoted following.

Leica is the name to conjure with here and a Leica from the 1920s with an Anastigmat lens will now sell for up to $30,000.

110

Horseman Press camera no. 403123, Tokyo Kogaku, Japan; 6 x cm. exposures on 120-rollfilm, with magazine back and a Tokyo Kogaku Topcor P.S f/3.5 10.5cm. lens. (Christie's) $475

Coronet Midget camera (red) Coronet Camera Co., England; 16mm. (cracked), in maker's box. (Christie's) $145

Makiflex SLR, gray-body, with a Carl Zeiss, Jena Tessar f/4.5 18cm. lens no. 507406. (Christie's) $397

Postage stamp camera, J. Lancaster & Son, Birmingham; 3 x 2in. carte de visite, mahogany body, with six brass bound lenses for Gem exposures. (Christie's) $4,491

A studio camera, Century No 2, mahogany body, square cut leather bellows, Stewart & Co Melbourne, Rapid Rectilinear, 12 x 10in. brass lens. (Christie's) $479

Tailboard camera no. 39172, G. & H. Hasselblad, Sweden; 18 x 24cm., wood-body, brass fittings, a Carl Zeiss, Jena Anastigmat f/9 230mm. lens and darkslides. (Christie's) $903

Nikon F Photomic FTN no. 7363471, black, with F-36 power-pack no. 97166 and motor winder no. 153102. (Christie's) $812

Ring camera, brass decorated body with sprung lion mask lens cover, single speed shutter. (Christie's) $4,023

Royal Mail postage stamp camera no. B31, W. Butcher & Sons, London; 3¼ x 4¼ plate, for fifteen exposures, polished wood body. (Christie's) $828

Compass II no. 4331, Le Coultre et Cie, Switzerland; with French engraving, tab engraved *F* and a CCL3B Anastigmat f/3.5 35mm. lens, in maker's box.
(Christie's) $3,347

Alfa-2 camera, WZFO, Poland; 35mm., pale blue painted body, with an Emitar f/4.5 45mm. lens.
(Christie's) $768

Primarflex SLR no. 27838, Curt Bentzin, Germany; 120-rollfilm, with a Meyer Trioplan f/2.8 10cm. lens.
(Christie's) $282

Kodak original camera no. 3039, Eastman Kodak Co., Rochester, N.Y.; rollfilm, 2½in. exposures, maroon leather-covered body, lacquered brass fittings, revolving exposure indicator.
(Christie's) $1,382

Petie handbook camera, W. Kunik, Germany; comprising a white lady's handbag with strap and metal clasp, a hinged panel revealing a 16mm. Petie camera.
(Christie's) $3,657

Daguerreotype stereoscopic camera, Home & Co., London, comprising a 2¾ x 3in. mahogany-body sliding-box camera with brass fittings, mahogany back with removable ground-glass focusing screen and wood shutter.
(Christie's) $21,305

MONEY MAKERS

With cameras becoming ever more computerised, there has been a certain backlash among collectors grown nostalgic for manual machines, where you have to set focus, aperture etc, yourself. One result of this is that good quality 1970s models are now being eagerly snapped up (excuse pun!). So pause before you ditch your old 'steam' model - it could be worth more than you think.

Royal Ruby Reflex camera, Thornton-Pickard Mfg., Co., England; quarter-plate, leather-covered wood-body, polished-wood interior and a Beck Isostigmar f/5.8 150mm. lens.(Christie's) $289

Bronica S2A no. CB117428, Zenza Bronica, Japan; 120-rollfilm, with magazine back and a Nikon Nikkor-P f/2.8 75mm. lens.
(Christie's) $483

Ticka camera, Houghton, London; 16 x 22mm., cassette film, bright metal plated body finish, meniscus lens, cap and reflex finder. (Christie's) $768

Brin's patent camera no. 621, Brin, London; 1-inch diameter, lacquered-brass body, spring shutter, metal plate holder with focusing screen. (Christie's) $26,438

Summa Report no. 0155, C. Tiranta, Rome; 6 x 9cm., with a rollfilm back, four-lens turret holding a Schneider Xenar f/3.5 105mm. lens. (Christie's) $4,485

Tessina automatic no. 63641, Concava S.A., Switzerland; 35mm., chrome, with a Tessinon f/2.8 25mm. lens, waistlevel finder and a removable accessory shoe-mounted Tessina photo-electric light meter.(Christie's) $1,467

Ben Akiba walking stick camera no. 664, Lehmann, Berlin; nickelled brass body, the exterior with decorative edge engraving, internal sprung shutter, winding handle, eleven brass film spools. (Christie's) $15,863

Sutton's Patent Panoramic lens no. 22, T. Ross, London; the brass bound lens engraved around the barrel *Sutton's Patent Panoramic Lens. Made by T. Ross, London No. 22*, in maker's brass cylinder case. (Christie's) $10,971

Noblex Panorama no. L24/55, Kamerawerke Noble GmbH, Dresden; 120-rollfilm, green-metal body finish, with a Tessar f/4.5 50mm. lens, strap and accessories, in a fitted case. (Christie's) $1,410

Contaflex 860/24 no. Z.42206, 35mm., with a Sucher-Objectiv f/2.8 8cm. viewing lens and with a Carl Zeiss, Jena f/2.5cm. taking lens. (Christie's) $1,083

MONEY MAKERS

The archetypical Volks-camera, the Box Brownie, was made from 1901 through to the 1930s and is virtually worthless as a collector's piece.

In the late 1920s, however, Kodak added an Art Deco color plate to the face and called it the Beau Brownie. One of these will now sell for $200 or more.

CAROUSEL FIGURES

A carved and painted wood carousel outside stander, Charles Looff, Brooklyn, New York, blue and gold bridle and harness inset with glass jewels above a red and blue scrolled saddle, 56in. long. (Christie's) $32,900

A Savages fairground ride of a galloping ostrich, with double seat, 57in. long. (Christie's) $1,316

A carved and painted carousel prancer, Charles Looff (active 1875-1918), Brooklyn, New York, the full-figured brown-painted bridle, leather reigns, blue and gold harness and saddle, 57½in. high. (Christie's) $8,000

A carved and painted wood carousel horse head, American, late 19th century, realistically carved with articulated features and open mouth, glass eyes and a faux leather harness, 20in. high. (Christie's) $2,350

A carved and painted wood carousel jumper, attributed to Charles Looff, Brooklyn, New York, the articulated full-bodied white-painted horse with glass eyes, black mane, green and black harness, 56in. long. (Christie's) $44,650

Carved and painted wood carousel lion stander, Charles Looff, Brooklyn, New York, with articulated mane and feet, open mouth and glass eyes, fitted with a red painted seat and stirrups, 57in. long. (Christie's) $28,200

Carved and painted carousel prancer, Charles Looff, Brooklyn, New York, embellished mane, saddle, horse shoes and jeweled harness with horse hair tail, 53in. long. (Christie's) $7,638

A carved and painted carousel figure of a dog, Charles Looff, Brooklyn, New York, the life size figure carved in the round on all fours with one paw raised, 55in. wide. (Christie's) $44,650

A carved and painted wood carousel figure of a jumper horse, stamped #37, C.W. Parker, Leavenworth, Kansas, circa 1917, 69in. long. (Sotheby's) $6,760

114

A Soumakh carpet, East Caucasus, circa 1900, 11ft.8in. x 10ft.5in. (Sotheby's) $4,008

A cotton and wool hooked rug, American, 20th century, fan-shaped, worked in red, yellow and green on a black ground featuring a central flower basket with five stemmed tulips, 27½ x 35in. (Christie's) $588

An Ushak carpet, West Anatolia, circa 1910, 14ft.8in. x 14ft.2in. (Sotheby's) $9,619

A fine Bakhtiari Garden carpet, West Persia, the field with multicolored square lattice containing polychrome angular flowering vine, bold palmettes, stylized trees and floral prayer arches, 314 x 208cm. (Christie's) $2,198

A fine unusual Tabriz carpet of Garden design, Northwest Persia, the field with six large rectangular panels containing polychrome shaped prayer panels containing bold pictorial boteh, scrolling flowering vine, various trees with occasional mythological figures, 368 x 271cm. (Christie's) $5,410

A fine tabriz carpet, North-West Persia, the light blue field with angular flowering vine issuing various bold polychrome palmettes, rosettes and hooked leaves around brick-red medallion with pendants containing similar design, 366 x 266cm. (Christie's) $3,043

A fine Continental quality Chinese carpet, the ivory field with central stylized polychrome open floral roundel, similar open spandrels, in an indigo border of meandering flowerhead and leafy vine, 414 x 335cm. (Christie's) $2,029

A wool hooked rug, American, late 19th century, worked in shades of red, orange, black and green wool, centering a bright red horse against a black background, 21 x 30½in. (Christie's) $8,225

An unusual antique cotton Agra rug, North India, the light rust field with angular vine in the shape of stylized cartouches containing polychrome floral vases and various floral motifs, 234 x 152cm. (Christie's) $1,860

1948 Chevrolet Fleetmaster 'Woody' station wagon, maroon with oak and mahogany panels and brown interior, engine: six cylinder with overhead valves with solid valve lifters, 216ci., gearbox: three speed manual; brakes: four wheel drums, left hand drive. (Christie's) $18,800

1927 Bugatti Type 37, French racing blue with brown leather seats, engine: four cylinder in-line, 1,496cc, single overhead camshaft, 70bhp at 4200rpm, gearbox: four speed with side change, brakes: mechanical cable, right hand drive. (Christie's) $79,500

1927 Rolls-Royce Phantom 1 Coupé, coachwork by George W. McNeer, gray with black leather interior for restoration, engine: six cylinder, two blocks of three, overhead valve, 7,668cc; gearbox: four-speed manual, brakes: four wheel drum, left hand drive. (Christie's) $47,000

1954 Allard K3 Three-Seater Roadster, duck-egg blue with gray leather interior, engine: Ford Pilot V8, 3622cc, 95bhp at 3800rpm, clutch: single plate, gearbox: manual three-speed with synchromesh, brakes: hydraulically operated drum, inboard at rear, right hand drive.(Christie's) $19,000

1935 Rolls-Royce 20/25hp Limousine, coachwork by Hooper & Co., cream over brown, with black and tan leather interior, engine: straight-six, overhead valve, 2699cc, gearbox: four speed manual with side change and synchromesh on top ratios, brakes: four wheel mechanically-operated servo-assisted drum, right hand drive. (Christie's) $17,273

1910 Rolls-Royce Silver Ghost "Balloon Car" Roadster, coachwork by Wilkinson & Sons, maroon with black wings with brown hide upholstery, engine: six cylinder, 7,248cc, side valves, 48bhp at 1,000rpm, gearbox: three speed manual, brakes: two wheel drum, right hand drive.

(Christie's) $244,500

1958 Bentley S1 Continental Four Door Sports Saloon, coachwork by James Young, Brewster green with magnolia interior, engine: six cylinder in line overhead inlet and side exhaust valves, right hand drive. (Christie's) $57,619

1973 Jaguar E-Type V12 Series III Roadster with hardtop, blue with beige leather interior, engine: V12, 5,343cc., 241bhp at 4,750rpm, gearbox: automatic transmission, brakes: hydraulic disc, left hand drive. (Christie's) $39,100

1929 Packard 645 Dual Cowl Phaeton, coachwork by Dietrich, blue with black fenders, green wheels and striping and tan leather interior, engine: straight eight, 384.8ci., gearbox: three-speed manual, brakes: four wheel drum, left hand drive.
(Christie's) $105,000

1965 Alfa Romeo 2600 Spider Superleggera, coachwork by Touring, red with black leather interior and a black convertible top, engine: six cylinder twin-cam, 2,582cc, 165 bhp at 5,900 rpm, gearbox: five-speed manual, brakes: front disk, rear drum, left hand drive. (Christie's) $10,675

1970 Dodge Challenger R/T Hemi Coupé, Plum Crazy Purple with black vinyl interior, engine: V8, 426ci., two 4-barrel Carter carburettors, 425 hp at 5,600 rpm, gearbox: four speed manual, brakes: hydraulically operated four wheel drums, left hand drive. (Christie's) $38,775

1968 Mercedes-Benz 600 SWB Limousine, dark blue with tan leather interior, engine: v8, single overhead camshaft per bank, fuel-injected, 6,332cc, 159bhp: gearbox: four-speed automatic, brakes: servo-assisted twin circuit disk, left hand drive. (Christie's) $47,000

1957 Mercedes-Benz 300 Sc Roadster, coachwork by Daimler Benz, Sindelfingen, maroon with tan leather interior and top, engine: six-cylinder in-line, single overhead camshaft, 2,996cc, 175bhp at 5,400rpm, gearbox: four speed manual, brakes: four-wheel hydraulic drum brakes with servo assistance. (Christie's) $442,500

1918 Hispano-Suiza Type 32 30 HP Landaulette, coachwork by Baltasar Fioly-Cia, Carrocerias Barcelona, dark brown with black fenders, light brown pinstriping, engine: four cylinder, 100 x 150mm. bore & stroke, 4,712cc (287ci.), monobloc, water-cooled, single overhead camshaft, gearbox: plate clutch with four-speed and reverse.(Christie's) $105,000

1954 Buick Skylark model-X100 Luxury Sports Car Convertible, black with blue leather interior, engine: fireball V8, 322ci., gearbox: Dynaflow three-speed automatic, brakes: hydraulic drums all around, left hand drive. (Christie's) $68,150

1953 Chevrolet Corvette Roadster, Polo white with Sportsman red interior, engine: Blue Flame six-cylinder, 235.5ci., 150bhp at 4,200rpm, gearbox: two speed automatic, brakes: front and rear drums, left hand drive. (Christie's) $68,500

1909 Rolls-Royce Silver Ghost Roi-Des-Belges Tourer, coachwork Barker style Roi-des-Belges, gray with blue leather upholstery, engine: six-cylinder, 7,036cc, side valves, gearbox: three speed manual, brakes: two wheel drum, right hand drive. (Christie's) $332,500

1902 Lambert 8hp Type G Two Seater Voiturette, dark green, with yellow chassis and black leather interior, engine: De Dion Bouton single cylinder, 100 x 120, 942cc, gearbox: three speed, brakes: rear wheel drum and contracting band on transmission, right hand drive. (Christie's) $44,909

Delage D8-120 Aerosport Coupé, coachwork by Letourneur et Marchand, bronze with burgundy leather upholstery, engine: eight cylinder, in-line, two overhead valves per cylinder, 4,300cc, gearbox: four-speed Cotal electro-magnetic; brakes: four wheel drum, right hand drive.(Christie's) $501,000

1902 Panhard-Levassor 7hp rear entrance tonneau, royal blue with red coachlining and upholstery, engine: two cylinder monobloc, 90 x 130mm. bore and stroke, 1654cc., 3 speed and reverse gearbox, Brakes: contracting bands on back wheels, right hand drive. (Christie's) $112,420

1949 Buick Roadmaster Estate Wagon, coachwork by Ionia, maroon with tan interior and white ash and mahogany woodwork, engine: in-line eight cylinder, 320.2ci, 150bhp at 3,600rpm, gearbox: Dynaflow automatic, brakes: four wheel drums, left hand drive. (Christie's) $24,675

1926 Bentley 3 litre four seater Sports Tourer, coachwork by Vanden Plas of Kingsbury, London, green with green leather interior, engine: four cylinder in-line, gearbox: four speed, brakes: four wheel drum, servo-assisted, right hand drive. (Christie's) $154,770

1922 Bentley 3 liter sports two seater, blue with brown leather interior, Engine: four cylinder in-line, Gearbox: four speed A type; brakes: rear wheel drum, right hand drive. (Christie's) $78,540

1910 Buick Model 17 Five-Seat Tourer, red with black upholstery and hood, engine: four-cylinder, cast in pairs, push-rod overhead valves, 2.7 liters, 22.5 bhp, gearbox: manual three-speed, cone clutch, brakes: rear two-wheel mechanical, right hand drive. (Christie's) $15,850

1929 Packard 645 Dual Cowl Phaeton, coachwork by Dietrich, gray over blue with black fenders and oyster white interior, engine: straight eight, 384.8ci., 120bhp at 3,200rpm; gearbox: three-speed manual, brakes four wheel drum, left hand drive. (Christie's) $116,000

1949 Jaguar XK 120 Roadster (Alloy), yellow and black with dark red leather interior, engine: six cylinder in-line, 3,442cc, compression ratio 7.8:1, 175bhp at 5,000rpm, gearbox: four speed manual, brakes: four-wheel hydraulic drum, left hand drive. (Christie's) $79,500

1933 Armstrong Siddeley 15HP Sports Saloon, cream and black with green leather interior, engine: six cylinders in line, side valves, single carburettor, 2.0 liter, gearbox: four speed pre-selector, brakes: four-wheel drum, right hand drive. (Christie's) $6,674

1904 Talbot 11hp Model CT2K two-seater, dark green with crimson coachlines, black upholstery, engine: 2-cylinder water-cooled, 1526cc, Transmission: cone-clutch, 3-speed & reverse gearbox, Brakes: internal expanding, on rear wheels. (Christie's) $56,518

Jaguar E-Type 3.8 Fixed Head Coupé, scarlet with tan leather interior, engine: six cylinders in-line, twin overhead camshaft, triple carburettors, 3781 cc, 265bhp at 5500 rpm, gearbox: four-speed manual with synchromesh, brakes: four-wheel servo assisted disk, right hand drive. (Christie's) $24,182

1915 Stutz Model 4F Bearcat, dark red with black fenders and black leather interior, engine: four cylinder, in-line, T-head, 390 ci., 50 bhp, gearbox: three speed manual, brakes: mechanical, internal expanding, right hand drive. (Christie's) $129,00

1963 Ferrari 250GTE 2 + 2 Pininfarina Coupé, Rosso Corso with tan leather interior, engine: V-12, overhead camshaft, 2953cc, triple Weber carburettors, 235bhp at 7,000rpm, gearbox: 4-speed manual, brakes: four-wheel hydraulic disk, left hand drive. (Christie's) $43,181

1911 Lion-Peugeot Type V2Y3 16HP Sports Two Seater, olive green – for restoration, engine: V-twin, 85mm x 150mm bore & stroke, 1,702cc (103ci) water-cooled with side valves and magneto ignition, gearbox: cone clutch, three speed and reverse gearbox, shaft drive, chassis: pressed steel, right hand drive. (Christie's) $19,975

1929 Chevrolet International AC Phaeton, green with black fenders and green vinyl interior, engine: in-line, six cylinder, pushrod operated overhead valves, 194ci, 46hp at 2,600 rpm, gearbox: three-speed manual, brakes: mechanically operated four wheel drums, left hand drive. (Christie's) $8,813

1921 Brewster Model 91 Town Car, green and cream with leather and cloth interior, engine: four cylinder in line Knight patent sleeve valve, cast en bloc 53bhp, gearbox: selective sliding three speeds forward and reverse, brakes: mechanical expanding on rear wheels, left hand drive. (Christie's) $19,97

1973 Ferrari 365/GT4 BB, coachwork by Pininfarina, yellow and black with black leather interior, engine: flat 12, twin overhead camshafts to each head, 4,390cc, 344bhp at 7,000rpm, gearbox: manual five-speed, brakes: four wheel power assisted hydraulically operated disk, left hand drive. (Christie's) $56,400

1935 Bugatti Type 57 Ventoux fixed head coupé, coachwork by Carrosserie Bugatti, two-tone black and yellow with beige leather upholstery, engine: straight eight, twin overhead camshafts, sixteen valve, 3257cc, gearbox: four-speed manual, brakes: finned drums front and rear, right hand drive. (Christie's) $171,00

1931 Lincoln Model K Convertible Coupé, coachwork by Le Baron, Jonquil yellow with red wings and brown leather interior, engine: V-8, side valve, 384ci, 120bhp at 2,900rpm; gearbox: three speed manual with free wheeling device; Brakes: four wheel drums, left hand drive. (Christie's) $61,600

1934 Reo Flying Cloud Convertible Coupé with rumble seat, olive green over cream with Piedmont green fenders and molding, green leather interior, engine: in-line six cylinder, 95hp; gearbox: three-speed manual, brakes: four wheel hydraulic drums, left hand drive. (Christie's) $88,125

1934 Packard V12 Dual Cowl Sport Phaeton, LeBaron replica coachwork, black with red leather interior, engine: V12, 445 ci., 160bhp at 3,200rpm, Stromberg dual downdraft carburettors, gearbox: three speed manual, brakes: four wheel, vacuum-assisted drums all around, left hand drive.
(Christie's) $266,500

1954 Bentley R-type Hooper Empress Sports Saloon, coachwork by Hooper & Co., two tone green with tan leather upholstery, engine: six cylinder in-line, overhead valve, twin carburettors, 4,566cc, 150bhp at 4,500rpm; gearbox: automatic; brakes: hydraulic front, mechanical rear, servo assisted, right hand drive. (Christie's) $18,800

1950 MG TD Sports two-seater, Clipper blue with a biscuit leather interior, engine: in-line four cylinder, pushrod overhead valves, 1,250cc, 57bhp, gearbox: four-speed manual with sychromesh on top three gears, brakes: four wheel hydraulic drums, right hand drive. (Christie's) $11,163

1938 Studebaker Model 84 State Commander Convertible Sedan, canary yellow with green leather upholstery, engine: six cylinder in-line, L-head, 226 ci., gearbox: three-speed manual, brakes: four wheel hydraulic drums. Right hand drive.
(Christie's) $30,550

1925 Lancia Lambda 4th Series Torpedo Tourer, red with black wings and black leather interior, engine: Tipo 67. Narrow Vee 4 cylinder, overhead camshaft, 2120cc, 50bhp at 3000rpm, Zenith Triple Diffuser carburettor, gearbox: four speed manual, brakes: four wheel mechanical, right hand drive.
(Christie's) $41,454

1951 Daimler DB18 Special Sports Three-Seater Drophead Coupé, Old English white, dark blue leather interior, engine: six cylinders in-line, push-rod overhead valve, 2.5 liter, twin carburettors, 85bhp at 4200 rpm, transmission: fluid flywheel with epicyclic preselector gearbox, brakes: four-wheel Girling hydro-mechanically operated drum, right hand drive. (Christie's) $17,273

1906 Reo Model B 8 HP Runabout, yellow with black leather seats, engine: horizontal single-cylinder, 106ci, water-cooled, side-valve with jump spark ignition, gearbox: planetary two-speed and reverse with final drive by central chain, brakes: external-contracting brakes on rear wheels, right hand drive. (Christie's) $12,925

1926 Kissel 8-75 Speedster, dark blue with black fenders and black leather interior, engine: in-line, L-head, 8-cylinder, 310ci, 71hp at 3,000rpm, gearbox: three-speed manual, brakes: four wheel hydraulic, left hand drive. (Christie's) $52,875

1937 BSA Scout Series IV Two Seater Sports, cream with maroon cloth interior, for restoration, engine: four cylinders, in-line, Solex carburettors, 1,203cc, 32bhp, gearbox: front-wheel drive, wet plate clutch, three-speed manual, brakes: four-wheel mechanically operated drum, right hand drive. (Christie's) $4,700

1903 Panhard-Levassor Type H 15hp Hotel Omnibus, gray bodywork, dark green mudguard and bonnet, black moldings, Panhard red wheels and coachlining, engine: four-cylinder, 90mm. 130mm bore & stroke, 3.3 liter, brakes: contracting bands on back wheels, right hand drive. (Christie's) $208,978

1901 Adler 4½ HP Vis-à-Vis, engine: front-mounted De Dion Bouton, 84 x 90mm. bore & stroke 498cc, transmission: cone clutch, 3-speed and reverse sliding gearbox, external contracting brakes on rear hubs from hand lever, right-hand drive. (Christie's) $42,504

1905 Oldsmobile Runabout "Curved Dash", black and red with black leather upholstery, engine: single horizontal cylinder, 1,565cc, 7hp, gearbox: two-speed epicyclic, suspension: semi-elliptic leaf front and rear with cantilever springs, brakes: rear contracting band, tiller steering. (Christie's) $15,275

1923 Buick Model 65 Five-Seat Tourer, burgundy with black wings, upholstery and hood, engine: six cylinders in line, overhead valves, 4.2 liters, 55bhp at 2800 rpm, gearbox: manual three-speed, brakes: mechanically-operated drum, left-hand drive. (Christie's) $23,924

1955 Mercedes-Benz 180 Ponton Saloon, black with dark green interior, engine: four cylinders in line, side-valve, 1767cc, 52bhp at 4000 rpm, gearbox: manual four speed all synchromesh, brakes: four wheel hydraulically operated drum, right hand drive. (Christie's) $7,254

1924 Ford Model T Doctor's Coupé, black with cloth interior trim, engine: four cylinders in line, side valves, 176.7 cubic inch (2890cc), 22bhp at 1800rpm, gearbox: two-speed and reverse epicyclic transmission, brakes: contracting band on transmission. (Christie's) $10,364

1937 Packard 8 Type 120-C 3-Position Drophead Coupé, coachwork by Chapron, pink with gray wings and with matching gray upholstery and trim, engine: eight cylinders in-line, side valves, 4.6 liters (282 cu inch) 120bhp at 3800 rpm, gearbox: manual three-speed with synchromesh, brakes: four wheel hydraulically operated drum, left hand drive. (Christie's) $39,292

1938 Rover 12 HP Saloon, complete car: engine runs, original tool kit, jack and starting handle, number plate elite value £1500, V5 Licence, dry stored for 17 years. (Brightwells) $2,660

1916 Overland Model 90 Country Club Roadster, green and black with black leatherette upholstery, engine: four cylinder, in-line, cast en bloc 35bhp; gearbox: selective sliding three speeds forward and reverse, brakes: mechanical contracting on rear wheels, left hand drive. (Christie's) $7,638

CARS

1910 Peugeot Type 134 22HP Tourer, cream paintwork – for restoration, engine: four cylinder, 108mm. x 130mm. bore & stroke, 4,763cc (290ci.), gearbox: cone clutch, shaft drive with four-speed and reverse, right hand drive. (Christie's) $38,775

1959 Chevrolet Apache 32 Long Stepside Pick Up, tartan turquoise and white with white interior, engine: in-line, overhead valve six cylinder, 235.5ci., four-speed manual; brakes: four wheel hydraulic drums, left hand drive. (Christie's) $21,150

1935 Bentley 3½ litre Sports Saloon, coachwork by Hooper & Co., black over cream with gray leather interior, engine: six cylinder-in-line, 3,669cc, gearbox: four speed manual, brakes: four wheel drum, right hand drive. (Christie's) $20,022

1940 Ford Deluxe V8 Convertible Coupé, maroon with maroon leather interior, engine: V8, L-head, 221ci., 85hp at 3,800rpm, gearbox: three-speed manual, brakes: four wheel hydraulic drums, left hand drive. (Christie's) $39,950

1910 Stevens-Duryea Model XXX Runabout Roadster, red with black fenders and black leather interior, engine: four cylinder L-head, 318ci., 35hp, gearbox: three speed manual, brakes: rear wheel drums, right hand drive. (Christie's) $79,500

1925 Morris Cowley Bullnose Four Seater Tourer, beige with black wings and dark red interior, engine: four cylinders in-line, side-valves, 11.9hp rating, gearbox: three-speed manual, brakes: four wheel mechanical drum. (Christie's) $13,348

1933 Pierce-Arrow V12 Convertible coupé, styled by LeBaron, built by Pierce-Arrow, pewter and blue with red leather interior, engine: V12 side valve, 462 ci., 175hp at 3,400rpm, gearbox: manual three speed, brakes: Stewart-Warner power assisted drums all around, left hand drive.(Christie's) $140,000

1937 Bentley 4¼-liter Four Door Allweather Tourer, coachwork by Vanden Plas, black with brown interior, and fawn hood, engine: six cylinder, 4,257cc, overhead valve, 125bhp at 4,500rpm, gearbox: four speed manual, brakes: four wheel drum, right hand drive. (Christie's) $45,138

1958 Edsel Pacer Coupé, two-tone green and white with green and white vinyl/cloth interior, engine: V-8, 361ci, 303bhp at 4,600rpm; gearbox: Teletouch three-speed automatic, brakes: four wheel drums, left hand drive. (Christie's) $11,750

1962 Fiat Jolly 600, coachwork by Ghia, white with wicker interior, engine: four cylinder, inline, overhead-valve, 633cc, gearbox: four speed manual, brakes: four-wheel drum, left hand drive. (Christie's) $39,100

1959 Corvette Roadster, Tuxedo black/silver coving with black soft top and red interior, engine, V8, single four-barrel carburetor, 283ci., 230bhp; gearbox: Powerglide automatic, brakes four wheel drum, left hand drive. (Christie's) $32,250

1955 Ford Thunderbird, red with black with white interior and white hardtop, engine: V8, 292ci, gearbox: four-speed manual, suspension: independent front with solid rear axle, brakes power assisted four wheel drums, left hand drive. (Christie's) $24,675

1930 Packard 745 Deluxe Eight Roadster, black with red leather interior, engine: side valve water cooled straight eight, 384 ci; gearbox: four speed manual; brakes: front and rear drums, left hand drive. (Christie's) $129,360

1939 Lasalle Coupé, coachwork by Fisher, tan with beige broadcloth interior, engine: eight cylinder L-head, 322ci, 125bhp at 3,400rpm, gearbox: three-speed manual, brakes: hydraulic drums all around, left hand drive. (Christie's) $14,100

1939 Bugatti Type 57 Stelvio Drophead Coupé, coachwork by Gangloff of Colmar, two tone blue with tan leather interior, engine: eight cylinders in-line, 135bhp at 4,500rpm. gearbox: four-speed manual; brakes: finned drum brakes with hydraulic actuation, right hand drive.(Christie's) $290,290

1936 Packard V12 Model 1407 Dual Cowl Phaeton, cream-yellow with tan leather interior and red wheels, engine: modified L-head V12, 473.3 ci., 175hp at 3,200rpm, gearbox: three speed manual, brakes: vacuum assisted hydraulic drums all around, left hand drive. (Christie's) $178,500

A late Victorian brass six light chandelier, late 19th century, with nozzles and drip pans about the pierced circlet and rod suspension, 24in. high.(Christie's) $1,097

A large hanging chandelier, designed by Hugo Gorge, circa 1925, large circular frame supporting three inset neon bulbs, 48in. diameter. (Christie's) $10,575

A late Victorian or Edwardian glass four branch gasolier, late 19th or early 20th century, F & C Osler, the part-faceted branches with swags of pendants below the writhen baluster stem, 38in. high. (Christie's) $2,011

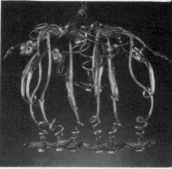

A clear cut and semi-opalescent blue glass nine light chandelier, early 20th century, the writhen s-scroll branches supporting petal cut candle sockets and conforming drip pans hung with faceted pendants, 42in. high. (Christie's) $5,851

A brass chandelier, designed by Dagobert Peche, circa 1918/1920, central bloom surrounded by six foliate tendrils, terminating in large blossoms, 40½in. approximate height. (Christie's) $16,743

A Gledstone Hall glass hanging shade, designed by Sir Edwin Lutyens, circa 1925, opalescent glass disk and three heads, suspended by entwined flex with three wire brackets supporting three further glass beads, 33in. high. (Christie's) $19,388

A hanging chandelier, retailed by E. Bakalowits Söhne, circa 1903, seven glass shades, suspended from large flat circular ceiling mount on cords threaded with emerald green beads, 49in. high. (Christie's) $16,743

A large brass chandelier, manufactured by A. Chertier, circa 1870, architectural form, four extending branches supporting candelabra, 73in. high. (Christie's) $5,252

'Boule De Gui', a molded glass ceiling light, designed by René Lalique, 1922, spherical form, modelled with mistletoe, 19¾in. diameter. (Christie's) $19,388

A gilt-bronze and cut glass chandelier, Paris, circa 1900, of basket form, filled with faceted drops with a foliate cast border surmounted by angels and medallions, approximately 145cm. high. (Sotheby's) $9,108

Giltwood and iron chandelier, probably Italy, late 18th /early 19th century, old surface, fitted with electrified sockets and external wiring, 39½in. high,46in. wide. (Skinner) $19,550

A Victorian cut-glass twelve-branch chandelier, of George III style, with central baluster column below two pendant palmed canopies, with serpentine branches hung with drops, 62in. high. (Christie's) $13,041

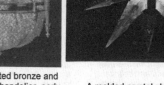

A gilt and patinated bronze and glass four light chandelier, early 20th century, the torchère branches about the circlet with ribbon crestings, 32in. high. (Christie's) $2,377

A molded crystal chandelier, by C.J. Weinstein, cica 1931, starburst form, gilt bronze mount, 27in. maximum length, diameter of star. (Christie's) $16,743

A gilt-bronze chandelier French, circa 1860, in Louis XV style, the leaf-cast corona suspended from a scrolled baluster standard with beading and gadrooning, issuing thirty scrolling foliate candlebranches, 143cm. high. (Sotheby's) $50,768

A brass twelve branch chandelier, late 19th or early 20th century, with nozzles and drip pans on scroll branches in two registers about the knopped bulbous stem, 26in., high. (Christie's) $1,646

A gilt brass and glass six branch chandelier, early 20th century, the branches issuing from the openwork frame of cartouche outline, with pear-shaped terminal and two tiers of subsidiary arms, 44in. high.(Christie's) $2,926

A unique carved chandelier, designed by Maurice Dufrene, circa 1913, three-tiered chandelier elaborately carved with eighteen graduated branches, cream opalescent tulip shades, 90½in. approximate height. (Christie's) $33,488

A Continental ormolu eighteen light chandelier, 19th century, the open scrolling frame applied with bearded masks and herms issuing two tiers of scrolling branches hung with faceted glass pendants, 34in. high. (Christie's) $2,944

A pair of Continental wrought-iron ten light chandeliers, of inverted trumpet outline, 34in. high. (Christie's) $2,608

A French gilt and patinated bronze twenty-four light chandelier, late 19th century, the entwined foliate cast branches issuing from the hexagonal base with gadrooned terminal to the underside, 40in. high. (Christie's) $3,312

A French gilt and patinated bronze six light chandelier, early 20th century, the fluted branches about the pierced domed underside with strings of graduated faceted beads, 24in. wide.(Christie's) $3,634

A French gilt brass and bronze three light chandelier, early 20th century, with glass petal shades on branches issuing from a lattice basket, 28in. high. (Christie's) $1,635

A six light antler chandelier, early 20th century, the frame of conjoined antlers with conforming corona and glass shades, 36in. wide. (Christie's) $2,776

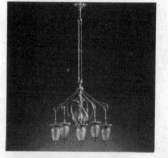

A large English gilt-bronze mounted brass twelve-light chandelier, early 20th century, the tapered tubular frame intersected by a projecting circular gallery with pierced lanceolate leaf decoration, 67¼in. high. (Christie's) $1,702

A copper and brass chandelier, designed by W.A.S. Benson, circa 1898, central stylized foliate stem, five tendril arms, yellow opalescent shades, 55in. approximate height. (Christie's) $38,775

A small brass and glass chandelier, designed by Koloman Moser, circa 1902, the glass shade attributed to Loetz Witwe, spherical glass shade decorated with dappled dot effect, 30½in. high. (Christie's) $5,640

cobalt-decorated stoneware vase,
nnsylvania, third quarter 19th
ntury, decorated all over with
lized blue flowers, height 18in.
otheby's) $11,400

A molded sewer tile bust,
American, late 19th century, the
molded form depicting Admiral
Dewey, 12¾in. high.
(Christie's) $4,113

A salt-glazed cobalt-decorated
stoneware jug Massachusetts,
second half 19th century, baluster
form with applied strap handle of 4
gallon capacity, 16½in. high.
(Christie's) $588

cobalt-decorated five-gallon
oneware jug, New York
oneware Company, mid-19th
ntury, and the body decorated
th crossed American flags above
stylised shield, height 18½in.
otheby's) $10,200

A molded and painted ceramic
figure of a spaniel, American, late
19th century, the seated figure with
articulated face, hair, legs and tail
on a molded base with stars and
gothic arch decoration, 11½in. high.
(Christie's) $1,500

A painted chalkware figure of a
fireman, American, 19th century,
the standing figure with painted
facial features, helmet, red shirt,
black pants and boots, 14in. high.
(Christie's) $15,275

glazed stoneware figure of a dog,
nnsylvania, 19th century, the
llow molded figure in the form of
eated spaniel with articulated
ad, body and fur, 11in. high.
hristie's) $1,000

A possibly Moravian, slip-decorated
bowl, Pennsylvania or Shenandoah
valley, 19th century, the interior
embellished with tow slip-decorated
scalloped lines with random copper
splash decoration, 13½in. diameter.
(Christie's) $1,175

A large salt-glazed stoneware
crock, American, 19th century,
wheel-turned baluster form with
wide mouth, flattened lip sloping
shoulder and irregularities in the
body shape enlivened with an
incised bird, 14in. high.
(Christie's) $470

Amphora centerpiece, with incised decoration and jewel style insets, 9¼in. high. (Skinner) $385

A large Amphora porcelain model of a lioness, standing on a rocky base with a deer at her feet, printed and impressed marks, 20th century, 44cm. long.
(Woolley & Wallis) $118

Amphora ceramic goat vase, Austria, early 20th century, the upper portion decorated with painted pastoral scene with goat reclining by trees, 10¾in. high. (Skinner) $92

ARITA

An Arita oviform jar and cover, late 17th century, decorated in underglaze blue with birds and insects among sprays of flower and foliage, the domed cover with a flattened knop finial, 9¾in.
(Christie's) $4,939

A pair of Arita blue and white kendi, early 18th century, painted in underglaze blue with flowering hydrangea bordered by foliate scroll and peonies around the shoulder, 24.3cm. high.
(Christie's) $6,580

A rare Arita model of a dog, late 17th century, decorated in iron-red green, yellow and black enamels, seated with its head raised and turned slightly to the left in an alert manner, 25cm. high.
(Christie's) $25,20

A Japanese Arita dish, circa 1710-25, painted in underglaze-blue, green and red enamels with two quail before chrysanthemums and foliage, 8¼in. diameter.
(Sotheby's) $1,080

A blue and white Arita vase, 17th century, finely decorated in underglaze blue with a bold design of a pair of herons perched in branches of wisteria, 15in. high.
(Christie's) $11,515

An Arita blue and white tureen, la 17th century, boldly decorated wit flowers and foliage among rocks and clouds with flattened knop finial, 13in. high.
(Christie's) $9,04

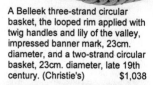

A Belleek 'Grass' pattern honey-pot and cover, modelled as a beehive, with basket-weave-molded handle issuing wild grasses, circa 1875, 16cm. high. (Christie's) $461

A Belleek three-strand circular basket, the looped rim applied with twig handles and lily of the valley, impressed banner mark, 23cm. diameter, and a two-strand circular basket, 23cm. diameter, late 19th century. (Christie's) $1,038

A Belleek oviform jug, with scroll handle terminating in a mask head, molded with scrolling foliage and enriched in shades of green, 25.5cm. high. (Christie's) $1,397

A Belleek shell-molded cornucopia vase, with a flared waved rim and spiral terminal, above two putti, painted to simulate bronze, circa 1880, 28cm. high. (Christie's) $2,632

A Belleek tete-à-tete, of hexagonal form with crimped borders, painted with butterflies among sprays of pink roses, circa 1900, the tray, 43cm. (Christie's) $7,402

A Belleek parian bust of Lord James Butler, quarter-length, modelled with his head turned, on waisted socle base, circa 1875, 30cm. high. (Christie's) $624

A Belleek hexagonal three strand basket, the rope-twist rim applied with sprigs of flowers to each tip, early 20th century, 15cm. wide. (Christie's) $656

A pair of Belleek 'Aberdeen' jugs, of reeded baluster form, with scroll handles, applied with loose sprays of flowers including roses and carnations, circa 1900, 23.5cm. high. (Christie's) $1,200

A Belleek two-strand circular basket, the looped rim applied with twig handles and flowers, impressed banner mark, circa 1880, 25cm. diameter. (Christie's) $1,250

A Berlin KPM plaque of Venus, circa 1880, painted after Titian, with the reclining Venus being crowned by a putto with a garland of flowers, 6¼in. (Sotheby's) $6,350

A Berlin (K.P.M.) oval plaque of the 'Queen of Roses', late 19th/early 20th century, signed *Wagner*, finely painted with a maiden wearing a hat of lace and roses tied with a large ribbon, 8¾ x 6½in. (Christie's) $5,875

An oval Berlin plaque, third quarter of 19th century, painted with the portrait of an exotic girl facing right, wearing an elaborately embroidered red and gold velvet dress, 10¼ x 8¼in. (Skinner) $3,66

A Berlin topographical vase, circa 1821-23, Kratervase, also known as Vase Medicis/Rheden'sche Sorte, each side painted with a named rectangular view of 'Das Opernhaus in Berlin' and 'Das neue Schauspielhaus in Berlin', 16in. (Sotheby's) $14,112

A pair of Berlin large white figures of Venus and Hercules, late 19th century, the scantily clad goddess seated on a conch-shell chariot, a wreath in her left hand, 40.2cm. high. (Christie's) $1,410

A Berlin (K.P.M.) rectangular plaque, circa 1880, signed *T. Sturm*, finely painted with a maiden serenading a youth holding a posy, attended by another fixing a ribbon in her hair, 33.2 x 28.4cm. (Christie's) $17,625

A Berlin (K.P.M.) rectangular plaque of 'Charitas', late 19th/20th century, painted with a seated bare-breasted woman embracing her four children, offering the bounties of Motherhood, 39.3 x 33.9cm. (Christie's) $12,925

A Berlin allegorical group of 'Astronomy' 19th century, modelled by Wilhelm Christian Meyer, as a putto leaning on a globe and holding a telescope to his right eye, seated figure holding a tablet, 5¼in. (Skinner) $2,900

A Berlin (K.P.M) oval plaque, late 19th/early 20th century, painted with Cupid aiming his arrow at a young beauty seated in a wooden garden, 18¼ x 14½in., within giltwood frame. (Christie's) $11,750

BERNARD MOORE _____ CHINA _____

An impressive Bernard Moore flambé luster jardinière, circa 1970, by Reginald Tomlinson, decorated with a dragon and three flying fish amongst foaming waves in ruby luster, height 28.9cm.
(Sotheby's) $2,700

A good Bernard Moore flambé plaque, circa 1910, painted with a Viking ship under sail in red and green amongst foaming waves with turquoise and gilt raised enamel detailing, diameter 13in.
(Sotheby's) $1,200

A Bernard Moore flambé ginger jar and cover, circa 1910, decorated with bats in flight against a night sky, height 6¼in.
(Sotheby's) $840

BESWICK

A Beswick model of Pigling Bland.
(Bonhams) $188

Minnie Mouse, a Beswick hand-painted figure of Minnie Mouse, 1950s printed in gilt *Minnie Mouse, Copyright Walt Disney, Beswick, England*, 4in. high.
(Christie's) $553

A Beswick model of Rupert The Bear, 11cm. high.
(Bonhams) $251

BÖTTGER

A Böttger polished red stoneware baluster flask, circa 1715, the shoulders applied with female masks with head-dresses and above foliate scrolls, 14.3cm. high.
(Christie's) $5,333

A rare Böttger stoneware plaque of Judith with the head of Holofernes, circa 1710, after Francis van Bossuit, of rectangular form pierced for hanging, 10.7cm. x 8.6cm.
(Sotheby's) $11,760

A Böttger polished red stoneware baluster flask, circa 1715, each recessed panel molded in low relief with birds of paradise in flight or perched among branches, 12.4cm. high.
(Christie's) $4,317

A Bow porcelain figure, 'Winter' from the Four Seasons, a hooded figure seated next to a brazier, 5in. high. (Bonhams) $1,232

A Bow cylindrical mug, flaring towards the base and with a loop handle, the body molded with three sprays of flowering prunus and painted in the famille verte palette, circa 1750-55, 12.3cm. (Woolley & Wallis) $500

A Bow baluster shaped milk jug, polychrome painted with three Chinese figures in a garden, no mark, circa 1760, 7.5cm. (Woolley & Wallis) $338

Two Bow figures of a huntsman and companion, modelled standing, each with a hound at their feet, on pierced scroll-molded bases, iron-red anchor and dagger marks, circa 1765, 16cm. high. (Christie's) $2,352

A Bow Commedia dell'Arte figural candlestick group, circa 1765, modelled with Harlequin and Columbine in dancing pose before a bocage, 11½in. (Skinner) $1,167

A rare small Bow figure of a squirrel, circa 1760, seated upright and eating a nut held in its forepaws, 5.5cm. (Bonhams) $7,350

BRITISH

A Caughley custard cup and cover, blue printed with the Fisherman pattern, 'S' mark, circa 1780, 8cm. (Woolley & Wallis) $368

Sylvac model of a seated terrier type dog, impressed marks and *no. 1380*, 11in. (G.A. Key) $139

An Aller Vale plate decorated with a black cat, inscribed *Actions speak louder than words*, 15cm. diameter. (Bonhams) $188

A 19th century pottery relief molded jug in pale blue glaze, the body modelled as a frieze of bacchanalian figures amongst trailing vines, 10in. high.
(Andrew Hartley) $70

A Jones & Son 'Death of Lord Nelson' blue and white shaped bowl, early 19th century, from the 'British History' series, the sides transfer printed with *Charles I ordering the speaker to give up the five members*, 28.6cm. wide.
(Bristol) $9,702

Wilson Pottery large ewer, molded with scenes of mythological charioteers and foliage on a treacle ground, impressed mark, 19th century, 8in.
(G.A. Key) $44

A Portobello Cottage moneybox, modelled with gothic windows and doors, inscribed *William Marshall Hemingly 1844*, flanked each side by oversized figures, 17cm. high.
(Bonhams) $1,323

A Leeds Fireclay Co Ltd Pottery vase, of gourd shape with bulbous elongated neck, painted in iridescent blue and bronze with scrolls and geometric banding, 7¼in. high.
(Andrew Hartley) $471

A 19th century pottery "Yorkshire Cricketing" mug, of cylindrical form with flattened loop handle, black printed with images of George H Hirst and Wilfred Rhodes, 4¼in. high. (Andrew Hartley) $251

An English blue jasper Stilton dish and cover, with the Muses and ivy borders, base diameter 26.5cm.
(Bristol) $188

Dorchester Pottery handled covered jar, mid 20th century, covered and raised rim on a bulbous body with C handle, signed *C.A.H.* under handle and on base N. Ricci Fecit, and circle stamp, 5¼in. (Skinner) $69

A C H Brannam fish spouted jug, incised mark, 1892, 18cm. high; and three others.
(Christie's) $295

A Newhall '425' pattern teapot, cover and stand, circa 1800, black printed and brightly enamelled with the 'Window' pattern.
(Bonhams) $515

A pottery figure of a seated cat wearing blue ribbon with brown painted details, 8in. high.
(Brightwells) $47

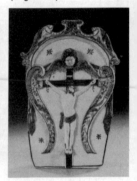

An Aynsley Limited Edition "Wedding Chalice" to commemorate the wedding of Charles and Diana 1981, with Caernarvon Castle etc, No. 34 of 150. (Brightwells) $434

An English porcelain Imari-pattern flared cylindrical small mug, circa 1758, attributed to Samuel Gilbody's factory, painted in underglaze-blue and overglaze iron-red with meandering flowering branch, 2¾in. high.
(Christie's) $1,382

A rare Prattware plaque of the Crucifixion, circa 1800, molded with the figure of Christ upon the Cross below a winged cherub's head in high relief, 9¾in.
(Sotheby's) $3,024

A Frank Brangwyn twin-handled vase, decorated with fruit and leaves, printed marks, 19cm. high.
(Christie's) $427

A large Adams blue and white jardinière, circa 1890, transfer printed with "Cattle Scenery", 20cm. high. (Bonhams) $140

A pottery bust of hooded infant, various marks, 35.5cm. high.
(Christie's) $101

A large English polychrome Farmers Arms jug, circa 1790, black printed and painted with the Farmers Arms' motto beneath *Robt Evans/ Alton Court Near Ross/ Herefordshire* 27.1cm. (Bonhams) $617

A pair of Derbyshire brown saltglaze stoneware models of spaniels, probably Brampton's, circa 1830, each modelled seated facing left and right with padlocked collars. (Sotheby's) $3,696

Donald Duck, a hand-painted porcelain toothbrush holder modelled as Donald Duck, printed *Maw of London Walt Disney Copyright Foreign*, 4in. high. (Christie's) $345

BURLEIGH

'Guardsmen' a Burleigh Ware jug, printed marks, 19.5cm. high. (Christie's) $1,809

A Burleigh Ware wall plate by Charlotte Rhead decorated with a lady's profile and foliate design, printed and painted marks, 25.5cm. diameter.(Christie's) $3,000

'Pied Piper' a Burleigh Ware novelty jug, impressed factory marks, 21.5cm. high. (Christie's) $329

BURMANTOFTS

A Burmantofts faience vase of baluster form, shape no. 2080, molded in parti-color with bands of stylized foliage in shades of blue, turquoise, green and brown, 8¾in. high. (Andrew Hartley) $400

A pair of Burmantofts faience green glaze tiles, relief molded, one depicting a heron, kingfisher and fish in water, the other depicting a rabbit and birds in an undergrowth, 11¾in. wide. (Andrew Hartley) $1,088

A massive Burmantoft's faience jardinière and stand, circa 1900, the jardinière molded with a continuous frieze of peacocks, height 40¾in. (Sotheby's) $12,000

A pair of Chinese Canton famille rose cylindrical vases, decorated with panels of figures and flowers, 19th century, 25cm. (Woolley & Wallis) $132

A Canton enamel saucer dish Yongzheng period, circa 1730, meticulously painted with stippling in the centre to depict a European setting with the Goddess Cybele, 14.4cm. diameter. (Sotheby's) $6,000

Pair of large 19th century Cantonese vases, each painted with two panels of numerous figures, and ground of figure-groups, insects, flowers and utensils, all in famille rose enamels, 24in. (Brightwells) $1,500

CAPODIMONTE

A French Capodimonte style vase and cover, late 19th/early 20th century, blue crowned *N* and gilt crossed arrows marks, with upright bracket handles the neck molded with mermen and sea sprites, 18¼in. high. (Christie's) $1,500

A Capodimonte cup and saucer, 1742-52, decorated by Giovanni Caselli, the cup with two figures by a fence and corner post. (Sotheby's) $13,728

A very rare Capodimonte group of 'Il Cavadenti', circa 1750, modelled by Giuseppe Gricci, the dentist holding pliers in his right hand and his seated patient's mouth open with the left, 19.5cm. (Sotheby's) $58,800

CARLTON WARE

'Red Devil' a conical Carlton Ware bowl mounted on three triangular feet, printed and painted in colors and gilt on a pale turquoise-green ground, 23cm. diameter. (Christie's) $6,000

A Carlton ware coffee set, decorated with the Mikado pattern, comprising: a coffee pot and cover, milk jug, sugar bowl, six cups and saucers and a Carlton ware soap dish. (Woolley & Wallis) $550

'Mandarins chatting' a Carlton Ware globular vase with strap handle, pattern 3653, printed and painted in colors and gilt on a black ground, 17.3cm. high. (Christie's) $1,000

'Floral Comets' a Carlton Ware
charger, pattern 3387, printed script
mark, 32cm. diameter.
(Christie's) $658

'Blackberry' a Carlton Ware
molded breakfast set, printed
script mark, height of teapot 11cm.
(Christie's) $410

Carlton Ware 'Red Devil' an ovoid
vase, pattern 3765, printed script
marks, 26.5cm. high.
(Christie's) $4,200

A large Carlton Ware luster ginger
jar and cover, 1920s, decorated
with cranes in flight before a large
stylized tree, picked out in gilding
and raised enamels on a matte pink
ground, blue printed factory mark,
12½in. (Sotheby's) $2,700

Carlton (Bains Patent) 'The
Marguerite Tea Infuser and
Separator', brightly decorated with
red poppies and flowers, enriched
with gilding and with cobalt blue
detail on a blush ground, circa early
20th century, 7in.
(G.A. Key) $189

Carltonware Rouge Royale baluster
vase, painted in colors with the
'Egyptian Fan' design, printed and
impressed marks and pattern
number 3695, 7in.
(G.A. Key) $2,356

A Carlton ware Guinness Toucan
lamp base and shade, printed
marks, 44cm.(Christie's) $575

Pair of Carlton Ware decorative
covered baluster vases, decorated
in colors with the 'Chinese Bird'
design, on a luster blue ground,
6½in. (G.A. Key) $225

'Rainbow Fan' a Carlton Ware
bulbous jug, pattern 3700, printed
marks, 15cm. high.
(Christie's) $5,264

139

A Castelli tondo, circa 1740, probably painted by Aurelio Grue, painted with pastoral scene before distant mountains, with figures and a farmhouse by a wooden bridge, 19.5cm. diameter.
(Christie's) $4,836

A Castelli oval two-handled tureen and cover, circa 1720, one side with Neptune embracing his wife Amphitrite pointing to fruit held by a Nereid, 13in. wide.
(Christie's) $4,836

A Castelli armorial berrettino-ground fluted tazza, mid 17th century, the central arms flanked by stylized foliage and surmounted by the crest of a bishop's miter, 10⅜in. diameter.(Christie's) $2,800

CHELSEA

A Chelsea dolphin salt, circa 1745, the decoration very slightly later, perhaps decorated in the workshop of William Duesbury, the shallow foliate bowl encrusted with moss and painted with shells, coral and waterweeds, 3¼in. wide.
(Christie's) $55,272

A pair of Chelsea groups of gallants and companions emblematic of the Seasons, circa 1760, each with Gold Anchor mark, Winter and Spring as a gentleman in fur-trimmed puce hat, Summer and Autumn as a gentleman in colored and gilt-patterned frock-coat.
(Christie's) $11,226

A rare Chelsea 'Goat and Bee' jug, circa 1745-49, the pear-shaped body molded on the backs of two goats with a spray of flowering branches beneath the spout, 4¼in.
(Sotheby's) $14,112

A Chelsea porcelain octagonal dish, circa 1753, painted in the Kakiemon style with two stylized oriental birds, one in flight, the other seated on the branch of a pine tree, 20.5cm.
(Bonhams) $1,205

A pair of Chelsea figures of musicians, circa 1758, each modelled seated, the male cellist wearing a gray hat, the female hurdy-gurdy player wearing a puce hat and bodice, 15.5cm.
(Sotheby's) $1,676

A Chelsea bonbonnière, Red Anchor period, circa 1755, modelled in the form of a woman's head, wearing a white lace cap trimmed with puce ribbons and an iron-red rose, 3in.
(Sotheby's) $1,176

A Chinese Export ox-head tureen and cover, 1750-70, naturalistically modelled, his yellow hide shaded in powdered russet, his horns striated in pale yellow, 15in. high. (Sotheby's) $110,000

A rare Chinese Export blue and white figure of 'Mr. Nobody' and a cover, late 17th century, holding a baluster-shaped wine ewer and goblet in his hands, 9in. high. (Sotheby's) $64,000

A Chinese Export 'Tobacco leaf' pattern jardinière, circa 1810, of flaring cylindrical form on four bracket feet, brightly painted with overlapping leaves and flowers beneath the gilt-edged rims, 10in. diameter. (Sotheby's) $9,600

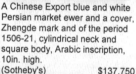

A Chinese Export blue and white Persian market ewer and a cover, Zhengde mark and of the period 1506-21, cylindrical neck and square body, Arabic inscription, 10in. high. (Sotheby's) $137,750

A Chinese Export blue and white 'Tea Cultivation' charger, circa 1740, finely painted with four Chinamen sampling tea in an open-sided building, diameter, 38.9cm. (Sotheby's) $5,400

A Chinese Export two-handled punch urn and cover, circa 1790, the octagonal vessel painted in brown monochrome on the front and reverse with an oval European landscape panel, 16in. high. (Sotheby's) $64,000

A Chinese Export 'Italian Comedy' coffee cup, circa 1740, delicately painted with a continuous scene depicting Scaramouche wooing Columbine seated in a garden, 6.6cm high. (Sotheby's) $2,100

A Chinese Export small mug, 1740-50, the bell-shaped body raised on a low foot, painted on the front with peonies and leaf sprays, 3¾in. high. (Sotheby's) $1,800

A large Chinese Export goose tureen and cover, 1760-80, seated with his head raised on his long neck and his wings swept back towards a short upturned tail, 16in. high. (Sotheby's) $148,750

A pair of Chinese porcelain vases of tapering form, with flared wave edged rim, the neck applied with Shishi and dragons, painted overall with scrolled lotus and foliage, the base with stiff leaf banding, 25¾in. high.(Andrew Hartley) $1,617

A pair of Chinese blue and white barbed dishes, Wanli, 1573-1619, each painted in underglaze-blue with lotus beneath an overhanging tree, the rim with 'The Three Friends of Winter', six character Chenghua marks.
(Sotheby's) $1,440

A pair of Chinese ceramic garden seats with floral decorated panels 19in. high.
(Lloyds International) $412

A Chinese blue and white elephant-form kendi, Wanli, 1573-1619, for the South-East Asian market, the stout rectangular body modelled with a short spout formed by his head and with a flared neck upon his back, 20cm. high.
(Sotheby's) $14,400

A pair of Chinese 'Baragon Tumed'-type bowls, 1830-50, each painted in vivid famille rose colors, the exterior with alternating figure and animal subjects, with a pair of shallow dishes en suite.
(Sotheby's) $6,600

A Chinese blue and white silver-mounted kettle and a cover, Wanli, 1573-1619, finely painted with alternating panels of scrolls, auspicious objects, birds and butterflies, flowers and foliage, height overall, 8½in.
(Sotheby's) $7,200

Chinese blanc de chine silver-gilt mounted globular teapot and cover, the porcelain late 17th century, the 'Gold Foil' decoration second quarter of the 18th century, the mounts Dutch or French Provincial circa 1735, the finial later.
(Christie's) $11,226

A Chinese blue and white ovoid mustard pot and related cover, decorated with panels of Lang Elizen, Artemisia mark, Kangxi, 1662-1722, 9cm.
(Woolley & Wallis) $118

A very rare Chinese octagonal Hausmaler beaker, the porcelain circa 1700, decorated circa 1720-30, the flared form painted in Schwarzlot with a continuous scene of a dancing couple, 1½in. high.
(Sotheby's) $1,680

ulia' a Royal Winton twin-handled sh, printed marks, 14cm. wide. hristie's) $329

'Sweetpea' a Royal Winton toast rack, printed factory marks, 18cm. wide. (Christie's) $245

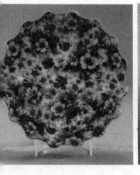

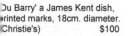

Du Barry' a James Kent dish, printed marks, 18cm. diameter. Christie's) $100

'June Roses' a Royal Winton teapot and cover and an 'Ascot' egg cruet set, printed marks, height of teapot 13cm. (Christie's) $420

'English Rose' a rare shaped Royal Winton jug, printed marks, 16.5cm. high. (Christie's) $350

Crocus' a Royal Winton box and over, printed marks, 8.5cm. high. Christie's) $140

'Queen Anne', Royal Winton sugar sifters, 16cm. high. (Christie's) $100

'Summertime' a Royal Winton tazza, printed factory marks, 9cm. high. (Christie's) $245

'Orange Trees and House', a 'Fantasque Bizarre' large conical jug, printed mark, 15cm. high. (Christie's) $1,233

'Egypt' a wall mask, printed mark, 11.5cm. high. (Christie's) $2,138

'Appliqué' Avignon, a 'Bizarre' plate printed and painted marks, 25cm. diameter. (Christie's) $2,961

'Summerhouse' a 'Fantasque Bizarre' single handled jug Isis printed mark, 25cm. high. (Christie's) $3,290

'Tibetan' a Wilkinson's large ginger jar and cover, painted in colors and gilt on an orange ground, printed mark, hand painted signature, exhibition labels, 35cm. high. (Christie's) $13,160

'Inspiration Persian' a 'Bizarre' twin-handled Lotus jug, printed and painted marks, 30cm. high. (Christie's) $4,606

'Circus' a 'Bizarre' plate designed by Dame Laura Knight, printed mark, 25.5cm. diameter. (Christie's) $1,397

'Blue Crocus' a 'Bizarre' Bon Jour biscuit barrel and cover, printed mark, 14cm. high. (Christie's) $1,068

'Inspiration Autumn' a 'Bizarre' wall plaque, printed and painted marks, 34cm. diameter. (Christie's) $2,961

A good Coalport trio, molded and painted with flowers on a blue and gilt ground, no marks, circa 1820. (Woolley & Wallis) $309

A Coalport pink and 'jeweled' gold ground baluster ewer, circa 1893, with foliate scroll spout and handle, the shoulder and lower body enamelled with turquoise 'jewels', 11¾in. high. (Christie's) $2,350

A good Coalport teapot, cover and stand, and a similar plate, all molded and painted with flowers on a blue and gilt ground, circa 1820. (Woolley & Wallis) $735

A pair of Coalport two-handled vases and covers, circa 1900, of slender tapering form, painted with titled views 'Ross Castle' and 'Old Weir Bridge Killarney', 13½in. (Skinner) $4,002

A Coalport yellow and 'jewelled' gold ground heart-shaped box and cover, circa 1893, the center finely painted with a brunette beauty within a seeded gilt cartouche incorporating cornucopiae on the yellow ground, 5½in. long. (Christie's) $2,350

A Coalport pot pourri vase and cover, the body painted with two rural vignettes and applied with flowers, a circular foot, no mark, circa 1840, 13.5cm. (Woolley & Wallis) $323

A Coalport ivory and 'jewelled' gold-ground topographical pot-pourri vase, cover and liner, circa 1910, the pierced domed cover with ball finial, the concave liner with gilt knop, finely painted with an oval view of Tintern Abbey, 6in. high. (Christie's) $2,350

A Coalport 'New embossed' plate, molded and painted with flowers with a blue and gilt border, 2 impressed, circa 1820, 22cm. (Woolley & Wallis) $235

A Coalport 'jewelled' green-ground gryphon-handled bottle vase, circa 1895, the bulbous body flanked by gryphon handles set with faux jewels and agate panels, the center painted with a brown eyed beauty, 18¼in. high. (Christie's) $4,935

A 19th century Copeland Parian ware vase and cover, the domed leaf molded lid with cherub finial flanked by cornucopia, 15¾in. high. (Andrew Hartley) $471

Copeland two handled covered soup tureen and stand and matching large platter, all decorated with an Indian Tree design, gilded detail, printed marks, 19th century. (G.A. Key) $193

A 19th century Copeland parian ware figure, 'Storm', in the form of a young girl wrapped in shawls, raised on circular base, inscribed *Wm Brodie R.S.A. 1858*, 18½in. high. (Andrew Hartley) $493

CREAMWARE

A creamware jug, probably Melbourne, with a double strap handle, one side painted in enamels with a head and shoulders portrait of a lady, circa 1770, 16cm. (Woolley & Wallis) $941

Cream ware large balustered milk jug, decorated with silver luster foliate design, 19th century, 6½in. (G.A. Key) $270

A creamware tankard, circa 1780, of cylindrical form molded with fluted panels enamelled with rough pink brush work, 12.7cm. (Bonhams) $882

An early 19th century cream ware botanical fruit dish, leaf shaped and painted with sweet pea, the rim with brown line banding, 8½in. wide. (Andrew Hartley) $280

A creamware model of a cow, modelled standing, sponged with ocher and brown glazes, on rectangular green base, circa 1800, 16.5cm. wide. (Christie's) $631

A late 18th century creamware tankard, straight sided with reeded loop handle, and printed and painted with cattle watering in a landscape, 5in. high. (Andrew Hartley) $450

Zeppelin Bomb, crest of Sheringham, a detail of the first one dropped from a Zeppelin on Sheringham on the 19th January 1915, made by Arcadian China Works. (Bosleys) $64

Carlton china busts of King Edward VII and Queen Alexandra, 135mm. high. (Lyle) $230

Unmarked crested china figure of a sitting cat with bow around neck, 105mm. (Lyle) $56

Military bell tent decorated with picture of RMS Lusitania, to the reverse text detail of the sinking on the 7th May 1915. (Bosleys) $99

The King's Own Yorkshire Light Infantry crested china teapot, decorated to the front with a Lance Corporal of the Regiment wearing scarlet tunic, dated 1914, S. Hancock & Sons. (Bosleys) $85

12th Lancers crested two-piece cheese dish, brightly decorated to the lid with a Trooper of the Regiment wearing full dress uniform and standing beside his mount, dated 1914, S. Hancock & Sons. (Bosleys) $170

Large pair of Great War military pattern binoculars with colored crest, Shelley factory, 3.5in. high. (Bosleys) $35

Pair of Carlton crested china stags with large antlers, on oval bases, 145mm. high. (Lyle) $650

A model of a sailor with Southsea crest, head and shoulder of a Jack Tar with cap tally HMS Queen Elizabeth. The color transfer of the crest is to the chest. (Bosleys) $71

A Crown Devon Fielding musical jug depicting Widdicombe fair with lyrics for song, 18cm. high. (Thomson Roddick & Medcalf) $218

Mickey Mouse, a rare early Crown Devon vase, modelled as Mickey Mouse seated in a wicker chair, painted in colors with red shorts and yellow gloves, early 1930s, 6¼in. (Christie's) $2,764

A Crown Devon ovoid vase, decorated with a flowering weeping tree on a blue ground, 20.5cm. (Woolley & Wallis) $191

CROWN DUCAL

A Crown Ducal charger by Charlotte Rhead, pattern 4318, printed and painted marks, 45cm. diameter. (Christie's) $461

A Crown Ducal coffee set, decorated with borders of orange trees, printed marks, circa 1920, comprising: a coffee pot and cover, a jug, a sugar bowl, six coffee cans and saucers and a tray. (Woolley & Wallis) $294

A Crown Ducal Charlotte Rhead jug, circa 1920, tubelined and decorated in orange and yellow with stylized flowers and geometric border, impressed 146, 22cm. high. (Bonhams) $143

DAVENPORT

A small Davenport circular basket, decorated in blue, green, gilt and red with an Imari pattern, pattern No. 6065, 1st half 19th century, 8.5cm. (Woolley & Wallis) $118

A Davenport rectangular plaque, painted with a portrait of a young man, signed *S. Chester*, and dated *1872*, 25.5 x 21cm. (Woolley & Wallis) $382

A Davenport bone china plate, painted with the view of a coastline within a gilt blue border, inscribed *Scanderoon* printed mark, 19th century, 22.5cm. (Woolley & Wallis) $382

good William De Morgan faience ☐arger, 1880s, painted by Charles ☐assenger, in Persian style with a ☐nd of reptiles amongst foliage, ☐ cm. diameter.
☐otheby's) $18,000

A large two-handled William De Morgan vase 1882-1888, decorated with Persian style panels of snakes amongst foliage below a foliate band on the neck, height 48.6cm.
(Sotheby's) $26,050

A William De Morgan ruby luster charger, painted by Charles Passenger, circa 1890, with a giant stylized fish against a yellow luster foliate ground, 30.8cm.
(Bonhams) $2,755

☐EDHAM

☐our Dedham Pottery rabbit plates, ☐ast Dedham, early 20th century, ☐reakfast plate with raised rabbit ☐order, together with three salad ☐lates, diameter 8½, 7½in.
☐kinner) $173

Dedham Pottery Iris breakfast plate, East Dedham, Massachusetts, pre-1932, marks include blue stamp and impressed rabbit, diameter 8³/₈in. (Skinner) $144

Three Dedham Pottery bread and butter plates, East Dedham, Massachusetts, before 1932, including border with Butterfly and Flower, Swan and Pond Lily, pattern, diameter 6in.
(Skinner) $690

☐ELFT

☐ 8th century delft circular plate, ☐ecorated in faience colors, ☐nderglazed blue detail with a bird ☐erched amidst foliage, 8½.
☐.A. Key) $193

A Lambeth Delft blue and white cylindrical mug, circa 1785, boldly painted with huts among trees and grasses on an elongated river island, 6in. high.
(Christie's) $1,640

An 18th century Dutch delft charger, polychrome painted with chinoiserie scene depicting a lady on a terrace, 13½in. wide.
(Andrew Hartley) $986

A London Delft blue and white fuddling-cup, circa 1650, modelled as three baluster two-handled vessels joined at the midpoint and with their handles entwined, each vessel painted with four fronds, 3½in. high. (Christie's) $6,909

A London Delft blue and white globular mug, circa 1685, the body painted in blue and outlined in manganese with an Oriental seated among boulders and grasses, 3¾in. high. (Christie's) $11,226

A rare and previously unrecorded English delftware model of a tabby cat, circa 1680, probably London, modelled reclining with its paws tucked under the tail curled around its side, length 13.7cm. (Sotheby's) $33,6

An English delftware plate, probably Bristol or London, circa 1710, painted in the center with Queen Anne wearing a crown and jeweled pendant flanked by the initials AR, 9in. diameter. (Sotheby's) $5,645

An English Delft puzzle jug, the bulbous body inscribed with a drinking verse in a panel flanked by landscape scenes, mid 18th century, 18cm. (Woolley & Wallis) $1,470

A rare and previously unrecorded London delftware oval polychrome pill tile, circa 1705-30, painted in blue, green, iron-red and yellow with the arms of The Worshipful Society of Apothecaries with unicorn supporters, length 32cm. (Sotheby's) $118,261

A London Delft polychrome Royalist caudle-cup, circa 1690, with a half-length portrait of William III in his coronation robes holding his orb and scepter, 3in. high. (Christie's) $41,454

A London delftware shield-shaped blue and white pill tile, circa 1705-30, painted in blue with the arms of the Worshipful Society of the Apothecaries with unicorn supporters, length 31.8cm. (Sotheby's) $22,094

A Bristol Delft blue-dash Adam and Eve charger, circa 1750, the unfortunate couple standing each holding a leaf and flanking the tree with the serpent about its trunk, 13in. diameter. (Christie's) $8,29

A Della Robbia Pottery wall charger, 1905, by Cassandia Annie Walker, incised with the head of a woman in profile within a spiral foliate border, 38.4cm. diameter. (Sotheby's) $5,700

A Della Robbia Pottery two-handled albarello, 1904, by Cassandia Annie Walker, incised with stylized bird heads amongst Celtic entwined strapwork, height 14¾in. (Sotheby's) $5,400

A fine Della Robbia Pottery plaque circa 1900, probably designed by Ellen Rope, painted by E.M. Wood, modelled with a boy riding a dolphin amongst waves, 15½in. diameter.(Sotheby's) $2,280

DERBY

A good pair of Bloor Derby figures of a Scotsman and his lass, attributed to William Coffee, he stands wearing a glengarry, she carries a basket of flowers, 30cm. (Woolley & Wallis) $1,176

A Derby botanical dessert dish, circa 1795-1800, attributed to William 'Quaker' Pegg, the shaped square dish finely painted with a flowering stem of China Astor, 9in. (Sotheby's) $5,998

A pair of Derby figures with 'Macaroni Dog and Cat', circa 1770, modelled as a young boy and girl, he kneeling upon a rocky mound with his arms encircling a spaniel, incised, 6in. (Sotheby's) $2,470

DERUTA

A Deruta pierced condiment stand, 17th century, of cruciform section, the pierced circular niches divided by four figures supporting scallop shells above their heads, 7½in. (Skinner) $1,334

A pair of Deruta armorial albarelli, late 17th century, each painted in polychrome enamels with a shield-shaped coat-of-arms within foliate cartouches. (Skinner) $2,835

A Deruta charger, circa 1540, painted in green, yellow, ocher and blue with a gentleman and a lady riding pillion on horseback in a landscape, 15¼in. diameter. (Christie's) $3,455

A pair of Doulton stoneware vases, tubelined with poppies by Emily Partington and Nelli Harrison, 27cm. high. (Bonhams) $298

Royal Doulton Watteau decorative toilet jug, printed in blue with romantic scene, applied with blue dolphin mask handle, printed mark, 9½in. (G.A. Key) $157

Hannah Barlow. A Doulton Lambeth stoneware pair of shouldered vases, incised with a girl, donkeys and geese between incised and colored bands, 22.5cm. (Bristol) $2,434

A Royal Doulton Lambeth stoneware three handled vase, by Emily Stormer, 1884, impressed marks, 15cm. high. (Christie's) $427

A Doulton Lambeth faiece moon-flask, painted by Ada Dennis with two girls picking primroses, initials of Josephine Durtnall and Mary Denley and no.823, circa 1890, 24cm. (Bristol) $2,867

A Doulton Lambeth stoneware planter, 1884, by Hannah Barlow, borders by Lucy Barlow, incised with a band of lions in shades of brown and green, 20cm. high. (Sotheby's) $3,600

John Barleycorn Old Lad, large size (style 1, handle inside jug), D5327, 6½in. (G.A. Key) $116

A pair of large Royal Doulton stoneware jardinières and pedestals, circa 1907. (Sotheby's) $19,150

'Winston Churchill' a rare character jug, 19cm. high. (Christie's) $5,264

A Dresden plate, decorated with two figures sitting beneath trees and four molded floral panels, a cross mark, late 19th century, 26.5cm.
(Woolley & Wallis) $147

A pair of Dresden flower-encrusted baluster vases and domed covers, the finial of each modelled as a seated putto holding a garland of flowers, 19th century, 48cm. high.
(Christie's) $1,480

A parcel-gilt white-ground Dresden porcelain jardinière, in the Louis XVI style, after the Sèvres model, 20th century, surmounted by four raised rectangular blocks and rams' masks, 17½in. diameter.
(Christie's) $5,527

EUROPEAN

A turquoise glazed Continental porcelain inkwell, formed as a juggling cherub balancing a drum on his knee, late 19th century, 12cm.
(Woolley & Wallis) $588

A pair of Continental vases, probably Bohemian, late 19th century, each piece of shouldered u-shape form finely painted with humming-birds flying amidst meandering garlands of yellow wisteria and leaves, 26¾in.
(Sotheby's) $9,173

A fine Copenhagen gilt-metal-mounted bonbonnière, circa 1790-95, naturalistically modelled as the head of a terrier with a white coat, gray ears, nose and muzzle and brown eyes, 2½in.
(Sotheby's) $1,323

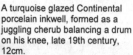

Heutschenreuter polychrome pottery figure, printed factory mark, 34cm. wide. (Christie's) $730

Pair of decorative Continental porcelain figurines, lady and gentleman in dancing poses, (flute or clarinet missing from his hands), painted in colors throughout, 9½in.
(G.A. Key) $116

A Keramos polychrome pottery figure, printed factory marks, 37cm. high. (Christie's) $174

A Chinese famille rose pillow, modelled as a smiling boy kneeling with his elbows on the ground, 18th century, 43cm. long.
(Woolley & Wallis) $5,880

A Chinese Export famille-rose teapot and cover and a tea canister, 1735-40, the spherical body painted on the shoulder with a black-edged ruyi-lappet border enclosing flowers, height of teapot 4¾in.
(Sotheby's) $840

A Chinese Export famille rose hexagonal jardinière, circa 1760, the body painted with vases of chrysanthemums, prunus blossoms, peacock feathers and coral, 15in. high.
(Sotheby's) $2,700

A Chinese Export famille rose ruby-backed soup plate, 1730-35, finely enamelled and gilded in the center with a leaf-shaped panel enclosing a lady seated between two boys, 21.1cm. diameter.
(Sotheby's) $4,800

A fine Chinese Export famille rose European subject square tea canister, 1730-35, painted on one side with a European gentleman seated before a rocky outcrop, height excluding cover 5½in.
(Sotheby's) $3,300

A Chinese Export famille rose triple-shell sweetmeat dish, circa 1765, after a Bow porcelain original, modelled with an iron-red and gilt central dolphin handle surrounded by three scallop shells, 7½in. wide.
(Sotheby's) $7,200

FAMILLE VERTE

A Chinese Export famille-verte biscuit Buddhist lion ewer and cover, late 17th century, the handle in the form of a Buddhist lion colored in aubergine and green, 8¼in. high.
(Sotheby's) $3,000

A Chinese Export famille-verte chamfered rectangular platter, 1700-20, painted in the center with two ladies on a fenced terrace overlooking a pond, 14in. long.
(Sotheby's) $1,920

A pair of large famille verte faceted vases, Kangxi six-character marks in underglaze blue, 19th century, decorated with military scenes below a figural scene on the neck, 34in. high.
(Christie's) $17,250

A Foley intarsio jardinière, printed marks, 14cm. high.
(Christie's) $279

A Foley Intarsio stick stand, decorated with herons, printed marks, 65cm. high.
(Christie's) $1,233

A Foley Intarsio twin-handled vase, decorated with fish, printed marks, 3169, 12cm. high.
(Christie's) $624

A Foley Intarsio twin-handled vase, printed mark, 3336, 25.3cm. high.
(Christie's) $460

A Wileman & Co. Foley Intarsio ware clockcase, circa 1900, by Frederick Rhead, painted with panels of maidens inscribed *DIES* and *NOX*, height 28.9cm.
(Sotheby's) $2,040

A Foley Intarsio Scotsman character jug, printed marks, 18cm. high. (Christie's) $493

FRANKENTHAL

A rare Frankenthal figure of a violinist, 1756-59, modelled by J.W. Lanz, his sheet music resting on a stand on a marbled plinth, 6¼in.
(Skinner) $2,501

A Frankenthal group, circa 1770, indistinct blue crowned lion mark, modelled by Karl Gottlieb Lück, with a mother cradling a sleeping infant in her lap after suckling, 20cm. high. (Christie's) $3,800

A Frankenthal figure of a cellist, 1759-62, modelled by J.W. Lanz, seated on a base modelled with gilt-edged scrollwork, 5¾in.
(Skinner) $2,501

A Longwy earthenware charger, printed factory mark, impressed numerals, 21cm. diameter. (Christie's) $1,137

Pair of Longwy ceramic pitchers, France, incised decoration of stylized polychrome flowering plants on a crackle glazed ground, 10in. (Skinner) $805

A polychrome pottery cat, modelled in the style of Gallé, unmarked, 32.5cm. high. (Christie's) $61?

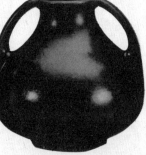

A French porcelain coffee pot and cover, with an urn shaped body, painted with figures before buildings, no mark, 19th century, 23cm. (Woolley & Wallis) $74

A pair of French Jacob Petit porcelain figural scent bottles, mid 19th century, modelled as the seated figures of a pasha and his lady, the stoppers inset in their turbans, 7¼in. high. (Christie's) $3,619

A pair of French biscuit porcelain figures of a gentleman and companion, each modelled gazing at a child seated on their shoulder, wearing 18th century dress, late 19th century, 59cm. high. (Christie's) $1,316

FULPER

Fulper crystalline glazed vase, Flemington, New Jersey, early 20th century, raised flared rim on bulbous body with flanking scrolled handles, 4¾in. (Skinner) $173

Fulper Pottery vase, Flemington, New Jersey, circa 1915, flared cylindrical form with swollen base with four raised buttress formations about the body, matte pink glaze with green vertical streaks, 8¼in. (Skinner) $288

Fulper Art Pottery two-handled vase, Flemington, New Jersey, raised rim on swollen base with two conforming handles, matte purple-blue glaze. (Skinner) $46?

A Fürstenberg group of Venus and Cupid, circa 1785, modelled by Hendler, scantily clad with a puce-ined flower-decorated robe, Cupid with gilt wings on her left, 21.2cm. (Sotheby's) $1,210

A rare Fürstenberg plate from the service for Duke Carl I of Brunswick, 1757-58, the well finely painted by Pascha Weitsch in purple camaïeu with a landscape scene depicting a shepherd and his flock in the foreground, 9¼in. (Sotheby's) $16,800

A Fürstenberg group of two children and a goat, circa 1770, modelled by Simon Feilner, one child seated on the goat feeding it a fruiting vine, the second child trying to dislodge the first, 13cm. (Sotheby's) $924

GEORGE JONES

A large George Jones majolica two-handled cup, circa 1871, the cylindrical body molded in relief with a hound chasing a game-bird through grass and a fox stalking a rabbit in a lair, 7in. (Sotheby's) $1,588

A pair of George Jones porcelain vases, with a pâte sur pâte panel depicting birds nesting in a river landscape and stiff leaf banding on green ground, 8in. high. (Andrew Hartley) $1,727

A George Jones majolica 'Double Dolphin and Cupids' sweetmeats dish, circa 1873, the central shell-molded dish supported by two cherubs seated on a rocky outcrop reclining against coral-molded branches, 11½in. high. (Sotheby's) $6,384

George Jones majolica cheese sh and cover molded in relief ith nasturtiums, painted in pink nd green on a blue basket weave round, 7½in. high. (Andrew Hartley) $2,590

A George Jones majolica garden seat, molded in high-relief with birds and dragonflies above water lilies on a turquoise ground, 17¾in. high. (Sotheby's) $7,800

A George Jones majolica game pie dish, cover and liner, the finial formed as a nesting woodcock above ferns and foliage, with branch handles and rim issuing oak leaves and acorns, 27cm. wide. (Christie's) $12,091

A Schleswig faience two-handled soup tureen, cover and stand, circa 1770, the tureen molded with a C-scroll cartouche containing flowers in manganese and green with scattered floral sprigs, the stand 17½in. (Skinner) $3,335

A pair of Gebrüder Heubach bisque figures of children, sitting on chairs, the girl knitting, the boy with cigar and glasses, 9in. high. (Christie's) $532

A Mettlach polychrome pottery plate, incised factory marks, impressed numerals, 18.5cm. (Christie's) $122

A WKW polychrome pottery figure, printed and impressed factory marks, incised *698*, 40cm. high. (Christie's) $350

A rare Fürstenberg Commedia dell'Arte figure of Pantalone, circa 1775-95, modelled by Anton Carl Luplau, standing with her hands behind her back leaning forwards, 11.3cm. (Sotheby's) $6,048

A Nymphenburg plate, circa 1770, painted in the well with a landscape vignette depicting two figures from the Commedia dell'arte, 10in. (Skinner) $2,668

A Fürstenberg figure of Cupid as a Pole, circa 1772-73, modelled by Johann Christoph Rombrich, wearing an iron-red tunic over a yellow shirt with a sword to one side, 3½in. (Sotheby's) $756

An extremely rare pair of Fürstenberg groups of a Sultan and Sultana, circa 1773-74, modelled by Anton Carl Luplau, the sultan offering a scarf with his left hand, wearing an ermine-lined puce coat, 25cm. and 22.5cm. (Sotheby's) $13,776

A Fulda pewter-mounted faience jug (Enghalskrug), circa 1741-58, painted in blue, yellow and outlined in manganese with flowers and foliage against a white ground, 13½in., restored. (Skinner) $4,669

A Goldscheider polychrome pottery figure from a model by Dakon, incised signature, printed factory marks, 18cm. high.
(Christie's) $437

A Goldscheider terracotta wall mask, modelled as a stylized female head with blue curls, holding a black mask, 11in. high.
(Andrew Hartley) $691

A Goldscheider polychrome pottery figure from a model by Dakon, printed factory marks, signed *Dakon*, 39cm. high.
(Christie's) $1,050

A Goldscheider figure, stamped factory marks, impressed numerals 187 90 11, 51cm. wide.
(Christie's) $298

A Goldscheider polychrome pottery figure from a model by Dakon, incised signature, printed factory marks, 37cm. high.
(Christie's) $3,326

A polychrome pottery mask, in the style of Goldscheider, unmarked, 25cm. high. (Christie's) $507

HAN

green-glazed pottery hu-form jar, an dynasty, the compressed lobular body supported on a high spreading foot, the tall waisted neck with grooved bands at the mouth nd base, 39.1cm.
Sotheby's) $480

A rare massive gray pottery figure of a 'flying horse', Han Dynasty, the gracefully proportioned horse modelled as if flying or galloping with head spiritedly raised and docked tail arched, 47in. long approximately,
(Christie's) $107,000

BUYER BEWARE

When inspecting ceramics or glass before purchase, first check any detachable parts such as lids and stoppers.

Pick the item up by the largest part, so that if anything falls off you will not be left just holding the handle!

(Woolley & Wallis)

Hans Coper, a small stoneware cup form, the sack-shaped body with oval rim and four dimples, incised with a spiral, on cylindrical stem and drum base, 12cm. high.
(Christie's) $1,725

Hans Coper, a stoneware spade form vase, the manganese brown body covered in a buff and bluish white slip burnished in areas to reveal brown body, circa 1972, impressed HC seal, 16.6cm. high.
(Christie's) $9,993

Hans Coper, a stoneware goblet vase, with waisted oval rim, the bulbous body covered in a bluish-white buff colored slip, impressed *HC* seal, 23.1cm.
(Christie's) $9,993

TOP TIP

Pieces by studio potters such as Hans Coper and Lucie Rie can now fetch phenomenal sums, but don't despair. They also turned out some often-repeated designs and cup and saucer sets for stores such as Heal's and Liberty's, to say nothing of the buttons they made just after the war. These can now be had for just a few hundred dollars.

A monumental Hans Coper thistle-form vase, circa 1975, the assembled thrown and altered sections glazed with stains and engobes, impressed *HC* monogram, height 17¾in. width 16in. (Sotheby's) $49,625

Hans Coper, a stoneware 'Cycladic' vase, of slender form with rounded lower section and mounted on drum base, covered in a matt black manganese glaze, impressed HC seal, 22cm. high.
(Christie's) $13,627

HÖCHST

A Höchst figure of a boy, circa 1771, modelled by J.P. Melchior, standing with an expression of alarm, holding a hat full of eggs on a rocky mound, 4¾in.
(Sotheby's) $1,008

A rare Höchst group of Amythas and Sylvia, circa 1770, modelled by J. P. Melchior, the naked young woman with long fair hair reclining in the grass with her arms tied to the tree behind her, Amythas approaching at the back, 27cm.
(Sotheby's) $8,820

A Höchst group of a vintner and children, modelled with a man seated on rockwork, surrounded by a girl wearing a flowered skirt and a boy in a pink-spotted suit, circa 1765, 18.5cm. high.
(Christie's) $1,727

A gilt bronze mounted Imari style porcelain pot pourri vase, late 19th century, the white ground with trailing flowers and foliage, the bulbous body with bifurcating foliate scroll handles, 12¼in. high. (Christie's) $3,454

A Japanese Imari circular charger, the center decorated with blue scrolling foliage encircled by four large panels, 19th century, 56cm. (Woolley & Wallis) $956

A pair of 19th century Imari pottery vases, of ovoid form with flared rim, painted with flowers and birds amongst scrolling foliage in iron red and blue over a blue stiff leaf banding, gilt embellished, 24¼in. high.(Andrew Hartley) $2,538

ITALIAN

A Cantagalli maiolica plaque, molded in high relief with the Annunciation in the style of Della Robbia, impressed and painted marks, 52.8 x 36cm. (Bristol) $393

A large pair of Italian faience models of dogs, 19th century, each modelled seated on its hind legs, each wearing a broad spiked collar, 32in. (Sotheby's) $11,760

A large Venice albarello, second half 16th century, painted with an oval medallion of a saint, possibly St. Valentine, edged in yellow and ocher. (Sotheby's) $5,040

Venice istoriato plate, 1570-1575, workshop of Domenico da Venezia, the reverse inscribed *Paris*, painted with Paris as a shepherd by a stream near a wooded shoreline, ?in. diameter. (Christie's) $3,455

Pair of Art Deco style porcelain heads, Italy, mid 20th century, the female heads with blond coiled hair wearing an ethnic sash, stamped Roman, made in Italy, 8¼in. high. (Skinner) $288

An Italian figural pottery candelabra, modelled as Columbine and Pierrot, painted and impressed numerals, 26cm. high. (Christie's) $447

A rare Arita dish with V.O.C. monogram, late 17th century, decorated in underglaze blue with sprays of finger citrus peaches and leaves, 12¾in. diameter. (Christie's) $16,450

A Japanese Hirado ewer, modelled as a figure astride a large fish, 19th century, 24cm. (Woolley & Wallis) $588

A Nabeshima dish, Edo period, late 17th century, decorated in iron-red, green, yellow enamels in underglaze blue with water hollyhock, the reverse with three sprays of flower heads and foliage, 8in. diam. (Christie's) $62,51●

A Shigaraki chatsubo [tea-jar], Edo Period (17th century), with a thin greenish glaze, partly worn, two fitted boxes and cover as well as an accompanying record and a red ink inscription on the bottom of the jar, old wear to the glaze, 13½in. high. (Christie's) $7,144

A Nabeshima dish, Edo Period (late 17th/early 18th century), decorated in colored enamels with cherry blossoms on scattered rafts amongst swirling waters, 8in. diameter. (Christie's) $35,720

A Japanese apothecary's bottle, the pear shaped body with a flange below the rim, decorated in underglaze blue with VOC, 19th century, 23.5cm. (Woolley & Wallis) $441

A kutani dish, Faku mark, late 17th century, decorated in Shonsui style in iron-red, green, yellow, black on underglaze with a bird in a flowering branch among rocks and bamboo, 11¾in. (Christie's) $50,995

An unusual Japanese Imari cistern and cover, with S-scroll handles and three gilt metal taps decorated with butterflies and foliage, circa 1700, 28.5cm. (Woolley & Wallis) $588

A late 19th century Imari porcelain charger, central square panel depicting a jardinière with flowering plant, in iron red and blue, 24¼in. wide. (Andrew Hartley) $1,044

A Kakiemon koro, late 17th/early 18th century, decorated in iron-red, yellow, blue, green and black enamels with Moso finding bamboo shoots in the snow, 2½in high. (Christie's) $4,935

A rare Kakiemon palette arita puppy, Edo Period (late 17th century), decorated in blue, black, yellow and green enamels, with colored patches, yellow eyes and a red ribbon collar, 10¼in. (Christie's) $39,216

A Kakiemon koro, Edo Period (late 17th century), decorated in iron-red, green, blue and black enamels, depicting symbols of longevity, 4in. diameter.(Christie's) $6,250

A Kakiemon vase, Edo Period (late 17th century), decorated in iron-red, green, yellow, blue and black enamels with a continuous design of butterflies above sprays of chrysanthemums and foliage, 8¼in. (Christie's) $30,362

KANGXI

A pair of Chinese Kangxi Imari baluster jars painted and gilt with broad bands of pavilions in flower-strewn gardens of peonies and pine, 16in. high. (Christie's) $3,000

A kangxi blanc de chine model of a cockerel standing on a simulated rockwork base, well molded to simulate the plumage, 8¼in. high. (Christie's) $3,000

TOP TIP

Everyone is looking for china in perfect or mint condition, while ceramic restoration is becoming more and more difficult to detect. Any potential purchases, therefore, should be very carefully inspected. Ideally, you need either good bright light or natural daylight, something not always available in a dim shop or saleroom. Ask if there is any damage or restoration and get a straight answer. Be suspicious of any fudging or evasions.

Always look closely at the areas most likely to attract damage, generally pro-truding areas like ears, tails, handles or spouts, and check these for changes of color or texture. If you are unsure, you can tap the area with a fingernail (teeth are even better) and compare the sound and feel to an unrestored part. Restored pieces have a softer or duller sound.

These basic actions should help most people, though many professionals carry a pin and scratch the area. If they can make a mark, the piece is definitely restored. However it is wise only to do this when you know exactly what you are dealing with. If you scratch enamelled Staffordshire figures, for example, you will damage them!

(Bearne's)

KUTANI _____ CHINA _____

A Kutani rectangular plaque painted and gilt with a lady at leisure on a terrace flanked by two children, all overlooking two mandarin ducks in a snow covered river landscape, 15¼in. x 11½in.
(Christie's) $549

A Kutani charger painted in green, brown, blue, ocher and cream enamels with chrysanthemums issuing from pierced rockwork, 15in. diameter, 19th century.
(Christie's) $600

LEACH

A large Bernard Leach faceted stoneware vase, circa 1950, impressed *BL* monogram and St. Ives Pottery mark, height 14in.
(Sotheby's) $4,500

Bernard Leach, 'Tree Vase' a screen print in colors, artist's proof, signed in pencil lower right *Bernard Leach* and inscribed A/P, 44.4 x 36.4cm.(Christie's) $545

A Bernard Leach temoku glazed stoneware vase, circa 1950, impressed *BL* monogram and St. Ives Pottery mark, height 12in.
(Sotheby's) $3,000

LEEDS

A creamware punch-kettle and cover, painted in a famille rose, palette with Orientals among furniture, vases and shrubs, probably Leeds, circa 1775, 21cm. high. (Christie's) $1,190

A Leeds creamware teapot and cover, circa 1780, of cylindrical form painted in pink, red, yellow and green with scattered floral sprays, 14.5cm.
(Bonhams) $588

A Leeds creamware plate, the center painted with the portraits of the Prince and Princess William V of Orange, 24.7cm.
(Bearne's) $420

Lenci (Italy) Art Deco period model of lady with her arm resting on an open book, naturalistically decorated in colors, dated 1932. (G.A. Key) $2,926

Lenci wall mask, modelled as the head of a young lady wearing black spotted green hood, the face decorated with puce naturalistic detail and blue eyeshadow, 11in. (G.A. Key) $1,727

A Lenci pottery jug in the form of a fierce rotund man with tall black hat being attacked by children, 30cm. high, 1930. (Bearne's) $1,050

LIVERPOOL

Liverpool pitcher, England, early 19th century, obverse with a reserve depicting a maiden on shore waving farewell to a trio of ships, one with American flag, 10^1/8in. (Skinner) $1,380

A documentary Liverpool Delft shipping bowl, dated 1752, the interior painted in blue and enriched in yellow and iron-red with a ship on the point of being launched, 10¼in. diameter. (Christie's) $112,500

Liverpool pitcher, England, 19th century, black transfer on a buff ground, one side depicts two portrait busts of John Hancock and Samuel Adams in an oval with a beehive and horn of plenty, 8in. (Skinner) $2,300

LOWESTOFT

A rare late Lowestoft teabowl and saucer, gilt decorated with leaf sprigs and garrya and scroll borders, no marks, circa 1780-90. (Woolley & Wallis) $294

A Lowestoft cylindrical mug, with an S-shaped handle, the body printed in blue with a pagoda landscape beneath a cell border, circa 1770-80, 14cm. (Woolley & Wallis) $691

A Lowestoft coffee can, with loop handle, painted with a tulip and three sprigs, a brown line rim, no mark, circa1765-75, 6.2cm. (Woolley & Wallis) $1,441

Dame Lucie Rie, a deep footed bowl of oval section, covered in a pitted buttercup yellow glaze, circa 1980, impressed *LR* seal, 16.8cm. wide. (Christie's) $6,541

Dame Lucie Rie, a porcelain sgraffito bowl, the unglazed white exterior with horizontal inlaid amethyst sgraffito, circa 1966, impressed *LR* seal, 21cm. diameter.(Christie's) $10,538

A Dame Lucie Rie glazed stoneware bowl, circa 1965, with palest blue and pink mottled glaze, impressed *LR* monogram, height 4½in. (Sotheby's) $7,200

LUDWIGSBURG

A Ludwigsburg silver-mounted circular snuff box, circa 1770-80, of bombé form, the side and base painted with vignettes of birds perched on branches, 8.5cm. (Sotheby's) $4,633

A very rare Ludwigsburg circular dish, circa 1775-80, the center painted with a single yellow flower and two oval panels enclosing river landscapes with figures, 20.8cm. (Sotheby's) $3,881

A Ludwigsburg figure of a horn player, circa 1764/1767, modelled by Nees, from the 'Kleine Musiksoli' series, seated on a stool by a round table with a cup, bottle and note sheet, 5in. (Skinner) $1,501

LUSTER

A pink luster jug, polychrome decorated and titled with The Agamemnon in Storm, and Ancient Order of Foresters, circa 1830, 14.2cm. (Woolley & Wallis) $235

A 19th century yellow ground silver luster jug, the body depicting scrolling foliage and fruiting vine, 4¾in. high. (Andrew Hartley) $261

A pink luster and relief molded jug, decorated with huntsmen, 1st half 19th century, 14.5cm. (Woolley & Wallis) $147

Unusual majolica ewer, modelled as a frog perched on a melon, naturalistically painted in colors, 6½in. (G.A. Key) $534

A majolica cheese bell and cover, probably English, molded with fern leaves between arched rope-twist sections, reserved on a lilac ground, circa 1880, 25cm. high. (Christie's) $431

19th century majolica basket formed vase, twisting branch handle joined on either side by foliate molded terminals, molded throughout with cream foliage on a mainly treacle ground, 6½in. (G.A. Key) $157

A Sicilian maiolica drug jar, 17th century, possibly Palermo, of ovoid form, painted with a full length figure of a crowned female against a yellow ground within a circular panel edged with C-scrolls, 12½in. (Sotheby's) $4,586

A pair of Italian maiolica wall brackets, late 19th century, each triform shelf supported by a putto with left arm raised and standing against elaborate foliate scrollwork, 15¾in. (Sotheby's) $1,764

A Caltagirone maiolica bottle vase, 17th century, painted in ocher with a classical bust within a circular reserve edged in ocher and reserved against a blue-washed ground, 9in. (Sotheby's) $2,470

A maiolica dish, the central well painted with a bearded man, the border molded with scrolls on a blue ground, 19th century, 23.8cm. (Woolley & Wallis) $147

Pair of unusual graduated majolica ewers modelled as owls, naturalistically painted in colors and applied with green trunk molded handles, 11½in. and 9in. (G.A. Key) $534

An Italian maiolica armorial charger, second half 17th century, possibly Savona, the central raised boss with an armorial painted in ocher, green, manganese and yellow, 43.5cm.(Sotheby's) $3,696

A Martin Brothers stoneware ribbed vase, incised marks, 1906, 12cm. high. (Christie's) $790

A Martin Brothers stoneware double-sided smiling face jug, dated 1885, the reverse with a stylized wide open mouth, height 8in. (Sotheby's) $5,700

A Martin Brothers stoneware bird jar, dated 1890, black-painted wood socle, height 8¾in. (Sotheby's) $20,300

A good Martin Brothers stoneware double bird jar, dated 1912, finely incised and colored, black-painted oval wood base, height 21.9cm. (Sotheby's) $38,125

A Martin Brothers stoneware monkey-bird jar, dated 1895, the body modelled with ape-like features surmounted by a long-beaked balding bird's head, 27.6cm.
(Sotheby's) $29,500

A very fine Martin Brothers stoneware vase, dated 1893, with highly amusing stylized birds posing amidst exuberate foliage, height 9¼in. (Sotheby's) $9,600

MASONS

Masons Ironstone circular bowl, decorated in colors with chinoiserie scene, printed and impressed marks, 19th century, 7½in. (G.A. Key) $44

Masons Ironstone large 19th century ewer of hexagonal baluster form, decorated in colors with vignettes of oriental scenes and applied with a gilded dolphin handle, printed mark, 10in. (G.A. Key) $659

A Masons Ironstone soup tureen, cover and stand, with a molded circular body and flower knop, richly decorated with panels of pagoda landscapes, circa 1830-40, 36cm. (Woolley & Wallis) $2,058

A Meissen figure group emblematic of 'Fire', circa 1880, from the series he Elements, Vulcan modelled eated wearing magenta drapery, ttended by four putti, 9in. across. Sotheby's) $4,032

A Meissen silver-mounted jug, circa 1750, with quatrefoil panel painted with Watteauesque figures in landscape.(Skinner) $2,835

A Meissen porcelain group of Count Bruhl's tailor, circa 1880, shown seated on a goat, with tailor's accoutrements, 17½in. high. (Christie's) $11,745

A Meissen cream jug and cover, circa 1735, the baluster-shape painted on each side with a Kauffahrtei scene in the manner of C.F. Herold depicting merchants and their wares by a quayside, 4¾in. (Sotheby's) $4,939

A Meissen (outside-decorated) group of 'The Surprise', after a model by J.J. Kändler from an engraving by Hogarth, modelled as a mother and child, accompanied by a lawyer, standing above three seated figures playing cards, 25.5cm. wide. (Christie's) $1,809

A Meissen padoda figure, circa 1730, the open-mouthed figure seated cross-legged with his paunch exposed and his right hand resting on his knee, wearing a gilt-lined red cloak, 3in. (Sotheby's) $9,702

Meissen figure group, late 19th entury, modelled with three herubs around a pierced pot-pourri rn, molded and painted with a lassical frieze, 6in. Sotheby's) $2,016

A Meissen figure of a farmer on horseback, circa 1745, modelled by J.J. Kändler, returning from the field, the horse's head bowed in fatigue and its harness loosely arranged, 8½in. (Sotheby's) $9,702

A Meissen cup and saucer, circa 1740, the exterior of the cup and underside of the saucer encrusted with applied flowerheads below a band of molded flowerheads at the rim. (Christie's) $5,329

A Minton's pâte-sur-pâte peacock-blue ground, circular plaque 'Le Collier', circa 1890, after the original by Louis Solon, the center with a nymph seated in a klismos, putting a collar and leash on a weeping putto, 17.5cm. diameter, the plaque. (Christie's) $2,350

A fine pair of Minton Kensington Gore Art Pottery pilgrim flasks 1870s, each delicately painted with female busts within stylized flower and foliate borders, height 13½in. (Sotheby's) $4,500

A Minton turquoise-ground candelabra, circa 1865, modelled with two parian putti circling a neo-classical column, supporting six S-scroll foliate-molded branches and a central sconce of turquoise ground, 24in.
(Sotheby's) $5,292

A Minton stoneware bread plate, circa 1880, designed by A.W.N. Pugin, inscribed *Waste not, Want not*, rust and blue encaustic glazes, 33cm. diameter.
(Bonhams) $277

A Minton majolica jardinière, circa 1866, molded with a turned over gadrooned rim above six lion-mask-and-ring handles on vertical strapwork terminating in paw feet, 11in. (Sotheby's) $2,520

A Mintons Art Pottery wall plate, decorated by Ellen Welby, with a maiden wearing pearls, before purple clematis, within a stylized border of foliage, 42.7cm.
(Bonhams) $798

A large Minton majolica figural urn, dated *1872*, modelled as two semi-clad putti, brown drapes covering their modesty, struggling to carry a blue urn supported on wooden rods, 37cm.
(Bonhams) $4,350

A pair of Minton's pâte-sur-pâte salmon-pink ground pilgrim bottles, circa 1890, impressed marks, one signed *L(ouis) Solon*, the fronts with putti tied to kites with foliate tails, 5½in. high.(Christie's) $9,400

A Minton's majolica Christmas charger, molded with a tudor rose within mistletoe below a cruciform border with pierced sections of holly between panels of putti at festive pursuits, 1859, 39.5cm. diameter.
(Christie's) $1,480

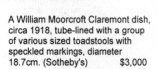

A Moorcroft Macintyre Florian ware part tea service, circa 1905, each piece finely tube-lined with stylized peacock feather motifs on a green ground height of teapot 6¾in. (Sotheby's) $6,600

A William Moorcroft Claremont dish, circa 1918, tube-lined with a group of various sized toadstools with speckled markings, diameter 18.7cm. (Sotheby's) $3,000

A rare Moorcroft Macintyre sterling silver-mounted part coffee service, circa 1910, each piece tube-lined with toadstools, overlaid with silver and pierced with stylised flowers and foliage, height 9½in. (Sotheby's) $21,450

A Moorcroft Macintyre Florian ware vase, circa 1900, finely tube-lined with large open poppies amongst elongated foliate panels, height 20cm. (Sotheby's) $1,800

A Moorcroft Macintyre Florian ware two-handled vase, circa 1900, finely tube-lined with stylized tulips and forget-me-not flowers repeated around the body, height 7½in. (Sotheby's) $3,000

A large Moorcroft flambé 'Orchid' vase, dated *1940*, tube-lined with orchids and spring flowers beneath a red, yellow and blue flambé glaze, 12½in. (Sotheby's) $3,360

A Moorcroft Macintyre Florian ware vase, circa 1900, finely tube-lined in white with large open poppy flowers and buds within stylized elongated foliate panels, in salmon pink and green, height 11in. (Sotheby's) $2,700

A Moorcroft Macintyre Florian ware jardinière, circa 1900-1902, finely tube-lined with stylized poppy flowerheads amongst elongated foliage, height 11½in. (Sotheby's) $3,000

A large William Moorcroft Plum vase, 1920, tube-lined with a broad band of fruits and foliage on a dark blue and mottled blue-green ground, painted script signature, III-1920 in green, height 38.4cm. (Sotheby's) $4,200

A Naples topographical wine cooler from the 'Fiordalisi Service', 1790-1800, each side painted with a named rectangular view, depicting 'Ved:^{ta} del Vesuvio, 7½in. (Sotheby's) $9,438

A pair of Naples maiolica blue and white pharmacy jars, date 1724, attributed to the workshop of Donato Massa, the twin handles with grotesque mask terminals, 18¼in. (Sotheby's) $8,467

A very rare Naples group of Moorish lovers, circa 1780, standing on a rocky base, the gentleman wearing a yellow and puce turban with puce stripes, his left arm around the waist of his companion, 19.5cm. (Sotheby's) $25,383

NYMPHENBURG

A Nymphenburg bust of Winter circa 1760, modelled by Franz Anton Bustelli, from a set of the Seasons, the old man wearing a fur-lined cap, puce robe, and black muff, 5¾in.(Skinner) $1,740

A rare pair of Nymphenburg plates probably circa 1755, each painted with an estuary scene within a green quatrelobe cartouche, 10¼in. (Sotheby's) $5,880

A rare Nymphenburg figure of a rat catcher, circa 1770, modelled standing wearing a black tricorn hat, pink coat and yellow breeches, 7½in. (Skinner) $4,350

PARIS

A Paris (Schœlcher) two-handled sugar-bowl, cover and stand, circa 1825, painted en grisaille with putti at various pursuits within a pale-blue ground, the stand 6¼in. diameter. (Christie's) $3,455

A pair of Paris portrait plates, first half 19th century, the first painted with a portrait of 'Marco Botzari', the second with 'Demetrio Ipsilanti', 9¼in. (Sotheby's) $1,680

A pair of ormolu-mounted Paris (Gille Jeune) figures of a Gallant and Companion, mid to late 19th century, each colored biscuit figure modelled standing holding a Bible, 84cm. high. (Christie's) $2,820

A pearlware 'Flight to Egypt' group, typically modelled, before a flowering bocage, on a mound base molded with scrolls, circa 1825, 18cm. high. (Christie's) $1,083

A pearlware jug, decorated with panels of birds and a building, no marks, circa 1830, 11.5cm. (Woolley & Wallis) $162

A pearlware figure of St. George and the Dragon, typically modelled impaling the dragon, mounted on a piebald charger, circa 1820, 32cm. (Christie's) $1,173

An unusual pearlware ovoid jug, the body painted in blue with flower sprays and sprigs, late 19th century, 20cm. (Woolley & Wallis) $176

A pair of Portobello pearlware figural spill vase groups, circa 1820, each modelled with a seated female figure holding a basket of fruit before a tree stump, 4¾in. (Skinner) $1,334

A pearlware flower vase, molded with swags, with three necks, and raised on twin dolphin supports, painted enamels, early19th century, 17.5cm. (Woolley & Wallis) $265

PILKINGTON

A Pilkington's Lancastrian two-handled vase, circa 1909, by Gordon Forsyth, decorated with mantled shields on either side, within foliate panels, height 9in. (Sotheby's) $4,500

An exceptional Pilkington's Royal Lancastrian luster charger, 1918, designed by Walter Crane, painted by Richard Joyce, inscribed *Un Chevalier Sans Peur Et Sans Reproche*, impressed factory mark. (Sotheby's) $27,200

A Pilkington's luster vase, circa 1908, by William Mycock, decorated with a frieze of three galleons, height 8in. (Sotheby's) $4,200

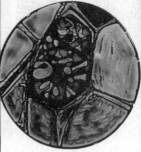

Poole (Carter Stabler & Adams) globular baluster jug with a blue speckled neck, decorated below in traditional colors with a panel of stylised foliage, embossed mark, 7½in. (G.A. Key) $145

A Carter Stabler Adams twin-handled vase by Ruth Pavely, pattern HE, impressed and painted marks, 17cm. high. (Christie's) $855

A Poole pottery Delphis charger painted with an abstract hexagonal design in blue, turquoise, yellow, red and green, printed and painted marks, 16½in. wide. (Andrew Hartley) $435

A CSA large Poole pottery vase by Anne Hatchard, pattern ZB, shape 220, impressed and painted marks, 26.8cm. high. (Christie's) $1,068

A large Carter Stabler Adams vase decorated with Aztec design by Mary Brown, pattern DK, shape 911, circa 1930s, 36cm. high. (Christie's) $5,757

A Carter Stabler Adams, twin-handled vase by Anne Hatchard, pattern BT, shape no. 973, impressed and painted marks, 17.7cm. high. (Christie's) $1,480

A Carter Stabler Adams vase by Eileen Prangnell, pattern EB, shaped no. 968, impressed marks, 17cm. high. (Christie's) $156

A Poole Pottery ovoid vase, decorated with the blue bird pattern in a wide band, impressed *Carter Stabler & Adams, HE* painted mark, 25cm. (Woolley & Wallis) $368

A CSA Poole pottery vase by Anne Hatchard, pattern EP, shape no. 116, impressed and painted marks, 21cm. high. (Christie's) $1,151

A large Ming-style blue and white Hu, Qianlong seal mark in underglaze blue and of the Period, shou medallions reserved on a wan fret ground and key pattern on the neck, 44.7cm. high.
(Christie's) $17,250

A pair of blue and white candle holders, Qianlong, circa 1740, well painted in the Ming style in rich tones of underglaze blue heightened by a 'heaped and piled' effect, 37.8cm. high.
(Christie's) $16,100

A copper-red-decorated blue and white moonflask, Qianlong seal mark in underglaze blue and of the Period, each side painted with a five-clawed dragon leaping in pursuit of a flaming pearl, 10¼in. high. (Christie's) $43,700

QUIMPER

Covered Quimper coffee pot with Breton female decoration, marked *Henriot Quimper France 744 ter.*, 10in. high. (Eldred's) $245

A pair of Quimper polychrome pottery jugs, painted marks *Henriot Quimper C. Maillard*, 26.5cm. high. (Christie's) $420

REDWARE

A green-glazed redware sitting dog, Pennsylvania, 19th century, articulated ears, snout and hair, on a rectangular base, 4in. high.
(Christie's) $3,055

A glazed redware jar, American, 19th century, the bulbous body with flared rim and two applied handles with reddish brown glaze and dark brown daubed decoration, 11in. high. (Christie's) $940

TOP TIP

In 1890 William McKinley, the President of the United States, introduced a high protective tariff, the McKinley Act, insisting that all imported items should be marked with the country of origin. The words *England*, *France* and *Germany* on ceramics therefore usually mean that they were produced in or after 1891.

In the early part of the 20th century, many factories in this country used the words *Made in England*.

On the other hand, this does not mean that all unmarked items will predate the McKinley Act, as many late pieces were produced with no thought of export, and left unmarked.

(Bearne's)

Rookwood Pottery flower vase, Cincinnati, 1947, short raised rim on tapered oval body decorated with large flower blossoms and leaves in relief, 9½in. high. (Skinner) $258

Rookwood standard glaze iris vase, Cincinnati, 1889, decorated by Amelia Browne Sprague, flared rim over wide neck and bulbous body, yellow iris and dark green leaves, 6½in. high. (Skinner) $575

Rookwood standard glaze two-handled vase, Cincinnati, 1891, decorated by Albert Valentien, flared rim on an extended neck over ovoid body, two loop handles at shoulder, 10in. high. (Skinner) $1,380

ROSEVILLE

Roseville Pottery Carnelian II vase, 1915, Zanesville, Ohio, raised flared rim on bulbous body with angled scrolled handles, mottled matte, mauve drip glaze, 8¼in. high. (Skinner) $546

Roseville Pottery woodland vase, Zanesville, Ohio, 1905, small raised rim above a tapered oval form with flared foot, incised and glazed floral and leaf decoration in brown and gold, 8⅞in. high. (Skinner) $172

A pair of Roseville Pottery 'Mostique' wall pockets, Zanesville, Ohio, circa 1915, tapered cone-shaped vessels with raised stylised flowers in yellow and brown, green leaves, and a blue band on a grey ground, approx. 10in. high. (Skinner) $500

ROYAL COPENHAGEN

A Royal Copenhagen bust from a model by Salto, incised signature, printed factory marks, numbered *20803*, 29.5cm. high. (Christie's) $420

A Royal Copenhagen Flora Danica part dinner and dessert service mainly 20th century, of conventional form, each piece with specimen flowers, within pink and gilt beaded and serrated rims, 68 pieces. (Christie's) $40,480

A Royal Copenhagen vase from a model by Salto, incised signature, printed factory marks, numbered *20664*, 29cm. high. (Christie's) $612

Czechoslovakian painted pottery figural group of a nymph on shell, after a Royal Dux model, painted in multicolors, factory marks, 20¼in. high. (Skinner) $863

A pair of Royal Dux porcelain figures of a setter and a pointer each carrying game in its mouth, in cream and green coloring with gilt embellishment, raised on oblong rustic base, 10¼in. wide. (Andrew Hartley) $1,130

A Royal Dux porcelain Art Deco figure of a lady in red evening dress, a pair of greyhounds at her feet, raised on oval green base with waved edge, 15in. high. (Andrew Hartley) $2,002

A pair of Royal Dux vases, applied pink triangle, 47.5cm. high. (Christie's) $894

Royal Dux Art Deco period wall mask, modelled as the head of a young woman in an outraged pose, painted in colors, 7in. (G.A. Key) $348

A pair of Royal Dux candlesticks, applied pink triangle, printed factory marks, stamped numerals, *3039*, 17cm. high. (Christie's) $420

A Royal Dux figure group from a model by Schaff, various marks, 28.5cm. high. (Christie's) $447

A pair of Royal Dux standing figures of lady and gentleman holding water vessels, with green flowing robes, tree trunk supports, 20in. high. (Brightwells) $1,078

A Royal Dux figure of a woman with two borzoi, applied pink triangle, stamped *Czechoslovakia*, 37cm. (Christie's) $1,024

A Ruskin Pottery high-fired stoneware flambé vase circa 1905, impressed oval mark *Ruskin Pottery West Smethwick* and *1905,* painted crossed swords mark, height 35.2cm.
(Sotheby's) $23,750

A Ruskin Pottery high-fired stoneware bowl and a stand, 1926 and 1933, the steep sided bowl covered with a sponged red and mauve glaze, repeated on the four leg table-form stand, diameter of bowl 25.7cm.
(Sotheby's) $1,680

A Ruskin high-fired stoneware baluster vase, shouldered form with collar rim, mottled voilet, purple and mint running glaze, printed factory marks, 1905, 21cm. high.
(Christie's) $5,175

SATSUMA

A pair of Japanese Satsuma ovoid vases, each decorated with Kwannon and other immortals, signed, Meiji 1868-1912, 37cm.
(Woolley & Wallis) $1,470

A Satsuma koro, signed *Dai Nihon Satsuma-yaki*, late 19th century, gilt with three panels on a floral and geometric ground, 6¾in. high.
(Christie's) $4,935

A pair of Satsuma vases, signed *Ryuzan*, Meiji period (late 19th century), the everted-neck vases decorated in colored enamels and gilt with scenes from the Gion Festival, 12¼in.
(Christie's) $4,286

A large Satsuma vase, signed *Shozan Tsukuru*, Meiji Period (late 19th century), decorated in colored enamels and gilt on a royal blue ground with panels depicting ladies in a village landscape and samurai, 15in. high.
(Christie's) $7,501

A 19th century Satsuma vase and cover of ovoid form, with ball finial on flattened lid, truncated branch handles, the body painted with birds in landscapes, 4½in. high.
(Andrew Hartley) $1,155

Fine late 19th century Japanese reticulated Satsuma censer, the domed cover of double pierced honeycomb form with gilt Greek key border, 11cm.
(T.R. & M) $3,770

An ormolu-mounted Sèvres style cobalt-blue ground pot-pourri vase and cover, late 19th century, signed *Deshelle,* painted with a scantily clad nymph in a garden attended by a putto and dove at an altar, 28½in. high. (Christie's) $5,875

A Sèvres style Louis Phillip monogramed cobalt-blue ground solitaire, late 19th/early 20th century, each gilt with a crowned LP monogram with a ribbon-tied laurel wreath flanked by putti wihtin a foliate surround, 17¾in. wide, the tray. (Christie's) $2,585

A 'Sèvres' porcelain and gilt-bronze centerpiece, French, circa 1890, with a reserve of lovers in a landscape signed *Henry,* opposed by a reserve with a landscape, 40.5cm. high.
(Sotheby's) $8,016

A rare Sèvres hard-paste clock base, circa 1786-87, probably after a design by Duplessis, in the white, as two naked children lifting drapery over the top of a column between them, 18.7cm.
(Sotheby's) $1,846

A fine pair of 'Sèvres-style' pink-ground gilt-metal-mounted vases and covers, late 19th century, each painted by C. Labarre, signed, with a continuous scene of nymphs at play with scantily clad putti in a forest setting, 16½in.
(Sotheby's) $20,020

A 'Sèvres-style' turquoise-ground gilt-metal-mounted jardinière, late 19th century, of 'U' form, painted with an oval panel of three children playing in parkland within a gilt scrollwork border, 10¼in.
(Sotheby's) $3,024

SPODE

A Spode bat-printed oviform jug, printed with three vignettes of fishermen before buildings and a bridge, circa 1815, 17cm. high.
(Christie's) $735

Early 19th century Spode ewer of spreading oval form, printed en grisaille with battle scenes of Sir George Brown at Alma and Sebastopol, 7½in.
(G.A. Key) $232

Decorative Spode vase of circular baluster form, brightly decorated in Imari colors in the oriental manner, the pedestal formed as a coiled snake, 5½in. (G.A. Key) $145

STAFFORDSHIRE _____ CHINA _____

A Staffordshire model of a black elephant, with a hunter and a dead tiger on its back, raised on a green and brown rocky base, 19th/early 20th century, 22.5cm.
(Woolley & Wallis) $647

A pair of Staffordshire models of pug dogs, seated on their haunches sparsely painted in shades of brown with black noses and collars, circa 1900, 28cm.
(Woolley & Wallis) $911

19th century Staffordshire treacle glazed character jug, modelled as a toper or drunkard, 7½in. high.
(G.A. Key) $79

TOP TIP

The dating of Victorian Staffordshire ornaments is difficult at the best of times, but a high shine to gilding will usually indicate that a piece may not have been made much before the end of the 19th century.

On earlier pieces, the finish to the gilding will be much more matt.

(Amersham Auction Rooms)

A rare Staffordshire creamware figure of a soldier, circa 1770-80, modelled standing holding his rifle to his right side, wearing a blue coat, manganese helmet, 6¼in.
(Sotheby's) $4,704

A model of a greyhound, modelled standing fore-square, with a hare at its feet, painted with black spots, 1880, 26cm. high.
(Christie's) $785

19th century Staffordshire model of a rider mounted on a black and white striped horse, (stylized zebra), painted in colors throughout, 6½in.
(G.A. Key) $174

A Staffordshire solid agate pecten-shell-molded teapot and cover, circa 1755, with serpent spout and lamprey handle, the cover with a lion knop, 14.4cm.
(Sotheby's) $2,856

A Staffordshire saltglaze pecten-shell-molded cream jug, circa 1750-60, each side molded with a shell, the spout with a pair of snails above two rows of small shells, 9.2cm.
(Sotheby's) $2,520

A Doulton Lambeth stoneware two-handled vase, by Hannah B. Barlow, incised with a frieze of deer and rabbits in a forest, 41.6cm. (Sotheby's) $7,800

A Royal Doulton Lambeth stoneware cache pot, by Mark V Marshall, 1884, impressed marks, 36cm. high. (Christie's) $987

A London brown salt-glazed stoneware tankard, dated 1766, applied with the 'Punch Party' beneath an inn sign of the Waggoner's Arms, 8in. (Skinner) $3,335

SUNDERLAND LUSTER

A named and dated Sunderland luster oviform jug, printed and painted in colors with a West View of the Iron Bridge, Sunderland, a panel of verse and the 'Sailor's Farewell', dated 1830, 20.5cm. high.
(Christie's) $759

19th century Sunderland luster plaque of rectangular form, puce border, center decorated with a religious message *Thou God, See'st Me*, within a garland, 8½in. (G.A. Key) $174

19th century Dixon Austin & Co Sunderland luster large globular jug, decorated with a scene, 'God Speed The Plough' to verse 'Here to the Wind That Blows...', early 19th century, 7in. (G.A. Key) $246

SWANSEA

A Swansea plate, brightly painted with a Chinoiserie pattern , red printed mark, circa 1820, 21.1cm. (Woolley & Wallis) $456

A pair of early 19th century porcelain two-handled urn-shaped fruit pails and covers finely painted with floral bouquets in colored enamels, 8in. high, possibly Swansea. (Brightwells) $309

One of a pair of early 19th century Swansea pottery blue and white plates printed with figures and animals etc in landscape, 10in. diameter.
(Brightwells)   (Two) $508

A straw and amber-glazed pottery figure of a horse, Tang Dynasty, the hogged mane, ears, divided forelock, well-modelled head, hoofs and tail glazed amber, 23in. long. (Christie's) $14,950

A Sancai-glazed pottery tripod censer, Tang Dynasty, decorated around the shoulder with chestnut-splashed cream dapples on a green ground, 12.4cm. high. (Sotheby's) $1,320

A large sancai-glazed pottery figure of a horse, Tang Dynasty, the cream-glazed mane swept to one side of the powerful neck and grooved to simulate thick hair, 28in. high.(Christie's) $244,500

THEODORE DECK

Théodore Deck charger, circa 1880, possibly by L. Descamps Sr., indistinctly signed, painted with a bee hovering over a spray of colorful wildflowers, 11¾in. diameter. (Sotheby's) $1,848

A pair of Théodore Deck chargers, one dated 1867, painted by J. Legarain, signed, with putti picking grapes from a vine and drinking wine from a carafe, 11½in. (Skinner) $4,350

AUCTIONEER'S ADVICE

If you buy ceramics or glass at auction, ask the auctioneer about the condition of pieces you are interested in, and preferably get an answer sent, faxed or emailed to you.

Good auction houses will be pleased to help, provided you don't leave it until the last minute or ask for too many reports.

(Woolley & Wallis)

URBINO

An Urbino Istoriato shallow footed dish, circa 1530, painted with a black-sailed ship approaching the shore before the fortified city of Athens, 11¼in. diameter. (Christie's) $14,163

An Italian maiolica tazza, circa 1540, School of Urbino, painted with a bust portrait of a woman three-quarters to left wearing a yellow turban, 6¾in. (Sotheby's) $18,805

An Urbino Istoriato dish, circa 1540-45, probably the workshop of Guido Durantino, painted with a coastal scene, the foreground with Marcus Curtius wearing a plumed helmet, 12¾in. diameter. (Christie's) $48,363

A Vienna style circular plaque, painted by P. Hoffmann with Dante, wearing Florentine dress, seated on a marble bench reading poetry to his seated companions, late 19th century, 50cm. diameter. (Christie's) $3,619

A Vienna style dark-blue-ground two-handled shaped oval dish, painted with quarter-length portraits of four Spring maidens, wearing loose robes, late 19th century, 29cm. wide. (Christie's) $2,250

A Vienna style coffee can and saucer, painted with a Classical woman and Cupid, a pair of lovebirds at their feet, 19th century. (Christie's) $658

A Vienna style green-luster ground Art Nouveau two-handled vase, late 19th/early 20th century, signed *Wagner*, with upright gilt scroll handles terminating in pink poppy blossoms, above a bust-length portrait of a long-haired beauty after Asti, 40.9cm. high. (Christie's) $8,225

A Vienna (Du Paquier) armorial two-handled beaker and trembleuse stand, circa 1735, the beaker of slightly flared form with molded scroll handles, each side painted and gilded with the arms of a Cardinal, the beaker 7.9cm. high. (Christie's) $13,818

A 19th century Vienna porcelain coffee can and saucer, the can depicting Jupiter and Calista, signed *Mathes*, within jeweled gilt border on lemon, blue and maroon banded ground, 2½in. high. (Andrew Hartley) $308

A large 'Vienna-style' circular plaque, circa 1880, by A.Beer, signed, painted with an apocalyptic scene of the Inferno, within a gilt rectangular frame, 24in. framed. (Sotheby's) $9,702

A pair of massive Vienna two-handled vases with reserves of classical figures on a puce and green ground with gilt rims on square bases, 33in. high. (Brightwells) $2,205

A large 'Vienna' charger, late 19th century, painted by Cirpriani, signed, with a circular scene depicting Hector's Farewell to Andromache, 15¾in. (Sotheby's) $3,360

A Vincennes cup and saucer, of 'Gobelet Hébert' shape modelled with five lobes and with a double twisted handle, date letter C for 1755, painter's mark of Denis Levé. (Phillips) $3,150

A Vincennes bleu lapis-ground butter tub, cover and stand, circa 1753, reserved on each side with two gilt birds in flight within gilt floral borders, the stand 20.5cm. (Sotheby's) $6,703

A Vincennes circular baluster sugar-bowl and cover painted with sprays of flowers including pink roses, date letter for 1754, 8cm. diameter. (Christie's) $980

VOLKSTEDT

A Volkstedt conversation group, modelled with a seated elderly lady and a gentleman, companion and three children in attendance, 20th century, 60cm. wide. (Christie's) $1,974

A pair of Volkstedt bookends, printed factory marks, 14.5cm. high. (Christie's) $735

Volkstedt Art Deco period figure, naked young woman on a lily pad, 6in. (G.A. Key) $157

VYSE

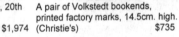

Charles Vyse (1882-1971), a stoneware vase, covered in a khaki glaze, decorated with running olive-green wide foliate band, incised *VYSE 1939*, 26.6cm. high. (Christie's) $816

Charles Vyse, a stoneware bowl on shallow foot with petal-like rim, covered in a lavender-blue glaze with areas of sage-green on the underside, 18.2cm. wide. (Christie's) $581

Charles Vyse, a stoneware ribbed, bulbous vase, covered in a translucent gray glaze revealing off-white banding, decorated with leaf and bird motifs between bands, 13.6cm. high. (Christie's) $508

A Wedgwood and majolica salmon platter, molded in low relief with a fish lying on foliage on a turquoise ground, 25¼in. long.
(Sotheby's) $5,400

A Wedgwood majolica circular Stilton dish and cover, decorated with band of tied flowers on lattice ground, with cheese finial, 28cm.
(Bristol) $1,005

A Wedgwood majolica game pie dish and cover, of oval form with rabbit finial, the cover and sides modelled with game and trailing vine, 14in. wide.
(Andrew Hartley) $942

A Wedgwood 'Willow Fairyland' luster vase, 1920s, painted in iridescent tones, enriched in gilding, with Chinese pagodas on islands joined by bridges with a 'Candle Lighthouse' in the distance, 22.5cm.
(Sotheby's) $4,234

A Wedgwood majolica circular charger, molded with the sea nymph Thetis riding a sea-serpent, the border molded with sea birds perched on dolphins, cypher for 1871, 39cm. diameter.
(Christie's) $950

A fine Wedgwood Fairyland luster jar, cover and stand, circa 1925, designed by Daisy Makeig-Jones, the ovoid form printed and gilt with a version of the Ghostly Wood pattern, 13in.
(Sotheby's) $25,383

A large Wedgwood charger, circa 1910, painted with a cockatoo amongst branches in blue within a lustrous border, impressed *Wedgwood*, diameter 22in.
(Sotheby's) $2,700

Wedgwood Portland vase of two handled baluster form, typically molded with pâte sur pâte with classical figures and putti, handles with mask terminals, 7in.
(G.A. Key) $174

A Wedgwood Fairyland luster octagonal bowl, the interior with 'Ship and Mermaid' pattern, the exterior with the 'Fiddler and Tree'.
(Bonhams) $4,350

A Wemyss Ware character jug modelled as a rotund sailor, painted in colors, impressed factory marks, 28cm. high. (Christie's) $276

Wemyss Ware claret glazed pig, Wemyss Ware R H & S, 6in. (G.A. Key) $361

'The Fair Maid of Perth', a Wemyss Ware character jug, modelled as a female figure, painted in colors, painted Wemyss Ware mark, 21cm. high. (Christie's) $430

A Wemyss spiral molded jardinière, painted with roses, impressed mark, 22cm., diameter. (Woolley & Wallis) $382

'Cherries', a Wemyss jug and bowl, painted and impressed marks, height of jug 23.5cm. (Christie's) $980

'Hen and Cock', a Wemyss three handled vase, impressed marks, (hairline cracks), 20cm. high. (Christie's) $352

A Wemyss large mug painted with birds, impressed mark, 14cm. high. (Christie's) $987

A Wemyss pottery figure by Plichta, modelled as a pig seated and painted with red roses, 15in. wide. (Andrew Hartley) $1,890

A Wemyss ovoid jug, painted with a band of black cockerels, *Wemyss* impressed, 25.5cm. (Woolley & Wallis) $529

A Royal Worcester pottery figure of a pug dog, depicted standing and looking upwards with an appealing expression, cream/brown coloring, 4¾in. high. (Andrew Hartley) $1,355

A Worcester blue and white globular teapot and cover, painted with the 'Mansfield' pattern of flowers below diaper panel and scroll borders, circa 1758, 11cm. high. (Christie's) $863

A Royal Worcester 'Grotesque Stork' ewer, circa 1887, of dramatic flaring form molded with four lobed panels painted in the manner of C.H.C. Baldwyn with swans in flight above grasses and gilt reeds, 11½in. (Sotheby's) $2,205

One of a pair of Royal Worcester scallop shape dishes painted, flowering branches in colors on an ivory ground with gilt rims, 8¾in. (Brightwells) (Two) $465

A Worcester yellow-ground cabbage-leaf-molded mask jug circa 1765, transfer-printed, colored and highlighted in gilding with three rural scenes after Robert Hancock depicting milking scenes and rural lovers, 17.5cm. (Sotheby's) $8,467

A Chamberlains Worcester porcelain plate from the Yeo service, the central crest motto and garter star with Japan patterned border No. 298 with gilt embellishment, 8¾in. wide. (Andrew Hartley) $508

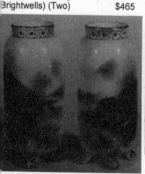

pair of Royal Worcester porcelain vases of cylindrical form, Shape No. 2/G with pierced necks painted with Highland cattle in landscapes, signed H Stinton, 6in. high. (Andrew Hartley) $2,828

A large Royal Worcester two-handled jardinière, circa 1908, by W. Jarman, signed, the quatrelobe body painted with pink cabbage roses, buds and green foliage on a cream ground, 11¾in. high. (Sotheby's) $6,385

Pair of Royal Worcester porcelain Chinese-style vases, England, circa 1883, square form with relief of egrets in landscapes, lion mask and ring handles, 11¼in. high. (Skinner) $2,990

Siemans ciné camera, Siemans, Germany; 16mm., nickel-fittings, top-mounted Leitz rangefinder, with three lenses mounted on a sliding track. (Christie's) $669

Cinematographic camera, Alfred Darling, Brighton; 35mm. wood-body, hand-cranked, with lens and crank. (Christie's) $433

JVC GR-C7E Video Movie no. 121E2143, Victor Corporation Ltd., Japan; VHS-C with an AF zoom 9-54mm. 1:1.6 lens, in maker's hard case. (Christie's) $293

Ciné camera no. 748, Newman & Sinclair, London; 35mm., duraluminum body, with an Angénieux Retrofocus f/2.2 18.5mm. lens. (Christie's) $686

Cinematographic camera, no. 755241, Ernemann-Werke A.G., Dresden; 35mm., hand-cranked, polished wood body, with crank, two film magazines and an Ernemann Ernon Series C f/3.5 50mm. lens. (Christie's) $1,410

Cinematographic camera, Moy and Bastie, London; 35mm. polished-wood body, black-painted metal fittings, two internal film magazines and a Busch Glauker Anastigmat f/3.1 7.5cm. lens, restored. (Christie's) $2,29

Bolex model B no. 5217, Paillard, Switzerland; 16mm., with a Hermagis Anastigmat f/3.5 25mm. (Christie's) $440

Parvo no. 620, J. Debrie, Paris; 35mm., polished wood body, hand-cranked, with crank, lens and two internal metal film magazines, in a leather case. (Christie's) $881

NS cinematographic camera no. 631, Newman & Sinclair, London; 35mm., metal-body, with a Ross Xpres 4 inch f/3.5 inch lens. (Christie's) $84

CINE CAMERAS

Cine Kodak Special II no. 10426, Eastman Kodak Co., Rochester, N.Y., 16mm. with a two-turret Ektar F/1.9 25mm. lens no. 1315, and other Ektar lenses two 15mm. viewfinders.
(Christie's) $686

Cinématographe no. 360, J. Carpentier, Paris; the wood body with metal fittings, top-mounted wood film magazine, hand-crank, internal film advance mechanism, brass-mounted lens.
(Christie's) $21,150

Cinematographic camera, B. J. Lynes Ltd., London NW1; 35mm., metal-body, hand-cranked, with a Dallmeyer Super-Six Anastigmat f/1.9 2in. taking lens and a Dallmeyer Triple Anastigmat f/2.9 2in. viewing lens.
(Christie's) $828

Chronophotographe no. 1, G. Demeny, Paris; 60mm., the wood casing with black-lacquered metal fittings, side door giving access to gears, top door giving access to upper film magazine.
(Christie's) $88,125

Ciné camera no. 162, Moy & Bastie; 35mm. wood-body, hand-cranked, with crank, two wood film magazines and lens; a ciné tripod.
(Christie's) $2,347

NS cinematographic camera no. 397, Newman & Sinclair Ltd., London; 35mm., polished duralinium body, with a Ross Xpres 1½in. f/1.9 lens, film magazine, reflex viewfinder and meter. (Christie's) $705

Eumig C16R camera, Eumig, Austria; 16mm., with two lenses, stand and instruction booklet, in maker's case.
(Christie's) $198

Bolex Auto ciné camera no. 6292, Paillard-Bolex, Switzerland; 16mm., with a Kern Anastigmat f/2.5 25mm. lens. (Christie's) $722

Bolex H16 Reflex no. 220428, Paillard-Bolex, Switzerland; 16mm., with three-lens turret mount holding a Kern Macro-Switar f/1.1 26mm. lens and two other Switar lenses.
(Christie's) $1,083

A Nema Type T-D post war example of the Enigma encoding machine, only 640 models of which were made for the Swiss Army, 1947.
(Auction Team Köln) $2,484

A very rare Enigma 10 rotor encoding machine, manufactured by Siemens & Halske as the Secret Writer T52a, 1935.
(Auction Team Köln)
$96,017

An Enigma Type A encoding machine, in original wooden case with plugs and additional row of lamps, 1940.
(Auction Team Köln)
$32,194

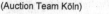

A filament lamp Enigma M Na 220 900 coding machine, 1944, with original wooden case, plugs and bulbs. (Auction Team Köln)
$36,713

Three original Enigma naval model rollers, and Enigma lamps.
(Auction Team Köln) $6,000

A Nema enciphering machine, Type T-D No. 648, with ten rotors, three-row keyboard with illuminated panel and German and French instruction leaflet dated *1947*.
(Christie's) $923

An Enigma Clock, rare accessory for the Enigma coding machine, for increasing the number of code possibilities. (Auction Team Köln)
$24,851

An early Hagelin Cryptos C-36 version of the Swedish encoding machine with 5 rotors, with print out on double strips of paper, 1929.
(Auction Team Köln) $3,276

An Enigma Type A encoding machine with additional row of special lamps, 1940,
(Auction Team Köln)
$24,287

A George III mahogany striking bracket clock, J. Northey, Spitalfields, the case with handle and pineapple finials to the bell top, later pierced mahogany sound frets to the sides, 18in. high.
(Christie's) $9,499

A mahogany chiming mantel clock German, circa 1911, 42cm.
(Bonhams) $588

A George II ebony quarter repeating small bracket clock with silent verge escapement, George Graham, London, the case with gilt-metal foliate-tied D-ended handle to the inverted bell top, 14¼in. high.
(Christie's) $105,766

Scottish George III mahogany striking bracket clock, James Allan, Kilmarnock, the case with handle to the caddy top, double-molded cornice above the front door inlaid with boxwood and ebony checker stringing, 18½in.
(Christie's) $5,329

A mahogany bracket clock with bracket, refinished painted dial with twin fusee bell striking movement in shaped case, Golding Plymouth, 19th century, 46cm.
(Bonhams) $544

A Victorian ormolu-mounted ebony small bracket timepiece, Payne, London, the case with inverted bell top applied with ribbon-tied floral garlands and surmounted by a flambeau urn finial, 13½in. high.
(Christie's) $2,073

n ebonized bracket clock with a ter movement, Charles Howe ondon, 18th and 19th century, 7in. rass dial with a silvered chapter ng and matted center, 20in.
Bonhams) $1,680

A mahogany cased bracket clock with round dial and carved foliage moldings, English, 19th century, 27cm.
(Bonhams) $393

A George II small ebonized striking bracket clock, Thomas Brass, London, the case with transverse-mounted gilt-brass baluster handle to the triple pad top, 11½in.
(Christie's) $5,527

An ebonized gilt basket top bracket clock, Payne & Co, London, nos 1923, circa 1880, twin fusee bell striking movement, in an ebonized case, 16in.
(Bonhams) $1,820

A Regency bracket clock with double-fusee 8-day repeater movement striking on bell, architectural case of ebony, inlaid brass swags and florets, 24in. high, by Handley & Moore, London.
(Brightwells) $2,025

A William and Mary olivewood sma striking bracket clock with pull quarter repeat, Jacobus Hasenus, London, the case with foliate cast basket top with dolphin handle, 12½in. high.
(Christie's) $5,88

A mahogany repeating bracket clock with enamel dial, Tutet, London, circa 1770, in a domed top with under curved top, brass panelled sides with drop handles, 17½in. (Bonhams & Brooks) $10,650

A Victorian bracket clock with triple fusee eight-day movement chiming on Cambridge & eight bells, in ormolu mounted ebonized case, 18½in. high.
(Brightwells) $2,175

A mahogany and brass inlaid bracket clock, circa 1870, 7½in. silvered dial signed *Shedden Pert* the twin fusee bell striking/repeati movement in a case with a gadrooned chamfered top, 19½in.
(Bonhams) $1,96

A 19th century ebonized bracket clock, 8-day movement by Haddack, Bath, in domed case with brass carry handle and pierced brass side panels, 18in. high.
(Brightwells) $3,542

A rare late 18th century bracket clock, by Thomas Berry, Ormskirk, Astronomical/Astrological, in mahogany case of Chippendale style, 31in. high.
(Brightwells) $70,000

A William and Mary ebony striking bracket clock with pull quarter repeat, Isaac Lowndes, London, t case with eagle-and-dolphin foliat tied handle to the cushion-molded top finials, 15¾in. high.
(Christie's) $18,13

A William and Mary ebony striking bracket clock, Jonathan Lowndes, London, the case with eagle and dolphin handle to the basket top, 12¾in. high.
(Christie's) $11,226

A William and Mary ebony quarter-striking miniature bracket clock with pull quarter repeat, Jonathan Puller, London, the case with small Tompion style foliate-tied handle to the cushion molded top, 10in. high. (Christie's) $134,873

A mahogany cased bracket clock, William Nicoll Junior, Great Portland Street, London, circa 1830, in a break arch case with top brass carrying handle, 16½in. (Bonhams) $3,500

A George III mahogany and ormolu-mounted musical automaton bracket clock, Thomas Wood, Tonbridge Wells, tune selection; Song/ Dance/ Gavot/ Air/ Song/ Gavot, 19¼in. high.
(Christie's) $31,105

An ebonized striking bracket clock with quarter repeating, Jonathan Lowndes, Att The Dyal in The Pall Mall London, circa 1695, 7in. dial, 14½in. (Bonhams & Brooks) $17.040

A small burr walnut and gilt chiming bracket clock, English, circa 1880, 6in. dial with a silvered chapter ring signed for Barnsdale 18 Brunswick Place, London, 17in.
(Bonhams & Brooks) $6,390

A George III ebonized and ormolu mounted musical bracket clock, Richard Templer, London, case with pineapple finials to the bell top applied with foliate ormolu mounts, 20in. high.
(Christie's) $11,745

A Regency rosewood small striking bracket clock, John Peterkin, London, the case with stepped chamfered top, foliate ring handles and fishscale sound frets to the sides, 11in.
(Christie's) $10,018

A Regency ebony small bracket timepiece, William Johnson, London, the case with brass-lined pad and handle to the breakarch top, brass line-inlaid sides and on bun feet, 7¾in. high.
(Christie's) $4,836

Early 19th century kingwood balloon formed large bracket clock, crested with gilt metal urn finial, by Johan Georg Wernle of Presburg, repeating movement, 20½in.
(G.A. Key) $3,625

A George II walnut striking bracket clock, John Ellicott, London, the case with brass handle to the inverted bell top, later fishscale soundfrets to the sides, 18in. high.
(Christie's) $51,876

A George III ebonized bracket timepiece, with silent verge escapement, Rainsford, London, the case with brass handle to inverted bell top, later pierced ebony frets to the sides, 15in.
(Christie's) $3,111

A red tortoiseshell bracket clock, the 8 day twin fusee movement with a verge escapement striking on a bell, with a foliage engraved back plate inscribed R Regard, London, 15½in. high.
(Woolley & Wallis) $9,580

An Edwardian inlaid mahogany bracket clock, of arched form, with a convex 15cm. circular enamel dial with Arabic numerals, fitted with a French movement, 38cm. high.
(Bonhams) $243

A magnificent mahogany and gilt mounted chiming bracket clock in the Eastern taste, English, 1900s, 7¼in. dial with a silvered chapter ring with raised Arabic numerals, 30in.
(Bonhams & Brooks) $6,390

A Regency figured mahogany bracket clock, the twin–fusee bell-striking movement with shaped backplate and 8in. white Roman numeral dial signed Tho's. Kidd, Manchester, 50.5cm.
(Bristol) $1,088

A George II ebonized striking bracket clock, Daniel & Thomas Grignion, London, the case with gilt-metal baluster handle to the inverted bell top, foliate pierced and engraved gilt-brass sound frets to the sides and front door, 16in. high.
(Christie's) $4,836

A burr yew striking bracket clock with pull quarter repeat, Christopher Gould, London, movement circa 1700, the 7¼in. re-gilt dial with silvered Roman and Arabic chapter ring and pierced blued steel hands, 16¼in. high.
(Christie's) $23,317

A Regency mahogany bracket clock, the 8 day twin fusee movement striking on a bell, with a pull repeat, back plate inscribed *Isaac Rogers, London*, 17¾in. high. (Woolley & Wallis) $2,464

A mahogany bracket clock, Robert Skinner, London, 19th century, in a refinished break arch case with top carrying handle, side brass sound frets, 18½in.(Bonhams) $1,190

A fine Regency brass inlaid mahogany lancet-top bracket clock dated *1823*, the 5-pillar twin-fusee bell-striking movement with trip hour repeat signed *Bentley & Beck, Royal Exchange, London*, 49.5cm. (Bristol) $3,969

A German walnut cased chiming bracket clock, circa 1900, Strike/Silent and regulation dials to arch, the break-arch case with brass acorn finials, backplate stamped *Lenzkiroh 414037*, 33.5cm. wide.(Bristol) $854

A 19th century bracket clock with triple fusee quarter chiming ebonized and gilt metal mounted oblong case, the domed top with putto and dragon surmounts, 21½in. high. (Andrew Hartley) $1,960

Late 19th century walnut and mahogany bracket clock, with pagoda top, applied with gilt metal mounts and caryatids etc., arched brass face with a silvered circular Roman chapter ring, plinth base, 8 day movement, 15in. (G.A. Key) $609

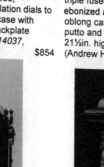

A fine Regency mahogany musical eight-day bracket clock, the substantial triple fusee movement with verge escapement, signed *Radford, Leeds*, 64cm. (Bristol) $6,468

An ebony veneered bracket clock formerly quarter repeating, Benjamin Willoughby, Bristol, circa 1695, 15½in. (Bonhams) $5,880

A Victorian bracket clock, the eight day fusee movement with Westminster and Whittington chimes, in mahogany architectural case, 22¾in. high. (Andrew Hartley) $3,360

A black lacquer & silver concealed sliding travelling watch, Omega, 1930s, silvered dial with black Arabic numerals.
(Bonhams & Brooks) $705

A French enamelled silver and agate minute repeating small travelling timepiece, Cartier, circa 1920, the rectangular case decorated overall with translucent cobalt blue guilloché enamel.
(Christie's) $20,722

A brass carriage timepiece, French, 1900s, enamel dial marked *Exm* by Frank Hyams Ltd New Bond St, with a plain gilt mask, 6in.
(Bonhams & Brooks) $426

A French engraved gilt-brass and porcelain mounted mignonnette carriage timepiece, the foliate engraved cannelee case with painted porcelain panels to the sides depicting a hunter and a peasant woman respectively, 3¼in. high. (Christie's) $5,145

A fine light blue guilloche enamel petite sonnerie repeating clock with a matching box, Cartier, Nos 4249, circa 1913, enamel dial with diamond set hands signed *Cartier*, 4in. (Bonhams & Brooks)
          $34,080

An engraved brass one piece case repeating carriage clock, French, circa 1860, enamel dial signed *Mottu Freres Paris*, the bell striking movement with a gilt platform escapement, 6¾in.
(Bonhams) $840

An engraved cased repeating carriage clock, French, circa 1880, gilt chapter and foliage engraved center with plain mask surround, 7½in.
(Bonhams & Brooks) $1,278

A Victorian gilt-brass striking giant carriage clock, Barraud & Lund, London, the case, in the style of James McCabe, with reeded handle to the top with push repeat button and large bevelled glass, 8½in. high. (Christie's) $18,135

A champlevé enamel repeating carriage clock, French, circa 1890, silvered dial with round reserves, pierced gilt center and plain gilt mask, 7in.
(Bonhams & Brooks) $1,562

A French gilt-brass and porcelain mounted bambu carriage timepiece, movement numbered *1233*, the case with panels to the sides and rear door painted à la Japonnais with pagodas within fanciful garden scenes, 3½in. high.
(Christie's) $6,909

A limited edition silver cased carriage clock, Mappin & Webb, 82/200, 1975, silver dial with an engraved foliage surround and center, 7in.
(Bonhams & Brooks) $2,272

A brass carriage clock with alarm, French, 1900s, enamel dial signed for Tiffany & Co, with an alarm setting dial below, 6½in.
(Bonhams & Brooks) $568

A Victorian gilt-brass striking carriage clock, Benjamin Lewis Vulliamy, London, No. 1357, the case with hinged baluster handle to the flat top, 6¼in. high.
(Christie's) $4,145

A silver miniature carriage timepiece and box, Swiss, 1900s, round enamel dial, the frost gilt 8 day lever movement in a rectangular polished case, 70mm.
(Bonhams) $560

A French gilt-brass and porcelain mounted mignonette carriage timepiece, retailed by Tiffany & Co, the foliate engraved cannelée case with porcelain panels, 3¼in. high.
(Christie's) $5,329

A silver cased carriage timepiece, Goldsmith & Silversmiths Ltd, 112 Regent St. W, 1910, enamel dial, the movement with a lever escapement in a case with engraved foliage top, 4in.
(Bonhams) $770

A French gilt and silvered brass musical and calendrical striking carriage clock, the enamel chapter disc with Roman chapters and blued spade hands painted in the center with clouds and with penny moonphase aperture beneath XII, 7½in.high.
(Christie's) $10,709

A small ormolu short duration quarter repeating travelling timepiece, late 18th century, 2½in. cracked blue glass dial, the verge watch movement signed *Tortell Paris*, with pull cord quarter repeating, 4½in.
(Bonhams) $532

Late Victorian brass and glass cased carriage clock, the shaped rectangular case with applied bands of carved foliage at top and base, masked dial, 5in. tall.
(G.A. Key) $174

Fine mid 19th century German/Austrian brass carriage clock with double wheel duplex escapement, grande and petite sonnerie movement, 5in. tall.
(G.A. Key) $1,540

A brass carriage timepiece with alarm, French, 1900s, enamel dial with alarm setting subsidiary below set within a pierced gilt foliage mask, 6in.
(Bonhams & Brooks) $454

A 19th century French oval carriage clock, the 8 day lever movement striking and repeating on a gong, the white enamel dial inscribed *Elkington & Co, Paris and Liverpool*, 6in. high.
(Woolley & Wallis) $955

A French engraved gilt-brass striking oval carriage clock, chapter disc with blued moon hands and subsidiary alarm disk below within a gilt mask pierced with a huntsman with two rabbits ahead within a wooded landscape.
(Christie's) $3,281

A grande sonnerie striking and repeating carriage clock with alarm, the gilded dial inscribed *Dent, London*, in glazed gilt metal case, 7½in. high, in maroon leather travelling case.
(Andrew Hartley) $2,310

An oval brass carriage timepiece, French, 1900s, enamel dial signed for Shepheard & Company 104 Regent St W, the movement with a lever escapement in a plain polished case with carrying handle, 6in.(Bonhams & Brooks) $369

A French ormolu-mounted ivory and marquetry carriage clock, the ormolu by Alphonse-Gustave Giroux, the marquetry by Duvinage & Harinckouk, Paris, circa 1877, 4½in. high.
(Christie's) $4,935

A paste set brass carriage timepiece with alarm, French, 1900s, enamel dial with lower alarm setting subsidiary and paste set surrounds the cylinder movement, 6in.(Bonhams & Brooks) $369

A Swedish bronzed and parcel-giltwood cartel clock, 20th century, in the Empire style with circular Roman and Arabic enamel dial with pierced gilt pointers inscribed *Exacta Sweden*, 23in. high. (Christie's) $1,006

A gilt-bronze cartel clock by H. Vian, Paris, circa 1870, in Louis XV style, the white enamel dial signed *h.Vian à Paris*, within pierced shaped foliage and scrolls, 45cm. high. (Sotheby's) $3,006

A French ormolu-mounted red 'Boulle' cartel d'applique, in the Louis XIV style, circa 1885, surmounted by a lyre centered by a female mask, above a shaped case centered to the top by a circular dial, 35½in. high. (Christie's) $4,410

A 19th century French cartel clock, the eight-day movement having white enamel dial in gilt metal rococo case cast with scrolling foliage, floral pendants and scroll work, 24in. high. (Andrew Hartley) $1,848

A French gilt-bronze and Jasperware cartel clock with its companion barometer, in the Louis XVI style, by Alfred Beurdeley Fils, Paris, circa 1885, each surmounted by a tied ribbon, each: 45¾in. high. (Christie's) $62,181

George III carved giltwood cartel clock, fourth quarter 18th century, with twin fusee striking movement, the signed silvered dial with subsidiary dials and date, 41½in. high. (Skinner) $12,650

Highly decorative gilded Scandinavian large wall clock, elaborately crested with ribbons, by John Manson of Norrkoping, the case signed verso, *G Boiardt*, 8 day movement, 30in. (G.A. Key) $841

A gilt ormolu cartel wall clock, French, mid 19th century, in an elaborately decorated case surmounted by a putti and trailing vine leaves, 21in. (Bonhams) $1,050

A French parcel-gilt and jeweled blue-ground Sèvres-pattern clock garniture, circa 1880, comprising a mantel clock and a pair of candlesticks; the clock surmounted by an urn, stamped *Japy Freres & Cie / above a pastoral scene,*14¼in. high.
(Christie's) $5,527

A Napoleon III gilt-bronze and white marble clock garniture, circa 1860, the clock surmounted by a knight menacing a Turk, in medieval costumes, above a circular white enamel dial *inscribed Potonié Léon / Paris,* the clock: 20¾in. high.
(Christie's) $5,880

A French bronze, ormolu and rouge griotte marble striking mantel clock and garniture, last quarter 19th century, the case surmounted by a bronze group of cavorting bacchantes, signed L. Gregoire, 32½in. high. (Christie's) $7,680

A gilt-bronze and white marble clock garniture, Paris, circa 1880, in Louis XVI style, the circular white enamel dial with Roman numerals, surmounted by a musical trophy flanked by two putti, flanked by a pair of five-light candelabra, candelabra 62cm. high. (Sotheby's) $10,246

A bluejohn and gilt-bronze clock garniture, French, circa 1860, comprising a clock and a pair of urns, the clock with two annular chapter rings enamelled with Roman and Arabic numerals, the hour indicated by the tongue of a coiled serpent, the clock: 53cm. high. (Sotheby's) $35,404

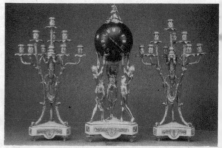

A French tôle-peinte, gilt-bronze and white marble clock garniture, in the Louis XVI style, circa 1920, the clock surmounted by a seated figure of an angel, holding a bow and an arrow, with a pomegranate lower terminal, supported by three graces, 30½in. high. (Christie's) $10,106

CLOCK SETS ———— CLOCKS & WATCHES

A French gilt bronze and porcelain mantel clock, late 19th century, the bleu de roi urn-shaped case with cherub surmount and waisted socle, mounted on a shaped platform with further cherub figures, 24in. wide, and a pair of associated candelabra en suite, 28½in. high. (Christie's) $7,402

A Louis Philippe gilt and patinated bronze mantel clock and garniture, second quarter 19th century, the rectangular case surmounted by a model of a cat seated on a cushion with foreclaw raised, hour hand lacking, 18½in. high, and a pair of conforming side urns en suite, later adapted as table lights, 15in. excluding fitment. (Christie's) $2,377

A gilt ormolu and sienna marble clock garniture, French, circa 1880, 4¾in. narrow chapter ring with a pierced spoke wheel center, drum case modelled as a chariot with a winged boy driving two lions, 17½in. (Bonhams & Brooks) $4,260

A Black Forest carved wood mantel clock and garniture, late 19th century, the case carved with a model of a stag standing over the drum case with naturalistic base, 28½in. high, and a pair of conforming side ornaments en suite, with etched glass vases, 15in. high. (Christie's) $10,057

A gilt ormolu and pink porcelain mounted clock with matched garniture, French, circa 1870, signed for Le Roy & Fils Palais Royal Paris, the bell striking movement in a drum case surmounted by a bird, together with a pair of four light candelabra, 16in. (Bonhams) $3,528

A French gilt and patinated-bronze clock garniture, circa 1880, compromising a mantel clock and two seven-light candelabra; the clock surmounted by a globe, centered to the front by a sunburst dial, the clock: 43½in. high. (Christie's) $19,000

201

A gilt-bronze clock garniture by Alfred Beurdeley, Paris, circa 1870, in Louis XVI style, the candelabra in the form of a putto and a satyr respectively, each supporting five foliate arms on a circular base with conforming decoration, the clock 55cm. high. (Sotheby's) $39,245

A gilt spelter and blue porcelain mounted clock garniture, French, 1880s, the bell striking movement in a cast case surmounted by doves and berried garlands, 15in. (Bonhams & Brooks) $781

A gilt ormolu and porcelain mounted mantel clock garniture, French, 1880s, 43cm., garniture 37cm. (Bonhams) $2,646

A French gilt, patinated-bronze and Cipollino Rosso marble clock garniture, circa 1880, comprising a mantel clock and two candlesticks; the clock surmounted by a cherub holding a torch, seated on a globe centered to the front by a dial, supported by a cloudborne cherub, the timepiece: 28¼in. high. (Christie's) $5,880

A 19th century Sèvres bisque porcelain clock garniture, with ormolu mounts, the body with sporting cherubs and classical maidens in low relief, 24½in. high, a pair of vases to match with cherub finials and goat mask handles.(Andrew Hartley) $7,065

A blue glazed Oriental style clock surmounted with mythical figure and a pair of lion garnitures, French, 1900s, clock 28cm., garnitures 15cm. (Bonhams) $544

A late 17th century style lantern clock, the 30-hour posted bell-striking movement with verge escapement and bob pendulum, signed William Gray, London, 38cm. approximately, with wall bracket and brass-cased weight. (Bristol) $628

Brass lantern clock, circa 1670, the brass dial with engraved chapter ring and alarm mechanism engraved with the maker's name *John Cotsworth Londini*, 6in. high. (Skinner) $5,175

A brass lantern clock, possibly part 17th century, the single fusee movement with passing strike, in typical case with Roman numeral chapter ring, 37cm. approximately. (Bristol) $377

A James I gilt-metal striking chamber clock, John Smith, Kings Lynn; dated *1610*, the elaborate case with four three quarter-columns to each angle supported on four gadrooned pad feet, 16in. high. (Christie's) $26,772

A brass lantern clock, unsigned, 18th/19th century, 9in. square brass dial with a chapter ring and corner foliage spandrels, the brass posted movement with a verge escapement, 16in. (Bonhams) $2,100

A brass lantern clock with a later movement, 18/19th century, 6½in. silvered chapter ring and polished center signed *Browning Bury*, later twin fusee movement, 15in. (Bonhams) $700

A brass lantern clock, John Bicknill of Cirencester, circa 1680, 6in. brass chapter ring with engraved minute ring, steel hands and matted center, 13¼in. (Bonhams) $1680

A brass lantern clock with a later movement, James Delance Froome Fecit, 17th/19th movement, 6½in. silvered chapter ring, the center engraved with tulips and signed, 16in. (Bonhams & Brooks) $1,207

A brass reproduction ting-tang quarter striking lantern clock, James Walker, London, circa 1880, 7½in. brass chapter ring and foliage engraved center, twin fusee movement striking on two bells, 17½in. (Bonhams) $1,750

A 19th century oak and mahogany longcase clock, dial inscribed *W. Herbert, Ludlow,* 8 day movement. (Brightwells) $3,148

A late 18th century longcase clock, cross-banded oak case, 8 day movement. (Brightwells) $2,926

A Georgian mahogany satinwood strung longcase clock, 8-day striking mechanism. (Brightwells) $7,350

A small mahogany longcase clock by William Green, Grantham, eight day movement 72½in. high. (Andrew Hartley) $3,925

An oak cased thirty hour longcase clock, the 30.5cm. square silvered dial, with Roman and Arabic numerals, signed *Pattison Halifax,* 219cm. high. (Bonhams) $1,288

An oak and mahogany cased eight day longcase clock, indistinctly signed and fitted with a seconds dial and calendar sector, 214cm. high. (Bonhams) $1,386

A French green onyx and champlevé enamel longcase clock, late 19th century, the twin barrel movement with strike on gong, 51½in. high overall. (Christie's) $6,580

An oak longcase clock, the eight day three train movement chiming on five tubular bells, 101½in. high. (Andrew Hartley) $3,140

A 19th century five glass wheel barometer and thermometer, with silvered dials, in mahogany case, 39in. high, dated *1898*. (Andrew Hartley) $672

An oak 30 hour longcase clock, English, 18th century, 182cm. (Bonhams) $695

A good Federal inlaid and figured mahogany tall-case clock, Warner & Schuyler, New York, circa 1795, 8ft.high. (Sotheby's) $21,850

An oak cased eight day chiming longcase clock, the four pillar movement striking on eight bells, 226cm. high. (Bonhams) $2,170

An early 19th century oak marquetry longcase clock with 30-hour movement, by John Nicholas, Daventry. (Brightwells) $1,654

A mahogany longcase with replaced brass dial, A . Dobble, Falkirk, 18th century, 203cm. (Bonhams) $755

An oak longcase clock, English, 18th century, Jn Symonds Reepham, 207cm. (Bonhams) $981

A Georgian mahogany longcase clock, eight day with date aperture, inscribed *Chorley Houghton.* (Brightwells) $9,996

Continental carved oak tall case clock, mid-19th century, the face signed Mezaize, orfeure, Horloger a Bacqueveille, 92½in. high.(Skinner) $1,495

A George III mahogany longcase clock, the 8 day movement Mattw. & Thos. Dutton, London, No. 257, 7ft.5in. high, circa 1785. (Woolley & Wallis) $55,440

Carved oak Renaissance Revival style tall case clock, late 19th century, three-train movement, 92in. high. (Sotheby's) $14,950

A red lacquered chinoiserie longcase clock, the eight day movement signed William *Luke Exon,* 75¾in. high.(Andrew Hartley) $2,926

George III faux tortoiseshell japanned tall case clock, 18th century, with two-train chiming movement, face signed *S. Boyce, Derenham,* 84¼in. high. (Skinner) $5,750

Cherry carved tall case clock, John Field, Cumberland, Rhode Island, 1760-80, 95in. high. (Skinner) $61,900

American tall case clock, late 19th century, by the Waterbury Clock Company, with two-train movement, set in rounded hood with C-scrolls to top, 90½in. high. (Skinner) $3,450

S. Jarvis, Birmingham, an 18th century longcase clock, the 30 hour movement with an outside countwheel striking on a bell, 6ft.6in. high. (Woolley & Wallis) $1,405

An unusual Shropshire oak 8-day longcase clock, signed *Newall, Cleobury*, 223cm. (Bristol) $4,704

A Victorian Irish mahogany longcase clock, the 8 day movement, C & C Sivel, Dublin, 6ft.7in. high. (Woolley & Wallis) $1,355

An 18th century Midlands oak longcase clock, the 8 day movement, James Green, Nantwich, 7ft.6½in. high. (Woolley & Wallis) $4,312

A good Federal birchwood thirty-hour tall-case clock, Riley Whiting, Winchester, Connecticut, circa 1800, 7ft.11in. high. (Sotheby's) $12,650

Dutch Rococo walnut and floral marquetry tall case clock, late 18th century, the two-train chiming movement signed *David Le Feure, Amsterdam*, 98in. high. (Skinner) $14,950

An oak and mahogany crossbanded longcase clock, 8-day bell-striking movement, by Barrett, Blandford, 215cm. (Bristol) $1,092

A mahogany longcase clock with eight-day movement, the moonphase with a sail ship, secondary dial and calendar aperture, 87½in. high. (Andrew Hartley) $7,700

American carved oak Renaissance-style tall case clock, circa 1890, works by Elliot of London, with two-train quarter striking movement, 104in. high. (Skinner) $13,800

A mahogany longcase clock, English, Sam Ballin, Wooten, 211cm. (Bonhams) $830

Curly maple tall case clock, Isaac Blasdel, Chester, New Hampshire, (1738-1791), 85in. high. (Skinner) $23,000

A mahogany longcase clock, German, 1900s, 198cm. (Bonhams) $750

A mahogany Georgian longcase clock with painted arched dial inscribed *John Parr, Liverpool,* 8-day movement.(Brightwells) $4,998

An 8 day oak longcase clock with turned columns on the hood, English, early 19th century, 204cm. (Bonhams) $1,176

A Louis XV ormolu-mounted tulipwood, amaranth, marquetry and parquetry regulateur, the case by Adrien Jérôme Jollain, 84¼in. high. (Christie's) $40,986

A 30 hour oak longcase with square silvered dial and plain trunk and base English, 18th century, Handcomb Ampthill, 197cm. (Bonhams) $680

An oak cased thirty hour longcase clock, the 31.5cm. square dial with Roman and Arabic numerals, signed *Helm Ormskirk,* 213cm. high. (Bonhams) $1,008

A Louis XIV ormolu-mounted tortoiseshell pendule, the later dial with an applied chapter ring set with white enamel Roman chapters with foliate pierced gilt-brass hands, 14½in. wide.
(Christie's) $2,236

A French ormolu, bronze and mahogany pendule aux cercles tournants, second quarter 19th century, with World time, of circular domed form with six female caryatids flanking an obelisk, 19in. high. (Christie's) $11,178

A Louis XVI gilt bronze mantel clock, circa 1780, the drum case flanked by goats and surmounted by a fruiting urn, the rectangular plinth with twin cherubs inscribed *Ragot A Paris,* 15½in. high.
(Christie's) $5,088

A Louis XVI style gilt bronze and white marble mantel clock, 19th century, the drum case flanked by dolphins spouting water, with a lion mask issuing from rushes below, inscribed *Leroy, Paris,* 16¼in. high.
(Christie's) $3,634

An Empire gilt bronze mantel clock 'The Ship of Time', early 19th century, the case modelled as a barge with a seated figure of Old Father Time and a cherub flanking the dial, 13½in. long.
(Christie's) $2,907

An Empire style ormolu pendule à cercles tournants mantel clock, second half 19th century, the shaped rectangular case with arched top flanked by a partially draped female figure, 19¼in. high.
(Christie's) $5,152

A Napoleon III gilt-bronze-mounted, parcel-gilt blue-ground Sèvres-pattern porcelain and white marble mantel clock, in the Louis XVI style, circa 1870, surmounted by flower branches, 16in. wide.
(Christie's) $7,350

A gilt bronze and porcelain mantel clock, late 19th century, the case as a clock tower with simulated basket-weave pagoda top and sides with bound bamboo stem, the oval plinth with a porcelain group of two Oriental figures, 19in. high.
(Christie's) $3,997

A Charles X gilt bronze mantel clock, second quarter 19th century, the rectangular case with pierced foliate mounts surmounted by a laurel wreath against two volumes and an oil lamp, 14½in. high.
(Christie's) $1,454

A gilt ormolu and marble mantel clock, French, circa 1870, the bell striking movement signed for G E Mylne London in a fluted drum case with a decorated bezel, 11¼in. (Bonhams) $896

A French ormolu and patinated bronze pendule à cercles tournants, mid-19th century, the splayed lotus-leaf wrapped lid surmounted by a pomegranate above an oak-leaf entwined reeded ring with winding holes and covers, 30½in. wide. (Christie's) $84,402

A carved beech cuckoo mantel clock, Black Forest, mid 19th century, the movement with pierced plates and a fusee for the going side, 19in. (Bonhams & Brooks) $369

A cast brass mantel clock with a scroll shape body and bell striking movement, French, 19th century, Henri Robert Paris. (Bonhams) $604

A gilt ormolu and blue porcelain mounted mantel clock French, circa 1880, 3¼in. porcelain dial decorated with flowers around the center,13in.(Bonhams) $1,050

A red tortoiseshell striking boulle clock with brass mounts, enamel dial signed *Goldsmiths Company, London*, French, Marti Paris, 19th century, 36cm. (Bonhams) $528

A 4 glass clock with mercury filled pendulum and visible Brocourt escapement, French, 19th century, 27cm. (Bonhams) $544

A gilt spelter and porcelain mounted mantel clock, French, early 19th century, 50cm. (Bonhams) $735

A mahogany mantel clock with box inlay decoration, J.C. Vickery, Regent St, 33cm. (Bonhams) $588

A Viennese silver-mounted green enamel timepiece, circa 1900, the hinged oval case centered to the top by a circular dial, the back with mirrored panel, flanked to each side by a herm figure, 4¼in. high. (Christie's) $1,382

A Louis XVI ormolu-mounted white marble mantel clock, by Jean-François Debelle, the dial surmounted and surrounded to the right by a nymph bearing garlands of flowers, 14¼in. wide. (Christie's) $2,981

Late 19th century English oak cased mantel clock, central circular Arabic chapter ring, crested above and below with blue printed neo classical ceramic panels, 8 day movement, 11in. (G.A. Key) $218

A finely made modern Congreve timepiece, English, late 20th century, central silvered minute chapter ring flanked by hour and seconds subsidiaries, 19in. (Bonhams & Brooks) $3,124

A French gilt-metal striking mantel clock, late 19th century, the naturalistic case surmounted by the reclining figure of a rustic youth picking grapes and the front supports modelled as entwined vine branches, 13¼in. wide. (Christie's) $373

An oak cased mantel timepiece with silvered chapter ring and brass dial, domed top case with brass mounts, French, 1890s, 38cm. (Bonhams) $483

A falling ball gravity timepiece, Thwaites & Reed, 20th century, 26cm. (Bonhams) $588

An ormolu and bronze figural mantel clock, French, mid 19th century. (Bonhams) $1,176

A gilt spelter and porcelain mounted mantel clock, French, 1860s, 41cm. (Bonhams) $515

Liberty & Co., 'Cymric' mantel clock, 1905, silver, set with a circular blue and green enamelled face, front and side panel framed in border. (Sotheby's) $6,384

An ormolu and red marble mantel clock, French, circa 1820, mounted in the body of a gilt chariot with a winged horseman driving two horses, 14½in. (Bonhams) $4,200

An ormolu and jeweled burgundy porcelain mounted mantel clock, French, circa 1875, 4¼in. porcelain dial, gilt decorated and a painted romantic scene in the centre, 16in. (Bonhams) $1,540

A French gilt bronze mantel clock, third quarter 19th century, the stepped rectangular case surmounted by a group of a seated maiden with cherub attendants, 22in. high. (Christie's) $3,619

A Victorian engraved gilt-brass calendrical strut timepiece, Wilhelm Vasel ; retailed by London and Ryder, London, the case in the style of Thomas Cole, finely engraved with formalized strap-work and flowerheads amongst foliate scrolls, 7in. high. (Christie's) $6,909

A gilt ormolu and blue porcelain mantel clock, French, circa 1880, 3¼in. enamel dial signed for Reid & Sons Paris, the bell striking movement in a dark blue vase shaped case, 22½in. (Bonhams) $2,240

A Turkish market gilt ormolu mantel clock, French circa 1880, 3½in. enamel dial with Turkish numerals signed *Hri Houdebine Ft de Bronzes Paris*, 22in. (Bonhams) $3,080

A Regency white marble cased mantel clock, the front carved with birds amidst foliage, mounted on later marmo portoro plinth, 13½in. wide. (Christie's) $1,974

A gilt ormolu mantel clock, French, circa 1820, 4in. enamel chapter with a blue border decorated with stars signed for Warnier Lnr A Paris, 17in. (Bonhams) $2,520

A mahogany and brass inlaid cased mantel clock, 8in. painted convex dial, the twin fusee bell striking movement in a case with a concave sided pediment, 19in. (Bonhams & Brooks) $1.988

A 20th century carved dog novelty timepiece, in the form of a terrier, the back plate stamped *Osuhr*, some restoration needed 13cm. high. (Bonhams) $323

An inlaid mahogany mantel clock, Rigby, Charing Cross, circa 1820, 7in. silvered dial, the twin fusee bell striking movement in an arched top case, 16½in. (Bonhams & Brooks) $2,698

A gilt-bronze and porcelain mantel clock, French, circa 1870, the circular dial painted with a winged Cupid within a case surmounted by a vignette of Marie Antoinette, flanked by cherubs, 52cm. high. (Sotheby's) $7,400

A bronze and gilt-bronze mantel clock by Henry Dasson, Paris, 1881, the enamel Roman numeral clock face surmounted by figures of a satyr and a nymph and flanked by a male and female satyr, 79cm. wide. (Sotheby's) $60,555

A French ormolu and ebonized hanging pendulum portico clock, Ledure, Paris, the ebonized case with rectangular stepped pediment applied with ormolu rosette and palmette mounts to the entablature, 26½in.high. (Christie's) $9,761

An Edwardian mahogany quarter chiming mantel clock, painted overall with trailing flowers and garlands of foliage, dial inscribed *John Wide, London*, 30½in. high. (Christie's) $3,290

A 19th century French gilt brass and porcelain mounted mantel clock, set in an architectural columned case, with pendulum and winding key, 30cm. wide. (Bonhams) $431

An ormolu and blue porcelain mounted mantel clock, French, circa 1880, dial with numeral reserves with a winged putti in the center, 19½in. (Bonhams & Brooks) $4,260

A brass skeleton timepiece, English, second half 19th century, single fusee movement with a half dead beat escapement, 16in. (Bonhams & Brooks) $710

A brass skeleton clock, in the gothic style, fitted with a single fusee movement, a shaped silvered 7in. dial with Roman numerals, set upon marbled base with a glass dome, 20th century.(Bonhams) $832

A brass skeleton timepiece, English second half 19th century, 5in. painted chapter ring, the single fusee movement with a half dead beat escapement 15in. (Bonhams & Brooks) $781

A gilt-brass year-going skeleton timepiece with calendar and world time, unsigned, probably French, circa 1860, the silvered regulator dial with calendar windows for the days within the hour ring, 17in. high. (Christie's) $19,000

Brass bill tray and skeleton clock of Lichfield Cathedral, by Thomas Simcock of Warrington, striking on a single gong and housed beneath a glass dome on a mahogany base, approximately 21in. overall. (G.A. Key) $4,239

An important English astronomical skeleton timepiece with mean solar and sidereal time, James Shearer, London, the movement frame secured at the angles by four columns with ball finials, radially pierced sides, 23in. wide. (Christie's) $425,930

A Victorian gilt-brass skeleton clock, Robert Leck, the pierced brass scroll frame with twin gut fusees, Harrison's maintaining power, deadbeat escape wheel with horizontal plane anchor escapement. (Christie's) $8,636

An English brass skeleton timepiece, 19th century, with a 6½in. dial and silvered chapter ring, the single fusee movement with passing strike,17in. high excluding dome. (Bonhams) $1,848

An Empire ormolu, marble and mahogany three month going and striking keyhole skeleton clock, the ormolu keyhole frame on chamfered pad feet, 18¾in. high. (Christie's) $18,135

A Charles II olivewood striking table
clock, William Knottesford, London,
the ebony-molded case, originally
on turntable base with ogee
molded narrow caddy to the top,
18¾in. high.
(Christie's) $86,377

An ormolu and porcelain mounted
table clock, French, circa 1880, the
bell striking movement in a cast
case surmounted by a blue
porcelain finial, waisted sides with
painted panels, 15in.
(Bonhams) $1,190

A Louis Philippe ormolu quarter
striking table regulator with coup
perdu escapement, calendar and
moonphase, Paul Garnier, Paris,
No. 1844, 19½in. high.
(Christie's) $32,818

An unusual light oak cased giant
triple calendar with a matching
table, F W Streeter, London, circa
1870, in a hump back case with a
French 8 day movement with a
small enamel dial controlling the
calendar above, 4ft.6in.
(Bonhams) $4,200

A Continental gilt-brass striking
hexagonal table clock, Carl Crems,
the dial with brass Roman and
Arabic chapter ring, gilt rosette-
engraved alarm disk to the center.
(Christie's) $6,564

A Napoleon III gilt-brass table
regulator with perpetual calendar
and equation of time, Achille
Brocot, retailed by J.W. Benson, the
arched case on molded base with
bevelled glasses to the front and
rear doors, 17½in. high.
(Christie's) $36,272

9th century oak large table clock
with a broken arch pediment,
central ball finial, the whole
molded with rosettes and foliage,
Barraud & Lunds, 41 Cornhill,
London, 25in.
(G.A. Key) $696

A brass bulkhead timepiece, early
20th century, the eight-day
movement with lever escapement
and white Roman numeral dial with
subsidiary seconds, in cylindrical
brass wall mounted case, diameter
20.5cm. (Bristol) $246

A gilt ormolu and porcelain
mounted table clock, French, circa
1870, 3¾in. enamel dial, in a case
with a stepped pediment
surmounted by a floral decorated
urn and flanked by cone finials,
16in. (Bonhams) $2,240

A Federal eglomisé and gilt mahogany banjo timepiece, the dial reads *warranted by Wm. Cummens,* Boston, Massachusetts, 1820s, 34in. high.
(Skinner) $6,325

A 19th century Vienna wall clock with circular dial, spring driven movement in glazed mahogany and stained wood case, 4ft.6in. high.Brightwells) $601

A walnut cased striking Vienna wall clock, 19th century, the 18cm. dial set in a carved and molded case with a glazed trunk door, 140cm. high.
(Bonhams) $756

Federal giltwood and eglomisé banjo timepiece, the dial reads *warranted by Curtis and Dunning,* *Concord, Massachusetts,* circa 1815, the 33½in. high.
(Skinner) $5,175

Classical carved mahogany veneer lyre wall clock, the dial signed *A. Chandler,* Concord, New Hampshire, 1825, encloses a striking brass eight-day weight-driven movement, 43in. high.
(Skinner) $17,250

A rosewood weight driven grand sonnerie wall clock, F Bruimann, mid 19th century, the three train movement striking on two gongs at quarters, 46in.
(Bonhams) $3,500

A German mahogany and maplewood observatory wall regulator, type A1 Sigmund Riefler, Munich, No. 117: dated *1905,* 59¼in. high.
(Christie's) $43,181

Classical mahogany carved and gilded eglomisé lyre clock, the dial signed *Swain and Dyer Boston,* mid 1820s, 40in.
(Skinner) $13,800

A mahogany cased single fusee dial clock, English, 20th century, 39cm. (Bonhams) $500

A large oak cased weight driven tavern wall timepiece, G Usmar, West Malling, circa 1800, movement with tapered plates in a case with a turned surround, 4ft.11in. (Bonhams) $5,320

A mahogany dial timepiece and a chrome pit clock, G. Baxter, Nottingham, 41cm. (Bonhams) $515

A short duration red lacquer weight driven wall timepiece, Maltese, mid 18th century, 12in painted chapter ring on a painted surround decorated with a picture of Cronus with a sickle together with putti, 37in. (Bonhams) $12,600

A mahogany cased dial timepiece with a 7in. painted dial, German movement, 19th century, 27cm. (Bonhams) $665

A French ebonized and Limoges enamel wall clock, the panels signed *Mausuy Dotin*, dated *1883*, the case of square shape with an arched pediment centered by an oval escutcheon, dial decorated with mythological beasts and foliage, 24in.wide. (Christie's) $7,350

A gilt framed short duration grand sonnerie wall clock, square gilt case with an oval pendulum aperture, Austrian, mid 19th century, 42cm. (Bonhams) $272

A French Comtois clock movement with brass weights, early 19th century. 38cm.(Bonhams) $441

A rosewood cased single fusee drop dial timepiece, 19th century, the 30.5cm. painted signed dial set in a case with mother of pearl and pewter inlays. (Bonhams) $504

19th century mahogany circular English dial clock, circular Roman chapter ring, by F J Reich of Folkestone, 12½in.
(G.A. Key) $345

A George III style mahogany dial timepiece, 20th century, with concave section brass bezel to concave mahogany surround screwed directly to the backbox, 8in. silvered brass dial, signed *G. Staples London*, 11¾in. high.
(Christie's) $1,646

A mahogany dial timepiece, English, 20th century, 12in. painted dial, the single fusee movement in a case with hinged back and turned surround.
(Bonhams & Brooks) $497

A mahogany striking drop dial wall clock, Adam Thomson, London, 19th century, twin fusee movement striking on bell in a later case with a turned surround and pegged back, 22in. (Bonhams) $910

Early 19th century mahogany cased circular dial clock, convex dial, brass bezel, circular Roman chapter ring, 14½in.
(G.A. Key) $1,160

A dark oak striking wall clock, English, 19th/20th century, 12½in. painted dial signed for Geo Whitehouse, Birmingham, twin fusee gong striking movement, 44in.
(Bonhams & Brooks) $1,470

19th century mahogany framed circular dial clock, circular Roman chapter ring by O Wehrle, Market Hill, Cambridge, 13½in.
(G.A. Key) $471

A mahogany drop dial wall timepiece, English, 19th century, 14in. painted dial signed for Keyser & Co 66 High St Boro, 26in.
(Bonhams & Brooks) $1,136

Circular mahogany cased dial clock, brass bezel, circular silvered Roman chapter ring by Saddleton of Lynn, circa late 18th/early 19th century, 14in.
(G.A. Key) $4,060

mahogany dial timepiece, John
Williams, Goodge St London, circa
1800, 12in painted dial with later
flower decoration, the movement
with tapered plates.
(Bonhams & Brooks) $1,207

A walnut spring driven Vienna wall
clock with barometer, German,
1900s, 7in. dial gong striking
movement in a case with a raised
pediment flanked by turned finials,
5ft. (Bonhams & Brooks) $639

A large Tower clock inscribed *J.H.
Wilkinson, Annan*, with Roman
numerals on a white enamel dial
within a molded stained beech
circular frame, German made,
82cm. diameter.(Thomson Roddick
& Medcalf) $1,088

mahogany and brass inlaid drop
dial wall timepiece, English, mid
19th century, the single fusee
movement in a case with a foliage
inlaid bezel and glazed trunk
aperture, 20in.(Bonhams) $420

A Scottish brass Arts and Crafts
wall clock, the square brass dial
with embossed Roman numerals
and Celtic banding, with brass
weights and pendulum, 27cm.
square.(Thomson Roddick &
Medcalf) $290

A mahogany drop dial wall
timepiece, Suggate, Halesworth,
circa 1790, the single fusee
movement with tapered shaped
plates in a case with turned
surround and cast bezel, 27in.
(Bonhams) $3,920

small size drop dial wall
timepiece, English, unsigned, early
19th century, the single fusee
movement in a case with an 8 sided
chamfered bezel, 14in.
(Bonhams) $2,100

19th century mahogany cased dial
clock, circular Roman chapter ring
by E J Perfitt of Wymondham, 14in.
(G.A. Key) $609

A mahogany cased striking drop
dial wall clock, F Gibbs,
Nottingham, circa 1870, the drop
trunk with a pendulum aperture with
a carved surround, 23in.
(Bonhams) $980

A silver repoussé pair cased calendar watch, James Shearwood, London late 18th century, enamel dial with gilt hands and calendar aperture, 47mm.
(Bonhams & Brooks) $426

A gold and enamel verge pendant watch in the form of a strawberry, Continental, circa 1800, white enamel dial with Arabic numerals, eccentric hole, moon hands, gilt fusee movement, 27mm.
(Christie's) $6,762

A silver open faced Masonic dialled verge watch, William Brownsword, Nottingham, 1882, enamel dial with subsidiary seconds and decorated with Masonic symbols, 52mm.
(Bonhams) $441

An 18ct. gold diamond set full hunter watch, International Watch Company, recent, the polished case with sapphire, diamond, ruby and emerald set applied crest, the reverse with an applied pavé set map of Oman, 54mm.
(Bonhams) $2.500

A rare early silver pre-hairspring verge pocket watch, Johann Sayller, Ulm, circa 1650, steel balance wheel without hairspring, pinned balance cock with small irregular foot, 37mm.
(Christie's) $9,499

An 18ct gold open-faced verge watch, Daniels, Liverpool, enamel dial with subsidiary seconds, the fully engraved full plate movement with the balance running in the top plate, 45mm.
(Bonhams) $470

A nickel open faced railway watch, English Watch Co, for Iraq State Railways, nos 1818, circa 1920, enamel dial, the full plate keyless movement in a hinged back case (lacking inner cover), 55mm.
(Bonhams) $162

A silver and tortoiseshell pair cased verge pocket watch with calendar, Le Maire, London, early 18th century, outer case overlaid with tortoiseshell and with pinwork decoration, 52mm. diameter.
(Christie's) $1,727

A silver and leather covered bag watch, Gruen, 1930s, silvered dial marked Alpina, the nickel movement in a case with a sliding front cover, 35 x 50mm.
(Bonhams) $176

gold quarter repeating Jaquemart verge watch, French, early 19th century, small white dial on dark blue guilloche surround, 55mm. (Bonhams & Brooks) $2,352

An 18ct. gold and diamond set clip watch, signed *Patek Philippe & Co., Geneve*, 1936-40, circular champagne dial with gilt baton markers and Arabic quarters, 32mm. (Christie's) $2,536

French Art Nouveau large coach-watch, and having subsidiary seconds dial, the back embossed with a young lady's head amongst trailing foliage, having a button wind anchor escapement, circa 1890. (G.A. Key) $290

yma, a Masonic automatic wristwatch, 1950s, enamel dial with Masonic symbols marking the hours and Masonic inscription, 21 jewel automatic movement, 38mm. (Christie's) $1,788

An Art Nouveau silver open faced keyless lever sector watch, Record Watch Co., Tramelan, circa 1900, off-white enamel dial signed *Sector Watch*, hour and minute sector, blued steel flyback hour and minute hands, 45 x 59mm. (Christie's) $2,590

A gold, enamel and seed pearl set quarter repeating keyless lever pocketwatch for the Chinese market, J. Ullmann & Co., Chaux de Fonds, circa 1900, gold case with painted enamel portrait on the front, 35mm. (Christie's) $2,936

gilt metal and painted shell pair cased verge watch J. Williamson, London late 18th century, the gilt movement with square baluster pillars and pierced balance cock, gilt metal case with matching red shell outer pair 50mm. (Bonhams & Brooks) $529

A 14ct. gold quarter repeating hunting cased keyless lever pocket watch with concealed erotic automaton, Swiss, circa 1910, cuvette with further hinged cover opening to reveal the erotic automata, diameter 50mm. (Christie's) $7,100

An 18ct. gold and enamel pair cased pocket chronometer, signed *Ilbery, London*, 1813, Earnshaw escapement, spring foot detent, cut bimetallic compensation balance, diameter 58mm. (Christie's) $14,369

A 14ct. gold and enamel hunting cased keyless lever pocket watch, Swiss, circa 1890, the front decorated with a peacock in a floral bower, 48mm. diameter. (Christie's)　　　　$1,233

Large Victorian silver cased pocket watch with gold Roman numerals to an engine turned silver dial, key wind, the case bearing the Birmingham hallmark for 1891. (G.A. Key)　　　　$80

A gold and enamel open faced verge pocket watch, Isaac Soret & Fils, circa 1780, eccentric winding hole, gilt fusee movement, chased case with paste set bezel, diameter 42mm. (Christie's)　　　　$1,225

A silver open faced verge pocket watch with center seconds and calendar, Continental, circa 1820, white enamel dial inscribed *Breguet a Paris*, subsidiary meantime and calendar dials, diameter 56mm. (Christie's)　　　　$658

A rare early gilt brass pre-balance spring octagonal clockwatch with stackfreed, German, maker's initials. *V.S.*, circa 1580, later silvered dial, octagonal case with molded band, 50 x 42mm. (Christie's)　　　　$11,515

Good large late Victorian 18ct gold half hunter pocket watch, the outer case with blue enamelled Roman numerals, button wind, 2in. diameter dial. (G.A. Key)　　　　$580

A precious metal open faced watch, L Le Roy & Cie, 13-15 Palais Royal, Paris, 1920s, silvered two tone dial with an engraved center and subsidiary seconds, 48mm. (Bonhams)　　　　$500

Nickel cased Goliath travelling watch with button wind, housed in a leather silver mounted travelling case, 4 x 3½in., Birmingham 1913. (G.A. Key)　　　　$73

A steel and gilt open faced pocket watch, Rolex, Prince Imperial, 1940s, nickel finished Observatory movement jeweled to the third with protected escapement, 37mm. (Christie's)　　　　$1,22

A gilt metal and under painted horn paircased verge watch John Curtis, Lonson circa 1790, the frosted gilt movement with cylindrical pillars, 48mm.
(Bonhams & Brooks) $588

Mickey Mouse, an Ingersoll Mickey pocket watch depicting Mickey Mouse on the face, the animated hour and minute hands shaped as Mickey's arms with orange painted hands, 1930s. 2in. diameter.
(Christie's) $310

A gold and enamel verge watch in the form of a mandolin, Continental, circa 1820, the case decorated with white, black and blue enamel, 67mm. (Christie's) $2,874

Swiss glass paperweight clock, etailed by Tiffany & Co., of typical orm, 4in. high. (Skinner) $460

A rare early silver pair cased pre-hairspring verge pocket watch with alarm, Charles Champion a Paris, circa 1675, outer case drilled for pinwork (now overlaid with fishskin), diameter 50mm.
(Christie's) $6,580

An 18ct. gold open faced watch together with a 2 color gold chain, Swiss, 1912, silvered dial with subsidiary seconds, the nickel movement in a polished case with a shaped aperture, 45mm.
(Bonhams) $265

magnificent gold, Dendritic agate, namel and pearl set duplex pocket atch for the Chinese market, ery, London, late 18th century, e front and back of the case set ith moss agate, 105 x 64mm. verall.(Christie's) $69,090

Victorian hallmarked silver cased pocket watch with key wind, the white enamelled dial inscribed *F Gibbs, Nottingham*, key wind.
(G.A. Key) $80

An unusual gold and enamel watch in the form of a shoe, Swiss/French, circa 1780, the gold body of the shoe decorated with yellow, green, red, pink and blue enamel, 48mm.
(Christie's) $6,424

A gold open faced quarter repeating jaquemart pocket watch with concealed erotic automata, Swiss, circa 1820, beneath the dial an automaton goat against a blued steel plate sliding to reveal the erotic automaton scene, diameter 54mm. (Christie's) $8,114

A gold, enamel and pearl set fob watch in the form of a padlock, Swiss/ French, early 19th century, case with seed pearl and enamel decoration, 30mm. (Christie's) $4,277

A very slim 18ct. gold cylinder pocket watch, signed *Courvoisier Freres,* Swiss, early 19th century, the border decorated with pale blue and pink lozenges decorated with gilt glowers and scrolls, diameter 53mm. (Christie's) $1,691

A silver triple cased quarter repeating verge pocket watch, William Gib, Rotterdam, early 18th century, pierced and engraved inner and second case, third outer case overlaid with shagreen and with pique decoration, diameter 64mm. (Christie's) $8,636

An 18ct. gold full hunting cased minute repeating keyless lever pocket watch with triple calendar and moon phase, Swiss, circa 1900, 57mm. (Christie's) $4,376

An interesting Napoleonic open faced verge pocket watch, Continental, circa 1807, the back set with an enamel plaque depicting Napoleon embracing Tsar Alexander I, diameter 56mm. (Christie's) $2,623

A gold, enamel and seed pearl set verge pocket watch, signed *Jaqs. Coulin & Amy Bry, a Geneve,* late 18th century, eccentric winding hole, seed pearl set hands, gilt fusee movement, diameter 41mm. (Christie's) $2,029

A silver and tortoiseshell pair cased verge pocket watch, P. Tollot, circa 1700, plain inner case, outer case overlaid with tortoiseshell and with pinwork decoration, 55mm. diameter (Christie's) $3,281

A gold and enamel pair cased verge pocket watch, signed *Fres. Bordier A Geneve,* circa 1770, outer case with paste set bezel, the back set with an enamel panel depicting the Madonna and child, diameter 38mm. (Christie's) $1,860

ange. A pink gold openface eyless pocketwatch, signed *A. ange & Söhne, Glashütte-SA,* 910s, the frosted gilt three-quarter late movement jeweled to the ird with bimetallic balance, 52mm. ameter. (Christie's) $3,381

A silver pair cased verge pocket watch, John Bushman, London, circa 1710, gilt fusee movement with divided Egyptian pillars, winged balance cock, 55mm. (Christie's) $3,281

A Louis XIV metal verge oignon pocket watch, I.Garnier à Partenay, circa 1710, cartouche dial with Roman numerals on white enamel grounds, profusely cast and chased case, diameter 57mm. (Christie's) $1,974

gold, enamel and pearl set open ced verge pocket watch, Ante. illiet & Ce, Geneve, circa 1790, e back enamelled with a neo-ssical scene and set with pearls, ameter 45mm. hristie's) $2,961

A rare 18ct. gold open faced minute repeating and split seconds keyless lever chronograph pocket watch, Patek Philippe & Co., circa 1918, champagne dial with Arabic numerals, subsidiary constant seconds, diameter 50mm. (Christie's) $23,924

A gold and enamel pearl set musical pocket watch for the Chinese market, unsigned, Swiss, circa 1820, the back cover finely painted and enamelled with a spray of flowers against a guilloche ground, diameter 61mm (Christie's)   **$12,259**

18ct. gold open faced keyless er pocket watch, signed *Patek ilippe,* 1910, frosted gilt ovement jeweled to the center d with Wolf's tooth winding. hristie's) $5,410

A gold and enamel pair cased cylinder pocket watch, Ellicott, London, 1780-81, enamelled case with oval scene en grisaille, diameter 47mm. (Christie's) $7,607

A gilt metal and enamel verge pocket watch, Continental, signed *Tarts, London,* case decorated with enamel and depicting a female nude, diameter 45mm. (Christie's) $1,575

Baume & Mercier, a stainless steel automatic wristwatch with chronograph and date, 1990s, white dial with luminous baton markers, 38mm. (Christie's) $638

An eight day silver wristwatch, 1930s, silvered dial with Breguet numerals, nickel finished movement jeweled to the center, 25mm. (Christie's) $1,001

A lady's 18ct. gold quartz wristwatch, signed *Patek Philippe*, recent, with quartz movement, integral tapered woven gold bracelet and clasp, 27mm. (Christie's) $3,212

Heuer, a gentleman's stainless steel chronograph wristwatch, 1970s, petrol blue dial with subsidiary constant seconds, date aperture, and minute recording dial, 36 x 42mm. max. (Christie's) $350

A gold and steel self winding and water resistant wristwatch, signed *Patek Philippe*, Model: Nautilus, recent, with self winding movement, the ribbed gilt dial with raised luminous baton indexes, date aperture, luminous hands, 38mm. diameter. (Christie's) $6,340

Universal, a stainless steel Aero-Compax chronograph wristwatch with second time-zone, 1950s, silvered dial with Arabic hours, subsidiary constant seconds, minute and hour recording dials, 37mm. (Christie's) $1,175

Patek Philippe, a rare stainless steel chronograph wristwatch, Model: Calatrava, 1938, 23-jewel movement with eight adjustments and bimetallic compensation balance, diameter 33mm. (Christie's) $42,770

Stewart Dawson & Co, a gentleman's silver cased curved wristwatch, 1920s, silvered dial with Breguet numerals, and blued hands, damascened nickel finished movement, 25 x 44mm. (Christie's) $1,050

A gentleman's stainless steel wristwatch, signed *Longines*, 1930s, frosted gilt movement jeweled to the third and with bimetallic compensation balance, diameter 35mm. (Christie's) $1,183

A gentleman's 18ct. gold automatic calendar wristwatch, signed *Ebel*, Model: 1911, recent, self winding movement, brushed case with polished bezel, 35mm. (Christie's) $5,410

Jaeger-Le Coultre, a gentleman's stainless steel cased center seconds wristwatch, 1940s, silvered dial with luminous Arabic numerals, frosted gilt movement, 33mm. (Christie's) $524

Omega, a gentleman's 18ct. gold diamond and coral set Constellation wristwatch, 1980s, machined 24 jewel automatic movement, adjusted 5 positions, 29 x 32mm. (Christie's) $2,101

Omega, a rare stainless steel limited edition, 'Apollo X' Speedmaster Professional chronograph wristwatch, recent, subsidiary constant seconds with Apollo X shield inscribed *Stafford, Young, Cernan*, 40mm. (Christie's) $2,138

An 18ct. gold one minute tourbillon chronograph wristwatch, Girard-Perregaux, No.1, recent, 46-jewel engraved nickel finished linear movement with yellow metal bridges, diameter 40mm. (Christie's) $27,636

A limited edition 18ct. gold self-winding retrograde sector watch with Chinese zodiac dial, Vacheron & Constantin, model: Gerard Mercator, recent, cloisonné enamel dial with hour and minute sectors, diameter 36mm. (Christie's) $14,681

A German Airman's large observation watch, Wempe, Hamburg, circa 1941, black dial with luminous baton and Arabic numerals, luminous hands and center seconds, 62mm. (Bonhams & Brooks) $1,470

An 18ct. gold self winding calendar chronograph wristwatch, signed *Audemars Piguet*, recent, with self winding movement, the silvered dial with raised gilt indexes, diameter 40mm. (Christie's) $5,410

A rare 18ct. gold chronograph wristwatch, Patek Philippe, circa 1948, applied gilt Arabic numerals, subsidiary constant seconds and thirty minute recording dials, diameter 33mm. (Christie's) $31,953

Chronoswiss, a gentleman's gilt cased five minute repeating automatic wristwatch, recent, white enamel dial with Breguet numerals, repeating on two gongs, 42mm. (Christie's) $2,801

A large WW II Aviator's wristwatch with a replaced movement, German, 1940s, black dial, **replaced movement in a gray metal case marked on the back** *RLM, Nav B Uhr, 1304*, 55mm. (Bonhams) $265

Longines, a gentleman's 18ct. gold Admiral chronograph wristwatch, recent, gilt dial with baton markers and XII, subsidiary seconds, dials for constant minutes and hours, diameter 40mm. (Christie's) $1,92

A square 18ct. gold wristwatch, Patek Philippe, ref 2488, 1940s, silvered dial with a subsidiary seconds, the fine damascened 18 jewel movement with a gyromax balance and wipe lash regulator, 28mm. (Bonhams) $4,116

A stainless steel and gold automatic calendar wristwatch with power reserve sector, Cartier, Model:Pasha, recent, gilt baton markers, Arabic quarters, date aperture between 4 & 5, diameter 39mm. (Christie's) $2,073

An 18ct. gold automatic center seconds calendar wristwatch, Breguet, Marine, recent, mother of pearl dial with Roman numerals, 18ct. gold bracelet with double deployant clasp, 35mm. (Christie's) $9,499

Longines, a lady's stainless steel gilt metal Lindbergh angle hour automatic wristwatch for navigational purposes, recent, diameter 32mm. (Christie's) $524

A large size stainless steel Aviator wristwatch, Longines, 1940s, black enamel dial with subsidiary seconds, the frosted gilt movement in a cushion shaped case, 40mm. (Bonhams) $412

A lady's 18ct. gold and diamond se automatic wristwatch, Cartier, Model: Pasha, recent, engine turned silvered dial signed *Cartier*, gilt Arabic quarters, sweep center seconds. (Christie's) $7,77

A 9ct. gold octagonal water resistant wristwatch Rolex, Oyster, 1929, the nickel 15 jewel movement timed to 6 positions and marked *Rolex Prima*, 32mm. (Bonhams) $2,646

Harwood, a gentleman's 9ct. gold self winding wristwatch, circa 1930s, silvered sunburst dial with luminous Arabic numerals, diameter 30mm. (Christie's) $437

A stainless steel center seconds alarm wristwatch, Jaeger Le Coultre, Memovox 1950s, silvered dial with central concentric setting disc, nickel movement, 35mm. (Bonhams) $956

Favre-Leuba, a gentleman's stainless steel Bivouac wristwatch with altimeter, circa 1970s, black dial with baton numerals, blue outer ring marked for barometric pressure, diameter 40mm. (Christie's) $350

A stainless steel tonneau shaped chronograph wristwatch, Franck Muller, Genève, Master of Complications, recent, orange dial, black seconds scale, subsidiary constant seconds, 40 x 29mm. (Christie's) $4,491

IWC, an 18ct. gold automatic calendar wristwatch, Model:Ingenieur, recent, baton markers, date aperture, sweep center seconds, sapphire crystal, 18ct. gold IWC bracelet with deployant clasp, 33mm. (Christie's) $4,836

A brushed stainless steel automatic chronograph bracelet watch with calendar, Breitling, Navitimer, Fighter Pilot Special Series, black dial with silvered subsidiaries for 12 hour, 30 minute and running seconds, 40mm. (Bonhams) $1,323

An 18ct. white gold rectangular quartz calendar chronograph wristwatch, Piaget, recent, 18ct. white gold bracelet with concealed double deployant clasp, 33 x 28mm. (Christie's) $4,836

A stainless steel chronograph wristwatch, Breitling, Long playing, 1970s, silvered dial with subsidiaries for running seconds, 30 minute and 12 hour recording with an outer timing scale, 38mm. (Bonhams) $353

A gentleman's 18ct. gold quartz calendar wristwatch, signed *Cartier, Model: Panthere*, recent, square silvered dial with Roman numerals, secret signature at 7, 27mm. (Christie's) $2,536

A platinum and pink gold tourbillon wristwatch, signed *Breguet Tourbillon*, recent, 20-second sector for use in conjunction with three armed seconds hand, diameter 35mm. (Christie's) $40,572

Cartier, a lady's gold tank wristwatch, 1960s, machined nickel 17 jewel mechanical movement, unsigned, 20mm. (Christie's) $2,467

Dodane, a stainless steel Type 21 military chronograph wristwatch, 1960s, black dial with luminous Arabic numerals, subsidiary constant seconds, and minute recording dial, 37mm. (Christie's) $755

A diver's early stainless steel self winding wristwatch, signed *Rolex*. Model: Oyster Perpetual Turn-O-Graph, 1954, black dial with luminous markers, Mercedes hands, sweep center seconds, diameter 35mm. (Christie's) $2,536

A gentleman's rare platinum tonneau shaped wristwatch, signed *Cartier Paris*, circa 1930, nickel finished 19-jewel movement signed *E.W & C. Co. Inc.*, with eight adjustments, 37 x 24mm. (Christie's) $10,143

A gentleman's 18ct. yellow gold reversible wristwatch, signed *Jaeger Le Coultre*, Model:Reverso, recent, with mechanical movement, 42 x 25mm. (Christie's) $3,381

A lady's 18ct. gold quartz calendar wristwatch, Corum, Admiral's Cup, recent, cream dial with flag markers, date aperture at 6, center seconds, quartz movement, diameter 27mm. (Christie's) $2,935

A gentleman's 18ct. gold rectangular wristwatch, signed *Patek Philippe*, 1945-50, damascened nickel finished movement jeweled to the center, 30 x 24mm. (Christie's) $7,100

Patek Philippe, a gentleman's 18ct. gold wristwatch, 1960s, 18-jewel movement adjusted to heat, cold, isochronism and five positions, 33mm. (Christie's) $3,024

Rolex, a gentleman's steel and gold self winding dual time zone calendar wristwatch, signed *Rolex*, Model: Oyster Perpetual GMT-Master, circa 1980, 39mm. (Christie's) $2,520

A 18ct. gold self winding water resistant world time calendar wristwatch, signed *Breguet*, recent, with self-winding movement, blued steel moon hands, 38mm diameter. (Christie's) $8,453

An 18ct. gold and diamond set quartz calendar wristwatch, Piaget, Model: Tanagra, recent, matt gilt dial with diamond set polished stripes, date aperture, quartz movement, 33mm. (Christie's) $6,045

An 18ct. white gold tonneau shaped automatic center seconds calendar wristwatch, Patek Philippe, recent, Arabic numerals, date aperture at 3, moon hands, sweep center seconds, self-winding movement, 40 x 34mm. (Christie's) $7,255

An 18ct. pink gold automatic calendar wristwatch, Audemars Piguet, circa 1990, gilt baton markers, outer Arabic five minutes, date aperture, sweep center seconds, self-winding movement, diameter 40mm. (Christie's) $3,626

A stainless steel automatic calendar wristwatch, Girard-Perregaux for Ferrari, recent, Arabic numerals, date aperture, dauphine hands, sweep center seconds, self-winding movement, 35mm. (Christie's) $691

A gentleman's stainless steel water resistant chronograph wristwatch, signed *Cartier*, Model: Pasha, circa 1990, subsidiary calendar dial and 30-minute and 12-hour recording dials, 36mm. (Christie's) $2,198

A gentleman's stainless steel chronograph wristwatch, signed *Franck Muller, Geneve*, Model: Endurance 24, recent, orange dial with Arabic 24-hour numerals, diameter 37mm. (Christie's) $5,410

A pair of Japanese plique a jour baluster vases decorated with a multitude of flowers amongst foliage on translucent pale green grounds, 7¹/₈in. high, 19th century. (Christie's) $5,896

An elaborate cloisonné and silver dish, signed *Hiratsuka Sei*, Meiji Period (late 19th century), the finely chased and engraved lobed dish with a wide band of chrysanthemums, supported by four dragons, 8¾in. wide. (Christie's) $17,860

A pair of Japanese cloisonné bottle vases with hexagonal bodies and slender flaring necks, decorated with birds perched amongst blossoming prunus branches, 9½in. high, 19th century. (Christie's) $1,843

A pair of cloisonné vases, impressed mark *Gonda Hirosuke*, Meiji Period (late 19th century), similarly decorated in various colored enamels and silver wire with a parrot perched on a leafy branch, 7½in. high. (Christie's) $2,143

A pair of large cloisonné enamel baluster vases, Qianlong, each ovoid body decorated with lotus scroll set between ruyi-head borders, with a band of pendant leaves alternating with butterflies encircling the spreading foot, 25in. high. (Christie's) $16,100

An unusual cloisonné and champlevé enamel figure of Guandi, 18th century, the immortal shown stiffly seated on a plinth decorated on top and the sides with foliate diaper and on the back with a large peony spray, 6½in. high. (Christie's) $17,250

Japanese cloisonné vase, early 20th century, one side depicting a perched bird, the reverse with foliage, 13½in. high. (Skinner) $1,265

A Chinese cloisonné dish, decorated with scrolls and a band of lotus on a turquoise ground, 17th century, 23cm. diameter. (Woolley & Wallis) $750

A pair of Japanese cloisonné baluster vases decorated with birds in flight amongst blossoming prunus branches above flowering kiku, 8½in. high, wood stands, 19th century. (Christie's) $774

232

CLOISONNÉ

A Japanese cloisonné tripod bowl and cover with flaring foliate rim, shaped feet and silver rims, decorated with prunus branches, 7⁷/₈in. wide, 19th/20th century, Hayashi Kodenji mark to base.
(Christie's) $11,977

A silver-gilt and cloisonné enamel coffee service, Moscow, 1896-1908, comprising a coffee pot with mother of pearl button, a milk jug and sugar basin, with a sugar basket and tongs.
(Sotheby's) $5,040

A Japanese cloisonné lobed quatrefoil vase and cover with coral knop finial, decorated with a multitude of butterflies above kiku heads on a black ground, 4¼in. high, 19th century.
(Christie's) $737

A pair of large cloisonné enamel crane incense burners, 18th/19th century, each shown standing on a tree stump, one with long neck twisted inquisitively to one side, the separately made wing section acting as a cover to the hollowed body, 30¾in. and 30in.
(Christie's) $9,775

A pair of cloisonné vases, Meiji Period (late 19th century), of globular form similarly decorated in various colored enamels and gold and silver wires on a pale blue ground with butterflies amongst sprays, 15½in. high.
(Christie's) $3,572

A pair of impressive Ota cloisonné vases, impressed mark of Ota Hyozo, Meiji Period (late 19th century), the large pair of blue ground vases, decorated in silver wire and colored cloisonné enamels, with cranes among a bamboo grove, 18½in. high.
(Christie's) $26,790

A Japanese cloisonné and gilt bronze ovoid jar and domed cover with kiku finial, decorated with ho-o in flight amongst flowers and foliage, 5¹/₈in. high, 19th century.
(Christie's) $1,474

A pair of large Japanese Meiji cloisonné enamel vases, late 19th century, the waisted necks decorated with entwined dragons and the bodies with birds amidst blossoming vases, 48½in. high.
(Christie's) $4,754

A Japanese cloisonné baluster vase, with slightly flaring neck,decorated with blossoming chrysanthemums and kiku on a bright yellow ground, 12in. high, 19th century. (Christie's) $774

A pair of mid Victorian brass door knockers, registration mark for 1872, each modelled as a lion mask with ring handle, the circular door plate stamped to the reverse *WT & S*, 9in. high. (Christie's) $1,829

Pair of Arts & Crafts period copper and brass candlesticks, central brass sconces and shafts, applied with copper drip trays, the shafts also joined by a treen handle, 7½in. (G.A. Key) $84

A fine and rare Newlyn copper cylindrical stick stand, decorated with a shoal of fish swimming downward through seaweed towards a crab, 22¼in. high. (David Lay) $1,287

A Swiss repoussé brass jardinière and cover 19th century, the bulbous body with domed cover and twin handles, with gadrooned ornament and impressed bosses to the foot, 16½in. high. (Christie's) $639

A 19th century brass footman. (Bonhams) $282

Decorative large copper Art Nouveau period coal shute, oval form, incised with stylized floral decoration on spreading circular foot, applied with cast metal wrythen swing handle, 17in. (G.A. Key) $139

A Regency copper samovar with lion mask and ring handles on reeded supports and paw feet, dolphin finial. (Brightwells) $574

Punch and Judy, two brass door porters. (Bonhams) $157

A Victorian brass door knocker, in the form of a hand, with circular backplate and doorplate, 8in. high. (Christie's) $914

Copper slave tax badge, Charleston, South Carolina, early 19th century, stamped, *CHARLESTON 1812 NO 500 SERVANT*, stamped on reverse *LAFAR* in a rectangle, 2 x 2in. (Skinner) $2,990

Fine and heavy copper and brass two handled oval covered log box, applied on either side with lion mask ring handles and raised on brass paw feet, 19th century, 18in. (G.A. Key) $493

Copper slave tax badge, Charleston, South Carolina, mid-19th century, stamped *CHARLSTON 12 PORTER 1852*, 1⅝ x 1⅝in.(Skinner) $1,725

A North Italian repoussé copper water ewer, late 17th or early 18th century, of tapering ovoid form with domed cover and loop handle, decorated with entwined flowers and foliage, 18½in. high. (Christie's) $878

Pair of brass petal base candlesticks, England, mid 18th century, conforming bobeche and swelling below the candle cup with push-up knob in the shaft, 8¼in. high. (Skinner) $1,380

A pair of brass andirons, late 19th century, in the Netherlandish 17th century style, the knopped standards with spherical intersections, on splayed feet with lion masks, 21¼in. high. (Christie's) $2,560

Unusual late Victorian Art Nouveau period brass and cast metal coal box modelled as a stylized flower pot, rosette formed cover, joined by black painted sconce, 25in. high. (G.A. Key) $435

A Nuremberg brass alms dish, 16th century, repoussé decorated with central writhen boss, within a band of script, the rim punched with foliate motifs, 16½in. diameter. (Christie's) $3,474

Unusual Arts & Crafts style copper and wrought iron coal box of oval form, with sloping lifting lid, the whole embossed with asterisk or star designs, with shovel, 15in. (G.A. Key) $204

Unusual copper square kettle, circa late 19th/early 20th century, 15in. (G.A. Key) $102

A pair of 17th century brass candlesticks, circa 1670, of trumpet form, with drip trays and set on spreading bases, 20.5cm. high. (Bonhams) $2,030

A repoussé brass jardinière, early 20th century, of oval outline, the sides raised and pierced with foliate designs, with lion mask and spiral-twist loop handles, 19½in. wide. (Christie's) $651

A pair of large floor standing brass candlesticks, dated *1636*, the bulbous knopped stems on domed circular bases inscribed *Sto. Cosmato Sor Anna Maria Della Croce Fecit Ano MDCXXXVI*, 62in. high. (Christie's) $9,994

A 19th century brass covered coal scuttle, with overhandle and matching scoop, 52cm. long. (Bonhams) $353

A North European brass square based candlestick, in the late 17th century style, 4¼in. high. (Christie's) $235

An Italian gilt brass casket, second half 19th century, of rectangular form with angled cover, the panels engraved with strapwork and entwined foliage, 6¼in. high. (Christie's) $4,600

Early 19th century copper samovar, applied on either side with ring turned treen handles and applied with a brass tap, 15in. (G.A. Key) $220

A Newlyn circular copper box and cover with stylized leafage design by John Pearson, 7'/5in. diameter. (Brightwells) $290

COPPER & BRASS

A brass alms dish, Nuremberg, probably 16th century, with central wrythen boss within double inscription bands, 16in. diameter. (Christie's) $690

19th century copper kettle on a spirit burner stand, applied throughout with stoneware handles, 15½in. (G.A. Key) $267

A brass warming pan, English, 17th century, the cover punch decorated and inscribed around the border *Live Well And Dy Never*, the center depicting a cockerel, 13¼in. diameter. (Christie's) $1,544

A pair of French paktong candlesticks, circa 1750, with hexagonal knopped shafts and conforming bases, the sockets and bases incised with monogramed crests, 9¼in. high. (Christie's) $4,361

A Netherlandish large copper and brass twin branch wall sconce, 19th century, the shaped rectangular backplate with canted angles, repoussé decorated with fruit and foliage with hearts to the angles, 60cm. high. (Christie's) $2,011

A brass square base candlestick, possibly late 17th century, 6in. high. (Christie's) $400

An Arts and Crafts copper charger, circa 1890, in the style of J Pearson, with embossed and hammered decoration, 61cm. diameter. (Bonhams) $728

A North Italian copper ewer, 17th century style, the bulbous body on a domed circular foot with cylindrical neck and cover, 18¼in. high. (Christie's) $696

A carved and painted "Flatty" yellowlegs, probably New England, early 20th century, the flat, almost silhouette-carved form with metal bill, 10¼in. high.
(Christie's) $353

Black duck decoy, A. Elmer Crowell (1862-1952), East Harwich, Massachusetts, bears the oval *CROWELL* brand on the underside, original paint, 17½in. long.
(Skinner) $1,380

Miniature sandpiper, A. Elmer Crowell stamp on the underside, 6in. long. (Skinner) $4,600

A carved and painted figure of a duck with three ducklings, American, late 19th-early 20th century, carved in the round each with painted head and body, orange beak and black eyes, 4½in. high.
(Christie's) $3,290

Miniature little blue heron, A. Elmer Crowell (1862-1952) East Harwich, Massachusetts, bears the rectangular *CROWELL* stamp, dated *1920* in ink on the underside, 6½in. long. (Skinner) $4,025

A large carved and painted Canada slat goose, signed *Elmer Crowell, East Harwich, Massachusetts*, the black and white painted carved head above a plank constructed black and white painted body, 42½in. long overall.
(Christie's) $3,760

Blue Jay mantel carving, A. Elmer Crowell (1862-1952), East Harwich, Massachusetts, bears hand-written signature A.E. Crowell Cape Cod, mounted on maple leaves, 7½in. long. (Skinner) $2,645

Carved and painted white swan decoy, America, late 19th century, two-piece hollow-form body, solid neck and head.
(Skinner) $4,888

Wilson's Snipe mantel carving, A. Elmer Crowell (1862-1952), East Harwick, Massachusetts, bears the rectangular CROWELL stamp, an ink signature, 9in. long.
(Skinner) $6,325

A J.D. Kestner character mold 211, with sleeping blue eyes, open/closed mouth, plaster pate, red mohair wig and jointed composition baby's body wearing blue cotton suit and white shoes, 12in. high.
(Christie's) $710

A Kathe Kruse boy doll No 1, with painted cloth head, brown hair, brown eyes, nettle-cloth covering stuffed body wearing original undergarment, 17in.
(Christie's) $1,419

A J. D. Kestner character baby, with blue sleeping eyes, open mouth with two upper teeth, blonde painted hair and jointed composition body wearing white cotton dress, 17in. high.
(Christie's) $3,020

An unusual painted wooden doll, with black painted eyes and brows, the jointed wooden body with flat carved arms, the legs painted from above the jointed knees, 12in. high, circa 1760, the clothes 1800.
(Christie's) $2,661

A pair of bisque shoulder-headed dolls' house dolls, with molded blonde ringlets, painted features and bisque limbs with pink luster boots and pink garters, in original lace frocks, 4½in. high, circa 1870.
(Christie's) $568

A fine Emile Jumeau A mold bébé, with pressed bisque head, closed mouth, brown yeux fibres, shaded brows, pierced applied ears, blonde mohair wig over cork pate, 25½in. high, circa 1880.
(Christie's) $7,402

A china-headed man doll, with molded short black curls, kid arms and original Norwegian clothes, 13in. high, circa 1880; and a bisque shoulder-headed doll, dressed as his wife, 13in. high.
(Christie's) $744

A Max Handwerck child doll, with brown sleeping eyes, short blonde mohair wig, open mouth and jointed composition body, 3in. high; and her red trunk containing garments.
(Christie's) $1,152

A bisque-headed male dolls' house doll, the cloth body and bisque limbs in original Hussar's uniform, 7in. high; and a bisque-headed doll with molded short blond curls, 7in. high. (Christie's) $975

A Bahr & Pröschild 109, shoulder-head, with brown sleeping eyes, jointed kid body and composition limbs, dressed in white, 22in. high. (Christie's) $624

A fine bébé Thuillier, blonde mohair wig over cork pate and jointed wood and papier mâché fixed-wrist body, 24in. high, circa 1880. (Christie's) $28,388

A Jumeau 1907 doll, with sleeping blue eyes, open mouth, pierced ears, blonde mohair wig and jointed composition body, 20in. high. (Christie's) $1,065

A Lenci series 109/48, with brown painted eyes glancing to the left, blonde mohair wig arranged in plaited coils over the ears and felt body, 21in. high, with original box, circa 1930/31. (Christie's) $987

An all-bisque Kestner Campbell Kid type googly-eyed doll, with molded fair hair, side-glancing gray eyes, watermelon mouth, joints at shoulder and hip and knitted clothes, 6¼in. high, circa 1914. (Christie's) $575

A Kammer & Reinhardt 114 with painted gray/blue eyes, short blonde mohair wig, jointed composition body, original cotton shift and homemade green smocked frock, 13in. (Christie's) $1,316

A Jumeau bébé, with fixed blue eyes, original auburn mohair wig, heavy brows, pierced ears and jointed papier mâché and wood body, 18in. (Christie's) $2,632

A Jumeau bébé with fixed brown eyes, closed mouth, pierced applied ears, fair hair wig and jointed wood and composition body wearing contemporary cream and yellow satin and buff silk frock, 22in. high. (Christie's) $5,593

A Kammer & Reinhardt child doll, with brown lashed sleeping eyes and jointed wood and composition body in original shoes and socks and later blue frock, 28in. high. (Christie's) $575

A Carrier-Belleuse Jumeau bébé, the long face with closed mouth, fixed brown eyes and pierced applied ears, with long blond hair wig. (Christie's) $14,805

A Shoenau & Hoffmeister character baby, with blue lashed sleeping eyes, short dark mohair wig, baby's body and knitted frock, 17¼in. high. (Christie's) $461

A Kestner all-bisque googlie 112, with brown sleeping eyes, closed mouth and neck, shoulder, elbow, thigh and knee joints, 4¾in. high. (Christie's) $1,645

A poured wax child doll, with fixed bright blue eyes, inset straight reddish hair, stuffed body, contemporary printed pink lawn tucked frock, straw bonnet and underclothes, 16in. high, circa 1840. (Christie's) $658

A pair of Lenci 300 series, modelled as a boy and a girl in original cream felt skirt and shorts with knitted cardigan, jersey and legwarmers, 16½in. high. (Christie's) $1,233

A Kammer & Reinhardt 117 character doll, with closed mouth, blue sleeping eyes, blonde mohair wig and jointed body, dressed in pink silk, underwear, shoes and socks, 21in. high, circa 1912. (Christie's) $2,661

A fine and rare bébé Halopeau, remains of blonde mohair wig and jointed wood and papier mâché body, dressed in dark purple silk outfit, 21in. high, circa 1880. (Christie's) $31,937

An Oriental dolls' house doll, with sleeping brown eyes, closed mouth, long black plait and jointed composition body wearing red print frock, hat and brown silk shorts, 5in. high. (Christie's) $568

A Schützmeister & Quendt 201 baby, with blue lashed sleeping eyes, short brown mohair wig and baby's body wearing later cream wool suit, 15½in. high. (Christie's) $329

A Tete Jumeau bébé, with fixed blue eyes, closed mouth, pierced ears, long brown hair wig and jointed adult body wearing cream silk frock and long coat, 24in.
(Christie's) $4,968

An Armand Marseille character mold 560, with solid dome, molded hair, painted blue eyes, jointed composition body wearing blonde mohair wig, 9in.
(Christie's) $568

A Kammer & Reinhardt 101 character mold, with painted blue eyes, closed mouth and jointed body, dressed in white muslin shirt, woollen trousers and leather shoes, 15in. high.
(Christie's) $2,129

A Jumeau bébé, with fixed brown eyes, open mouth, pierced ears, long brown hair wig and jointed composition body wearing pale green silk with lace trim coat, 22in. high.
(Christie's) $1,507

A rare Simon & Halbig 151 character doll, with open/closed smiling mouth showing teeth, painted features, brown mohair wig and jointed body, 15in. high, circa 1912.
(Christie's) $2,484

A fine Bébé Schmitt, with closed mouth, blue yeux fibres, shaded brows, pierced ears and blonde mohair wig over papier mâché pate, 15½in. high, circa 1880.
(Christie's) $4,968

A Pierrotti wax child doll, with fixed pale blue eyes, inset short blonde curls, stuffed body and wax limbs dressed in red spotted frock and underclothes, 17in. high.
(Christie's) $710

A Kammer & Reinhardt character mold 112, with painted blue eyes, short blonde wig, open/closed mouth with two upper teeth and jointed composition body, 13in. high.
(Christie's) $886

A rare Bébé Bru Gourmande with open mouth showing tips of teeth, brown yeux fibres, skin wig over cork pate, bisque shoulder plate with nipples and kid body, 17½in. high, circa 1880.
(Christie's) $19,517

A Gaultier fashionable doll, with fixed blue eyes, closed mouth, pierced ears, short blonde mohair wig, bisque breast-plate and stuffed kid body wearing blue with lace frock and bonnet, 28in. high. (Christie's) $4,613

A rare Kammer & Reinhardt Moritz character doll, with impish expression, wide grinning mouth, blue sleeping and flirting eyes, brown mohair wig, jointed fixed wrist body, 15½in. high, circa 1913.(Christie's) $2,839

A fine Emile Jumeau A mold Bébé, with pressed bisque head, blonde mohair wig over cork pate and fixed-wrist jointed wood and papier Mâché body, 25½in. high circa 1880.
(Christie's) $11,532

An Armand Marseille character mold 560, with solid dome, molded hair, painted blue eyes, jointed composition body wearing blonde mohair wig, 9in. (Christie's) $3,015

An early child doll mold 224 with blue sleeping eyes, blonde wig, pierced ears fixed-wrist jointed body and quilted blue dressing gown, 16½in. high. (Christie's) $744

A Jumeau long face doll, long brown hair wig, cork pate with remains of original skin wig and eight ball jointed composition body, 20in. high. (Christie's) $15,968

A bisque doll dressed as an 18th century man, with fixed blue eyes, closed mouth, short blonde mohair wig and jointed composition body, 10in. high.(Christie's) $568

A fine Bru Jeune, with closed mouth, brown yeux bres, blonde mohair wig over cork pate and jointed wood and papier mâché body, 16in. high, circa 875. (Christie's) $8,516

A Tête Jumeau, with fixed blue eyes, long blonde mohair wig, closed mouth, pierced applied ears and jointed composition body wearing white frock and bonnet, 19½in. high. (Christie's) $2,306

A Kammer & Reinhardt mold 117, with blue lashed sleeping and side glancing eyes, open mouth, short blonde wig and jointed composition body, 27½in. (Christie's) $1,065

A kicking crying Steiner dome, short blonde mohair wig, composition arms and lower legs with voice box and original red with lace trim frock, shoes and hat, 18in. high. (Christie's) $2,484

Jumeau bébé with fixed lue eyes, open mouth, ong blonde hair wig and inted composition body earing white cotton nder-garments, frock and onnet, 32in. high, npressed 1907. Christie's) $1,685

A Kammer & Reinhardt 115 character doll, original brown mohair wig and jointed toddler body, dressed as a boy in red and white checked cotton romper, 14½in. high, circa 1911. (Christie's) $2,839

An S.F.B.J. mold 252, with blue lashed sleeping eyes, closed mouth, short blonde mohair wig and jointed composition body wearing white with blue flowers print frock, 20in. high. (Christie's) $2,129

A large Steiff body doll, with blue glass eyes, center face seam, set in mouth, mohair wig, separated fingers and original Lederhosen, 19in. high, with button circa 1913. (Christie's) $975

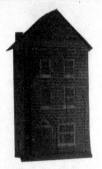

A home-made dolls' town house, painted dark red, the windows and doors picked out in cream, the front opening to reveal four rooms, 18½in. wide. (Christie's) $337

An unusual dolls' house of one bay and one story with attic, loggia, garage, steeply pitched curving roof and hinged dormer side windows opening to reveal the attic, 14in. wide, probably Gottschalck, circa 1910. (Christie's) $1,065

A Gottschalck red roofed dolls' house, of three bays and two store with dormer window, sun and front porches, opening to reveal two rooms with original floor papers, 17½in. wide. (Christie's) $886

A Gottschalck red roof dolls' house, opening at the front to reveal two rooms, hall with staircase and landing, 22½in. wide. (Christie's) $2,306

A red roof German farm house, with stencilled "tiles", painted half-timbering, hay loft, tools, horses and stalls, 19in. long, possibly Wagner. (Christie's) $797

A Christian Hacker printed paper o wood dolls' house, the central front door flanked by window bays, the roof simulating tiles, opening at the front to reveal two rooms, 18½in. wide. (Christie's) $1,774

A painted wood dolls' house with fine detailing in mahogany, of three bays and two storey, opening at the front to reveal two rooms, 19½in. wide. (Christie's) $2,839

A painted wood dolls' house, simulating half-timbering with "slate" roof and decorated barge boards, opening at the front to reveal five rooms with interior and three exterior doors, 59in. long. (Christie's) $4,613

A Lines' box-back dolls' house, with brick printed paper and two storeys, opening to reveal two rooms with fireplace and shaped front, 23in. high. (Christie's) $987

244

A Pifco British teasmade with clock and alarm, white bakelite with two chromed water boilers, circa 1958. (Auction Team Köln) $102

A steel Universal E945 American toaster by L.F. & C., with integral toast rack for keeping the toast warm, circa 1918. (Auction Team Köln) $99

A Westinghouse oscillating single speed fan with level adjustment, brass rotor blades and cage, 33cm. diameter. (Auction Team Köln) $42

A Universal E941 two-slice folding toaster with early three row heating bars, by Landers Frary & Clark, New Britain, USA, circa 1915. (Auction Team Köln) $68

A Bunting designer radiant heater, the two chromed tin sails acting as heat reflectors, the mast as the heating rod, English, 1930. (Auction Team Köln) $451

A Universal D-12 porcelain toaster with floral decoration and wire basket over, circa 1920. (Auction Team Köln) $367

An Art Nouveau style brass electric fire with three vertical 'bars', with label *Robertson 220 GEC,* circa 1910, 25cm. wide. (Auction Team Köln) $282

A Toastrite toaster by the Pan Electric Co., Cleveland, in shaded orange porcelain. (Auction Team Köln) $593

A Thomas A Edison early electric fan, brass cage, circa 1898. (Auction Team Köln) $2,710

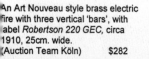

A large Viennese gilt-metal-mounted enamel octagonal casket, circa 1890, the hinged top centered by a goddess walking a lion ridden by a cherub, 21¼in. wide.
(Christie's) $38,000

An enamel belt buckle with jeweled two-color gold mounts, unmarked, probably Fabergé, circa 1900, oval, the reverse enamelled in translucent oyster white over wavy engine-turning, length 7.2cm.
(Sotheby's) $2,940

A Viennese silver-gilt, gem-set enamel and rock crystal tray, the design attributed to Josef von Storck, Vienna, circa 1880, set with engraved crystal medallions flanked by female caryatids and masks, 58cm. wide.
(Christie's) $27,636

A pair of Swiss enamelled gold zarfi for the Turkish market, Geneva, circa 1830/40, cups enamelled with tapering reserves painted with floral swags on salmon pink or turquoise blue grounds, each 62mm. high.
(Christie's) $5,339

A good pair of Battersea mirror knobs depicting Dr. (Benjamin) Franklin and Governeer Morris Esq., late 18th century, 2 x 1½in.
(Sotheby's) $5,462

A Viennese silver-gilt and enamel miniature model of a barrel, circa 1880, surmounted by a conical finial, the barrel with a tap to one side, supported by two seated jesters, 4½in. high.
(Christie's) $2,936

A Viennese gilt-metal and enamel covered tankard, circa 1880, surmounted by a standing figure in costume, the domed lid above a cylindrical neck on an ovoid body, 5½in. high.
(Christie's) $1,467

Russian enamel and gold washed charka, 1881, tapered cylindrical form, on low base, enamelled with quatrefoils and geometric bands, the ear handle with enamel striping, 2⅝in. approximately 4 troy oz.
(Skinner) $431

A Viennese silver and enamel ewer, circa 1880, with a shaped and cut spreading rim above a tapering ovoid body, with a saytr mask terminal, 7½in. high.
(Christie's) $2,590

A Gunsen or War fan, the stiff paper leaf painted recto with a red sun on gold and verso two characters against a silver ground, with bamboo sticks and metal guardsticks, all lacquered black, 10.5in., Japanese, late 19th century. (Christie's) $1,335

Marat, a printed fan, the leaf with an oval stipple engraving printed in color, with wooden sticks, the pin concealed with a bone fillet, 10in., French, circa 1793. (Christie's) $1,335

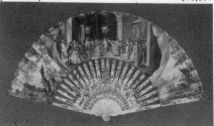

Pierrots observing the Moon through a telescope, signed *Van Garten*, a fan, the leaf painted on black gauze, the verso inscribed *Duvelleroy, Paris*, with smoky gray mother of pearl sticks, 10½in. circa 1900. (Christie's) $917

A rare straw-work fan with pagoda sticks, the chickenskin leaf with three colored straw-work vignettes, the verso of paper painted with a shepherd in a landscape, the ivory sticks decorated with three straw-work vignettes, 10in., circa 1750. (Christie's) $10,011

A Venetian Masquerade, a fine fan painted with elegant masked couples dancing, the verso with a couple wearing a black and a white mask, the ivory sticks carved and pierced with flowers and painted with Harlequin, Punchinello and Pierrot, and with shells and music, 10.5in., English, circa 1760. (Christie's) $23,359

Eventail Point de Hongrie, by Duvelleroy, the leaf embroidered overall in pink sequins, inscribed *Duvelleroy Paris* on verso, the smoky gray mother of pearl sticks carved and pierced to resemble feathers, 10½in., circa 1908. (Christie's) $1,001

A fan, the leaf painted with travellers and cattle, with a fortified village beyond, the ivory sticks carved with a wild boar hunt, 10.5in. circa 1740. (Christie's) $667

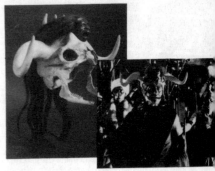

Harrison Ford/Indiana Jones And The Temple Of Doom, 1984, a hand-made sixteen-plait bull-whip of kangaroo hide with 106in. long lash, used by Harrison Ford as Indiana Jones in Indiana Jones And The Temple of Doom, 1984.(Christie's) $18,095

Indiana Jones And The Temple of Doom, a ceremonial head dress of fiber-glass painted to simulate bone in the shape of a ram's skull with curly ram's horns and extending lower jaw, 13in. high (Christie's) $9,341

Superman II, 1980, a prop newspaper with the headline Inside Story of Superman, one of the images of Superman drawn over in black felt pen with a hat, glasses, shirt and tie; another prop Daily Planet newspaper, 23½ x 17in.(Christie's) $1,151

Michelle Pfeiffer and Al Pacino's costumes from 'Frankie & Johnny', circa 1991, peach dress and blouse, green tank top and light gray trousers together with letters of authenticity. (Bonhams) $67.

Tyrone Power, 1940/The Mark of Zorro, an open neck shirt of black silk, a triangle mask of black silk with cut-out eye holes, both made for Tyrone Power as Zorro.(Christie's) $4,935

Julia Roberts/Notting Hill, 1999, a pale blue satin evening jacket with floral embroidery in brightly colored silks with frogged fastening, lined in pale blue silk.(Christie's) $6,352

Marlon Brando overcoat and hat from "The Godfather", Part 1", Paramount, 1972, a brown wool single-breasted overcoat with a three-button front closure and two flap pockets.
(Christie's) $19,975

Diane Keaton dress and hat from "The Godfather, Part 1", Paramount, 1972, a long dress with a white squared collar, an empire waist, short puffy sleeves and a matching self-belt made of orange cotton. (Christie's) $4,465

Indiana Jones And The Last Crusade, 1989, a rare prop facsimile manuscript book known as the 'Grail Diary', contained within the pages of the book a prop train ticket Pacific Electricity Ry. Cash Fare and Joint Ticket and a prop U.S. dollar bill.
(Christie's) $24,675

Leonardo Dicaprio/The Man in The Iron Mask, 1997, pair of brown woollen fleece 18th century style breeches, two loose-fitting shirts of loosely woven wool, and a pair of men's high tongued suede shoes.
(Christie's) $6,251

Judy Garland wedding gown from "The Harvey Girls", MGM, 1946, a creme-colored silk wedding gown with ornate puffy shoulders, lace sleeves and lace trim.
(Christie's) $3,525

Clark Gable, a navy blue wool ¾ length one button jacket, having label in the interior breast pocket reading *Metro Goldwyn Mayer Name Clark Gable No. 732 82 56.*
(Bonhams) $2,355

FILM ARTIFACTS

The Curse Of The Pink Panther, 1983, a gentleman's white leather left hand glove embroidered in 'gold' thread with the letter *P*, framed with a piece of paper bearing the director Blake Edwards' facsimile signature, overall measurements, 16 x 14in. (Christie's) $2,615

Tom Cruise/Mission: Impossible, 1995, a costume comprising: a t-shirt, jogging pants, shoes of black suede. (Christie's) $12,140

Madonna/Dick Tracey, 1990, a cigarette holder of imitation ivory, inset with red rhinestones, with lipstick traces on mouth piece, 5¾in., in common mount with a color publicity photograph of Madonna as Breathless Mahoney using the holder, 10 x 8in. (Christie's) $2,467

Ben-Hur, 1969, a centurion's tunic of brown brushed cotton to simulate suede, labelled inside *Angelo Di Pippo, Roma...*, the label inscribed in black ink *Centurions*. (Christie's) $493

Tom Cruise/ Legend, 1985, an 'armored' tunic of brown suede with gold painted metal disks stitched on to brown jersey, the sleeves made up of strips of brown suede. (Christie's) $12,145

Robocop, 1987, a highly detailed futuristic replica Robocop costume, a padded body of contoured black foam with velcro fastening at the back. (Christie's) $6,909

Titanic, 1997, a prop lifejacket of cream linen, hung on a brass rail on a piece of wood, with a brass plaque engraved *Titanic, 20th Century Fox, 1997.* (Christie's) $1,401

Star Trek, pair of Spock's rubber ears from the original series created by Phillips using the original molds. (Christie's) $3,290

John Wayne, The Duke's famous costume from 'True Grit', wine colored cotton long sleeve shirt with fabric-backed, lined suede vest, with collars. (Christie's) $16,275

The Curse Of The Pink Panther, 1983, Inspector Clouseau's painted plaster 'death mask' mounted on a wooden wall plaque covered in blue velvet, overall measurements, 11 x 8in. (Christie's) $933

Austin Powers: The Spy Who Shagged Me, 1999, a prop car licence plate SWINGER 2, black with white lettering, 5 x 20in., and a Basil Hero File. (Christie's) $933

A circa 1940 menu for Walt Disney's Studio Restaurant, Burbank, California, the front cover signed by Walt Disney, unframed. (Christie's) $2,585

Greta Garbo, a stylish travelling hat designed by 'Adrian', worn by Greta Garbo in the 1937 MGM movie, 'Conquest'. The taupe-colored hat has a matching silk chiffon ribbon tied around the rim. (Christie's) $2,350

Moira Shearer/The Red Shoes, 1948, a pair of red satin ballet shoes, one shoe signed and inscribed on the sole in black ink, additionally signed by Anton Walbrook and Leonide Massine. (Christie's) $19,740

Indiana Jones And The Temple Of Doom, 1984, a prop chalice in the form of decaying skull, the shrunken head of molded resin with applied surface decoration to simulate decomposition,11½in. (Christie's) $6,580

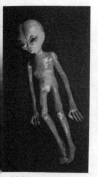

The X-files, 1995, a prop alien creature of latex-covered foam with enlarged head, almond-shaped eyes and elongated arms and fingers, 48in., 121.9cm. long. (Christie's) $904

Hugh Grant/Notting Hill, 1999, a single breasted jacket of olive green corduroy, lined with brown 'art' silk, worn by Hugh Grant as William Thackery. (Christie's) $821

Combat vest, camouflage shirt, and military web belt worn by Arnold Schwarzenegger in "Predator". The vest in brown suede, with buckles, ties, pockets, and velcro straps. (Christie's) $3,625

David Niven, signed sepia 5 x 7, head and shoulders smiling wearing tie. (Vennett Smith) $77

Gary Cooper, signed sepia 8 x 10, head and shoulders. (Vennett Smith) $231

Dorothy Dandridge, signed postcard, half-length wearing low-cut dress. (Vennett Smith) $77

Alastair Sim, signed 7 x 10, head and shoulders wearing suit, photo by Howard Coster, rare in this larger format. (Vennett Smith) $196

Grace Kelly, signed 7.5 x 10.5 magazine photo, head and shoulders in headscarf, close-up, centerfolds. (Vennett Smith) $262

Klaus Kinski, signed and inscribed color 7.5 x 11 heavyweight magazine photo, portrait, 1984, signed to images on both sides. (Vennett Smith) $92

Joan Crawford, signed and inscribed sepia, half-length, conclusion of signature a little weak. (Vennett Smith) $246

Betty Grable, signed 5 x 7, full length seated wearing elaborate costume and fishnet tights. (Vennett Smith) $185

W.C. Fields, signed 5.5 x 7, *Sincerely W.C. Fields*, head and shoulders. (Vennett Smith) $585

Gloria Swanson, signed 8 x 10, half-length smiling. (Vennett Smith) $62

Mel Gibson, signed color 8 x 10, half-length in kilt from Braveheart. (Vennett Smith) $188

Vivien Leigh, signed 4.5 x 6, head and shoulders early. (Vennett Smith) $431

Montgomery Clift, signed 6 x 9 Picturegoer's Gallery photo, weak signature in parts. (Vennett Smith) $431

Grease, signed color 8 x 10 by both John Travolta and Olivia Newton John, full-length in dance pose together from Grease. (Vennett Smith) $154

Claude Rains, signed and inscribed 8 x 10, head and shoulders wearing spectacles, in later years, partially signed in dark portion. (Vennett Smith) $154

Peter Sellers, signed and inscribed 8 x 10, head and shoulders wearing black spectacles. (Vennett Smith) $157

Mae West, signed 8 x 10, three quarter length seated in later years wearing white dress and large white hat. (Vennett Smith) $100

Edward G. Robinson, signed and inscribed 8 x 10, three quarter length wearing suit. (Vennett Smith) $92

Boris Karloff, signed 8 x 10, half-length in suit and hat, reading newspaper clippings. (Vennett Smith) $400

Lancaster & Dru, an 8 x 10 still from Vengence Valley, signed by both Burt Lancaster and Joanne Dru. (Vennett Smith) $156

Noel Coward, signed 5 x 7, to lowe white border, head and shoulders with one hand raised to his chin. (Vennett Smith) $182

Rogers & Evans, signed 8 x 10, by both Roy Rogers and Dale Evans, three quarter length standing together in cowboy costumes. (Vennett Smith) $77

Friends, signed color 8 x 10 of each of the female stars, Jennifer Aniston, Courtney Cox and Lisa Kudrow, full-length standing together in short skirts pulling ropes. (Vennett Smith) $105

Harold Lloyd, signed and inscribed 8 x 10, full length in a scene with a pretty dancer in elaborate costume from 'Professor, Beware!', with additional sketch of spectacles to image. (Vennett Smith) $22

Orson Wells, signed 8 x 10, head and shoulders in later years smoking large cigar. (Vennett Smith) $279

Rudolph Valentino, a signed sepia 13 x 18, to photographer's mount, head and shoulders in profile, framed and glazed in Art Nouveau design frame. (Vennett Smith) $750

Gloria Swanson, signed and inscribed sepia 10 x 13, half-length wearing white blouse and looking away over her shoulder, 1941. (Vennett Smith) $1,278

Katharine Hepburn, signed color postcard, portrait, neatly trimmed to lower edge. (Vennett Smith) $216

Marilyn Monroe, signed and inscribed album page, with four attached magazine portraits (three color), together with a similar signed and inscribed album page by Arthur Miller. (Vennett Smith) $980

Edward G. Robinson, signed and inscribed 8 x 10, half-length showing the bearded Robinson in costume as a scientist. (Vennett Smith) $139

Fred Astaire, signed 8 x 10 head and shoulders in naval uniform, modern reproduction signed in later years. (Vennett Smith) $169

Laurel & Hardy, signed and inscribed postcard by both Stan Laurel and Oliver Hardy individually, to lower white border, head and shoulders, together with an unsigned theater program for their appearance at the Bradford Alhambra, 1952. (Vennett Smith) $524

David Niven, signed and inscribed 7.5 x 9.5, head and shoulders in military uniform as Sir Arthur Robertson, the British Envoy to Peking, from the film 55 Days At Peking. (Vennett Smith) $298

Audrey Hepburn, signed and inscribed 8 x 10, head and shoulders smiling. (Vennett Smith) $262

Public Enemy, signed 10 x 8, by both James Cagney and Mae Clarke, half-length seated at a table in the classic 'grapefruit' scene. (Vennett Smith) $140

Judy Garland, signed irregularly clipped piece, laid down to front of 6.25 x 8.25 photo, half-length in negligee. (Vennett Smith) $162

Phil Silvers, signed 5 x 7, head and shoulders smoking cigarette, in costume as Sargant Bilko, modern reproduction signed in later years. (Vennett Smith) $154

John Wayne, signed and inscribed 9.5 x 7, also signed by Ray Milland and Wee Willie Davis, half-length together in a scene from Reap The Wild Wind. (Vennett Smith) $431

Marlon Brando, signed postcard, head and shoulders, wearing military uniform, from Sayonara. (Vennett Smith) $293

The Munsters, 8 x 10, signed Fred by Fred Gwynne, Yvonne de Carlo, Al Lewis, Butch Patrick and Pat Priest, full-length in costume. (Vennett Smith) $277

The Marx Brothers, signed album pages, 4.5 x 2.25 and smaller, by Groucho (first name only), Chico (inscribed) and Harpo (inscribed with self-caricature), overmounted in blue beneath 10.5 x 7 photo, showing all three head and shoulders. (Vennett Smith) $616

Laurel & Hardy, a fine signed and inscribed 8 x 10, by both Stan Laurel and Oliver Hardy, showing them full-length in characteristic poses. (Vennett Smith) $1,176

Lee Brandon, signed and inscribed color 13 x 20 poster advertising Rapid Fire, some creasing. (Vennett Smith) $254

Witches of Eastwick, signed color 10 x 8, by Cher, Susan Sarandon and Michele Pfeiffer, half-length from The Witches of Eastwick. (Vennett Smith) $185

Vivien Lee, signed postcard to lower white border, head and shoulders resting her chin on one hand. (Vennett Smith) $169

ae West, signed and inscribed
pia 8 x 7, head and shoulders
earing white furs.
'ennett Smith) $123

Harrison Ford, signed color 10 x 8,
head and shoulders leaning on
computer. (Vennett Smith) $75

Dorothy Dandridge, signed
postcard, three quarter length
seated on small table alongside
typewriter, smiling.
(Vennett Smith) $191

urel & Hardy, signed and
scribed postcard by both Stan
aurel and Oliver Hardy, half-length
characteristic pose wearing
wler hats.
ennett Smith) $539

Judy Garland, a black and white
head and shoulders publicity
photograph, signed in blue ballpoint
pen *Best Wishes Judy Garland*, 8½
x 6½in. and signed program for
the Glasgow Empire, May, 1951.
(Christie's) $658

Buster Keaton, an excellent signed
8 x 10, full-length seated on a film
set alongside another actor and a
director, with camera and umbrella
in background.
(Vennett Smith) $644

ela Lugosi, signed postcard to
wer white border, in red ink, head
nd shoulders in costume as
racula.(Vennett Smith) $832

Star Wars, signed color 10 x 8, by
Harrison Ford, Carrie Fisher and
Mark Hamill.
(Vennett Smith) $200

Ingrid Bergman, signed 4 x 6 head
and shoulders in later years,
smiling. (Vennett Smith) $139

Marlene Dietrich, signed and inscribed 10.5 x 11.5, with first name only, 1949, head and shoulders looking back over one shoulder.(Vennett Smith) $277

Judy Garland, photograph signed and inscribed *To Julie / from / Judy Garland*, 8 x 10in. (Christie's) $764

Jayne Mansfield, photograph signed and inscribed *To Ray Jr. / Best Wishes / Jane Mansfield*, 8 x 10in. sepia. (Christie's) $28?

Charles Chaplin, photograph inscribed and signed, 6½ x 9in. sepia by Hartsook of San Francisco and Los Angeles, elegantly matted and framed with a plaque to 14 x 21in. (Christie's) $3,760

Laurel and Hardy, a full length black and white portrait, signed in blue ink *Stan Laurel* and *Oliver Hardy*, additionally inscribed in Laurel's hand *Kindest Regards & Best Wishes Always Tom! Sincerely, Oct. 24th 1953*, 11¾ x 9½in. (Christie's) $1,068

Johnny Weissmuller, signed 6 x bookweight photo, three quarter length seated in safari gear in costume as Jungle Jim alongsid? chimpanzee Kimba. (Vennett Smith) $1?

Errol Flynn, signed and inscribed 7.5 x 9.5, head and shoulders wearing leather jacket, signed in white ink, weak in places, photo by Hurrell, 1940. (Vennett Smith) $456

Bela Lugosi, a half-length publicity photograph circa 1932, signed and inscribed in blue ink *Betty Williams, Faithfully, Bela Lugosi*, 10 x 8in. (Christie's) $526

Star Trek, Leonard Nimoy, photograph signed and inscribed *Fred/An artist & a friend / with gratitude / Leonard Nimoy / ' 78*. Color, 15 x 20in. (Christie's) $7?

FILM STAR AUTOGRAPHS

Frank Sinatra, signed postcard, head and shoulders, early. (Vennett Smith) $431

Greta Garbo, a mimeographed typescript document, addressed to Saul Rittenberg at Metro Goldwyn Mayer, 10202 W. Washington Boulevard, Culver City, California, 6½ x 8in. (Christie's) $1,809

Emil Jannings, signed postcard, head and shoulders as Kruger, pub. by Ross, signed to darker portion, slight silvering. (Vennett Smith) $92

Burns and Allen, signed and inscribed sepia 10 x 8 by both George Burns and Gracie Allen individually, head and shoulders laughing together. (Vennett Smith) $132

Gloria Swanson, signed 7 x 9 of a bust of Swanson, signed to lower white border *G.S. by Gloria Swanson*. (Vennett Smith) $54

Abbott & Costello, signed and inscribed sepia 10 x 8, showing them half-length. (Vennett Smith) $518

Clark Gable, signed postcard, head and shoulders smiling, Picturegoer No. 737C, signed across darker portion although reasonable contrast.(Vennett Smith) $336

Monroe, Marilyn and Miller, Arthur, Certificate of Conversion To Judaism, signed document, also signed by her husband, Rabbi Robert E. Goldberg, and two witnesses. 1 page, quarto, Lewisboro, New York, July 1, 1956. (Christie's) $28,200

Brigitte Bardot, signed and inscribed postcard, three quarter length smiling, early photo by Harcourt of Paris, partially signed in darker portion. (Vennett Smith) $77

Brighton Rock, 1947, A.B.P., British one sheet, 40 x 27in. (Christie's) $673

I'm No Angel, 1933, Paramount, U.S. window card, 22 x 14in. framed. (Christie's) $1,240

Frankenstein, 1931, Universal, Swedish, 39 x 28in., unfolded. (Christie's) $1,990

My Fair Lady, Style B, Warner Brothers, 1964, Italy, Due, 39 x 55in., linen backed. Artist; Guillano Nistri. (Christie's) $1,998

Lawrence Of Arabia, Columbia, 1962, 6 sheet, 81 x 81in., linen backed. Roadshow (first run, hard ticket) version. Less than 200 posters were produced in this size for the initial engagement. (Christie's) $4,935

Affair In Trinidad/Trinidad, Columbia, 1952, Italy, Quattro, 55 x 77in., linen backed. Artist: Anselmo Ballester. (Christie's) $5,22

Revenge Of The Creature, Universal, 1955, 1 sheet, 27 x 41in., linen backed. (Christie's) $1,175

Gigi, 1958, M.G.M., French, 63 x 47in., linen backed. (Christie's) $354

Flesh, 1968, Factory, German, 33 x 23in., signed in black felt pen by Andy Warhol. (Christie's) $1,594

Salomé, 1918, Fox, French, 63 x 47in., linen backed, Art by Vila. (Christie's) $1,682

Gilda, 1946, Columbia, Belgian, 18½ x 14in. (Christie's) $1,417

Bus Stop, 1956, T.C.F., British double crown, 30 x 20in., unfolded, framed. (Christie's) $1,150

The Cowboy Millionaire, Selig, 1910, 1 sheet, 29½ x 40in., period cloth backing. (Christie's) $2,350

The Dawn Patrol, 1938, Warner Bros., U.S. jumbo window card, 28 x 22in., framed. (Christie's) $5,667

Metropolis, 1927, U.F.A., British première program, Monday, March 21st 1927, 10 x 7½in. (Christie's) $1,417

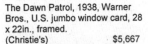

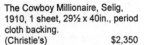

Words And Music, 1929, Fox, Swedish, 39 x 28in., linen backed, Art by Eric Rohman. (Christie's) $673

Shanghai Express, 1932, Paramount, U.S. printed cloth banner with braid fringe, 29 x 22½in. (Christie's) $2,479

Rose-Marie, 1936, M.G.M., U.S. one sheet, 41 x 27in., Leader Press, linen backed. (Christie's) $248

Terror By Night (Sherlock Holmes), Universal, 1946, 1 sheet, 27 x 41in, linen backed. (Christie's) $940

Lawrence Of Arabia, 1962, Columbia, British quad, 27¼ x 39in., linen-backed, timmed. (Christie's) $3,896

Godzilla, Toho, 1956, Italy, Due, 39 x 55in., linen backed. (Christie's) $2,820

Combat America, 1944, 20 x 28in. folded. Technicolor propaganda film featuring Clark Gable promoting the sale of war bonds. (Christie's) $363

One Hundred And One Dalmations, Buena Vista, 1961, 6 sheet, 81 x 81in., linen backed. (Christie's) $1,528

TOP TIP

When repairing paper ephemera, boxes etc., always avoid the use of sellotape. It devalues the item and is difficult to remove without leaving tears or stains.

If mounting or framing posters, handbills and so on, do not have them glued in place. Leave them 'loose mounted' to avoid devaluing them.

(Collector's Corner)

The Lone Ranger And The Lost City of Gold, United Artists, 1958, one-sheet, linen backed, 41 x 27in. (Christie's) $470

Cinematographe de Salon "KOK", circa 1899, Pathé, French, 47 x 63in., linen backed. (Christie's) $6,198

This Gun For Hire, 1942, Paramount, U.S., one sheet, 41 x 27in., linen backed. (Christie's) $4,250

Gone With The Wind, 1939, M.G.M., U.S. window card, 22 x 14in. (Christie's) $1,417

The Ipcress File, 1965, Rank, British quad, 30 x 40in. (Christie's) $1,948

Casablanca, 1942, Warner Bros., French, 47 x 33in., framed. (Christie's) $83,622

The Prisoner Of Zenda, 1937, United Artists, U.S., one sheet, 41 x 27in., framed. (Christie's) $9,741

Rain, re-release, 1938, half sheet, 28 x 22in. rolled. (Christie's) $1,880

The Rounders, Keystone/Mutual, 1914, 1 sheet, 27 x 41in, linen backed. This is the earliest known poster for a Chaplin film. (Christie's) $7,050

Bullitt, 1968, Warner Bros, Italian advance two-foglio, 55 x 39in. Art by R. Ferrini. (Christie's) $708

The Glen Miller Story, 1953, Universal, British quad, 30 x 40in., linen backed, art by Eric Pulford. (Christie's) $796

The Adventures Of Robin Hood, 1938, Warner Bros., U.S., one sheet, 41 x 27in., linen backed, framed.(Christie's) $19,481

Point Blank, 1967, M.G.M., U.S. three-sheet, 81 x 41in., linen backed. (Christie's) $973

Can-Can, 1960, T.C.F., German, 34 x 46½in., linen backed. (Christie's) $496

The African Queen, United Artists, 1951, three-sheet, linen backed, 81 x 41in. (Christie's) $4,465

The Ploughboy/Mickey Laboureur, 1929, Walt Disney, French, 47 x 31in., linen backed, art by Roger Cartier. (Christie's) $4,959

The Graduate, 1968, Embassy, British quad, 30 x 40in. (Christie's) $708

The Lone Ranger And The Lost City of Gold, United Artists, 1958, one-sheet, linen backed, 41 x 27in. (Christie's) $470

Psycho, Paramount, 1960, one sheet, linen backed, 41 x 27in. (Christie's) $2,115

Yellow Submarine, 1968, United Artists, British quad, 30 x 40in., linen backed. (Christie's) $3,542

Some Like It Hot, United Artists, 1959, one sheet, linen backed, 41 x 27in. (Christie's) $3,878

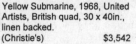

The Great Escape, 1970 re-release, United Artists, U.S. three-sheet, 81 x 41in. (Christie's) $531

Alfie, 1966, Paramount, U.S. half sheet, 22 x 28in., paper backed, unfolded. (Christie's) $744

Planet of the Apes, 20th century Fox, 1974, festival poster, 41 x 27in. (Christie's) $2,350

Piccadilly, 1929, B.I.P., Austrian, 110 x 49in., líned with japan paper. (Christie's) $7,084

Johnny Guitar, 1953, Republic, British quad, 30 x 40in., linen backed., art by Eric Pulford. (Christie's) $425

2001: A Space Odyssey, 1968, M.G.M., style D U.S. one sheet, 41 x 27in., linen backed. (Christie's) $16,285

Fatty And Mabel At The San Diego Exposition, Keystone/Mutual, 1915, 3 sheet, 36½ x 74½in., linen backed. (Christie's) $6,463

How To Steal The World, 1968, M.G.M., British quad, 30 x 40in., linen backed. (Christie's) $336

Whipshaw/En Äventyrerska, 1935, M.G.M., Swedish, 39 x 27½in., linen backed. (Christie's) $265

A pair of French bronze and ormolu chenets, 19th century, after a design by Caffieri, one in the form of a poodle, the other a cat, both seated on a cushion, 11½in. wide. (Christie's) $13,041

A pair of Louis XV style gilt bronze chenets, late 19th century, of naturalistic form with openwork scroll bases; each surmounted by figures of bacchic cherubs, 11¾in. high. (Christie's) $1,646

A pair of Napoleon III gilt bronze chenets, the flambeau urn finials above openwork bases with boldly cast foliate capped scrolls above waisted shaped bases, 16in. wide. (Christie's) $1,068

A pair of French bronze chenets, late 19th century, the urn surmounts with finials modelled as an eagle and owl respectively, on pierced stepped plinths with female masks, 20¾in. high. (Christie's) $1,104

A pair of Louis XVI style gilt bronze chenets, late 19th century, the flambeau urn standards with bearded masks and berried swags flanked by foliate capped scrolls, 12½in. wide. (Christie's) $2,726

A pair of wrought-iron goose-head andirons, American, early 20th century, each with an abstracted goose head and beak above a curvilinear neck, 18in. high. (Christie's) $1,88[

A pair of German andirons, probably circa 1600, the square section tapering uprights incised with panels of strapwork and foliate ornament, 24½in. high. (Christie's) $5,451

A pair of French gilt bronze chenets, early 20th century, modelled with classical maidens holding flambeau torchères, on foliate capped scroll bases, 19in. high. (Christie's) $2,743

A pair of wrought iron andirons, French, late 19th century, the wrythen standards with spherica[finials above scroll feet, 12¼in. high. (Christie's) $291

An English polished steel firegrate, early 20th century in the George II style, the serpentine railed basket above a conforming latticed pierced apron, flanked by incised tapering standards with urn finials, 29in. wide. (Christie's) $1,829

A George III style cast-iron basket fire grate, 20th century, the curved front rail mounted with snake handles to the sides and drapery swags to the front, 22½in. high. (Christie's) $1,500

A Regency brass-mounted cast-iron grate, the back with stylized foliate frieze, above a barred grate, and the front with foliate-cast cross cornucopia, 29¾in. wide. (Christie's) $8,384

A George III style brass and steel firegrate, early 20th century, the serpentine railed basket with urn finials, with beaded flanges and pierced frieze to the outset tapering legs with further urns, 32in. (Christie's) $3,496

Cast iron parlour stove, Wager, Richmond & Smith, Troy N.Y., 1853/4, the "S" form fire box embellished by cast "S" scrolls flanking the central tripartite arch with trefoil design, 38in. high. (Christie's) $1,175

A steel and cast iron firegrate, early 20th century, the tapering railed basket with foliate finials and mounts to the angles, on scroll feet, 26in. high.(Christie's) $1,196

A Victorian cast iron firegrate, 19th century, the railed basket with lattice frieze flanked by griffin monopodiae, with later arched backplate, 25in. wide. (Christie's) $3,474

A George III brass and steel basket grate, the arched rectangular cast-iron backplate above a slatted grate with serpentine bowed front with three bars, 33½in. wide. (Christie's) $3,337

A Franklin-style cast iron stove, stamped *WF*, Wilson's Forge possibly Poughkeepsie, New York, early 19th century, 41½in. wide. (Christie's) $1,410

FIRE IRONS

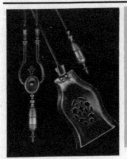

A set of three steel and brass fireirons, the associated lanceolate leaf cast urn handles on faceted shafts, the shovel with a pierced oval, 30in.(Christie's) $3,680

A set of Victorian polished steel fire irons, second half 19th century, the grips with faceted pommels, with plain shafts, the pierced shovel, 26½in. high. (Christie's) $511

A set of three William IV polished steel and brass fire-irons, circa 1840, the handles cast as stylized camels, on faceted shafts, the flared shovel with a pierced oval 30in. (Christie's) $2,576

A set of three polished steel fire irons, 19th century, with silver plated pommels modelled as camel's heads on plain cylindrical shafts, with pierced flared shovel, 31½in. long. (Christie's) $2,725

A set of Victorian brass and steel fire irons, second half 19th century, with foliate cast waisted grips, the pierced shovel, 30¼in. long. (Christie's) $1,000

A set of three polished steel fire irons, 19th century, with gadrooned pommels and knopped grips and shafts, the rectangular shovel with a border of pierced hearts, the shovel, 29¼in. long. (Christie's) $1,635

FIRE SIDE FENDERS

A gilt bronze fender, possibly English, early 19th century, the plinth standards with winged sphinx flanking the balustraded rail, on molded plinth, 34½in. wide. (Christie's) $2,377

A George III brass serpentine fender, early 19th century, the pierced frieze with beaded border and molded foot, raised on ball feet, with iron base plate, 43in. wide. (Christie's) $2,926

An English steel club fender, 20th century, of rectangular form, the button down leather covered padded seats to the corners on square section and part spiral twist supports descending to the molded base, 67in. wide. (Christie's) $1,371

A French gilt bronze fender, late 19th century, the flambeau urn standards with foliate capped paw feet on shaped stepped plinths flanking the adjustable pierced arcaded rail, 48in. long. (Christie's) $3,089

A George III style hardstone inlaid white marble chimneypiece, 19th century, the stepped breakfront shelf above a frieze with pietre dure panel depicting two ducks flanked by a partly stop-fluted Siena frieze, the jambs carved with classical vases above further fluting, 77in. high. (Christie's) $13,160

A carved carrara marble fire-surround, possibly American, circa 1870, the serpentine-shaped shelf with stepped edge, above a triangle-molded front, the arched opening with rope-twist edge, centered by a scrolled cartouche carved with a young girl on a swing, 78in. wide. (Christie's) $49,350

One of a pair of late Victorian bronze mounted white marble chimneypieces, in the Louis XV style, each with serpentine shelf with molded border above a frieze with boldly cast foliate capped cartouches with trailing flowerheads to the side panels, 64in. wide. (Christie's)   (Two) $19,740

Louis Majorelle, fireplace and overmantel, circa 1900, the fireplace within bronze frame enclosing tiled green border, cream marble base, 246cm. high by 112cm. wide. (Sotheby's) $20,020

A carved carrara marble fire-surround, possibly American, circa 1870, the serpentine-shaped shelf with stepped edge, above a triangle-molded front, the arched opening with rope-twist edge, centred by a scrolled cartouche carved with a boy and girl on a vine-garlanded swing, 82in. wide. (Christie's) $25,850

A Scottish 4in. pirn or winch, with an iron handle and foot, revolving wooden 4in. drum.
(Christie's) $3,611

A carved wood model of a fish, 19th century, with chip carved scales, the back fitted with a wrought iron suspension loop, 17in. long.
(Christie's) $397

An unusual willow creel, with leather strap, curved back to sit around the waist and lid with fastening catch.
(Bonhams) $283

J.J. Hardy, Salmon Fishing 1907 black cloth binding with gilt decoration.
(Bonhams) $180

A framed display of quill floats, including porcupine, goose, wood and other materials, with painted tops and whipped banding, arranged in graduated form, 22¾in., 32¼in. high, overall.
(Christie's) $7,222

A scarce Hardy 'Perfect' brown wicker creel, 17in. wide with reverse opening lid, leather strapped front net and canvas shoulder strap.
(Bonhams) $195

A framed display of lures, centered with an Invincible Brand line from Wyers Frères, Paris and surrounded by Wyers Frères spoons and spinners etc., the mount 18½ x 23½in.
(Christie's) $7,222

A rare cut glass bait attributed to Allcock, late 19th century, 2½in. long, with cut glass to both sides held onto fish shaped nickel silver body by tiny claws.
(Bonhams) $628

A framed display of baits and lures, in the form of minnows, eels, insects and others, arranged on a paper mount and later glazed, 21¼in. wide.
(Christie's) $14,444

A Scottish turned wood trolling winch with a wide drum, wooden handle, crack winding arm, pierced hole for rod and wooden spars. (Christie's) $1,986

A rare 4½in. brass "Superior Flexible Jointed Bait" attributed to Gregory, circa 1890, glass-eyed, stamped *Patent* to each fin. (Bonhams) $1,884

An early leather pot bellied trout fisherman's creel, 12in. wide, hinged lid with oval fish hole and simple embossed decoration to borders. (Bonhams) $1,960

A Chevalier Bowness & Son 3¾in. brass crankwind winch, 1866-1882, with quadruple pillared cage, raised constant check housing, ivory handle to 'S' crank and riveted brass foot. (Bonhams) $283

A framed exhibition display of flies and baits centered with two oval prints of a young trout, salmon, par or smelt in one and grilse in the other, later glazed, 31½in. high. (Christie's) $18,055

A framed display of fishing weights, all lead and some green painted, many with different stamps or labels with Patent names and No's, mounted on paper and later glazed, 22in. high. (Christie's) $4,514

A 'Hardy's Anglers Guide', 1923, illustrated, front cover untidy, 383 pages. (Bonhams) $126

A wrought iron weather vane, mid 19th century, modelled as a silhouette fish, surmounted by a crown motif and pierced with a heart shape, on a tapering shaft with foliate sprays, 38in. long. (Christie's) $5,417

A 19th century part calf bound folding trade display card of salmon flies. (Bonhams) $540

Two perch by W. Dennis in a wrap-around case, mounted in a setting of reeds and grasses against a green background, inscribed *Taken 10.3.1901, 1lb. 4oz., 1lb. 1oz.* and with W. Dennis of Dalston label, case 24½ x 11½in. (Bonhams) $754

A fine barbel by Cooper, mounted against a turquoise background in a gilt lined bow front case with gilt inscription *"Barbel 5½lbs. Caught by W. Carse 19th June 1934 at Marlow*, case 31³/₁₆ x 41½in. (Bonhams) $3,140

Two chubb by Cooper, mounted amongst a setting of fern and grasses, with card to interior *P. Brook-Hughes, 'The Royalty' Weight 7lb. 6oz. 4. Dec. 1951.* and with J.Cooper & Sons label. Case 30⁵/₈ x 20¾in., (Bonhams) $1,570

A roach by Cooper, mounted in a setting of reeds and grasses against a blue background in a gilt lined bow front case with J. Cooper & Sons label to case interior, case 19⁷/₈ x 12¼in. (Bonhams) $785

A fine bream by Homer, mounted in a setting of reeds and grasses with gilt inscription *Bream. Caught in the 'Witham' by S. F Fletcher. 9th August 1910, wgt. 6lbs.* and with W.F Homer label to case interior. Case 28¾ x 16³/₈in. (Bonhams) $1,099

A rare gudgeon, mounted in a setting of grasses against a turquoise background in a gilt lined bow front case, *Gudgeon 4ozs. 2drms. Caught by R S Wilson in the River Nene 16-2-38.* Case 10³/₁₆in. x 5¼in. (Bonhams) $1,413

A tench by Homer, mounted in a setting of reeds and grasses, *Caught by E.C Hartnell, Aug 31st 1941. Weight 3½lbs,* with Homers label, case 25¾ x 12⅝in. (Bonhams) $1,099

A perch by Cooper, mounted in a setting of reeds and grasses, in a gilt lined bow front case inscribed *Perch Caught by Mr. J. Griffiths at Patshull Park, June 16th 1914.* and with J. Cooper & Sons label, case 20⁷/₈in. x12³/₈in.(Bonhams) $864

A fine cased pike, the 10lb. fish *Taken by Mr. J. Courcha, in the river Lea, Jany. 20th. 1880, Preserved by J. Cooper & Sons*, framed and glazed with curved glass. (Christie's) $1,313

A fine cased trout, the 2lb. 10oz. fish *Caught by W. Elsworthy, at Ware, May 30th. 1898, Preserved by J. Cooper & Sons.* (Christie's) $1,313

Vintage preserved pike, clutching a smaller fish in its jaws, in a mahogany framed bow fronted display case, 33in. (G.A. Key) $1,885

A pike by Parker, mounted in a setting of reeds and grasses against a blue reed painted background, *Pike. Caught at Nailsea Ponds by S.A.E. Lowe. 1st Nov 1914. Wgt. 13lbs.* Case 39 x 16³⁄₈in. (Bonhams) $1,099

Three roach in a wrap around case, in the style of Cooper, with gilt inscription *Roach. Caught by Miss E.M.D Andridge. 1899.* Case 36½ x 15½in. (Bonhams) $1,884

A fine cased chubb, the 3lb. 4oz. fish *Caught by M. Maybury with a tight line, at Sandy Dec. 6th. 1900* and realistically presented, framed and glazed with curved glass. (Christie's) $1,225

A fine cased group of perch, the combined 5lb. 2oz weight of fish *caught by E. Elsworthy at Bures. Oct. 1879, Preserved by J. Cooper & Sons.* (Christie's) $1,137

Two dace by Cooper, mounted in a setting of reeds and grasses inscribed *Dace Weighing 11 & 10ozs. taken by Mr. Ellins from the River Kennett, 25th Febr. 1894.* and with J. Cooper & Son label, case 23 x 12½in. (Bonhams) $1,256

A fine large cased pike realistically presented and *Preserved by J. Cooper & Sons, 28, Radnor Street, S. Luke's, London, E.C.*, framed and glazed. (Christie's) $700

A fine top quality J.Bernard & Son of London 5½in. walnut and brass starback Nottingham reel with counterbalanced, rosewood handle. (Bonhams)　$840

A Hardy 'Jock Scott' bait casting reel with chrome foot black anodized duraluminum frame, hiduminum drum, chromed rim tension. (Bonhams)　$644

A 19th century brass crank wind reel, the face plate engraved R.F. straight arm with turned folding ivory knob, cut out rim. (Bonhams)　$266

A Hardy The "Sea Silex" 5in. ocean reel, an early model with the backplate stamped The "Silex" No. 2 and patent number 2206, twin bulbous horn handles mounted to circular alloy receivers. (Bonhams)　$393

A.J. Bernard & Son 5in. walnut starback center pin reel with Bickerdyke line guide, optional check, brass drum flange and back plate lining. (Bonhams)　$280

A rare Hardy "Cascapedia" 2/0 Multiplying salmon fly reel, 2.5:1 gear ratio, ebonite and nickel silver construction, backplate with seven point drag selector. (Bonhams)　$4,082

A scarce F. Cox ebonite and brass 2/3in. Scottish pattern fly reel, with nickel silver rims, wasted horn handle and constant check winding plate. (Bonhams)　$98

A rare 3in. Allcock "Coxon Aerial" centerpin reel, six spoke model with spoke tension regulator, ebonite drum, mahogany backplate. (Bonhams)　$1,020

A Geo. Wilkinson 'Perfection Flick-em' 4¼in. alloy center pin reel with brass foot, shallow perforated drum (Bonhams)　$84

A Julius Vom Hofe 4¼in. 6/0 salmon fly reel, nickel silver rims and fittings, ebonite handle to counterbalanced crank set in anti-foul rim. (Bonhams) $659

A black japanned fly reservoir with five removable trays, four with graduated clips for salmon/trout flies. (Bonhams) $196

A Hardy 4¼in. half ebonite and brass plate wind salmon fly reel with nickel silver rims, constant check and ivorine winding knob. (Bonhams) $238

A Hardy The "Sea Silex" 5in. alloy ocean reel, with twin reverse tapered ebonite handles, three rim control model with brass compression check lever and corresponding ivorine rim lever. (Bonhams) $471

A Hardy St. Andrew 4in. alloy fly reel, ribbed alloy foot, rim check, regulator screw, u shaped nickel line guard in Hardy zip case. (Bonhams) $105

A fine Hardy The "Hercules" 4½in. Special Pattern fly reel, with raised constant check housing, ivorine handle, handleplate stamped with 'Rod-in-Hand' trade mark and bordered oval logo, retaining most of original bronzing, circa 1890. (Bonhams) $502

A scarce Hardy "Saint George" multiplying fly reel, alloy construction with ribbed brass foot, agate line guide, rim mounted regulator screw. (Bonhams) $980

A 19th century 2¼in., reel with brass clamp foot winch, curved winding arm and bone winding knob. (Bonhams) $140

A scarce Hardy The "Triumph" 3½in. alloy bait casting reel, circa 1925-1927, with four position nickel silver regulator, nickel silver brake withdrawal stud to back plate. (Bonhams) $864

Grain painted stencil-decorated low post bed, probably Northern New England, 1825-35, the scrolled head and foot boards flanked by ball topped ring-turned posts ending in ring-turned tapering legs, 52¼in. wide. (Skinner) $1,495

Joined and panelled oak cradle, New England, late 17th/early 18th century, the panelled head and foot boards, with finials, joined to the recessed panelled sides, all on rockers, 39in. long. (Skinner) $1,840

Anon, French, bed with original drawing, circa 1939, rosewood and mahogany frame, the head and footboard modelled as stylized shells and upholstered in caramel leather, 158.5cm. wide by 202cm. long. (Sotheby's) $6,384

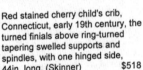

Charles II style carved oak full tester bed, of typical 17th style, with molded cornice top, raised on turned supports, with panelled headboard and foot posts. (Skinner) $1,725

Red stained cherry child's crib, Connecticut, early 19th century, the turned finials above ring-turned tapering swelled supports and spindles, with one hinged side, 44in. long. (Skinner) $518

A carved oak and marquetry tester bedstead, English, late 16th/ early 17th century and later, the nine panel tester profusely carved overall with foliate whirls, guilloche and lion masks, 66in. wide. (Christie's) $38,258

An extremely rare figured maple and pine child's pencil-post bedstead, New England, 1780-1800, the foot posts and head posts faceted and tapering, 34in. wide. (Sotheby's) $12,650

Paint decorated cradle, probably Connecticut River Valley, Massachusetts, early 19th century, the shaped sides joining arched head and footboards on scrolled rockers, 40½in. long. (Skinner) $1,500

A 17th century carved oak joined tester bed, with two-part four-panel headboard carved with bird and tulip design with scroll frieze beneath panel roof-board, 128 x 185cm. (Bristol) $4,928

William IV mahogany tester bed, double size, the turned front columns carved with petal borders, the foot and upper frieze carved with leafage scrolls, 5ft.6in. wide. (Brightwells) $3,850

A George I style giltwood bed, circa 1900, the arched headboard decorated with floral arabesques on a punched ground within a floral border, 58in. wide. (Bonhams) $2,002

A 17th century style oak full tester bed, 19th century and later, a full height carved bedhead decorated with Romanesque arches and lozenges, 166cm. wide. (Bonhams) $2,380

An oak and inlaid tester bedstead, English, 17th century and later, the nine panel tester with molded and scratch carved cornice raised on ring-turned and square section column supports, 52in. wide. (Christie's) $5,851

A George III style four-poster bed, circa 1920, with lobed and acanthus carved columns and a panelled bed head and ends, 58½in. wide. (Bonhams) $647

An oak and inlaid tester bedstead, English, 17th century and later, the headboard with an upper row of three lozenge-filled panels, the central one arcaded and flanked by figures, 60in. wide. (Christie's) $11,885

A mid Victorian mahogany double bed, the headboard with a molded cornice above an arched panel flanked by plain uprights, 64in. wide. (Bonhams) $552

A George III mahogany metamorphic bureau bed, the hinged slope above four simulated drawers enclosing a later fold-out bedframe, on later bracket feet, 44½in. wide. (Christie's) $2,385

A Regency mahogany and polychrome-painted four-post bed, by Gillows, the rectangular canopy with cavetto cornice painted in ocher, brown and green with lappeted frieze, the frame 98½in. high. (Christie's) $22,356

A mahogany breakfront library bookcase, 19th century, the upper part with a molded dentil cornice and enclosed by four glazed astragal doors, 104in. wide. (Christie's) $12,434

A Victorian mahogany breakfront bookcase with molded cornice over three glazed doors enclosing shelving, protuding base with central frieze drawer, 60in. wide. (Andrew Hartley) $2,079

An oak bookcase, Victorian; circa 1870, in Gothic Revival style, with a battlemented cornice above tracery panels and two sections with adjustable shelves, 277cm. wide. (Sotheby's) $12,024

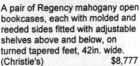

A late Georgian mahogany bookcase press, the upper section fitted with adjustable shelves with arched astragal glazed doors on base, 4ft.5in. wide. (Brightwells) $2,499

A pair of Regency mahogany open bookcases, each with molded and reeded sides fitted with adjustable shelves above and below, on turned tapered feet, 42in. wide. (Christie's) $8,777

An associated Regency bookcase, the molded top above a pair of glazed doors set on a base fitted with two short and three long graduated drawers, 115cm. wide. (Bonhams) $1,386

A fine Victorian mahogany bookcase, circa 1850, the breakfront cornice above four glazed doors divided by molded pilasters headed by bellflower and lattice carved scrolled corbels, 113¼in. wide. (Bonhams) $15,400

A mahogany triple tier circular open revolving bookcase, 19th century, in the Regency style, with graduated circular tops with molded edges, on rectangular uprights and central column. (Christie's) $1,809

A mahogany breakfront library bookcase, parts George III and later, the lower part with a molded edge containing a central fitted frieze drawer with hinged leather lined surface concealing four drawers to the sides, 80in. wide. (Christie's) $12,337

Regency mahogany breakfront bookcase, first quarter 19th century, molded cornice above glazed mullioned doors enclosing shelves, the base with oval raised panel doors, 107in. wide.
(Skinner) $42,550

A late Victorian mahogany revolving bookcase, circa 1890, with a Maple & Company Ltd applied circular label, 50cm. wide.
(Bonhams) $952

A mahogany breakfront bookcase, the molded cornice above three glazed doors, originally the upper section to a mid Victorian breakfront bookcase, 72¼ x 76½in.
(Bonhams) $1,540

A mahogany and brass bureau bookcase, French, circa 1840, in Louis XVI style, of break-front form with overhanging cornice above three glazed doors enclosing shelves, 148cm. wide.
(Sotheby's) $14,028

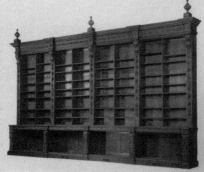

A carved walnut and pine open library bookcase, late 19th century, of massive proportions, in the Georgian style; the molded dentil cornice surmounted by neo classical urns and frieze with fluted and flowerhead ornament, 265in. wide. (Christie's) $36,190

A Regency rosewood and bird's eye maple bookcase, the upper part with a triangular pediment centered by a roundel with brass Apollo mask, fitted with shelves and enclosed by a pair of glazed panel doors, 39¾in. wide.
(Christie's) $13,165

A late Victorian oak bookcase, the glazed upper section fitted with three doors, the base having three drawers and panelled cupboards under, 6ft. wide.
(Brightwells) $3,419

A George IV rosewood open bookcase, circa 1830, the rectangular top and band frieze above a single shelf, held by turned columns, 33in. wide.
(Bonhams) $1,924

A French ebonized boulle bookcase, circa 1860, the arched cornice centered with a grotesque mask, above two glazed cupboard doors flanked by gilt metal capitals, 52in. wide.(Bonhams) $3,588

279

An oak and inlaid court cup-board, English, early 17th century, with molded plank top and frieze drawer, checker inlaid and flanked by marblewood panels, supported by angled lions, 46in. wide.
(Christie's) $30,889

An Edwardian oak two drawer buffet, 107cm. wide.
(Bonhams) $277

Late 19th century mahogany two tier buffet, the tray top crested at the four corners with finials, the lower tier fitted with a drawer, 24in.
(G.A. Key) $522

A Victorian buffet, veneered in pollarded oak on mahogany, the molded edge top shelf with a raised back, having dog's tooth molding flanked by pierced panels, 4ft.6in. wide.
(Woolley & Wallis) $1,570

A French Provinçial carved oak and possibly chestnut buffet a deux corps, late 18th/early 19th century, the upper part with a stylized foliate overhanging molded cornice and guilloche carved frieze, 64½in. wide. (Christie's) $4,935

A late Victorian walnut three-tier buffet, with elevating rectangular shelves, on fluted standard end columns and dual inswept scroll supports and castors joined by a spindle arched stretcher below, 39in. wide. (Christie's) $1,106

A Victorian mahogany dinner wagon, the three shelves with molded edges, missing the galleried borders, the melon panelled fluted supports with fielded panels, 4ft.3in. wide.
(Woolley & Wallis) $1,386

Victorian mahogany buffet on porcelain castors, the base with two door cupboard with shelf above, with further tier above this, turned standards with rosette carved finials to the top, 3ft.3in. wide.
(G.A. Key) $816

A Victorian mahogany three tier buffet of oblong form, the ledge back with arched center carved with a vine roundel, cantilevered shelves, 48in. wide.
(Andrew Hartley) $1,295

Queen Anne Revival mahogany bureau bookcase, late 19th century, the upper section fitted with doors and candleslides, the lower section fitted with a slant-lid bureau, 36½in. wide. (Skinner) $5,175

A George I blue and gilt-japanned double-domed bureau-cabinet, attributed to John Belchier, 44in. wide. (Christie's) $567,645

Classical carved and glazed mahogany veneer cylinder fall desk and bookcase, Baltimore, 1825-35, the cornice flares above the veneered frieze and doors with arched glass panels, 46in. wide. (Skinner) $2,070

An Irish George II mahogany writing-cabinet, the broken cornice with egg-and-dart, dentilled and lappeted moldings above a pair of shaped panelled doors with foliate and C-scroll moldings, 64in. wide. (Christie's) $317,725

A Chippendale figured cherrywood secretary bookcase, Pennsylvania, 1760-80, in two parts; the upper section with overhanging cornice and panelled doors, opening to shelves, pigeonholes, and short drawers, 38in. wide. (Sotheby's) $9,775

A George II oak bureau cabinet with mahogany crossbanding, molded cornice over two arched ogee welded panel doors, the fall front revealing fitted interior, 42½in. wide.(Andrew Hartley) $3,920

A French walnut cylinder bureau bookcase, 20th century, with a molded cornice above a glazed cabinet enclosing shelves, the roll-top with carved foliate decoration, 46½in. wide. (Christie's) $4,959

A mahogany bureau bookcase, the top with a dentil and pendant detachable cornice, above adjustable shelves enclosed by a pair of glazed tracery doors, associated bureau, 3ft.5in. wide. (Woolley & Wallis) $2,002

A German walnut bureau cabinet, circa 1750, the arched plinth top with carved foliate crest above a pair of well figured line inlaid doors, above a rectangular fall with conforming inlay, 54in. wide. (Bonhams) $5,624

A 19th century oak bureau cabinet with parquetry stringing, double domed top with molded cornice over two glazed doors, 24½in. wide. (Andrew Hartley) $8,008

A Regency mahogany and ebony strung cylinder bureau bookcase, the upper part with a molded cornice, on swept bracket feet, 44½in. wide. (Christie's) $5,264

An oak bureau cabinet, English, late 18th century, the molded cornice above a pair of panelled cupboard doors, the top and base associated, 43in wide. (Bonhams) $3,234

A Dutch walnut and floral marquetry bombé bureau bookcase, circa 1780, of small proportions, the domed cornice centered by a carved floral cartouche above an arched glazed door, 41in. wide. (Bonhams) $21,000

A burr-walnut, crossbanded and feather strung bureau cabinet, early 18th century and later, the upper part with a molded cornice and enclosed by ogee cushion molded arched panelled doors, 42½in. wide. (Christie's) $6,251

A George III mahogany bureau cabinet with dentil and pendant carved cornice above a pair of solid panelled doors enclosing adjustable shelves. (Brightwells) $4,000

A Victorian Gothic Revival walnut bureau bookcase, in the style of C.L. Eastlake, the arched back above a fall front, with a single long drawer and two panelled cabinet doors, 96cm. wide. (Bonhams) $1,694

An early 18th century oak bureau bookcase having molded top above a pair of fielded panelled doors, above two short and two long drawers, 6ft.9in. high. (Brightwells) $1,885

oak bureau, English, early 18th
ntury, the fall enclosing a fitted
terior above a well, with two short
d two long frieze drawers, 36¼in.
de. (Bonhams) $4,410

A 19th century Louis XV style
walnut bonheur du jour of bombé
form with bird and floral marquetry,
fall enclosing three small drawers,
2ft. 5in. wide.
(Brightwells) $2,860

A George II oak bureau with
stepped fitted interior and well, two
small drawers and two others
beneath, 3ft.2in.
(Brightwells) $1,972

Louis XV period kingwood,
rossbanded, marquetry and
uitwood bombé fronted bureau,
ossibly Provincial, with panels of
oral marquetry within borders of
roken outline, 39in. wide.
Christie's) $4,200

A scarlet japanned and chinoiserie
decorated bureau de dame, 19th
century and later, the sloping fall
decorated with figures in pagoda
landscapes with lattice and floral
spandrels, 41in. wide.
(Christie's) $4,023

A George III mahogany bureau,
circa 1770, of narrow proportions,
the fall enclosing a fitted interior of
drawers and pigeon holes, 29½in.
wide. (Bonhams) $3,404

Dutch mahogany and floral
arquetry cylinder bureau, 19th
ntury, in two sections, with aller panels of flowers and foliage,
e superstructure fitted with three
awers, 53in. wide.
hristie's) $6,948

A George I walnut bureau, the front
inlaid with featherbanding, the
rectangular top above a hinged flap
enclosing a red baize-lined writing-
surface, 33¼in. wide.
(Christie's) $7,079

A Continental cream japanned and
gilt chinoiserie decorated bureau,
late 18th/early 19th century,
probably Dutch, the sloping fall with
book ledge decorated with figures
in landscapes, 43½in. wide.
(Christie's) $3,619

A French kingwood, rosewood and marquetry cylinder bureau, 19th century, in the Louis XVI style, the gallery top with cornucopiae inlay and pierced ornament, 56in. wide.
(Christie's) $8,225

Red painted pine desk, New England, 19th century, the rectangular top above an interior of sixteen drawers and flanking shaped sides, 36in. wide.
(Skinner) $5,750

A south German walnut bureau, circa 1760, the rectangular top and fall inlaid with geometric crossbandings and enclosing a simple interior of drawers and pigeonholes, 47½in. wide.
(Bonhams) $4,44

A Queen Anne carved and figured mahogany slant-front desk, Goddard-Townsend School, Newport, Rhode Island, 1740-60, the hinged lid opening to an interior with two stacks of blocked short drawers, 37in. wide.
(Sotheby's) $8,625

A Queen Anne walnut bureau, featherbanded to the top, front and interior, the hinged slope enclosing a fitted interior, with two secret drawers, above two short and two long graduated drawers.
(Christie's) $41,713

A late 18th century Dutch bureau, walnut veneered, later cut in two halves, the later crossbanded top a burr veneered hinged flap to a stepped fitted serpentine interior, 3ft.8in. wide.
(Woolley & Wallis) $4,31

A mid 18th century mahogany bureau, the figured veneered fall flap opening to a fitted interior with a fielded panel cupboard door, 3ft.5in. wide.
(Woolley & Wallis) $2,512

Chippendale reverse serpentine slant-lid desk, Boston, 1760-80, the slant lid opens to a fitted interior, the cockbeaded case with an arched top drawer over three graduated drawers, 41½in. wide.
(Skinner) $6,900

A small walnut veneered bureau, George I style, having herringbone inlay, the stepped interior with drawers and pigeon holes above a well, 25in. wide.
(Woolley & Wallis) $2,61

Chippendale tiger maple slant lid desk, New England, mid 18th century, the slant lid opens to a two-stepped interior of valanced compartments over small drawers, 35in. wide. (Skinner) $6,325

A late 19th century French bureau de dame, veneered in faded rosewood with floral marquetry panels, the top with a pierced gilt bronze gallery, 28¾in. overall. (Woolley & Wallis) $1,068

A George III mahogany bureau, the fall front enclosing fitted interior, four long drawers with oval brass handles, shaped apron and splayed feet, 42in. wide. (Andrew Hartley) $1,309

A Dutch walnut and floral marquetry bombé bureau, fall decorated with an inlaid urn issuing floral garlands enclosing a later arrangement of drawers, pigeonholes, secret compartments and a well, 42in. wide. (Bonhams) $4,440

A Louis Philippe mahogany ormolu mounted bureau à cylindre, the rectangular verde antico marble top above three small frieze drawers, the roll top embellished with a putto standing on a carriage, 56in. wide. (Christie's) $3,657

Italian Baroque-style ivory and fruitwood marquetry inlaid walnut slant-lid desk, late 19th century, with fitted interior and three long drawers, inlaid with hunt scenes, 29½in. wide. (Skinner) $1,725

Chippendale birch slant-lid desk, Northern New England, mid to late 18th century, the slant lid opens to two-stepped interior on a molded base with shaped bracket feet, 39in. wide. (Skinner) $3,105

A Dutch walnut and marquetry bureau of bombé form, circa 1800, with the inlaid fall enclosing a fitted interior of drawers and secret compartments above a well, the shaped front of three long drawers inlaid with foliage,134cm. wide. (Bonhams) $8,140

A George III oak bureau, the fall front opening to reveal fitted interior with drawers and pigeon holes, central frieze drawer flanked on either side by a small drawer, 42in. wide. (Andrew Hartley) $1,617

A carved oak cabinet-on-stand, possibly German, 19th century, the upper part with ledge back and enclosing a pair of panelled doors, 46½in. wide.(Christie's) $4,606

An early 19th century rosewood side cabinet, the rectangular gadrooned top above two panelled arched cabinet doors, 104cm. wide. (Bonhams) $372

A Victorian rosewood mirror backed side cabinet of serpentine form, the arched mirror within molded frame carved with trailing leaves, 64in. (Andrew Hartley) $2,610

A Continental walnut and brass studded side cabinet, 17th century, Italian probably Bolognese, elements of a later date, applied with brass stellar flowerhead and roundel ornament, 61in. wide. (Christie's) $8,225

An Italian marquetry, ebonized, fruitwood and inlaid side cupboard, 19th century, incorporating elements of an earlier date, in the Baroque style, of recessed angular form, the top inlaid with a female figure with a cross bow, 33in. wide. (Christie's) $3,619

A French ebonized, brass marquetry scarlet tortoishell and ormolu-mounted side cabinet, 19th century, with panelled door, centered by a female mask with fan headdress, 34½in. wide. (Christie's) $2,632

A Continental ebonized and silver-painted table cabinet-on-stand, the cabinet 17th /18th century with later elements, with a hinged cavetto frieze top with portrait roundels, the cabinet, 27½in. wide. (Christie's) $3,657

A Maples mahogany office cabinet with sixteen drawers, circa 1890, by repute from the Earl of Balfour, Whittingham House, East Lothian, 80cm. wide. (Bonhams) $2,100

An oak and mahogany crossbanded cabinet on chest, early 19th century, married, the molded cornice above a pair of panelled cupboard doors, 44in. wide. (Bonhams) $955

A Dutch mahogany cabinet, late 18th century, the arched and molded cornice with canted angles centered by a ribbon-tied cartouche depicting the head of a woman and flanked by foliate scrolls, 76in. wide. (Christie's) $6,251

A joined oak side cabinet Westmorland, late 17th century, the rectangular overhanging top above a single panelled door carved to the top with a geometric design incorporating stylized foliage, 33in. wide. (Bonhams) $764

An early Victorian mahogany entomologist's cabinet, the top with a floral and butterfly carved edge, with forty- two drawers which contain British Geometridae moths, British and exotic butterflies, 100cm wide. (Bonhams) $5,236

An Edwardian inlaid mahogany enclosed desk cabinet, the hinged lid and drop front enclosing numerous fitted pigeon holes and drawers.
(Brightwells) $2,174

A pair of Victorian French style walnut and floral marquetry side cabinets each with single solid panelled door having floral design and cross-banding, 2ft.11in.
(Brightwells) $8,526

A 19th century Continental carved walnut specimen cabinet, the upper section of oblong form with waisted top on caryatid supports, flower and dragon finials, single door carved with niche figure, 46in. wide.
(Andrew Hartley) $6,468

A fine George III mahogany cabinet on stand, circa 1785, the cabinet with a full arcaded gallery surmounted at the corners with leaf carved urn finials with oval paterae to the plinths, 26¼in. wide.
(Bonhams) $22,200

A Victorian oak coin collector's cabinet, second half 19th century, with rectangular top above two panelled doors, on separate stepped and molded plinth, the interior with thirty gilt numbered trays, 24¼in. wide.
(Christie's) $6,583

An Edwardian mahogany music cabinet, crossbanded with stringing, the raised mirrored back with molded cornice and shaped shelf, 25in. wide.
(Andrew Hartley) $906

A 19th century breakfront cabinet, burr walnut veneered, the top edge crossbanded and inlaid with stringing, 6ft.7½in. wide, circa 1880. (Woolley & Wallis) $3,611

Renaissance Revival carved walnut side cabinet, circa 1860-80, with marble top above a canted case elaborately carved with figural stiles, foliage and putti, 34½in. wide. (Skinner) $4,313

A gilt metal mounted boulle breakfront side cabinet, 19th century, the ebonized top above inverted cavetto molded frieze and central door flanked by female mask gilt metal mounts, 176.5cm. wide. (Bristol) $1,016

An Italian walnut side cabinet, circa 1600, the later hinged rectangular top with molded edge enclosing a well above a dentil molded frieze and stepped edge above a pair of panelled doors, 36in. wide. (Bonhams) $2,520

Continental Baroque walnut two-part side cabinet, composed of antique elements, each section fitted with doors, elaborately carved with foliage, figures, and architectural elements, 39½in. (Skinner) $2,990

A good Edwardian mahogany and satinwood crossbanded drinks cabinet, retailed by Mappin and Webb, the rectangular top dividing to reveal a rising fitted interior with a tantalus, a humidor and twenty seven cut glass drinking glasses, 28¾in. wide. (Bonhams) $6,160

Edwardian rosewood purdonium, arched pediment, inlaid throughout with boxwood and ivorine stringing and neo-classical designs, open shelf over compartment, 15½in. (G.A. Key) $691

A 19th century breakfront side cabinet, veneered in burr and figured walnut, the frieze marquetry inlaid and having gilt bronze mounts, 4ft.6¼in. (Woolley & Wallis) $3,542

A late Victorian ebonized and amboyna gilt metal mounted side cabinet, the back upstand with jasperware plaque inset pediment above shelf with mirror behind, 81cm. wide. (Bristol) $617

A Victorian mahogany parlour cabinet, the stepped upper section with arched surmount centered by a mask, glazed door below enclosing shelving, 52½in. wide. (Andrew Hartley) $2,310

A mid Victorian walnut and tulipwood parquetry side cabinet, circa 1870, inlaid overall with parquetry geometric panels an applied with gilt metal figural and floral mounts, 69in. wide. (Bonhams) $4,774

British pine hutch/cabinet, with rounded cornice and three open shelves flanked by carved pilasters, the lower section fitted with a door, 43½in. wide. (Skinner) $863

mahogany cabinet, the rectangular veneered top inlaid with stringing and rosewood crossbanding; above shelves enclosed by a pair of recess panel doors, 3ft.4¾in. wide. (Woolley & Wallis) $990

French Louis XIV style boullework and bronze mounted and ebonized side cabinet, third quarter 19th century, with brass and tortoiseshell marquetry, with satyr and foliate bronze mounts, 32in. wide. (Skinner) $1,265

A 19th century North Italian small pier cabinet, with old alteration, veneered in rosewood, banded in tulipwood and inlaid marquetry, 21in. (Woolley & Wallis) $1,820

ne of a pair of Italian enaissance-style walnut cabinets, te 19th century, carved ctangular top above a pair of abinet doors flanked by herms, in. wide. kinner) (Two) $4,313

Napoleon III fruitwood marquetry and gilt bronze mounted side cabinet, circa 1850-70, with serpentine crest and shelved superstructure above a serpentine case fitted with a drawer and two doors. (Skinner) $4,025

Fine Wedgwood and gilt bronze mounted amboyna and ebony side cabinet, England, circa 1870, the stepped superstructure with mirrored back and side cabinets above a rectangular top. (Skinner) $6,325

A brass-bound black lacquer and gilt japanned cabinet-on-stand, 19th century, decorated overall with Oriental courtly figures, pagodas foliage and birds, with a pierced brass gallery above a pair of doors, 51in. wide.(Christie's) $3,452

An American sycamore and mahogany cabinet-on-stand, late 18th century, crossbanded overall in tulipwood, the rectangular top with simulated baluster galleried frieze, above a pair of panelled doors with inset ovals, 38in. wide. (Christie's) $5,339

An oak collector's cabinet, late 19th century, a shallow drawer, three deep drawers modelled as two drawers and three further graduated shallow drawers below, 29in. wide.(Christie's) $2,236

A North European mother of pearl inlaid black, gilt and silver-japanned cabinet-on-stand, early 18th century, probably Dutch, decorated overall with landscapes, animals and figures, 47½in. wide. (Christie's) $35,397

A pair of limed oak and polychrome decorated cabinets, late 19th/early 20th century, in the Gothic style, each with dentil molded cornice above a pair of Gothic tracery carved and linen fold panelled cupboard doors, 38in. wide. (Christie's) $3,291

A brass-mounted black, red and gilt-japanned cabinet-on-stand, the cabinet late 17th/early 18th century, the base George II, decorated overall with figures, birds, animals and foliage, the cabinet with a pair of doors enclosing a fitted interior, 41in. wide.(Christie's) $3,671

A kingwood, gilt-bronze and enamelled cabinet, French, circa 1860, the upper part with overhanging cornice above a door with central blue and turquoise enamelled panel with grotesque work, 68.5cm. wide.
(Sotheby's) $5,010

A satinwood, rosewood-banded and parcel-gilt side cabinet, 20th century, in the Regency style, the shaped crossbanded top within a gilt guilloche-carved edge, above two freize drawers and a pair of silk lined grille applied cupboard doors, 56in. wide.
(Christie's) $2,236

A late Victorian rosewood, satinwood-line and inlaid breakfront side cabinet, the upper section with urn finial capped, pierced trellis work gallery above a bowed molded cornice and inlaid frieze between three arched recesses, 72in. (Christie's) $15,277

A Victorian walnut canterbury with scroll carved cresting rail to shaped shelf, pierced scroll divisions and turned fluted column supports, 2ft.6in. wide. (Brightwells) $3,150

A mid Victorian walnut canterbury/games table, circa 1880, hinged games board above a frieze drawer, on turned legs, 61cm. wide. (Bonhams) $868

A fine early Victorian burr walnut and satinwood crossbanded canterbury music stand, circa 1850, the rectangular top with gilt metal baluster gallery opening to reveal an adjustable music stand, 25¼in. wide. (Bonhams) $3,080

A Regency mahogany canterbury, circa 1815, with three folio sections held by turned spindles, the corner spindles surmounted by acorn finials, 21in. wide. (Bonhams) $4,144

A Victorian burr-walnut canterbury whatnot, with a pair of graduated open tiers with foliate pierced gallery backs and a drawer above a three division canterbury, 23½in. wide. (Christie's) $1,884

A Regency brass-mounted mahogany canterbury, the dished pierced four-section top with spirally-turned baluster columns, above two drawers, 20in. wide. (Christie's) $6,674

A William IV rosewood canterbury, with three divisions, after a design by John C. Loudon, separated by diagonal splats and turned ends with pierced anthemion and garland to the center, 21in. wide. (Christie's) $3,271

A Victorian walnut canterbury, low brass gallery above four vertical shaped fret-carved divisions, on a raised plinth with a drawer, 22in. wide. (Christie's) $1,884

A George III mahogany four-division canterbury, with pierced carrying handle and slatted divisions containing a drawer below, 18in. wide. (Christie's) $2,467

An early Victorian mahogany music canterbury, the shaped open divisions with turned side stretcher rails, a frieze drawer, cedar lined, 21½in.
(Woolley & Wallis) $1,260

A Regency mahogany three-division music canterbury, with curved and slatted divisions and ring-turned reeded uprights containing a drawer, 19½in. wide.
(Christie's) $3,089

A Victorian walnut canterbury with turned tapering spindle divisions and similar corner supports with turned finials, 19in. wide.
(Andrew Hartley) $1,848

An early 19th century mahogany music canterbury, the dipped divisions with vertical supports and turned corner supports and a frieze drawer, 20in.
(Woolley & Wallis) $1,771

A Victorian burr walnut corner canterbury whatnot, the fretwork gallery above shaped-front shelf with further fretwork supports above shaped-front platform, 76cm. wide.
(Bristol) $2,464

A William IV mahogany music canterbury, the criss cross divisions with turned hand grips as side stretchers and centered carved lyres, 19¾in. wide.
(Woolley & Wallis) $2,660

Federal mahogany canterbury, probably Boston, 1815-25, the curving tops of the three sections divided by the flat column-like supports and flanked by ring-turned tapering corners, 18⅛in. wide.
(Skinner) $4,600

A fine early Victorian burr walnut canterbury whatnot, circa 1850, the shelf superstructure above a rectangular top and frieze drawer on fluted and baluster turned supports, 23½in. wide.
(Bonhams) $3,388

A mid Victorian walnut canterbury whatnot of large size, circa 1855, the rectangular top with shaped foliate pierced three-quarter gallery on c-scroll and barley-twist end supports above a three tier canterbury base, 34in. wide.
(Bonhams) $2,175

Edwardian mahogany corner chair, splayed back inlaid with boxwood stringing and supported by two similarly inlaid and scrolled pierced splats, on cabriole supports. (G.A. Key) $217

A George III mahogany corner armchair, with curved bar back, top-rail and outswept flattened scroll arm supports, having vase shaped splats, on column supports. (Christie's) $7,680

Roundabout maple chair, New England, late 18th century, the crest with shaped terminals above cyma curved horizontal splats, rush seat. (Skinner) $2,185

Painted maple corner chair, Connecticut, Rhode Island border region, 1790-1800, the spindled crest above the pillow back lower crest ending in scrolled terminals over shaped horizontal splats. (Skinner) $4,600

Queen Anne walnut roundabout chair, Boston, circa 1740-60, the shaped crest above outscrolled arms on vase and ring-turned supports flanking two vasiform splats. (Skinner) $6,900

Chippendale mahogany roundabout chair, 18th century, New England or New York State, the scrolled crest above pierced splats, and a molded seat frame. (Skinner) $2,645

Painted maple corner chair, New England, circa 1780, the pillow back crest ending in scrolled terminals above three vase and ring-turned supports. (Skinner) $345

Queen Anne maple roundabout commode chair, New England, late 18th / early 19th century, the molded seat frame with slip seat over shaped skirt, and a frontal cabriole leg ending in pad foot. (Skinner) $2,185

Chippendale cherry roundabout chair, probably Connecticut, circa 1770-80, the shaped crest above outscrolled arms on vase and ring-turned supports. (Skinner) $5,175

One of a set of five Regency mahogany dining chairs, brass inlaid curved top rail with scrolled surmount and carved with scrolling foliage.
(Andrew Hartley) (Five) $725

Two of a set of four George III mahogany chairs, the channelled back with arched crest, pierced vase shaped splat, drop in seat, raised on chamfered square legs.
(Andrew Hartley)(Four) $1,201

One of a set of six Victorian walnut balloon back dining chairs with arched, scrolled bar back, overstuffed seat, raised on cabriole front legs with pad feet.
(Andrew Hartley) (Six) $1,040

Two of a set of six William IV mahogany dining chairs, the carved bar backs above upholstered drop in seats, the carvers with scrolled open arms.
(Bonhams) (Six) $2,233

One of a set of six elm dining chairs, East Anglia, late 18th century, each with a slatted back and solid seat, on square section legs tied by stretchers.
(Bonhams) (Six) $1,205

Two of a set of four late Victorian mahogany dining chairs, the waisted backs with pierced baluster splats, on turned tapered legs.
(Bonhams) (Four) $647

Two of a set of six early Victorian dining chairs, the waisted backs with scrolled horizontal bar splats, above drop in seats.
(Bonhams) (Six) $1,540

Two of a set of five mid Victorian dining chairs, circa 1870, the carved backs above serpentine upholstered seats and raised on cabriole legs.
(Bonhams) (Five) $644

Two of a set of six mid Victorian mahogany dining chairs, the open waisted backs above overstuffed seats, on molded cabriole legs.
(Bonhams) (Six) $1,386

One of a set of six mid Victorian rosewood chairs, circa 1860, the heart shaped back with a pierced floral cabochon crest and a conforming splat.
(Bonhams)   (Six) $1,386

Two of a set of ten Regency mahogany dining-chairs, each with a foliage-scrolled tablet toprail above a spirally-reeded horizontal splat and drop-in seat, on reeded saber legs.
(Christie's) (Ten) $15,836

One of a set of four oak Arts and Crafts dining chairs.
(Bonhams)   (Four) $572

Two of a set of six oak Arts and Crafts dining chairs, circa 1905, attributed to a design by Ernest Archibald Taylor, probably made by Wylie & Lochhead.
(Bonhams)   (Six) $1,260

Two of a set of four mid 19th century rosewood framed dining chairs, the carved shaped hoop backs above a horizontal splat, stuffed over seat and turned front legs.(Bonhams)(Four) $529

Two of a set of eight Arts and Crafts oak dining chairs, attributed to a design by Ernest Archibald Taylor, the crest rail with pierced crescent molding above three shaped vertical rails.
(Bonhams) $2,000

One of a set of four George III mahogany dining chairs, circa 1760, shaped backs above upholstered seats and raised on square chamfered legs.
(Bonhams)   (Four) $1,960

Two of a set of eight William IV mahogany dining chairs, including two armchairs, with bowed toprails and scrolled horizontal bar splats.
(Bonhams)   (Eight) $4,620

One of a set of ten early Victorian mahogany dining chairs with scroll carved central horizontal splats, stuff-over seats on turned and fluted tapering front supports.
(Brightwells) (Ten) $7,350

Two of a set of eight Regency mahogany dining chairs, the open backs with rope twist rails and veneered crest panels, molded side supports. (Woolley & Wallis)   (Eight) $10,857

Two of a set of six Regency mahogany chairs with scrolled reeded uprights, curved crest, pierced bar back centered by a roundel.
(Andrew Hartley)   (Six) $3,062

Two of a set of six 19th century mahogany dining chairs, the curved crest with inscribed line and carved florette, scrolled and wrythen uprights.
(Andrew Hartley)   (Six) $924

Two of a set of six George III mahogany dining chairs including two carvers, in the Sheraton style, the channelled back with curved crest, four bar back with three carved roundels.
(Andrew Hartley)   (Six) $4,200

Two of a set of four 19th century mahogany chairs including two carvers, in the Sheraton style, curved crest over three pierced and leaf carved splats.
(Andrew Hartley)   (Four) $314

Eight antique spindle-back country dining chairs in beech etc, with rush seats, three with arms and three-tier backs. (Brightwells) $1,950

Two of a set of eight early 19th century mahogany dining chairs, of Hepplewhite design, the pierced splat backs carved with a band of leaf ties with wheat sprays and bellflower pediments.
(Woolley & Wallis)   (Eight) $4,710

A pair of Irish mahogany side chairs, with pierced splat backs, scroll carving to a dipped crest, the drop in seats to molded edge frames, one 18th century, the other 19th century.(Woolley & Wallis) $1,386

Two of a set of eight Italian Neo-classical parcel-gilt fruitwood dining chairs, circa 1810, each backrest with curved figureheads above a faux bamboo and rope twist lattice, carved birdhead handholds.
(Skinner)   (Eight) $48,300

Two of a set of seven Sheraton period mahogany dining chairs, the reeded edge curved top rails with scroll ends and carved tassel pendants to a central tied acanthus shaped open splat.
(Woolley & Wallis)   (Seven) $2,380

Edwardian painted and caned satinwood armchair and side chair, circa 1895, each with oval backrest inset with a portrait roundel, with foliate painted frame. (Christie's) $2,185

Two of a set of six Edwardian mahogany dining chairs of Hepplewhite design, the shield backs finely carved with Prince-of-Wales plumes and pendants to the pierced splat. (Brightwells)   (Six) $1,110

Two of a set of eight 'Clissett' chairs, circa 1910, stained ash, open ladder backs, rush seat above turned legs with conforming stretchers. (Sotheby's) $3,024

Two of a set of twelve George III style mahogany dining chairs, including two armchairs, the arched top rails with acanthus carving above pierced vase shaped splats. (Bonhams) (Twelve) $7,452

Two of a set of six mahogany dining chairs, 19th century, in the Hepplewhite style, including a pair of armchairs, each with undulating arched top-rail and pierced vase splats with trailing flowerheads and bellflowers. (Christie's) (Six) $5,520

Two of a set of fourteen mahogany and marquetry dining chairs, of George III style, eight late Victorian six of later date, including two open armchairs, each with a double-arched back centered by a marquetry fan medallion. (Christie's) (Fourteen) $35,397

Two of a set of two of seven mahogany dining chairs, early 19th century, in the Hepplewhite style, including a pair of armchairs, each with serpentine arched back with pierced Gothic vase splat. (Christie's) (Seven) $2,560

Two of a set of ten mahogany dining chairs, 19th century and later, including a pair of armchairs, in the Hepplewhite style, each shield-shaped back with pierced vase shaped splats. (Christie's) (Ten) $6,62...

Two of a set of six William IV mahogany dining chairs with deep curved bar backs, upholstered drop-in seats in turned and carved front supports. (Brightwells)   (Six) $1,890

Pair of antique Country yew-wood side chairs with pierced splats, rush seats and turned stretchers to the cabriole legs. (Brightwells) $1,525

Two of a set of five Regency mahogany and brass inlaid dining chairs, with bar backs above stuffed over later leathered seats set on saber legs. (Bonhams)   (Five) $1,287

Two of a set of nine Victorian mahogany dining chairs, including a pair of scroll armchairs, each molded balloon-shaped back with curved horizontal splats with lotus ornament. (Christie's)   (Nine) $7,360

Two of a set of mahogany dining chairs, comprising a set of five George III chairs including an armchair, two of a later 19th century date including one armchair and another single chair of recent manufacture. (Christie's)   (Eight) $4,600

A George III style mahogany dining suite, by Waring & Gillow, early 20th century, comprising a set of eight Chippendale style dining chairs, an extending dining table, 240cm. long extended and a matching sideboard, 183cm. wide. (Bonhams) $3,360

Regency period mahogany bergère elbow chair, splayed back, cresting rail incised with bell flowers and scrolls, joined by reeded slightly splayed arm rests.
(G.A. Key) $6,314

Regency period mahogany nursing chair, arched splayed back, raised on saber front supports.
(G.A. Key) $2,748

An oak barrel chair, formed from a cut out oak banded cask, the seat fitted with a hinged lid, 62cm. diameter. (Bonhams) $200

An early Victorian mahogany show frame armchair, the button back and arms with leaf carved terminals, the arm fronts with leaf scroll sprays.
(Woolley & Wallis) $1,109

A pair of stained beechwood and gilt embellished open armchairs, 20th century, in the Baroque taste, after Andrea Brustolon, the serpentine stuff-over shaped backs with foliate C-scroll finials and stuff-over seats, 56in. wide.
(Christie's) $4,023

Victorian steer horn and upholstered armchair, circa 1870, arched back, with original upholstery, curved legs ending in casters, 36½in. high.
(Skinner) $1,035

A Victorian walnut low salon tub armchair, the arched back with scroll carved arm terminals above shaped front rail, on cabriole supports with upturned knurl feet, 89cm. (Bristol) $345

Early Victorian stained beech bergère tub chair, the arched back molded with scroll, plain apron and raised on fluted tapering circular front supports.(G.A. Key) $609

A good Regency mahogany armchair with square upholstered back and upholstered arms, supported by fluted scrolls and turned balusters.
(David Lay) $2,041

Regency mahogany bergère, with reeded frame and deep-buttoned padded cushions covered in green leather, above ring-turned baluster arm-supports.
(Christie's) $8,942

An early Victorian mahogany reclining armchair, the arms with reclining mechanism to the underside, the seat with sliding ratcheted foot-rest.
(Christie's) $2,795

Jacobean-style oak armchair, late 19th century, with simulated tapestry upholstery.
(Skinner) $345

Louis XVI beechwood bergère, late 18th/19th century, arched rectangular crest, padded scrolled arms on fluted supports, raised on circular tapering stop fluted legs, 35in. high. (Skinner) $1,840

A pair of Anglo-Indian metal-mounted armchairs, probably circa 1860, each with a toprail centered by the monogram CMR, above an oval back decorated with foliage and flowers.
(Christie's) $15,545

An Egg chair designed by Arne Jacobsen, manufactured by Fritz Hansen, the shaped shell covered in black naughhyde with a loose cushion, on a swivelling cast aluminum base.
(Woolley & Wallis) $2,240

A mid Victorian mahogany framed gentleman's armchair, circa 1880, the later upholstery above scrolled arms and raised on cabriole legs.
(Bonhams) $392

A William IV grained and parcel gilt desk chair, with curved padded back covered in close-nailed green suede, above a bracket and rail splat and a padded seat.
(Christie's) $5,589

A Victorian button back armchair, upholstered with a sprung seat, the front turned legs on original brass sunken panel capped castors.
(Woolley & Wallis) $448

A mid Victorian mahogany framed armchair, circa 1890, the shaped back above scrolled arms and raised on turned legs with castors. (Bonhams) $392

A Louis XV beechwood fauteuil à la reine, with cartouche upholstered panel back with floral posy cresting, having padded scroll arm supports and serpentine seat-rail. (Christie's) $2,743

A Regency mahogany caned bergère, circa 1810, the shaped and gadrooned back above sweeping arms, and raised on saber front legs. (Bonhams) $1,509

A Regency gentleman's reclining chair with mahogany frame having green leather and studded upholstery, fold-out foot rest. (Brightwells) $2,100

A mid Victorian mahogany three piece salon suite, comprising a chaise longue, a lady's and a gent's chair, with foliate carving and baluster turnings, the chaise 80in. wide. (Bonhams) $718

An Italian walnut open armchair, mid 18th century and later, in the Louis XV style, the cartouche shaped upholstered panel back with floral cresting and scroll arm supports. (Christie's) $1,480

A George III giltwood open armchair, circa 1780, the shaped padded back with molded frame continuing to scrolled arms, the serpentine seat on conforming cabriole legs. (Bonhams) $592

A George IV mahogany reclining armchair, by Robert Daws, with a padded back and seat and padded scrolled arms, above a pull out foot rest. (Bonhams) $2,464

An Anglo-Flemish oak and hide Burgomaster's chair, late 19th century, formerly owned by Sir William Gilbert, the Victorian lyricist. (Bonhams) $5,390

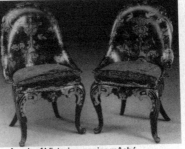

A mid Victorian walnut framed prayer chair, circa 1880, the scrolled and upholstered back above upholstered seat and raised on turned and twisted legs. (Bonhams) $266

A pair of Victorian papier-mâché and parcel gilt mother of pearl inlaid chairs, dated *1843*, each with an arched back and a scalloped edge above a drop-in padded seat with scrolled arm rests above a serpentine apron on cabriole legs. (Christie's) $4,388

A silvered throne chair, Indian, circa 1900, the arched crest with two rampant lions flanking an inscription *R.S. KABRA* surmounted by an urn finial. (Sotheby's) $20,040

A George IV mahogany framed gentleman's armchair with scroll arms, leather upholstered back, seat and arms on turned tapering front supports. (Brightwells) $1,848

A pair of mahogany caned bergères, 19th century, channelled overall with an ebonized line, each with curved back, sides and buttoned squab covered in simulated suede. (Christie's) $13,041

A carved giltwood bergère, 19th century, in the Louis XV style, with pierced foliate cresting and panelled upholstered back with Aubusson tapestry of putti. (Christie's) $2,743

An early 19th century mahogany elbow chair with shaped and buttoned leather upholstered back, scrolled arms and raised on slender cabriole front supports. (Brightwells) $1,294

A pair of carved giltwood and needlework upholstered open armchairs, late 19th /early 20th century, in the Louis XIV style, with rectangular panelled upholstered backs in gros and petit point needlework. (Christie's) $3,474

An unusual Victorian period carved walnut, possibly mahogany, adjustable sliding armchair, on sliding base and curved scroll carved front supports with brass castors. (Christie's) $2,961

Victorian walnut elbow chair with short splayed back, molded with rosettes, scroll etc, upholstered back seat and arm rests, serpentined apron molded with 'C' scrolls. (G.A. Key) $493

A Howard and Son armchair, the upholstered back, arms and seat above ring turned front legs and castors. (Bonhams) $678

A William IV rosewood library bergère chair, tub shaped with scrolled leaf and flower carved crest, downswept arms with scroll and leaf terminals. (Andrew Hartley) $9,73

Federal mahogany circular easy chair, New England, circa 1815-20, the arched crest above a curving back and out-scrolling arms on four vase and ring-turned frontal legs. (Skinner) $3,450

Georges de Feure for the salon of Madeleine Vionnet, low seat, 1924, faceted wood seat with traces of white paint, molded legs with angled H-form stretcher, 25¼in. (Sotheby's) $14,280

An Anglo-Indian metal-mounted armchair, in the George IV style, probably circa 1830, the back with a curved rectangular toprail above a deeply-buttoned back, flanked by a pair of scrolled armrests. (Christie's) $5,527

A Howard and Sons upholstered armchair, late 19th century, on turned legs with brass castors, the castors stamped Howard & Sons Ltd London. (Bonhams) $1,372

A Regency giltwood bergère, in the manner of Gillows, the arm-supports carved scrolling acanthus and floral patera, on leaf-wrapped tapering legs. (Christie's) $6,521

A Regency mahogany bergère, in the manner of Gillows, bowed top rail and molded arms, one with a later adjustable reading rest, the caned seat above a molded frieze. (Bonhams) $7,400

Queen Anne maple armchair, New England, circa 1740-60, the yoked crest over vasiform splat and molded stay-rail, flanked by raked stiles. (Skinner) $9,200

A Regency simulated rosewood library chair, in the manner of Henry Holland, with green leather and brass upholstered panelled back, with scroll apron below. (Christie's) $7,680

A carved mahogany open armchair, 19th century, in the Chippendale style, of generous proportions, the foliate scroll-carved top-rail and pierced interlaced Gothic splat having a stuff-over seat. (Christie's) $1,646

One of a set of three George III mahogany and inlaid armchairs, with curved bar top-rails inlaid with ebonized lines and reeded horizontal and pierced foliate elliptical oval rope-twist central splats. (Christie's) (Three) $2,303

Queen Anne carved walnut compass-seat armchair, in the Philadelphia manner, the shell- and volute-carved crest above a vasiform splat flanked by shepherd's-crook arms. (Sotheby's) $9,775

A beechwood and alder box seat armchair, East Anglia, early 19th century, the rectangular back with reeded vertical splats, the outswept arms on incurved supports, the box seat with hinged lid. (Christie's) $293

An Edwardian satinwood elbow chair, painted with trailing flowers, foliage and paterae within ebony stringing, the shield back with pierced interwoven splat.
(Andrew Hartley) $1,740

One of a pair of George II mahogany 'cockpen' open armchairs, circa 1760, each with a rectangular back and drop in seat, on square section chamfered legs.
(Bonhams) (Two) $29,400

One of a pair of silver and silver gilt armchairs and foot stools, Indian, circa 1880, the chairs with pierced scrolled cartouche-form back, the padded arms in the form of lions.
(Sotheby's) (Two) $14,231

An Arts & Crafts oak open armchair with outsplayed arms, rush back and seat, on H frame.
(Brightwells) $285

A pair of Scottish George III mahogany cockpen armchairs, each with a pierced latticework rectangular back, dished seat, on turned splayed legs joined by stretchers.
(Christie's) $10,247

An Edwardian painted satinwood elbow chair, in the manner of George Seddon, the shield back with pierced and waisted splat painted with a vase of flowers.
(Andrew Hartley) $4,350

A 17th century oak armchair with guilloche carved cresting rail above plain panel back, solid seat on baluster turned and square front supports.
(Brightwells) $2,503

A George III mahogany open armchair, circa 1760, the shaped and acanthus carved top rail above a pierced 'owl back' splat, the shaped arms joining a button leather drop in seat.
(Bonhams) $5,180

A Regency mahogany framed elbow chair, the curved crest with arched and gadrooned surmount, pierced and scroll carved bar back
(Andrew Hartley) $693

erre Chareau, armchair, circa
24, walnut, the shaped tapering
ck with open side panels, the
at upholstered in brown leather,
pering square section legs,
½in. (Sotheby's) $4,704

A pair of Chinese-Export bamboo
armchairs, early 19th century, each
with pierced geometric panels, on
six legs joined by stretchers.
(Christie's) $5,216

A George III mahogany library
reading chair, in the manner of
Morgan and Saunders, with a
curved top-rail and sliding rest with
ratcheted adjustable book slope.
(Christie's) $9,047

17th century oak monk's bench
ith adjustable top/back, solid seat
n baluster turned and square
upports with square stretchers,
t.3in. wide.
rightwells) $406

A pair of 17th century style oak
armchairs with mask and scroll
carved cresting rails above
guilloche frieze and floral inlaid
panel, solid seats.
(Brightwells) $1,478

One of a set of four carved
mahogany armchairs, early 19th
century, in the manner of Gillows,
the shield-shaped backs with foliate
splats radiating from a floral lunette.
(Christie's)   (Four) $2,961

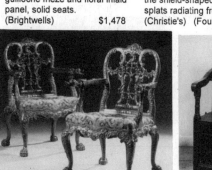

Regency mahogany and ebony
rung open armchair, circa 1815,
e bowed top rail and scrolled
rms above a leather drop in seat,
n saber legs.
Bonhams) $1,260

A pair of carved mahogany
armchairs, English, circa 1900, in
mid-eighteenth century style, backs
with pierced foliate splats crowned
by a bird, the out-curved arms
carved with bird's heads,
(Sotheby's) $10,020

A 17th century oak armchair with
rosette carved top rail bearing date
5 rosette and scroll carved panel
boxed seat with hinged lid, 20in.
wide.
(Brightwells) $1,940

18th century oak and fruit wood elbow chair, with arched cresting rail, vase shaped central splat joined by slightly splayed arms, solid seat and plain apron.
(G.A. Key) $597

Queen Victoria's personal travelling chair, believed used by Her Majesty when travelling between Windsor Castle and her retreat at Osborne House. Polished mahogany folding chair, shield shaped blue velvet padded back.
(Bosleys) $5,320

A Hepplewhite period mahogany elbow chair, the pierced splat ba with a carved honeysuckle and I pendant motif to a serpentine cr
(Woolley & Wallis) $1,

A George III elm elbow chair with arched crest, pierced waisted splat, out curved arms with scrolled ends on shaped supports, drop in upholstered seat, on chamfered square section legs.
(Andrew Hartley) $1,335

A pair of late 19th century Chinese carved hardwood armchairs, the open backs with a circular splat of a vase of flowers, deer, a bat and foliage to a shaped cresting.
(Woolley & Wallis) $308

Painted slat-back arm chair, Ne England, 18th century, the turn finials, arched slats, and down-turned scrolled handholds abo vase and ring turned legs.
(Skinner) $1,0

BUYER BEWARE
The value of a set of chairs increases exponentially (a set of eight can be worth twice as much as a set of six). The buyer should therefore pay attention to whether they are indeed an original set. If armchairs are included, compare the width of the front seat rails with the side chairs. It should be an inch or two wider, otherwise it may be a made up standard chair.
(Cotswold Auction Co.)

18th century mahogany tub elbow chair, scrolled pediment terminating in similar arm rests and raised on ring turned spindle back with central pierced splat.
(G.A. Key) $2,355

An Irish Chippendale mahogany elbow chair, the pierced carved splat back decorated with leaf sprays and florets and a serpent crest.
(Woolley & Wallis) $1,8

A Welsh oak and lipwork chair, early 20th century, the shaped back above drop in seat and raised on square tapered legs.
(Bonhams) $1,330

Set of early 19th century jockey scales, circular silvered dial, raised on fluted ring turned support, adjacent seat with slightly splayed back, by Henry Pooley & Son, Liverpool and Fleet Street, London, 37½in. (G.A. Key) $6,930

A mahogany framed open armchair, 19th century, the reeded frame and legs united by turned stretchers with a caned back and seat.
(Bonhams) $448

Maple slat-back armchair, Delaware River Valley, 18th century, turned stiles with turned ball finials joining reverse graduated arched slats on the shaped and scrolled handholds.
(Skinner) $9,200

Pair of painted hickory armchairs, possibly New York, early 20th century, the chairs with seven spindles, trapezoidal splint seats, and double stretchers, crackled white paint over earlier green.
(Skinner) $805

Child's Queen Anne maple armchair, probably Connecticut, 1775-1800, the serpentine crest with central scallop ending in angled ears above a vasiform splat.
(Skinner) $863

A George III mahogany open armchair, circa 1780, the straight top above a pierced 'owl eye' splat and shaped arms.
(Bonhams) $672

Painted and decorated pine chair table, possibly upstate New York, early 19th century, the rectangular overhanging top above bench seat joining cut-out ends with recessed panels, 52¼in. long.
(Skinner) $3,335

A George IV mahogany elbow chair, the shaped top rail with a gadroon crest and leaf carved ends above an open scroll and shell horizontal bar.
(Woolley & Wallis) $490

A pair of Regency mahogany hall chairs, each with a shield-shaped back with a pair of eagle-heads on a waisted support, with bowed solid seat. (Christie's) $21,691

A George III mahogany hall armchair, the waved toprail above a pierced Chinese-fretwork splat, with outcurved arms flanking a solid dished seat. (Christie's) $19,187

A matched pair of Regency mahogany hall chairs, attributed to Gillows, each with shell-carved back above a shaped seat on reeded tapering saber legs. (Christie's) $4,004

Two of a set of five George III oak hall chairs with oval backs painted with central panels of wild boars and initials, solid seats on square tapering front supports. (Brightwells) (Five) $3,430

A Victorian Gothic Revival oak hall chair, the pierced pointed-arch top surmounted by florette above panel back and wooden seat, 104cm. (Bristol) $262

A pair of George II oak and walnut hall chairs, each with a cartouche-shaped pierced back above a solid seat, on solid shaped supports, with plugged holes to seat, restorations. (Christie's) $3,167

A pair of Regency mahogany hall chairs, circa 1810, each with an oval molded back joining a scrolled waisted support centred by a painted oval panel. (Bonhams) $4,144

A pair of Victorian oak hall chairs, in the Gothic taste, the shaped trefoil arched backs with recessed arched shield with initials K in gilt, on square tapering legs. (Christie's) $945

A pair of mid Victorian mahogany hall chairs, each with an arched waisted back and solid seat, on ring turned tapering legs. (Bonhams) $493

A Victorian ebony and green leather upholstered reclining library armchair, padded seat and with a sliding ratcheted caned footrest below the seat.
(Christie's) $635

A George III mahogany open armchair, the rectangular padded back, scrolled arms and seat covered in deep-buttoned beige leather, on square legs.
(Christie's) $3,353

A George III mahogany library open armchair, with serpentine-crested rectangular padded back, armrests and seat covered in later petit-point needlework of flowers.
(Christie's) $13,348

A Victorian carved rosewood library bergère, with buttondown rectangular back and padded arm supports with buttondown seat and molded foliate uprights with flowerheads.
(Christie's) $2,961

An early Victorian rosewood and simulated-rosewood library reading-chair, the U-shaped back, arms and seat covered in close-nailed buttoned brown leather, with adjustable book-stand on turned reeded baluster legs.
(Christie's) $9,176

A George III carved mahogany open arm library chair, of Gainsborough design, with rectangular stuff-over back and padded splayed arm supports with scale and foliate scroll ornament.
(Christie's) $4,935

A mid 18th century walnut library armchair, upholstered in needlework, the back with a serpentine crest, open panelled arms with acanthus and shell fluted carved terminals, probably German.
(Woolley & Wallis) $4,200

A George III mahogany Gainsborough armchair, the open arms with downswept front to a later sprung seat.
(Woolley & Wallis) $1,916

A George II mahogany library open armchair, with stop-fluted serpentine arm-supports, on stop-fluted cabriole legs with foliage-carved ears and scrolled feet.
(Christie's) $63,403

A birch and elm high-back rocking chair, North Country, late 19th century, with curved and arcaded top-rail, wavy square section splats. (Christie's) $635

An oak and elm rocking armchair, Lake District, early 18th century, the twin panelled back with shaped top-rail initialled and dated *H.I.K. 1722*, with arms on turned supports, solid seat. (Christie's) $1,817

Painted Windsor comb-back rocking arm chair, New England, early 19th century, the curving rectangular crest above the tapering spindles. (Skinner) $230

Shaker painted armed rocker, Canterbury, New Hampshire, circa 1840, the shaped pommels above the lightly tapering stiles flanking the arched splats with bevelled top edges. (Skinner) $2,185

A 19th century American rocker, with turned supports. (Bonhams) $185

Shaker maple No. 7 production armless rocking chair, Mount Lebanon, New York, late 19th/early 20th century, the stiles surmounted by acorn form finials joined by taped back. (Skinner) $575

A 19th century child's ash and elm rocking chair, straight crest on reeded five bar back, shaped arms on baluster turned supports. (Andrew Hartley) $308

A yew-wood and elm rocking Windsor armchair, South Yorkshire/North Nottinghamshire, late 19th century, with a burr-yew pierced fret-carved central splat and outswept arms. (Christie's) $2,544

Bow-back Windsor rocking chair, New England, early 19th century, the bowed crest rail above eight spindles on a shaped pommel seat and bamboo turned legs, rockers added mid 19th century. (Skinner) $690

Queen Anne maple side chair, Massachusetts, circa 1740-60, the oked crest rail over vasiform splat nd molded shoe flanked by raked nd chamfered stiles. (Skinner) $4,313

Pair of Portuguese Colonial carved walnut side chairs, 18th century, each with foliate and C-scroll carved high backrest and slip seat on foliate carved cabriole legs ending in hoof feet. (Skinner) $1,150

One of a pair of mahogany side chairs, the pierced carved splat backs with rococo decoration, serpentine crests and molded carved rails, 18th century but later carved. (Woolley & Wallis) (Two) $1,078

Cherry turned and carved side chair, probably Amherst, Massachusetts area, late 18th century, the shaped crest rail ending in carved terminals over a vasiform splat and raked styles. (Skinner) $1,265

Pair of American Renaissance Revival carved rosewood side chairs, attributed to John Jeliff, circa 1865-70, with high scroll and architectural carved cresting centered by a maidenhead, (Skinner) $978

Victorian Wedgwood mounted black painted side chair, circa 1860, with open splat and circular splayed legs, inset with neoclassical jasperware medallions, 34in. high. (Skinner) $431

Chippendale carved mahogany side hair, Boston, Massachusetts, 760-80, the serpentine crest rail nds in raked molded terminals bove chip carving and a diamond nterlaced splat with C-scrolls. Skinner) $10,925

Two of five early 19th century cottage side chairs, with interlaced hooped ash backs, elm seats on turned legs with 'H' stretchers. (Woolley & Wallis) (Five) $2,541

Painted maple side chair, Portsmouth, New Hampshire, 1735-50, the carved yoke crest on a vasiform splat flanked by molded raked stiles above an over-upholstered seat. (Skinner) $3,738

A fruitwood, elm and beech
Windsor armchair, probably
Lincolnshire, mid 19th century, with
a pierced central splat, flattened
arms with inswept front supports.
(Christie's) $382

Late 18th/early 19th century comb
back elbow chair, elm seat, ring
turned splayed supports joined by a
crinoline stretcher.
(G.A. Key) $370

A yew-wood and elm Windsor
armchair, North East, early 19th
century, with a pierced and rounded
decorated splat, ring-turned front
arm supports, ring-turned legs and
crinoline stretchers.
(Christie's) $781

A yew-wood and elm "Gothic"
Windsor armchair, English, mid
18th century, with pointed arched
back and Gothic tracery splats,
incurved front arm supports.
(Christie's) $6,086

A yew-wood, elm and walnut
Windsor armchair, Thames Valley,
late 18th century, with a pierced
central splat and outswept arms
with incurved front arm supports.
(Christie's) $10,902

Windsor painted braced bow-back
side chair, New England, circa
1780, the bowed crest rail above
eight swelled spindles and shaped
saddle seat on splayed vase and
ring-turned legs.
(Skinner) $748

A 19th century yew wood Windsor
armchair, the low hooped back with
pierced shaped splat, scrolled arms
on turned supports, elm saddle seat
with scribe line.
(Andrew Hartley) $1,570

Early 19th century
fruitwood/oak/elm Windsor stick
back elbow chair, central pierced
splat, solid seat, raised on ring
turned splayed spindle supports.
(G.A. Key) $483

Dark-stained child's combed fan-
back Windsor armchair, labelled
Wallace Nutting, Saugus, Mass.
20th century, the serpentine crest
with scrolled ends above spindles
(Skinner) $1,380

A late Federal turned mahogany easy chair, probably New England, circa 1810, the serpentine crest flanked by ogival wings and outscrolled arms. (Sotheby's) $3,450

A George I style walnut framed upholstered wing armchair. (Bonhams) $708

English mid-Georgian mahogany wing armchair, mid-18th century, of typical form, with shaped wings, scrolled arms, and shell carved cabriole legs. (Skinner) $978

A wing armchair, in early 18th century style, the front walnut short cabriole legs with a turned and block 'H' stretcher to scroll block walnut back legs. (Woolley & Wallis) $616

Chippendale mahogany upholstered easy chair, late 18th century, New England, the serpentine crest above shaped wings and scrolled arms on square front legs. (Skinner) $3,738

Chippendale mahogany upholstered easy chair, New England, late 18th century, the arched crest above shaped wings continuing to outscrolled arms on down-sweeping supports. (Skinner) $2,760

A late 18th century wing armchair, the shaped back with a serpentine crest, with a cushion to the seat, on front mahogany square chamfered legs. (Woolley & Wallis) $2,669

Federal mahogany upholstered easy chair, New England, late 18th/early 19th century, the serpentine crest above scrolled arms and serpentine front seat rail. (Skinner) $4,888

A wing armchair, upholstered yellow ground hessian with applied pieces of old floral needlework. (Woolley & Wallis) $1,676

A Chippendale mahogany easy chair, Philadelphia, circa 1770, the arched serpentine crest flanked by ogival wings on rolled arms. (Sotheby's) $20,700

A George I style walnut framed wing arm chair, the shaped upholstered wing back, arms and seat above shell carved cabriole legs with claw and ball feet. (Bonhams) $1,417

A green leather upholstered wing armchair, parts George III, with a shaped back, out-turned arms and a padded seat, on channelled and chamfered square section legs. (Christie's) $2,544

A good Chippendale carved mahogany easy chair, New York, circa 1780, the arched crest flanked by ogival wings with outscrolled arms on cabriole legs. (Sotheby's) $21,850

A Queen Anne walnut wing armchair, the tapestry Flemish verdure, mid-16th century, the shaped arched top above projecting eared sides and outscrolled arms. (Christie's) $20,493

A George II walnut wing armchair, the rectangular padded back with projecting ears, outscrolled arms and loose squab cushion covered in later needlework, on scrolled slightly cabriole legs. (Christie's) $8,34:

A George III mahogany wing armchair, with ogee shaped sides and serpentine arched back, padded seat and cushion, on square chamfered legs joined by H-stretchers.(Christie's) $4,361

A George I elm wingback armchair, circa 1720, the down swept wings and scrolled arms above a loose cushion seat, on cabriole legs and castors. (Bonhams) $8,140

A walnut wing armchair, 20th century, with a high-back, arched top-rail, out-turned arms and loose cushion to the seat, on square cabriole legs. (Christie's) $1,02

18th century walnut silver chest, lifting lid over a dummy drawer, with two further full width drawers below and raised on bracket feet, 25in. (G.A. Key) $4,553

A carved oak bible box on stand, with molded edged plank lid, carved strap work front and side panels, the stand with similar drawer, 25in. wide. (Andrew Hartley) $6,776

A red-painted pine and poplar blanket chest, New York, 1720-50, the hinged cleated top above a well and a drawer with a mid-molding and shaped apron, 38in. wide. (Sotheby's) $5,462

Painted pine storage box, possibly Ohio, early 19th century, the rectangular hinged molded top opening to shallow and deep compartments above a dovetail constructed tapering box, 47¾in. wide. (Skinner) $3,450

Goanese crème painted and parcel-gilt coffer on stand, 18th century, the two-train chiming movement signed *David Le Feure, Amsterdam,* lift-top, scrolled base with leafy detail, paw feet. (Skinner) $1,553

A painted iron strongbox on stand, German, early 17th century, painted overall with flower heads and small vignettes, the hinged lid with pierced lock plate and seven bolts, with a smaller interior lockable compartment, 32½in. wide. (Christie's) $5,486

Grain painted pine chest over drawers, northern New England, circa 1830, molded top lifts above a cavity over two drawers, original putty painting using red, green, and yellow with umber tones, 38in. wide. (Skinner) $16,100

A Spanish leather covered coffer, 17th century, of rectangular form with domed cover, with iron lockplate and twin handles, decorated overall with iron studwork, 39in. wide. (Christie's) $914

Blue painted pine chest over drawer, New England, early 19th century, the hinged pine top lifts above a cavity and a single drawer, on frontal shaped bracket feet and bootjack ends, 36in. wide. (Skinner) $1,840

A Continental cream japanned and gilt chinoiserie decorated chest, late 18th/early 19th century, probably Dutch, of arc en arbalette outline, with an overhanging molded top, 36¼in. wide.
(Christie's) $3,619

A William and Mary oak chest, of two short and three long graduated drawers with brass bail drop handles on bracket feet, 37in. wide.
(Bonhams) $770

A fine Chippendale figured cherrywood blocked reverse-serpentine chest of drawers, Connecticut, circa 1780, the shaped thumb-molded top above four graduated long drawers 37in. wide.
(Sotheby's) $24,15

A George III mahogany serpentine fronted chest of three long graduated drawers, having satinwood stringing and cross-banded edge, shaped under with splay feet, 3ft.7in. wide.
(Brightwells) $5,100

A late Victorian walnut tool chest and contents, circa 1882, with brass stamp, *RD Melhuish & Sons London, Prize 1884 Technical Schools*, 112cm. wide.
(Bonhams) $1,064

Federal mahogany and flame birch veneer birch bowfront chest of drawers, Portsmouth, New Hampshire, 1805-15, the edge of the birch top is outlined with patterned inlay above a case of fou cockbeaded drawers, 40¼in. wide.
(Skinner) $83,90

A George III mahogany bachelor's chest fitted with brushing slide above two short and three long drawers, on bracket feet, 2ft.9in. wide.
(Brightwells) $3,080

A walnut bachelor's chest, the folding half-top above a small drawer and three graduated long drawers, on bracket feet, late 19th/early 20th century, 27¼in. wide.
(Christie's) $7,825

A walnut and seaweed marquetry banded chest, early 18th century and later, the quarter veneered top crossbanded and bordered with foliate banding, with stylized foliate inlay, 40in. wide.
(Christie's) $11,337

A George III mahogany chest of serpentine shape fitted with two short and three long graduated drawers, 3ft.9in. wide. (Brightwells) $7,938

Chippendale mahogany serpentine chest of drawers, Boston, circa 1760-80, the overhanging molded top with serpentine front and serpentine sides over conforming cockbeaded case of four graduated drawers, 36in. wide. (Skinner) $34,500

A George II mahogany chest of drawers, circa 1750, the rectangular top with molded edge above four long graduated drawers, 30½in. wide. (Bonhams) $6,216

A Dutch walnut and marquetry bombé fronted chest, late 18th/early 19th century, inlaid overall with floral marquetry, the undulating overhanging top with a vase of flowers with birds and butterflies, 36½in. wide. (Christie's) $7,314

A fruitwood press chest, East Anglia, late 18th century, the press section with an arched top centered by a carved scallop shell, above a chest with two short drawers flanking a molded front drawer above three further long drawers, 36in. wide.(Bonhams) $3,822

A mahogany bachelor's chest, the associated hinged top above two short and three long drawers, basically 18th century converted from a four drawer chest of drawers, 32½in. wide. (Bonhams) $3,256

A George III mahogany bowfront chest, of small size, with a molded edge and fitted with a slide containing four long drawers below, 35½in. wide. (Christie's) $7,680

A late Regency mahogany bowfront chest, with four long graduated drawers, flanked by gadrooned moldings, on later bun feet, 98cm. wide. (Bonhams) $678

A fine Queen Anne figured mahogany block-front chest of drawers, Boston, Massachusetts, 1750-70, the shaped molded top above four graduated long drawers within beaded surrounds, 34½in. wide. (Sotheby's) $37,375

A late 17th century oak two-section block-front chest of four long drawers, with applied molded drawer fronts, on later plinth base, width 100cm. (Bristol) $879

Good Regency period mahogany Scotch chest, the central deep drawer inlaid with ebonized stringing and flanked on either side by two shorter drawers, three further full width graduated drawers below, 51in.(G.A. Key) $1,491

Victorian campaign chest of drawers, of polished mahogany, mounted with brass bound corners and angles, breaking into two sections for transportation, 45in. wide. (Bosleys) $1,278

Classical mahogany carved and mahogany veneer bureau, Massachusetts, circa 1825, the scrolled back above two cock-beaded swelled short drawers, flanked by ovolo corners and ring-turned quarter engaged posts, 42in. wide. (Skinner) $1,955

A good Federal mahogany and figured maple-inlaid birchwood chest of drawers, probably Vermont, circa 1810, the oblong top with outset corners above four long drawers, 44in. wide. (Sotheby's) $8,050

Federal wavy birch and grained cherry chest of drawers, North Shore, Massachusetts, early 19th century, the curving splash board with scrolled terminals above the top with ovolo front corners, 39½in. wide. (Skinner) $1,380

A good Regency mahogany bowfront chest, the top with a reeded edge above four long graduated drawers, mahogany lined, 3ft.3½in. wide. (Woolley & Wallis) $2,395

Painted and decorated pine child's classical chest of drawers, New England, 1835-45, original brown and red paint with gold and olive highlights, original turned pulls, 22in. wide. (Skinner) $748

An 18th century oak chest with walnut crossbanding, two short over three long drawers, later brass drop handles, on bracket feet, 30¼in. wide. (Andrew Hartley) $1,386

English Jacobean oak chest of drawers, circa 1680, with rectangular case fitted with four panelled drawers on bun feet, 37½in. wide.
(Skinner)　　　　$3,450

British Colonial brass-bound camphorwood campaign chest, mid-19th century, of typical form, pair of drawers over three graduated drawers, raised on turned feet, 49in. wide.
(Skinner)　　　　$920

arly 19th century mahogany bow-
nt chest of two short and three
ng drawers, flanked on either side
wrythen pilasters, 39in. wide.
.A. Key)　　　　$1,885

:lassical faux bois chest of
:rawers, Massachusetts, 1825-35,
e splashboard with scrolled and
ourred ends over four drawers, top
ith red satin, the drawers with
arly graining simulating
nahogany, 43in. wide.
Skinner)　　　　$546

A small Dutch marquetry bombé chest, veneered in walnut, the top inlaid with an urn of flowers, foliage spray and stringing, 34in. wide.
(Woolley & Wallis)　　$2,874

Federal mahogany carved and mahogany veneer bureau, Massachusetts, circa 1825, the scrolled backboard above a swelled case of two cockbeaded short drawers on projecting lower case of drawers, 40in. wide.
(Skinner)　　　　$2,415

late 17th century stained pine and
uitwood joined block fronted chest
three drawers, the molded edge
ne top above twin geometric
nel molded drawer fronts, 87cm.
de. (Bristol)　　　$1,441

A George III mahogany bow fronted chest, with beaded edged top, two short over three long drawers with turned wood handles, shaped apron and splayed feet, 45½in. wide.
(Andrew Hartley)　　$1,020

Painted pine chest over drawers, New England, early 19th century, molded lift top over deep well case of two thumb-molded drawers with incised beading on cut-out legs, 39½in. wide.
(Skinner)　　　　$1,495

A good Queen Anne carved and figured cherrywood bonnet-top chest on chest, Connecticut, circa 1740, in two parts; the swan's neck pediment surmounted by an urn-and-corkscrew finial above three short drawers, 42½in. wide. (Sotheby's) $19,550

A George III mahogany chest on chest, with molded cornice, two short over three long drawers above, 47½in. wide. (Andrew Hartley) $2,683

A George I burr-elm tallboy, with fruitwood cornice, waist and apron moldings, the cavetto cornice above three short drawers one with secret drawers to the back, 38½in. wide. (Christie's) $20,493

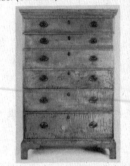

Chippendale cherry and maple carved tall chest of drawers, probably Connecticut, 18th century, the flat molded cornice above a case of central fan carved short drawer flanked by two sets of small drawers, 37in. wide. (Skinner) $46,000

A George III mahogany chest on chest, circa 1790, the molded cornice above two short and three long graduated drawers, set on a base with three long graduated drawers, 114cm. wide. (Bonhams) $2,380

Chippendale tiger maple tall chest, southeastern New England, circa 1780, the molded cornice over a case of six graduated thumb-molded long drawers on bracket feet, 36in. wide. (Skinner) $5,750

A George III mahogany chest on chest, with molded and dentil cornice, two short over three long drawers flanked by inlaid canted corners, 45in. wide. (Andrew Hartley) $2,590

An 18th century walnut chest on chest, the molded cornice above three frieze drawers, with three long graduated drawers under, 106cm. wide. (Bonhams) $7,700

Chippendale cherry chest-on-chest, Delaware River Valley, circa 1770-90, in two sections, the upper with a case fitted with three thumbmolded short drawers over two thumbmolded short drawers and three graduated long drawers, 40in. wide.(Skinner) $12,650

An early Georgian oak chest on stand, with crossbanding, molded cornice, two short over three long drawers, 38¾in. wide. (Andrew Hartley) $3,080

A Jacobean style oak chest of two short and three long drawers with molded fronts, on stand fitted with drawer with turned supports and flat stretchers, 3ft.5in. (Brightwells) $2,475

A good Queen Anne figured maple high chest of drawers, Connecticut or Rhode Island, circa 1750, in two parts; the overhanging cornice above two short and three graduated long drawers, 39¼in. wide. (Sotheby's) $17,250

The Adams and Cranch Family important William and Mary japanned pine high chest of drawers, the case by 'Park,' the japanning probably by Nehemiah Partridge, Boston, Massachusetts 1712-25, 40¼in. wide. (Sotheby's) $1,597,500

A Queen Anne walnut and line inlaid chest on stand, the double domed cornice with molded edge raised on later cabriole legs and claw and ball feet, 41in. wide. (Bonhams) $4,144

A late 18th century oak chest of two short and three long drawers, crossbanded in mahogany, on base fitted with single drawer with cabriole supports carved shell knees and hoof feet, 3ft.3in. (Brightwells) $9,000

An early 18th century walnut chest of two small and three graduated drawers with crossbanding and drawer-fronts of seaweed marquetry, on later stand with five twist-turned supports, 3ft.1in. wide. (Brightwells) $2,250

Queen Anne carved and figured cherrywood bonnet-top high chest of drawers, Connecticut River Valley, 1740-60, in two parts; the swan's neck pediment with flower terminals, 44½in. wide. (Sotheby's) $25,300

A rare Queen Anne burl maple-veneered flat-top high chest of drawers, Boston, Massachusetts, 1730-50, the shaped apron below hung with pendant acorns, on cabriole legs, 37in. wide. (Sotheby's) $16,100

A Regency mahogany and inlaid secrétaire chiffonier, inlaid with ebony lines, the shelved galleried superstructure with S-scroll uprights containing four drawers, 36in. wide. (Christie's) $5,520

A mid Victorian mahogany chiffonier of small size, 89cm. wide. (Bonhams) $265

A Victorian mahogany chiffonier, the shelved superstructure with triangular pediment ledge back and ring-turned uprights, 36in. wide. (Christie's) $2,024

A 19th century mahogany chiffonier, the raised back with spindle turned gallery and two shelves on baluster turned supports, 54in. wide. (Andrew Hartley) $1,274

A Victorian brass-mounted black and gold-japanned chiffonier, adapted, superstructure with a square platform cresting on a spreading support, above two cupboards flanking a mirror, 48½in. wide. (Christie's) $5,589

A Regency mahogany chiffonier, with molded edged oblong top, two dummy freize drawers with turned handles over two shaped panelled doors enclosing shelving, 37¼in. wide. (Andrew Hartley) $1,453

A simulated rosewood and parcel-gilt chiffonier, in the Regency style, with a superstructure of open shelves supported by S-scroll uprights above two frieze drawers and cupboards, 42½in wide. (Christie's) $1,570

A mid Victorian mahogany chiffonier, circa 1860, fitted with a concealed frieze drawer and raised on a plinth base, some restorations, 81cm. wide. (Bonhams) $1,120

A William IV rosewood chiffonier, with a shelved and mirrored back superstructure with triangular pediment with lotus scrolls and scroll fret supports, on a plinth base, 39½in. wide. (Christie's) $2,528

An early 19th century faded mahogany clothes press, the molded dentil cornice above an interior with a brass hanging rail and two sliding trays, 4ft.2in. wide. (Woolley & Wallis) $3,375

A late Victorian mahogany gentleman's clothes press, by Howard and Sons Ltd, London, the rectangular gadrooned top above two acanthus molded panelled doors, 49½in. wide. (Bonhams) $1,311

A George II Cuban mahogany clothes press, the cavetto molded cornice above an interior with oak sliding trays, 3ft.8in. wide. (Woolley & Wallis) $3,992

A 19th century Jersey mahogany clothes press, the detachable gadroon cornice to a plain frieze with a bead edge, above adjustable shelves enclosed by a pair of rectangular panel doors, 4ft.5¼in. wide. (Woolley & Wallis) $1,492

A George II mahogany clothes-press, in the manner of Giles Grendey, the rectangular dentilled cornice above a pair of shaped fielded-panelled doors enclosing seven later slides, 49½in. wide. (Christie's) $7,000

A Scottish Regency mahogany clothes-press, crossbanded in rosewood to the front, the inverted breakfront cornice above a plain frieze and a pair of panelled doors enclosing four slides and a later hanging-rail, 57in. wide. (Christie's) $3,003

A good early Victorian mahogany bowfront clothes press, the interior with sliding trays and a later brass hanging rail, enclosed by a pair of well figured veneered doors, 4ft.5in. wide. (Woolley & Wallis) $2,310

An 18th century oak press cupboard on chest, with molded and dentil cornice, two ogee arched, fielded panel doors, 48½in. wide. (Andrew Hartley) $4,060

A George III mahogany campaign hanging press, the molded and dentil cornice over two panelled doors, two drawers below, 57½in. wide.(Andrew Hartley) $2,320

A small Cape Dutch commode, 20th century, with a shaped top and cartouche panelled sides, with three serpentine fronted drawers, 28in. wide. (Christie's) $1,295

A bowfront commode, mahogany veneered, the top crossbanded in kingwood with fine stringing, the front with four drawers, oak and cedar lined, 3ft.6in. (Woolley & Wallis) $4,151

A late Louis XV ormolu-mounted kingwood, tulipwood and marquetry breakfront commode, by Jean Chrysostome Stumpff and Martin Ohneberg, breccia marble top, 43½in. wide. (Christie's) $24,219

A Russian mahogany commode, early 19th century, inlaid overall with checker line inlay, the rectangular top with canted front corners above four graduated long drawers, 35½in. wide. (Christie's) $14,904

Louis XV kingwood-style marquetry inlaid tulipwood and marble-top two-drawer commode, 20th century, serpentine top and case on angular cabriole legs, 27½in. wide. (Skinner) $1,265

A gilt-bronze and parquetry commode after Leleu, Paris, circa 1880, the rouge Languedoc marble top above a frieze drawer applied with foliage and two drawers, sans travers, centered by a crossbanded diamond reserve, 89cm. wide. (Sotheby's) $13,627

A South German rosewood and tulipwood marquetry bombé commode, 18th century, surmounted by a serpentine, containing two long drawers with quarter veneered scroll cartouche panes, 48in. wide. (Christie's) $5,451

A George III satinwood and marquetry bowfront commode, attributed to Mayhew and Ince, crossbanded overall in rosewood, the rectangular top with a central tablet in a fan medallion surrounded by swag husks, 34in. wide. (Christie's) $130,285

A Louis XIV ormolu-mounted and brass-inlaid tortoiseshell and ebony boulle commode, by Nicolas Sageot, in première partie, inlaid overall with scrolling foliage, the rounded rectangular top centered by Venus with attendants, 52in. wide.(Christie's) $465,750

black and gilt-lacquered, panned and parcel-gilt commode, corated overall with foliate rders and with Chinese dscape panels with figures, the mi-lune top with figures, 47½in. de. (Christie's) $13,041

A Dutch walnut and marquetry commode, late 18th century, the **shaped quartered top centered by a bird and urn of flowers above four** graduated waved drawers decorated with floral sprays, 41in. wide. (Bonhams) $7,000

A George III mahogany elliptical commode, late 18th century, with a single drawer, two cupboards, with some later green wash, 95cm. wide. (Bonhams) $2,940

Transitional kingwood, tulipwood nd fruitwood marquetry petite ommode, circa 1770, the reakfront gray fossil marble top vith molded edge above canted orners above two inlaid long rawers, 33in. wide. Bonhams) $5,920

A Swedish tulipwood and palisander bombé commode, in the manner of Christian Linning, mid 18th century, the associated red-brown marble top above three parquetry inlaid crossbanded drawers, 46½in. wide. (Bonhams) $7,000

A French rosewood, crossbanded and marquetry serpentine commode, 18th century and later, surmounted by a molded rance marble top, containing two short and two long drawers, 37½in. wide. (Christie's) $5,851

n Austrian satinwood, rosewood arquetry and parcel-gilt ommode, circa 1840, of serpentine rm, shaped carrara marble top oon a serpentine front with five rawers inlaid with rosewood rabesques, 54½in. wide. onhams) $2,002

A Lombardy walnut bombé commode, 18th century, surmounted by a later green veined marble top, the ogee hipped form containing three long drawers and applied with pierced gilt metal rococo handles, 48½in. wide. (Christie's) $18,095

A George III satinwood, harewood, rosewood and burr ash demi-lune commode, circa 1800, the later pink and white veined marble top above a central frieze drawer and two flanking over a cupboard door, 50½in. wide. (Bonhams) $4,900

A George III mahogany tray topped commode, the square galleried top above two inlaid cabinet doors with two drawers under, 50cm. wide.
(Bonhams) $1,463

A George III mahogany and line-inlaid commode, with a hinged top and front inlaid in imitation of panelled doors and six short drawers, 24½in. wide.
(Christie's) $1,090

A late 18th century mahogany Lancashire night commode, the hinged flap top to down scroll supports to a hinged seat flap revealing a pierced interior.
(Woolley & Wallis) $700

George III period mahogany night cupboard with tray top over two doors enclosing cupboard, double dummy drawer front below enclosing a fitted pot, 20in.
(G.A. Key) $3,456

A matched pair of George III mahogany bedside commodes, each with rectangular pierced gallery with serpentine front edge above a frieze drawer and a pair of doors, 22in. wide.
(Christie's) $36,707

A Charles X maple and amaranth-inlaid bedside commode, by Cordier, circa 1832, the eared top with inset variegated gray marble tablet above a tambour shutter inlaid with concentric stars and rosettes, 17½in. wide.
(Christie's) $3,089

A George III mahogany crossbanded and checker-strung bedside commode, applied with ebony and boxwood lines, with a hinged lidded top and lidded compartment below, 24in. wide.
(Christie's) $1,656

George III period mahogany tray top night cupboard, the roller shutter front applied below with a lion mask ring handle, enclosing original pot, 19½in.
(G.A. Key) $1,450

A late 18th century mahogany night commode, the rectangular top with a shaped gallery pierced with hand grips, above a tambour shuttered compartment and a pull out pot holder, 19¾in.
(Woolley & Wallis) $1,400

An 18th century hanging corner cupboard, the walnut front with a key cavetto molded cornice and swan neck pediment terminating in gilt florets, 28½in. wide. (Woolley & Wallis) $894

A German inlaid walnut bowfront corner cabinet, 18th century style, the twin doors inlaid with ebony and boxwood panels over conforming full-width drawer, 89.5cm. wide. (Bristol) $570

Biedermeier willowwood corner cabinet, mid-19th century, with shaped molded top above a frieze drawer over a panelled cabinet door, on shaped feet, 36in. long. (Skinner) $1,380

A George III oak standing corner cupboard with breakfront molded cornice, two arched panelled doors enclosing shaped shelving, 50in. wide. (Andrew Hartley) $2,156

A George III oak corner cupboard with mahogany crossbanding, molded and dentil cornice over a blind fret frieze, arched fielded panel door, 31in. wide. (Andrew Hartley) $910

A bowfront corner cupboard, with a shaped back fitted with a shelf to the top, a cavetto cornice and three shelves to the interior, enclosed by a pair of black and gold lacquer doors, 24in. (Woolley & Wallis) $770

George III black japanned hanging corner cabinet, 18th century, bowfronted design fitted with two doors opening to shelves, decorated all over with Chinese scenes, 24in. wide. (Skinner) $1,265

An early 19th century bowfront corner cupboard, mahogany veneered, the painted interior enclosed by a pair of doors inlaid stringing and elliptical marquetry panels, 28in. (Woolley & Wallis) $840

An oak standing corner cupboard, English, early 19th century, with molded cornice and a pair of doors with applied panels (locked), above a smaller similar pair of doors, 44in. wide. (Christie's) $3,657

A George III mahogany bow fronted corner cupboard, crossbanded with shell marquetry patera and checker banding, molded cornice, 29in. wide.(Andrew Hartley) $1,668

A George III mahogany bowfronted corner cupboard, circa 1780, the pair of cupboard doors open to reveal three shelves and three drawers, 76cm. wide. (Bonhams) $1,316

A George III mahogany bow front hanging corner cupboard with pair of solid doors having H hinges enclosing shelves, 3ft.9in. (Brightwells) $1,680

An ormolu mounted, tulipwood, rosewood, fruitwood, harewood, marquetry and parquetry encoignure, 19th century, in the Louis XV style, with shaped red and white mottled marble top, 29in. wide. (Christie's) $4,754

A pair of south German walnut fruit wood and marquetry upright corner cabinets, late 19th /early 20th century, each upper part with a molded cornice enclosed by a pair of glazed panelled doors between canted angles, 34½in. wide. (Christie's) $4,023

A George III oak corner cupboard, the molded cornice over mahogany veneered frieze with inlaid checker banding, ogee panelled door with marquetry shell patera, 33¼ x 45¼in. (Andrew Hartley) $616

An antique oak corner cupboard, the upper section fitted with a pair of glazed doors with pair of solid double panel doors under, 4ft.1in. x 7ft.4in. high. (Brightwells) $2,775

An oak and mahogany corner cupboard, basically 18th century, the dentil molded cornice above a glazed door, 30¼in. wide. (Bonhams) $400

A Louis XV ormolu-mounted tulipwood and parquetry encoignure, diagonally-banded overall, with later serpentine-fronted white marble top, 24in. wide. (Christie's) $33,534

330

A George III mahogany standing corner cupboard, crossbanded with stringing, molded cornice, two panelled doors with reeded banding, 49½in. wide. (Andrew Hartley) $3,140

A Dutch walnut corner table, 19th century, of serpentine outline, with a molded top above a shaped conforming frieze, on scroll carved hocked cabriole legs, 41in. wide. (Christie's) $2,726

A painted corner cupboard, North/Central European, 19th century, decorated overall with flowers and doves, with an upper astragal glazed door above a small drawer and further cupboard door below, 31in. wide. (Christie's) $1,463

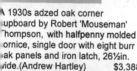
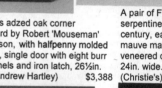
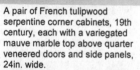

A 1930s adzed oak corner cupboard by Robert 'Mouseman' Thompson, with halfpenny molded cornice, single door with eight burr oak panels and iron latch, 26½in. wide. (Andrew Hartley) $3,388

A pair of French tulipwood serpentine corner cabinets, 19th century, each with a variegated mauve marble top above quarter veneered doors and side panels, 24in. wide. (Christie's) $2,220

A fine south German fruitwood and silvered corner cabinet, circa 1760, of tapered form, the scrolled plinth top carved with grapes, acanthus scrolls and rocaille above an arched tapering triple glazed door, 38½in. wide. (Bonhams) $4,736

George III mahogany upright corner cupboard, early 19th century, with canted angles, the upper part with a molded cornice and enclosed by a pair of panelled doors, 44in. wide. (Christie's) $3,108

A Louis XV ormolu-mounted tulipwood, kingwood and marquetry encoignure, by BVRB, the shaped molded triangular rouge griotte marble top above a shaped panelled door with inlaid floral spray, 27¼in. wide. (Christie's) $20,493

A George III oak and mahogany corner cupboard with scrolled pediment, single astragal glazed door enclosing shaped shelving, canted corners and molded base, 26in. wide, 43in. high. (Andrew Hartley) $1,201

A late Victorian ebonized, amboyna and marquetry credenza, the stepped superstructure with a cavetto frieze with incised decoration, the deep frieze with stylized anthemion ornament, 76in. wide. (Christie's) $2,250

A Lombardy walnut and marquetry credenza and prie-dieu or Inginocchiatio, 17th century with later restoration, of angular concave outline, with geometric lines and crossbanded, 28¾in. wide. (Christie's) $9,200

A Victorian burr-walnut and gilt-metal mounted credenza, with foliate molded edge and frieze enclosed by an ogee arched glazed panel door headed with female mask and foliate spray, 67in. wide. (Christie's) $4,935

A mid Victorian walnut credenza with mirror back, circa 1880, the later back above a bowfronted base, both with boxwood inlays and stringing, 150cm. wide. (Bonhams) $2,240

An Italian carved walnut credenza, 17th century and later, with a **rectangular molded top** fitted with a drawer between drawers with masks enclosed by a panel door below, 27½in. wide. (Christie's) $2,944

A late Victorian, amboyna, marquetry and gilt-metal mounted credenza, of breakfront outline, in the Aesthetic Movement taste, surmounted by an arched divided and mirrored shelved mirror back, 68in. wide.(Christie's) $1,829

A Victorian parquetry and amboyna inlaid ebonized gilt metal mounted credenza, the central cupboard applied with oval parquetry panel within amboyna borders, 152cm. wide. (Bristol) $1,470

Renaissance Revival walnut, burl walnut, marquetry, part ebonized, and gilt incised credenza, third quarter 19th century, shaped removable pediment over a shaped top with central cabinet door, 21in. wide. (Skinner) $7,475

Italian Renaissance-style inlaid walnut credenza, late 19th century, the canted rectangular case fitted with frieze drawers and doors and inlaid allover with foliate marquetry, 84 long. (Skinner) $978

An oak cupboard, English, late 17th century, with a foliate filled lunette carved frieze and a pair of twin panel doors, 42½in. wide.
(Christie's) $3,478

A red-stained pine hanging cupboard, American, 19th century, the rectangular top above a conforming case over glazed door with molded mullions, 30½in. wide.
(Christie's) $3,760

An oak livery cupboard with carved cornice, two doors below each with two small over a large raised and fielded panel, 18th century, 57¼in. wide.
(Andrew Hartley) $2,800

An oak tridarn, North Wales, mid 18th century, the upper section with molded cornice and frieze with cup hooks, on ring-turned column supports, the center section with a pair of arched fielded panelled doors, 54in. wide.
(Christie's) $11,885

A George III satinwood bowfront cupboard, the shaped eared rectangular top above a pair of panelled doors enclosing a shelf to each side, between reeded columns, 43½in. wide.
(Christie's) $10,845

A grain-painted pine hanging cupboard, American, 19th century, the rectangle top above a conforming case with rectangular glazed door with mullions revealing a shelved interior, 22½in. wide.
(Christie's) $2,350

An oak standing cupboard, English or Flemish, early 16th century, five sided and profusely carved, with a molded frieze and Romayne heads within Renaissance grotesquework, 40in. wide.
(Christie's) $11,811

An oak cwpwrdd deuddarn, North Wales, 1721, the overhanging top section with a molded cornice above a frieze bearing the letters *CAE* and dated *1721*, on block feet, 70½in. wide.
(Bonhams) $8,085

An oak and mahogany crossbanded housekeeper's, cupboard, West Midlands, early 19th century, the upper section with a later molded cornice and enclosed by a pair of four panel doors, 71in. wide.
(Christie's) $3,826

An 18th century oak cupboard with dentil cornice, gouge carved frieze, fluted corner pilasters, fitted with three short and two long drawers on bracket feet, 3ft.11in. wide.
(Brightwells) $5,600

A painted two door cupboard, English, late 17th century, with a molded top and continuous sides with metal carrying handles, the front with an overall checker pattern, 42½in. wide.
(Christie's) $5,486

An oak deuddarn, North Wales, 19th century, the upper section with molded cornice and plain frieze with drop pendants, above three ogee pointed arched fielded panel doors, 55in. wide.
(Christie's) $5,486

An oak and marquetry press cupboard, English, late 19th/early 20th century, in the 17th century style, with an arcaded frieze supported on bulbous gadrooned ionic style columns and flanking a central cupboard, 45in. wide.
(Christie's) $4,571

An oak livery cupboard, English, early 17th century, with a molded top and a whirl filled guilloche frieze raised on turned column supports, with a pair of panelled doors, 49in. wide. (Christie's) $5,120

A German walnut, ebonized and seaweed marquetry Schrank, first half 17th century, the molded cornice above a panelled marquetry inlaid frieze and a pair of molded cupboard doors, 64¼in. wide.
(Bonhams) $7,280

A George III oak housekeeper's cupboard, the molded cornice above a pair of panelled cupboard doors, raised on bracket feet, 135cm. wide.
(Bonhams) $2,464

An Elizabethan style oak cupboard, the rectangular top above a guilloche carved frieze drawer above a cupboard door with an arched foliate inlaid panel, 49¾in. wide. (Bonhams) $1,263

A late Georgian oak hall cupboard, the six-panel front fitted with two doors beneath a fluted cornice, and six drawers below, 6ft.6in. wide.
(Brightwells) $2,426

mid Victorian rosewood
davenport, the mirrored back above
sloping fall, the exterior with a
ng pen drawer with a cupboard
nder, 56cm. wide.
Bonhams) $2,310

A Chinese export camphorwood
and ebony strung davenport, early
19th century, the top with a lidded
compartment for stationery with
molded glass inkwell, 29½in. wide.
(Christie's) $2,860

A Victorian burr-walnut piano top
davenport with pop-up stationery
compartment, slide out writing
surface with interior drawers, side
doors enclosing four drawers,
2ft.3in. wide.
(Brightwells) $5,880

A William IV flame mahogany
davenport, possibly satinwood, with
pierced spindle gallery, parts
missing, and hinged green leather
ined slope enclosing a satinwood
nterior, 20in. wide.
Christie's) $5,486

A mid Victorian walnut davenport,
the exterior with four short drawers,
front turned supports missing,
54cm. wide.
(Bonhams) $1,463

An early 19th century rosewood
davenport with ormolu gallery,
leather inset slope, four drawers
and pen drawer to side, 19in. wide.
(Brightwells) $3,360

A Victorian walnut davenport, the
satinwood interior fitted with three
small drawers and three drawer-
fronts concealing a pull-out pen
compartment, 22in. wide.
(Brightwells) $1,232

A Victorian rosewood davenport
with raised gallery, with tapering
octagonal front columns, fitted with
four side drawers and pen drawer,
27in. wide. (Brightwells)
                           $2,541

A Regency rosewood davenport
with pierced brass gallery, red
leather inset writing slope, the one
side with fitted pen drawer, writing
slide and four graduated drawers,
20in. wide.
(Brightwells) $9,540

A George IV mahogany davenport, with a low three-quarter gallery, leather-lined molded writing slope and concealed stationery drawer, four drawers to the right-hand side and opposing false drawers, 24in. wide. (Christie's) $2,213

A mid Victorian rosewood davenport, the mirrored back above a sloping fall, the exterior with a long pen drawer with a cupboard under, 56cm. wide. (Bonhams) $1,764

An early Victorian Irish arbutus-wood and marquetry davenport, Killarney, inlaid overall with scrolling rose, thistle and shamrock motifs, the hinged flap with flowers and two ruins, 25in. wide. (Christie's) $3,475

Victorian walnut pop-up davenport, the rising top inset with stationery compartments, over a lifting lid enclosing a sliding writing surface, fitted on either side with drawers and dummy drawers, 23in. (G.A. Key) $5,809

A mid-Victorian walnut davenport, the rectangular hinged stationery compartment with gilt gallery rail above a fall front with inset leather, 55cm. wide. (Bonhams) $1,264

A Victorian mahogany adjustable davenport, the top with a tooled leather inset slope with a gallery, the section lifts up on a ratchet support, 22in. wide. (Woolley & Wallis) $4,000

Late 19th century mahogany davenport, the upper section fitted with a stationery compartment, galleried surround, applied at the corners with finials, 22in. wide. (G.A. Key) $1,130

A Victorian davenport, veneered in burr walnut, the top with a pierced fret gallery, the flap inset with green gilt tooled leather, boxwood fitted interior, 21in. (Woolley & Wallis) $1,756

A Victorian burr walnut davenport desk, with hinged stationery compartment above leather inset fall with carved serpentine supports and four true and four false drawers to sides, width 53cm. (Bristol) $1,225

n Edwardian mahogany and polychrome decorated display abinet, the arched molded ornice above a floral decorated rieze and an astragal glazed door, 6in. wide.
Christie's) $3,657

A Dutch walnut bombé display cabinet, 19th century, the glazed upper section with a molded shaped pediment centered by a foliate carved tablet and, 71in. wide.
(Christie's) $6,127

A Continental walnut and marquetry display or china cabinet, 19th century, possibly Italian, in the Goanese style, inlaid overall with geometric ebony and ivory designs, 50½in. wide.
(Christie's) $3,128

A kingwood, Vernis Martin and gilt-bronze vitrine, French, circa 1890, the arched top with pierced foliate scrolled crest above the glazed door with a Vernis Martin panel depicting lovers in a landscape, 85cm. wide.
(Sotheby's) $11,385

A pair of French kingwood, tulipwood crossbanded and purplewood veneered vitrines, in the Louis XVI transitional style, each with ormolu mounts surmounted by molded rance marble tops, 34in. wide.
(Christie's) $5,152

A French kingwood, tulipwood-crossbanded and ormolu-mounted vitrine, 19th century, in the Louis XV/XVI Transitional style, the upper part with a cavetto frieze, a bevelled glazed panel door between canted angles, 28½in. wide.
(Christie's) $3,634

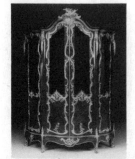

A French ormolu-mounted kingwood vitrine, in the Louis XV style, circa 1890, of serpentine outline, surmounted by a broken pediment, the central glazed door flanked by female caryatids, 51¼in. wide. (Christie's) $17,273

A French gilt-bronze mounted kingwood vitrine, in the Louis XV style, circa 1890, of serpentine shape with an arched pediment, above a pair of central glazed doors, flanked to each side by a glazed door, 74in. wide.
(Christie's) $27,636

A French ormolu-mounted kingwood and marquetry vitrine, in the Louis XV style, by François Linke, Paris, circa 1885, central waisted pediment, surmounted by a serpentine brèche jaune marble top, 66in. high.
(Christie's) $38,000

A Victorian mahogany display pier cabinet, of serpentine form with satinwood floral marquetry panels, raised scrolled back, 48in. wide. (Andrew Hartley) $2,800

A mid Victorian walnut display cabinet, circa 1870, the inlaid frieze above glazed door flanked with gilt mounts and floral inlays, 81cm. wide. (Bonhams) $1,316

A rare Classical figured maple and carved mahogany secretary, attributed to John Needles, Baltimore, Maryland, circa 1815, in three parts; 4ft.3in. (Sotheby's) $13,800

A good late Victorian satinwood, marquetry and painted display cabinet, circa 1900, the arched panelled back surmounted by a painted urn and swag finial above a central astragal glazed door and frieze drawer, 49½in. wide. (Bonhams) $4,004

A Victorian ebonized and burr walnut display cabinet, with a pair of arch top plain glazed doors with ormolu mounts, raised on turned feet, 48½in. wide. (Bonhams) $1,540

A Dutch walnut and floral marquetry display cabinet, late 18th century, the arched top above a trailing flower inlaid frieze above a single astragal glazed door and canted panelled glazed sides, 53½in. wide. (Bonhams) $4,480

An oak display cabinet circa 1930, with a pair of astragal glazed doors above a pair of panelled doors, on turned legs, 39³/₈in. wide. (Bonhams) $539

A mahogany bowfront display cabinet, circa 1920, with an astragal glazed door, on cabriole legs and claw and ball feet, 42in. wide. (Bonhams) $339

An oak display cabinet, English, circa 1900, of rectangular form, with a domed top enclosing glass shelves, the lower part with a Greek-key pattern frieze, 146cm. wide. (Sotheby's) $14,028

A mid Victorian gilt and composition open display cabinet, the arched mirrored superstructure with four flanking bijouterie shelves, 53in. wide. (Bonhams) $3,850

A mid Victorian walnut display cabinet, circa 1870, set with gilt metal mounts and boxwood inlays, 119cm. wide. (Bonhams) $1,820

A breakfront mahogany display cabinet with pierced fret surmount, central astragal glazed panel flanked on either side by a similar door, 51½in. wide. (Andrew Hartley) $2,310

A fine late Victorian satinwood and marquetry inlaid display cabinet in the Adam taste, the broken pediment with an ogee cornice above a ribbon and drape swagged frieze above a single glazed door enclosing shelves, 130cm. wide. (Bonhams) $12,012

A Dutch oak and marquetry vitrine, early 19th century, the arched **cavetto cornice centered by a foliate carved plinth above a rectangular astragal glazed door flanked by canted sides, 63in. wide.** (Bonhams) $10,360

One of a pair of Edwardian mahogany and marquetry inlaid demi-lune display cabinets, the molded dentil cornice above a rosette ribbon and husk chain swagged frieze, 42in. wide. (Bonhams) (Two) $7,065

A kingwood, gilt-bronze and Vernis Martin vitrine, French, circa 1890, of bombé form, the top surmounted by pierced foliate crest and two female busts, 142cm. wide. (Sotheby's) $14,429

A Louis XV style kingwood and Vernis Martin vitrine, circa 1890, the shaped cushioned top with a gilt metal rocaille crest above two female espangnolettes over a bombé panelled painted door, 55in. wide. (Bonhams) $8,470

A Regency rosewood display cabinet, circa 1820, the shelf superstructure with mirrored back and scrolled supports, above a glass topped frieze drawer, 38½in. wide. (Bonhams) $4,292

A fine and rare walnut Dutch cupboard, Pennsylvania, 1750-70, in two parts; the upper section with an overhanging stepped cornice above glazed doors, 5ft.3½in. wide. (Sotheby's) $20,700

A 1930s adzed oak enclosed dresser by Robert 'Mouseman' Thompson, with ledge back, two short over three long central drawers with turned wood handles, 68in. wide. (Andrew Hartley) $5,655

An oak dresser, North West, late 18th/ early 19th century, the plate rack with dentil molded cornice and wavy frieze, with three open shelves and fluted uprights, later boarded, 84in. wide. (Christie's) $9,143

An oak dresser, South Wales, early 19th century, the later-boarded plate rack with molded cornice and wavy frieze, above three shelves and a row of five small drawers, 61½in. wide. (Christie's) $11,337

A George III oak dresser and open rack, circa 1780, the shaped cornice above an open rack fitted with two panelled cupboard doors, and set on a base fitted with three frieze drawers, 201cm. wide. (Bonhams) $3,500

A Georgian fruitwood dresser, shelves over with three shelves with cupboards either side, the base fitted with four central drawers flanked by a pair of double panel doors, 5ft.6in. wide. (Brightwells) $6,900

An antique oak dresser and shelves, the associated upper section fitted with a central cupboard door, the base having four central drawers, 5ft.6in. wide. (Brightwells) $5,145

An oak enclosed dresser, English, late 18th century, the top section with a molded cornice and a pair of astragal glazed cupboard doors, the base with three frieze drawers, 68¼in. wide. (Bonhams) $5,439

An 18th century oak dresser with molded cornice above a rack with boarded back, the base fitted with five drawers around arched frieze, 6ft.2in. wide. (Brightwells) $8,268

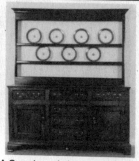

n oak Pembrokeshire dresser and ssociated rack, circa 18th century, he open rack above a base fitted with drawers and pot board, 151cm. ide. (Bonhams) $2,380

An antique oak dresser base fitted with three drawers raised on chamfered square supports, 5ft.11in. wide. (Brightwells) $3,339

A Georgian oak dresser with open shelves above an enclosed base fitted with six drawers and pair of solid panelled doors, 5ft.9in. wide. (Brightwells) $6,027

A George III oak dresser, the associated delft rack with molded cornice and waved frieze over two molded edged shelves flanked on either side by three small arched shelves, 82½in. wide. (Andrew Hartley) $5,544

A Georgian elm dresser, the boarded rack with shaped frieze, the base fitted with three large and two small drawers, on square tapering legs, 6ft.9in. wide. (Brightwells) $5,077

An oak open dresser, South Wales, late 18th century, the plate rack with molded cornice above three open shelves, the base with three frieze drawers and a shaped apron, 55in. wide. (Bonhams) $3,528

A beechwood and pine dresser, Swiss, 19th century, with a molded cornice and a pair of panelled doors with arcaded apron and above an open section, 49in. wide. (Christie's) $1,739

An antique oak dresser with shelves over, fitted with two small cupboards, the top altered to make sloping cornice, on square supports, 6ft.8in. (Brightwells) $2,867

A George III oak dresser, crossbanded in yew and with checker banding, the delft rack with molded cornice and ogee waved frieze, 75½in. wide. (Andrew Hartley) $5,800

A George III mahogany dumb waiter, circa 1770, with three graduated tiers, with turned columns and downswept cabriole legs and pad feet, 43¾in. high. (Bonhams) $2,800

A George III mahogany two tier dumb waiter, each dished circular top with a molded edge, on baluster-turned column supports and downswept legs with pad feet and inset castors, 34in. high. (Christie's) $1,454

A George III mahogany dumb waiter, circa 1760, with three graduated dished tiers, held by turned supports on a tripod base, 40½in. high. (Bonhams) $3,552

A 19th century dumb waiter of Georgian style, each of the three tiers fitted with drop leaves, on baluster turned stem, 22in. diameter. (Brightwells) $735

A pair of George III mahogany three-tier tripod dumb-waiters, each with circular graduating tiers with ropetwist edges, on fluted and spirally-turned supports, 24¾in. diameter. (Christie's) $21,300

A George III mahogany tripod dumbwaiter, with two circular graduated dished tiers on a turned baluster column, on cabriole legs, 35¾in. high. (Christie's) $4,658

A George III mahogany three-tier dumb waiter, with circular graduating tiers on turned and spirally-fluted columns, on cabriole legs, 41in. high. (Christie's) $4,099

A George III mahogany two tier dumb waiter, circa 1810, fitted with two graduated revolving reeded tiers, with drop sides, set on a turned and gadrooned column, 66cm. diameter. (Bonhams) $2,660

A George III mahogany circular three-tier graduated dumb waiter on turned column and tripod base with casters, 3ft.5in. high. (Brightwells) $2,385

An adzed oak jardiniére by Robert Mouseman' Thompson, of oblong form with tin liner, raised on shaped end supports, 48in. long.
(Andrew Hartley) $2,233

A 19th century Dutch mahogany jardinière of waisted circular slatted form with molded rim, swing loop handle, detachable brass liner, 15in. wide.
(Andrew Hartley) $1,595

A 19th century French kingwood and veneered jardinière of serpentine oval form with gilt metal mounts and loop handles, metal liner and bun feet, 17½in. wide.
(Andrew Hartley) $637

A rosewood floor standing jardinière, 19th century, the sides inset with painted panels of flowers and foliage, on wrythen legs and splayed feet, 37in. high.
(Christie's) $2,370

Late 19th/early 20th century mahogany jardinière stand of rectangular form, inset on one side with tiled frieze, raised on lyre type supports, 37in.(G.A. Key) $290

Napoleon III tulipwood marquetry and gilt-metal mounted jardiniére, circa 1870, serpentine case on cabriole legs joined by a shelf stretcher, 28in. wide.
(Skinner) $1,265

Bronze jardinière, late 19th century, of tapering hexagonal form, with foliate capped volute scrolls to the angles and on claw feet, 26in. wide.
(Christie's) $3,125

A late 19th century jardinière of Louis XV style, veneered in satinwood and kingwood with gilt metal mounts of flowers and leafage, on cabriole legs, 27in.
(Brightwells) $1,530

A large brass bound oak jardinière, early 20th century, of tapering coopered construction, with foliate cast loop handles and scroll feet, 22in. wide.
(Christie's) $2,138

A mid Victorian mahogany barrel front pedestal desk, circa 1870, the interior fitted with pigeon holes and drawers and a pull out writing surface, 152cm. wide.
(Bonhams) $1,400

A George III mahogany kneehole desk fitted with frieze drawer above six drawers flanking a recessed cupboard, 2ft.9in. wide.
(Brightwells) $3,260

A Queen Anne carved and figured mahogany kneehole dressing bureau, Goddard-Townsend School, Newport, Rhode Island, circa 1760, long drawer carved with one concave shelf with two convex shells flanking, 36in. wide.
(Sotheby's) $46,000

A rosewood cylinder pedestal bureau cabinet, late 19th/early 20th century, applied with silvered mounts, the superstructure with pierced gallery containing three drawers enclosed by a locking stile, 73in. wide.(Christie's) $8,280

A George III mahogany kneehole desk, the rectangular molded top with re-entrant front corners above a slide and frieze drawer and with three further drawers to each side of the kneehole.
(Christie's) $6,674

A late Victorian rosewood kneehole writing desk, the raised superstructure with a bobbin-turned gallery and two banks of three drawers around a mirror backed recess, 54in. wide.
(Christie's) $3,634

A George II walnut kneehole desk, featherbanded to the top and front, the quarter-veneered rectangular top with re-entrant corners above a frieze drawer and a kneehole with a drawer and a cupboard, 31¾in. wide. (Christie's) $15,017

A George III mahogany architect's pedestal desk, attributed to Gillows, with green leather-lined double-ratcheted hinged top above a fitted frieze drawer with green leather-lined writing-surface and lidded compartments, 49¾in. wide.
(Christie's) $35,039

A Venetian blue and gilt-japanned bombé bureau, decorated overall with Chinese court figures and pagodas amidst landscapes with birds and foliate C-scrolls, probably 19th century, 45¾in. wide.
(Christie's) $13,973

A mahogany pedestal desk, 20th century, of serpentine outline, the green leather lined top with a molded edge and three frieze drawers, 61in. wide.
(Christie's) $8,722

An American walnut "Shannon" roll top desk, late 19th century, made by the Shannon File Co. Ltd. with swing cupboards and multiple drawers, 150cm. wide.
(Bonhams) $3,080

A Victorian carved mahogany, possibly walnut, partner's pedestal desk, the crossbanded top inset with a panel of tooled leather with ribband and paterae carved edge containing six drawers in the frieze with beaded molding below, 54½in. wide.
(Christie's) $8,225

Dutch mahogany and marquetry secrétaire pedestal desk, 19th century, in sections, with carved foliate, ripple and spirally-turned ornament inlaid overall with fan and shell inlay, 62in. wide.
Christie's $5,451

A George IV mahogany architect's pedestal desk, the rounded rectangular double-ratcheted top with two later book-stops, above a fitted frieze drawer with a fall-flap and a green baize-lined writing-surface, 51½in. wide.
(Christie's) $15,017

A George III mahogany kneehole desk, the rectangular top above a fitted secrétaire-drawer with drawers and pigeon-holes, above a kneehole with a cupboard enclosing a shelf, 33¾in. wide.
(Christie's) $3,003

late Victorian mahogany pedestal desk, circa 1890, top with two cupboards and three drawers set in pedestals with eight drawers, 142cm. wide.
Bonhams $1,008

A rare George III mahogany bow end pedestal desk with a leather inset top, molded edge and shaped three-quarter detachable gallery fitted with a bowed cockbeaded drawer, 1.53m.
(T.R. & M) $24,650

A George III mahogany architect's pedestal desk, attributed to Gillows, the later rectangular hinged top above a fitted drawer with leather-lined slide and six wells, 49in. wide.
(Christie's) $6,400

A George III mahogany linen press, the molded and dentil cornice over blind fret frieze, two panelled cupboard doors applied with brass flowerheads, 50in. wide. (Andrew Hartley) $1,256

A Regency mahogany and crossbanded linen press, the molded cornice above a pair of flame veneered panelled cross banded cupboard doors, 52in. wide. (T.R. & M) $3,625

A Victorian figured mahogany linen press, with projecting cornice above twin shaped top, the base with two short and two long graduated drawers, 131.5cm. wide. (Bristol) $942

A George III mahogany linen press, the dentil molded cornice over twin oval panelled doors enclosing four slides, the base fitted with two short over two long drawers, on bracket feet, 137.5cm. wide. (Bristol) $1,806

A George III mahogany linen press, in the manner of Giles Grendy, the upper part with a molded dentil cornice and fitted with trays with labels, 49½in. wide. (Christie's) $7,680

A George III figured mahogany linen press, with later ogee cornice above twin oval banded panel doors enclosing later rail, 150cm. wide. (Bristol) $1,963

Federal mahogany veneer linen press, New York, labelled *Thomas Burling*, circa 1840, the flaring cornice above the veneered frieze over the recessed panel doors, 49in. wide. (Skinner) $1,840

A George III mahogany linen press, circa 1790, fitted with slides, the whole with stringing and inlays, 134cm. wide. (Bonhams) $1,176

A George III mahogany linen press, with dentil cornice above twin panel doors enclosing five linen trays, over two short and two long drawers with original brass swan neck handles, on bracket supports, 147cm. wide.(Bristol) $2,240

An 18th century oak low boy, the molded edged top with cusped corners, the fascia with four small drawers, shaped apron, panelled sides, 33in. wide.
(Andrew Hartley) $2,310

A Georgian oak lowboy fitted with a single drawer on cabriole supports and hoof feet, 2ft.5in. wide.
(Brightwells) $1,400

A George I walnut, crossbanded and feather-strung lowboy, the quarter veneered top feather strung and crossbanded with a molded edge and re-entrant corners, 31½in. wide. (Christie's) $6,909

An 18th century lowboy, the walnut figured veneered top with herringbone banding and a crossbanded edge, the shaped walnut veneered frieze with three drawers, 30in. wide.
(Woolley & Wallis) $1,540

An oak and mahogany crossbanded side table, English, mid 18th century, the rectangular top above three drawers to the shaped frieze, on cabriole legs and pad feet, 35½in. wide.
(Bonhams) $2,058

A George I walnut lowboy, the molded rectangular quarter-veneered and crossbanded top with re-entrant corners above a small frieze drawer and a shaped arch, 29in wide.(Christie's) $5,679

An early Georgian blue and gilt japanned lowboy, with lions, flowers and foliage, molded rectangular top with central raised Chinese scene, one short drawer and two deep drawers, 30¾in. wide.
(Christie's) $5,486

A George II mahogany lowboy, the rounded rectangular projecting molded top above three short drawers, on lambrequin-headed club legs and pad feet, 27¼in. wide.
(Christie's) $4,260

A George I walnut lowboy, circa 1720, the rectangular top above a long frieze drawer with two short deep drawers and a shaped apron under, 74cm. wide.
(Bonhams) $14,700

347

A mahogany tray top night table, 19th century, the panelled door above a shaped apron and raised on square tapered legs, 38cm. wide. (Bonhams) $448

19th century mahogany cylindrical commode, marble inset over a lifting lid, with a cupboard below, raised on a square plinth base, 31in. (G.A. Key) $769

An Edwardian mahogany bedside table, with drop leaf top over two cabinet doors, 47cm. wide. (Bonhams) $262

A Milanese walnut and marquetry bedside cabinet, 19th century, in the manner of Maggiolini, the rectangular top inlaid with scrolling leaves and centered by a bowl of fruit flanked by putti, 21¾in. wide. (Christie's) $4,023

An Italian tulipwood commode, Genoese, circa 1770, of serpentine form, the brèche violette inset marble top with a three quarter shaped gallery above a pair of cupboard doors and sides with simple parquetry decoration, 22in. wide. (Bonhams) $5,920

A George III mahogany pot cupboard, circa 1770, the galleried top with pierced carrying handles, above a sliding fall, on chamfered square section legs, 20in. wide. (Bonhams) $3,256

An early George III mahogany bedside cupboard, the rectangular galleried top with pierced hand grips, the fall front reveals a frieze drawer, 23¼in. wide. (Woolley & Wallis) $2,310

A Regency mahogany night cupboard, crossbanded with gilt metal mounts and ebony inlaid panelling, two doors over a deep drawer, 22in. wide. (Andrew Hartley) $2,175

A George III mahogany bedside cupboard, the rectangular tray top above a tambour shutter and a drawer with a simulated suede top 23¾in. wide. (Christie's) $4,844

French gilt bronze fire screen, te 19th or early 20th century, the liate cast cartouche shaped frame n splayed feet, the mesh ground entered with a flambeau urn ount, 29in. wide. Christie's) $4,023

A brass fan-shaped folding firescreen, early 20th century, the openwork frame with lion masks and trophies and on claw feet, with radiating pierced brass leaves, 29½in. high. (Christie's) $2,377

A Louis XV style bronze firescreen, early 20th century, the naturalistic scrolling border with loop handle and splayed feet, 28¾in. high. (Christie's) $1,090

Dutch polychrome-painted and arcel-gilt four-leaf leather screen, 8th/19th century, each leaf with ree sections, depicting chinoiserie astoral scenes, within close-nailed ilt borders, 20in. wide, each leaf. Christie's) $5,339

A giltwood cheval screen, 19th century, inset with an 18th century petit and gros point needlework panel of cartouche outline, depicting mythological figures, 30½in. wide. (Christie's) $2,208

A Chinese polychrome-decorated six-leaf lacquer screen, decorated overall on a black ground, the central rectangular scene depicting various figures and warriors in a landscape, each leaf 79in. high,16in. wide. (Christie's) $1,532

French bronze firescreen, early th century, the oval frame flanked fluted tapering standards twined with foliage, centered with rced mount, 33½in. high. hristie's) $1,272

An early Victorian lacquered and gilt painted pole screen, mid 19th century, the oval glazed frame inset with a classical scene of vases and fruit against a landscape. (Bonhams) $744

A French gilt bronze firescreen, late 19th or early 20th century, the mesh ground applied with foliate mounts within the cartouche shaped frame, on scroll feet, 31½in. wide. (Christie's) $1,974

A 19th century German Biedermeier type escritoire in walnut, the interior cupboard and drawers in burr-maple, enclosed by sliding fall-front, 3ft.9in. wide. (Brightwells) $1,800

A George III mahogany secrétaire chest, the rectangular top above a secrétaire drawer and three long graduated drawers, on splayed bracket feet, 39in. wide. (Bonhams) $552

A 19th century mahogany escritoire with top drawer with molded front, hinged secrétaire fitted interior, three drawers below on turned supports, 3ft.5in. wide. (Brightwells) $1,940

A south German walnut secrétaire cabinet, circa 1760, the arched crossbanded breakfront cavetto **cornice centered by a rocaille crest** above a panelled door flanked by ten shaped drawers above a rectangular fall, 49in. wide. (Bonhams) $3,700

A Regency mahogany secrétaire, circa 1820, the fitted secrétaire flanked by two short and three long drawers, 111cm. wide. (Bonhams) $1,092

A Queen Anne walnut and crossbanded secrétaire on chest, the upper part with a molded cornice and fitted with a cushion molded frieze drawer, the crossbanded fall enclosing a fitted interior, 45½in. wide. (Christie's) $12,337

A Dutch walnut and marquetry semainier, circa 1830, inlaid overall with floral marquetry, distressed, lacking marble top, 39in. wide. (Bonhams) $2,664

A Regency mahogany bow front secrétaire chest with well fitted top drawer above three graduated long drawers having ebonized stringing, 4ft. wide. (Brightwells) $3,790

A Transitional tulipwood, bois satiné, amaranth, bois de violette and palisander marquetry secrétaire à abattant, by Jean Georges Schlichtig, gray and white fossil marble top, 37¾in. wide. (Bonhams) $10,360

Continental Neo-classical secrétaire à abattant, mid-19th century, molded cornice above a fall-front enclosing a fitted writing compartment above drawers, 41¼in. wide.
(Skinner) $2,070

A George III mahogany secrétaire-chest, the molded rectangular top above a secrétaire-drawer, enclosing small drawers, each inlaid alphabetically, 53in. wide.
(Christie's) $9,315

Biedermeier fruitwood part-ebonized and ivory secrétaire à abattant, early 19th century, top with molded cornice over a cupboard door flanked by drawers over a drawer, 43in. wide.
(Skinner) $7,188

...non, French, secrétaire, circa 1930, walnut, of slightly bowed rectangular form, fall front flap inlaid with ivory diamond patterned banding, 97cm. wide.
(Sotheby's) $6,720

A camphorwood military secrétaire chest, early 19th century, of two sections, with ebony outlines, recessed brasswork and fitted interior, on turned wood supports, 103.5cm. wide.
(Bristol) $3,454

Emile-Jacques Ruhlmann, secrétaire, circa 1925, bois de violette veneer, of slightly swollen rectangular section, fall-front flap inset with beige leather writing surface, 27in. wide.
(Sotheby's) $77,980

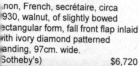

...rare William and Mary cedar fall-...nt secretary, Bermuda, 1700-...25, in two parts; the upper ...ction with overhanging cornice ...d hinged front fitted with an ...justable writing surface, 43½in. ...de. (Sotheby's) $6,900

A George III mahogany secrétaire chest with molded edged top, the fall front as two long drawers enclosing fitted interior, three long drawers below, 40in. wide.
(Andrew Hartley) $1,348

An early Victorian mahogany secrétaire, the galleried top above a fitted interior with drawers and pigeon holes, enclosed by a panelled fall front, 3ft.8in. wide.
(Woolley & Wallis) $4,340

A mahogany secrétaire bookcase, late 18th/early 19th century, of small size, the top and bottom possibly associated, the upper part with a molded cornice with lines to the crossbanded frieze, 54¾in. wide. (Christie's) $18,095

An English mahogany secrétaire bookcase, both sections late 18th century, associated, the molded cornice above a pair of astragal glazed doors, 44in. wide. (Bonhams) $2,464

A mahogany secrétaire bookcase, early 19th century, the twin glazed door upper section over fitted secrétaire above three long drawers, on turned bun feet, 11cm. wide. (Bristol) $2,983

A late George III faded mahogany secrétaire bookcase, the top with a dentil cornice and architectural pediment, the base with a well figured veneered front. (Woolley & Wallis) $3,193

A large Victorian mahogany breakfront secrétaire bookcase, with cavetto cornice over three arched glazed doors, rounded stiles headed by leafy brackets, 161in. wide. (Andrew Hartley) $11,932

A 19th century secrétaire bookcase molded cornice over two astragal glazed doors enclosing shelving, the base with secrétaire drawer, two arched panelled doors below, on turned feet, 47½in. wide (Andrew Hartley) $2,041

A George III mahogany secrétaire bookcase, the associated upper section with pair of astragal glazed doors enclosing adjustable shelves, the base with well fitted interior above three long graduated drawers on splay feet, 3ft.6in. wide. (Brightwells) $3,000

A George III inlaid mahogany secrétaire bookcase, the arched pierced pediment centered by a tablet with an applied cast lion's head above a pair of astragal glazed doors, 46½in. wide. (Bonhams) $5,328

A George III mahogany and inlaid secrétaire bookcase, inlaid with lines, the upper part with a molded cornice, crossbanded frieze and fitted with three drawers below enclosed by a pair of glazed astragal doors, 43¼in. wide. (Christie's) $9,870

ileen Gray, bench, circa 1923,
ood, the top and underside
cquered in red, the edges in
lack, the slightly concave seat
pholstered in black leather,
epped at base, 19½in. high.
Sotheby's) $143,500

An unusual early Victorian oak,
fruitwood and ebonised parquetry
chaise longue, circa 1840-50, the
shaped back inlaid with a running
band of thistles and clover leaves,
77in. wide.
(Bonhams) $2,310

A Scandinavian style bent plywood
lounger with walnut veneer arms,
circa 1950s x, 50 x 32in.
(Brightwells) $4,500

painted pine settle, probably Irish,
te 18th/early 19th century, the
ctangular boarded back with
uare section struts to simulate
nelling, the arms on square
ction supports continuing to the
nt leg, 56in. wide.
hristie's) $1,097

A pine high back settle, West
Country, late 19th century, with
covered and recessed seat, one
side with shepherd's crook type
armrest, with boarded front, the
reverse with a full length door
enclosing a shallow cupboard, 37in.
wide. (Christie's) $1,463

19th century Queen Anne style
double hoop wing back sofa, high
back, splayed armrests, apron
molded with shells and scrolls and
raised on five scroll and acanthus
leaf molded short cabriole
supports with claw and ball feet,
59in. (G.A. Key) $3,003

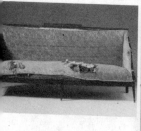

ne Federal inlaid mahogany
a, New York, signed *Nicholas
derson* and dated *May 14, 1799,*
horizontal crest with projecting
let inlaid with swags and fleur de
flanked by downswept arms, by
10in. overall length.
otheby's) $17,250

A Continental walnut framed double
ended sofa, circa 1880, the
upholstered back and seat above
shaped legs with castors, 162cm.
wide. (Bonhams) $700

Emile-Jacques Ruhlmann, two-
seater sofa, possibly for the Yardley
showroom in Bond Street, London,
circa 1930, macassar ebony frame,
gently curved back and arm rests,
the underside with branded mark
Ruhlmann, 52in. wide.
(Sotheby's) $23,240

Classical mahogany carved sofa, probably New York, circa 1830, the shaped scrolling water leaf-carved crest with circular bosses centering a veneered and cross-banded panel surmounted by leaf-carved tablet joining out-scrolled reeded arms and supports with circular bosses, 82in. wide. (Skinner) $1,955

Federal mahogany inlaid sofa, probably Boston or North Shore, Massachusetts, circa 1800-10, the arched crest flanked by shaped sides and molded arms continuing to vase and ring-turned, reeded and swelled posts, 80½in. wide.(Skinner) $17,25

Jacobean oak settle, late 17th century, with rectangular panelled backrest and scrolled arms above rope seat and plank legs joined by stretchers, 75in. long. (Skinner) $6,325

An early 19th century mahogany show frame sofa, the scroll and channelled back with a central veneered tablet, the scroll arm supports applied with rondels to a tablet veneered front, on turned legs to later china castors, 6ft.6in. (Woolley & Wallis) $1,33(

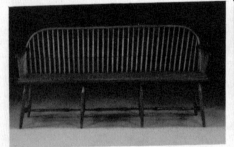

A bamboo-turned Windsor settee, Pennsylvania, 1800-1820, the moulded arched crest above thirty-five bamboo-turned spindles over shaped downscrolling arms above a shaped plank seat, on bamboo-turned legs, 75¾in. wide. (Christie's) $9,775

A fine settee, in a mid 18th century style, the upholstery in a floral crewelwork design, the serpentine crest back to scroll arms, the sprung seat with a squab cushion on walnut cabriole legs to pad feet, 5ft.3in. (Woolley & Wallis) $1,400

Osvaldo Borsani for Tecno, 'D70' adjustable tilting divan bed, designed 1954, black painted pressed steel frame, original striped fabric upholstery, 187cm. wide. (Sotheby's) $4,048

Rococo Revival walnut and upholstered recamie third quarter 19th century, scrolled back on scrolle support, raised on cabriole legs ending in scrolle toes, 34in. high, 77in. long. (Skinner) $2,30(

A Victorian walnut framed sofa, the double ended button upholstered back with flower carved crests and joined by a central oval padded panel surround, 72in. wide. (Andrew Hartley) $1,491

an early Georgian walnut chair back settee, with arched crest, two shaped solid splats, scrolled arms on shaped supports, 51½in. wide. (Andrew Hartley) $1,960

painted faux bamboo turned tête à tête, probably Boston, early 19th century, each crest rail above four spindles and splint seat on legs joined by double stretchers, old black paint, 37in. long. (Skinner) $1,380

Classical carved mahogany veneer sleigh bed, New York area, the scrolled head and foot boards with foliate carving over the gadrooned sides and rails above leaf carved shaped legs, 103½in. long. (Skinner) $31,050

A William IV carved mahogany scroll arm sofa, with central shaped panel flanked by foliate carved scrolls above shaped arms and panelled frieze, on four reeded turned tapering supports with brass castors, 216cm. wide. (Bristol) $2,079

Federal mahogany and mahogany veneer sofa, Boston or North Shore, Massachusetts, circa 1815-20, the reeded crest rail above the molded arms continuing to reeded arm supports above the veneered seat rail, 76 in. (Skinner) $7,475

A Victorian carved walnut settee, the back with central low section and button upholstered twin back panels above well-carved scroll arms and conforming seat with carved apron, on scroll supports with brass castors, 77cm. (Bristol) $840

355

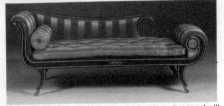

A Regency brass-mounted, grained and parcel-gilt daybed, with scrolled ends, on rectangular tapering legs, brass caps and castors, inscribed in paint to the underside *his a.Junel*, redecorated 84in. long. (Christie's) $9,315

Painted and decorated child's Windsor arrow-back settee, New England, early 19th century, the square crest above shaped spindles, the incised plank seat and raked legs joined by a rectangular stretcher, 25¾in. long. (Skinner) $12,650

A joined oak panelled settle, English, late 17th century, the rectangular back with six fielded panels, the shaped arms and plank seat on ball turned baluster legs tied by stretchers, 73in. wide. (Bonhams) $2,058

Baroque paint decorated day bed, Europe, early 18th century, the molded and scrolling crest above shaped foliate-carved panel joining block, vase and ring-turned stiles. (Skinner) $2,415

A Regency mahogany sofa, with stepped padded back, outscrolled arms, bolsters and seat cushions covered in striped watered green silk, on splayed reeded legs with castors, restorations, 80in. wide. (Christie's) $9,315

A French duchesse brisé, 19th century, each chair with curved padded backs and scrolled top rail continuing to arms with acanthus carving, the bowed padded seats on scrolled legs and a concave sided stool, 220cm. long in total. (Bonhams) $5,040

An Anglo-Indian metal-mounted sofa, probably circa 1920, the deeply buttoned arched rectangular back with a frieze centered by a figure of Lord Shiva seated on his tiger, 64in. wide. (Christie's) $7,254

Victorian mahogany chaise longue, galleried armrest and the back molded with scrolls and foliage, over a plain apron and raised on ring turned tapering cylindrical supports, 73in.(G.A. Key) $722

Federal fancy settee, probably Massachusetts, circa 1815-25, the five crest rails decorated with anthemia, acanthus leaves, and scrolled vines with five horizontal spindles below separated by spherules joining six raked thumb-back stiles, 76in. wide. (Skinner) $13,800

A 19th century mahogany framed sofa with scrolled leaf carved padded back, similar raised ends with carved rosettes, on wrythen turned legs with brass castors, 80in. wide. (Andrew Hartley) $1,386

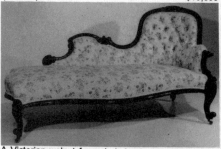

A Victorian walnut framed chaise longue, the arched serpentine button upholstered back with leaf and scroll carving, carved cabriole front legs, 69in. wide. (Andrew Hartley) $2,198

A white painted and giltwood sofa, 19th century, in the Louis XVI style, with beaded and molded frame, the rectangular upholstered panel back with foliate scroll cresting and paterae, 84¼in. wide. (Christie's) $4,571

A late Regency oak and mahogany crossbanded settle, the rectangular four panelled back above downswept arms, on turned tapering legs. 72in. wide. (Bonhams) $924

An early Victorian mahogany chaise longue, the foliate carved scrolled back and arm above a squab cushion and molded seat rail, 82in. wide. (Bonhams) $1,232

A good Chippendale mahogany camel-back sofa, Massachusetts, circa 1780, the serpentine back flanked by outscrolled arms, overupholstered serpentine-fronted seat on square molded legs joined by stretchers, 7ft. long. (Sotheby's) $29,900

Regency diminutive caned, painted, and ebonised triple chair-back settee, circa 1810, painted with reserves of putti and foliage, on circular splayed legs, 45½in. long. (Skinner) $2,530

An oak and polychrome three seat choir stall, North European, early 17th century, each hinged seat with foliate miserichord detail flanked by molded arched divides, 91in. long. (Christie's) $2,608

A good mid Victorian rosewood sofa, the shaped button upholstered back carved with rosettes and s-scrolls continuing to knurled arms, 193cm. long. (Bonhams) $1,540

A mid Victorian mahogany framed three-seater sofa, the button upholstered back above upholstered arms and seat with carved and scrolled arm terminals, 165cm. wide. (Bonhams) $1,109

An ash and oak boxed seat cupboard settle, English or Welsh, late 18th/early 19th century, the high back with molded cornice and a twin fielded panel door, the seat with hinged lid and fielded panel front, 34in. wide. (Christie's) $3,657

Edwardian mahogany two seater cottage sofa, the back inlaid with boxwood neo-classical urns and garlands etc, raised on tapering square supports with spade feet, 43in. (G.A. Key) $524

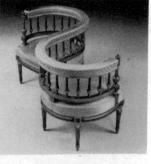

A late 18th century provincial elm settle of concave shape with a panelled back, shaped sides, solid seat, the base with a pair of panelled cupboard doors, probably Welsh, 75in. wide.(Thomson Roddick & Medcalf) $2,175

A French giltwood confidante, in the Louis XV style, circa 1875, of 'S' – shape, each section surmounted by a serpentine back rail centered by foliage, above a three-section padded back with scroll armrest, 57in. wide.(Christie's) $3,281

A French gilt-wood confidante, in the Louis XVI style, circa 1875, of 'S' –shape, surmounted by an upholstered back-rail, supported by a baluster gallery, 55in. wide. (Christie's) $3,455

pair of North European ormolu-mounted ebony wall-brackets, third quarter 18th century, each with rectangular molded cornice above shaped edge and incurved foliate-wreathed lower section, 8½in. and in. high.(Christie's) $10,247

Pierre Chareau, bureau murale, 1932, mahogany, the rectangular top with wrought iron supports and wall fixings, 33¼in. wide. (Sotheby's) $45,780

An Italian beechwood wall bracket, late 19th century, the platform modelled as a scallop-shell, tapering down to a putto amongst pierced scrolling foliage, 11in. high. (Christie's) $812

A pair of carved pine console wall brackets, probably Italian, 19th century, modelled as cherubs, some damage, 61cm. high. (Bonhams) $4,312

An English giltwood wall bracket, second quarter 19th century, of tapering semi-circular form, the fluted body rising to fixed tongue molding, 16in. high. (Christie's) $400

A pair of Central European polychrome and parcel-giltwood wall brackets, 18th century, modelled with stylized foliate scrolling ornament and scallop-shells, distressed, 34½in. high, (Christie's) $1,652

pair of Victorian carved oak wall brackets, late 19th century, of semi-circular form, with everted rims, the bodies with richly scrolling acanthus and pineapple terminals, 9¾in. high. (Christie's) $951

Gilt carved wooden eagle wall bracket, America, 19th century, oval shelf with beaded trim on carved eagle perched on rockery, 16in. high. (Skinner) $2,185

A pair of French giltwood wall brackets, late 19th century, the lobed platform above foliate backplates, 10¾in. high. (Christie's) $690

A George III mahogany sideboard, the later rectangular top above a **fluted frieze centered by a panel**, above a drawer and an arch, 58¼in. wide.
(Christie's) $7,825

A mid Victorian mahogany sideboard, the arched back with central cartouche, above four arched panel cupboard doors, 90in. wide. (Bonhams) $2,070

A Regency mahogany pedestal sideboard with three quarter gallery back, on reeded edged top, the fascia having concave center with incised panel, flanked on either side by a drawer over a cupboard, 84½in. wide.
(Andrew Hartley) $6,090

A George III mahogany, inlaid and marquetry bowfront sideboard, the fiddle back veneered top banded in satinwood with ebony lines containing a central drawer in the arched apron, 48in. wide.
(Christie's) $4,023

An early Victorian mahogany pedestal sideboard, the rectangular top surmounted by an arched mirror glazed panel carved with foliate scrolls, 74½in. wide.
(Bonhams) $1,232

A Sheraton style mahogany sideboard with shaped concave central drawer flanked by a pair of bowed drawers.
(Brightwells) $2,240

An Edwardian mahogany and satinwood banded breakfront **sideboard, the dentil molded and** bowed top of stepped form, with a brass gallery above the central drawer, 65¾in. wide.
(Bonhams) $483

A good Federal inlaid birchwood-inlaid mahogany bowfront sideboard, North Shore, Massachusetts, circa 1810, the shaped inlaid top above three frieze drawers, repairs to inlay, 6ft. long.
(Sotheby's) $16,100

A Regency mahogany bowfronted sideboard, circa 1780, decorated with rosewood crossbanding, boxwood stringing and thistle corner inlays, 122cm wide.
(Bonhams) $22,330

A 1930s adzed oak sideboard by Robert 'Mouseman' Thompson with edge back, six central small drawers over a long drawer with turned wood handles, 64in. wide. (Andrew Hartley) $5,698

A mid Victorian oak pedestal sideboard, the back carved with the Bullock family armorial, together with scrolls, fruits of the vine and assorted other fruits, set on an inverted breakfront top, 236cm. wide. (Bonhams) $1,263

An adzed oak sideboard by Robert 'Mouseman' Thompson, with slightly raised back, three central drawers, flanked on either side by a panelled cupboard door, 54¾in. long. (Andrew Hartley) $924

George III mahogany sideboard, the breakfront D-shaped top with reeded edge, above two curved cupboard doors to each side and a central drawer, 43½in. wide. (Christie's) $5,589

A small George III mahogany serpentine sideboard, the shaped top above two central drawers flanked by a further drawer and cupboard door, 41¼ wide. (Bonhams) $3,360

> **TOP TIPS**
> Auctioneers advice - take a torch to view sales and a UV light is also very useful to show up restoration on both pictures and porcelain. If light is poor, take a piece of furniture into the daylight, this will show up marriages where pieces have been put together at a later date, different colors and finishes on wood and other faults.
> Color photographs in catalogs often improve the color of a piece of antique furniture and should be treated circumspectly.
> (Thomson Roddick & Medcalf.)

George III mahogany breakfront sideboard, inlaid with boxwood lines, the rounded rectangular top with a reeded edge containing two frieze drawers flanked by cupboard doors, 84in. wide. (Christie's) $4,754

An Arts & Crafts oak sideboard, the raised mirror back with overhanging cornice, inlaid and stained wood floral panels above candle stand, 5ft.4in. wide. (Brightwells) $1,290

A Victorian mahogany large mirror back sideboard, the mirror surround finely carved with leafage scrolls and fruiting vines the inverted breakfront base with pair of panelled doors, 7ft.10in. wide. (Brightwells) $3,000

An antique miniature spinning wheel in fruitwood with baluster turned spokes to the 9in. wheel and frame, 16in. high.
(Brightwells) $397

A mahogany pipe stand, early 20th century, the folding brass mounted frame with two tiers of rests, frieze drawer below with shield shaped escutcheon, 21in. high extended.
(Christie's) $2,743

A Victorian mahogany "A Frame" gallery easel with carved foliate decoration and pierced and scrolled surmount, adjustable supports, scrolled feet and china castors.
(Andrew Hartley) $2,120

A late Victorian or Edwardian oak music sheet stand, circa 1900, the lyre-shaped frame with twin divisions on a revolving oval base raised on four turned feet, 22¾in. high. (Christie's) $2,743

A pair of cast iron walking stick stands, early 20th century, the rectangular frames each cast with twenty-eight apertures, with baluster upright supports and drip pan inserts, 32¾in. wide.
(Christie's) $4,571

A pair of green onyx stands with gilt metal mounts, the square top on Ionic style column applied with festoons and collar, 41½in. high.
(Andrew Hartley) $3,915

An Edwardian turned wood walking stick stand, early 20th century, the frame with three circular apertures, the rectangular base with a later drip tray, 24in. wide.
(Christie's) $1,280

A Coalbrookdale pattern cast iron walking stick stand, late 19th or early 20th century, modelled as a chihuahua, with riding crop retaining rail to its mouth, 23in. high. (Christie's) $3,619

Charlotte Perriand, coat rack, 1950s, oak, rectangular frame with laddered center with six adjustable iron and oak coat hooks and vide-poche, 32in. wide.
(Sotheby's) $12,600

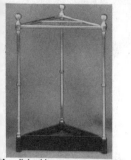

A polished brass corner walking stick stand, early 20th century, the tubular frame with sphere finials, the top with six divisions, with retractable drip tray, 24¼in. high. (Christie's) $1,280

A George II gilt-gesso stand, the associated drop-in brown breccia marble top above an acanthus and foliate-carved frieze and apron, 33in. wide.(Christie's) $6,521

A mid-Victorian mahogany and brass-mounted stick-stand, the galleried top above a panelled back with pierced slats and flanked by finials, 22¼in. wide. (Christie's) $5,962

A mahogany kettle-stand, of George III style, the pierced galleried square top above a plain frieze, on later square tapering legs with brackets, 11½in. square. (Christie's) $1,304

A Portuguese red painted and parcel-gilt corner stand, mid 18th century, the triangular top with molded front edge above a plain frieze with waved and carved apron, 39½in. wide. (Bonhams) $2,800

A Chinese hardwood two-tier stand, 19th century, with pierced geometric friezes, the rectangular top with rectangular superstructure inset with an amboyna panel, on square legs joined by an undertier, 23¼in. wide. (Christie's) $1,677

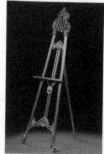

An Edwardian turned wood walking stick stand, early 20th century, the divided top with twelve apertures, the base with later retractable drip tray, 24in. wide. (Christie's) $1,134

Jean Dunand, table gong, circa 1925, circular hammered metal gong, decorated in dinanderie with geometric motifs, 45.5cm. (Sotheby's) $28,070

A gilt-wood easel, French, circa 1900, in the Rococo style, of typical form with a pierced basket weave crest interspersed with flowerheads, framed by foliate C-scrolls, 194.5cm. high. (Sotheby's) $5,313

A rare Queen Anne carved and figured mahogany tilt-top candlestand, Philadelphia, circa 1740, the circular molded top tilting and revolving above a birdcage support, 23¾in. diameter. (Sotheby's) $34,500

A pair of brass hall stands, early 20th century the tubular cylindrical frames with baluster finials and beaded borders, with retractable drip trays, 28½in. high. (Christie's) $1,817

Chippendale mahogany tilt-top stand, Boston or coastal Essex County, Massachusetts, 1775-1800, the serpentine-folding top above the block, incised *I Young*, 21¾in. wide. (Skinner) $2,185

Classical mahogany and veneer basin stand, probably Northshore Massachusetts, circa 1825, the cyma-curved splash board above the cut-outs and the bowed veneered skirt flanked by small drawers, 20½in. wide. (Skinner) $1,150

A very fine and rare Federal inlaid mahogany candlestand, New York, 1790-1810, the square crossbanded top with astragal corners, string and diamond-inlay, and centering a spread-winged eagle, 22in. wide. (Sotheby's) $31,050

Classical tiger maple one-drawer stand, New England, circa 1830, the overhanging square top on conforming base with single drawer on ring-turned and swelled legs, 20in. wide. (Skinner) $2,070

A 19th century mahogany boot rack, with turned finials on ring turned end supports, on scrolled down curved legs with bun feet, 22in. wide. (Andrew Hartley) $616

Classical tiger maple candlestand, New England, circa 1825, the rectangular top with canted corners on a vase and ring-turned post and tripod base, 16¾in. wide. (Skinner) $1,380

A Victorian burr walnut hexagonal sculpture stand, with well-figured top above shaped rosette applied frieze and four bobbin turned uprights, 75.5cm. (Bristol) $1,016

An early 19th century mahogany stool/library steps, the rectangular hinged padded seat reveals treads on hinged supports on square tapering legs, 28½in.
(Woolley & Wallis) $840

A late Victorian mahogany metamorphic library steps chair, the shaped back pierced an upside down heart to the crest, ebony corner blocks, the hinged seat converts to treads.
(Woolley & Wallis) $647

A Regency mahogany patent metamorphic library step armchair, after a design by Morgan and Saunders, with curved uprights and channelled molded curved bar top-rail and reeded horizontal splat, 34¼in. high.
(Christie's) $6,680

Regency mahogany metamorphic orary armchair, after a design by Morgan & Sanders, the curved anelled table toprail above a orizontal splat and downscrolled rms, caned seat and reeded ounded frontrail, 30in. high, open.
Christie's) $9,176

A set of Victorian oak library steps, with bowed balcony and conforming projecting rest, on shaped brackets and ten treads and square section balustrades and arm rest, the front with double X-frame supports, 119in. high.
(Christie's) $1,646

A set of George IV mahogany crossbanded bedside steps, with two tooled leather inset crossbanded top treads and enclosing panel door, with ring-turned column rail above, 17½in. wide. (Christie's) $1,974

set of mahogany commode steps, arly 19th century, of three leather ned bowfronted treads, the center tep with a hinged top on turned gs, 18½in. wide.
Christie's) $992

A rare set of mid 19th century walnut library steps, in the form of a Gothic settle, with pierced tracery back and upholstered seat, 24½in. wide. (Bonhams) $2,156

A set of 19th century mahogany folding library steps "The Simplex Ladder" with self acting stop, 3ft.10in. high.
(Brightwells) $1,980

A pair of early 19th century simulated rosewood foot stools of scrolled oblong form with leather covering, scroll carved sides with central roundel, 15½in. wide. (Andrew Hartley) $4,312

A William IV rosewood piano stool, square padded seat with rosewood molded edge, on a veneered and leaf carved stem with a gilt brass trellis patterned collar, 13½in. (Woolley & Wallis) $524

A 19th century mahogany framed piano stool, the circular top with damask carving, raised on turned and wrythen turned legs with splayed feet, 13¼in. wide. (Andrew Hartley) $693

A pair of Victorian walnut stools, circa 1850, the square overstuffed seat upon X shaped supports carved with acanthus scrolls and centered by a flower paterae, 17in. wide. (Bonhams) $1,540

A pair of 'X' frame stools, in Grecian style, veneered in satinwood, the scroll legs with panelled tied and petal carved side rail lifts, 22½in. (Woolley & Wallis) $4,620

An Edwardian satinwood piano stool of oblong form painted with flowers, husking and trailing foliage, 22½in. wide. (Andrew Hartley) $756

A George II style carved giltwood window stool, 19th century, later upholstered top, some damage, 82cm. wide.
(Bonhams) $229

A mid Victorian walnut revolving piano stool, with later gilt decoration, 48cm. high.
(Bonhams) $191

Queen Anne style mahogany window seat, incorporating 18th century elements, with scrolled arms and cabriole legs ending in pad feet, 33in.
(Skinner) $1,540

A fine stool after Giles Grendey, the rectangular stuffed over seat with a floral needlework cartouche, on well carved channelled cabriole legs, 27in.
(Woolley & Wallis) $1,570

A Swiss pine milking stool, 19th century, in the form of a small table with hinged side panels and a frieze drawer below, 13½in. high.
(Christie's) $608

Italian Neo-classical green painted and parcel gilt tabouret, circa 1800, rectangular upholstered top over a Greek key decorated frieze, raised on circular stop fluted legs ending in leaf-carved feet, 17½in. wide.
(Skinner) $2,990

A French giltwood stool, late 19th/early 20th century, in the Louis XV style, with serpentine padded seat upholstered in Aubusson tapestry, with ribband and floral scroll-work. (Christie's) $552

A Victorian rosewood music stool with stringing, the button upholstered circular adjustable top on four shaped square section supports headed by foliate marquetry and ivory inlaid panels, 15in. wide.
(Andrew Hartley) $440

A good early Victorian rosewood piano stool, circa 1840, the rectangular padded top opening to accommodate sheet music above pierced fretwork sides.
(Bonhams) $924

A rosewood X frame stool, 19th century, possibly French, the wool and beadwork cover depicting a dog above rectangular frame with twin reeded X shaped end supports, 20½in. wide.
(Bonhams) $539

A 17th century style joined oak stool, the rectangular seat above a lunette carved frieze on turned baluster legs tied by stretchers, 18in. wide.
(Bonhams) $470

A George III mahogany window seat, circa 1780, with scrolled arms and a rectangular seat, on square section chamfered legs with beaded front corners.
(Bonhams) $5,180

A Regency rosewood 'X' frame stool, by Gillows, circa 1827, the padded drop in seat on twin scrolled end supports, tied by a turned stretcher on bun feet.
(Bonhams) $4,144

A mid Victorian walnut framed stool, the shaped upholstered tapestry top above a carved frieze and raised on carved foliate scrolled legs, 37cm. wide. (Bonhams) $293

A walnut stool, incorporating some 18th century elements, the serpentine top with drop-in padded seatabove a plain frieze centered by a shell, 21in. wide.
(Christie's) $5,962

A pair of upholstered giltwood stools, French, circa 1900, in the Art Nouveau style, each with incurved padded sides and padded seat above the apron carved with stylized flowers and ribbons, 81cm. wide. (Sotheby's) $9,867

A Regency mahogany piano-stool, by Gillows, the padded circular seat above a turned spiral shaft, on ring-turned and tapering legs joined by a stretcher.(Christie's) $2,981

A Queen Anne style window stool, the rectangular upholstered top above shell carved cabriole legs with claw and ball feet, 64cm. wide. (Bonhams) $585

An Art Deco maple dining suite with satinwood inlay, comprising an oblong table, 72 x 36in., six chairs to match, and a breakfront sideboard with frieze drawer, 47¾in. wide. (Andrew Hartley) $2,355

An Italian cream-painted and giltwood salon suite, late 19th century, possibly Tuscan or Venetian, in the neoclassical style, comprising a sofa, a pair of armchairs and six single chairs, each back of broken and splayed outline with beaded ornament hung with drapery and flowerheads, (Christie's) $10,971

A reproduction walnut dining room suite in the early Georgian style, comprising extending dining table, 10ft., eight chairs and a sideboard, all raised on scallop carved cabriole supports. (Brightwells) $11,200

A carved gilt-wood and Aubusson salon suite, Paris, circa 1870, in Louis XV style, comprising a canapé, four fauteuils, and four side chairs, each with an arched padded back and outcurved padded arms, on stylised foliate carved supports, the canapé 176cm. long. (Sotheby's) $58,450

A carved giltwood salon suite, Paris, circa 1880, in Louis XV style, comprising a canapé and four fauteuils, each with serpentine cresting centrally carved with a shell, above the upholstered back and out-curved arms on incurved supports, canapé 186cm. long. (Sotheby's) $31,563

Classical carved mahogany diminutive window bench and back stools, Boston, 1825, the upholstered window bench with fan-carved shaped crests above two upholstered arms with panelled fronts, bench 43in. wide. (Skinner) $2,185

An aluminum clad eight-piece bedroom suite by P B Crow & Co for Hunting Aviation Ltd, late 1940s, of double wardrobe, double bed frame, tallboy, dressing table, corner cabinet, pair bedside lockers and circular table, each clad in anodized light green aluminum and with orange bakelite handles. (Bristol) $722

An Edwardian mahogany part bedroom suite, with stringing and checker banding, triple wardrobe, 84in. wide, matching dressing table, writing table, bedside cupboard and chair. (Andrew Hartley) $1,960

An Art Deco walnut dining suite, quarter veneered and crossbanded, comprising a canted oblong dining table, 73½ x 37¾in. , six tub chairs in cream leather covering with arched backs, a sideboard and a serving table to match. (Andrew Hartley) $5,320

A Biedermeier fruitwood suite, circa 1820, comprising a sofa, four chairs, with bowed top rails, a centre table, with circular oyster veneered top, a rectangular wall mirror and a plant stand of tapering octagonal form. (Bonhams) $5,600

mahogany four-piece bergère suite, 1920s settee and three chairs, with shaped fluted toprails over woven cane panel backs and scroll profile arms carved with rosettes and overlapping scales, on acanthus carved outswept bracket supports, 75cm. (Bristol) $816

Art Deco maple dinette set, National Chair Co., Boston, Massachusetts, circa 1938, cut-corner table on U-shaped fluted base with extension leaves, accompanied by four stepped panel-back chairs with plank seats, table 42in. wide. (Skinner) $345

A Victorian carved walnut salon suite, in the Rococo Revival style, comprising a pair of elbow chairs with scrolled and leaf carved arched crest and matching sofa with padded back, 54in. wide. (Andrew Hartley) $2,100

A mid 20th century burr walnut dining suite. (John Maxwell) $4,000

371

An unusual late Victorian maple draughtsman's table, the rectangular drop leaf top, on a ratcheted easel and swivelling above a frieze drawer, and further shallower drawers, 30in. wide. (Woolley & Wallis) $840

A mahogany kneehole architect's table, early 19th century, the rectangular molded top with molded book rest and adjustable ratchet, with candle slides to the sides, 49½in. wide. (Christie's) $6,583

A George II walnut architect's desk, the rectangular top with re-entrant corners and rising book-stop, with a pair of circular candleslides, 30in. wide. (Christie's) $14,200

A Victorian oak architect's or draughtsman's folio cabinet, in the manner of Gillows, the sliding superstructure with elevating double ratcheted adjustable top with a pair of hinged leather-lined panels, 41¾in. wide. (Christie's) $36,800

A George III mahogany and inlaid architect's or draughtsman's table, with double ratcheted adjustable top, having a sliding frieze compartment inlaid with lines, with a fitted interior, 39½in. wide. (Christie's) $4,441

A George III mahogany architect's table, the rectangular hinged top with retractable book-rest, with candle-slides to each side, above a frieze drawer, 34¼in. wide. (Christie's) $5,679

A Charles X mahogany architect's table, the double adjustable ratcheted top inset with a panel of tooled leather, with bookrest containing a frieze drawer, 38¾in. wide. (Christie's) $7,402

A George III mahogany architect's table, the rectangular molded hinged adjustable top with mahogany crossbanding, above a full length carved deep drawer, 92cm. wide. (Bonhams) $2,772

A George III mahogany architect's table, the rectangular double-ratcheted hinged top above a fitted frieze drawer with a red leather-lined writing-surface above divisions, 52in. wide. (Christie's) $3,500

A George IV mahogany rosewood crossbanded and ebony strung breakfast table, the circular tilt-top with a reeded frieze on a turned column and four reeded splayed legs, 52in. wide. (Thomson Roddick & Medcalf) $2,248

A fine and rare Queen Anne figured mahogany diminutive breakfast table, Boston, Massachusetts, circa 1750, of rare small size, the oblong top flanked by rectangular leaves, depth open 30in. (Sotheby's) $55,375

A Victorian rosewood breakfast table, the molded edged circular tip up top on lobed baluster stem, tripod base with leaf carved downswept legs, 59½in. wide. (Andrew Hartley) $1,848

An early Victorian rosewood circular breakfast table, the well-figured tilting top with shallow frieze over faceted baluster upright and triform concave-sided platform base with bun feet and brass castors, diameter 122cm. (Bristol) $1256

A good mid Victorian walnut and marquetry breakfast table, the circular segmentally veneered top centered by a floral reserve and with a broad outer border of floral arabesques, 137cm. diameter. (Bonhams) $10,205

A Regency mahogany breakfast-table, the rounded rectangular tilt-top crossbanded in goncalo alves above a plain frieze with beaded lower edge, on a ring-turned shaft, 54in. wide.(Christie's) $6,340

A Victorian style mahogany circular tilt-top breakfast table, the molded top above turned upright and three downswept cabriole supports with brass castors, 121cm. wide. (Bristol) $550

Federal tiger maple breakfast table, New England, circa 1810, the rectangular overhanging drop leaf top with ovolo corners above a straight skirt, 36¼in. wide. (Skinner) $3,738

An early Victorian rosewood breakfast table, the dodecahedral molded tilt top set on a faceted pedestal base, with concave tripartite base, 127cm. diameter. (Bonhams) $339

An early Victorian mahogany breakfast-table, the circular molded top above a frieze and a baluster shaft with fluted plinth base, on scrolling legs bearing hunting trophy masks, 66in. diameter.(Christie's) $13,041

A Victorian rosewood oval breakfast table on bulbous column and leafage carved quadruple splay base, 4ft.10in. x 3ft.8in. (Brightwells) $2,250

A George IV mahogany breakfast table, the circular top above a turned column with lotus leaf carve collar, 48in. diameter. (Bonhams) $1,17

A Regency plum-pudding mahogany breakfast-table, the canted rectangular tilt-top inlaid with boxwood, ebony and satinwood bands, above a ring-turned shaft, 48in. wide.(Christie's) $5,962

An Anglo-Indian padouk breakfast table, circa 1870, the circular top with ripple cut edge, above a pierced foliate frieze and triform base heavily carved with foliage and berries, 53in. diameter. (Bonhams) $2,464

A polychrome decorated breakfast table, 19th century, the oval top painted in the manner of Landseer, with recumbent spaniels, within a gilt decorated border, 28½in. high. (Christie's) $4,571

A Victorian burr-walnut, kingwood crossbanded and marquetry breakfast table, the circular snap top centered by a crossbanded panel with strapwork and garlands of flowers, 58in. diameter. (Christie's) $21,385

A Regency mahogany breakfast table having later drop leaves, the top with rosewood and satinwood cross-banding on four baluster turned columns, 4ft.1in. x 4ft.10in. fully extended. (Brightwells) $3,225

A William IV mahogany tilt top breakfast table, circa 1835, the circular crossbanded top above triangular pedestal, set on a platform base, 30cm. diameter. (Bonhams) $2,24

Louis XV style kingwood and
ormolu mounted card table, circa
1860, the quarter veneered and
crossbanded serpentine top above
shaped frieze centered by an
oval Sèvres style porcelain plaque,
on square section cabriole legs,
34in. wide. (Bonhams) $1,242

A William IV card table, the
rosewood veneered 'D' shape
swivel top baize lined, on a frieze
with scroll borders to a well and
turned side rails, 3ft.¼in.
(Woolley & Wallis) $1,617

A mid Victorian walnut swivel top
card table, circa 1880, serpentine
top above a bulbous column set on
four scrolled legs, 89cm. wide.
(Bonhams) $1,064

William IV rosewood swivel top
card table, circa 1830, the rounded
rectangular top above a turned
bulbous column and set on a
concave platform base, 92cm. wide.
(Bonhams) $1,540

A Regency brass inlaid rosewood
and brass mounted patent card
table, circa 1815, the inlaid fold
over top with a shaped apron and
corner brackets, 36¼in. wide.
(Bonhams) $6,440

A Regency mahogany swivel top
card table, circa 1820, raised on
four carved outswept legs with
brass caps and castors, 91cm. wide
and 74cm. high.
(Bonhams) $1,036

George IV mahogany card table,
circa 1830, the swivel top above an
outswept base, and fitted with brass
caps and castors, 89cm. wide.
(Bonhams) $952

A George III rosewood and
satinwood crossbanded card table,
circa 1800, the inverted breakfront
top above a line inlaid band frieze,
on conforming square section
tapered legs, 36¼in. wide.
(Bonhams) $2,072

A mid Victorian mahogany and
walnut card table, circa 1880, the
hinged swivel top above a turned
column set on four outswept legs,
98cm. wide.
(Bonhams) $756

A Victorian rosewood center table, circa 1840, the rounded rectangular top with molded edge above a band frieze centered to each side with a cartouche and scroll carved motif and conforming corner decoration, 54¼in. wide.
(Bonhams) $3,640

A Victorian oak octagonal center table, the top crossbanded with geometric lines with a molded edge and frieze applied with geometric rectangular boss and roundel ornament, 57in. diameter.
(Christie's) $5,757

A George II style mahogany center table, 19th century, the rectangular top above a molded band frieze, on cabriole legs carved with acanthus leaves and scroll decoration, 72½in. wide.
(Bonhams) $14,800

A kingwood and gilt-bronze center table, Paris, circa 1890, the shaped circular top inlaid with veneer au soleil, above the frieze with central shell mount, 84cm. diameter.
(Sotheby's) $5,210

A gilt-bronze center table, French, circa 1870, with circular white marble top within a border cast with Vitruvian scrolls and lambrequin, 102cm. diameter.
(Sotheby's) $14,028

A Dutch walnut and marquetry center table, early 19th century, the circular top inlaid with a musician playing a cello bordered by floral reserves within concentric line inla 28¼in. diameter.
(Bonhams) $1,18

A Milanese ebony veneered, ebonized and ivory inlaid center table, 19th century, the rectangular top with projecting angular corners centered by a mythological group of Venus in her chariot surrounded by mermaids and armorini, 42in. wide.
(Christie's) $8,228

An oriental padouk wood center table of cylindrical form, the top carved with emblems and with beaded edge, raised on square section supports, 25in. wide.
(Andrew Hartley) $700

A William & Mary walnut center table with boxwood stringing and cross-banding, having shaped frieze with acorn drops raised on chamfered cabriole legs, 30 x 20ir
(Brightwells) $6,20

One of a pair of George II style giltwood and marble topped console table, after a design by William Kent, each with a top with outset square corners, above an egg and dart edge and wave carved frieze, 55½in. wide. (Bonhams) (Two) $28,120

Classical bird's-eye maple and mahogany console table, probably Vermont, circa 1825-30, the rectangular white marble top with molded edge above a straight skirt centering a mahogany panel with ovolo corners, 40in. wide. (Skinner) $2,875

A Victorian white-painted cast-iron serpentine console table, the white marble top above a pierced floral and shell-decorated frieze, on cabriole legs with scroll feet, 57½in. wide. (Christie's) $2,961

carved giltwood console table, Victorian, circa 1880, the serpentine variegated marble top above the shell and C-scroll carved apron on foliate scrolled supports joined by a putto, 92cm. wide. (Sotheby's) $3,006

A pair of Austrian mahogany corner bowfront console tables, 19th century, each with gray marble top, the ebony inlaid and painted frieze on scrolling legs, with a mirror back, 26in. wide. (Christie's) $1,327

A George II ebonized and gilt gesso console table, the later marble top with brass edge above a frieze decorated with scrolling foliage, on acanthus carved cabriole legs and scrolled feet, distressed, 36¼in. wide. (Bonhams) $4,480

giltwood console table, of George style, late 19th / early 20th century, the later rectangular pink-veined marble top above an egg-and-dart molding and pounced frieze, 52in. wide. (Christie's) $6,007

A console table, veneered in oyster walnut with figured ebony star and checker circle inlay to the top, the frieze drawer inlaid with a star and mosaic banded, 31¾in. wide. (Woolley & Wallis) $1,309

A George III style mahogany console table, 20th century, the demi-lune top with a drawer, the back stamped 7903/199, 122cm. wide. (Bonhams) $2,940

A fine George IV mahogany concentric extending circular dining table, circa 1825, the circular top with molded edge above a panelled frieze with eight retractable lopers, 106in. extended.
(Bonhams) $148,000

A William IV mahogany extending dining table with drop leaves pulling out to accommodate two extra leaves on five turned and fluted tapering supports and casters, 8ft full extension.
(Brightwells) $6,027

A Regency extending dining table, of patent design, in the manner of Morgan and Saunders, the hinged D-shaped tops with reeded edges opening to accommodate three extra leaves, 100¾in. long.
(Christie's) $4,937

A Louis Philippe mahogany extending dining table, the rounded top with a molded edge and five additonal leaves, above a conforming ripple molded frieze, 148in. extended.
(Christie's) $6,808

An Edwardian walnut extending dining table, the rectangular top with two extra leaves, the molded edge with rounded corners, the frieze with a wind out action, 6ft.10in. extended.
(Woolley & Wallis) $1,540

A large mahogany oval drop leaf dining table, with an arcaded frieze, a hinged underframe, on six turned tapering legs to pad feet, 5ft.9in.
(Woolley & Wallis) $10,640

An Italian white marble, scagliola and giltwood circular table, in the baroque style, the circular table top centered by a star, with stylized floral motifs, above a serpentine apron, each side centered by a cartouche, 39in. diameter.
(Christie's) $10,364

A French mahogany drop-leaf dining table, 19th century, with three additional later leaves, plain friezes and faceted tapering legs with brass caps and castors, 132in. extended.(Christie's) $3,455

A Regency mahogany concertina dining table, circa 1820, the rounded rectangular top fitted with four leaves, set on a concertina body with brass mounts and raised on six turned and twisted legs, 312cm. long.
(Bonhams) $16,800

A Victorian mahogany extending dining table, the rounded rectangular top including three additional leaves with a molded edge above a plain frieze, with a simulated oak panelled leaf box, 121in. extended.
(Christie's) $7,452

A Regency mahogany campaign patent extending dining table, in the manner of Morgan and Saunders, circa 1810, the rectangular top with reeded edge above a band frieze opening to support the leaves, 91¼in. long.
(Bonhams) $7,000

Victorian mahogany extending
ining table, the rounded
ctangular top with a molded
dge and two additional leaves, on
ulbous turned and boldly reeded
gs, 94in. extended.
Christie's) $3,574

Queen Anne Santo Domingo
mahogany dining table, Rhode
Island, circa 1750-60, the
rectangular overhanging drop-leaf
top on cabriole legs ending in pad
feet, 47¾in. wide.
(Skinner) $10,925

A mahogany extending dining table,
late 19th/early 20th century, the
rectangular top with a gadrooned
edge and two additional leaves,
above a stop-fluted and rosette
carved frieze, 128in. extended.
(Christie's) $4,085

George II mahogany large drop-
af table, the oval twin-flap top
bove a drawer to each end, on
abriole legs and pad feet, two ears
eplaced, 72½in. wide, open.
Christie's) $15,850

A Victorian burr oak, possibly
pollard oak and ebonized extending
dining table, including six extra
leaves, the D-shaped ends with a
molded ovolo edge and molded
frieze, 59in wide.
(Christie's) $13,982

early 19th century mahogany
ar dining table, the circular top
ending outwards with four sliding
pports (segment leaves missing),
turned stem and four saber
ports, 5ft.3in. diameter.
ightwells) $109,710

A George II mahogany circular
tripod table, the circular tilt-top
above a bird-cage support and a
ring-turned column, on cabriole legs
with pierced angles, 38¼in.
diameter.
(Christie's) $25,028

A mahogany Cumberland action
dining table, early 19th century and
parts later, the hinged top with
rounded molded edge raised on
ring-turned column supports, the
top 50¾in. extended.
(Christie's) $1,817

brown oak and oak extending
ing table, early 20th century, the
xagonally shaped stellar inlaid
above a stepped and acanthus-
rved edge including two
ditional leaves, 138in. fully
tended.
hristie's) $5,216

A George II mahogany oval twin
flap dining table, the solid top above
shaped end aprons, on four
cabriole supports with ball-and-claw
feet and single swing action to each
side. 140 x 121cm.
(Bristol) $1,382

Queen Anne maple drop-leaf table,
Massachusetts, 1750-75, the
rectangular leaves flank the scrolled
ends over cabriole legs, full
extension 45½in.
(Skinner) $2,070

A Louis IV style vitrine table, the glass panelled hinged top above side windows, and raised on slender cabriole legs united by a platform stretcher, 80cm. wide.
(Bonhams) $1,694

A French bronze, marble and oak shop display cabinet, late 19th century, in the Art Nouveau taste, the rectangular glazed top with stylized decoration to the corners, raised on mottled green and white marble slab, 42in. wide.
(Christie's) $2,560

A walnut kidney shaped display table, late 19th century, fitted with a glazed top and sides, the whole with gilt metal applied mounts, 69cm. wide.
(Bonhams) $2,170

An Edwardian mahogany kidney shaped display cabinet, with satinwood crossbanding, stringing and marquetry floral pendants, glazed top and sides, 23½in. wide.
(Andrew Hartley) $1,365

A pair of George IV rosewood cabinets-on-stands, attributed to Gillows, each with a glazed rectangular cabinet with three-quarter pierced brass gallery and enclosing a shelf, on a stand with rounded rectangular top, 29in. wide.
(Christie's) $17,519

A Victorian mahogany display cabinet, the upper section with pierced broken pediment on molded and dentil cornice, glazed doors and sides, 29½in. wide.
(Andrew Hartley) $2,59

A 19th century Louis XV style kingwood display table of shaped oblong form with gilt metal mounts, the hinged top with glazed insert, 23¾in. wide.
(Andrew Hartley) $1,270

A Regency satinwood and tulipwood crossbanded vitrine table, circa 1815, the hinged glazed top above a band frieze, on ring turned legs and castors, 34¼in. wide.
(Bonhams) $1,260

A George III style mahogany and boxwood inlaid bijouterie table, circa 1890, the rectangular glazed display case top enclosing a velve lined interior above square tapere legs, 16in. wide.
(Bonhams) $647

hippendale mahogany carved
ressing table, Philadelphia, 1760-
5, the rectangular top with
olded edge overhangs a case
ith quarter columns above four
umb-molded drawers, 35in. wide.
Skinner) $13,800

A Regency mahogany dressing-
table, attributed to Gillows, the
rectangular three-quarter galleried
top above a concave-fronted freize
drawer, 42in. wide.
(Christie's) $11,178

A Regency mahogany dressing-
table, the rectangular three-quarter
galleried top above two frieze
drawers, on square tapering legs.
(Christie's) $3,726

ueen Anne carved cherry
ressing table, coastal
Massachusetts, New Hampshire or
aine, 1750-80, the thumbmolded
op overhangs a case of drawers
ith cockbeaded surrounds and a
entral fan-carved drawer, 33in.
ide. (Skinner) $29,900

An Edwardian satinwood dressing-
table, with mahogany and
satinwood serpentine slatted sliding
top revealing three panels inlaid
with ebony, the central panel
banded to both sides in tulipwood
and enclosing a hinged mirror, 32in.
wide. (Christie's) $5,589

A fine Queen Anne carved and
figured mahogany dressing table,
Wethersfield area, Connecticut,
circa 1750, one long and three
short drawers, the center one fan-
carved, 35½in.
(Sotheby's) $68,500

good mid Victorian burr walnut,
ngwood and tulipwood inlaid
ressing table, by Holland & Sons,
e figured rectangular top with
utset rounded corners and a
olded edge, 23¼in. wide.
Bonhams) $3,454

A Queen Anne burl maple-
veneered dressing table, Boston,
Massachusetts, 1730-50, the
rectangular top above one long and
three short drawers, 32¼in.
(Sotheby's) $8,337

A mahogany and gilt-bronze
dressing table, French, circa 1890,
the rectangular gray and white
veined marble top surmounted by
an octagonal adjustable mirror
within a band of palmettes, 117cm.
wide. (Sotheby's) $20,873

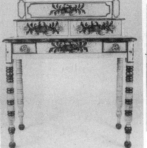

Queen Anne maple dressing table, New England, circa 1740-60, the molded rectangular top overhangs a case of a single drawer with a three-drawer facade joined by a shaped skirt with two acorn-form pendants, 32¾in. wide. (Skinner) $12,000

Federal painted and decorated dressing table, Newburyport, Massachusetts, circa 1820-30, the backsplash above two small indented drawers and one long drawer, 35⅜in. wide. (Skinner) $4,600

Queen Anne walnut carved dressing table, Massachusetts, 1730-50, one long above three short drawers, the central one of which is fan-carved, above a skirt with flat-headed arches, 34½in. wide. (Skinner) $28,750

Classical faux dressing table, New England, circa 1820, the scrolled backboard and chamfered top on conforming base containing a single long drawer, allover red fanciful graining, 29¼in. wide. (Skinner) $575

A late Victorian inlaid satinwood dressing table, by Gillows of Lancaster, circa 1885, the shaped-top swing mirror with inlaid inverted cavetto frieze flanked by shaped side supports, 104cm. wide. (Bristol) $1,727

An Italian walnut, fruitwood, burr yew and marquetry inlaid poudreuse, late 18th century, the rectangular top with three panels centered by an oval medallion depicting a female bust flanked by two oval reserves, 35¾in. wide. (Bonhams) $4,480

A kingwood, marquetry and gilt-bronze poudreuse, French, circa 1850, in Louis XV style, the hinged serpentine top centered by two lovebirds within a stylized floral border, 66cm. wide. (Sotheby's) $3,960

Louis XV style painted dressing table, 19th century, the top enclosing lift-up mirror flanked by wells, with central drawer flanked by two small drawers, 33in. long. (Skinner) $1,610

Grain painted dressing stand, labelled J.G. Briggs, Charlestown, New Hampshire, 1830-33, the shaped splashboard above two small drawers and a long drawer on four ring-turned tapering legs, 36⅜in. wide. (Skinner) $920

ak drop leaf dining table, 2 drop
aves, raised on central support
th shaped frieze at either end,
ised on cabriole supports with
d and ball feet, 18th century and
er, 48in. (G.A. Key) $1,001

A late Victorian walnut drop-leaf
occasional table, the square cleated
top with four rounded leaves, on
cluster column supports joined by a
shaped undertier, 31in. wide.
(Christie's) $1,454

A mahogany gateleg dining table,
the rectangular drop leaf top above
a frame with six fluted tapering legs
on tassel feet, 5ft.4in. x 4ft.
(Woolley & Wallis) $1,355

Regency mahogany and inlaid
op flap worktable, the top
ossbanded in rosewood
ontaining two drawers in the
onized strung frieze with sliding
ell below, 26¾in. wide, extended.
hristie's) $1,747

A William IV oak drop-leaf work
table, the hinged top and reeded
edge containing a drawer to either
side having a sliding well below,
31¾in. wide.
(Christie's) $4,048

A George IV mahogany and
fiddleback-mahogany work-table,
the rounded rectangular twin-flap
top above two panelled drawers,
the top drawer fitted with a green
leather-lined writing-slope and a
mahogany-lined pen drawer, 33½in.
wide. (Christie's) $4,171

9th century mahogany side
e, the rectangular drop side
ves above a single frieze drawer,
m. wide.
nhams) $862

A George II mahogany drop leaf
dining table, circa 1740, the oval
hinged top above a slight arcaded
frieze, on scrolled cabriole legs and
claw and ball feet, 59in. wide,
leaves open.
(Bonhams) $3,500

A George III mahogany spider-
gateleg table, the rectangular twin-
flap top on turned legs joined by
stretchers, on pad feet with double-
gateleg action, 26¾in. wide.
(Christie's) $5,839

A Regency kingwood, crossbanded and inlaid drum top library table, the circular rotating top crossbanded and inset with a panel of tooled leather, containing five cedar lined drawers in the frieze, 42in. diameter.
(Christie's) $21,942

A Regency mahogany drum table, circa 1815, the circular rotating top above four short drawers and four dummy drawers, set on a ring turned pillar with a concave platform base, 107cm. diameter.
(Bonhams) $11,760

A mahogany drum table, early 19th century, the tan leather-lined top with a reeded edge above a frieze with four drawers and four false drawers, 42in. diameter.
(Christie's) $12,954

A George III mahogany drum top library table, circa 1800, the circular later leather inset top above four sliding frieze drawers and four hinged drawers, 48¼in. diameter.
(Bonhams) $14,800

A 19th century drum table, leather top with hinged reading slope, five drawers and three dummy drawers, with satinwood stringing turned stem, by Edwards & Roberts, 3ft. diameter.
(Brightwells) $8,008

An early Victorian oak library drum table, the circular revolving radialling-veneered top above four drawers and four simulated drawers, on an octagonal tapering column, 41½in. diameter.
(Christie's) $5,600

George III style mahogany drum library table, second half 19th century, circular top with inset green gilt tooled leather, over series of working and sham drawers, 35in. diameter. (Skinner) $4,313

A George III mahogany circular drum table, the green leather-lined top above four drawers and four simulated drawers, on a turned baluster support and three square downswept legs, 36¼in. diameter.
(Christie's) $10,011

A mahogany drum top library table, 19th century, the crossbanded top inset with a panel of red tooled leather, containing four drawers in the frieze, the top 49in. diameter.
(Christie's) $5,851

ak circular gate leg dining table,
ne drop leaf and raised on ball and
let supports, joined by plain
tretchers, 18th century and later,
0in. (G.A. Key) $400

Baroque maple gate-leg table,
Massachusetts, 1720-80, the
hinged leaves flank the single
drawer, the gate and the block,
vase and ring-turned legs are joined
by similar stretchers, with leaves
47½in. deep.
(Skinner) $19,550

A walnut gateleg table, English, late
17th century, the oval hinged top
above a single end frieze drawer,
on ball and fillet turned baluster
legs, 51½in. wide, open.
(Bonhams) $8,085

n early 18th century oak gateleg
able, the rounded rectangular top
bove elliptical leaves, set on a
ase with a single drawer, 139cm.
ully extended.
Bonhams) $1,463

A George III mahogany gate leg
table, the rectangular hinged top
containing a later frieze drawer to
one end, on turned legs, 33¾in.
wide extended.
(Christie's) $1,974

An oak corner gateleg table,
English, early 18th century, the
panelled top above a band frieze,
on turned baluster legs tied by
stretchers, the top 24½in. square.
(Bonhams) $1,323

A late 17th century gateleg table
with yew wood top, on oak base
with turned baluster supports and
squared stretchers, fitted with two
drawers, 35in. square.
(Brightwells) $5,145

An 18th century oak gateleg table,
the rounded rectangular top above
elliptical leaves and raised on
bobbin turned legs, 120cm. deep
fully extended.
(Bonhams) $277

A small oak gateleg table, the oval
top raised on baluster turned and
block legs, scrolled frieze with
drawer, 30¼in. wide, early 18th
century.
(Andrew Hartley) $2,079

A Spanish walnut refectory table, 19th century, with possible earlier elements, the rectangular top possibly of an earlier date, on ring-turned splayed legs joined by undulating stretchers, 75in. wide.
(Christie's) $5,851

Federal mahogany veneer two-part dining table, Massachusetts, 1820s, the two ends each rounded and with a hinged leaf supported from beneath, above a skirt on ring-turned spiral carved legs ending in ring-turned feet on castors, 78¾in. long.
(Skinner) $1,840

An oak and inlaid six leg refectory table, Dutch, 19th century, with a cleated plank top and chequer strung edge, above molded and ebonized raised panel frieze, 95in. long. (Christie's) $3,826

Pine painted harvest table, New England, late 18th/19th century, the scrubbed top with hinged leaves which flank the painted base with its ring-turned tapering legs, 102¾in. long.
(Skinner) $11,500

Good reproduction mahogany oval extending wind ou dining table, in the Gillows manner gadroon molded rim over a plain frieze and raised on C scroll molded supports, extends to 96in. including two loose leaves
(G.A. Key) $2,175

A fine and rare Classical carved, gilded, ormolu-mounted, and stencil-decorated mahogany three-part banquet table, Duncan Phyfe or one of his contemporaries, New York, circa 1825, leaf-carved animal-paw legs, 10ft. 5in. open.
(Sotheby's) $37,375

A substantial Victorian pollard oak extending dining table, the molded-edge top with four original leaves with well-figured burr veneers above four substantial reeded vase supports with ceramic castors, 362 x 138cm. extended. (Bristol) $4,340

Irish mahogany wake table, 18/19th century, the al twin-flap top on eight square legs, the top and se associated, the top reshaped, 79in. wide. hristie's) $10,011

A Victorian pollard oak extending dining table, of large proportions, the extending top with a molded edge raised on bulbous and fluted turned legs terminating in brass caps and porcelain castors, the caps engraved *Cope and Collinson*, 189¾in. fully extended. (Christie's) $9,448

Victorian walnut extending dining table, with D-aped ends and single leaf, on four tapered faceted pports with wooden castors, 190 x 130cm. tended; and a later pine leaf. (Bristol) $1,250

A late Georgian mahogany three-section dining table with drop leaves, semi-circular ends raised on twelve squared tapering legs, 4ft. wide x 9ft. full extension. (Brightwells) $2,279

A walnut and pine draw-leaf slate top table, Swiss, late 18th/early 19th century, with later pull-out leaves, the slate top within cleats, above a plain frieze, 93in. fully extended. (Christie's) $2,956

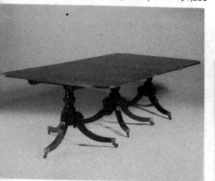

Regency mahogany three-pedestal dining-table, mprising three tilt-top sections and a later leaf, the unded rectangular top with reeded edge, on baluster pports and square tapering reeded legs, below a own, 117½in. long, without later leaf. hristie's) $25,028

A mahogany D-end extending dining table, parts early 19th century, including two additional leaves, the ends each with a shaped conforming frieze and with chamfered square section legs, 104in. extended. (Christie's) $2,528

A late Victorian oak library table with a leather-lined top and three drawers to each side, on turned tapering legs, 72in. wide.
(Christie's) $1,208

A George IV mahogany library table or desk, the green leather-lined rectangular top with two ratcheted sections to one half, above two frieze drawers and a kneehole flanked by five further drawers, 57½in. wide.
(Christie's) $5,589

An early Victorian mahogany library table, the rectangular leather-lined top above three simulated frieze drawers to each side, with a drawer to each end, 76in. wide.
(Christie's) $10,84[?]

A Louis XV ormolu and brass-mounted kingwood bureau plat, the featherbanded red leather-lined rectangular top with foliate corners above three red paper-lined frieze drawers, 58in. wide.
(Christie's) $12,110

A Regency ormolu-mounted rosewood library table, crossbanded overall in goncalo alves, the rectangular top with flap to each end, the underside lined with gilt-tooled brown leather, 55¼in. wide, open.
(Christie's) $8,343

A Victorian mahogany partner's library table, circa 1840, the rectangular tooled leather inset top above three frieze drawers to each side, on reeded turned tapered legs and brass castors, 59in. wide.
(Bonhams) $7,104

A William IV rosewood library table of rounded oblong form, the panelled frieze with drawers and dummy drawers having beaded edging and centered by carved flower heads, 54in. wide.
(Andrew Hartley) $2,772

A matched pair of George IV mahogany writing-tables, in the manner of Gillows, each with molded rounded rectangular top above a bead-and-reel frieze, on reeded and ring-turned baluster legs, both 47½in. wide.
(Christie's) $10,011

Gillow of Lancaster, library table, circa 1880, oak chamfered rectangular top inset with black leather writing surface, raised on Gothic manner supports, 47¼in. wide. (Sotheby's) $4,200

A Victorian rosewood loo table, the molded edged top on lobed baluster stem, scrolled quadruple base, 51in. wide. (Andrew Hartley) $1,617

A Victorian walnut, burr-walnut and marquetry loo table, the oval quarter-veneered top with a foliate-carved edge inlaid with boxwood lines, foliate arabesques and cartouches of exotic woods, 52in. wide. (Christie's) $1,986

A Victorian walnut loo table, the quarter veneered burr walnut top, on carved baluster stem, quadripartite base with down curved legs, 42 x 54in. (Andrew Hartley) $1,848

A mid Victorian walnut loo table, the oval top with boxwood stringing and central foliate scrolls, set on a turned column, 120cm. wide. (Bonhams) $739

An early Victorian mahogany loo table, circa 1840, the tilt top above a turned and gadrooned stem set on a concave platform base, 112cm. diameter. (Bonhams) $1,470

A mid 19th century rosewood loo table, the molded circular tilt top set on a baluster pedestal, fitted with three outswept legs, 135cm. diameter. (Bonhams) $2,772

A Victorian rosewood loo table, the oval veneered tilt top with a frieze and a veneered block with leaf petal carving to the vase shape stem, 34in. x 4ft. (Woolley & Wallis) $1,201

A Victorian figured walnut oval loo table, the quarter veneered tilting top over foliate carved baluster upright and four downswept supports with scroll feet, width 137cm. (Bristol) $1,130

A Victorian loo table, the circular top veneered in faded rosewood with a molded edge, the rosewood veneered panelled vase shape stem on three rosewood molded cabriole legs, 4ft.5½in. diameter. (Woolley & Wallis) $1,836

A rustic brown-painted twig table, 19th century, the elliptical radially-veneered top with lambrequin frieze, above a tripartite base, 29in. high. (Christie's) $1,335

A George III Irish mahogany tripod table, with plain circular tip up revolving top, on gadrooned baluster stem, 38in. wide. (Andrew Hartley) $3,080

An Anglo-Indian metal-mounted circular occasional table, 20th century, the top decorated with acanthus leaves, above a shaped scroll and acanthus frieze, 64cm. diameter. (Christie's) $2,245

A George III mahogany folding table, the inlaid triangular top hinged to reveal a compartment, plain frieze, on four cabriole legs with shaped pointed pad feet, 35in. wide.
(Andrew Hartley) $3,234

A set of four Victorian papier mâché and mother of pearl inlaid quartetto tables, the largest with a serpentine rectangular top painted with horses watering, the others of plain rectangular form, one with a chessboard, 24½in. wide.
(Bonhams) $942

A French ormolu-mounted tulipwood and amaranth occasional table, in the Louis XV style, circa 1895, surmounted by a serpentine rectangular top, the frieze fitted with a side drawer, on four cabriole legs, 23in. wide.(Christie's) $3,455

A Sheraton period pole screen table, the adjustable pole with a tilting rosewood glazed angled frame top with a needlework panel of roses, 16½in.
(Woolley & Wallis) $1,540

A good William and Mary turned walnut tavern table, Pennsylvania, 1720-30, the removable shaped rectangular top above a frieze drawer on turned legs, 34½in. wide.
(Sotheby's) $4,600

An 18th century elm cricket table with circular top on three slightly splayed legs, joined by a triangular tray shelf, diameter 28½in.
(David Lay) $1,335

A mahogany supper table, the circular tilt top with a cut out border of dishes on a revolving birdcage to an open carved triform base, 26in. (Woolley & Wallis) $8,302

A pair of mid 19th century mahogany hall tables, the rectangular reeded edge tops with rounded front corners, the veneered frieze with applied moldings, 3ft.10in. wide. (Woolley & Wallis) $5,040

A George II mahogany occasional table, the circular tilt top on a revolving birdcage action, with turned pilasters to the block, 3ft.1in.diameter. (Woolley & Wallis) $1,038

Classical bird's-eye maple table, probably Vermont, circa 1830, the octagonal top on tapered octagonal ogee-molded pedestal surmounting four scrolled legs, 29in. wide. (Skinner) $1,610

An Edwardian inlaid mahogany oval occasional table, the oval top with central inlaid fan cartouche and raised lip to edge, 68cm. wide. (Bonhams) $343

Napoleon III fruitwood marquetry and gilt-metal mounted drop-leaf table, circa 1870, with floral marquetry and frieze drawer raised on circular fluted legs, 24in. wide. (Skinner) $978

A 19th century walnut tricoteuse, crossbanded and with gilt metal mounts, the hinged lid with marquetry panel depicting a musical trophy on an inlaid trellis ground, 29½in. wide. (Andrew Hartley) $2,079

A Victorian oak hall table, the brass galleried top above a single frieze drawer, stamped *JAS Shoolbred & Co. /6005*, with galleried undertier, 51cm. wide. (Bonhams) $585

A William IV Irish mahogany occasional table, the rectangular drop leaf top above a deep frieze drawer, oak lined, on a ring turned and acanthus carved stem, 26¾in. (Woolley & Wallis) $392

19th century mahogany circular pedestal table, segmented veneered top with molded edge, over a blind fret work molded frieze, 27in. (G.A. Key) $479

An Edwardian satinwood occasional table, crossbanded with string and parquetry banding, the circular top inlaid with husks and flowerheads, 18in. wide. (Andrew Hartley) $1,335

A 19th century mahogany occasional table with circular dropleaf top on turned column with quadruple splay base, 2ft.9in. diameter.(Brightwells) $2,695

An Edwardian satinwood two tier tricoteuse of oval form with mahogany crossbanding and stringing, removable glass tray top with parquetry edging and brass loop handles, 34¾in. (Andrew Hartley) $3,542

A George III marquetry inlaid tulipwood occasional table, circa 1790, of oval form, with a Greek key pierced brass gallery, the central panel inlaid with flowers, 19in. wide. (Bonhams) $7,696

A George III mahogany serpentine silver table, circa 1760, the shaped top with a later pierced fretwork gallery, above a blind fretwork frieze, the legs with incised geometric decoration, 33½in. wide. (Bonhams) $16,280

Adolphe Chanaux, incised geometric motif occasional table, late 1920s, oak, overall worked to create variously textured surfaces imitating galuchat or snakeskin arranged in geometric patterns, 20½in..(Sotheby's) $13,440

An elm tripod table, English, late 18th century, the oval hinged top on a ring turned column and outswept legs, 25¼in. wide. (Bonhams) $5,586

An unusual mahogany folding top table, 19th century and later, possibly Irish, the rectangular hinged top with a reeded edge and fitted with dummy drawer fronts to the front and reverse, swivel dish holders, 75in. wide extended. (Christie's) $2,560

Federal mahogany veneer Pembroke table, New York, early 19th century, the hinged shaped leaves flank the single drawer at each end, one working, one faux, 42½in. wide.
(Skinner) $1,380

Chippendale mahogany Pembroke table, New England, 1760-90, the serpentine top with similarly shaped leaves flanking straight skirts with beaded edges, 30½in. wide.
(Skinner) $6,325

Federal mahogany veneer Pembroke table, New York, circa 1815, with rectangular top flanked by shaped drop leaves and two drawers, one working, one faux, 22¼in. wide.
(Skinner) $3,105

George III string inlaid satinwood, Pembroke table, 1790, with oval inlaid top and crossbanded border, on square tapered legs ending in spade feet, 43½in. wide.
(Skinner) $2,185

A very fine and rare Federal inlaid and highly figured mahogany Pembroke table, New York, circa 1795, on square tapering line-and husk-inlaid legs, 40¾in. open.
(Sotheby's) $51,750

A George III satinwood and palisander crossbanded Pembroke table, circa 1790, with a single end frieze drawer, on line inlaid square section tapered legs and lotus casts brass cap castors, 39½in. wide open. (Bonhams) $5,320

A Federal inlaid cherrywood Pembroke table, probably Connecticut, circa 1805, the rectangular top flanked by shaped leaves above a hidden frieze drawer, 40¼in. wide open.
(Sotheby's) $3,737

A Regency mahogany Pembroke table with reeded top with satinwood stringing, fitted with a single drawer on four turned columns and quadruple splay base, 3ft. x 3ft.5in. open.
(Brightwells) $1,200

Federal mahogany inlaid Pembroke table, probably New York, circa 1790-1800, the rectangular drop leaf top with ovoid corners and string inlaid edge above a straight skirt with inlaid stringing and cockbeaded drawer, 22¾in. wide.
(Skinner) $5,463

A good Federal inlaid cherrywood Pembroke table, branded *E. Swift*, probably Connecticut, circa 1800, the oblong top flanked by shaped leaves above a hidden frieze drawer, 33½in. open.
(Sotheby's) $11,500

A George III Sheraton-style satinwood banded Pembroke table, the shaped rectangular top above one true and one false frieze drawer with twin oval panel inlaid fronts, 92 x 91.5cm. extended.
(Bristol) $973

A George III harewood and marquetry oval Pembroke table, the oval top banded in satinwood and inlaid with laurel, the main field with an oval medallion of palms and acanthus, 37in. wide, open.
(Christie's) $26,696

A George III satinwood Pembroke table, inlaid overall with boxwood and ebonized lines, the rounded rectangular twin-flap top crossbanded in rosewood, 39in. wide open.
(Christie's) $5,216

A George III padouk Pembroke table, the rectangular twin-flap diagonally-banded in goncalo alvez, above a frieze drawer and a simulated drawer to the reverse, on square chamfered legs, 41½in. wide, open.
(Christie's) $14,182

A George III satinwood and polychrome-decorated Pembroke table, inlaid overall with ebonized lines, the canted rectangular top with later decorated floral border depicting roses, lilies, and other flowers, 35½in. wide.
(Christie's) $4,672

A George III crossbanded and ebony strung satinwood Pembroke table, the crossbanded twin flap top with lily engraved border above true and opposing false drawer, 97 x 81cm. extended.
(Bristol) $2,277

A George III mahogany pedestal Pembroke table, the top and base associated, crossbanded twin-flap top above a frieze drawer, on a ring-turned baluster tripartite base, 37in. wide.(Christie's) $2,502

A George III mahogany and marquetry Pembroke table, the oval top with a molded edge above a frieze drawer inlaid with boxwood lines, 41in. wide.
(Christie's) $1,047

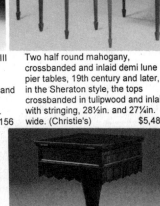

A giltwood pier table, of George III style, probably 19th century and reconstructed, the later siena marble top above a fluted frieze and ribbon-tied border, on ram monopodia cabriole legs, 48½in. wide. (Christie's) $14,156

Two half round mahogany, crossbanded and inlaid demi lune pier tables, 19th century and later, in the Sheraton style, the tops crossbanded in tulipwood and inlaid with stringing, 28½in. and 27¼in. wide. (Christie's) $5,486

A giltwood pier table, late 20th century, in the neo-classical taste, surmounted by a green marble top with a molded white marble edge, 49½in. wide. (Christie's) $3,291

READING TABLES

An unusual mid Victorian amboyna, rosewood and marquetry inlaid two tier lady's reading table, circa 1870, the rectangular top inlaid with a basket of flowers and mounted with a brass three-quarter gallery, 48cm. wide. (Bonhams) $1,848

A Scottish Victorian yew wood writing/reading table, circa 1840, the double hinged top sloping for a reading rest and lifting to reveal a writing surface, above a single drawer with arcaded friezes running to all sides. 20in. square. (Bonhams) $2,664

An unusual mid Victorian walnut reader's companion, the circular top with a revolving candlestick above a multiple baluster column and a triform galleried book shelf, 90cm. high. (Bonhams) $1,540

SERVING TABLES

A good Victorian carved oak serving table, the back carved with central shell motif flanked by S-scrolls above molded top and ogee shaped frieze drawer, 145cm. wide. (Bristol) $1,649

A Victorian mahogany metamorphic buffet table, the rectangular rising molded edge top with molded lifts revealing two further tiers, 3ft.4½in. wide. (Woolley & Wallis) $2,310

A George IV mahogany sideboard table, the solid top and applied molded edge above a figured veneered stepped frieze, on waisted turned and ribbed tapering legs, 7ft.11in. wide. (Woolley & Wallis) $8,680

A side table, in late 17th century style, the rectangular molded edge top in hardwood, the frieze drawer veneered in rosewood, on bun feet, 3ft.10½in.
(Woolley & Wallis) $3,388

A Dutch walnut side table, basically late 17th century, the later rectangular top above a frieze drawer on six baluster turned supports united by a shaped platform stretcher, 36in. wide.
(Bonhams) $980

A black lacquered side table of 17th century design, painted and gilded with chinoiserie river scenes and flowers, single long frieze drawer, 36¼in. wide, 19th century.
(Andrew Hartley) $1,771

A Louis XVI style inlaid ebonized and parcel gilt marble topped side table, converted from a stand, circa 1880, the later marble top with molded edge above a spring loaded frieze drawer, 27¼in. wide.
(Bonhams) $2,516

Fine pair of Edwardian style fruitwood and harewood inlaid satinwood marble-top side tables, circa 1890, each with three-quarter gallery and white marble top above three drawers, 19½in. wide.
(Skinner) $4,888

A George III style rosewood and satinwood crossbanded and marquetry inlaid side table, stamped *Liberty & Co., Regent Street*, the demi-lune top inlaid with an urn and rinceau motif above a frieze drawer.
(Bonhams) $2,512

A giltwood marble top side table, 20th century, in the manner of William Kent, surmounted by a rectangular green marble top, the frieze with Vitruvian scrolls and punched ornament, 40½in. wide.
(Christie's) $6,909

Two mahogany and gilt-bronze side tables, French, in the Transitional style, one with doors opening to shelves, the other with a platform stretcher, larger: 53.5cm. wide.
(Sotheby's) $7,210

An inlaid oak side table, Dutch, part 17th century, the later angled top with thick molded edge above a panelled frieze inlaid with a geometric 'dog tooth' design, 39½in. wide.
(Bonhams) $1,249

Regency mahogany sofa table, inlaid overall with boxwood and ebony lines, the rounded rectangle twin-flap top crossbanded in rosewood, 63½in. wide. (Christie's) $4,672

A Regency padouk and rosewood sofa table, the rounded rectangular twin-flap top banded in partridgewood and boxwood, above two mahogany-lined drawers to each side, 60in. wide, open. (Christie's) $9,176

A Regency rosewood sofa table, the rounded rectangular twin-flap top crossbanded in satinwood above two frieze drawers to the front and two simulated drawers to the reverse, 57in. wide open. (Christie's) $15,017

A Regency rosewood sofa table of unusually small proportions fitted with a single drawer, on cheval frame with fluted quarter roundels, 1ft.6in. wide. (Brightwells) $5,700

A George III burr ash and burr yew sofa table, circa 1790, the crossbanded double hinged top with reeded edge, inlaid with a central oval above a pair of true frieze drawers, 57¼in. wide open. (Bonhams) $60,680

A Regency camphorwood sofa table, the rectangular top with hinged flaps above two frieze drawers, one fitted to one side and simulated drawers to the other, 40¾. wide, open. (Christie's) $4,388

A fine sofa table, veneered in rosewood, the top with satinwood and kingwood banding, the end flaps with rounded corners, 5ft.1½in. (Woolley & Wallis) $6,160

A fine sofa table, mahogany veneered, the rectangular twin flap top crossbanded and inlaid with stringing, above two frieze drawers. (Woolley & Wallis) $3,672

Sheraton period faded mahogany sofa table, rectangular drop leaf top, the side flaps with rounded corners, key inlaid banded frieze with drawers, 35in. wide, circa 1800. (Woolley & Wallis) $1,355

A mid Victorian walnut veneer Sutherland table, 91cm. wide. (Bonhams) $408

A Victorian rosewood Sutherland table with marquetry and stringing, shaped canted oblong top, on twin turned tapering end supports and trestles, jointed by a pole stretcher, 21¼in. wide. (Andrew Hartley) $1,178

Edwardian mahogany Sutherland table, boxwood banded and ebonized strung border, two drop flaps with canted corners and raised on ring turned spindle supports terminating in splayed feet, 24in. (G.A. Key) $464

A Victorian walnut and burr-walnut Sutherland table, with a molded edge, on turned, fluted and boldly reeded standard end supports joined by a turned stretcher, 41in. wide. (Christie's) $1,191

An Edwardian mahogany Sutherland table, the oval satinwood banded top above pierced end supports and outswept legs tied by a platform stretcher, 28¾in. wide. (Bonhams) $524

A late Victorian mahogany and satinwood banded Sutherland table, outlined in boxwood stringing, the rectangular top with canted corners, 24¼in. wide. (Bonhams) $370

A Regency rosewood line inlaid Sutherland table, circa 1810, the hinged top above a pair of end frieze drawers, on ring turned legs and peg feet, 43¼in wide, leaves open. (Bonhams) $5,320

A late Victorian walnut two tier Sutherland table, the burr veneered twin flaps with molded edges and canted corners, on twin turned supports, 61cm. (Woolley & Wallis) $910

A Victorian walnut Sutherland table, the rectangular top with a molded edge, on paired bobbin-turned end supports and shaped feet, 30in. wide. (Christie's) $471

Queen Anne mahogany tea table, coastal northern Massachusetts or New Hampshire, 1730-60, the molded tray top overhangs a straight molded frieze above a scrolled skirt, 23in. wide. (Skinner) $41,400

A William and Mary walnut demi-lune tea-table, featherbanded overall, the hinged top enclosing a veneered surface, above a pair of candle-slides and three frieze drawers, 28in. wide. (Christie's) $21,691

An Irish George II mahogany tea-table, the shaped rectangular eared top above a waved frieze with a drawer, on cabriole legs headed by shells and scrolls, 32½in. wide. (Christie's) $13,348

A fine and rare Queen Anne mahogany one-drawer tea table, Rhode Island, 1740-60, the **rectangular molded top above a** frieze drawer, top 30in. wide. (Sotheby's) $27,600

A Continental walnut and inlaid tea table, 18th century, possibly Italian, the hinged crossbanded top with projecting re-entrant corners, similar inlaid and quarter-veneered inside, 39½in. wide. (Christie's) $2,377

An early Victorian amboyna tea-table, the rounded rectangular hinged swivel top, above a concave-sided panelled plinth shaft, and scrolling plinth base, 39½in. wide. (Christie's) $5,216

A Regency mahogany tea-table, possibly Scottish, inlaid overall with ebony lines, the hinged crossbanded sliding top, enclosing a crossbanded, figured interior, above a frieze drawer, 40¼in. wide. (Christie's) $2,422

Queen Anne figured cherry tilt-top tea table, Massachusetts, 18th century, the three-board top tilts over a pedestal on cabriole legs, 31in. diameter. (Skinner) $1,150

A 19th century rosewood folding tea table, the beaded edged swivel D shaped top, on baluster turned stem with carved leaf banding, 34¼in. wide. (Andrew Hartley) $2,541

A Victorian rosewood sewing table of rounded oblong form, the hinged lid with foliate marquetry and inlaid beaded edging, 20½in. wide. (Andrew Hartley) $1,386

A Norwegian teak sewing table, the half hinged circular top with a rotating shelf, leather lined material store on turned legs and stretchers, (First prize in Norwegian design competition 1962), 23in., diameter. (Thomson Roddick & Medcalf) $305

19th century mahogany work table, two drop flaps, the frieze fitted at either end with two drawers and two dummy drawers, 19in. (G.A. Key) $1,309

A mid-19th century oak Revivalist work table, the hinged rectangular top opening onto a sliding fitted drawer, the front of which is carved with dolphin head scrolls, at the center a wrought iron handle. (David Lay) $471

Classical mahogany and mahogany veneer carved work table, New England, 1820-30, the crossbanded rectangular top over veneered case of two drawers above four turned drops, 24in. wide. (Skinner) $1,265

Victorian walnut sewing games table, the lid inset with checkered board over a fitted interior, the box with fret work and embroidered panel, raised on short tulip balustered support, 19in. (G.A. Key) $1,386

A rare Louis XV/XVI straw-work marquetry work table, late 18th century, the serpentine shaped top, enclosing a fitted interior, overlaid with stained straw parquetry and floral marquetry banding, 20in. wide. (Bonhams) $1,820

A Victorian mahogany veneered and fruitwood work table, the rectangular top above a pair of frieze drawers, each with a turned wood knob handle, 23½in. (Woolley & Wallis) $420

A 19th century walnut marquetry game tables, the shaped top decorated with floral and bird designs, opening with shell inlay on cabriole supports and pad feet, 2ft.5in. wide. (Brightwells) $3,927

400

Victorian fruitwood inlaid parquetry walnut worktable, mid-19th century, with circular checkerboard inlaid top and fitted interior above a tapered standard, 18in. diameter. (Skinner) $690

Victorian mahogany oval sewing table, lifting lid enclosing a fitted interior with bag below, raised on ring turned foliate molded balustered supports, 24½in. (G.A. Key) $653

William IV period rosewood work table, two drop flaps, flanking a frieze fitted on either side with two drawers and two dummy drawers, 18in. (G.A. Key) $1,201

Classical mahogany carved and mahogany veneer work table, attributed to Isaac Vose and Son, Boston, circa 1825, the rectangular top with rounded rectangular leaves above two convex working and two faux drawers, 22in. wide closed. (Skinner) $2,875

A copper inlaid oak games table, designed by C.A. Voysey for J. S. Henry, circa 1900, square, with the suits inlaid in copper, each side with hinged shaped extension, green baize top, height 89cm. (Bonhams) $10,150

A Victorian walnut work table, burr veneered and inlaid with stringing, the serpentine edge rectangular top above a frieze drawer, on ring turned baluster supports, 22¾in. wide. (Woolley & Wallis) $2,030

Bird's-eye maple, tiger maple and cherry worktable, possibly Pennsylvania, circa 1825, the rectangular top above two drawers and straight skirt, 21½in. wide. (Skinner) $1,610

Classical mahogany veneer work table, Boston, 1830's, the top with hinged leaves which flank the veneered drawers, the top drawer with fittings, 18¹/₈in. wide. (Skinner) $1,380

An early 19th century faded mahogany work table, the rectangular twin flap top with a molded edge and rounded corners above two drawers one end, 21in. (Woolley & Wallis) $2,618

A walnut veneered writing table, the rectangular molded edge top baize inset, the shaped frieze with a main drawer above two small drawers, 30in.
(Woolley & Wallis) $2,772

A French mahogany and brass mounted bonheur du jour, early 19th century, in the Empire style, the superstructure with pierced three quarter brass trellis gallery and marble top, 33in. wide.
(Christie's) $2,743

A Victorian rosewood bonheur du jour with stringing and marquetry depicting putti and scrolling foliage, the oblong top with rounded flaps, 41½in. wide.
(Andrew Hartley) $2,618

A Louis XV style mahogany and parquetry kidney-shaped bureau plat, the leather inset kidney shaped top with a gilt metal mounted edge above three shaped drawers veneered with cube parquetry, 118cm. wide.
(Bonhams) $2,926

An Edwardian mahogany and marquetry kidney-shaped desk, inlaid with panels heightened in ivory, the curved superstructure with central pierced gallery and cupboard, 44in. wide.
(Christie's) $4,754

A kingwood and gilt-bronze bureau de dame, French, circa 1880, the upper part of ogee arched form centered by a clock with a white enamel dial, flanked by two deep drawers, 99cm. wide.
(Sotheby's) $14,028

A Victorian walnut bonheur du jour, of shaped oval form with floral marquetry and stringing, raised stationery compartment with hinged lid having gallery surmount, 37in. wide.(Andrew Hartley) $1,727

Emile-Jacques Ruhlmann, bureau de dame, circa 1925, macassar ebony, the sides of the slightly receding rectangular top banded with ivory, the top inset with cream galuchat writing surface, 92.5cm. wide.(Sotheby's) $112,700

A 19th century mahogany and floral marquetry writing table in the Louis XV style, with stringing and applied gilt metal mounts, shaped frieze drawer with gilt metal handles, 38in. wide.
(Andrew Hartley) $1,423

A good American walnut, burr walnut, bird's eye maple and ebonised Wooton clerk's desk, manufactured by the Wooton Desk Company, Indianapolis, the plain top above a hinged frieze with applied ebonized tablets, 46½in. wide. (Bonhams) $6,160

A mahogany writing slope on stand, the hinged slope opening to a fitted interior with side drawer and exterior book rest, 46cm. wide. (Bonhams) $832

Edwardian satinwood and inlay writing desk, circa 1900, stamped *Edwards & Roberts*, shaped leather inset top over a central drawer flanked by banks of three graduated drawers, 42in. wide. (Skinner) $3,105

A kingwood parquetry bureau de dame, Paris, circa 1900, the curved top with six small drawers flanked by two gilt-bronze acanthus scrolled candlearms, 125cm. wide. (Sotheby's) $9,867

An oriental padouk wood desk, the raised back with carved and pierced surmount depicting dragons amongst clouds, two frieze drawers, pierced foliate apron, 37¼in. wide. (Andrew Hartley) $840

A Regency 'gothic' oak writing table, circa 1805, the quatrefoil line inlaid top above a frieze with blind fretwork carving, incorporating one long and two short drawers to the front, 33in. wide. (Bonhams) $11,900

An oak desk on stand, English, late 17th century, the slope top box with book rest and fitted with three drawers within, flanked by a lower shelf enclosing a drawer, 30½in. wide. (Christie's) $2,743

An early Victorian mahogany writing table, possibly Scottish, the rectangular top with green-leather writing-surface, above a frieze drawer with stylized foliate pattern, 39¼in. wide. (Christie's) $4,844

Edwardian mahogany small cylinder desk, pediment fitted with two central mirror back shelves, flanked on either side by two further smaller shelves, over a roller shutter front, 30½in. (G.A. Key) $1,201

403

A Regency rosewood and specimen wood parquetry teapoy, the hinged rounded rectangular top enclosing a fitted interior with two lidded caddies and openings for two mixing bowls, 15in. wide. (Christie's) $8,050

A Victorian Tunbridge ware teapoy, the sarcophagus shaped top enclosing four lidded compartments with bird and butterfly designs on tapering octagonal stem, 19in. (Brightwells) $4,925

A George III mahogany teapoy with octagonal hinged lid enclosing three lidded boxes, the reeded spreading legs headed by lotus leaves, 16¾in wide. (Christie's) $4,900

A Victorian walnut teapoy, of oval form, crossbanded with stringing, hinged lid revealing fitted interior with a pair of glass bowls and a pair of removable oval caddies, 20in. wide.(Andrew Hartley) $1,523

A Regency rosewood teapoy, the shaped top with hinged lid set on a hexagonal pillar with quatrafoil base, fitted on a sewing table, 43cm. wide. (Bonhams) $658

A Regency rosewood teapoy, with hinged ebonized molded lid enclosing a fitted interior with brass inlaid lidded compartment, one canister lid missing, 20in. wide. (Christie's) $3,125

William IV rosewood teapoy, second quarter 19th century, rectangular molded hinged top enclosing an interior fitted with compartments and spaces for mixing bowls, 29 x 14 x 12½in. (Skinner) $862

A mahogany teapoy, early 19th century, of sarcophagus design, with cavetto hinged lid enclosing a fitted interior with tin lidded compartments and liner, 22in. wide. (Christie's) $2,550

William IV rosewood teapoy, second quarter 19th century, rectangular molded hinged top enclosing an interior fitted with compartments and spaces for mixing bowls, 15¼in. wide. (Skinner) $1,092

... mahogany gentleman's ...ardrobe, converted from Regency ...othes press, with ebony stringing, ...e molded cornice with outline ...ringing to the frieze, 4ft.2in. wide. ...Voolley & Wallis) $2,475

A Victorian satin walnut breakfront triple door wardrobe, the ogee molded cornice over shape top mirror panel door, 210cm. (Bristol) $1,015

A Victorian figured walnut wardrobe, the shaped cornice with turned corner finials above twin arch panel carved crest doors enclosing hanging space, 134in. wide. (Bristol) $1,441

...umwood and poplar Kasten, New ...ork, circa 1740, the molded ...rnice above two doors and with ...lded panels surrounded by ...plied moldings, 55½in. wide. ...kinner) $13,800

A good early Victorian mahogany double door wardrobe, the molded cornice with applied bead and disk carving, over twin panelled doors, later block feet, 148in. wide. (Bristol) $1,413

A Victorian burr walnut and satin birch Greek Revival breakfront triple wardrobe, circa 1880, with anthemion incised ebonized cavetto cornice above shaped mirror door, 228cm. wide. (Bristol) $1,120

...uis XVI style oak armoire, with ...f tip carved cresting, the frieze ...rved with a flower-filled basket, ...e panelled doors similarly carved, ...on cabriole legs, 52½in. wide. ...kinner) $1,610

A Victorian limed oak and inlaid wardrobe, in Aesthetic taste, the detachable dog's tooth molded cornice with a wavy cloud top inlaid with dots, 8ft.2½in. wide, circa 1880. (Woolley & Wallis) $958

A Regency mahogany gentleman's wardrobe, the molded cornice above a hanging space with later hat pegs and a brass rail, enclosed by a pair of outline molded well figured panel doors, 4ft.7½in. wide. (Woolley & Wallis) $2,464

405

An adzed oak wardrobe by Robert 'Mouseman' Thompson, the straight top with halfpenny molding, two panelled doors with iron hinges and latch, 48in. wide.
(Andrew Hartley) $4,930

A Regency mahogany gentleman's breakfront wardrobe, the pediment central section with molded cornice, two brass trimmed panelled doors enclosing slides, 101in. x 90in.
(Andrew Hartley) $9,106

A late 18th century Dutch walnut marquetry armoire with pair of arched doors having bird, merma and floral designs enclosing shelves and four small drawers, wide (Brightwells) $5,96

A south German fruitwood, walnut, crossbanded and marquetry wardrobe or Schrank, late 19th century, of serpentine and broken undulating outline, 73½in. wide.
(Christie's) $6,948

Jean Prouvé, armoire, circa 1945, oak and green painted metal frame, of rectangular form with two sliding doors each with full length chamfered handles, 63in. wide.
(Sotheby's) $9,240

A Dutch mahogany and marquet gentleman's wardrobe, 19th century, inlaid with checker lines with arched cornice and enclose by a pair of mirror panelled doors containing three long drawers below, 53¾in. wide.
(Christie's) $4,02

A George III mahogany gentleman's wardrobe, with some alteration, the upper part with a molded dentil broken pediment with central platform and dentil cornice, 52½in. wide.
(Christie's) $4,606

A late Victorian walnut wardrobe, the molded cornice above a pair of panelled cupboard doors flanking a mirror glazed door on a plinth base, 75in. wide. (Bonhams) $339

A Dutch walnut armoire, circa 18 the arched molded cornice cente by a crest above two arched panelled doors carved with rocail ornament and portrait profiles, 77 wide. (Bonhams) $8,4

George IV mahogany washstand, e rectangular top with three uarter gallery above two frieze rawers, on turned tapering legs, 3in. wide. (Bonhams) $308

An early 19th century mahogany washstand of square form, the molded edged top with dished compartments and aperture containing a Minton pottery jug and bowl, 12¼in. wide. (Andrew Hartley) $377

A George III gentleman's mahogany washstand, circa 1770, fitted with a mirror and box compartments set on legs with leather castors, 27cm. wide. (Bonhams) $1,120

A George III mahogany corner washstand, the arched gallery above a top fitted for a bowl and two cups, the mid tier with a drawer, 22in. wide. (Bonhams) $431

An early 19th century quadrant washstand crossbanded with stringing, the molded edged top with three apertures and raised back, 22in. wide. (Andrew Hartley) $551

A fine George III mahogany enclosed gentleman's washstand, circa 1770, the concave shaped double hinged top enclosing three circular fittings, above a deep frieze with fluted canted corners, 17½in. square. (Bonhams) $16,280

A Regency style mahogany corner washstand, the shaped back and top above a platform shelf, fitted with a single drawer and two dummy drawers, 58cm. wide. (Bonhams) $339

A George III mahogany, inlaid and decorated washstand or side cabinet, possibly converted, the central bowed part with hinged top inset with mirror to the reverse enclosing a fitted interior to receive bowls, 51¼in. wide. (Christie's) $4,606

A Regency mahogany corner washstand, the shaped back and top above a platform shelf, fitted with a single drawer and two dummy drawers, 61cm. wide. (Bonhams) $339

Victorian mahogany washstand, **pediment molded with rosettes and bell flowers**, frieze below fitted with two drawers and raised on ring turned tapering cylindrical supports with ball feet, 41in. (G.A. Key) $1,201

Red painted pine dry sink, New England, early 19th century, the rectangular well with projecting splashboard above two cupboard doors on cut-out feet, old red paint, 42in. wide. (Skinner) $633

A George III mahogany washstand, crossbanded with stringing, the **center split top hinged to reveal** interior now fitted with writing slope and rising stationery compartment, 21¼in. wide. (Andrew Hartley) $1,540

Classical mahogany and mahogany veneer chamber washstand, Maryland, the sides with scrolled terminals above a marble top and single drawer over a mahogany veneer platform, 29⅝in. (Skinner) $1,495

A George III mahogany and boxwood lined bowfront washstand, the hinged divided top revealing pierced rings and a rising mirror with a cupboard below, 20in. wide. (Christie's) $1,150

Shaker double washstand, 1820-30, probably Enfield, Connecticut, South family, the ogee shaped sides flanking a work surface with a backsplash above two recessed panel doors, 38½in. wide. (Skinner) $4,600

A Victorian mahogany washstand, of breakfront outline, with raised back and shaped top above a frieze drawer, 42in. wide; and a Victorian mahogany toilet mirror, of similar form. (Christie's) $628

A late Victorian mahogany wash—stand, of George II style, the rectangular three-quarter galleried top, with shaped sides, above two frieze drawers, 47½in. wide. (Christie's) $1,501

Federal stained wash stand, New England, early 19th century, the flaring scrolled splashboard above a solid board and straight skirt flanked by turned supports, 20½in. wide. (Skinner) $460

poleon III boullework d ebony three-tier gère, circa 1870, with pentine shelves and gular supports, 16in. e. (Skinner) $633

A 19th century inlaid marquetry three-tier étagère with ormolu gallery and finials to the turned scrolled supports. (Brightwells) $801

An early Victorian mahogany what-not, circa 1840, united by turned supports and a base drawer, 50cm. wide. (Bonhams) $784

A Regency mahogany square four-tier what not fitted with single drawer on turned supports and casters, 19 x 17in. (Brightwells) $2,240

et of 19th century hogany hanging elves with gilded ounts, the raised panel ck with applied beading er four oblong mirror cked shelves, 8½in. e. (Andrew Hartley) $753

A Georgian mahogany four-tier whatnot, the top shelf fitted with shaped gallery, turned baluster column supports the two lower shelves fitted with single drawers, 5in. square. (Brightwells) $1,323

A good mid Victorian burr walnut what-not, circa 1860, the three shaped tiers and outset corners joined by opposing foliate C-scroll supports, the top with an applied waved gallery, 25¼in. wide. (Bonhams) $847

A fine Regency four-tier whatnot with reading slide, the galleried platforms with ring-turned uprights and pull-out adjustable reading slope above single drawer base, 48.5cm. (Bristol) $4,116

hogany music stand, land or America, circa 0-10, the square stand molded edge and ped support bar tilting r shaped ratchet chanism, 17¾in. wide. inner) $2,875

Good early Victorian rosewood three tier whatnot, the fret work and scrolled pierced gallery top raised on four tulip balustered uprights, 29in. (G.A. Key) $2,574

An early Victorian rosewood three tier what-not, circa 1830, fitted with gadrooned finials and raised on legs with brass caps and castors, 35.5cm. wide. (Bonhams) $1,610

A Regency mahogany four-tier square whatnot fitted with single drawer on baluster turned and square supports and casters, 19in. wide.(Brightwells) $1,781

A George III mahogany oval wine cooler on stand, the coopered oval cistern with two brass bands (lacking liner), on separate stand, 58cm. wide. (Bristol) $952

A pair of Edwardian japanned metal wine coolers, G.Peak & Co, London, each with four apertures to the tapering angular body above a domed circular base, 12¼in. wide. (Christie's) $7,238

A George III brass-bound mahogany cellaret, the octagonal hinged top centered by a marquetry star surrounded by radiating panels, enclosing a later metal liner, 18in. diameter. (Christie's) $5,589

A George III mahogany and brass-bound oval cellaret, the hinged top enclosing a lead lined interior with a tap below, having brass ring handles to the sides, 24¾in. wide. (Christie's) $4,609

A Regency style mahogany wine cooler, the domed hinged top above plain sides with brass carrying handles, 59cm. wide. (Bonhams) $686

A rare Federal inlaid mahogany cellaret, probably New York, circa 1795, the oval brass-banded top opening to a divided well above a conforming case, 29½in. wide. (Sotheby's) $10,925

An early 19th century mahogany cellaret of oblong form with reeded edged hinged lid, the fascia with applied molding over a drawer, 21¾in. wide. (Andrew Hartley) $1,570

An early Victorian sarcophagus shape wine cooler, figured faded mahogany veneered, the stepped tablet hinged lid to a divided and zinc lined interior, 30½in. wide. (Woolley & Wallis) $3,513

A mahogany, crossbanded and ebony strung oval cellaret, late 18th century, enclosing a metal lined interior, concealing a tap below with re-entrant ebony strung panels to the sides, 23in wide. (Christie's) $4,112

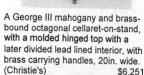

Regency mahogany sarcophagus laret, the gently sloping ramidal-shaped rectangular ged top above a panelled ering body, 32¾in. wide. ristie's) $1,501

A George III mahogany, tulipwood crossbanded and inlaid cellaret, the hinged top and front with oval figured crossbanded panels, with fitted interior, 20in. wide. (Christie's) $3,128

A George III mahogany and brass-bound octagonal cellaret-on-stand, with a molded hinged top with a later divided lead lined interior, with brass carrying handles, 20in. wide. (Christie's) $6,251

egency mahogany cellaret, the ed square top with reeded edge with inset oval panel, enclosing ad-lined interior, the tapering y with two oval panels to the t, 17in. square. ristie's) $4,171

A George II brass-bound mahogany wine-cooler, the oval slatted top with scrolled handles and later base, with a metal liner, on a stand with cabriole legs, 28½in. wide. (Christie's) $21,691

A George III ormolu-mounted and brass-bound mahogany wine-cooler, of oval form with gadrooned and removable later lead liner, each end with ram-mask carrying-handles, on a guilloche and fluted frieze.(Christie's) $75,083

te George III mahogany, inlaid brass bound cellaret-on-stand, ed lid with crossbanded and decoration centered by conch l inlay, 25½in. wide. istie's) $2,362

A George III mahogany wine-cooler, of rectangular tapering form with reeded edge enclosing two later lead liners the ends with carrying-handles, on a rectangular stand with plain frieze, 26¼in. wide. (Christie's) $6,340

A mahogany and line-inlaid cellaret, 19th century, of octagonal form, the patera centered line-inlaid top enclosing a lead lined interior above a panelled body, 18in. wide. (Christie's) $2,362

A carved architectural clock holder, American, late 19th century, the crescent-shaped molded top above the gilt inscription "Tempus Fugit" on one side and a carved angel's head and wings on the other, 8in. wide.
(Christie's) $3,525

A pair of lead figures of a shepherdess and a shepherd, late 20th century, after the models by John Cheere, 52in. and 50in., on reconstituted stone pedestals.
(Christie's) $6,909

A pair of lead figures of nymphs, early 20th century, Bromsgrove Guild, Worcestershire, each shown standing with floral garlands and entwined trailing vines, 44in. high.
(Christie's) $15,627

A pair of Coalbrookdale fern and blackberry pattern cast iron chairs, circa 1870, the backs and sides pierced with ferns and clusters of blackberries above wooden slatted seats, 26½in. wide.
(Christie's) $6,909

A reconstituted stone urn and pedestal, late 20th century, the shallow bowl with molded egg and dart rim and part lobed underside, 49in. high. overall.
(Christie's) $1,382

A cast iron table, Coalbrookdale, circa 1860, the pierced circular top on three winged griffin supports, with trefoil-shaped stretcher and foliate cast feet, 20½in. diameter.
(Christie's) $9,499

A pair of sandstone garden urns of campana form with ovolo molded rim, the body with foliate banding, 45½in. high.
(Andrew Hartley) $899

A Coalbrookdale medallion patte cast iron seat, circa 1870, the arched pierced back with a centr oval panel of a classical maiden, 65in. wide.
(Christie's) $55,2

A pair of large reconstituted stone urns, late 20th century, in the manner of a William Kent design, the knopped acorn finials on stepped domed covers, mounted on stepped rectangular plinths, 98in. high overall. (Christie's) $6,564

A Coalbrookdale nasturtium pattern cast iron seat, circa 1870, circa 1870, the back with panels of flowers and foliage above a wooden slatted seat, the legs with conforming decoration, 72in. wide. (Christie's) $12,091

A pair of reconstituted stone urns, late 20th century, in the manner of a William Kent design, the ovoid bodies with sphere finials and Greek key banding, 82½in. high. overall. (Christie's) $4,836

A pair of lead models of herons, late 20th century, in the Japanese Meiji period style, shown standing on pierced shaped bases cast with fish, 60in. high. (Christie's) $6,564

A set of four lead models of the Seasons, late 20th century, each young girl with her attribute, 51in. high and smaller and four reconstituted stone circular pedestals. (Christie's) $25,909

Cast iron painted fountain, attributed to J.W. Fiske, New York, late 19th century, the basin with cast leaf exterior on base of cranes and cat-o'-nine tails, 46¾in. high. (Skinner) $2,875

A Victorian cast iron plant stand, mid 19th century, with six plant holders about a central raised fitting, the stem as a tree trunk above a conforming spreading base modelled with lizards, 42½in. high. (Christie's) $3,626

A pair of terracotta urns and pedestals, Somerset Trading Company, Bridgwater, early 20th century, the flared rims with egg and dart borders, 43½in. high overall. (Christie's) $5,527

A lead figure of a laborer, possibly 18th century, in the manner of John Cheere, the base with a modern lead figure of a hound, the axe also later, on a rectangular stone plinth, the figure 53½in. high. (Christie's) $3,948

A Portland stone pedestal, the inverted stepped top above two recessed molded panels and molded stepped base, 33in. high. (Christie's) $1,467

One of a pair of reconstituted stone models of the Medici lion, 20th century, 48in. long. (Christie's) (Two) $8,982

A lead figure of the Young Bacchus, mid 20th century, shown standing clasping a bunch of grapes, with toga style drapery, his hair entwined with further grapes, 30½in. high. (Christie's) $950

A Continental white painted wrought iron flower vendor's cart, early 20th century, of tapering rectangular outline, the opening to one side modelled with 'S' scrolls and flanked by scrolled uprights, 43in. wide. (Christie's) $3,281

A lead figure of a dancing girl, late 20th century, playing with a billowing scarf, on a square base 36in. high, on a reconstituted stone pedestal. (Christie's) $1,070

A Coalbrookdale cast iron stick stand, third quarter 19th century, of rectangular form, the plateau pierced with thirty-two circular apertures, the sides with trefoil pendant frieze, 37¼in. wide. (Christie's) $4,491

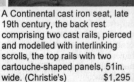

A Victorian cast iron seat, John Finch Foundry, late 19th century, the back rest pierced with panels of stylized foliage, the side panels pierced with conforming ornament, with wood slatted seat, 67½in. wide. (Christie's) $6,564

Pair of decorative green painted wrought iron garden elbow chairs, slatted backs and seats, slightly splayed arms, terminating in scrolls, raised on slightly splayed feet, circa late 19th century. (G.A. Key) $290

A Continental cast iron seat, late 19th century, the back rest comprising two cast rails, pierced and modelled with interlinking scrolls, the top rails with two cartouche-shaped panels, 51in. wide. (Christie's) $1,295

A rare Victorian commemorative wrought iron conversation seat, 19th century, of serpentine form, the opposing arched backs pierced with asymmetrical scrolling tendrils inscribing the initials P.A. and V.R. for Prince Albert and Victoria Regina, 59in. wide.
(Christie's) $31,088

A pair of reconstituted stone gate or pier finials, late 20th century, modelled as pineapples, on waisted and knopped socles above square bases, 32¾in. high.
(Christie's) $1,208

Painted arrow-back garden seat, 19th century, the curving crest above arrow-back spindles, shaped arm supports a plank seat and square splayed legs.
(Skinner) $1,725

A Victorian cast iron seat, Bradshaw & Sansom Foundry, circa 1870, the pierced back with central roundel cast with a pointing labrador, the sides with bird's head terminals and further roundels, 70in. wide.
Christie's) $8,982

A Scottish cast iron seat, Carron Foundry, mid 19th century, the foliate scrolling crested back rest pierced with conjoined hoops, the sides with 'C' scrolls, 63¼in. wide.
(Christie's) $14,681

An English lead urn, early 20th century, the knopped acanthus clasped finial and domed cover above body with twin cherubs, floral swags and stiff-leaf decoration, 36in. high.(Christie's) $2,537

Coalbrookdale passion flower pattern cast iron seat, circa 1870, of scrolling curved form, cast with blossoming and interweaving passion flower vines, 42in. wide.
Christie's) $24,182

A carved stone bust of George Washington, indistinctly signed *S. Woro..*, and dated *1830*, carved in the round, the forward-facing figure with articulated facial features, 22in. high. (Christie's) $14,100

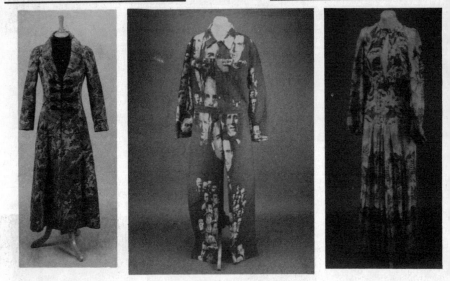

A full-length machine woven tapestry coat, worked with a dense design of scrolling flowers and acanthus leaves, with four frogged fastenings at the front, Biba, circa 1970. (Christie's) $517

A man's denim suit, comprising jeans and jacket woven with newsprint-style male figures, labelled *Gaultier Jeans*, 1993/1994. (Christie's) $484

A summer dress of cotton voile, with a Persian-style print of women on horseback with hounds, labelled *THEA PORTER*, 1970s. (Christie's) $553

A fine Pearly King's costume, comprising coat, waistcoat, trousers and cap of black wool decorated overall with mother of pearl buttons, late 19th century. (Christie's) $1,554

A pair of blue denim Levi jeans, with flared legs, applied with bands of brightly embroidered, printed and woven bands and patches, circa 1972-5. (Christie's) $345

A Valentino scarlet wool sable trimmed red coat, Italian, winter 1969/70, the 'Anna Karenina' ankle length coat with wrap-over effect fitted bodice, bust 34¾in. (Sotheby's) $3,192

A man's couture smoking jacket, of pink and old gold silk decorated with flower and bird-filled roundels, labelled *Christian Dior Monsieur Mai 69*. (Christie's) $345

A rare lady's riding habit jacket and waistcoat, of crimson broadcloth, the jacket with turn-down collar and facings buttoned-back to simulate double-breasted fastening, English, circa 1775.
(Christie's) $12,954

A parachute top, of burgandy, gray and blue denim, applied with a patch printed with Karl Marx upside down, circa 1979.
(Christie's) $2,245

A pair of tartan bondage trousers, of blue, yellow, red, black and green wool, with black belt and purple towelling loin cloth, labelled *SEX ORIGINAL 430 Kings Road Chelsea*, late 1970s.
Christie's) $2,245

Diaghilev Ballet Russe 'Mourner' costume, designed by Henri Matisse for 'Le Chant du Rossignol' French, 1920, of voluminous cream felt of large rectangular form, applied with midnight blue velvet triangles.(Sotheby's) $9,240

A fine black sequinned ball or court gown, French, circa 1909, labelled *Charlotte Duclos, 12 Rue de l'Arcade, Paris*, the curvaceous gown of dazzling graduated sequins that enlarge to 1cm. diameter at the hem. (Sotheby's) $840

A short sleeved dress of bright orange wool with belt and faux pockets of black vinyl – labelled *Courreges Paris*, and an associated sleeveless dress, labelled as above. (Christie's) $863

A dress, the green-gray ground woven with bronze and gold lamé with a spot motif, 1920s, possibly Poiret. (Christie's) $950

An ensemble of burgundy, orange, gray and ivory tweed coat, with fur trimmed collar and cuffs, and matching skirt, labelled *CHANEL*. (Christie's) $5,182

A silk evening coat, the black ground woven with stylized flowers in red, orange and green silks and with palm trees in gold lamé, possibly Jenny, circa 1930.(Christie's) $65

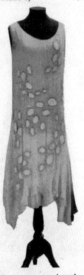

A champagne colored chiffon bias cut flapper dress, circa 1927, with an integral chiffon slip, with a pair of pink silk combinations and a gold lamé turban with ostrich plume, 34in. (Sotheby's) $924

An Yves Saint Laurent Picasso Collection ball gown, French, Autumn/Winter collection, 1979-80, deep coral pink moiré skirt appliquéd with brilliantly covered random abstract swirls and stars, bust 36in. (Sotheby's) $2,856

A Delphos dress by Fortuny, of pleated black silk slotted front and back with a satin lace, to make the dress cling to the body, trimmed with black and white Venetian glass beads, circa 1910. (Christie's) $1,554

A Valentino black silk dress with gilt embroidery, Italian, circa 1969, profusely embroidered with flowers and foliage in colored metal gilt threads and coral colored beads, bust 37½in. (Sotheby's) $50

A sleeveless cocktail dress of ivory muslin, embroidered with silvered bugle beads forming a vermicular pattern, mid 1920s.
(Christie's) $758

A coat of white, gray and black mohair tweed, the collar and cuffs trimmed with white fur, labelled *CHANEL*.
(Christie's) $1,122

A sleeveless cocktail dress of lemon yellow muslin, embroidered in silvered bugle beads, forming a vermicular pattern, hem shaped, mid 1920s.
(Christie's) $325

An ensemble of lime green wool, of double breasted jacket with side pockets, straight leg trousers and short sleeved vest, labelled – *Courreges Paris.*
(Christie's) $863

Biba striped satin evening ensemble, English, circa 1970, with a diagonal fastening to the jacket, tie belt, long pointed sleeves striped bronze, brown and copper.
(Sotheby's) $672

A dress, of chintz printed with passion flowers, roses and convulvulus against a black ground, the material circa 1795, the dress made up in the early 19th century.
(Christie's) $1,297

A Jeanne Lanvin black satin silk evening dress, French, 1926, the knee length tubular shaped sleeveless dress with two crepe self colored ribbons over the left shoulder, 36in. (Sotheby's)
                 $1,596

An Yves Saint Laurent shot-taffeta evening gown, French, Spring-Summer 1985, the strapless bodice with pleats of ruched fabric that culminates in a large puff-ball bustle and train, bust 36in.
(Sotheby's) $1,428

BASKETS

Sterling silver overlay glass basket, early 20th century, angular handle over a narrow waisted basket of transparent lime green, silver overlay of roses and foliate border, 11¾in. high.(Skinner) $2,415

A façon de Venise glass basket, the ogee body panel molded, the rim with applied loops and a twist swing handle, 18cm. diameter. (Woolley & Wallis) $441

J & L. Lobmeyr enamelled glass basket, Austria, late 19th century, colorless thorn handle over a shallow squared and footed bowl of transparent pink, enamelled with multi-colored foliate scroll work, engraved Lobmeyr grid mark, 6in. high. (Skinner) $500

BEAKERS

A façon de Venise latticinio beaker, possibly Liège, 17th century, in vetro a fili, the flared form inset with spiralling translucent cobalt-blue and white threads, kick-in base, 9.3cm. (Sotheby's) $1,680

An interesting Bohemian engraved beaker, perhaps Riesengebirge, circa 1690, perhaps by the Master of the Koula beaker, the faceted thick-walled flared form engraved in Tiefschnitt with a hand, 5¼in. (Skinner) $1,740

A fine Nuremberg engraved three-footed beaker, circa 1690, attributed to Hermann Schwinger, the deep u-shaped form engraved with a continuous scene of birds and insects flanking a perched owl amidst shrubbery, 4in. (Sotheby's) $4,704

BOTTLES

An unrecorded sealed wine bottle, circa 1700, the squat onion form of dark green olive glass with short tapering neck and string rim, 15cm. (Sotheby's) $10,584

A pair of 19th century deep green bulbous shaped apothecary bottles, with gilt labels inscribed in black TR:CARD.CO: and D:PAREIR; Conc., 13in. high. (Christie's) $1,001

An early serving-bottle, circa 1715 the squat onion form with short tapering neck and string rim, applied with a scroll handle with thumbpiece, kick-in base, 13.8cm. (Sotheby's) $4,368

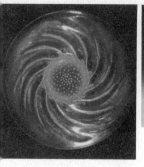

'Poissons No.1' No.3262, a clear and opalescent bowl, molded mark *R.Lalique*, 29.5cm. diameter. (Christie's) $490

An Irish cut-glass canoe-shaped bowl, probably Cork, circa 1790, the large ovoid bowl cut with a narrow band of stars and prismatic lines between stylized leaf ornament, 20.6cm. (Sotheby's) $2,205

An Art Deco Verlys glass bowl, factory mark *A Verlys France*, 39cm. diameter. (Christie's) $420

Daum Nancy Art Glass footed bowl, France, circa 1925, colorless glass cased to amber and decorated internally with mottled brown and gold foil, 8¼in. (Skinner) $345

A shallow opalescent Lalique bowl, circa 1920, decorated with three jellyfish, 21.5cm. diameter. (Bonhams) $404

The Angle of Descent, a Laurence Whistler stipple-engraved bowl, dated *1990*, engraved in diamond-point with two large buildings shrouded in moonlight, the sky with a jetstream, an owl to one side, 21.8cm. high. (Sotheby's) $3,175

A Lalique glass 'Marguerites' bowl and frosted shallow circular form, the everted rim molded with overlapping daisies, traces of green staining, 13in. wide. (Andrew Hartley) $393

An interesting gilt opaque-white glass water bowl, circa 1765, the waisted globular form decorated in gilding and tooled with the figure of a man standing amidst shrubbery, 3¾in. (Sotheby's) $1,260

A Lalique 'Poisson' opalescent shallow bowl, after 1931, the underside molded with fish swirling around a pool of bubbles, 29.2cm. (Bonhams) $508

An interesting Queen Anne commemorative amber-tinted wine-taster, possibly circa 1702-1714, stone-chipped on the side with *God save Queen Anne*, 11.3cm. long. (Sotheby's) $1,260

A Monart 'Paisley Shawl' glass bowl, 19cm. diameter. (Christie's) $316

A Sabino opalescent glass bowl, incised *Sabino Paris*, 32.5cm. diameter. (Christie's) $700

An early footed bowl, circa 1700, the wide shallow rib-molded with folded rim, 18cm. diameter. (Sotheby's) $2,352

A Daum cameo glass bowl, with quatrefoil rim, acid-etched mark *Daum Nancy* with a cross of Lorraine, 15cm. diameter. (Christie's) $1,050

A Beijing blue glass floriform flaring bowl on short foot, 9¾in. diameter, incised Qianlong four character mark, 19th century. (Christie's) $2,900

A rare gilt emerald-green-tinted bowl and stand, circa 1770, possibly from the atelier of James Giles, the cup form with gilt-edged scalloped rim, height of bowl 6.8cm. (Skinner) $1,334

A pair of Beijing white glass with red overlay flaring bowls with everted foliate rims, carved in low relief to the exterior with scrolling lotus, 4½in. diameter, 19th century. (Christie's) $1,206

Tiffany Favrile lobed bowl, New York, early 20th century, pronounced scalloped rim on a ten ribbed shallow bowl, stepped base surface with strong gold iridescence, base inscribed *X-129 L.C.T. Favrile*, 2½in. high, diameter 7¼in. (Skinner) $489

A Gallé cameo glass bowl, decorated with cherry blossoms, cameo mark *Gallé*, 20cm. diameter. (Christie's) $1,575

Steuben blue Aurene bowl, early 20th century, undulating ruffled rim, polished pontil marked Aurene Haviland within, diameter 6in. (Skinner) $460

A Loetz bowl, the clear bubbled glass with branching blue iridescence, 22cm. diameter. (Christie's) $1,024

A Daum cameo glass box and cover, the clear glass overlaid in emerald etched with stylized mistletoe, with enamel and gilt highlights, 13.8cm. (Bonhams) $726

'Quatre Scarabées' No.15, a clear, frosted, and gray-stained box and cover, molded mark R. Lalique, 15cm. diameter. (Christie's) $1,050

Continental gilt-metal mounted rectangular glass box and cover, late 19th/20th century, the hinged cover with rounded gilt-metal rim above the conforming base fitted with a demi-shield-shaped escutcheon and with allover diamond cutting, 20.9 x 12.6cm. (Christie's) $1,175

'Vegas' No.66 a clear, frosted, sepia-stained, and slightly opalescent box, molded mark R. Lalique, 8cm. diameter. (Christie's) $612

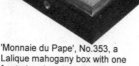

'Monnaie du Pape', No.353, a Lalique mahogany box with one frosted and sepia-stained inset panel, engraved R. Lalique, 31cm. wide. (Christie's) $3,725

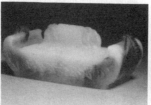

An Almaric Walter pâte-de-verre cigarette box and cover, impressed signature A. Walter-Nancy, 23cm. diameter. (Christie's) $2,976

A Palme-Konig iridescent glass hinged box, egg-shape, in gilt-metal mount, 16.5cm. high. (Christie's) $70

'D'Orsay 2' a clear, frosted, and opalescent box cover with later box, molded mark R. Lalique D'Orsay, 8.5cm. diameter. (Christie's) $612

Val St. Lambert cameo covered box, Belgium, circa 1920, faceted knob applied to a cylindrical covered box of colorless glass, 6½in. diameter. (Skinner) $862

A Beijing ruby glass circular box and domed cover, carved in low relief with a central shou character surrounded by bats in flight, 4in. diameter. (Christie's) $884

A French gilt-brass mounted 'Aesthetic' glass coffer, late 19th century, probably Baccarat, with hinged domed cover, ball and ring handles and lappet escutcheon, 6½ x 8⁵⁄₈in. x 4½in. (Christie's) $2,630

'Premier Désir', Lalique for Jean de Parys, circa 1926, a clear, frosted and silver-stained scent bottle and cover, flattened sphere of box-like shape, the cover molded with flowerheads, 6.5cm. high. (Christie's) $7,878

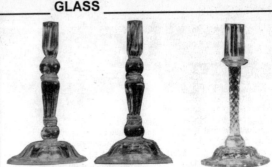

A fine pair of molded pedestal-stemmed tapersticks, circa 1740, each vertically-ribbed sconce set on a beaded knop between collars above a wrythen octagonal molded stem, 16cm., 6¼in.
(Sotheby's) $6,720

A fine faceted candlestick, circa 1750, the vertically-ribbed sconce with collar set on a tall slender diamond-cut stem, 10in.
(Sotheby's) $1,26◼

A pair of composite cut candelabra, each with a gadrooned vase finial above a flat cut turnover collar and tapering stem above auricular branches and twin scroll branches, late 18th century and later, 55cm.
(Christie's) $1,295

'Volutes' No.2120, a pair of clear and frosted candlesticks, stencil marks *R. Lalique*, 20.5cm. high.
(Christie's) $2,975

A pair of Charles X gilt metal and glass luster candlesticks, 40.5cm. high.
(Bonhams & Brooks) $450

A pair of assembled French frosted glass candelabra, late 19th/20th century, the dolphin stems probably Baccarat, with waisted urn-form candleholders above dished drip-pans hung with bead and teardrop prisms, 22¼in. high.
(Christie's) $2,820

A near pair of Regency glass and ormolu twin light candelabra, the gilt bronze sun-burst masks with radiating faceted graduated pendants, the tapering hob-nail cut stems with twin foliate cast branches, 17¾in. high.
(Christie's) $8,228

Pair of Tiffany gold Favrile glass candlesticks, New York, early 20th century, broad flared cups over spiral ribbed shaft flaring to base, amber glass with gold iridescent surface, 7in. high.
(Skinner) $2,500

'Faucon' No. 1124, a Lalique clear and frosted car mascot, molded mark R. Lalique, 15.5cm. high. (Christie's) $1,925

'Tête D'Aigle' No.1138, a clear and frosted car mascot, molded mark R. Lalique, 11cm. high. (Christie's) $3,501

'Tête de Coq' a clear and frosted car mascot, intaglio molded mark Lalique France, 18cm. high. (Christie's) $840

CENTERPIECES

A cut glass circular center dish, the turnover rim with hobnail and fan cutting, raised on a knopped stem, circa 1830, 19cm. high. (Woolley & Wallis) $330

An Italian glass figural fountain, comprising a blue glass wrythen cone with female figure and swan surmount, rising from a deep blue glass bowl with pink flowerheads, 31in. high, early to mid 20th century. (Andrew Hartley) $385

'Fauvettes A' No.1171 a clear and frosted surtout de table, wheel-engraved R.Lalique France, 39.5cm. long. (Christie's) $9,628

COUPES

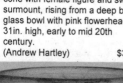

Gabriel Argy-Rousseau, coupe 'Etoiles', 1924, pâte-de-verre, in shades of pink, mauve and brown, molded with overlapping star-shaped flowerheads, 3¾in. (Sotheby's) $4,200

A Daum Nancy glass comport, the circular satin and green veined top molded in relief with corn ears, raised on gilt metal circular stem cast with foliage, molded foot and scrolled feet, signed, 8½in. wide. (Andrew Hartley) $615

> **FASCINATING FACT**
> Cut glass was first used by Caspar Lehmann in late 16th century Prague and its use was developed in England in the mid 1700s. It is a method of decorating glass with faceted slices to catch the light. Lead glass was very suitable for this as it has light dispersing qualities. 19th century examples can be very elaborate with many prisms.
> (Cotswold Auction Co.)

A Regency silver four bottle decanter stand, Paul Storr, London, 1811, square cut-cornered with egg-and-dart border and lotus leaf supports, 8¼in. square.
(Sotheby's) $12,516

A pair of green faceted and gilt decorated decanters and stoppers, facet cut overall with diamonds, the shoulders cut with extending flutes and richly gilt in the atelier of James Giles, 1765-70, 31cm. high.
(Christie's) $13,130

Three blue mallet-shaped decanters and stoppers, named in gilt for Brandy and Rum and Hollands, within octagonal panels suspended from gilt lines, mounts, 19th century, 25cm. high max.
(Christie's) $863

A pair of green cut ship's decanters and stoppers, with two silver labels formed as vine leaves, pierced with the names SHERRY and PORT, Rawlings & Summers, London, 1837, the glass 19th century, 25cm. high. (Christie's) $1,208

A fine and unusual Stourbridge 'rock crystal' engraved decanter and stopper, probably Stevens and Williams, circa 1885, molded with diagonal pillar flutes with a short angled neck and loop handle, 7½in.
(Sotheby's) $2,470

A George III three-bottle decanter stand, Rebecca Eames & Edward Barnard, 1809, the loaded base with a pillar and lion paw footed three bottle guard, engraved Hollands, Brandy and Rum, height 9¾in. (Christie's) $1,447

A pair of cut glass mallet shaped decanters and stoppers, diamond cut bands to the shoulders and fan shaped panels to the sides, early 19th century, 26cm.
(Woolley & Wallis) $500

An ormolu and Baccarat glass spirit decanter set, late 19th century, including three small tapering panelled decanters with trefoil stoppers and double ringed necks, 12¾in. diameter, the stand.
(Christie's) $3,525

A Daum enamelled glass decanter and six glasses, gilt-enamelled marks Daum Nancy with a cross of Lorraine, decanter 20cm. high.
(Christie's) $1,192

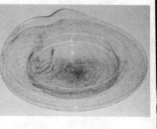

A Schneider tazza, acid-etched mark *Schneider*, 20.2cm. diameter. (Christie's) $314

A Clutha glass dish with one upturned section, green with flecked gold and other colorings, 20cm. diameter. (Thomson Roddick & Medcalf) $160

A Daum enamelled glass dish, the underside with gilt mark *Daum Nancy*, with a cross of Lorraine, 29.2cm. diameter. (Christie's) $1,575

An early Venetian circular dish, the wide, shallow ribbed bowl with a border of iron red, opaque white and blue small oval dots and a gilded band, early 16th century, 23.5cm. (Woolley & Wallis) $588

A large Venetian armorial dish, 16th century with later armorial decoration, the wide shallow form with wide everted folded rim, molded on the underside with nipt diamond waies, gilt with a scale band painted with four rows of blue enamel dots, 39cm. (Sotheby's) $16,758

A rare Irish gilded and crested dish circa 1785, attributed to John Grahl of Dublin, of deep form, the center painted on the underside with a spray of fruit, the narrow everted rim with a moor's head crest in profile, 24cm. (Sotheby's) $5,376

ÉPERGNES

A green Vaseline glass épergne, comprising one central and three smaller trumpets, each applied with spiral trailed decoration, 44cm. high. (Bonhams) $447

A green Vaseline glass épergne, comprising a large central trumpet flanked by two smaller examples, each with applied trails, alternating with two clear crook-shaped supports suspending baskets, 51cm. high. (Bonhams) $441

A large Vaseline glass épergne, with wavy edges and applied green rims, the three suspended baskets and four trumpets applied with crimped green tails, 2nd half 19th century, 59cm. high. (Woolley & Wallis) $1,029

Silver mounted pressed glass pitcher, German, .800 fine silver, 20th century, tapered cylindrical form with cross-cut diamonds, cross-hatching, 11in.
(Skinner) $633

A Bohemian pale-ruby ewer and two goblets, the oviform ewer entwined with an emerald green serpent handle with aventurine inclusions, 32.5cm. high.
(Christie's) $1,122

Art Glass and foil pitcher, attributed to Schneider, France, circa 1925, pulled spout on a swollen vessel of mottled pink and yellow cased glass, 8¼in. high.
(Skinner) $1,000

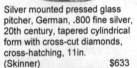

A French blue-tinted ewer, 17th/18th century, the ovoid shouldered form with overall honeycomb molding below a slender neck and three-sided rim, 9in. (Sotheby's) $3,675

Seventeen Lobmeyr clear glass punch cups and two ewers, late 19th/early 20th century, engraved monogram marks, each with panelled body engraved with *Laub-und-Bandelwerk*, 7½in. high, the ewers. (Christie's) $3,000

A small German engraved 'Goldrubinglas' jug, probably Nuremberg, circa 1700, probably Hermann Schwinger, engraved with a continuous landscape and riverscape scene of figures, buildings and trees, 12.4cm.
(Sotheby's) $3,024

FLASKS

A Clichy gilt latticinio scent flask and stopper, circa 1850, the squat hexagonal form cut with arched lobes of alternating panels of diamonds and stylized leaves below a hexagonal neck, 4¾in.
(Sotheby's) $1,764

A pewter-mounted Saxon enamelled armorial flask and cover, dated *1699*, the square form with canted corners, painted with a coat-of-arms and *1699* on one side, 15cm. (Sotheby's) $2,470

A signed and engraved blown glass flask, Oneida County, Dunbarton, New York, early 19th century, the flattened circular flask of natural green glass engraved on both surfaces, 6in. high.
(Sotheby's) $3,737

A Bohemian amber-flashed and clear goblet, the generous bucket bowl cut with a raised oval panel engraved with deer 1860, 17.5cm. high. (Christie's) $840

A Hessen engraved armorial goblet, Paderborn, Emde or Altmündener Glashütte, circa 1760, 21.5cm. (Sotheby's) $5,376

A previously unrecorded large early lead glass façon de Venise goblet, circa 1685, perhaps Hawley-Bishopp, 25.7cm. (Sotheby's) $20,449

A large drawn-trumpet goblet, circa 1740, the flared bowl above a teared plain stem and folded conical foot, 10in. (Sotheby's) $1,512

An early heavy baluster goblet, circa 1700, the large funnel bowl with solid base, set on an inverted baluster stem and folded conical foot, 7¼in. (Sotheby's) $2,520

A baluster goblet, circa 1725, the funnel bowl set on two bladed knops above a plain section between annular collars, 8¼in. (Sotheby's) $1,092

A Hessen or Lauenstein engraved goblet, perhaps Paderborn, Emde or Altmündener Glashütte, circa 1770, 23cm. (Sotheby's) $2,016

A fine mammoth heavy baluster goblet, the generous funnel bowl with solid base above an inverted baluster with large tear, 28.2cm. (Sotheby's) $4,368

A Northern Dutch façon de Venise wheel engraved goblet, circa 1680, the funnel bowl engraved with swags of fruit and laurel pendant from tied ribbons, 20cm. (Sotheby's) $1,270

A fine façon de Venise winged goblet, 17th century, supported by a pair of incised scrolls applied with two turquoise-blue tinted pinched scrolls, 20.7cm. (Sotheby's) $12,035

A Saxon engraved goblet for the Dutch market, the thistle-shaped bowl engraved with a figure of Flora holding a floral cornucopia and a bouquet, mid 18th century, 21.5cm. high.(Christie's) $560

Bohemian enamelled and gilt portrait goblet, Harrach Glasshouse, Neuwelt, after 1896, the thistle-shaped bowl painted with the half-length portrait of Graf von Harrach, 21.4cm. (Skinner) $5,002

A circular glass inkwell, with a silver hinged cap, bearing a monogram, circa 1897, 11.5cm. diameter. (Woolley & Wallis) $162

Iridescent gold glass and bronze inkwell, attributed to Tiffany, early 20th century, iridescent gold glass lid on a hinged bronze inkwell, 6¼in. high. (Skinner) $3,450

A clear, frosted, and blue-stained inkwell, molded with octopus legs, molded *Luzia Deposé*, 8cm. high. (Christie's) $373

JARS

A set of four deep amethyst drug rounds, with red bordered gilt labels, gilded glass covers, each approximately 13in. high. (Christie's) $1,835

A Venetian armorial waisted jar and cover, painted with a coat of arms on an enamelled and gilt scale pattern ground between wreaths, late 19th century, 22cm. high. (Christie's) $588

A Continental glass jar and cover, formed as a barrel with three applied rings and horizontal ribbing, 18th century, 23cm. (Woolley & Wallis) $147

JUGS

A Stevens & Williams 'Transparent Cameo' silver-gilt-mounted lemonade jug and hinged cover of tapered cylindrical form, clear overlaid in green and intaglio-cut with fan panels between sprays of mimosa, 28.5cm. high. (Christie's) $1,401

A Daum glass sauce-boat, wheel cut mark *Daum Nancy France* incorporating a cross of Lorraine, 9cm. high. (Christie's) $447

An American silver-mounted cranberry-stained cut-glass claret jug, Gorham Manufacturing Corporation, Providence, Rhode Island, 1880, with hobnails, lattice and fan-shaped ornament, 12in. high. (Sotheby's) $3,880

A silver-mounted cut green jug, after the antique, cut with flutes, the mounts formed as a branch handle issuing fruiting vines, John Figg, London, 1840, 20.5cm. high. (Christie's) $5,527

A silver-mounted cut novelty jug, in the form of a carp, naturalistically modelled, the glass cut with hexagonal facets and gilt to imitate scales, William Leuchars, London, 1883, 24cm. long. (Christie's) $9,499

A Victorian novelty silver mounted glass claret jug, Alexander Crichton, London, 1881, in the form of a resting duck, tail feather and finely modelled head mounts, cranberry glass handle, 10¾in. long. (Sotheby's) $23,240

A French gilt-metal-mounted filigree jug, probably Clichy, circa 1850, everted foot and hinged cover encasing alternate spiralling amethyst and opaque-white bands, 20cm. (Skinner) $1,740

An English cut glass water jug, the wide rim with fine diamond cut panels, the body with a wide diamond cut band, 1st half 19th century, 18cm. (Woolley & Wallis) $323

A fine engraved claret jug probably Stourbridge, possibly Thomas Webb, circa 1870, the flattened ovoid form engraved with the Triumph of Amphitrite in intaglio, 11in. (Skinner) $15,010

LUSTERS

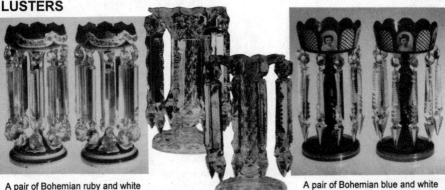

A pair of Bohemian ruby and white overlay lusters, the shallow bowls cut with swags painted with flowers below crenellated rims, late 19th century, 32.5cm. high. (Christie's) $1,899

A pair of clear cut-glass table lusters with fluted edges, baluster stems and circular bases, with drops. (Brightwells) $652

A pair of Bohemian blue and white overlay lusters, the bowls cut with arched panels painted with portraits of young girls between diamond-cut panels, late 19th century, 33.5cm high. (Christie's) $1,323

'Wingen' No.5108, a clear and frosted carafe, molded mark *R. Lalique*, 20.5cm. high. (Christie's) $700

A Leerdam yellow glass egg cup set, designed by H.P. Berlage, circa 1924, molded HB monogram to each piece, tray 19.5cm. diameter. (Christie's) $1,400

A Murano lamp, sticker label, 28cm. high. (Christie's) $101

Clear etched blown glass tumbler, John Frederick Amelung, New Bremen Glass Manufactory, circa 1788-89, brilliant grayish color, decorated with copper-wheel engraved floral and vine wreath encircling the word *Federal*, 6¹/₈in. (Skinner) $51,750

A Bohemian silver-gilt-mounted Travelling Apothecary, early 18th century, fitted with three octagonal turquoise-blue tinted bottles, two with silver-gilt mounted screw covers, and a small silver-gilt funnel, 10cm. by 7.5cm. (Sotheby's) $2,520

A late 19th century Storer's patent fountain, the decorative brass frame with cranberry and crackle-finished shaped bowl, the axis with mounting points for the two cranberry glass bulbs, 51.8cm. high. (Christie's) $4,836

Three French yellow opaline glass graduated toilette bottles and stoppers, late 19th/early 20th century, each cylindrical, with short neck and flaring rim, fitted with hollow ball stoppers, the largest 7¼in. high.(Christie's) $2,585

A pair of Continental cut urns and covers, in the Georgian style, the bowls cut with a band of ovals above gadrooning, on socle bases, the covers with similar bands above fluting, 33.5cm. (Bonhams) $1,326

A rare bullet-shaped glass teapot and cover, circa 1740, of spherical form with narrow neck, scroll handle, 5¼in. (Sotheby's) $1,848

A post-war statue, modelled as two fish, engraved *Lalique France*, 30cm. high. (Christie's) $1,313

A Sabino opalescent glass model of a female torso, raised on a circular base, 20cm. (Woolley & Wallis) $382

Kristian Klepsch glass elephant sculpture, Germany, late 20th century, a domed receding rectangular form of cast colorless glass, internally decorated with an elephant, 6½in. wide. (Skinner) $2,300

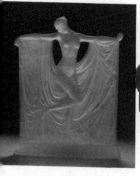

'Suzanne' No.833, a clear frosted, and opalescent figure, molded mark *R. Lalique*, inscribed *France*, 22.5cm. high. (Christie's) $10,505

A pair of Sabino clear and frosted glass marks, molded marks *Sabino 4684 Paris Depose*, 25.5cm high. (Christie's) $2,275

A post-war statue modelled as three children, stencil mark Lalique France, 21cm. high. (Christie's) $910

MUGS

A baluster mug, possibly first quarter 18th century, of waisted cylindrical form with folded everted rim and gadroon-molded base, 3½in. (Sotheby's) $1,848

A Continental Milchglas mug, painted with a man drinking and inscribed *Fuego*, 18th century, 10.5cm. (Woolley & Wallis) $168

A clear and red overlay cylindrical mug with coin insert, probably English, the base with an 1812 Imperial French Kingdom of Italy 5 Lire coin insert, mid 19th century, 12.5cm. high. (Christie's) $700

A St. Louis blue double-clematis paperweight, circa 1850, the central yellow stamen cane surrounded by two rows of blue pointed and striped petals with five leaves, 8cm. (Sotheby's) $2,293

A rare Baccarat faceted bouquet paperweight, circa 1850, the central coral pink flower surrounded by a small white and blue flower and bud, 9cm. diameter. (Sotheby's) $8,820

A St. Louis garlanded bouquet paperweight, circa 1850, the three small blue flowers with yellow stamens and five leaves, 6.8cm. diameter. (Sotheby's) $2,822

A Clichy spaced-millefiori paperweight, circa 1850, set with a variety of colorful canes including two pink, green and white rose and one white rose cane, 8.1cm. diameter.(Sotheby's) $2,822

'Perche' No.1158. a clear and frosted paperweight, molded mark *R. Lalique*, 17cm. (Christie's) $700

A Baccarat garlanded butterfly weight, the insect with an amethyst body, turquoise eyes and marbled millefiori wings, mid 19th century 7cm. diameter. (Christie's) $2,245

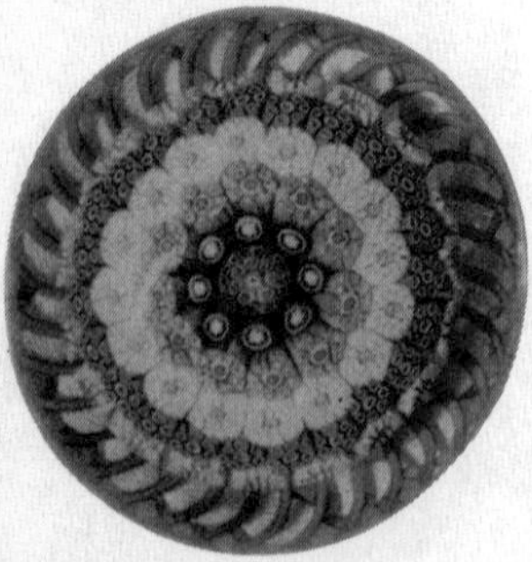

A St. Louis concentric millefiori mushroom paperweight, circa 1850, the tuft comprising five rows of assorted canes, predominantly in salmon pink, green, blue and white, 7cm. diameter. (Sotheby's) $4,234

Lundberg Studios paperweight, design by Daniel Salazar, California, 1988, white flowering tree branch with delicate scalloped petals and green leaves over a cobalt blue ground, diameter 2¾in. (Skinner) $259

A Venetian scrambled millefiori paperweight, Pietro Bigaglia, signed and dated *1846*, set with assorted silhouette canes, short lengths of latticinio tubes and areas of aventurine, 7.2cm. diameter. (Sotheby's) $8,800

A Baccarat garlanded pink pom-pom paperweight, circa 1850, the large flower with cane stamen, pink bud and leaves, 7.2cm. (Sotheby's) $5,645

A St. Louis crown paperweight, circa 1850, the central millefiori cane with radiating twisted red and green ribbons outlined in opaque-white, 7.4cm. (Sotheby's) $2,016

A St. Louis faceted garlanded flat bouquet paperweight, circa 1850, the four cane flowers set within five leaves all within a garland of white and blue canes, 8.5cm. diameter. (Sotheby's) $1,764

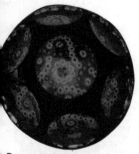

A Baccarat ruby flash overlay patterned millefiori weight, the central canes set within two interlocking trefoil garlands in blue and white canes, enclosing six silhouette canes of alternating cockerels and goats, mid 19th century, 8cm. diameter. (Christie's) $3,800

Modern Saint Louis King Tutankhamun paperweight, France, 1979, gold mask of the Pharaoh in the center of a ring of red, yellow, blue and white canes, diameter 3in. (Skinner) $316

A Baccarat butterfly and white clematis paperweight, circa 1850, the insect with brightly colored wings hovering over a white double-clematis flower, 2¾in. x 1¾in. (Sotheby's) $2,646

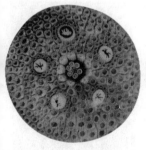

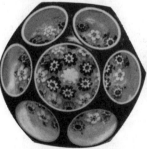

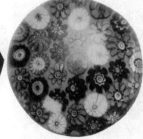

St. Louis green carpet-ground paperweight, circa 1850, with central cane arrangement surrounded by five silhouette canes of three dancing devils, a lady and camel, 7.2cm. diameter. (Sotheby's) $7,056

A ruby double-overlay paperweight, possibly Bohemian or Gillinder, 19th century, the central mushroom two rows of canes around a central white cane all on a bed of white latticinio tubing, 6.7cm. diameter by 5cm. (Sotheby's) $4,410

A Clichy turquoise-blue ground millefiori paperweight, circa 1850, set with a variety of canes including two green, pink and white rose canes on an opaque turquoise-blue ground, 3¼in. (Sotheby's) $3,864

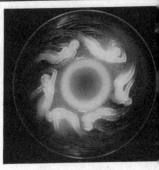

A Schneider plate with mottled blue and yellow glass, etched factory mark, 40cm. diameter.
(Christie's) $894

A Lalique 'Ondines' clear and opalescent plate, after 1921, the underside molded with naiads amongst bubbles, 27.2cm.
(Bonhams) $1,813

'Ondines' No.3003, a clear, frosted, and opalescent plate, molded mark *R.Lalique*, 28cm. diameter.
(Christie's) $2,451

SAND GLASSES

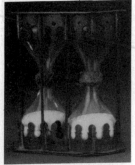

An 18th century double bulb sandglass, the upper and lower plates with decorative freeze, united by seven (of ten) supports, 5in. high. (Christie's) $2,670

A late 17th/early 18th century four-bulb sand-glass, each double-bulb joined with wax, the upper and lower plates joined by brass rods, 10½in. wide.
(Christie's) $5,339

An unusual sandglass, mounted in a cylindrical brass frame with bayonet catch top, modelled as a crown (possibly originally used as a bailiff's tipstaff), 8in. high.
(Christie's) $1,680

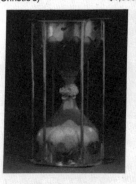

A rare late 17th/early 18th century four-bulb church sand-glass, the elongated bulbs united with wax covered with silk, cord-bound, fitted with fine white, gray and pale brown sand, 9½in. wide.
(Christie's) $5,339

A Regency period rosewood hour glass, the two turned end plates united by bobbin-turned columns, with bun feet, the two phials united by a silver metal collar, 8½in. high.
(Christie's) $1,501

A 17th century sand-glass, the two bulbs joined with wax covered with cord-bound silk, filled with fine-grained pale brown and black sand, 8in. high.(Christie's) $3,671

'Vers Le Jour', Lalique for Worth, circa 1926, a clear and frosted scent bottle and stoppper, in graduating red to yellow hues, molded with chevron pattern, 10.6cm. high.(Christie's) $963

'Lunaria' No.482 Lalique for Maison Lalique, circa 1912, a clear, frosted and dark-gray stained scent bottle and stopper, with branching monnaie-du-pape pattern, 7cm. high. (Christie's) $3,852

'Serpent' No.502, Lalique for Maison Lalique, circa 1920, a clear, frosted and gray-stained scent bottle and stopper, molded with sinuous snake-scale body, 8.4cm. high. (Christie's) $3,502

'Styx' Lalique for Coty, circa 1911, a clear, frosted and sepia-stained scent bottle and stopper, the topper molded with a quartet of wasps and outspread wings touching, 11.5cm. high. (Christie's) $1,788

'Cigalia' Lalique for Roger et Gallet, circa 1911, a clear, frosted and dark green-stained scent bottle and stopper, the four corners molded with cicadas, 12.7cm. high. (Christie's) $2,980

'Bouchons Mûres' No.495 for Maison Lalique, circa 1920, a clear and blue-enamelled scent bottle, the tiara stopper molded in blue-frosted and polished opaque glass as a spray of mulberries, 11.5cm. high. (Christie's) $24,510

'A Coeur Joie' a clear and frosted perfume bottle, made for Nina Ricci, stencil mark bottle made by Lalique France, 12cm. high. (Christie's) $384

'Les Yeux Bleus' Lalique for Canarina, circa 1928, a sapphire blue glass scent bottle and stopper with white-staining, molded in low relief with eyes, 5cm. high. (Christie's) $2,975

'Triomphe', Lalique for D'Orsay, circa 1920, a clear, frosted and sepia-stained scent bottle and stopper, molded with vertical bands of foliage, 11.7cm. high. (Christie's) $1,751

'Parfum des Anges' a clear glass perfume bottle, made for Oviatt, molded mark *R.Lalique* Paris *France,* 9cm. high.
(Christie's) $742

A large post-war scent bottle, in clear and frosted glass made for Nina Ricci, wheel-engraved *Lalique*, 31cm. high.(Christie's) $612

Dubarry 'A Toi', a clear, frosted an enamelled perfume bottle, circa 1919, 17cm. high.
(Christie's) $4

'La Phalène' Lalique for D'Héraud, circa 1925, a clear and frosted scent bottle and stopper in graduating red to amber hues, molded in low relief with the shape of a butterfly, 9.5cm. high.
(Christie's) $5,252

'La Belle Saison' Lalique for Houbigant, circa 1925, a clear, frosted and sepia-stained scent bottle and stopper, concave front with center panel molded in low relief with a maiden head, bottle 10cm. high.
(Christie's) $3,853

'Orée', Lalique for Coty, circa 1930 a clear, frosted and sepia-stained scent bottle and stopper, central panels to front and reverse molded in low relief with draped female figure amid foliage, 8cm. high. (Christie's) $2,979

'Bouchons Fleurs de Pommiers' No.493 for Maison Lalique, circa 1919, a clear and frosted pink-stained scent bottle and stopper, the tiara stopper molded and pierced as spray of branching flowers, 13.8cm. high.
(Christie's) $12,255

'Flausa' Lalique for Roger et Gallet, circa 1914, a clear, frosted and orange-stained scent bottle and stopper, molded in relief with seated robed maiden among blossoms, 12cm. high.
(Christie's) $9,628

'Ambre de Siam', Lalique for Volnay, circa 1920, a clear, frosted and black-enamelled scent bottle and stopper, the vertical bands terminating either end with animalistic heads, 14.8cm. high.
(Christie's) $26,26

pair of frosted glass and bronze eiling lights, 20th century, the omed shades issuing from pierced ttice frames with entwined foliage, 2¼in. high. hristie's) $2,544

Art Glass shade, possibly Luster Art, circa 1920, bud form shade of opal glass with scalloped rim with five pulled gold feathers to exterior, 4⁷/₈in. (Skinner) $115

A silver plated and cut-glass plafonnier, early 20th century, the domed shade cut with diamond and lanceolate leaf designs, mounted within a spreading circlet with ribbon-tied reeded border, 17in. diameter. (Christie's) $1,280

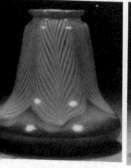

n Art Nouveau American idescent glass shade, 12.8cm. gh. (Christie's) $350

Gabriel Argy-Rousseau, pair of Veilleuse shades 'Rosaces', 1923, pâte-de-verre, in shades of blue, green and purple, molded with panels above a frieze of roses, 6¼in. (Sotheby's) $6,720

A Sabino plafonnier, molded marks *Sabino Paris Depose 4389*, incised *Made in France*, 47.2cm. diameter. (Christie's) $437

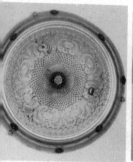

pair of French molded glass and t metal plafonniers; early 20th ntury, the domed, hobnail cut ass with foliate terminal, the rrounds with applied flower ads, 15¾in. diameter. hristie's) $999

A gilt-bronze and frosted glass plafonnier, early 20th century, the domed shade cut with lanceolate leaf and stellar designs, with hinge to the ribbon-tied berried laurel circlet, 13in. diameter. (Christie's) $822

Emile Gallé, pomegranate plafonnier, circa 1900, slightly opalescent pale yellow glass, overlaid with dark red and etched with flowering branches laden with pomegranate fruits, 52.4cm. diameter. (Sotheby's) $10,416

A pedestal-stemmed sweetmeat glass, the vertically ribbed double-ogee bowl with everted rim, circa 1750, 15cm. high.
(Christie's) $980

A baluster sweetmeat glass, circa 1725, the wide double-ogee bowl with everted rim and applied trail, 6½in. (Sotheby's) $2,352

An opaque-twist sweetmeat glass, the flared vertically ribbed bowl with waved rim, on a double-series stem and conical foot, circa 1775, 11cm. high. (Christie's) $700

A sweetmeat glass, circa 1745, the double ogee bowl with everted rim, on an eight-pointed pedestal stem with diamonds on the shoulders between collars, 16.5cm.
(Bonhams) $412

An English sweetmeat glass, mid 18th century, with flared bowl raised on a double teared ball knop stem and slight conical foot, 14.7cm.
(Bonhams) $441

An early baluster stem sweetmeat glass, circa 1730, the ogee bowl with everted rim, on a double collar a beaded ball knop, a triple-ringed annulated knop and short inverted baluster section, 14.2cm.
(Bonhams) $911

TANTALUS

An oak three bottle tantalus, with silver plated mounts and three plated wine labels, 39cm. wide.
(Bonhams) $323

An oak and electroplated three bottle tantalus, 38cm. wide.
(Bonhams & Brooks) $450

A tantalus, raised on ball feet to an open bar frame, holding three similar cut glass square decanters with stoppers, 14½in. James Dixon & Sons.(Woolley & Wallis) $279

Czechoslovakian red glass vase, circa 1930, raised rim on a flattened spherical form of red cased to colorless glass, decorated internally with lavender windings, 4in. high. (Skinner) $115

A pair of semi-opaque oviform vases, possibly French, acid-etched, silvered and gilt with vignettes of classical maidens decorating vases, circa 1880, 30cm. high.
(Christie's) $517

A Marcel Goupy enamelled vase, of globular form with short neck, the amethyst body enamelled in blue and green with a trellis of heartsease, enamelled signature to base, 15cm.
(Bonhams) $464

A French opaline glass baluster vase, circa 1835, atelier of Jean-François Robert, the body finely painted with a garland of entwined garden flowers, 20in. high.
(Christie's) $8, 225

A fine and rare Thomas Webb imitation 'rock cyrstal' marine vase, circa 1885, by William Fritsche, signed, deeply engraved and polished overall with a variety of large and small fish swimming amidst flowing waves, shells and marine life, 12in.
(Sotheby's) $23,738

A fine Lobmeyr enamelled and gilt 'Persian-style' two-handled vase, circa 1875, painted and gilt with a shaped panel of stylized flowers below an Arabic inscription, 6¾in.
(Sotheby's) $5,040

A Lalique 'Prunes' clear and opalescent vase, after 1930, of flared cylindrical form molded in relief with a garland of plums and foliage, 17.5cm.
(Bonhams) $4,350

A pair of Victorian cranberry glass vases, enamelled with Mary Gregory style scenes depicting children in a garden, with gilt embellishment, 8in. high.
(Andrew Hartley) $462

Steuben green jade swirl vase, wide mouth on cylindrical form raised on circular foot, polished pontil, Steuben fleur-de-lis marks on base, 6⅞in. high.
(Skinner) $374

441

A Gallé mold-blown glass vase, cameo mark *Gallé*, 32cm. high. (Christie's) $4,202

A pair of Bohemian cranberry ground and overlay vases each depicting a circular bust portrait of a young girl, 26 and 24cm. (Thomson Roddick & Medcalf) $943

A Gallé cameo glass vase, decorated with pink flowers, cameo mark *Gallé*, 30.5cm. high. (Christie's) $7,003

Daum, vase, circa 1925, blue/smoky glass, deeply etched with a zigzag frieze and geometric motifs, 23.2cm. (Sotheby's) $4,704

A pair of Loetz silvered metal mounted vases, the pale green glass with turquoise iridescence, 20cm. high. (Christie's) $5,602

'Camargue' No.10-937, a clear, frosted, and sepia-stained vase, engraved *Lalique France*, 29cm. high. (Christie's) $3,151

An Art Deco glass vase by Henri Navarre, incised signature *H.Navarre*, 16cm. high. (Christie's) $989

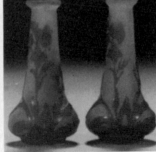

A pair of Gallé cameo glass vases, cameo marks *Gallé*, each 8.5cm. (Christie's) $1,050

A Gallé cameo glass vase, cameo mark *Gallé* with a star, 10cm. high. (Christie's) $700

chneider vase of flattened ovoid
n, the clear glass internally
tled with yellow, deep red and
ethyst, etched *Schneider*
navera, 26cm. high.
ristie's) $1,788

'Marisa' No.1002, an olive green
glass vase, engraved *R.Lalique
France*, 24cm. high.
(Christie's) $4,202

A Daum enamelled vase decorated
with a winter landscape, enamelled
mark *Daum Nancy BJ* with a cross
of Lorraine, 11.5cm. high.
(Christie's) $5,252

allé enamelled glass vase, in
Islamic style, painted signature
é, 20cm. high.
ristie's) $6,127

An Austrian Art Nouveau glass
vase, the peppermint glass
decorated in various enamels,
applied yellow rim, 11.5cm. high.
(Christie's) $490

'Saint-François' No.1055, a clear,
frosted blue-stained opalescent
vase, stencil mark *R.Lalique
France*, 17.8cm. high.
(Christie's) $2,424

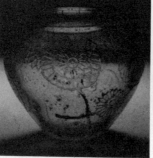

lique blue stained frosted glass
, of tapering form with five
ontal protruding bands edged
molded flowerheads, 6½in.
(Andrew Hartley) $1,276

A Daum vase, the clear glass
engraved and with gilt foil
inclusions, gilt engraved mark
Daum Nancy France with cross of
Lorraine, 13cm. high.
(Christie's) $2,980

René Lalique, vase 'Nanking', after
1925, clear glass, the sides faceted
with triangles molded with
geometric motifs and heightened
with black staining, 32.7cm.
(Sotheby's) $7,056

A Schneider vase, factory mark, 21.7cm. high.
(Christie's) $596

A Gallé cameo glass vase, cameo mark *Gallé*, 9.8cm. high.
(Christie's) $875

A Sabino amber glass vase, incise *Sabino France*, 17.5cm. high.
(Christie's) $74

Rene Lalique Cariatides vase, France, raised rim on an ovoid vessel of colorless glass, decorated with eight female torso columns on a leafy ground, 7¾in. high. (Skinner) $4,600

A pair of Stourbridge yellow, blue and white cameo vases, possibly Thomas Webb, pear-shaped with waisted necks, carved with trailing branches, circa 1885, 25cm. high.
(Christie's) $5,527

French molded Art Glass vase, André Hunebelle, circa 1920, stepped bulbous form of colorless glass, molded with raised decoration of angel fish among seaweed, 8½in.
(Skinner) $345

René Lalique, vase 'Gros Scarabées', after 1923, deep partly frosted amber glass, molded with scarabs, 28.9cm.
(Sotheby's) $9,240

Legras enamelled cameo glass vase, France, early 20th century, elongated ovoid vessel of olive green glass etched with trailing leaves and tassel seed pods, 8⅛in. high. (Skinner) $460

'Saint-François' No.1055, a clea and frosted vase with feint turquoise-staining, stencil mark *R.Lalique France*, 17.5cm. high.
(Christie's) $1,78

Loetz vase, the cased orange
glass with amethyst rim and base,
3cm. high.(Christie's) $596

A Gallé mold-blown glass vase,
cameo mark *Gallé*, 39.5cm. high.
(Christie's) $4,902

A Gallé cameo glass vase, cameo
mark *Gallé*, 13cm. high.
(Christie's) $1,050

important Lalique 'Quatres
geons' cire perdue frosted vase,
23, of ovoid form molded with
ur pigeons facing dexter with
ffed chests and wings sweeping
wn into the tail feathers forming
et, 25cm.
onhams) $137,750

A pair of French opaque glass
oviform vases, late 19th century,
probably Baccarat, each with gilt
flaring rim and painted in colors
with roosters and hens walking in
an extensive grisaille landscape,
30.8cm. high.
(Christie's) $3,525

Murano Art Glass vase, attributed
to Archimede Seguso, Italy, mid
20th century, cylindrical vessel
tapering to the base of red glass,
decorated with a grid of white and
rust lines, 11in.
(Skinner) $1,380

rder Steuben Wisteria glass pillar
e, Corning, New York, circa
25, raised on a knob and domed
t of dichroic pink/blue glass,
in. high. (Skinner) $633

A Deguy frosted vase, of footed
flared form, etched and enamelled
in deep purple with three phoenix,
etched mark *Deguy*, 29.2cm.
(Bonhams) $1,015

An etched Daum glass vase,
factory mark *Daum Nancy France*
with a cross of Lorraine, 26cm.
high. (Christie's) $700

A facet stem wine glass, circa 1780-90, the ogee bowl cut at the base and engraved round the rim with a border of egg-and-dart motifs, 13.7cm.
(Bonhams) $250

A rare early wine-glass, circa 1700, the funnel bowl with molded gadroons and pincered flammiform edge, 15.7cm.
(Sotheby's) $8,064

A Dutch engraved light-baluster wine glass, the funnel bowl engraved with a mother and two children standing on a continuous narrow tiled floor, 19.2cm.
(Skinner) $4,669

A fine deceptive baluster wineglass, circa 1700, the flared bowl set on a short inverted baluster with central tear, 11.3cm.
(Sotheby's) $4,23

A Beilby enamelled opaque-twist wine glass, circa 1765, the funnel bowl painted with fruiting vine in opaque-white above a band of molded flutes, 14.2cm.
(Sotheby's) $1,512

An Anglo-Venetian wine glass, late 17th century, the flared bowl set on a collar above a hollow flattened quatrefoil knop between mereses and plain sections, 14.4cm.
(Sotheby's) $1,176

A fine Venetian or façon de Venise filigree wine glass, late 16th century, in vetro a fili and a retorti, the trumpet bowl with vertical ribs below two trailed bands, 16.2cm.
(Sotheby's) $4,704

An engraved air twist wine glass, circa 1755, the ogee bowl engraved with a border of flowers above molded vertical fluting, the stem with a central mercurial twist cable, 15cm.
(Bonhams) $50

A rare opalescent opaque-twist cordial glass, circa 1765, the small funnel bowl set on a double-series opaque-twist stem of opalescent tint and a conical foot, 15.6cm.
(Sotheby's) $2,352

A color-twist wine glass, circa 1765, with bell-shaped bowl, the stem with a central core of translucent blue, brown and opaque entwined threads, 6½in.
(Sotheby's) $4,057

A color-twist wine glass, late 18th century, the ovoid bowl set on a stem enclosing a pink, blue and opaque-white corkscrew spiral edged in emerald-green, 5¼in.
(Skinner) $3,335

A Dutch engraved light-baluster wine glass, circ 1760, the funnel bowl engraved with an equestrian portrait, inscribed below the rim, 21.2cm.
(Skinner) $4,66

A balustroid wine glass with bell bowl, the solid lower section with an air inclusion, the stem with a triple-annulated knop, circa 1730, 16.5cm. high.
(Christie's) $1,052

An air twist wine glass, circa 1750, the bell bowl with solid base, on a shoulder knopped multi-ply air twist stem and conical foot, 16.7cm.
(Bonhams) $470

A plain-stemmed wine glass in the 18th century style, the flared thistle-shaped bowl with a tear to the solid lower part, 17.5cm. high.
(Christie's) $350

A Beilby enamelled opaque-twist wine glass, circa 1770, the funnel bowl painted with a band of fruiting vine in opaque-white , 15.5cm.
(Skinner) $2,168

An engraved 'Jacobite' portrait airtwist wine glass, circa 1750, the generous funnel bowl engraved with the bust portrait of Prince Charles Edward Stuart within an oval line panel, 18.2cm.
(Skinner) $6,337

A façon de Venise winged wine glass, possibly Venetian or North Italian, 17th century, of straw tint, the hexagonal lobed cup-shaped bowl, set on a stem applied with blue double-scroll, 12cm.
(Skinner) $1,666

A façon de Venise winged wine glass, probably Lowlands, 17th century, the octagonal bowl set on a closely coiled incised spiral stem, above a short section and wide conical foot, 13.5cm.
(Skinner) $3,167

A Venetian filigree wine glass 17th century, in vetro a retorti, the ribbed conical bowl set on a knopped and inverted baluster stem flanked by clear glass mereses, above a wide conical foot, 16.2cm.
(Skinner) $2,834

A fine heavy baluster wine-glass, circa 1700, the funnel bowl with solid base set on an everted baluster knot and folded conical foot, 17cm.
(Sotheby's) $3,024

An air twist ale glass, circa 1750, with deep rounded funnel bowl, on a shoulder and center-knopped multiply air twist stem terminating in a conical foot, 19.5cm.
(Bonhams) $559

A opaque twist firing glass, circa 1760, with ogee bowl, the stem composed of four solid intertwined spiral, within an eight-ply spiral strand, on a terraced foot, 9.8cm.
(Bonhams) $441

A drop-knop baluster wine glass, circa 1720, the funnel bowl with teared solid base set on a half knop above a drop knop with central tear over a true baluster, 19.5cm.
(Sotheby's) $2,856

A Regency mahogany celestial globe on stand, by J & W Cary, dated *1820,* with a brass meridian circle and mahogany stand, with a ring turned column and downswept legs. (Bonhams) $7,104

Franz Xavier Schönninger, Vienna, 1864, 9¼in. diameter terrestrial table globe made up of twelve hand-colored engraved gores, on an ornate ebonized wooden tripod stand, 15in. high. (Christie's) $6,045

Matthäus Albrecht Lotter (1741-1810, Augsburg, a rare 12in. diameter celestial globe made up of twelve finely-engraved hand-colored gores, 19in. high. (Christie's) $11,22

Heinrich Kiepert, Berlin, 1870, a 13¾in. diameter terrestrial table globe, made up of twelve chromolithographed gores and two polar calottes, raised on a cast bronze stand, 23½in. high. (Christie's) $1,554

A pair of early 19th century library globes, 12in. diameter, 35in. high, each made up of twelve hand colored gores, reticulated for 1830, Newton, Son & Berry, Chancery Lane, Fleet St, London. (Woolley & Wallis) $12,773

Josiah Loring, Boston, 1833, a fine 12in. diameter celestial table globe made up of twelve hand-colored engraved gores laid to the ecliptic poles, on four baluster turned mahogany legs, 18in. high. (Christie's) $6,909

Rand McNally, Chicago, a 12in. diameter terrestrial table globe made up of twelve chromolithographed paper gores, raised on four carved quadrant supports to decoratively carved and channelled column, 25in. high. (Christie's) $4,836

Nicolas Lane, London, 1776 [after 1779], a fine 2¾in. diameter pocket terrestrial globe, made up of twelve copper plate engraved paper gores, the equator graduated in degrees 1-180º (x2), in the original spherical fishskin covered case. (Christie's) $4,836

Schropp & Co., Simon (1757-1817) Berlin, 1827, a rare 4½in. diameter miniature terrestrial table globe made up of twelve hand-colored engraved gores and two polar calottes, in an unstained mahogany stand, 6¾in. high. (Christie's) $7,254

A Swiss enamelled gold snuffbox, by François Joanin, marked, Geneva, circa 1800, the center of the cover enamelled en plein with a rectangular scene depicting four gypsy women in front of a seated young gentleman, 85mm. wide. (Christie's) $6,045

A fine Louis XV vari-color gold and enamel snuffbox, by Claude Perron (fl. 1750-1777), the cover inset with a cartouche-shaped enamel plaque finely painted with a flower still-life, 81mm. wide. (Bonhams) $30,033

A Swiss jewelled and enamelled gold snuff-box with musical movement, by Sené & Détalla, marked, Geneva, circa 1820, the central panel on the cover later applied with pierced rose-cut diamond inscription Belle, 85mm. wide. (Christie's) $12,954

An Italian gold-mounted hardstone snuffbox set with a micro-mosaic, probably Rome, circa 1820, the lid inset with a gold-mounted micro-mosaic plaque depicting Pliny's Doves, 58mm. diameter. (Bonhams) $10,011

A German rococo jeweled and gold-mounted hardstone snuffbox, probably Dresden, circa 1740/1750, the lid applied with a silver-mounted jeweled bouquet tied with a ribbon, 58mm. wide. (Bonhams) $7,508

A George IV gold-lined composition boîte-à-surprise, English, circa 1830, the three miniatures French School, late 18th century, the hinged inner secret lid containing miniature of an Abbé caught in the act by a cuckold warrior, 86mm. diameter. (Christie's) $5,839

A fine Louis XV gold-mounted burgau and lacquer snuffbox, by Jacques-Michel Lemaire (fl. 1722-1776), all over inlaid with a paperwork pattern of shimmering burgau and gold in the Japanese nomada technique, 54mm. diameter. (Christie's) $19,000

A very fine Saxon hardstone and gold snuffbox, by Johann Christian Neuber, Dresden, circa 1780; the lid centered with an oval mocha-colored hardstone panel applied with a flower composition, 3¼in. wide.(Christie's) $442,685

A German rococo gold-mounted mother of pearl and burgau 'chinoiserie' snuff box, probably Dresden, circa 1740/1750, cartouche-shaped reserve painted in black with a Chinaman seated on a swing, 69mm. wide. (Bonhams) $2,502

A fine Louis XV enamelled three-color gold snuffbox, by Jean-Joseph Barrière (fl. 1763-1793), the cover centered with an oval reserve painted in brown camaïeu with an allegory of Music, 3¼in. wide. (Christie's) $63,403

A Swiss enamelled silver-gilt singing-bird box, by Charles Bruguier (1788-1862), colorfully plumed singing bird rotating on its axis, flapping its wings, turning its head, 92mm. wide. (Christie's) $12,954

A Continental jeweled and enamelled hardstone and gold cagework snuffbox set with an enamel miniature, possibly Germa or Swiss, late 19th century, 81mm wide. (Christie's) $43,18

A Louis XVI enamelled gold snuffbox set with a miniature, by Jean-Joseph Barrière (fl.1763-1793), the miniature of a young Lady in curled centered with a glazed oval portrait miniature of a young lady in curled Louis XIV hairdress, 3¼in. wide. (Bonhams) $12,513

A George III hardstone and gold snuffbox set with a miniature, English, circa 1780/1790, the miniature late 19th century, cover centered with an oval portrait miniature of Peter the Great of Russia (1672-1725), 85mm. wide. (Bonhams) $6,340

An early Louis XV gold snuffbox se with an enamel and a miniature, Paris, 1727/1728, the miniature attributed to Carl-Gustav Klingsted (1657-1734), a rectangular ename plaque finely painted with Vertumnus seducing Pomona, 85mm. wide. (Bonhams) $18,354

A Swiss enamelled two-color gold snuffbox set with an enamel miniature, Geneva or Neuchatel, circa 1820/1830, the cover inset with a rectangular enamel plaque painted with kneeling Cupid blowing into flame a bonfire of trophies of War, 3½in. wide. (Christie's) $10,011

A Louis XVI Japanese lacquer and vari-color gold snuffbox, by Barthélémy Pillieux (fl.1774-1790), the cover, sides, corners and base inset with panels of Japanese hiramaki-e gold and silver lacquer on a nashiji ground applied with kirikane, 2½in. wide. (Bonhams) $76,751

An unusual French jeweled and enamelled gold snuffbox for the Indian market, by Louis-François Tronquoy, enamelled in turquoise blue, the cover applied with an Indian elephant cast in gold and studded with a sapphire and diamonds, 97mm. wide. (Christie's) $10,01

An Art Nouveau two-handled cup presented to Harry Vardon during his tour of the United States, 1900, of hammered copper, with silver trimming and antler handles. (Sotheby's) $6,840

A silver plated tea set presented to Harry Vardon by the South Herts, G.C. in 1903, on the occasion of his fourth Open Championship victory. (Sotheby's) $4,140

Royal Doulton Proverb mug, a mug decorated with Charles Crombie style characters playing golf with the proverb 'Promise Little and Do Much', 6in. high. (Bonhams & Brooks) $458

Copeland Spode jardinière, a blue ground jardinière with a continuous center band of relief decoration of golfing figures, impressed factory mark and stamp, 8in. (Bonhams & Brooks) $1,359

Harry Vardon figure, a silver figure of Harry Vardon, after Hal Ludlow, mounted on a marble base, 6in. high. (Bonhams & Brooks) $715

Roy Ullyet original cartoon, used 11 October 1963, relating to Arnold Palmer's boast 'My Boys are unbeatable', framed, 17 x 17in. (Bonhams & Brooks) $143

Edwardian golfer's what-not stand, in oak, brass mounted golfer's stand with divisions for golf clubs and rack for balls and hooks for cap and shoes, 32in. high. (Bonhams & Brooks) $629

A rare 18th century Honourable Company Membership Certificate, dated 22 of May 1784 from Golf House, Links of Leith, signed by James Balfour, Secretary 10½ x 14½in. (Bonhams & Doyle) $18,400

An Open Championship Programme for Hoylake, June 16th to 20th 1930, in gray paper covers, the First Round scores printed and the second filled out in pencil. (Bonhams) $5,024

R & R Clark Golf A Royal and Ancient Game, First edition, Edinburgh 1875, 284 pp., green cloth. (Bonhams) $864

A superb silver bowl presented to Harry Vardon by South Herts. G.C. on the occasion of his record sixth Open Championship victory, hallmarked London, 1883, 11¼in. diameter.(Sotheby's) $8,100

Charles Smith Aberdeen Golfers Record And Reminiscences London: Privately printed Ltd editio (150 copies) 1909, 167pp, illustrated decorative cloth, 24.5cm (Bonhams & Doyle) $3,45◼

A hand colored photograph after James Arthur of a Lady Golfing, in ebonized oak frame, carved golfing emblems, entitled 'Queen of the Links'. 28 x 24in. overall. (Bonhams & Doyle) $1,840

A pair of plated open book and golfer bookends, 9in. (Bonhams) $464

Thomas Mathison, The Goff, An Heroi-Comical Poem in Three Cantos, Second Edition, Edinburgh 1793, with appendices, 32pp in good original uncut condition boun◼ half tooled morocco, 19th century. (Bonhams & Doyle) $63.00◼

A Dunlop 65 advertising ball, in painted plaster, of massive size, the dimple ball on triangular green painted plinth, 20in. high. (Bonhams) $406

A plated figure of Bobby Jones, by WB (USA), Jones is putting, on oblong base with plinth, 8¼in. max. (Bonhams) $435

A very heavy gutta percha ball mold, circa 1875, of iron approximately 4½in. diameter, 5k◼ weight. (Sotheby's) $5,40◼

Rowland Hilder, Come To Britain For Golf, lithograph printed in colors, circa 1950, printed by W.S. Cowell Ltd., London & Ipswich, for the Travel Association of Great Britain and Northern Ireland, framed and glazed, 29½ x 19½in.
(Sotheby's) $1,080

A brass two part bramble ball mold. "The Forresters Ruby", the mold stamped *505* and *Patent 11917* for a 27½ ball complete with 2 spare cups.
(Bonhams & Doyle) $3,680

A photographic portrait of Harry Vardon and James Braid, dated *June 7th 1912*, signed by both golfers, print 7¾ x 6½in., framed.
(Bonhams) $2,041

A Doulton Seriesware quart jug, no D5716 in pale brown decorated with Crombie type golfers, 9½in. high.
(Bonhams) $435

A gilt metal and simulated tortoiseshell mantel clock, the square case with scrolled corners, surmounted by an Edwardian golfer addressing the ball, 9in. high.
(Bonhams) $435

A chromed metal figurine of a golfer, in jacket and breeches at the end of his swing, on ebonized turned wood base, 8¾in.
(Bonhams) $406

A fine golfing vesta case, Sampson Mordan & Co., London, 1894, in hallmarked silver with painted enamel scene of a golfer at the top of his backswing, 2¼ by 1¼in.
(Sotheby's) $2,880

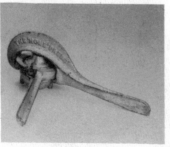

A Ross's Patent The 'Home' Press ball mold, circa 1900.
(Sotheby's) $1,260

Rev J. Kerr, The Golf Book Of East Lothian, large paper edition 4/250, Edinburgh 1896, 516 pp. plus index, green cloth and half morocco, signed by the author.
(Bonhams) $2,277

An Army and Navy No 2 bramble, with 90% paint and 3 hacks.
(Bonhams) $247

A 'The Vail', with concentric dotted quadrilateral markings.
(Bonhams) $2,030

A hand hammered gutta in the Forgan mesh style, near mint.
(Bonhams & Doyle) $6,325

A very rare gutta hammered longitudinally in the Dunn style, with equator line and some hacks and 98% paint.
(Bonhams & Doyle) $20,125

A feather ball in fairly good condition indistinctly stamped *T Robertson*.
(Bonhams & Doyle) $13,800

A John Gourlay feather ball circa 1850, marked *J. Gourlay*, approximately 1 13/16ths in., 47mm. diameter, in used condition.
(Sotheby's) $3,960

A Crane Junior, with sunbursts to the poles and horseshoe motifs.
(Bonhams) $870

A US Nobby No 31, with rows of rice grain motifs.
(Bonhams) $522

A Duplex, with alternating triangle markings.
(Bonhams) $4,495

An Arch Colonel, with double crescent markings, near mint. (Bonhams) $609

A rare Tom Morris hand hammered gutty, circa 1855, in style very similar to Forgan, stamped *T. Morris 27*. (Sotheby's) $11,700

A Lunar, with dot and bracket markings. (Bonhams) $609

A D Marshall Featherball, circa 1820/ 1830, in good condition. (Bonhams) $20,300

The Link Ball, with chain link moldings, red painted for use in frosty conditions. (Bonhams) $943

Allan Robertson, a mint feather ball, stamped *Allan* and ink written weight *29*. (Bonhams & Doyle) $10,925

The Tit-Bit, with 'C' and ring markings, very good. (Bonhams) $1,450

A W and J Gourlay feather ball, circa 1840 with ink written weight, good condition. (Bonhams) $5,510

An Eclipse gutty, with mesh markings. (Bonhams & Doyle) $508

A rare R Ferguson midspoon in dark stained beech stamped with owner's initials *JAJ*, 37in overall. (Bonhams & Doyle) $4,485

A William Dunn midspoon, with golden thornwood head 1in. deep face, 39in. overall. (Bonhams & Doyle) $8,050

An H Philp putter with thornwood head, 36in. overall with natural knot above the head, and 1in. deep face (Bonhams & Doyle) $5,520

A Charlie Hunter, Prestwick, short spoon, circa 1880, with golden beech head and hickory shaft. (Sotheby's) $4,140

A good early rut iron, mid 19th century, with circular face and 6in. hosel engraved owner's initials *JT*, 38in. overall. (Bonhams & Doyle) $6,900

A Tom Morris, St. Andrews, long nosed driver, circa 1875, the golden beech head also stamped *F.B. Elliot,* with hickory shaft. (Sotheby's) $6,300

A Willie Dunn, Musselburgh, long nosed putter, circa 1850, with fruitwood head, stamped *Wm. Dunn* in large letters, and hickory shaft. (Sotheby's) $3,240

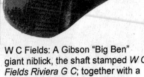

W C Fields: A Gibson "Big Ben" giant niblick, the shaft stamped *W C Fields Riviera G C*; together with a cloth head cover, with metal tag inscribed *M G M Studios, WC Fields.* (Bonhams & Doyle) $4,140

An early general iron, circa 1820, the heavy iron head with slightly concave face, with hickory shaft. (Sotheby's) $18,000

A very rare McEwan thornwood spoon head, circa 1840, bearing the McEwan stamp six times with at least four different stamps. (Bonhams) $1,595

A rare Philp putter with golden thornwood head 1in. face 37in., overall and with engraved silver band to the top of the shaft inscribed *Presented by Captain H Armytage 1927.* (Bonhams & Doyle) $10,350

A rare Cochranes patent driver, with iron head shell and persimmon head. (Bonhams) $1,233

An early iron, circa 1810, the very heavy head with rounded sole at heel end, heavily nicked large hosel, very thick replacement hickory shaft. (Sotheby's) $24,900

A scarce T. Travers putter circa 1920, with long rectangular persimmon head, rounded down to the toe, with four round lead weights in back and seven in sole. (Sotheby's) $1,260

A fine McEwan longspoon, in golden brown thornwood, bearing an additonal monogram above, of *MC* conjoined, 42in. long. (Bonhams) $4,350

Jackson playclub with golden
ornwood head, 1in. deep face,
3in. overall.
Bonhams & Doyle) $13,800

A T Morris putter, in dark stained
beech.
(Bonhams & Doyle) $2,415

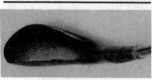

An A. Somervile long nosed driver
circa 1885, with stained, probably
holly head and hickory shaft.
(Sotheby's) $1,440

early track iron, circa 1820, with
rticularly small, heavy head with
ongly curved face, and extremely
e and thin African macassar
ony shaft.
otheby's) $8,100

An extremely rare cleek with 5in.
hosel, the blade inscribed *Bruce*
with lancewood shaft and stout grip,
38in. overall.
(Bonhams & Doyle) $2,530

A rare Robert Kirk, St. Andrews,
short spoon, circa 1875, with thorn
head and hickory shaft.
(Sotheby's) $7,560

particularly fine Robert Forgan,
. Andrews, child's long nosed
ver, circa 1885, with stained
ech head stamped with Prince of
ales feathers, 30½in.
otheby's) $3,060

An early 19th century oval dish-
faced "sand" iron, with 5½in. hosel,
deep nicking and with hickory shaft,
period grip, 38in. overall.
(Bonhams & Doyle) $18,400

A Brown's of Montrose Patent rake
iron, circa 1905, major model with
Brown's oval stamp, the six 'teeth'
with ornate face markings, with
hickory shaft.
(Sotheby's) $6,840

rare Josh Taylor's Non-Skid cleek
rca 1913, with most unusual
ramble' face pimples; together
th a Bakspin Mashie, circa 1923,
nd a Dedstop patent mashie, circa
920. (Sotheby's) $5,040

An extremely rare McEwan
midspoon, the head also stamped *J
Gourlay*, with dark stained
thornwood head and 1in. face, 38in.
overall.
(Bonhams & Doyle) $6,900

A rare Pope's Short-Head putter
circa 1905, with hickory shaft, 31in.
(Sotheby's) $1,440

A good T Morris shortspoon, in dark
stained beech, the shaft with 3in. of
whipping. (Bonhams) $8,120

A G S Sprague & Co Boston Patent
adjustable head putter, the block
head with 2 lofts stamped with
patent date *1904*, adjustable by
means of ball foot to hosel.
(Bonhams & Doyle) $2,530

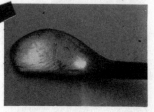

An A Patrick transitional driver, in
beech with composition face insert.
(Bonhams) $493

Large Lindström Parlograph swan-neck coin operated gramophone, by Carl Lindström, Berlin, with original Art Nouveau horn and classical ornament to the front of oak case, 1910.
(Auction Team Köln) $1,864

A Swiss Triumph gramophone with automatically swivelling tin horn, in working order, circa 1915.
(Auction Team Köln) $6,212

A Hammond gramophone with large swan-neck horn, in brown wooden case with bevelled glass sides, enamel picture to front, 191
(Auction Team Köln) $1,8

An EMG Mark X hand-made gramophone with papier mâché horn, four-spring EMG sound box on swan neck tone-arm, quarter-veneered oak case, the horn 26in. diameter.
(Christie's) $6,332

The Aladdin Gramophone Lamp, the mahogany standard lamp and shade enclosing an oak gramophone with a Rexophonic sound box and fittings, 80in. high.
(Christie's) $3,297

A Monarch Junior Gramophone, b the Gramophone & Typewriter Ltd with single-spring worm-drive mot in oak case, HMV Exhibition soundbox and later full-size Morning Glory horn, repainted bright red, 23in. diameter.
(Christie's) $77

A French Pathéphone Reflex gramophone, with wood and tin case, integral tin horn in the head, for round needles, 1925.
(Auction Team Köln) $226

A German red Nirona Nirophon tin gramophone, with original sound box, wind-up drive and crank, in original box, circa 1920.
(Auction Team Köln) $253

An unattributed brass horn gramophone, the front with glas plate to reveal the mechanism, 45cm. diameter horn, circa 191
(Auction Team Köln) $62

An HMV Model 460 table grand gramophone, with Lumière pleated diaphragm and gilt fittings in a quarter veneered oak case on a contemporary oak trolley stand. (Christie's) $1,437

A Mignonphone de Luxe Model D small portable gramophone by Walker Products, New York, with unattributed pick-up and speaker in lid. (Auction Team Köln) $113

A compact Pathéphone No. 1 table gramophone with integral aluminum horn, original sound box, 1910. (Auction Team Köln) $903

A Sheraton B Gramophone by the Gramophone & Typewriter Ltd, in mahogany case, the sides inlaid with ribbon-and-harebell swags, and fluted mahogany horn, the horn 21¼in. diameter. (Christie's) $2,590

An HMV Model 460 gramophone with Lumière pleated diaphragm and double-spring motor, in quarter-veneered oak case with gilt internal fittings, 1924-5 (diaphragm torn near rim). (Christie's) $1,176

An HMV Model IIa gramophone, with mahogany horn, No. 4 soundbox on gooseneck tone-arm and single-spring motor in mahogany case with Nipper transfer on case and horn, the horn 17½ x 17½in. diameter, circa 1912. (Christie's) $1,467

A horn gramophone with shaded gray and purple horn, Veni, Vidi, Vici soundbox and walnut case, the horn 19½in. diameter. (Christie's) $484

A Cascade II gramophone by W.J.Bond & Sons, Harlesden, with long papier mâché horn emerging from the side of the stained beech cabinet, the cabinet 39in. high, the horn projecting 65¼in. (Christie's) $1,467

An HMV gramophone, the mahogany cabinet gramophone with 5a sound box and other fittings, internal horn, fall front door missing, on square tapering legs, 45cm. wide. (Christie's) $110

459

A Hermès beige crocodile leather Kelly handbag, French, the khaki leather interior with three compartment pockets, 14in. (Sotheby's) $8,738

A clutch bag of maroon leather, the interior lined with maroon kid leather and fitted with pockets, stamped *HERMES PARIS MADE IN FRANCE*, 9¼in. (Christie's) $431

A handbag of olive green ostrich skin, with short rigid handle and detachable strap, opening up concertina style to reveal various pockets, stamped *Asprey*, 9½in. base. (Christie's) $450

A handbag of black ostrich skin, with two rigid handles, detachable strap and exterior pocket, the interior fitted with pockets and with a matching mirror and purse, stamped *Asprey London*, 12¼in. base. (Christie's) $450

A "Constance" handbag of navy blue leather, the interior lined with navy blue kid leather and fitted with pockets, stamped *HERMES PARIS MADE IN FRANCE*, 9½in. (Christie's) $1,175

A Hermès chaîne d'ancre brown leather handbag that belonged to Wallis Simpson, French, circa 1956, the shaped flap with chain link gilt clasp surmounted by the gilt metal cypher *WE* of the Duke and Duchess of Windsor, 10 x 6in. (Sotheby's) $3,192

A Hermès brown crocodile leather Kelly handbag, French, the brown leather lined interior with three compartments, 14in. (Sotheby's) $9,072

A "Market" drawstring bag of black morocco leather, the base stamped *Hermes, Paris, Made in France*, 10½in. (Christie's) $553

A Hermès black crocodile handbag French, circa 1960, with short strap, gilt metal square lock, 9½ x 8in. (Sotheby's) $1,344

A three-case inro, signed Kanshosai, Edo Period (late 18th/19th century), on one side a male courtier in a robe decorated with a turnip motif, 3in. long.
(Christie's) $1,586

A singe-case inro, signed Kanshosai, Edo Period (late 18th/19th century), polished wood ground, on one side a traveller in disguise, with a face-cloth and large hat, 6.2cm. high.
(Christie's) $2,678

A single-case inro, signed Masaru, Edo Period (18th century), black lacquer ground; decoration in shell overlay with gold takamaki-e and engraving; 2¼in. long.
(Christie's) $7,050

A three-case inro, signed Shiomi Masanari (Seisei), Edo Period (late 18th/19th century), black lacquer ground, the front with a leafy branch bearing two mikan [Japanese oranges], 3¼in. high.
(Christie's) $7,144

A three-case inro, with seal Kan, Edo Period (19th century), black lacquer ground, caparisoned elephant, 2¾in. long.
(Christie's) $9,960

A four-case inro, unsigned, in Somada style, Edo Period (19th century), black lacquer ground; the entire surface minutely inlaid in shell and gold foil with a variety of geometric and stylized floral grounds, 8.5cm. long.
(Christie's) $4,230

A fine four-case inro, signed Shiomi Masanari, Edo Period (19th century), black lacquered ground, decoration in gold, aokin, silver and red togidashi-e and gold flakes and dust, 8cm. high.
(Christie's) $5,000

A four-case inro, unsigned, Edo Period (late 18th/19th century), black lacquer ground. The Chinese Song-dynasty poet Toba riding into exile on his mule, 6.6cm. long.
(Christie's) $6,169

A four-case inro, signed Koma Kyuhaku, Edo Period (late 18th/19th century), shibuichi-nuri ground; decoration in gold takamaki-e with overlay of shell and lead, 7.3cm. long.
(Christie's) $4,406

461

A late 18th century brass universal equinoctial ring dial, unsigned, the equinoctial ring divided I-XII (x2) on one side, the meridian ring with punched names and latitudes of Continental cities, 8cm. diameter. (Christie's) $2,336

An unusual 18th century double-wheel waywiser, signed on the finely engraved silvered dial *B. Martin, London*, 55in. long. (Christie's) $4,338

A Continental painted wrought-iron and copper armillary sphere, 19th century, with gilt lead dragon finial on a green-painted wood baluster-turned plinth, 38½in. high. (Christie's) $2,435

An 18th century 2½in. reflecting telescope, signed on the back plate *Watkins, Charing Cross London*, the body-tube with screw-rod focusing for the secondary speculum mirrors, eyepiece extension with shade cap, 16½in. (Christie's) $1,669

An 18th century lacquered-brass surveying theodolite, signed on the horizontal plate *Troughton, London*, the telescope with draw-tube focusing, mounted with a bubble level, the axis located on twin inverted V supports, 5¾in. long. (Christie's) $917

An 18th century brass 4in. reflecting telescope, signed on the back plate *H. Pyefinch London*, the 24in. long body-tube with starfinder, lens cap, primary and secondary speculum mirrors, 27in. wide. (Christie's) $4,830

TOP TIP

If you want to set your aneroid barometer accurately, phone your local weather center, who will give you the barometric pressure for your locality.

You can then adjust the instrument via the small screw on the reverse of the case.

(Dee Atkinson Harrison)

A 19th century lacquered-brass drum sextant, signed *Elliott Brothers, 30 Strand London*, with silvered scale, vernier, magnifier, two-draw telescope, two shades, 3in. diameter. (Christie's) $267

A 19th century lacquered-brass Wenham's Compound binocular microscope, signed on the Y-shaped stand *Ross, London*, 10½in. wide, and a compound monocular microscope by Henry Crouch. (Christie's) $1,585

A lacquered brass improved compound microscope by Carpenter with all original accessories, circa 1820, in original mahogany case, 16in. wide.
(Charles Tomlinson) $3,234

18th century silver octagonal compass sundial, signed *Pre Le Maine Paris*, the underside with the names and latitudes of nineteen Continental cities and towns, 7.3cm. long.
(Christie's) $1,835

A Lownes Patent Anemometer by Stanley, London, circa 1890, 7in. high, in original green felt lined mahogany case.
(Charles Tomlinson) $441

A 19th century miner's theodolite, signed on the silvered compass dial *W & S Jones, 30, Holborn London*, the vertical half-circle with rack and pinion adjustment for the fore and aft sights, 13¾in. high.
(Christie's) $1,001

A lacquered brass binocular microscope, with rack and pinion and fine focusing to a rectangular stage on a 'Y' shaped base, inscribed *E Wheeler, London*, 13¾in.
(Woolley & Wallis) $1,540

A rare mid 19th century lacquered-brass theodolite, signed on the silvered dial *E. Kraft & Sohn in Wien No. 357*, the telescope with rack and pinion adjustment, four spider's web adjusters, 13¼in. high.
(Christie's) $6,340

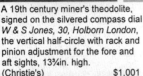

A mahogany cased 2 day marine chronometer, Charles Frodsham, London, circa 1850, silvered dial with subsidiary seconds and power reserve indicator, bezel diameter 115cm.
(Bonhams & Brooks) $2,698

A late 18th century octagonal compass sundial, signed on the horizontal plate *Langlois Paris aux Galleries du Louvre*, the engraved broken hour ring with Roman numerals on the upper surface, 8cm. long.
(Christie's) $2,002

A George IV mahogany waywiser, by Thomas Jones, with spoked wheel and engraved dial with miles and furlongs and links of chains, 50½in. high.
(Christie's) $2,981

Cast iron gate, America, circa 1860, the vine cresting centering a banner *EDWARD R. DOLAN* above a willow tree with doves in the branches with flanking lambs, 41in. high x 29in. wide. (Skinner) $1,380

A pair of cast iron andirons in the shape of baseball players, American, early 20th century, cast in the half round in the shape of standing baseball players, 19¼in. high. (Sotheby's) $4,600

A Victorian steel door knocker, modelled as a hand clasping a pomegranate, with square backplate and circular door plate, 4¼in. high. (Christie's) $458

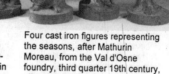

A pair of cast-iron horse-head hitching posts, attributed to J.W. Fiske and Company (active 1870-1893), New York City, each cast in the full round with articulated mane, eyes, nostrils and mouth, 48in. high.(Christie's) $4,465

Four cast iron figures representing the seasons, after Mathurin Moreau, from the Val d'Osne foundry, third quarter 19th century, all on integral bases cast with the maker's name, 63½in. high. (Christie's) $72,345

A black-painted cast-iron hitching post finial, American, late 19th century, cast in the full round with clasped digits and applied chain above a ruffled cuff, on a modern base, 9¼in. high with base. (Christie's) $3,760

Cast iron rooster windmill weight, attributed to Elgin Co., America, late 19th century, the full-bodied rooster with a number of coats of old paint, 15in. high, 19in. long. (Skinner) $2,185

A pair of cast-iron hitching post finials, American, early 20th century, each cast in the full round as footmen with an articulated hat and facial features, with outstretched arms, 13in. high. (Christie's) $1,645

A cast-iron lion's-head architectural ornament, Rochester Iron Works, late 19th century, cast in the half round with articulated mane, brow, eyes, snout and jaw, 11in. wide. (Christie's) $1,528

A red-painted cast-iron rooster mill weight, American, early 20th century, cast in the full round, the Mogul form with articulated orange-painted comb, eyes, wattle and white-painted beak, 23in. high, with stand. (Christie's) $8,813

A cast-iron hitching post finial, American, 9th century, cast in the full round depicting Napoleon's head with articulated hair, ears and facial features, 8in. high. (Christie's) $4,465

Cast iron Punch and Judy doorstop, America, 19th century, polychrome decoration in red, blue, black, and white, 12in. high. (Skinner) $1,725

A brown-painted cast-iron eagle counterweight, Columbia Printing Press, Philadelphia, 1813, cast in the full round with articulated eyes, beak, feathered spreadwinged body, on a modern base 18¼in. high, with stand. (Christie's) $1,410

A cast-iron horse-head hitching post finial, American, late 19th century, cast in the full round, mouth pierced with a double-ring attachment, 10in. high. (Christie's) $1,058

A painted cast-iron shooting gallery, American, early 20th century, steel bar uprights centering six similar horizontal bars, each with six white-painted targets of birds in profile swinging back on cotterpin hinges, 33¾in. wide. (Christie's) $6,463

A pair of cast iron and gilt gates French, circa 1890, the two sides creating an arched gate centering an urn with Greek key decoration and issuing flowers, 209cm. high, 161cm. wide. (Sotheby's) $18,975

A painted cast-iron Massachusetts State seal, American, late 19th-early 20th century, cast in the half round, the scrolled cartouche headed by a raised arm with sword enclosing a standing figure of a Native American, 13in. wide. (Christie's) $588

A Victorian painted cast iron walking stick stand, late 19th century, with a cherub standing amidst rushes, representing the youthful Hercules, entwined with a snake to form the retaining rail, 33in. high.(Christie's) $1,646

A Danish cast-iron flat iron stove by C.M. Mess, Veil, for twelve irons, 38 x 64 x 40cm., circa 1900.
(Auction Team Köln) $423

An 'Egg-laying Hen' automatic chocolate dispenser, cast iron, by MUM-Automaten, Dresden, circa 1920, 58cm. high.
(Auction Team Köln) $3,049

A Hegaard flat iron stove for six irons, with lion feet and four irons present, circa 1900.
(Auction Team Köln) $480

A cast iron trough, J.W. Fiske and Company, New York City, the conforming back splash plate with maker's inscription, centering a lion mask spout over a grilled overflow drain, 35½in. wide.
(Christie's) $1,293

A monumental French cast-iron vase on pedestal, by Val d'Osne, Paris, circa 1890, the vase with foliate-cast overhanging rim and stepped neck, the fluted body applied with a pair of Greek key handles, 75¼in. high.
(Christie's) $23,500

A North European cast-iron fire-back, 18th century, cast with two armorial shields flanked by hound supporters with visor cresting and Latin inscription to the ribbon cartouche, 32 x 35in.
(Christie's) $6,956

A Continental cast-iron fire-back, early 18th century, cast with an armorial device above figures of blacksmiths and with the date 1701, 32½in. square.
(Christie's) $1,129

A Continental sheet-iron sign, part 19th century, modelled as a crowned spread eagle, head restored, 41in. high.
(Christie's) $835

A chocolate and postcard dispenser with applied cast iron Art Nouveau decoration by Ges. Neubert & Co., Dresden, circa 1910, 98cm. high.
(Auction Team Köln) $2,146

A Danish cast brass box type slug iron with pointed sole, walnut handle on baluster supports, horizontal hinged gate, lozenge shaped slug, circa 1880. (Auction Team Köln) $141

A small cast iron flat iron, tear-drop sole, the top surface with decoration of a courting couple in high relief, Belgian, circa 1850. (Auction Team Köln) $124

An Omega silvered spirit iron with transverse reservoir, with wooden handle and hand protector, old wooden case with brass handle, circa 1900. (Auction Team Köln) $112

A Scottish cast steel slug iron, with brass columns, turned wood handle with brass finials, sole plate 15cm. long, circa 1880. (Auction Team Köln) $1,355

A small cast metal flat iron in the shape of a swan, with applied handle, sole 12cm. long. (Auction Team Köln) $508

A triangular slug iron, turned wooden handle, decorative backplate, circa 1800, German, sole plate 19cm. long. (Auction Team Köln) $2,823

An unusual small cast iron slug iron, with column supports, turned wood handle, the top decorated with a small amphora on a brass plate, circa 1700. (Auction Team Köln) $3,389

A brass ox-tongue slug iron with long walnut handle and single baluster pillar, circa 1820, 21cm. long. (Auction Team Köln) $158

A heavy cast iron spirit chimney iron with stand, possibly a prototype by Husqvarna, Sweden, brass tank and heating parts, dated 1895, weighing 12kg. (Auction Team Köln) $1,863

A German multifunction slug iron, cast iron with welded hoop iron band, cool tip, Wuppertal region, circa 1850, 19cm. long.
(Auction Team Köln) $508

An early European gothic cast metal flat iron of teardrop form with twisted handle, 15th/16th century, 18cm. long.
(Auction Team Köln) $3,106

A German ox-tongue silvered cast metal slug iron with ceramic handle, black with floral decoration, circa 1900.
(Auction Team Köln) $310

A cast iron German charcoal iron with pointed sole, dolphin posts, ash handle and front latch in the form of a bearded man's head, damper at rear, circa 1900, 21cm. long.
(Auction Team Köln) $101

A cast brass Austrian miniature slug iron, with iron slug and pointed sole, walnut handle and straight columns, vertical gate, floral decoration, dated *1883*.
(Auction Team Köln) $101

A cast iron charcoal iron, Austro-Hungarian, semi-circular beech handle on cast iron front post with griffin finial, rear damper, circa 1880, 21cm. long.
(Auction Team Köln) $158

An American soapstone topped iron by Phineas E. Hood, Milford, NH, metal handle and iron sole, 1887, 17 x 11 x 14cm.
(Auction Team Köln) $169

A dragon-form charcoal chimney iron, with smoke vent front right, cast iron, lever closure for the lid and rosette slide for ventilation, 1880.
(Auction Team Köln) $3,106

A German cast brass box type slug iron with pointed sole plate and walnut handle, circa 1860.
(Auction Team Köln) $79

Kholmogory walrus ivory casket, rly 19th century, of rectangular rm with rising top, inset with etwork panels and penwork ecorated in red and green inks, in. wide.
hristie's) $585

A Burmese ivory model of an oxen-driven cart, circa 1900, the cart supporting four figures, on a rectangular onyx plinth, the ivory group 7in. long.
(Christie's) $1,038

A French gilt-metal-mounted ivory casket, circa 1890, decorated all-over with hunting scenes; surmounted by a rectangular spreading hinged top, 12¾in. wide.
(Christie's) $9,499

Continental carved ivory bust of elamonian Ajax, mid 19th century, ter the Antique, with integral quare waisted socle and later one base, the ivory element 7in. gh. (Christie's) $3,619

A set of six late Victorian ivory pepper mills, the waisted cylindrical bodies with dentil borders to the covers and finials, engraved with a crest of a griffin head holding a feather, 4in. high.
(Christie's) $4,724

A French silver-mounted ivory tankard, circa 1880, the oval hinged lid surmounted by a figure of Hercules fighting the Lion, the cylindrical body carved with mythological scenes, 13¾in. high.
(Christie's) $12,090

19th century Oriental carved ivory ure of a standing fisherman rrying a child on his back, a asshopper on his shoulder, 7¼in. gh. (Andrew Hartley) $672

A pair of French ivory figures of cherubs, circa 1875, one with a quiver and arrows, the other tensing his bow, each seated on a tree-trunk, on a velvet-covered plinth, the ivories: each 9½in. high.
(Christie's) $10,364

A French ivory tankard, circa 1890, the body carved with the scene of lions attacking horsemen, 11in. high. (Christie's) $6,876

A large Chinese celadon jade brushwasher in the form of an open lotus, the interior carved with a frog, 9½in. wide, early 19th century. (Christie's) $9,000

A Chinese yellow jade model of an elephant standing with its head turned to its left, the folds of the hide well delineated, 6¼in. long, 20th century. (Christie's) $3,080

A Chinese pale celadon jade tea and cover with lotus-pod finial, branch handle and animal-head spout, 7½in. wide, 18th/19th century. (Christie's) $2,2

A pale greenish-white jade lotus leaf-form vase, 17th/18th century, carved as a deep, upright lotus leaf borne on a stem which forms part of the openwork base, 8½in. high, wood stand. (Christie's) $3,450

A pair of unusual mottled jadette vases, carved from a semi-translucent stone of whitish colour with green and russet markings, one carved with two hollowed, tapering ribbed horns rising from outcroppings of rock, 11in. high. (Christie's) $23,000

A Chinese pale celadon jade vas of flattened baluster form, carved with a band of archaic design to mid section and with pheonix standing among rockwork and plantain to the sides, 3¾in. high, 18th century. (Christie's) $8

A pair of Chinese celadon jade boxes and covers modelled as seated quail with incised plumage, facing left and right, 4⅝in. long, 19th/20th century. (Christie's) $1,450

A Chinese celadon and gray jade group carved and pierced with three monkeys clambering on a large peach spray, 3¾in. long, 18th/19th century. (Christie's) $1,290

A Chinese mottled jade model of elephant, 20th century, the recumbent figure carved with clou scrolls and Buddhistic symbols issuing from its trunk over its back 5⅞in. long. (Christie's) $4

Tourmaline, ebony and diamond brooch, designed as a blackamoor, the ebony head wearing diamond earrings, the headdress set with carved tourmalines and brilliant-cut diamonds.(Sotheby's) $5,040

Ruby and diamond earclips, 1940s, of stylized furled ribbon design, each decorated with calibré-cut rubies and single-cut diamonds. (Sotheby's) $1,344

Sapphire and diamond brooch, designed as a flower, the center and the leaf set with brilliant-cut diamonds, the petals decorated with calibré-cut sapphires. (Sotheby's) $5,376

Tourmaline and diamond pendant, designed as a cross set with step-cut tourmalines and brilliant-cut diamonds. (Sotheby's) $1,260

A Victorian oval brooch, the center with bust cameo of gentlemen, within blue enamelled border and gold mount with rope twist detail. (Brightwells) $406

TOP TIP
Jet jewelry, so beloved of the Victorians, is made from fossilized wood. It therefore feels light and fairly warm to the touch.
One very effective test of authenticity which can be carried out on the reverse of a piece is to apply a heated needle - true jet will smell like coal burning.
Glass or onyx would be unaffected, while bakelite would smell strongly of plastic.   (Cotswold)

A 19th century openwork enamelled pendant in the manner of Carlo Giuliano, set with two garnets, the central stone surrounded by twelve rose-cut diamonds, 2½in. (Brightwells) $1,764

A diamond clip by Van Cleef & Arpels, French, circa 1950, designed as a spray of leaves, buds and flowers set throughout with brilliant-cut diamonds; and a pair of matching earclips. (Sotheby's) $8,736

An antique silver, diamond, ruby and emerald openwork pendant with tulip motif suspending pierced heart-shape with flower to the center, 9ct gold chain. (Brightwells) $711

Covered wooden storage barrel, America, 19th century, tapered round form with stave and metal band construction, single finger-lapped rim on cover, painted red, 21½in. high. (Skinner) $1,150

A lignum vitae coffee grinder, late 18th century, the iron handle issuing from a two tiered turned body with reeded banding, 5½in. high. (Christie's) $2,362

A late Victorian or Edwardian mahogany and sheet metal coffee grinder, with frieze drawer to the base, with crank handle to the top over the covered hopper, 6½in. wide. (Christie's) $329

A four segment spice tower, 19th century of turned form with paper labels, 20cm. high. (Bonhams) $168

A large lignum vitae mortar and pestle, 19th century, with reeded banding and waisted foot, the pestle with baluster handle, 22.5cm. high. (Christie's) $2,726

A Carmarthenshire spoon rack, 18th century style, of shaped form fitted with ten spoons, 39cm. wide. (Bonhams) $61

A 19th century Thomason's patent Ne Plus Ultra corkscrew, the turned bone handle fitted with a brush, turning a double screw with a cylindrical barrel, 17cm. long. (Bonhams) $431

A Regency mahogany coffee grinder, of square outline with a frieze drawer, the top with sheet iron hopper and crank handle, 5½in. wide. (Christie's) $731

A carved stained wood fruit press, the base modelled as a recumbent ram, with a twin handled plunger above, possibly associated, 13½in. wide. (Christie's) $34

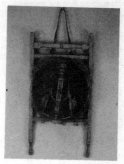

A Welsh oak combined spoon and candle rack, 18th century, the shaped backplate with spoon rails, with candle tray to the base, 27½in. high. (Christie's)　　$1,043

A pair of brass and oak mechanical bellows, 19th century, of typical form, 24in. long. (Christie's)　　$1,129

A Swiss fruitwood sauerkraut machine, 19th century, 37in. long. (Christie's)　　$278

A late George III lignum vitae coffee grinder of triple baluster form, 9in. high. (Christie's)　　$4,023

A pair of iron bound oak jugs, 19th century, of coopered construction, with loop handles, 14½in. high. (Christie's)　　$639

A late Victorian or Edwardian stained oak hearth brush, carved with a caricature face, 24½in. long. (Christie's)　　$639

A Christopher Dresser, manufactured by Benham & Froud, a pot, circa 1882, black patinated tin, tapering square section body with studded decoration raised on integral base cut with stylized cloud motifs, 8¼in. (Sotheby's)　　$7,728

A fine Negoro lacquer yuto (hot-water ewer), Momoyama Period (late 16th/early 17th century), of turned wood covered in red lacquer, the black undercoat just visible in places, 14½in. high. (Christie's)　　$55,100

A Regency style japanned wood coal box, early 20th century, of polygonal form and with domed top, decorated against a black ground with chinoiserie figures and flowers, 17¼in. wide.(Christie's)　　$1,118

A pair of Oriental famille rose vases, early 20th century, later gilt bronze mounted and adapted as table lamps, baluster bodies with pierced handles, 19in.
(Christie's) $1,656

A chromed single arm desk lamp, by Edouard-Wilfrid Buquet, circa 1930, mirrored shade, adjustable arm, wooden base, 27½in. maximum height.
(Christie's) $10,575

A pair of French bronze and ormolu lamp bases, mid 19th century, modelled with male and female Bacchic youths respectively, each supporting a foliate cast cornucopia shaped branch, 19½in. high.
(Christie's) $4,38

A pair of Chinese porcelain Buddhistic lions, late 19th century, the green glazed lions on raised yellow plinths, with later gilt bronze mounts and adapted as table lamps, 13½cm. excluding fitment.
(Christie's) $2,208

Two painted wooden table lamps, the design attributed to the Omega Workshops, circa 1915, the central square section column on four brightly painted cylinders, central column on palette shaped base, 14¾in. high.
(Christie's) $6,698

A gilt bronze and carved cameo glass 'water-lily' lamp, by Louis Majorelle and Daum, circa 1900, the gilt bronze base cast in the form of three water-lily stems terminating in three lily pads each with a seated frog, 18½in. high.
(Christie's) $52,875

An early Anglepoise desk lamp, designed by George Cawardine, 1932, for Herbert Terry & Sons Ltd, perforated aluminum shade with bakelite fitting, 36½in. high.
(Christie's) $1,938

An Alpacca table lamp, Austrian, circa 1905, Industrial grid design, original gas fittings adapted for electricity, 16¾in. high.
(Christie's) $16,012

A pair of late Victorian gilt bronze mounted Bohemian glass table lamps, late 19th century, the ruby glass and opaque columns with star-cut decoration, 18in.
(Christie's) $2,37

n Empire style gilt bronze
ouillotte lamp, 20th century, the
djustable gilt tooled leather
neered shade above the three
ht fitting, 26¾in. high.
hristie's) $1,974

A 'PH' table lamp, designed by Poul
Henningson, 1927, for Louis
Poulsen, Copenhagen, domed
yellow enamelled shade, cylindrical
stem, round foot, 21½in. high.
(Christie's) $12,338

A Victorian ebony and ivory table oil
lamp, with an associated spherical
reservoir, stamped to the collar
*Manufactured in Germany by the
Lampe Veritas Works*, 20½in. high.
(Christie's) $1,380

arcel Bouraine, 'Harlequin' table
np, 1920s, cold-painted bronze
d ivory figure of a dancer in a
eckered harlequin costume
ised on one foot, the other
sed, arms outstretched holding
lanterns, 21¾in.
otheby's) $28,070

Emile-Jacques Ruhlmann, pair of
table lamps, 1913, silvered bronze,
the fluted tapering stems above
circular base, panelled cream silk
swivel shades, 43cm.
(Sotheby's) $26,460

An Alpacca table lamp, the design
attributed to Josef Hoffmann, circa
1907/1908, circular base with
beaded decoration, oval carrying
handle, original yellow silk shade,
14½in. high.
(Christie's) $14,981

hromed metal and glass table
np by Desny, circa 1935, square
ction stem intersected with plate
glass 6½in. high.
ristie's) $4,583

A gilded bronze sculptural lamp, by
Hubert Le Gall, 1998, the lamp
emerging from a rectangular cube,
36.5cm. high.
(Christie's) $4,935

An Art Nouveau bronzed metal
lamp with six openwork stems
supporting a domed shade frame
cast with ribbon and tassel drops,
21in. high. (Brightwells) $924

A large bronze glass hall lantern, 20th century, of tapering form with canted angles, the openwork scroll frame with loop suspension, 46¾in. high. (Christie's) $5,486

A mahogany wall lantern, of George III style, probably late 19th century, with downswept pagoda roof above a glazed door with hinged pierced brass panel to the top, 19½in. high. (Christie's) $11,680

A late Victorian or Edwardian glass hall lantern, early 20th century, the ovoid cut bowl with tapering facete cover, with silver plated mounts, terminal lacking, 19in. high. (Christie's) $2,194

A large Louis XVI style gilt bronze hall lantern, of recent manufacture, the cylindrical frame with pierced balustraded gallery and ribbon tied tasselled beaded swags, 48½in. high. (Christie's) $3,271

A pair of Venetian gilt repoussé copper pole lanterns, basically 18th century, of hexagonal tapering form, the frame modelled with rocaille ornament below the lobed top with rising pierced chimney, 37in. high.(Christie's) $4,869

A set of four polished steel and brass hall lanterns, early 20th century, of hexagonal outline, the sloping covers with loop suspension, with twin light fitment 24¾in. high. (Christie's) $2,94

A gilt bronze chinoiserie rectangular hall lantern, early 20th century, the simulated bamboo frame with openwork suspension issuing a single fitting, 14½in. high. (Christie's) $920

A pair of Gothic bronze hall lanterns, late 19th century, the hexagonal frames cast with berried laurel and outset crocketed spire finials, 35in. high. (Christie's) $9,200

A Victorian bronze hexagonal ha lantern, in the gothic manner, the arched panels with quatrefoil banding and castellated cresting 27½in. high. (Christie's) $5,52

Louis Vuitton trunk, covered in striped canvas and bound in leather and brass with wooden banding, interior fitted with a divided tray, 9½ x 23 x 27½in., circa 1880. Christie's) $2.766

A Louis Vuitton shoe case, covered in LV monogram canvas and bound in leather and brass, the interior lined in orange Vuittonite and brown felt, 23½ x 15 x 13½in., mid 20th century. (Christie's) $2,766

A Louis Vuitton courier trunk, covered in monogram LV canvas and bound in leather and brass with wooden banding, 32 x 20 x 22½in., circa 1890. (Christie's) $1,845

A Louis Vuitton shaped case, covered in tan canvas, the interior fitted with a dividing section with a compartment for papers and with straps, 24 x 17 x 9½in. (Christie's) $542

A Louis Vuitton suitcase, covered in LV monogram fabric, bound in leather and brass, with leather handle and painted with the name C.M.Thomas., 26 x 16½ x 8½in. (Christie's) $903

Louis Vuitton trunk, covered in LV monogram fabric, bound in leather nd brass, with wooden banding, with two leather handles, 35½ x 20 19¼in. (Christie's) $6,319

A Louis Vuitton wardrobe trunk, covered in LV monogram fabric, bound in leather and brass and with wooden banding, on castors, 44½ x 21½ x 21½in., with one key. (Christie's) $3,000

A Louis Vuitton trunk, covered in tan canvas, bound in white metal with brass rivets and with wooden banding, 35½ x 19½ x 12½in. (Christie's) $866

n orange Vuittonite hat trunk, monogramed D V on either side, e interior fitted with two ribbon ays, the lid with ivory ribbon ttice, 26 x 25 x 25½in., circa 1900. Christie's) $4,058

A Hermès briefcase of black leather, the front stamped G.H., the interior lined in maroon leather, the lid fitted with a concertina style document holder, 19 x 13 x 6in., mid 20th century. (Christie's) $1,291

A Louis Vuitton hatbox, covered in LV monogram fabric, bound in leather, with leather handle and monogramed E.M, the lid with straps, 16 x 15 x 13½in. (Christie's) $2,347

An Italian sculpted white marble bust of venus, late 19th century, after the Antique, 20in. high, on a later associated green marble pedestal, 42½in. high.
(Christie's) $4,023

A French white marble bust of Bacchus, late 17th/early 18th century, looking slightly downward, with long curling hair, on an associated waisted portor marble plinth, 16in. high.
(Christie's) $18,630

A 19th century white marble bust of a young woman, her head bowed, with long hair tied with ribbons, unsigned, 20½in. high.
(Andrew Hartley) $924

One of a pair of French carved white marble busts of children, 19th century, after Jean Baptiste Pigalle, the girl with a flower in her hair and loosely draped, the boy with a strap across his shoulder, on circular waisted socles, 44.2cm. high.
(Christie's)   (Two) $4,112

A large Continental carved white marble bust of Diana, 19th century, in the manner of the Diane Chasseuresse, portrayed wearing the half-moon tiara, weathered overall. 30in. high.
(Christie's) $21,385

A Continental carved white marble bust of a togate Roman, late 18th century, heavily draped, the head detached, with old restorations, weathered overall; and an associated stone columnar pedestal, 19th century, 26¼in. high.
(Christie's) $4,935

A 19th century white marble bust of a naked young woman, her head turned and bowed, on socle and gray marble plinth, unsigned, 17in. high. (Andrew Hartley) $1,078

An Italian marble bust of a young gentleman in the Florentine 15th century style, 19th century, modelled looking straight ahead, his tunic buttoned to the neck, 19in. high overall.(Christie's) $1,188

An Italian white marble bust of a young maiden, chained, signed G Gambogi, in the Art Nouveau style, raised on square tapering black marble inscribed Schiava, 20¼in. high.(Andrew Hartley) $1,925

An Italian carved green serpentine marble male torso, early 19th century, chipped overall, 17¾in. high. (Christie's) $8,225

A broccatello marble basin, 20th century, modelled as a scallop shell, on associated fluted white marble socle with square base, 31in. wide. (Christie's) $3,291

An Italian carved marble bust of Vitellius, probably first half 18th century, the head and neck in white marble, the breastplate and drapery in variegated gray and yellow marbles, 32½in. high overall. (Christie's) $14,805

An English sculpted white marble bust of an Elizabethan Gentleman, 19th century, shown bearded with head slightly to dexter, semi-cuirassed with ruff collar, right shoulder draped, 32in. high. (Christie's) $2,936

A pair of Indian parcel-gilt white marble figures of Buddha, 20th century, each wearing drapery, seated cross-legged, on a triangular base: one with a waisted base with foliate decoration, 36½in. high. (Christie's) $6,564

An Austrian white marble bust of a young girl wearing a head scarf, signed *Blasche*, raised on veined marble square tapering plinth, 10¾in. high. (Andrew Hartley) $462

An Amercian white marble bust of Proserpina, by Hiram Powers, circa 1870, shown looking to her right, on foliate base, signed to the front *H. Powers Sculp.*, 22in. high. (Christie's) $41,454

An Italian marble figure of a young girl, entitled 'Volere E Potere' by Cesare Lapini, Florence, dated *1889*, the naturalistic base inscribed to the side *C. Lapini/Firenze 1889* and with title to the front, 27½in. high. (Christie's) $12,925

A Continental carved white marble bust of a Roman Emperor, 19th century, with laurel wreath in his hair, a cloak draped around him with a brooch to his right shoulder, the bust 33¼in. high. (Christie's) $11,515

A Herophon organette table barrel organ by the Euphonia Musikwerke, Leipzig, for square cardboard disks, 24 reeds, black wooden case, organ mechanism beneath the fixed disk, 1905.
(Auction Team Köln) $734

A Kalliope Gloriosa musical Christmas tree stand, brass mounted walnut case, for 18cm. tin disks, 36-tone comb, 1903.
(Auction Team Köln) $1,472

An Ariston Organette, the twenty-four note organette in an incised ebonized case with nineteen 13in cardboard disks, 16¼in. wide.
(Christie's) $542

A twenty-six key barrel organ by G. Bacigalupo, Berlin, playing eight tunes, in walnut case with painted decoration and fifteen visible brass pipes to the front, 19¼in. wide, mid-20th century, with four-wheel rubber-tyred cart.
(Christie's) $8,142

A Harmonipan thirty-three-note portable barrel organ by Frati & Co, Schoenhauser Allee 73, Berlin, late 19th century, the facade with nineteen visible flute pipes screened with interlaced colored ribbons, 22in. wide.
(Christie's) $14,681

An oak cased Welte No. 2 'Cottage Orchestrion, with 146 pipes including eighteen trumpets and thirty-three metal pipes (twenty-nir with red, blue and gilt stylized flower decoration), 107½in. high, with fifty-seven red rolls.
(Christie's) $69,09

An Orpheus Grand Piano Zither, the twenty-four note mechanical zither with disk mechanism in a mahogany case with incised decoration, on baluster turned legs, and twelve cardboard disks, 89cm. long. (Christie's) $2,277

A J.P. Seeburg 'Style F' Upright Grand Piano, circa 1920, the coin operated electric piano with flute pipes and mandolin including additional castanets, triangle and tambourine, the oak case with eight illuminated leadlight panels across the top section, 62¾in. wide.
(Christie's) $14,915

A revolving musical necéssaire, 19th century, with six revolving doors, each faced with a gilt harp, enclosing a set of crocheting implements, thread spools, scent bottles etc, rosewood case, 11in.
(Christie's) $1,02

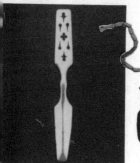

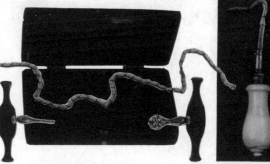

A 19th century silver tongue-depresser, unmarked, with spade-shaped blades, one with pierced decoration, 15.6cm. long. (Christie's) $467

A 19th century small hand operated surgeon's amputating chain saw, by Mayer and Meltzer with ebony handles, leather case, length of chain, 12in. (Brightwells) $1,147

An early 19th century burnished iron dental elevator, the shaped shank and claw, with decorative brass ferrule and baluster turned ivory handle, 5in. long. (Christie's) $416

A 19th century molded plaster model of the human male, signed on the base *Stein* and dated *1869;* the figure standing with one arm gesturing, finished with a waxed and polished surface, 27in. high. (Christie's) $1,669

A pair of deep amethyst globular drug bottles, with gilt and black labels numbered *26* and *27,* the necks with folded tops, 28.2cm. high. (Christie's) $1,501

An aluminum leather and steel artificial leg, with label on the calf inscribed *Hanger Nov 27 NcNM Edinburgh,* with copper rivets, the lower leg pierced for ventilation, with suspension strap, 31in. long overall. (Christie's) $250

rare 18th century wax model of e human hand, designed to ustrate the nerves, veins and tructure, complete with finger nails, an ebonized oval wood plinth se, 11½in. high. Christie's) $13,348

An instructional anatomical model of the human male head and neck, sectioned and colored by M. Augier and P. Roux, the brain, muscles, veins colored, 16½in. wide. (Christie's) $2,168

A late 19th century Fowler's phrenological bust, the cranium delineated with areas of the sentiment, 11½in. high. (Christie's) $1,034

A Dutch style bird and floral marquetry apprentice armoire with pair of solid panelled doors enclosing small drawers and cupboard, 30in. wide. (Brightwells) $2,035

Empire-style brass and ivory mounted rosewood sideboard-form tea caddy, 19th century, with ivory pulls and feet, the interior fitted with three wells, 14½in. wide. (Skinner) $2,415

Whimsical late Georgian mahogany miniature "Bedsteps" box, 19th century, with lidded well on each tread and on turned legs, 4¾in. high. (Skinner) $40

A north Italian walnut miniature bureau, circa 1770, the fall enclosing two drawers above a well, with three long graduating drawers below, inlaid overall with boxwood stringing, 16½in. wide. (Bonhams) $2,516

A very fine Chippendale carved and figured walnut diminutive chest of drawers with bonnet top, Lancaster-Area, Pennsylvania, circa 1760, the swan's neck dentil-molded pediment surmounted by three urn-and-acorn finials, width 26½in. (Sotheby's) $104,250

An Italian red lacquer miniature serpentine commode, circa 1770, the superstructure with three drawers above a base with three further drawers, 10¼in. wide. (Bonhams) $2,664

A South German walnut miniature serpentine commode, late 18th or early 19th century, with cross banding to the borders, fitted with three drawers, 11¾in. wide. (Christie's) $4,416

A miniature Dutch mahogany and floral marquetry bureau cabinet, 19th century, in the 18th century style, 19in. wide. (Christie's) $6,909

An "Apprentice" style chest, 20th century, predominantly mahogany and rosewood, with five graduated drawers and bone handles, 37cm wide. (Bonhams) $323

George III giltwood mirror, the
cresting missing, the rectangular
plate in a beaded slip and egg-and
dart beaded surround,
17½ x 32½in.
(Christie's) $3,128

A Regency mahogany dressing-
mirror, the rectangular plate within a
crossbanded and boxwood-strung
frame between reeded supports
surmounted by ball finials, 24½in.
wide.(Christie's) $1,335

Rococo-style giltwood mirror, 19th
century, the shaped surround
carved with rocaille, C-scrolls,
shells, and flowers, 48in. long x
29in. wide.
(Skinner) $2,875

large early 19th century gilt frame
convex mirror, the original plate
with an ebonized reeded slip, a
band of gesso foliage tied raised
back, a gesso leaf bracket edge, a
carved dragon surmount, 4ft.6in.
Woolley & Wallis) $7,392

A carved and gilt composition
overmantel mirror, early 20th
century, of Chinese Chippendale
style, with a C-scroll and acanthus
cresting and ho-ho birds to the
upper corners, 61in. wide.
(Christie's) $5,814

A William IV giltwood and
composition convex mirror, the
circular plate within a reeded and
ebonized frame, the leaf carved
cylindrical molding with eagle
perched on a rockwork cresting,
38in. high.
(Christie's) $2,194

George II giltwood overmantel
mirror of large size, with shaped
rectangular frame carved with C-
scrolls, rock-work, acanthus, palm
sprays and swags of fruiting floral
garlands, 62in. wide.
(Christie's) $25,760

A French gilt bronze mounted
mahogany toilet mirror, late 19th
century, the circular plate with
ribbon cresting above a rectangular
platform with frieze drawer, 17¼in.
wide. (Christie's) $1,472

One of a pair of Continental carton
pierre gilt frame mirrors, the
scrolling foliage oval frames set
with cherub masks with crown
surmounts, 20in. x 23½in.
(Woolley & Wallis)
                     (Two) $1,469

A mahogany fret frame mirror, the glass with a gilt gesso edge, the surmount with a gesso ho-ho bird, 22½ x 35in.
(Woolley & Wallis) $639

A George II walnut and parcel-gilt mirror, the rectangular bevelled plate within an eared rectangular frame, the sides hung with foliage and flowerheads, surmounted by a molded cornice, 52¾ x 31in.
(Christie's) $9,677

An Italian gray-painted and parcel-gilt cheval mirror, 19th century, in the rococo taste, surmounted by pierced foliate and floral crestings with putti masks, 51in. wide.
(Christie's) $17,480

Courting mirror, Northern Europe, late 18th century, molded rectangular frame with shaped crest enclosing reverse-painted glass panels and etched mirror glass, 18½ x 11¼in.
(Skinner) $3,738

A walnut, oyster-veneered cushion frame mirror, late 17th/early 18th century, inset with a later mirror plate within a molded and projecting rectangular surround, 18in. wide.
(Christie's) $2,208

A 19th century carved gilt wood mirror, in the Rococo Revival taste, small circular plate over two shaped plates within a frame carved with acanthus leaves, floral swags and a pair of applied ho ho birds, 30in. wide. (Andrew Hartley) $597

Chippendale mahogany looking glass, Pennsylvania, circa 1770, the shaped and scrolled crest above mirror glass with molded frame on shaped and scrolled pendant, 35in. high x 18in. wide.
(Skinner) $1,093

A Chinese-Export black and two-tone gilt-lacquer dressing-mirror, late 18th century, the oval plate with floral-decorated edge between shaped supports, above a serpentine base with two long drawers, 21¼in. wide.
(Christie's) $4,838

A Continental silvered wood and tapestry applied mirror, 19th century style, the cushioned frame with a foliate needlework border and conforming roundel to the arched top, 33¾ x 19¾in.
(Christie's) $2,435

A stationary hot air engine after Heinrici, Zwickau, with two 20cm. diameter flywheels, air cooled, lacking spirit burner, on wooden plinth, 1900.
(Auction Team Köln) $508

An unattributed steam engine, cast iron base, working regulator, stationary cylinder, 29 x 20 x 18cm.
(Auction Team Köln) $339

An unattributed steam locomotive, painted tin with some wooden parts, clockwork, with cast wheels, 1925, 24cm. long.
(Auction Team Köln) $282

A mid 19th century brass and ferrous metal model single cylinder overcrank engine, with brass cylinder approximately 1¼in. bore x x 1½in. stroke, draincocks and pipes, centrally mounted valve chest, the whole mounted on a cast iron bed with railings, 21 x 13in.
(Christie's) $6,909

A mid 19th century, probably instrument maker's brass model stationary steam set, the riveted and soldered center flute boiler with fittings including water pressure gauges, weight and lever safety valve, finished in maroon and lacquered-brass, 14 x 13½in.
(Christie's) $1,641

An early 19th century brass and ferrous metal model single cylinder table engine, with brass cylinder 1½in. bore x 3in. stroke mounted on a metal floor supported by decoratively pierced frames, measurements overall, 17¼ x 22in.
(Christie's) $4,145

A well engineered model Stuart Victoria single cylinder horizontal mill engine, built by Modelcraft with brass-bound mahogany lagged cylinder 1in. bore x 2in. stroke, overmounted valve chest, 8½ x 16¾in. (Christie's) $517

A well engineered model Stuart 'Real' single cylinder overcrank engine, with brass-bound, mahogany lagged cylinder 1in. bore x 2in. stroke, 15¼ x 5in. wood. (Christie's) $431

A live-steam model of a traction engine, coal-fired with 4.5in. six-spoked flywheel, the rear axle with wire coil drum and roof over driver's cabin, 45cm. long
(Bristol) $1,805

DR Class BR78 4-6-4T (2-3-2T) No. 78002, Gauge 1 spirit-fired live steam, Aster, 18½in. long. (Christie's) $2,352

Alisan RR "Shay" 2-truck No. 6 Gauge 1, spirit-fired live steam, Aster, 1977 (clack valve re-caulked), 17in. (Christie's) $3,166

B.R. (ex. LNER) Class A4 4-6-2 No. 60007 Sir Nigel Gresley, Gauge 1, spirit-fired live steam, Aster 1984, 27½in. long. (Christie's) $6,876

J.N.R. "Mogul" 2-6-0 No. 8550, Gauge 1 spirit-fired live steam, Aster, 1976 (ex Kyusbu Railway), 21in. long. (Christie's) $1,628

A Bassett-Lowke/Winteringham 'Mobiloil-Gargoyle' Tank Wagon, lithographed in gray with ivory and red oval emblem, 1935. (Christie's) $534

Western Maryland RR "Shay" 3-truck No. 6, Gauge 1, spirit-fired live steam, Aster, 1984, Cat. Ref. 1207/1, 25¼in. long. (Christie's) $7,600

SBB Be 4/6 No. 12336, Gauge 0, Toby, 1971, Cat.Ref. 2503. (Christie's) $1,266

A Märklin Electric 2.C.1. Swiss Type Electric Locomotive, Cat. Ref. HS64 13020 painted in lined green and tan, 1929. (Christie's) $4,672

DR Class BR 18 4-6-2 (2-3-1) Rekolok No. 18201, Gauge 1 Electric, GT International, 1999 with full inside motion, 31½in. long. (Christie's) $8,142

DR Class BR 05 4-6-4 (2-3-2) No. 05001, Gauge 1 Electric, Bockholt, 1982, 22in. long. (Christie's) $17,189

A Bassett-Lowke steam LMS 4-6-0 Super Enterprise Locomotive and Tender No. 5794, painted in lined lake, with guarantee and fillers, in original box, 1950. (Christie's) $467

A Hornby Series Electric E220 Special LMS Compound Locomotive and No. 2 Special Tender, painted in lined lake, 1936. (Christie's) $1,335

G.W.R. "City" Class 4-4-0 No. 3717, City of Truro, Gauge 1, spirit-fired live steam, built from some Aster parts, by Baker, 22½in. long. (Christie's) $3,981

DR Class BR96 0-4-0 + 0-4-0T Maffei "Mallet" No. 96018 Gauge 1 Electric, Bockholt, 1976, Cat. Ref. 2580, 23in. long. (Christie's) $8,686

L.N.E.R. Class A4 4-6-2 No. 4468 Mallard, Gauge 1, spirit-fired live steam, cut-away for exhibition purposes, Aster, 1984, 27½in. long. (Christie's) $5,067

DR "Mitropa" 4-axle (twin bogie) sleeping car, Gauge 1, another lot, similar Wilag, (Märklin style), (two ventilators missing), 57cm. long. (Christie's) $724

A German painted tin train set, including model buildings of Waiting Room and Central Station, two platforms with tin roof, quantity of track, coal wagon and figures, circa 1900. (Brightwells) $9,860

A Märklin early 30cm. LNWR Four-Axle Bogie 'Corridor Car', Cat.Ref 1841 LNW, hand-painted in gold lined chocolate and ivory, with hinged roof and detailed interior, 1905.
(Christie's) $2,502

A 5.25in. gauge spirit-fired 4-4-0 locomotive, painted in lime green and black, mainly finished, length 86cm.
(Bristol) $1,015

Nord 2-3-1 (4-6-2) C No. 3:1280 Super Pacific "Collin de Caso", electric, Bockholt, 1993, Cat.Ref. 3709, 28in. long. Display track. This prototype pulled the Royal Train from the depot at Batignolles to Bois de Boulogne Station, carrying the King and Queen of England on a State visit to France in 1938.
(Christie's) $13,570

Hornby Series freight stock, GWR Gunpowder Van, No. 0 GW Refrigerator Van, in original boxes, No. 2 GW bogie Cattle Wagon, in original box, four other wagons, mostly in original boxes.
(Christie's) $1,417

Bassett-Lowke, a Bassett-Lowke Electric BR 'Duchess of Montrose' Locomotive and Tender No. 46232, painted in lined dark green, fitted with double chimney and smoke deflectors, 1957.(Christie's) $2,670

A 5in. gauge live-steam model of an LMS 0-6-0 tank locomotive, No. 15697, coal-fired with twin inside cylinders, water and pressure gauges, spring mounts and finished in black, length 85cm.; on display track.
(Bristol) $3,140

A Märklin Stuttgart Hauptbahnhof Station, Cat. Ref. 2038 G/O Station Hall, 35.5 x 20.5 x 19.5cm. high and Cat. Ref. 2039 G/O Main Building with tower, 35.5cm. high, painted in shades of stone with green and copper roofs.
(Christie's) $4,672

A Märklin Gauge III (75mm) Steam Würtemberg 2 B (4-4-0) Locomotive and Four-Axle Bogie Tender, Cat. Ref. 4023W, repainted in black and red, fitted with twin double-acting cylinders with drain cocks, reversing from track or cab, steam fittings, tender fitted with water tank and valve for locomotive pump, battery holder for locomotive electric light, circa 1912.
(Christie's) $23,359

A Bill E Grin cast metal mechanical bank by J & E Stevens, Cromwell, CT, designed by John W Schmitt, circa 1900, 11cm. high. (Auction Team Köln) $678

A J. & E. Stevens 'Teddy and the Bear' money bank, painted cast-iron, President Roosevelt with rounded hat, standing firing, 10¼in. long. (Christie's) $1,050

A Humpty Dumpty mechanical savings bank by Shepard & Adams, beige, red and yellow painted cast metal, patented 1884, 19cm. high. (Auction Team Köln) $282

A 19th century redware high glazed money bank, in the form of a house, the window detail and center picked out in cream, the reverse molded with a recumbent dog, 6½ x 3½ x 3¼in. high. (Diamond Mills) $720

A polychrome-painted cast-iron toy bank, Hubley Manufacturing Company, Lancaster, Pennsylvania, early 20th century, in the form of an elephant with open howdah, coin slot behind head and tail-pull and raised-trunk mechanism, 5½in. high. (Christie's) $999

A polychrome-painted cast-iron Tammany bank, patented by Russel Frisbie, Cromwell, Connecticut, circa 1875, the seated figure of a man with coin slot in breast and raised-arm and nodding-head mechanism, 5½in. high. (Christie's) $353

A mechanical Calamity Bank (Football) by J. & E. Stevens, Cromwell CT, cast iron, 18cm. wide, post 1905. (Auction Team Köln) $700

Saalheimer and Strauss Bonzo Bank, lithographed tinplate with key, late 1920s, 7½in. (Christie's) $2,590

Cast iron 'State Bank' still bank, by Kenton, circa 1900, 8in. high. (Eldred's) $315

1912 Indian 1,000 cc motorcycle, Indian Red, 1901 by George Hendee, a bicycling enthusiast, auxiliary pedal starter, leaf spring front suspension, long handle bars and Bosch magneto.(Christie's) $29,900

1886 Benz ¾HP Two Seater tricycle Replica, green frame, natural wood finish and black upholstery engine: single horizontal cylinder, four stroke, 970cc giving ¾hp, brake: transmission only, center tiller steering. (Christie's) $26,450

The Whizzer, a motorised bicycle having a two-stroke power unit with belt-drive assisting chain-drive pedal propulsion, black enamelled frame with red flashes to headstock, circa 1950s. (Christie's) $4,370

1947 Indian Chief, Indian red with black leather seat engine: V-Twin, 74ci, 20hp, gearbox: three-speed with left hand throttle and right hand shift, brakes: front and rear drum hidden disks. (Christie's) $30,650

1914 Indian 3½ hp motorcycle with coronet sidecar, blue with blue interior to sidecar and black tonneau, Engine: single-cylinder 494cc, mechanical exhaust, automatic inlet valves, single speed chain drive with optional frictional clutch, sprung front forks. (Christie's) $14,168

1942 Harley-Davidson WLA, black and red, engine: 750cc (45ci.), four stroke two cylinder, 25hp at 4,700rpm, gearshift: 3-speed with suicide clutch, suspension: coil sprung front and rear, brakes: front and rear. (Christie's) $28,750

1954 MV Agusta Monoalbero 123.5cc racing motorcycle, red, Engine: Single cylinder 4-stroke, air cooled, 53 x 56mm., 123.5cc, Dell'Orto carburettor and magneto ignition, transmission: four speeds with wet multiplate clutch; brakes central drums. (Christie's) $24,794

1899 De Dion-Bouton 2½ HP Tricycle, black with nickel-plated brightwork, engine: single cylinder, air-cooled, 70 x 70mm. bore & stroke, 270cc. (16½ci.), frame: tubular with direct drive and beaded-edge pneumatic tyres. (Christie's) $25,300

A Mandoline Expressive musical box, probably by Paillard, playing eight airs including The Mikado, associated burr veneered case, 20in. wide, the cylinder 11in. (Christie's) $2,205

A Kalliope Panorama coin operated music box with rare horse racing automaton, 154 tone double comb and 12 bells, circa 1900. (Auction Team Köln)
                                        $20,898

A musical box by Ami Rivenc, No. 44277, playing eight dance and popular operatic airs, walnut-veneered case with carrying handles, 20¾in. wide. (Christie's) $2,590

A musical box with seven bells, playing eight ballads, the engraved bells with on/off lever, in crossbanded rosewood case with inlaid lid and front, 19¼in. wide, the cylinder 9⅛in. (Christie's) $3,257

An interchangeable cylinder musical box on table, with double-spring motor, mandoline expression, inlaid rosewood case, 34½in. wide. overall, the cylinders 11in. (Christie's) $11,226

A 19th century Swiss music box on stand, playing twelve airs with 13in. cylinder and tune indicator, in walnut and ebonized case with feather banding and stringing, 29in. wide.(Andrew Hartley) $2,198

A mandolin musical box, probably by Bremond, No. 12920, playing six airs, with full-length zither attachment marked Nicole Frères, in walnut case, 20½in. wide. (Christie's) $3,437

A walnut 'Fortissimo' interchangeable cylinder musical box by Mojon Manger, with three cylinders playing eight airs each, double-spring motor, zither attachment, 30½in. wide. (Christie's) $6,564

A walnut Mandolin-Harpe and Bells musical box, by B.A. Bremond, playing eight airs with zither attachment and ten bells with on/off levers and gilt brass bracket formed as the Bremond lyre, 24in. wide. (Christie's) $2,748

An ivory netsuke, signed *Masateru*, Edo/Meiji Period (late 19th century), of Kiyohime turning into a demon, holding a staff and coiled around the bronze Bell of the Dojoji temple, 5.4cm. high.
(Christie's) $1,674

A fine boxwood netsuke, Showa period (20th century), of a natamame [long sword bean] and vine, signed on the bottom *Soko*, with a wood box, 2¼in. long.
(Christie's) $9,062

A tall ivory netsuke, unsigned, Edo Period (18th century), of a Dutchman holding a cockerel in both arms, 5in. high.
(Christie's) $2,291

A finely carved stagshorn netsuke, signed *Masatada?*, 19th century, of a seated monkey devouring a peach which he grasps in both hands, eyes inlaid in dark horn, 2in. long. (Christie's) $2,467

An inlaid wood and ivory netsuke, sealed Bairyu, late 19th century, of Hotei with his hands raised above his head, the robe of dark wood, the face, torso, hands, feet and sash of ivory, 1½in. high.
(Christie's) $3,619

A stained boxwood netsuke, Showa period (20th century), of a standing shishimai dancer, signed on the side *Soko*, with a wood box, 1¾in. high. (Christie's) $14,805

A large ivory netsuke, signed *Masamori*, Edo/Meiji Period (late 19th century) of Hotei holding his large sack from which emerges a child holding in his hands a gunbai [general's fan], 7.2cm. high.
(Christie's) $4,935

An ivory netsuke, unsigned, Edo Period (18th century), of two karako back to back, one playing the trumpet and the other holding a gong 1½in. long.
(Christie's) $4,935

A lacquered wood netsuke, unsigned, Edo Period (18th century), of a laughing riverporter crouched and cross-legged, his haori pulled up over his back revealing his posterior, 2in.
(Christie's) $33,488

An ivory netsuke, unsigned, Edo Period (17th/early 18th century) of a large and powerful figure of Shoki seated on an oni and holding a sword in his right hand, black, 3¼in. high. (Christie's) $12,338

A stained boxwood netsuke, signed *Tomotada*, Edo Period (late 18th century), of an octopus with its eight tentacles raised to its head, eyes and pupils inlaid, 1¼in. high. (Christie's) $3,619

A wood netsuke, signed *SHUYA*, Edo Period (19th century) of an octopus tying a hachimaki [headband], 2in. high. (Christie's) $3,878

A compact and fine boxwood netsuke, signed *Toyomasa*, 19th century, of a fugu [Tetrodon historix] fully inflated as he senses danger, eyes inlaid in ebony, 2¼in. long. (Christie's) $32,900

An ivory netsuke, unsigned, Edo Period (18th century), of a fox affectionately resting on the right shoulder of a seated nun, stained and well patinated, 2in. high. (Christie's) $3,348

An ivory netsuke, unsigned, Edo Period (circa 1800), of a reclining shishi holding a loose ball in his mouth, 4.8cm. long. (Christie's) $2,858

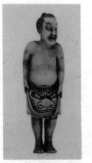

An ivory netsuke, unsigned, Edo Period (19th century), of a Sumo wrestler standing and smiling, his loincloth decorated with the face of a shishi, 8.5cm. high. (Christie's) $2,820

A stained boxwood netsuke, unsigned, late 18th century, of a dog lying and curled up to lick the back of his tail, with wood box signed *Takamura Koun Shirusu*, 2in. long. (Christie's) $23,030

A large and powerful ivory netsuke, unsigned, Edo Period (late 17th/18th century), of Ikkaku Sennin standing and carrying his wife on his back, 11cm. high. (Christie's) $7,050

An F & E Lightning Check Writer by the Hedman Mfg. Co. Chicago.
(Auction Team Köln) $186

A Peerless Senior check writer by the Peerless Check Protecting Co., Rochester, NY.
(Auction Team Köln) $96

An American New Era Check Writer of unusual design, 1915.
(Auction Team Köln) $226

A Pathé Salon No. 3 talking machine with (repainted) pink flower horn, ebonite soundbox and 8in. turntable, in stained beech case, 24½in. high.
(Christie's) $1,036

A Gestetner Rotary Cyclostyle No. 6 two-cylinder wax stencil copier, with original metal cover, circa 1920.
(Auction Team Köln) $186

An Edison model E dictating machine, with dual record and play reproducers, headphones and speaking tube in a tambour oak cabinet on stand.
(Christie's) $298

Williams Automatic Bank Punch, a very decorative early perforating machine by the Automatic Bank Punch Co., New York, black with gold decoration, 1885.
(Auction Team Köln) $395

The Un-Official Presidential Pencil Sharpener, and unused Bill Clinton 'Scandal' pencil sharpener.
(Auction Team Köln) $79

A US Automatic Pencil Sharpener, with three rotating blades, tin housing on wooden base, 1906-7 patents.
(Auction Team Köln) $339

A French Taxiphote stereo viewer by Richard, Paris for 45 x 107mm slides, in hardwood case, with black wooden eyepieces, circa 1910, 49cm. high.
(Auction Team Köln) $734

A Brewster-pattern hand-held stereoscope with hinged top and pair of focusing lenses, with a matching stereograph box with hinged top and internal divider; extensive gilt, green and red-painted decoration on a black lacquer base.
(Christie's) $84,600

A 19th century rosewood stereoscope viewer with indented lenses to top, concave sides and silvered back flap, together with a collection of stereoscope cards.
(Thomson Roddick & Medcalf) $123

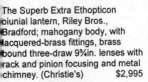

The Superb Extra Ethopticon oiunial lantern, Riley Bros., Bradford; mahogany body, with lacquered-brass fittings, brass bound three-draw 9¾in. lenses with rack and pinion focusing and metal chimney. (Christie's) $2,995

Magic lantern, Georges Carette & Co., Germany; building-style lantern, with brickwork chimney, roof with pressed metal gallery, painted base, with lens, condenser and reflector, 15¼in. high.
(Christie's) $2,996

Achromatic Stereoscope no. 258, R. & J. Beck, London; polished-wood body, lacquered-brass lens panel with a pair of focusing lenses and hinged top, inverting into box; contained within a matching cabinet, 13½in. high.
(Christie's) $863

The Terpuoscope Patent lantern, tin-lamphouse, the brass bound 7-inch lens with rack and pinion focusing. (Christie's) $198

Praxinoscope, the metal body with turned wood stand and turning mechanism with eight picture strips, candle holder.(Christie's) $722

Stereoscope, Brewster-pattern, the black-lacquered body with painted and inlaid mother of pearl decoration. (Christie's) $776

Lantern, J. Brown, Glasgow; mahogany body, with plaque *J. Brown. 76 St Vincent St. Glasgow*, lacquered-brass fittings, metal chimney, lens, condenser, in a wood case. (Christie's) $440

A French mutoscope, by L. Gaumont & Cie Paris No 1332, for the Mutoscope and Biograph Syndicate Ltd London, circa 1900, of typical form with crank handle and coin mechanism. (Christie's) $4,498

A magic lantern, with mahogany body, lacquered brass fittings, brass lens section, tin lamp house, fitted with a later electric illuminant, in a fitted wooden box. (Christie's) $345

A Model E Mutoscope, by the American Mutoscope and biograph Co, New York, USA, circa 1906, of typical barrel form with crank handle, coin mechanism, decorated with eagles and American Indians. (Christie's) $5,095

Praxinoscope, Ernst Plankl, Germany; the 15cm. diameter drum with hand-crank mechanism, viewing lens set in to the box and a quantity of paper strips. (Christie's) $3,525

A Peerless Peep Show Viewer, by Peerless Company, Canvey, England circa 1950, the upright metal cabinet with coin mechanism showing forty-eight erotic photographs in six series, 162cm. high. (Christie's) $1,319

Magic stereoscopic no. 202, Negretti and Zambra, London; the viewer covered in tooled leather, hinged top, rack and pinion focusing, two internal pairs of supplementary lenses. (Christie's) $4,935

Roul'scope praxinoscope, French; the drum with red-paint and gilt decoration, with stand on a wood base and a quantity of paper strips, in maker's box. (Christie's) $669

Achromatic Stereoscope no. 2423, R. & J. Beck, London & New York; polished-mahogany body, with lacquered-brass fittings, hinged top, reflector, a pair of rack and pinion focusing lenses. (Christie's) $3,348

Russian papier mâché cigar box, late 19th century, the cover slightly ised in molded relief, depicting vo maidens carrying a basket and wer respectively, 13cm. wide. Christie's) $204

A Victorian papier mâché tilt top side table, the oval pie crust top with a mother of pearl inlaid and gilt decorated landscape of an abbey ruin, 30in. high.
(Christie's) $2,392

An English black and polychrome-japanned papier-mâché tea-caddy, early 19th century, decorated overall with scrolling foliage, flowerheads and birds, the rectangular stepped hinged top enclosing a fitted interior, 7¾in. wide. (Christie's) $1,335

Victorian wood and papier-mâché ork table, rectangular top with ntral collage of various metals d on silvered metal sheet under a ass panel, 27½in. wide. hristie's) $1,840

A late Victorian papier mâché paper bin, late 19th century, of tapering cylindrical form, the black ground painted with figures shooting in a landscape, 10¼in. high.
(Christie's) $2,180

A pair of Victorian wood and papier, mâché chairs, with a curved and scalloped edged back, black ground with inlaid mother of pearl and gilt scrolling foliate decoration, 35in. high. (Christie's) $4,784

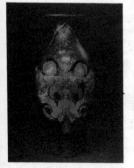

Victorian papier mâché vase, lay & Co, of baluster form with aring rim, black ground with floral ecoration inlaid in mother of pearl,)½in. high.
hristie's) $1,747

A Victorian papier mâché tea caddy, mid 19th century, the cover painted with a rustic scene entitled View in Wales, the interior with twin subsidiary covers with mother of pearl handles, 7½in. wide.
(Christie's) $878

A Victorian double stereoscope in a papier-mâché case, with hinged opening top doors and two pairs of viewing lenses, black ground case with borders outlined in mother of pearl, 19¾in. high.
(Christie's) $4,048

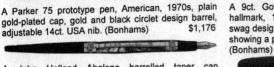

A Parker 75 prototype pen, American, 1970s, plain gold-plated cap, gold and black circlet design barrel, adjustable 14ct. USA nib. (Bonhams) $1,176

A John Holland Abalone barrelled taper cap eyedropper, American, circa 1905, over black hard rubber, two gold-plated chased bands, John Holland '12' nib. (Bonhams) $279

A Pilot yellow metal stylus pen, Japanese, 1970s, marked *Pilot 18k-750*, Pilot nib, in lined velvet box with leaflet and card outer.
(Bonhams) $13,230

A Dunhill namiki maki-e lacquer balance decorated with a squirrel, Japanese, circa 1930, in gold and silver hiramaki-e with mura nashiji on a roiro-nuri ground showing a squirrel seated beneath a fruiting vine. (Bonhams) $4,998

A Montblanc yellow metal 1M safety, German, circa 1920, alternating plain and diamond-striped pattern, clip stamped *18 ct.,* '1'nib. (Bonhams) $3,258

A Montblanc gold-plated 4-size safety, German-Italian circa 1920, barrel and cap decorated with brocade vine panels, three floral and foliate decorated bands, clip and cap crown, 14ct. '4' nib.
(Bonhams) $1,176

A Montblanc No. 4 lever-filler with contemporary filigree overlay, German with English overlay hallmarked *1923*, black hard rubber, delicate sterling silver Art Nouveau overlay, overlay on cap crown.
(Bonhams) $2,058

A Pullman gold-plated octagonal automatic pen, English, 1930s, barley and geometric pattern, Pullman 14ct. nib. (Bonhams) $2,205

A Waterman's No. 42 'Luca Della Robbia' safety, Italian, 1930s, gold-plated overlay, one band on cap and barrel decorated with a riot of dancing putti, remainder of pen decorated in pierced and floral/foliate panels. (Bonhams) $1,911

A De La Rue Onoto filigree pen, English, circa 1910, white metal over black hard rubber long plunger-filler, barrel marked *Sterling*, 14ct. over/under fed nib, in Onoto presentation case. (Bonhams) $662

A 9ct. Gold De La Rue Onoto, English, London hallmark, 1908, fully-covered repoussé flower and swag design, cartouche engraved with a heraldic crest showing a phoenix rising from the flames.
(Bonhams) $1,250

An important Dunhill-Namiki maki-e lacquer pen by Kasui decorated with a sparrow flying over a rice field and bird scarer, Japanese, early 1930s, the cap decorated with two swooping sparrows in gold and silver hira maki-e on a roiro-nuri ground.
(Bonhams) $64,680

A platinum leather-covered pen, Japanese, mid 1970s, cream textured leather decorated with flowers, 18ct. platinum nib in a cream section.
(Bonhams) $88

A set of Dunhill namiki maki-e lacquer bridge pencils, Japanese for the French market, 1930s, each conical pencil decorated in iroe-taka maki-e and hira maki-e on a roiro-nuri ground, signed in Kanji, *Namiki....Shozan and Kakihan*, comprising: seahorse, sea bream, Medaka (type of freshwater fish), and geese, in a leather Dunhill pouch.
(Bonhams) $6,468

A platinum maki-e lacquer balance by Rosui, Japanese, 1930s, cap and barrel depicting an autumn scape with mountains, decorated in iroe-hira- maki-e and nashiji on a roiro-nuri ground.
(Bonhams) $3,234

A Kaweco gold-plated safety, German circa 1915, decorated in wavy line design with two relief bands, the band on the cap inlaid with five blue-stone cabochons, 14ct. '585' nib. (Bonhams) $382

PENS

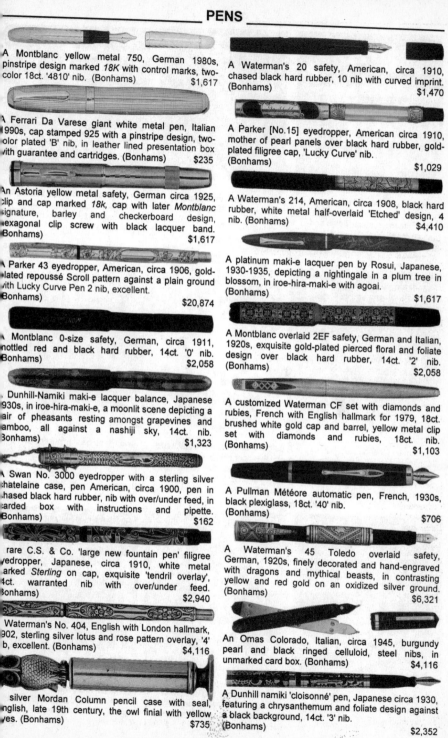

A Montblanc yellow metal 750, German 1980s, pinstripe design marked *18K* with control marks, two-color 18ct. '4810' nib. (Bonhams) $1,617

A Ferrari Da Varese giant white metal pen, Italian 1990s, cap stamped 925 with a pinstripe design, two-color plated 'B' nib, in leather lined presentation box with guarantee and cartridges. (Bonhams) $235

An Astoria yellow metal safety, German circa 1925, clip and cap marked *18k,* cap with later *Montblanc* signature, barley and checkerboard design, hexagonal clip screw with black lacquer band. (Bonhams) $1,617

A Parker 43 eyedropper, American, circa 1906, gold-plated repoussé Scroll pattern against a plain ground with Lucky Curve Pen 2 nib, excellent. (Bonhams) $20,874

A Montblanc 0-size safety, German, circa 1911, mottled red and black hard rubber, 14ct. '0' nib. (Bonhams) $2,058

A Dunhill-Namiki maki-e lacquer balance, Japanese 1930s, in iroe-hira-maki-e, a moonlit scene depicting a pair of pheasants resting amongst grapevines and bamboo, all against a nashiji sky, 14ct. nib. (Bonhams) $1,323

A Swan No. 3000 eyedropper with a sterling silver chatelaine case, pen American, circa 1900, pen in chased black hard rubber, nib with over/under feed, in carded box with instructions and pipette. (Bonhams) $162

A rare C.S. & Co. 'large new fountain pen' filigree eyedropper, Japanese, circa 1910, white metal marked *Sterling* on cap, exquisite 'tendril overlay', 14ct. warranted nib with over/under feed. (Bonhams) $2,940

A Waterman's No. 404, English with London hallmark, 1902, sterling silver lotus and rose pattern overlay, '4' nib, excellent. (Bonhams) $4,116

A silver Mordan Column pencil case with seal, English, late 19th century, the owl finial with yellow eyes. (Bonhams) $735

A Waterman's 20 safety, American, circa 1910, chased black hard rubber, 10 nib with curved imprint. (Bonhams) $1,470

A Parker [No.15] eyedropper, American circa 1910, mother of pearl panels over black hard rubber, gold-plated filigree cap, 'Lucky Curve' nib. (Bonhams) $1,029

A Waterman's 214, American, circa 1908, black hard rubber, white metal half-overlaid 'Etched' design, 4 nib. (Bonhams) $4,410

A platinum maki-e lacquer pen by Rosui, Japanese, 1930-1935, depicting a nightingale in a plum tree in blossom, in iroe-hira-maki-e with agoai. (Bonhams) $1,617

A Montblanc overlaid 2EF safety, German and Italian, 1920s, exquisite gold-plated pierced floral and foliate design over black hard rubber, 14ct. '2' nib. (Bonhams) $2,058

A customized Waterman CF set with diamonds and rubies, French with English hallmark for 1979, 18ct. brushed white gold cap and barrel, yellow metal clip set with diamonds and rubies, 18ct. nib. (Bonhams) $1,103

A Pullman Météore automatic pen, French, 1930s, black plexiglass, 18ct. '40' nib. (Bonhams) $706

A Waterman's 45 Toledo overlaid safety, German, 1920s, finely decorated and hand-engraved with dragons and mythical beasts, in contrasting yellow and red gold on an oxidized silver ground. (Bonhams) $6,321

An Omas Colorado, Italian, circa 1945, burgundy pearl and black ringed celluloid, steel nibs, in unmarked card box. (Bonhams) $4,116

A Dunhill namiki 'cloisonné' pen, Japanese circa 1930, featuring a chrysanthemum and foliate design against a black background, 14ct. '3' nib. (Bonhams) $2,352

499

A WMF silvered metal tea and coffee set comprising coffee-pot, teapot, creamer, sugar basin and tray, stamped factory marks, tray 42cm. diameter.
(Christie's) $454

A WMF pewter vase stamped factory marks, 35cm. high.
(Christie's) $745

A WMF silvered metal figural tray stamped factory mark, stamped numerals, *169/4*, 25.5cm. high.
(Christie's) $1,400

Two similar Charles I pewter flagons, the covers with conical-shaped knops, the thumbpieces pierced with heart-shaped motifs, 14½in. and 14¼in. high.
(Christie's) $6,905

A pair of modern Continental white metal five-light candelabrum, circular bases with five scroll stems meeting at a central point, height 14cm. (Bonhams) $2,233

Two Swiss pewter prisemkanns, late 18th century, the hexagonal sided flasks with wriggle work engraved decoration surrounding the lidded spouts, 14in. high.
(Christie's) $869

A WMF silvered metal dish cast with Art Nouveau maiden, stamped factory marks, 32cm.
(Christie's) $894

A set of six pewter plates, mid 18th century, the rims engraved with armorials, the undersides with the touch mark of Jonas Durand, 9¾in. diameter. (Christie's) $1,391

A WMF silvered metal jardinière with later metal liner, printed facto marks, 26.5cm. diameter.
(Christie's) $59

An Austrian carafe in pewter and green glass, 35.5cm. high. (Christie's) $560

A George II single reeded pewter charger, the underside with the touch marks of William Smith of York or Leeds, 16¾in. diameter. (Christie's) $363

A WMF silvered metal and glass liqueur set comprising decanter, four glasses and stand, stamped factory marks and numbered 168, stand 33cm. diameter. (Christie's) $490

A Tudric pewter twin handled vase inscribed *For Old Times Sake* and decorated with elongated trees, 20cm. high. (T.R. & M) $290

A group of four silvered metal candlesticks, two with WMF printed factory marks, 15cm. high. (Christie's) $665

A straight sided pewter flagon in the James I style, restorations, 15in. high. (Christie's) $5,486

A pair of silvered metal vases, signed in the metal *Bl Poccard* and *V. Olivier*, 30cm. high. (Christie's) $745

A German pewter plate, late 18th or early 19th century, decorated to the center with the Star of David within animals and foliage, 8¼in. diameter. (Christie's) $730

Six modern Jean Puiforcat metalware and rosewood gravy dishes, stamped factory marks, 17cm. diameter. (Christie's) $3,852

An early American Graphophone phonograph, decorative wooden case with lid and silvered horn, in working order.
(Auction Team Köln) $620

A Columbia Graphophone Style Q, with silvered cast metal plinth, the glass horn possibly replaced, 1904.
(Auction Team Köln) $1,016

A Phonograph by Chardin Paris with 7 part convolvulus horn and a lion's head decorated lyre, with Edison cylinder, circa 1900.
(Auction Team Köln) $564

An Edison S19 disk phonograph, No SM 133 871, the upright mahogany case with gilt sound box and fittings, adjustable settings, automatic brake, internal swivel horn, cupboard below with a collection of needles and 78rpm records, 20in. wide.
(Christie's) $157

An Edison Long Playing Disk Phonograph, Model 3-c, No. 1159, with Long Playing attachment, standard, long-play and lateral-cut reproducers and dark mahogany console case with central cloth mask, 44in. wide.
(Christie's) $604

A Capitol Model EA phonolamp in Art Nouveau style by the Burus Pollock Electric Mfg. Co., Indiana Harbor, on brass mounted copper horn base, octagonal shape with two pink shaded lamps, 1919.
(Auction Team Köln) $3,388

An early Edison Amberola 30 No 41231, with nickel diamond reproducer, black bedplate and governor housing and oak case with metal grille.
(Christie's) $597

An Edison Red Gem Phonograph, Model D No 326 724D, with K combination reproducer, maroon fireside horn and crane.
(Christie's) $1,437

An Edison Amberola cylinder phonograph with integral horn, circa 1915, in working order.
(Auction Team Köln) $480

Pamela Hanson, Paris, French Vogue, 1989, two gelatin silver prints, 9½ x 14in., each signed in ink in margin, matted and framed. (Christie's) $329

Marilyn Monroe unpublished baby photograph, circa 1930, black and white snapshot of a young Norma Jeane who appears to be three or four years old, by Julian Arnold Smith who was an extra in Hollywood films and who knew one of Marilyn's early guardians, 3½ x 2½in. (Christie's) $1,293

Michael Kenna, 'Wave, Scarborough, Yorkshire, England', 1981, printed 1983, toned gelatin silver print, 6⅝ x 8⅞in., mounted, signed, dated and editioned 74/90 in pencil on mount, matted, studio stamp on reverse. (Christie's) $3,619

Terry O'Neill, Michael Douglas in Hollywood, circa 1989, printed later, cibachrome print, 13 x 11¾in., signed, matted and framed. (Christie's) $246

Attributed to Thomas R. Williams, The Royal and Imperial Visit to the Crystal Palace, 20 April 1855, stereoscopic daguerreotype, black card mount, paper-taped, printed paper label, inscription in pencil Crystal Palace 20 Aout 1855. (Christie's) $4,523

Herb Ritts (b.1952), Waterfall, Hollywood, 1988, gelatin silver print, 18½ x 14¾in., signed, titled and numbered 8/25 on the reverse, matted and framed. (Christie's) $3,125

Philippe Halsman (1906-1979), Albert Einstein, 1947, printed circa 1979, gelatin silver print, 13½ x 10³/₈in. (Christie's) $1,628

Henry White (1819-1903), Old house with extension, 1850s, albumen print, 7⁵/₈ x 9⁵/₈in., mounted on card, matted and framed. (Christie's) $4,523

Brian Aris, Queen at Live Aid Concert, 1985, gelatin silver print, 14¼ x 12in., artist's stamp on reverse, matted and framed. (Christie's) $329

Lewis Carroll [Charles Lutwidge Dodgson] Xie with violin, 1876, albumen print mounted as cabinet card, 5¼ x 4¼in., inscribed *Mrs. Kitchin, from the Artist, July/76* in purple ink in Carroll's hand on reverse.(Christie's) $17,189

Brassaï [Gyula Halasz] (1899-1984), The Sunbather, 1930s, glossy gelatin silver print, 6³/₈ x 9³/₁₆in., photographer's ink copyright stamp on reverse. (Christie's) $8,142

J.R.H. Weaver, 'Frederick Evans', 1914, platinum print, 7¾ x 4⁷/₈in., mounted on card, titled, dated and initialled in pencil in margin. (Christie's) $81

Joseph-Philibert Girault de Prangey, Central Pavilion of the Tuileries Palace, Paris, circa 1841, daguerreotype, 4¾ x 3¾in., later glass mount. (Christie's) $9,951

Norman Parkinson, David Bowie, 1982, printed later, dye-destruction color print, 19 x 19¼in., signed on image and reverse, matted and framed. (Christie's) $1,316

Wall & Co, portrait of a man drinking beer, circa 1850s, quarter-plate ambrotype, gilt mount, stamped *Wall & Co., 559B Way, N.Y.,* in folding case. (Christie's) $1,628

John Chillingworth (b. 1928), The Boy and the distorting mirror, Rotherham, July 1960, gelatin silver print, approximately 12 x 10in., signed in pencil on the reverse. (Christie's) $1,316

Ida Kar, Georges Braques, 1960, gelatin silver print, 9⅜ x 9½in., signed in white crayon on image. (Christie's) $1,316

Eugene Atget, 'Boulanger', 1899, albumen print, 8¾ x 6⅜in., numbered *3208* in the negative, mounted on green card. (Christie's) $2,895

Bill Brandt (1906-1984), Northumbrian Miner at his Evening Meal, 1930s, printed 1970s-80s, gelatin silver print, 13½ x 11⅜in., mounted on card, signed in ink on mount. (Christie's) $1,316

Michel Comte (b. 1949), Darryl Hannah, 1992, toned gelatin silver print, 15¼ x 15¼in., signed. (Christie's) $739

Attributed to William Edward Kilburn, Victoria, Princess Royal, 1847, quarter-plate daguerreotype, arched mount with gilt slip, paper surround, approximately 5¾ x 4¾in. (Christie's) $15,924

Roger Fenton, portrait of a lady, circa mid 1850s, salt print, 5⅞ x 4¾in. It has been suggested that this sitter may be Fenton's wife, Grace Maynard whom he married in 1847. (Christie's) $2,895

Hippolyte Bayard (1801-87), Chateau, 1839, direct positive, approximately 3¹/₁₆ x 3¹/₈in., inscribed in two or possibly three separate hands in pencil. (Christie's) $225,995

Walker Evans, Alabama Tenant Farmer's Wife (Allie Mae Burroughs), 1936, possibly printed 1950s, gelatin silver print, 7½ x 9¼in., signed and inscribed. (Christie's) $9,951

E.E. Haynes, World record parachute attempt, 1932, ten gelatin silver prints, 6³/₈ x 8¾in. to 6⁷/₈ x 9½in.
(Christie's) $1,809

Walker Evans (1903-1975), Lucien Freud circa 1960s, four gelatin silver prints, each approximately 4¾ x 4¾in. to 7 x 9in.
(Christie's) $7,402

André Kertész, 'Ecoliers', circa 1931-36, gelatin silver print, 9¼ x 7in., photographer's studio and copyright stamp.
(Christie's) $13,570

Bill Brandt (1904-83), Nude, 1951, gelatin silver print, 17 x 14½in., hinge-mounted, signed later on the mount, framed.
(Christie's) $11,761

The Douglas Brothers (Andrew b. 1952; Stuart b. 1962), Tilda Swinton, 1993, printed later, platinum/palladium print, 20 x 15¾in., signed, titled, dated and numbered.
(Christie's) $739

Julia Margaret Cameron, Dejátch Alámáyou, King Theodore's Son, 1868, albumen print, 10⁷/₈ x 9⁷/₈in., mounted on card, signed, titled and inscribed.(Christie's) $7,23▮

Norman Parkinson (1913-1990), Audrey Hepburn and donkey, 1955, gelatin silver print, 14½ x 11¾in., inscribed CV84-16 in red crayon on reverse. (Christie's) $3,980

Robert Mapplethorpe, Ron Simms, 1978, gelatin silver print, 13¾ x 13¾in., signed, dated and numbered 4/10, framed.
(Christie's) $4,705

Oscar Gustave Rejlander, portrait of young woman, circa 1862-68, printed circa 1890-1900, carbon print, 7⁷/₈ x 6in.
(Christie's) $72▮

onymous, British Suffragettes, 08-1909, album of twenty-two latin silver prints, 6 x 4¼in. to 9½ in., dark brown mounts, green th, 9 x 11½in. hristie's) $5,067

Anonymous, Orientalist portrait, circa 1850s-60s, albumen print, 8 x 10in., mounted on card, mount trimmed to image size. (Christie's) $658

Alfred Eisenstaedt (b. 1898), V-J Day, Times Square, New York, 1945, printed later, gelatin silver print, 12¾ x 8¾in., signed in ink in margin. (Christie's) $5,429

da McCartney, Jimi Hendrix, NY, 0s, printed 1992, gelatin silver t, 16 x 11in., signed and dated 12/92.(Christie's) $7,402

Manuel Alvarez-Bravo (b. 1902), 'La buena fama durmiendo' [Good reputation sleeping] 1939, printed later, gelatin silver print, 7¹/₈ x 9½in., signed in pencil on verso, matted. (Christie's) $5,790

Willy Kessels, Nude with drapery, circa 1930s, gelatin silver print, 4⁷/₈ x 3¹/₈in., photographer's studio stamp on the reverse, mounted. (Christie's) $1,316

old Newman, 'Arp', 1949, gelatin r print, 9½ x 7in., signed, unted, titled and dated in pencil mount.(Christie's) $2,352

Eugene Atget, 'Place du Tertre', 1922, matt gelatin silver print, 7 x 9in., numbered in the negative 6307, photographer's ink credit stamp. (Christie's) $2,533

Rudolf Koppitz (1884-1936), 'Bewegungsstudie' [Movement study], circa 1926, photogravure print, 9¼ x 6¾in., mounted on gray card. (Christie's) $822

Josef Koudelka (b. 1938), Ireland, 1972, printed 1982, gelatin silver print, 13⁷/8 x 21¹/8in., signed in ink, matted. (Christie's) $1,448

Adrien Tournachon (1825-1903), 'Bois-Robert', c 1859, salt print 6¾ x 8⁷/8in., mounted on card, card with printed photographer's credit. (Christie's) $2,3

Anonymous, farmer with bull, 1850s – 60s, half-plate ambrotype, hand-tinted, gilt-metal mount, plain wooden frame. (Christie's) $1,448

Herbert Ponting, Lieutenant Gran Skiing, Bri Antarctic Expedition, 1910-1912, gelatin silver p 13¹/8 x 17⁷/8in., title, number 702 in (Christie's) $1,6

Norman Parkinson, Fashion, Harpers Bazaar, circa 1930s, printed later, two gelatin silver prints, 11¼ x 15in., signed on image and 14¼ x 11in., signed on mount, each matted and framed. (Christie's) $1,974

Henri Cartier-Bresson, Portrait of Alberto Giacom 1963, printed later, gelatin silver print, 9½ x 1 signed in ink in margin.(Christie's) $1,

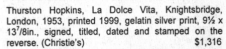

ngus McBean (1904-1990), Quentin Crisp, 1941, gelatin silver print, 11³/₈ x 14¹/₈in., mounted on card, signed in pencil in margin, matted and framed. Christie's) **$658**

Thurston Hopkins, La Dolce Vita, Knightsbridge, London, 1953, printed 1999, gelatin silver print, 9½ x 13⁷/₈in., signed, titled, dated and stamped on the reverse. (Christie's) **$1,316**

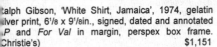

Ralph Gibson, 'White Shirt, Jamaica', 1974, gelatin silver print, 6¹/₈ x 9¹/₈in., signed, dated and annotated P and *For Val* in margin, perspex box frame. Christie's) **$1,151**

Roger Mayne (b. 1929), 'Children, Southam St.', 1957, gelatin silver print, 5⁵/₈ x 7¹/₈in., titled, signed, annotated, dated and photographer's stamp on reverse, matted. (Christie's) **$493**

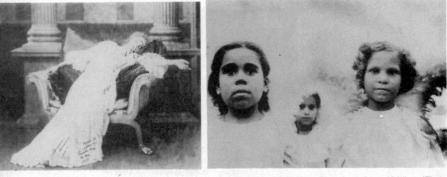

W. & D. Downey, autograph portrait of Sarah Bernhardt, 1907, albumen print, approximately 9 x 11³/₈in., signed, inscribed and dated on image by sitter. (Christie's) **$395**

Sabastiao Ribeiro Sagado (b. 1944), 'First Communion in Juazeiro Do Norte, Brazil, 1986', printed 1990, platinum print, approximately 8½ x 13in., matted, framed, titled and dated. (Christie's) **$1,990**

A late 19th century grand piano forte with rectangular ebonized base, 6ft. 6in. wide, especially made for the climate of India, by Schiedmayer, 7 octaves overstrung.
(Brightwells) $630

A Régence style ormolu-mounted mahogany grand piano, the movement by Gaveau, Paris, circa 1880, the top with ribbon-bound reeded edge above panelled sides centered to the base by shell and acanthus mounts, 57½in. wide.
(Christie's) $58,750

Classical mahogany carved veneer and stencilled piano forte, labelled *Patent Thomas Gibson 61 Barclay New York,* the cross-banded rosewood veneer in outline with gilt fruit and flower stencilling on the case front, 67½in. wide.
(Skinner) $1,380

A Victorian burr-walnut upright piano, by John Bunting, London, the case with a molded top above a damask panel framed by foliate scrolls, 53in. wide.
(Christie's) $886

A George III mahogany and rosewood crossbanded box piano by Clementi & Co., Cheapside, London, brass and ebony stringing, gilt brass acanthus motif to the frieze, 68in. wide.
(T.R. & M) $1,276

An Italian harpsichord in a painted wooden case, depicting landscape vignettes and scrolling foliate panels within red and green strap work, late 19th century and probably by Leopold Franciolini, 51in. long.
(Andrew Hartley) $3,925

A John Broadwood & Sons rosewood framed grand parlor piano, mid 19th century, with a straight strung metal frame, turned and fluted legs with brass caps and castors and a lyre foot pedal support, 127cm. wide.
(Bonhams) $1,029

Mackay Hugh Baillie Scott for John Broadwood & Sons, 'Manxman' piano, circa 1890, oak, the hinged two-panel doors opening to reveal painted interior depicting elfin children by a pastoral wooded shoreline, 149cm. wide.
(Sotheby's) $16,800

An ebonized and gilt metal mounted upright piano, mid 19th century, attributable to Erard, the later iron framed mechanism by Steinway and Sons, 65in. wide.
(Bonhams) $4,620

A French Art Deco plaster urn, on a pedestal foot, the body with diagonal flutes, incised *acrapole*, 49cm. high.
(Christie's) $700

A 19th century molded plaster phrenology head, with label corresponding to the delineated areas of the sentiments, the label inscribed *Gall's System*, 5½in. high.
(Christie's) $917

A tinted plaster portrait bust, entitled 'Le Boudeur' by Jean-Baptiste Carpeaux, circa 1875, the reading socle inscribed *JB Carpeaux*, 11½in. high.
(Christie's) $1,200

A molded and painted plaster portrait bust of John Paul Jones, stamped by Caproni Brothers, Boston, late 19th-early 20th century, cast in the half round with articulated hair, ears, facial features and neck scarf, 10in. high.
(Christie's) $588

A French plaster bust entitled 'L'Espiegle' by Jean-Baptiste Carpeaux, circa 1871, inscribed *J B Carpeaux [18]71*, on a waisted plinth, 20in. high, overall.
(Christie's) $3,000

A Calor shop window advertising display for the Belgian Calor electric razor, colored plaster, 40cm. high.
(Auction Team Köln) $395

John Gibson, English, 1791-1866, Hylas and the Naiades, painted plaster, 164 x 121 x 73cm.
(Sotheby's) $17,078

A plaster bust of George II, his hair dressed with laurels, 27in. high.
(Christie's) $1,050

A Polyphon No. 42 music box for 28.1cm. disks, with 108-tone double comb, walnut case inlaid floral decoration on lid, lithographed underside.
(Auction Team Köln) $819

A 19⁵/₈in. upright Polyphon with two combs, pediment, coin mechanism and shallow-fronted drawer and transfer of Joseph Riley, Birmingham, 49in. high, with twelve disks. (Christie's) $6,876

An 11in. Polyphon disk musical box, the walnut and marquetry case with a colored print inside the hinged lid, retail label, Hugo Wertheim, Melbourne & Adelaide, with nine disks, 15¾in.
(Christie's) $1,13

A 19⁵/₈in. upright Polyphon, with two combs, spring-loaded sprocket teeth, coin mechanism with slots on each side, transfers of Nicole Frères and Jas. Lowe, Darwen, 39in. high, with ten disks.
(Christie's) $5,182

A 15⁵/₈in. table Polyphon with comb-and-a-third movement, in quarter-veneered walnut case, 21in. wide, with forty disks in a wood box.
(Christie's) $3,109

A Polyphon No 104 player for 50cm. tin disks by Polyphon Musikwerke, Leipzig, 120-tone double comb, coin operated, 1895
(Auction Team Köln) $4,5

A Polyphon No. 104 coin operated player for 50cm. disks by Polyphon, Leipzig, 120-tone double comb.
(Auction Team Köln) $4,385

A 15⁵/₈in. table Polyphon with single comb, in walnut case with monochrome print and Archer, Liverpool plaque inside lid, 19¼in. wide, with twenty-six disks.
(Christie's) $1,554

A 19th century "Penny in the Slot" Polyphon by Nicole Frères, Leipz playing 19½in. disks, in walnut case, with molded cornice on turned columns, 27in. wide.
(Andrew Hartley) $5,65

Circle of Christian Friedrich Zincke, circa 1720, a young Gentleman, facing left in gold-bordered green velvet jacket with gold buttons, white cravat, enamel on copper, oval, 46mm. high. (Bonhams) $1,835

Attributed to Charles Beale, circa 1680, an extremely fine pair of portraits of Mr and Mrs Caswal, on vellum, backed with loose playing cards, original 22ct gold lockets, with original crystal, ovals, 60mm. high. (Bonhams) $7,350

Nathaniel Hone, R.A. (1718-1784), a young Lady, facing left in lace-bordered white silk dress, signed with monogram and dated *NH./1751*, enamel on copper, 47mm. high. (Bonhams) $4,672

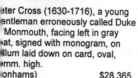

Peter Cross (1630-1716), a young Gentleman erroneously called Duke of Monmouth, facing left in gray coat, signed with monogram, on vellum laid down on card, oval, mm. high. (Bonhams) $28,365

Attributed to Domenico di Costanzo (circa 1795/1800), a double-sided miniature of Ferdinand IV of Bourbon (1751-1825), King of Naples and his wife Queen Maria Carolina of Habsburg (1752-1814), 1¾in. diameter. (Christie's) $12,954

John Simpson (1811- d. after 1871), Queen Victoria (1819-1901), in profile to the left in off the shoulder yellow dress, signed and dated in full, enamel on copper, oval 34mm. high. (Bonhams) $2,502

Samuel Cooper (1609-1672), a Gentleman called Sir Henry Vane facing right in black doublet, signed with monogram, on vellum laid down on card, oval, 79mm. (Bonhams) $31,702

English School, circa 1790, Clement Drake, with powdered hair en queue, wearing blue coat with white piping, the finely executed reverse with plaited hair, oval, 1¾in. high. (Bonhams) $1,470

Charles Guillaume Alexandre Bourgeois, (1759-1832), a young Lady, facing right in lilac-colored dress with white underslip, signed with initials and dated, oval, 64mm. high. (Christie's) $2,502

Frédéric Dubois (fl. c. 1780-1819), a young Lady holding a posy of pink roses and forget-me-nots to her chest, signed, 2¾in. diameter. (Christie's) $4,317

Pierre Adolphe Hall (1739-1793), a young Gentleman, facing right in green shot silk coat, 59mm. diameter. (Christie's) $12,090

J. Doucet De Suriny (b. c. 1770 – after 1806), a Gentleman, facing right in brown coat, signed in penc 2½in. diameter, gold mount. (Christie's) $9,49

Jean-Antoine Laurent (1763-1832), the artist's Daughters as young girls, signed, 65mm. diameter, gold mount, set on the cover of a composition bonbonnière. (Christie's) $32,819

Samuel Cooper (1609-1672), a very fine miniature of a young Gentleman, facing right in black doublet and cloak, signed with monogram; on vellum, oval, 67mm. high. (Bonhams) $60,066

MONEY MAKERS

There's a pecking order in portrait miniatures as elsewhere. Where two female portraits exist by the same artist, the prettier one will always fetch more, perhaps even twice as much, as the plain Jane.

In the case of similar male portraits however, a dashing blade will only fetch one and a half times as much as his less handsome counterpart.

Not fair, is it?

French School, circa 1790, a young Gentleman holding a quill in his right hand, facing right in brown coat, 84mm. diameter. (Christie's) $6,340

François Dumont (1751-1831), a fine miniature of a young Gentleman, full face in dark gray coat and blue bordered white waistcoat, signed, 2¾in. diameter. (Christie's) $30,033

Louis André Fabre (1750-1814), young Lady called Madame de Genlis, embracing her young son 3in. diameter, gilt-metal frame. (Bonhams) $9,176

Pierre Rouvier (after 1742-after 1815), a young Officer seated at a table, signed, 66mm. diameter. (Bonhams) $3,169

François Dumont (1751-1831), a young Citoyen, facing right in brown coat and waistcoat, signed and dated, 69mm. (Christie's) $12,090

Busset (fl. c. 1810), a Child, full face in white robes, fair hair, signed, 2¾in. diameter. (Christie's) $3,109

French School, circa 1800, two nude young children playing in a pond; one boy holding a mallard, the other holding a fishing rod, 2¾in. diameter. (Christie's) $1,641

John Smart (1742-1811), a young Gentleman, facing left in dark brown coat with gold buttons, signed with initials and dated, 78mm. high. (Christie's) $36,707

School of Jean-Baptiste Jacques Augustin (circa 1800), a young Gentleman holding his right hand to his chest, 69mm. diameter, gilt-metal mount. (Christie's) $1,382

Jean-François Soiron (1756-1813), Madame Popp, facing right in low-cut black dress with short white sprigged sleeves, signed enamel on copper, 2½in. diameter. (Christie's) $4,317

Jean-Baptiste Joseph Le Tellier (1759-d. after 1812), a Mother and Child; she, in black sleeveless gown with white underdress, signed, 3in. diameter. (Christie's) $10,364

François Dumont (1751-1831), a young Lady called Mademoiselle Duchesnois, full face in the guise of Hebe, signed and dated, 79mm. diameter. (Christie's) $6,909

Chocolat Pailhasson, lithograph in colors, printed by Camis, Paris, backed on linen, 53½ x 29½in.. (Christie's) $863

La Syphilis, lithograph in colors, circa 1925, printed by Tolmer, Paris, backed on linen, 24 x 32in. (Christie's) $1,727

Pal, (Jean de Paléologue), Rayon d'Or, lithograph in colors, circa 1895, printed by Paul Dupont, Paris, backed on linen, 47½ x 31½in. (Christie's) $2,528

J. Michielssen, La Panne, lithograph in colors, 1924, printed by F. de Smet, Anvers, framed, 39 x 25½in. (Christie's) $345

Myrhaflor, Les Boules Mysterieuses, lithograph in colors, circa 1910, printed by Louis Galice, Paris, backed on linen, 29½ x 41in. (Christie's) $942

Adrien Barrère (1877-1931), La Famille du Brosseur, lithograph in colors, printed by Ch. Wall & Cie., Paris, 54 x 38in. (Christie's) $638

Jules Chéret, A la Place Clichy, Paris, lithograph in colors, 1883, printed by Chaix, Paris, backed on linen, 68 x 47½in. (Christie's) $588

Iu Mokhor, Sports competition of the Ukraine, offset lithograph in colors, 1955, printed by Mistetstvo, Kiev, backed on linen, 23½ x 32in. (Christie's) $588

Jules Chéret, Baldu Moulin Rouge, lithograph in colors, 1892, printed by Chaix, Paris, backed on linen, 32 x 23in. (Christie's) $1,848

Luciano Achille Mauzan, (1883-1952) Bertozzi, lithograph in colors, 1930, printed by Mauzan Morzenti, Milano, 55 x 39½in. (Christie's) $4,705

Hans Rudi Erdt, (1883-1918) Engelhards, lithograph in colors, 1915, printed by Hollerbaum & Schmidt, Berlin, 27½ x 37½in. (Christie's) $2,688

Da Capo, lithograph in colors, 1917, printed by J.Aberle & Co., Berlin, 48 x 36in. (Christie's) $705

Roger Broders (after), Villard de Lans, SNCF, lithograph in colors, 1936, printed by Lucien Serre & Cie., Paris, 39 x 24½in. (Christie's) $973

E Tollim, Café Thiers, lithograph in colors, printed by Bergeret & Cie, Nancy, backed on linen, 37 x 52in. (Christie's) $1,763

David Hockney, Parade, Metropolitan Opera, offset lithograph in colors, 1981, countersigned in ink, lower right, 38 x 24in. (Christie's) $1,427

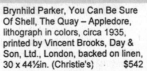

Wilton Williams, "Ensign" Cameras & Films, lithograph in colors, printed by David Allen & Sons Ltd., London, backed on linen, 29½ x 19in. (Christie's) $839

Brynhild Parker, You Can Be Sure Of Shell, The Quay – Appledore, lithograph in colors, circa 1935, printed by Vincent Brooks, Day & Son, Ltd., London, backed on linen, 30 x 44½in. (Christie's) $542

Engelhardt, Steinebach Wörthsee, lithograph in colors, circa 1930, printed by H. Sonntag & Co., München, on two sheets, 67 x47in. (Christie's) $735

Galoches, lithograph in colors, circa 1910, printed by A. Trüb & Cie., Aarau, 39½ x 31½in. (Christie's) $686

Jean Carlu (1900-1977), Gifrer, lithograph in colors, circa 1930, printed by Giraud & Rivoire, Lyon, backed on linen, 12 x 18½in. (Christie's) $451

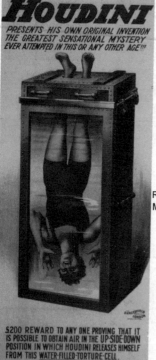

Robys, Bitter Secrestat, lithograph in colors, 1935, printed by L Marboeuf, Paris, 49½ x 77in. (Christie's) $1,680

H.H. Houdini, lithograph in colors, circa 1912, printed by The Dangerfield Printing Co., Ltd., London, on two sheets, laid on board, framed, 87½ x 39½in. (Christie's) $51,818

Richard T Cooper, The Boat Race Centenary, lithograph in colors, 1929, printed by The Baynard Press, backed on linen, 11½ x 18½in. (Christie's) $1,974

Paul Colin, Bal Fleuri, lithograph in colors, 1927, printed by H. Chachoin, Paris, backed on linen, 62 x 47½in. (Christie's) $15,347

M Pathe, Peter Pathe, lithograph in colors, 1919, printed by Oscar Consée, München, 49 x 35½in. (Christie's) $1,467

Francisco Tamagno, (1851-?) Cachou Lajaunie, lithograph in colors, circa 1890, printed by B. Sirven, Paris, backed on linen, 51 x 39in. (Christie's) $1,444

Robert Falcucci (1900-1989) Pastilles Valda, lithograph in colors, 1939, printed by Bedos & Cie., Paris, 63 x 47in. (Christie's) $722

Roger Pérot (1908-1976), Corsets Le Furet, lithograph in colors, 1933, printed by Delattre, Paris, backed on linen, 55½ x 40in. (Christie's) $903

Emil Cardinaux, Bally, Sportschuhe, lithograph in colors, 1924, printed by Wolfsberg, Zürich, 50 x 35in. (Christie's) $772

Alfred Roller, (1864-1935), Secession 16 Ausstellung Vereinigung Bild Künstler Österreichs 1903... Ver Sacrum 6 Jahr, lithograph in colors, 1902, printed by A. Berger, Wien, on two sheets, 74.4 x 24.9in. (Christie's) $60,489

Portola Amerika, lithograph in colors, 1926, printed by Zimmer & Munte, Magdeburg, 34 x 22in. (Christie's) $1,208

Alan Rogers, Imperial Airways, lithograph in colors, circa 1932, printed by Baynard Press, London, 30 x 20in. (Christie's) $1,382

Lucerne, lithograph in colors, printed by Institut Orell Füssli, Zürich, backed on paper, 27 x 38½in. (Christie's) $839

Melai, Far East, KLM Royal Dutch Airlines, 1954, 99 x 60cm. (Onslows) $63

Air France vers des Ciels Nouveaux, pub Perceval Paris, framed, 100 x 65cm. (Onslows) $377

A Sorel, Port-Aviation, lithograph in colors, 1909, printed by Société Générale d'Impression, Paris, backed on linen, 30 x 45½in. (Christie's) $5,417

A Solon, Air France, lithograph in colors, 1933, printed by France-Affiches, Paris, 38½ x 23½in. (Christie's) $1,122

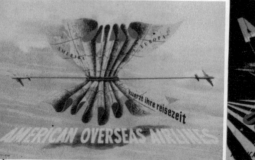

Ernest Montaut, (1879-1936), Grande Semaine d'Aviation, lithograph in colors, 1909, printed by Montaut & Mabileau, Paris, backed on linen, 64 x 47in. (Christie's) $3,455

Lewitt-Him (Jan Lewitt:) American Overseas Airlines, lithograph in colors, circa 1948, printed by W.R. Royle & Sons, Ltd., London, 24 x 38in. (Christie's) $506

Lewitt-Him (Jan Lewitt, (1907-1991); George Him, 1900-1982), AOA USA, lithograph in colors, circa 1949, printed by W.R. Royle & Son, Ltd., London, 38 x 24in. (Christie's) $431

Ottomer Anton (1895-1976), Nach Südamerika in 3 Tagen! Lithograph in colors, circa 1934, 46½ x 33in. (Christie's) $4,836

BEA Comet 4B, cutaway poster brochure, pub November 1959 –78 x 106cm. (Onslows) $63

Aquila Airways, Madeira, 1950, printed in Portugal, 99 x 60cm. (Onslows) $283

Julius Ussy Engelhard, (1883-1964), Münchener-Flieger-Tag, lithograph in colors, 1918, on two sheets, 52½ x 35½in. (Christie's) $2,184

V Römer, Zug Spitze, lithograph in colors, printed by Himmer, Augsburg, 41½ x 31in. (Christie's) $638

Hermann Schütz, Konstanz, lithograph in colors, 1913, printed by Propaganda, Stuttgart, 38½ x 27½in. (Christie's) $923

Lewitt-Him (Jan Lewitt; George Him), AOA, lithograph in colors, 1948, printed by W.R.Royle & Sons, Ltd., 37½ x 24in. (Christie's) $310

Ernest Gabard, (1879-1957), Pau-Aviation, lithograph in colors, circa 1912, printed by Garet & Haristoy, Pau, backed on linen, 31 x 47in. (Christie's) $1,899

Klotz & Kienast, Luftfahrt-Werbetage, lithograph in colors, 1932, 44 x 33in. (Christie's) $638

20o Gran Premio D'Europa, offset lithograph, 1960, printed by Industrie Grafiche Fratelli Azzimonti S.P.A., Milano, backed on linen, 53 x 37½in. (Christie's) $924

Walter Thor (1870-1929), Automobiles Barré, lithograph in colors, circa 1910, printed by Affiches Kossuth, Paris, backed on linen, 46½ x 62in. (Christie's) $2,708

Fell, Delahaye, lithograph in colors, circa 1925, printed by Riegel, Paris, backed on linen, 63 x 47in. (Christie's) $1,727

Roger Broders, Le Tour du Mt.Blanc, PLM, lithograph in colors, 1927, printed by Lucien Serre & Cie., Paris, 42½ x 31in. (Christie's) $3,719

Otto Ludwig Naegele (1880-1952), Forstenriederpark, lithograph in colors, 1909, printed by J.G. Velisch, München, 47 x 35in. (Christie's) $1,727

Le Trèfle, lithograph in colors, circa 1905, backed on linen, 54½ x 39in. (Christie's) $1,264

"British Dominions" Authorised Service Agent Eagle Star Free Towing Instant Repairs, enamel sign, 153 x 102cm. (Onslows) $1,335

M Leigh, Vauxhall Victor Estate car, offset lithograph in colors, circa 1950, printed by Hudson & Son Ltd., Birmingham, 19½ x 29½. (Christie's) $1,714

You cannot buy a stronger car – L.S.D., lithograph in colors, printed by Pictorial Publicity Co., London, backed on linen, 30 x 19½in. (Christie's) $863

Arthur, Peuget, lithograph in colors, circa 1924, printed by Affiches Adalta, Genève, backed on linen, 50 x 35½in. (Christie's) $1,036

Cottereau, lithograph in colors, 1906, printed by Belleville, Paris, backed on linen, 46½ x 62in. (Christie's) $2,205

Geo Ham (Georges Hamel, 1900-1972), 24 Heures du Mans, 11-12 Juin 1955 silkscreen in colors, 1955, backed on linen, 17½ x 11½in. (Christie's) $1,036

Jack Le Breton, Fiat, lithograph in colors, 1928, printed by McLay London, backed on linen, 60 x 40in. (Christie's) $1,470

Permis de Conduire, lithograph in colors, circa 1930, printed by Marchand, Thoissey, backed on linen, 33 x 48in. (Christie's) $903

Geo Bric, Circuit de Dieppe 1908, lithograph in colors, 1908, printed by B. Chapellier, Jeune, 41 x 29½in. (Christie's) $1,344

Fabien Fabiano, (1883-1962), Michelin, Enveloppe Vélo, lithograph in colors, 1916, printed by Chaix, Paris, backed on linen, 46 x 30in. (Christie's) $948

Bombled (?), Clément, lithograph in colors, printed by Kossuth & Cie., Paris, backed on linen, 37 x 50½in. (Christie's) $1,036

Geo Ham (Georges Hamel, 1900-1972) Prix De Paris, 29 Avril 1956, lithograph in colors, 1956, printed by A.A.T. Thivillier, Paris, backed on linen, 30½ x 20½in. (Christie's) $672

Pal (Jean de Paléologue), Phébus, lithograph in colors, circa 1898, printed by Paul Dupont, Paris, backed on linen, 59 x 43½in. (Christie's) $5,417

Cycles & Automobiles Cottereau, lithograph in colors, printed by P. Vercasson & Cie., Paris, backed on linen, 62½ x 45½in. (Christie's) $1,727

Humber Cycles, 99 x 69cm., on old linen with restorations. (Onslows) $46

Cycles Lea, lithograph in colors, printed by La Lithographie Artistique, Bruges, backed on linen, 39 x 25½in. (Christie's) $515

Walter Thor, Pneu Vital, lithograph in colors, circa 1905, printed by Kossuth, Paris, backed on linen, 35 x 49in. (Christie's) $839

O'Galop (Marius Rossillon) (Unsigned), Pneu Vélo Michelin, lithograph in colors, 1913, printed by Chaix, Paris, backed on linen, 47 x 31in. (Christie's) $1,175

Philippe Chapellier, Petit, Cycles and Automobiles, lithograph in colors, circa 1900, printed by P. Chapellier, Paris, backed on linen, 50 x 36½in. (Christie's) $470

E Clouet, Liberator, lithograph in colors, circa 1900, printed by J. Simon, Paris, backed on linen, 59 x 43in. (Christie's) $1,083

Noel Dorville, Société La Française, lithograph in colors, printed by Weyl and Sevestre, Paris, backed on linen, 60½ x 48½in. (Christie's) $839

Hurtu, lithograph in colors, printed by Verneau, Paris, backed on linen, 58½ x 39½in.(Christie's) $638

Gladiator, lithograph in colors printed by Gener, Paris, backed on linen, 50 x 35in. (Christie's) $470

Cycles Georges Richard, lithograph in colors, printed by P. Chapellier & Cie., Paris, backed on linen, 59½ x 41½in. (Christie's) $572

Dam (Agency) Peugeot, lithograph in colors, printed by ET. & L.Damour, Paris, backed on linen, 46½ x 30½in. (Christie's) $503

J. Matet, "Griffon", lithograph in colors, printed by G. Elleaume, Paris, backed on linen, 46 x 62in. (Christie's) $839

Emile Vidal, Cycles Omnium, lithograph in colors, printed by Vidal and Regnault, Paris, backed on linen, 49 x 33in. (Christie's) $807

Charles Tichon, Acatène Métropole, lithograph in colors, circa 1900, printed by Kossuth, Paris, backed on linen, 53 x 39in. (Christie's) $588

E Vulliemin, (d'après), Cycles Peugeot, lithograph in colors, 1905, printed by L.Revon & Cie., Paris, backed on linen, 63 x 46in. (Christie's) $903

Pal, (Jean de Paléologue, 1860-1942), La Péoria, lithograph in colors, circa 1898, printed by P.Lemènil, Asnières, backed on linen, 63 x 43in. (Christie's) $5,055

Orient Line Cruises, 20,000 ton Steamers, folds, 101 x 61cm. (Onslows) $678

S. Rowles P&O To Australia, lithograph in colors, circa 1930, printed by De La Rue, London, 40 x 25in. (Christie's) $686

Andrew Johnson, Orient Cruises, lithograph in colors, backed on linen, 40 x 25in. (Christie's) $1,986

Fernand Le Quesne, Cie. Gle. Transatlantique Havre-New York, lithograph in colors, 1910, printed by Ch. Verneau, Paris, backed on linen, 39 x 26½in. (Christie's) $1,382

Cunard Line, Liverpool to New York and Boston, also mentions Lusitania and Mauretania Largest and Fastest Ships in the World, and other detailed information, mono photographic, 65 x 39.5cm. (Onslows) $157

Andre Wilquin, (1899-?) Cie. Gle. Transatlanique, Normandie, lithograph in colors, 1935, printed by J. Barreau & Cie., Paris, cover and longitudinal cross section of the Normandie, 12½ x 8in. (Christie's) $691

W J Aylward, (1875-1958), Majestic, White Star Line, lithograph in colors, circa 1928, printed by O.de Rycker, Brussels, 29½ x 19½in. (Christie's) $394

Frank Newbould, White Star to New York (Olympic) printed by Baynard Press no. L125A, mounted on linen, 50 x 33cm. (Onslows) $1,178

William McDowell, The Call of the Sea, White Star to USA & Canada, printed by Charles Birchall no. PW2, mounted on linen, 49 x 33cm. (Onslows) $1,178

Albert Fuss, Nach New York, lithograph in colors, printed by Kunst & Werbedruck G.m.b.H., Frankfurt, 47 x 33in. (Christie's) $976

Kück, An Die Nordsee Über Bremen, lithograph in colors, 1933, printed by Wilhm Jötzen, Bremen, 34 x 24in. (Christie's) $776

Willy Hanke, Bremen-New York, lithograph in colors, circa 1935, 47 x 33in. (Christie's) $1,382

LMS Express & Cunard Liner, lithograph in colors, printed by Thos. Forman & Sons, Nottingham, 40 x 25in. (Christie's) $2,688

Ligne Allan Au Canada Du Havre, lithograph in colors, circa 1910, backed on linen, 25 x 40in. (Christie's) $419

Greig, Pleasure Cruises by P&O (Strathaird), printed by Lamson Agency, 101 x 63cm. (Onslows) $973

Hugo Feldtmann, Lloyd Ostasien Express, lithograph in colors, 1935, printed by Wilhm Jöntzen, Bremen, 33 x 23½in. (Christie's) $1,122

Atlantic Transport Line, New York to London, lithograph in colors, circa 1920, printed by The Liverpool Printing & Stationery Co., Ltd., 34 x 23½in. (Christie's) $1,625

Montague B Black, White Star Line, Europe to America (RMS Olympic), 64 x 102cm. (Onslows) $3,140

Rapnicki, Olimpiada W Tokio, 1964, lithograph in colors, 1964, printed by Prasa, backed on linen, 32½ x 22½in. (Christie's) $1,554

Henry Mayer, (1868-1953), Scribner's, lithograph in colors, 1896, backed on linen 18 x 14in. (Christie's) $1,467

Jano, Olimpiada de Tokio, offset lithograph in colors, 1964, backed on paper, 39 x 26½in. (Christie's) $588

Joseph Johannes Rovers, (1893-1973), 1928 IXe. Olympiade Amsterdam, Officielee Feestuitgave, lithograph in colors, 1928, printed by Joh.Mulder, Gouda, front cover of magazine and contents, 13 x 9½in. (Christie's) $735

Jean Droit, (1884-1961), Jeux Olympiques, VIIIe Olympiade, lithograph in colors, 1924, printed by Hachard & Cie., new margins, backed on linen, 39 x 28in. (Christie's) $5,880

Edouard Elzingre (1880-1966), XXième Anniversaire du Rétablessement des Jeux Olympiques 1894-1914, lithograph in colors, 1914, printed by Atar, Genève, backed on japan, 40½ x 29in. (Christie's) $1,264

Martha Van Kuyck, (1884-1923), VIIe Olympiade, Anvers, 1920, lithograph in colors, 1920, printed by J.E. Goossens, Bruxelles, backed on linen, 33 x 23in. (Christie's) $2,418

Walter Herz, (1909-), Olympic Games, London 1948, lithograph in colors, 1948, printed by McCorquodale & Co., Ltd., London, framed, 30 x 20in. (Christie's) $3,947

Philips Radio, London 1948, offset lithograph in colors, 1948, mounted on display card, 18½ x 13in. and two other 'Philips Radio London 1948' display cards. (Christie's) $656

Friedel Dzubas, (1915-) & Krauss, XIth Olympiad Berlin 1936, offset lithograph in colors, 1936, backed on linen, 39½ x 25½in. (Christie's) $2,205

H. Meyer, Jeux Olympiques à Athènes, letterpress in colors, 1896, backed on linen, 16 x 11½in. (Christie's) $553

Frugier-Fem, Macon, lithograph in colors, 1928, backed on linen, 47 x 31in. (Christie's) $1,010

Ilmari Sysimetsä, (1912-1955), XVes Jeux Olympiques Helsinki Finlande, offset lithograph in colors, 1952, printed by OY. Tilgmann AB., 39½ x 24½in. (Christie's) $882

Olympiska Speleni, Antwerpen, a 5 volume Swedish report of the 1920 Olympic Games, 11 x 14in. and 19 photographs from the 1920 Olympic Games. (Christie's) $1,122

John Sjövärd, (1890-1958) Jeux Equestres de La XVIeme Olympiade, offset lithograph in colors, 1956, printed by Esselte, Stockholm, backed on linen, 39 x 24½in. (Christie's) $3,947

Pati Nunez, Games Of The XXV Olympiad, Barcelona 1992, offset lithograph in colors, 1992, 27½ x 19½in. and 18 other different posters for the 1992 Olympics. (Christie's) $471

Les Dieux du Stade, Le Film des Olympiades, photography and offset lithography in colors, circa 1938, printed by L.F. de Vos & Co., Anvers, backed on linen, 32 x 23½in. (Christie's) $1,382

La Grande Olympiade, offset lithograph in colors, 1960, printed by Vecchioni & Guadagno, Roma, backed on linen, 53½ x 36in. (Christie's) $882

Visit Garhmukhtesar, printed by
East Indian Railway Press,
Calcutta, 101 x 63cm.
(Onslows) $246

Terence Cuneo, On Early Shift,
British Railways, lithograph in
colors, 1948, printed by waterlow
& Sons Ltd., London, 40 x 50in.
(Christie's) $1,645

D Newsome, Delhi, The Iron Pillar
East Indian Railway printed by
Norbury Natzio, 101 x 63cm.
(Onslows) $216

Les Trains du Soleil Côted'Azur,
printed by Dehon Paris, on linen,
100 x 64cm., 1931.
(Onslows) $628

Helen Madeleine Mckie, (d.1957),
Waterloo Station, Southern
Railway, lithograph in colors,
1947, printed by The Baynard
Press, London, 40 x 50in.
(Christie's) $7,402

Philip S Brown, Westward! GWR,
lithograph in colors, 1932, printed
by S.C. Allen & Company Ltd.,
London, backed on linen, 39½ x
24½in.(Christie's) $1,068

Nunney, Holidays By LMS,
lithograph in colors, circa 1930,
printed by John Horn, Limited,
London, backed on plasticized
linen, 40 x 25in.
(Christie's) $987

Doris Zinkeisen, The Coronation
Stream-Lined Train 1937, pub. by
LNER printed by Baynard, 102 x
127cm.
(Onslows) $4,004

Gert Sellheim, (1901-1970), The
Seaside Calls, Go By Train,
lithograph in colors, printed by
F.W.Niven Pty., Ltd., Melbourne,
backed on linen, 39½ x 24½in.
(Christie's) $2,016

Nowell M Edwards, Southern, lithograph in colors, 1935, printed by McCorquodale & Co., Ltd., London, backed on linen, 40 x 25in. (Christie's) $904

W S Bagdatopoulos, Bombay – Delhi, Bombay & Baroda Central Indian Rly, printed by The Avenue Press, 103 x 127cm. (Onslows) $2,669

Davies, Ease The Strain Go By Train, pub by BR/ER, printed by Jordison, double royal on linen. (Onslows) $487

Alfred Nicholls, The Most Interesting Route To Scotland, Midland Railway, lithograph in colors, 1907, printed by Nathaniel Lloyd & Co., London, backed on japan, 39 x 24in. (Christie's) $1,986

Alfred Choubrac (1853-1902), Trianon Concert, Orient Express, Wagons Lits, lithograph in colors, circa 1900, printed by G. Massias, Paris, backed on linen, framed, 16 x 24in. (Christie's) $1,256

Tourist Resorts Of The Peak Of Derbyshire, Midland Railway, lithograph in colors, circa 1905, backed on japan, 37 x 22½in. (Christie's) $1,353

Via Hull & Zeebrugge, Lancashire & Yorkshire & North Eastern Railway, lithograph in colors, 1907, printed by McCaw Stevenson & Orr, Ltd., Belfast, backed on linen, 28 x 39½in. (Christie's) $2,798

Terence Cuneo, Giants Refreshed, *Pacifics in the LNER Locomotive Works Doncaster* pub. LNER, printed by Waterlow, 102 x 127cm. (Onslows) $3,140

Moy-Thomas, Canadian National Railways, lithograph in colors, printed by Waterlow & Sons Ltd., London, 40 x 25in. (Christie's) $1,596

Jean-Gabriel Domergue, Monte-Carlo, lithograph in colors, circa 1960, printed by Nationale, Monaco, backed on linen, 39 x 25in. (Christie's) $776

Alphonse Mucha, Monaco Monte-Carlo, lithograph in colors, 1897, printed by F. Champenois, Paris, 43½ x 30in. (Christie's) $9,499

Vacances en Suisse, lithograph in colors, circa 1938, 40 x 25in. (Christie's) $336

Roger Broders, (1883-1953), Marseille, PLM, lithograph in colors, 1930, printed by Lucien Serre & Cie., Paris, backed on linen, 39½ x 25in. (Christie's) $3,800

Arthur C Michael, The Belgian Coast, LNER, lithograph in colors, circa 1935, printed by R.H. Perry, backed on linen, 40 x 50in. (Christie's) $4,705

Cie, Gle. Transatlantique Marseille-Algier In 20 Stunden, lithograph in colors, printed by Mühlmeister & Johler, Hamburg, backed on japan, 41½ x 27in. (Christie's) $1,344

Roger Broders, Agay, PLM, lithograph in colors, 1928, printed by Lucien Serre & Cie., Paris, backed on linen, 41½ x 30in. (Christie's) $2,764

Emil Cardinaux, Palace Hotel, St. Moritz, lithograph in colors, 1920, printed by Wolfsberg, Zürich, 50 x 35½in. (Christie's) $14,168

Otto Baumberger, (1889-1961), Zürich, lithograph in colors, circa 1916, printed by J.E. Wolfensberger, Zürich, 50½ x 35½in. (Christie's) $1,554

Leonard Richmond, Canadian Pacific, Riding, Mountaineering, Fishing Holidays in Canada, 101 x 63cm. (Onslows) $924

Louis Icart, Monte-Carlo, lithograph in colors, circa 1948, printed by Monégasque, Monte-Carlo, 30½ x 45in. (Christie's) $2,764

M Couchaud, Val d'Esquieres, printed by Lucien Serre, on linen, 102 x 63cm. (Onslows) $550

Roger Broders, Sante-Maxime Plage d'Hiver et d'Eté Côte d'Azure a Côte des Maures, pub by PLM, printed by Lucien Sere, 102 x 65cm., on linen. (Onslows) $1,021

Sem (Georges Goursat, 1863-1934), Monte Carlo Beach, lithograph in colors, circa 1950, printed by Draeger, Paris, 31½ x 47in. (Christie's) $903

André Bermond, Agadir, Maroc, lithograph in colors, 1950, printed by Société Marseillaise de Publicité, backed on linen, 39½ x 24½in. (Christie's) $656

René Gruau, (Renato de Zavagli) Relax..., offset lithograph in colors, printed by Editions Bonsch, backed on linen, 38½ x 25in. (Christie's) $1,295

Candido Aragonese de Faria (1849-1911, atelier), Chachat's Majestic, lithograph in colors, 1914, printed by Atelier Faria, Paris, backed on linen, 46 x 62in. (Christie's) $2,889

Jules Grün Alexandre, (1868-1934), Monaco, lithograph in colors, 1905, printed by F. Daubenbis & Cie., Paris, 49 x 34½in. (Christie's) $4,145

Lu Néva, lithograph in colors, circa
1900, printed by F. Champenois,
Paris, backed on linen, 59 x 39½in.
(Christie's) $803

Walter Herdeg, St. Moritz, Fis,
lithograph in colors, 1933, printed
by Orell Füssli, Zürich, backed on
linen, 50½ x 36in.
(Christie's) $3,542

Oke Oksanen, Finland for Winter
Sports, Finnish State Railways, 100
x 62cm. (Onslows) $157

Roger Broders, Chamonix,
Mt.Blanc, PLM, lithograph in
colors, 1930, printed by Lucien
Serre & Cie., Paris, backed on
linen, 39½ x 24½in.
(Christie's) $3,896

Alfred Marxer (1876-1945), Winter
Sport, Zürcher-Oberland, lithograph
in colors, 1905, printed by J.E.
Wolfensberger, Zürich, backed on
linen, 38½ x 30½in.
(Christie's) $3,188

Roger Broders, Funiculaire,
Chamonix-Planpraz, PLM,
lithograph in colors, 1931, printed
by Lucien Serre & Cie., Paris, 42½
x 31in. (Christie's) $2,302

ALO (Charles Hallo) (1884-1969),
Chamonix-Mont Blanc, PLM,
lithograph in colors, circa 1924,
printed by Cornille & Serre, Paris,
43 x 31in.
(Christie's) $2,125

Walter Koch (1875-1915), Davos 27
& 28 Januar 1906, lithograph in
colors, 1906, printed by Wolf,
Basel, backed on japan, 35½ x
25in. (Christie's) $2,479

G Flemwell, Villars-Chesières-
Arveyes, lithograph in colors, circa
1925, printed by Simplon,
Lausanne, backed on linen, 40 x
29in. (Christie's) $7,970

Roger Broders, Winter Sports In The French Alpes, lithograph in colors, circa 1930, printed by L.Serre & Cie., Paris, 40 x 25in. (Christie's) $5,313

Grindelwald, Switzerland, color photographic, 100 x 62. (Onslows) $283

Draim, Flêche des Neiges, lithograph in colors, printed by H. Caudoux, Lille, backed on linen, 28½ x 20in. (Christie's) $691

Alois Carigiet, St. Moritz, lithograph in colors, circa 1935, printed by Wolfsberg, Zürich, backed on japan 50½ x 35½in. (Christie's) $3,896

C G Bsor, Sports d'Hiver Concours du Ski Club, Peira-Cava, lithograph in colors, 1911, printed by G.Mathieu, Nice, backed on linen, 26 x 18in.(Christie's) $6,730

Kama, Megéve, lithograph in colors, circa 1932, printed by H.Truan, Paris, backed on linen, 38 x 26in. (Christie's) $1,382

Bernard Villemot, Sports d'Hiver, France, lithograph in colors, 1954, printed by S.A. Courbet, Paris, backed on linen, 39½x 24½in. (Christie's) $2,889

Guy Dollian, Rivalité, lithograph in colors, 1942, printed by Bedos et Cie., Paris, backed on linen, 62½ x 46in. (Christie's) $973

Roger Broders, Mont-Revard, PLM, lithograph in colors, circa 1927, printed by Lucien Serre & Cie., Paris, backed on linen, 42½ x 31in. (Christie's) $483

Currier and Ives (Publishers), Winter Morning, hand colored lithograph, 1861, F.F. Palmer del., image 287 x 388mm. (Sotheby's) $1,400

Currier and Ives, publishers (American, 1857-1907 John Cameron, lithographer (American, circa 1828 1860), The Life of a Fireman/The Metropolitan System, 1866, lithograph with hand-coloring heightened with gum arabic on paper, sheet size 22⁷/₁₆ x 30in., framed. (Skinner) $2,645

Edward Savage (Engraver), The Washington Family, stipple engraving, 1798, after the painting by Savage, published by Edward Savage and Robert Wilkinson, London, image 18¼ x 24½in. (Sotheby's) $1,190

'Ecstasy' by Louis Icart, drypoint, etching, and aquatint, printed in colors, signed in pencil copyright mark, 42.8 x 37.8cm. (Christie's) $78

Currier and Ives, publishers, The Mill-Dam at "Sleepy Hollow", lithograph with hand-coloring and gum arabic, on wove paper, with margins, framed, 406 x 517mm. (Christie's) $575

Louis Icart, Coursing III, 1930, etching with drypoint printed in colors with touches of pochoir on wove paper, signed in pencil, 15¹⁵/₁₆ x 25¹¹/₁₆ in. (Christie's) $4,200

Mourning' by M. Millière, drypoint and etching, printed n colors, signed in pencil, numbered *15*, dated *1914*, 3.5 x 56cm. (Christie's) $787

Gray Lithograph Co., American, 19th century, *"Maine Steamship Company...S.S. 'Horatio Hall' 4000 Tons."* Chromolithographed on paper, 28 x 42in., in an oak frame. (Skinner) $2,000

Currier and Ives, publishers (American, 1857-1907), American Hunting Scenes- An Early Start," 1863, lithograph with hand-coloring on paper, sheet size 0½ x 28in. (sight), framed. Skinner) $3,565

'Resonance' by Louis Icart drypoint, signed in pencil, 59 x 48.5cm. (Christie's) $1,192

ouis Icart, Perfect Harmony, 1932, drypoint and quatint printed in colors with touches of hand-ploring on wove paper, signed in pencil, with the tist's blindstamp, 13⁵/₁₆ x 17¼in. Christie's) $3,500

Currier and Ives, publishers, American Railroad Scene, Snow Bound, lithograph with hand-coloring, 1871, on wove paper, with margins, framed, 9¼ x 12½in. (Christie's) $5,175

An Amish pieced wool coverlet, Lancaster County, Pennsylvania, 1920-1930, the rectangular form worked in various red, blue, green, yellow, brown, and gray wools in a Chinese Coins pattern on a gray wool ground with brown binding, 60 x 48⅜in. (Christie's) $6,900

An appliquéd cotton quilted coverlet, Kansas, circa 1866, worked in blue and red cotton in a Whig's Defeat pattern, featuring ten blue diamonds with scalloped tips overlaid on red squares and alternating with white squares, 84¾ x 68¼in. (Christie's) $3,450

A fine pieced, appliquéd, reverse appliquéd and button hole stitched cotton quilt, signed *Mary Price, Barnsville Ohio,* dated 1850, composed of brightly colored red, green and yellow fabrics arranged in a Princess Feather pattern surrounded by peacocks, doves and floral motifs, approximately 96in. x 80in. (Sotheby's) $3,450

A pieced and embroidered velvet coverlet, American, late 19th-early 20th century, worked in blue, red, yellow, gray, green, black, cream, brown and purple velvet centering a star within a diamond medallion inside a variation Diamond-in-the-Square, 70 x 70in. (Christie's) $3,450

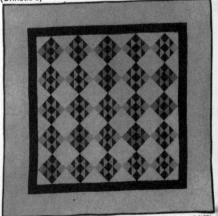

A pieced wool quilted coverlet, New York State, circa 1880, worked in green and blue patterned wools, the green wool squares with blue borders on a moss-green ground with sunflowers, shell and diamond quilting, 91¾ x 85½in. (Christie's) $1,380

An Amish pieced cotton quilted coverlet, Mifflin County, Pennsylvania, 1910-1930, initialled *L.A.Y.,* the rectangular form worked in blue, purple, brown and green cotton in a Nine-Patch pattern, 73¼ x 71in. (Christie's) $5,175

538

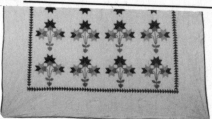

stuffed and appliquéd cotton quilted coverlet, central New Jersey, mid-19th century worked in yellow, pink and green cotton and calicos appliquéd with large central stylized flowers surrounded by leaves and smaller flowers, 87½ x 82in. (Christie's) $3,680

A pieced and appliquéd cotton quilted coverlet, American, 19th century, rectangular worked in yellow, red, and green cotton and calico in the North Carolina Lily pattern centering sixteen floral pieced and appliquéd diamonds, 77½ x 76¾in. (Christie's) $1,380

pieced and appliquéd cotton quilted coverlet, American, third quarter 19th century, the rectangular form worked in repeating blocks of red, green and orange sunbursts separated by meandering oak and flower-set sashing, 85½ x 88½in. (Christie's) $3,525

A pieced and appliquéd cotton quilted coverlet, Pennsylvania, circa 1890, the rectangular form worked in white, red, green, and orange cotton centering nine channel-quilted and machine appliquéd Dove of Peace squares, 80 x 77½in. (Christie's) $3,680

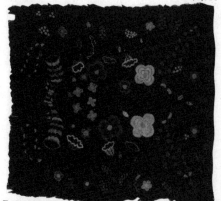

pieced cotton quilted coverlet, Cincinnati, Ohio, 1890-1910, the rectangular form worked in red plain-woven cotton centering a star issuing appliquéd Princess Feathers surrounded by similar smaller stars and pinwheels, 86½ x 84in. (Christie's) $4,370

Embroidered woven wool coverlet, probably Franklin County, Massachusetts, early 19th century a large central bouquet of flowers extending upwards from a pair of flanking cornucopiae, 80in. wide x 83in. long. (Skinner) $25,300

A pieced cotton coverlet, American, dated *1923*, rectangular and worked in red, white and various blue cotton, in repeating red disks centering white five-point stars on medium and dark blue stripes, 90 x 67in. (Christie's) $588

A fine and rare appliquéd and pieced cotton, flann and velvet African-American Baltimore memorial quil probably Baltimore, 1900-1910, at center a shape 'frame' sewn with fabric tape enclosing the figures two young girls wearing white clothing and beade pearl necklaces, approximately 68 x 84in. (Sotheby's) $31,80

A pieced, appliquéd and embroidered cotton quilted coverlet, American, mid-19th century, the square form worked in red, green, orange and teal cotton centering Rose of Sharon variation blocks separated by red and green striped sashing, 87 x 87in. (Christie's) $4,113

A fine appliquéd cotton and chintz 'broderie pers quilt, probably Southern late 18th-early 19th centu appliquéd with a large and elegantly wrought tree life with spade-shaped leaves and floweri blossoms, 92 x 100in. (Sotheby's) $7,800

Appliqué quilt, late 19th/early 20th century, a rose pattern, orange and red flowers, green leaves and stems, white ground, wide red and white striped border, 104 x 102in. (Skinner) $1,265

A wool and cotton doublecloth coverlet, American, mi 19th century, woven in two widths from cotton yarn rust and indigo wool, featuring paired peacocks an turkeys separated by rosettes, 82 x 70in. withou fringe. (Christie's) $1,175

A cotton appliquéd and embroidered album quilt, American, dated *1865*, worked as a square comprising sixteen different pattern blocks employing plain and printed cottons on a white cotton ground set with red sashing, most blocks signed in ink, 80 x 80in. (Christie's) $4,465

A wool and cotton jacquard-woven coverlet, Harry Tyler, Jefferson County, New York, dated 1842, hand-woven in two widths in ivory cotton and red wool for Sophia A Clark 1842, featuring foliate cartouches enclosing flowers and diamonds, 93 x 88in. (Christie's) $6,463

A pieced flannel Amish Bar quilt, probably Lancaster County, Pennsylvania, circa 1910, composed of three wide green stripes within a red frame with purple block corners, 70 x 81in. (Sotheby's) $4,800

A pieced cotton American flag quilt, American, circa 1930, composed of red, white and blue printed and solid cotton patches in a stylized checkerboard of American flags, 72 x 85in. (Sotheby's) $5,700

A pieced cotton Amish Star quilt, American early 20th century, composed of red, white and blue polka dot cotton patches arranged in a concentric star pattern, with stars and arrows in the corners, 90 x 90in. (Sotheby's) $3,000

Cotton patchwork quilt, America, mid-19th century, initialled *E.C.R. 1867*, calico print of rust and white in a geometric pattern with alternating triangles of various sizes, sawtooth border, 90 x 90in. (Skinner) $1,840

A 2-valve battery radio, single wave receiver, perhaps home-made, in wormed wooden case, circa 1925. (Auction Team Köln) $169

A very rare Rondo Magic Box ceramic vase-shaped radio by LTP of Tübingen, circa 1950. (Auction Team Köln) $1,863

A Telefunken 343W bakelite radio in good condition. (Auction Team Köln) $282

A Fisk Radiolette receiver, Model 38B, in veined ivory Radelac with matching grille and backplate, by Amalgamated Wireless (Australasia) Limited, circa 1937. (Christie's) $1,640

A Gecophone 'smoker's cabinet' two-valve receiver, type BC 2001, in mahogany cabinet, 16½in. high, circa 1923; and a horn speaker with non-metallic straight-stemmed curved horn, 29¼in. high. (Christie's) $604

A Fisk Radiolette 'Empire State' receiver, in veined ivory Radelac case of Art Deco architectural style with reeded central motif incorporating square dial, 11in. high, circa 1935. (Christie's) $2,418

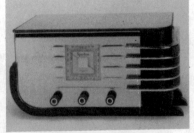

An unusual Telefunken VE301N radio with Kaco wave trap, 1935, in working order. (Auction Team Köln) $395

A Sparton Model 557 radio receiver, designed by Walter Teague, in rectangular case with blue mirror-glass to the front and top, ebonized right-hand end with chrome-plated wrap-around straps, 16in. wide, circa 1937. (Christie's) $1,036

A Wega 301GW multi-wave receiver, in decorative brown case. in working order, 1934. (Auction Team Köln) $152

A KO-Yoshiba, Japan, Planet Robot, blue painted tinplate with wind-up mechanism, rubber hands, and chrome additions, with stop lever, circa 1960, 22cm. high. (Auction Team Köln) $339

Nomura for Fairylight Batman, battery operated, blue and light blue lithographed tinplate with cloth cape, 12in. (Christie's) $987

A tinplate Robby The Robot by Nomura, Japan, bakelite arms and legs, clear plastic head, with separate battery box, 22cm. high, 1950. (Auction Team Köln) $494

A Super Hero Japanese lithographed tinplate robot, with plastic head and wind-up mechanism, in original box, circa 1975, 24cm. high. (Auction Team Köln) $124

Yonezawa for Cragstan Mr. Robot, battery operated, red and black lithographed tinplate, in original box. (Christie's) $624

A battery-operated lithographed tinplate Mars King robot by Horikawa, Japan, circa 1965, 24cm. high. (Auction Team Köln) $395

A red lithographed tinplate Cragstan Astronaut robot by Yonezawa, Japan, with flywheel drive, circa 1955. (Auction Team Köln) $423

A Strenco clockwork robot, painted in silver with red detailing and chrome strip down chest, with sparkling flint action, in original box, 1950s, 19cm. high excluding aerial. (Christie's) $461

A red lithographed tinplate Super Hero robot, clockwork mechanism, by ST, Japan, with original box, circa 1975, 23cm. high. (Auction Team Köln) $135

TRICKS OF THE TRADE

When cleaning your guitar, avoid polishes that are paraffin based, as they will dull the finish. Wax polishes should also be avoided as they will leave the guitar greasy, as will silicon.

Wipe your guitar with a damp cloth and regularly replace the strings.

A rare single of 'Blue Days – Black Nights' by Buddy Holly, Brunswick, 05581, 1956, 'Love Me' on side B, with two Brunswick sleeves.
(Bonhams & Brooks) $801

Oasis, signed color 8.5 x 10 cover to Q Magazine, Jan. 1988, featuring portraits of each.
(Vennett Smith) $60

Gene Vincent, signed postcard, half-length holding guitar, promotional image by Capitol Records.
(Vennett Smith) $57

Help!, 1965, United Artists, British quad, 30 x 40in. (76.2 x 101.6cm.)
(Christie's) $1,150

Elvis Presley, signed postcard, to lower white border, head and shoulders smiling, 1959.
(Vennett Smith) $676

The Beatles, signed 6.5 x 8.5, by all four individually, full-length standing and seated in group pose wearing suits and drinking tea.
(Vennett Smith) $1,470

The Rolling Stones, signed 10 x 8, by all five, Mick Jagger, Brian Jones, Bill Wyman, Keith Richards, Charlie Watts, head and shoulders in group pose together, promotional photo by Decca Records.
(Vennett Smith) $312

Jerry Lee Lewis, a scarce 10 x 15 poster, for Lewis's Show at the Gaumont Doncaster, with the Treniers as backup.
(Vennett Smith) $216

Bruce Springsteen, signed color 8 x 10, three quarter length playing guitar, (Vennett Smith) $116

Paul McCartney, signed 8 x 10, half-length holding his hands in the air. (Vennett Smith) $323

Bob Dylan, signed color 8 x 10, head and shoulders. (Vennett Smith) $339

Marc Bolan, a silver T.Rex/Marc Bolan scarf, signed and inscribed by Marc Bolan, apparently obtained in person at a meeting with him following a competition win with Top of The Pops magazine, Nov 1975. (Vennett Smith) $210

George Harrison, signed 6 x 5 magazine photo, half-length playing guitar, laid down to heavy card. (Vennett Smith) $339

Elvis Presley, signed postcard, half-length leaning on stepladders, from Jailhouse Rock, weaker contrast to signature. (Vennett Smith) $435

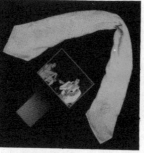

Ringo Starr, signed 8 x 10 Apple records promotional photo, slight paperclip indentation. (Vennett Smith) $111

Elvis Presley, yellow silk scarf, inscribed and signed *Best Wishes / Elvis Presley*, with gold colored brooch in shape of piano with treble clef, approximately 36in. long. (Christie's) $1,880

The Animals concert poster,
Rhodes Centre, November 27
1965, 'Limelight Promotions present
The Animals plus Dave and the
Strollers', black lettering on yellow
background, 75.5 x 49.5cm.
(Bonhams) $210

The Beatles, a rare early concert
poster The Beatles, Gerry And the
Pacemakers and From The United
States, Roy Orbison; and others,
the Gaumont, Ipswich, Wednesday,
22nd May, 1963, 29 x 39in.
(Christie's) $6,580

The Beatles, the front cover of a
souvenir booklet The Beatles, 1964
signed in black ballpoint pen by all
four members of the group, 9½ x
7in. (Christie's) $3,61

Albert Lee's Gibson Super 400 Ces
Serial No. A28256, 1958, sunburst
carved spruce top blonde binding to
top of body, ebony fret board with
pearl/abalone block inlays.
(Bonhams) $13,230

A 1956 Gibson Super 400
CES/Scotty Moore, Serial No. A-
24672, Factory Order No. V7370 7,
in natural finish, maple body with
round cutaway, arched spruce top
with bound f-holes, maple neck.
(Christie's) $106,054

Elvis Presley, a black and white
publicity postcard signed and
inscribed on the reverse in blue
ballpoint pen Elvis Presley "59", 3¼
x 5in., in common mount with a
color machine-print photograph.
(Christie's) $507

A jacket owned and worn by Tom
Jones on his television show 'This
is Tom Jones', January 8 1971, the
brown jacket with inner lining and
four front pockets, with a letter of
authenticity. (Bonhams) $252

Mick Jagger, a blue cotton shirt with
ruffled front and cuffs, labelled
inside Peculiar To Mr. Fish, 17
Clifford Street, London W.1.15,
worn by Mick Jagger for a photo
session with David Bailey.
(Christie's) $5,922

A postcard autographed by Dire
Straits, 1980s, signed Mark
Knopfler, Alan Clark, Guy Fletcher,
Terry Williams, Jack Sonni and
John Illesey in blue ballpoint, 14.7 x
10cm. (Bonhams) $147

Madonna, a color machine-print photograph of subject, circa 1986, signed and inscribed by subject in red felt pen *love Madonna*, 14 x 11in. (Christie's) $239

The Beatles/Brian Epstein, a large black and white photograph of The Beatles performing at the Empire Theatre, Liverpool, October 28th, 1962, 30½ x 47in., formerly belonging to Brian Epstein. (Christie's) $25,827

Autographed photograph of Elvis Presley, 1960s, signed *Sincerely Elvis Presley* in blue ballpoint, 31.5 x 31.5cm. (Bonhams) $364

John Lennon's tax check, dated *July 26th 1971*, a Lennon Productions Ltd. check drawn on the District Bank Limited and payable to the Inland Revenue for £593.40, signed *John Lennon*. (Bonhams) $1,985

Elvis Presley, a 'sailor's' cap of white cotton with black plastic peak, signed and inscribed in blue ballpoint pen *To Maile from Elvis Presley*; accompanied by a color photograph of Presley wearing the cap, 6¼ x 5in. (Christie's) $1,974

Freddie Mercury's 'FLASH' T-shirt, 1980, the white T-shirt with red *FLASH* on front and red thunderbolt on back, red rimmed neck and sleeves, worn on stage by Freddie. (Bonhams) $853

A shell necklace owned and worn by John Lennon, 1960s, 126 small Indian Ocean Volute shells, 67cm. long. (Bonhams) $2,058

A black wool 'Poor Boy' cap owned by John Lennon and worn in the 1965 film 'Help', labelled inside, *M* and *Made In England*. (Bonhams) $3,925

Elvis Presley, a black and white RCA Victor publicity postcard, signed in blue ballpoint pen *Elvis Presley*, 12 x 8cm. framed. (Christie's) $774

Janis Joplin, a black and white machine-print photograph signed and inscribed in blue felt pen *Love, Janis Joplin*, 5½ x 8in. (Christie's) $1,068

A black and white machine-print publicity photograph of the group signed by Ginger Baker, Jack Bruce, Eric Clapton '94, 11¼ x 18¾in. (Christie's) $1,233

A signed Buddy Holly and The Crickets UK tour programme, 1958. (Sotheby's) $1,512

Cliff Richard's stage suit, 1967, the cream elephant cord suit with Robert Valentine tailor's label *Cliff Richard June 67* and possibly the suit worn in the '68 Eurovision Song Contest. (Bonhams) $658

Elvis Presley, an Elac Miraphon 12 portable record player with four speed turntable in a duotone carrying case, signed and inscribed on top of the case, in blue ballpoint pen *To Karin thanks from Elvis Presley "59"*, also signed and inscribed inside the lid. (Christie's) $1,645

A programme and two tickets for the Jimi Hendrix Experience's First UK Tour, English Astoria Finsbury Park March 13 1967, headlined by The Walker Brothers with support from Cat Stevens and Engelbert Humperdinck, 26 x 20cm. (Bonhams) $255

A programme for The Beatles concert at Winter Gardens Margate Thursday 11th July 1963 signed on the cover *Paul McCartney, John Lennon, George Harrison and Ringo Starr*. (Bonhams) $4,710

The Beatles, a rare British EMI promotional poster for an album Sgt. Pepper's Lonely Hearts Club Band, 1967, 17¾ x 24¼in. (Christie's) $987

The Beatles, a printed black and white Swedish press advertisement for the group, 1963, signed in blue ball point pen by all four members of the group, 8 x 5½in. (Christie's) $2,766

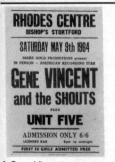

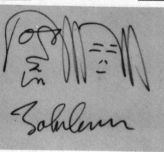

A Gene Vincent concert poster, Rhodes Centre, May 9 1964, 'Mark Gold Promotions present In Person – American Recording Star Gene Vincent and the Shouts plus Unit Five',76 x 50cm. (Bonhams) $364

John Lennon, a self-portrait caricature of John and Yoko in black felt pen on paper, signed by John Lennon, 4 x 5½in. laminated. (Christie's) $4,277

Autographs of Elvis, Scotty, Bill & D.J. Fontana, dated *8/7/56*, signed *To Sandy- Elvis Presley, Scotty Moore, Bill Black "Bass"* and *D. J. Fontana Drums* in blue ballpoint, 12.5 x 10cm. framed. (Bonhams) $1,050

Pink Floyd, the reverse of an album record sleeve signed by Roger Waters, Nick Mason, Dave Gilmour and Rick Wright, above a 7 x 5.5 photo of the band and two tickets for Pink Floyd: The Wall Concert. (Vennett Smith) $493

Freddie Mercury's sunglasses, 1985, worn for many years and on the front cover of his 'Mr. Bad Guy' solo album, together with the case and a color photograph. (Bonhams) $1,176

Britney Spears' autographed silver shoes, 1999, the silver high heels owned and worn by the star, signed *Love Britney* in black marker, together with a letter of authenticity, size 6½. (Bonhams) $809

A black and white print of Elvis on stage, circa 1973/74 signed *Thanks Elvis Presley*, in blue felt tip pen, mounted, framed and glazed, 12. x 15in. (Bonhams) $628

The Sex Pistols, a promotional poster designed by Jamie Reid God Save The Queen, 1977, 27 x 39in; and corresponding banner, 10½ x 37½in. (Christie's) $369

The Who, a black and white publicity photograph circa 1970, signed in black ballpoint pen by Roger Daltrey, Pete Townsend, Keith Moon and by John Entwistle 10¾ x 8¾in. (Christie's) $590

An autographed photograph of Elvis Presley, circa 1969, signed *Elvis Presley* on a color photo of Elvis at Las Vegas in 1969, together with a letter of authenticity, 20 x 25cm. (Bonhams) $412

Jim Morrison/ The Doors, a black and white machine print photograph of Jim Morrison, signed and inscribed in black felt pen, *To Terry, Morrison The Doors*, 10¾ x 8in. (Christie's) $1,151

A rare early handbill for a cancelled date Elvis Presley, The Atomic Powered Singer, New Frontier Hotel, Las Vegas, Sunday, 6th May, 1956, signed and inscribed by subject in blue ballpoint pen *Elvis Presley "1956"*, 10 x 6in. (Christie's) $6,251

A rare set of four Royal Doulton Beatles character jugs, English circa 1984, showing the Beatles in 'Sgt. Pepper'-style costume, from the 1987 Limited Edition of 1000 pieces in Royal Doulton box. (Bonhams) $1,125

A glass Evian mineral water bottle, the label signed in black felt pen, *Madonna*, the neck with traces of pink lipstick, 12¾in. high. (Christie's) $493

A rare proof poster for the 'Butcher' cover 'Yesterday and Today' album, American, circa 1966, sheet 63.5 x 45cm. (Bonhams) $4,704

The Beach Boys, an album sleeve Best Of The Beach Boys, signed recently on the front in blue felt pen by Brian Wilson, Carl Wilson, Mike Love, Al Jardine and Bruce Johnston. (Christie's) $410

Linda McCartney, signed 7.5 x 10, head and shoulders portrait, smiling. (Vennett Smith) $98

Love Me Tender, 20th Century Fox,1956, U.K. 30 x 40in. poster. (Bonhams) $154

A page from an autograph album signed in blue ballpoint pen by Buddy Holly, Joe Mauldin, and Jerry Allison, 4½ x 4in. (Christie's) $1,290

Elvis Presley, signed 6 x 4, head and shoulders wearing shirt and tie. (Vennett Smith) $764

Eric Clapton/Paul Kossoff/Cream/Blind Faith/Free, a 1958 Gibson Les Paul Standard, Serial No. 8 2453, in sunburst finish, mahogany body with single cutaway, maple top, mahogany neck, twenty-two fret bound rosewood fingerboard with crown inlays. (Christie's) $65,800

Elvis Presley, a black and white polka dot shirt fastening with white buttons, labelled inside *Cutler and Company Quality Shirts* framed, 35½ x 28in., accompanied by a document from the Elvis Presley Museum. (Christie's) $2,961

Buddy Holly and the Crickets Autographs, 1958, signed *Buddy Holly* and *Jerry Allison* in black ballpoint and *Joe Maudlin* in blue ballpoint, on the front of a promotional Coral Recording Artist card, 14.5 x 8.5cm. (Bonhams) $1,029

An early black and white publicity photograph of The Who as The High Numbers, 1964, signed in blue ballpoint pen by Roger Daltry, Pete Townsend, Keith Moon and John Entwistle, 8½ x 6¼in. (Christie's) $2,632

Elton John's piano stool used on tour, 1992, the black padded stool with leatherette cover and round cogs at both sides, made by Paul L. Jansen & Son, 59cm. wide. (Bonhams) $382

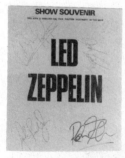

Led Zeppelin, a concert programme circa 1973 signed on the cover in blue ballpoint pen *Jimmy Page, John Paul Jones, John Bonham and Robert Plant*, approximately 8½ x 11in. (Bonhams) $550

A fine needlework sampler, Marcy Hay, probably Boston, dated *1777*, executed in a variety of pink, green, yellow and blue stitches on a canvas ground, 12½in. high. (Sotheby's) $18,400

A 19th century woolwork sampler worked by Martha Wood depicting a child with a cat feeding birds under an arch of trees with floral border, 20¾ x 20¼in. unframed. (Andrew Hartley) $862

A George IV needlework sampler, circa 1823, signed and dated in the center *Mary Braithwaite, 1823*, framed, 42cm. x 31cm. (Bonhams) $728

Sampler, wool or silk stitched on gauze, trees and house by Sarah Pattinson, aged 11 years, April 8th, 1815, 19 x 13in. (G.A. Key) $1,068

A sampler by Sarah Earnshaw at Mrs Wetherell's School, South Emsall, worked with Don Quixote chasing at a windmill, 26 x 15½in., 19th century. (Christie's) $1,752

A fine sampler by Dorothy Roberts, worked mainly in cross stitch and Algerian eye with pious verses, floral decoration, fruiting trees, flower-filled vases, 1770, framed and glazed, 17½ x 12in. (Christie's) $740

Needlework family register, 1828, *wrought by Louisa Wright, age 10 years,* register above a pious verse, a basket of flowers, and a willow tree, 17 x 17in. (Skinner) $3,105

A sampler by Mary Martin 1827, worked in colored silks, the center with a red brick house, the verse "Jesus permit thy gracious name..." above, 15¼ x 19¾in. (Christie's) $5,778

Samper, silk stitched on gauze, central bible verses, geometric foliate border, by Sarah Sandford, 1767, 17½ x 17. (G.A. Key) $1,256

Sampler, wool stitched on gauze, verse bordered by figures, scene of an oasis, by Anna Barnes, Aged 12, September 29th, 18 x 17in. (G.A. Key) $371

A William IV sampler, *Ann Snow Aged 14 Years – 1836*, with central verse and flanked by rabbits, parrots, bouquets and vases of flowers, 51.5 x 63cm. (Bristol) $1,890

19th century sampler, silk and wool stitched on gauze, house, verse, trees and design etc. by Mary Ann Rodgers, Aged 12 years, 1844, 17 x 14in. (G.A. Key) $659

Needlework sampler, America, early 19th century, *Sarah Jubb Aged 9 Dec 4. 1809*, inspirational verse above a panel with a geometric flowering vine border, framed, 20 x 16in. (Skinner) $690

A William IV sampler worked by Mary Ann Gray, dated *1832*, and featuring a country house with peacocks, flowers and animals and stanza within a trailing border, 23 x 23in., unframed. (Andrew Hartley) $1,109

Needlework sampler, *Martha Mary Miller Newport August 25 1823*, with alphabet panels above a verse above the maker's identification, surrounded by stylized floral border, 17¼ x 17¼in. (Skinner) $1,955

A sampler by Louisa Sarah Smith, 1830, finely worked in colored silks with alphabets and numerals, with a central verse On Industry, 24 x 20in. (Christie's) $1,321

Needlework family register, America, 1833, *Wrought by Harriet A. Newall Aged 11 Pluma Loomis Instructress,* alphabet panels above family register above a scenic panel, 17 x 18in. (Skinner) $2,760

A finely worked sampler by Emma Bailey 1820, embroidered in colored silks with the verse "Make God the beginning...", a brick house with a tree lined vista below, 13½ x 16¼in. (Christie's) $2,528

SCRIMSHAW

A scrimshawed whalebone box, American, 19th century, the circular lid with pinprick decoration in the form of two interlocking hearts, 4in. diam. (Christie's) $1,680

A fine engraved and scrimshawed sperm whale's tooth, probably American, mid 19th century, the obverse engraved with two full-rigged ships engaged in battle, 7½in. long. (Sotheby's) $1,955

A scrimshawed whalebone and baleen box, American, 19th century, the circular baleen lid engraved with a fully rigged ship, 5¾in. diameter. (Christie's) $1,190

Carved and polychrome decorated whale's tooth, mid 19th century, obverse depicting a classical domed building with columns, probably a state capitol, flying an American flag, 8¼in. long. (Skinner) $600

An early 19th century scrimshaw whale's tooth, one face engraved with the full length portrait of a lady, inscribed 1804, 16cm. high. (Bonhams) $400

A fine engraved and scrimshawed sperm whale's tooth, mid 19th century, the tooth engraved in the round with a woman holding a broom pointing a scolding finger at a sailor with duffle bags, 4¾in. long (Sotheby's) $1,725

Engraved whale's tooth, mid-19th century, depicting various figures including a woman seated on a sea serpent and a banner inscribed The Queen of the Sea, 6in. long. (Skinner) $2,415

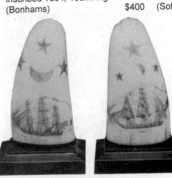

A pair of polychrome engraved whale's teeth, 19th century, each decorated with square-rigged ships under full sail, 4¼in. high. (Skinner) $3,750

Engraved whale's tooth, 19th century, both sides depicting the British ship "Calliope" at sea with flags flying, 5¾in. long. (Skinner) $3,450

A Willcox & Gibbs type domestic chain-stitch sewing machine, signed *American S.M. Co. London*, circa 1890.
(Auction Team Köln) $96

An English Jones hand sewing machine on decorative cast socle, circa 1880.
(Auction Team Köln) $214

An unusual Clark's Foliage American chainstitch machine in original condition, lacking needle, circa 1859.
(Auction Team Köln) $4,236

An American Little Comfort Improved child's chainstitch sewing machine, circa 1905.
(Auction Team Köln) $395

An American Florence standard long shuttle sewing machine, with shuttle and finely decorated, circa 1870.
(Auction Team Köln) $1,412

A Grant Brothers Philadelphia New England type sewing machine with hand painted decoration, circa 1865.
(Auction Team Köln) $2,259

A French Avrial Legat domestic sewing machine with unusual pump drive, complete with shuttle, circa 1885.
(Auction Team Köln) $1,976

A Müller No. 2 child's chain stitch sewing machine, circa 1930.
(Auction Team Köln) $902

A Casige Nr. 2/2 gray cast metal and tinplate child's chain stitch sewing machine with gold and red decoration, circa 1935
(Auction Team Köln) $135

A Colibri sewing machine by
Bremer & Brückmann, Brunswick,
early German child's chain-stitch
machine, circa 1890.
(Auction Team Köln) $197

An Arm and Platform sewing
machine, no 16792, with shuttle
and gilt decoration.
(Christie's) $462

The head of a very rare Osborn A
American domestic sewing
machine, lacking shuttle, spool
case and foot, circa 1875.
(Auction Team Köln) $169

A Soezy child's sewing machine by
Batchelor & Stevenson, NY, with
unusual needle action, circa 1902.
(Auction Team Köln) $1,468

An Improved Little Stranger sewing
machine, by Nussey & Pilling,
Leeds, with C-frame with gilt
transfer and blue lining and circular
stitch-plate and base, 12in. wide.
(Christie's) $829

A 'skinny pillar' sewing machine by
Shaw & Clarke, traces of original
decoration, circa 1864.
(Auction Team Köln) $4,230

A Shaw & Clarke 'skinny pillar'
American chainstitch sewing
machine, circa 1864.
(Auction Team Köln) $6,212

A 'Little Hereford' sewing machine
by A.W. Bezant, Widemarsh St. of
Starley 'Queen of Hearts' design,
with gilt decoration highlighted in
white, mark for 1874, 13½in. wide.
(Christie's) $1,208

La Canadienne, an unusual
domestic sewing machine by
Vigneron, Paris, mounted on a new
board, with oscillating shuttle, circa
1885.
(Auction Team Köln) $299

SILHOUETTES

Arthur Lea, circa 1800, Admiral Sir Roger Curtis G.C.B., profile to the right, his hair en queue, painted on convex glass backed with plaster, oval 3in. high.
(Bonhams) $3,675

An early 19th century silhouette picture depicting a family group in interior, with painted drapes and floor, the background in pencil and crayon on paper giving a three dimensional effect, unsigned, 8½ x 10in., gilt frame.
(Andrew Hartley) $1,232

John Woodhouse, 1842, a fine profile of Matthew Plummer, full-length, facing left, painted on flat glass backed with card, 303mm. high. (Bonhams) $882

English School, circa 1830, a Gentleman, full-length, profile to the right, with side-whiskers, wearing top-hat, cut-out on card with details in Chinese white, 244mm. high.
(Bonhams) $220

American School, 19th century, a pair of silhouette portraits of a man and woman, each hollow-cut with ink details, 3¾ x 2⅝in.
(Christie's) $1,058

Royal Victoria Gallery, probably H.A. Frith, 1848, a Gentleman, full-length, profile to the left, his hands in his pockets, cut-out on card with details in ochre and Chinese white, rectangular, 16¼in. high
(Bonhams) $294

German School, circa 1745, a Lady, profile to the right, standing full-length holding a vase of pink tulips, cut-out on card, the sitter's face in black and costume of collaged fabric, rectangular, 9¾in. high.
(Bonhams) $529

American School, 19th century, silhouette of a man holding a whip, inscribed faintly in pencil on right *Samuel Pyle*, dated *1828*, hollow-cut with water-color and ink details, 5 x 5¾in.
(Christie's) $1,645

MONEY MAKERS

Right since their inception silhouettes have always been the poor relations of full color portrait miniatures, and they remain so to this day.

A first-quality 17th century portrait of a minor lord might now be worth around $15,000 while a silhouette of the same person would fetch only $3,000.

557

SILHOUETTES

Samuel Metford, circa 1843, a fine portrait of a Lady and Gentleman standing on a balcony, cut-out on card with details in gold, rectangular, 9¾in. high. (Bonhams) $1,029

German School, possibly Christine Marie Haflingerin, circa 1790, a fine conversation piece of a Gentleman, said to be Joseph Haydn, instructing a Lady, seated at a piano, painted on flat glass in verre églomisé, rectangular 5½in. high. (Bonhams) $1,323

William Wellings, 1783, Captain William Affleck R.N., full-length, profile to the left, his powdered hair en queue, wearing Naval uniform, painted on card, rectangular, 10in. high. (Bonhams) $956

John Field, circa 1825, Jane Elliot, profile to the right, her hair in a plaited bun, with comb and ringlets at the front, painted on plaster and bronzed, oval, 80mm. high. (Bonhams) $1,250

German School, circa 1745, a conversation piece of a Lady and boy, standing full-length, in profile, cut-out on card, the sitters' faces in black and costumes of collaged fabric, rectangular, 8¾in. high. (Bonhams) $515

John Field, circa 1815, a Gentleman, profile to the right, wearing double-breasted coat, painted on plaster and bronzed, oval, 80mm. high. (Bonhams) $515

Augustin Edouart, 1841, a fine profile of a young Gentleman standing, full-length facing left, at a harbor entrance, cut-out on card on a lithographed background, rectangular, 10½in. high. (Bonhams) $1,029

Hill's Gallery, circa 1833, a fine conversation piece of Samuel and Eliza Hollins with their five children, cut-outs on card and bronzed on a pencilled background, rectangular, 14⅛in. high. (Bonhams) $2,793

Mr. Raper, circa 1830, a fine portrait of Great Aunt Denys, profile to the left, full-length, painted on card, the sitters' faces in black and costumes in color, 258mm. high. (Bonhams) $1,250

A George III silver cake-basket,
William Plummer, London, 1763,
the body pierced and chased with
diaperwork, scrolls and beading,
14¾in. long, 45oz.
(Christie's) $3,799

A George III cake basket, John
Edward Terrey, 1817, the
rectangular basket with a
gadrooned rim and lobed well,
raised on a conforming foot,
31.5cm., 32oz.
(Christie's) $1,208

A George II silver-gilt basket,
Thomas Farren, London, 1735,
base later armorial engraved, raffia
side with strap bound reeded girdle,
14¾in. long, 1940gm.
(Sotheby's) $11,622

A George III swing handled sugar
basket, London 1781, maker's mark
of Robert Hennell, pierced with
vertical slats, scroll decoration and
urns, engraved swags, beaded
borders, with a blue glass liner,
approximate weight 2.5oz., 7.4cm.
high. (Bonhams) $1,029

A George III silver-gilt cake basket,
John Edward Terrey, London, 1819,
shaped oval and on four cast
openwork dolphin and rocaille feet,
the body pierced with scrolls and
diaperwork, 15¼in. long, 83oz.
(Christie's) $14,838

A George III swing handled sugar
basket, London 1792, maker's mark
of Duncan Urquhart and Napthali
Hart, bright cut decoration, with two
cartouches, monogramed,
approximate weight 6oz., 12.4cm.
long. (Bonhams) $617

A George III silver cake basket,
William Vincent, London, 1769, the
lower body embossed with beading
and scrolls, the wire-work sides
applied with flower sprays, 13in.
long, 23oz.(Christie's) $3,619

An Edwardian silver fruit basket of
oval dished form, the flared rim
above a fretwork body, London
1912, Stewart Dawson Ltd,
approximately 9oz., 33cm. wide.
(Bonhams) $353

A George III cake basket, maker's
mark *RM*, 1775, the oval basket
with a gadroon motif rim decorated
with urn motif medallions, with
pieced lattice motif sides, 34.7cm.,
31oz. (Christie's) $2,073

559

A 19th century American beaker, of slightly tapering cylindrical form, engraved with the name, *John S. Sinead*, marked underneath twice *Kitts*, 8.5cm. high.
(Christie's) $923

A German silver-gilt beaker and cover, Christian Friedrich Winger, Dresden, 1731, the detachable domed cover with baluster finial, 7in. high, 8oz.
(Christie's) $10,495

A Russian beaker, maker's mark *BA*, Moscow, 18th century, the circular section beaker with exotic bird and rocaille cartouche motifs, 3in., 2.25oz. (Christie's) $431

A Norweigan silver beaker, Hans Jörgen Michaelsen Blytt, Bergen, 1796, the body applied with two chased bands, the upper with hanging ornaments, 6in. high, 5oz.
(Christie's) $2,422

A Cape beaker, Gerhardus Lotter, Capetown, circa 1820, the circular section beaker of slightly tapering form with a central reeded band and a reeded foot, height 8.5cm., 5.5oz. (Christie's) $5,264

A 19th century Russian silver and enamel beaker, Moscow 1881, assay master unknown, maker's mark of Maria Adler, tapering circular form, ropework borders, 8oz., 12cm. high.
(Bonhams) $1,103

An early 18th century German parcel-gilt beaker, Ohlau pre-1717, maker's mark of George Kahlert, embossed and engraved with shell and foliate scroll decoration, later inscribed, approximate weight 3oz., 10.2cm. (Bonhams) $1,176

A German silver Roemmer, probably North Germany, circa 1580, maker's mark *HCT*, the lower part of the body chased with indented lobes on matted ground with wriggle band above, 7cm. high, 67gm. (Christie's) $9,315

An American silver beaker, Myer Myers, New York, circa 1775, of tapered cylindrical form with molded rim, engraved with a contemporary foliate cypher *AB* sprouting flowers, 187gm, 9.8cm.
(Sotheby's) $14,400

A Swedish parcel-gilt silver beaker, Lorens Stabeus, Stockholm, 1747, the upper part of the body engraved with scrolls and rocaille and with stamped border of foliage, 8¼in. high, 19oz.
(Christie's) $4,844

A Louis XV silver-gilt beaker, Strasbourg, circa 1725, probably Johan Jacob Frey, bell-shaped on gadrooned spreading foot, the upper part of the cup engraved with strapwork, 3¼in. high, 3oz.
(Christie's) $3,726

A Baltic parcel-gilt silver beaker, Johann Mürmann, Riga, dated *1747*, the body chased and repoussé with a scene of Darius' family before Alexander the Great, 21.5cm. high, 17oz.
(Christie's) $5,589

BELLS

George III silver table bell, London, 1805, maker's mark indistinct, of typical form with molded rim and baluster handle, with plain clapper, 5¼in., 5oz.
(Christie's) $2,430

A novelty nickel-plated table bell, unmarked, early 20th century, modelled as a tortoise, nickel plated body mounted with a tortoiseshell, 18cm. long. (Bonhams) $706

An electroplated novelty table bell, maker's mark of Elkington and Co., modelled as an old lady, holding a dog and a cane, with a nodding head, 11.2cm. high.
(Bonhams) $382

BISCUIT BOXES

late Victorian silver plated biscuit box of folding type within a scrolled frame, 10in. tall.
(G.A. Key) $408

A late Victorian double biscuit box, the shell molded hinged body with two compartments, rococo chasing, sprays and scrolls pierced fret hinged covers, laurel wreath hinged ring handles, 11½in.
(Woolley & Wallis) $368

A Victorian silver plated folding biscuit box, with naturalistic central carrying handles and frame supporting two hinged scalloped shaped bowls, 9½in. high.
(Bonhams) $370

A late Victorian silver rose bowl, London 1891, John Newton Mappin, part fluted and beaded decoration, gilt interior, approximate total weight 30oz., diameter of bowl 25.5cm. (Bonhams) $739

Late Victorian silver plated pedestal fruit bowl, circular shaped with pierced and embossed floral and scrolled decoration, engraved solid swing handle, 10in. diameter. (G.A. Key) $87

A Chinese silver rosebowl, maker's mark of Woshing, embossed with butterflies and peonies, wavy edge border, approximate weight 20oz., diameter 20.8cm. (Bonhams) $808

An Edwardian bowl, R.H. Halford & Sons, 1907, the oval bowl with a leaf decorated rim, with two applied scroll handles, the body decorated with further leaf motifs, length 46cm., 57oz. (Christie's) $2,467

A large Edwardian silver rosebowl, the plain circular bowl set on a short pedestal base, with gadrooned borders, Sheffield 1928, 25cm. diameter, approximate weight 45oz. (Bonhams) $617

A Spanish Colonial Holy Water Stoup, stamped *AMAT*, possibly South America, presentation date *1779*, the circular section vessel with robust lobes separated by leaf capped cartouches, 22.4cm., 16oz. (Christie's) $1,974

An Edwardian silver rose bowl, London 1904, William Hutton and Sons. Ltd., fluted decoration, on a spread circular foot also with fluted decoration, approximate weight 20oz., 23in. diameter. (Bonhams) $462

Good quality pedestal silver fruit bowl, the top well pierced with foliate garlands to shaped oval panels, 9in. diameter, Sheffield 1911 by Joseph Round, 20oz. (G.A. Key) $681

A modern two-handled rose bowl, with shaped border of stylized foliage, the handles leaf-capped and with mask terminals, Goldsmiths & Silversmiths Co., 1911, 35cm. long, 59oz. (Bonhams) $1,467

George III silver rose bowl, London 1789, the whole with later embossed floral, scroll and berry decoration, approximate total weight 26oz., diameter of bowl ...cm. (Bonhams) $882

A modern monteith, Arthur & Frank Parsons, 1919, the lobed circular section bowl with alternating matted panels and lion drop ring handles, 28.2cm., 68oz. (Christie's) $2,590

A silver bowl, Birmingham 1938, Barker Bros, Ltd., the whole body pierced with vertical slats and stylized scroll and floral decoration, glass liner, approximate weighable 21oz., diameter of bowl 23.5cm. (Bonhams) $801

George I silver bowl and cover, Gabriel Sleath, London, circa 1715, stepped domed cover with baluster finial, engraved with a coat-of-arms within a baroque cartouche, 3½in., ... (Christie's) $7,079

A modern Scottish bowl, John Fetter, Glasgow, 1916, the oval bowl of boat-form raised on a conforming oval base by four Art Nouveau style leaf form supports, 6¾in., 11.25oz. (Christie's) $545

A George II silver sugar bowl and cover, Pezé Pilleau, London, 1750, bombé, engraved with rococo armorials below chased flower and scroll shoulder, 5in. high, 389gm. (Sotheby's) $5,006

...th century Dutch sugar bowl, ...our ram's mask and scroll supporters, the body pierced with bands of scrolling foliage and ...te draping swags, Amsterdam, ... century, 10.5cm. high. ...istie's) $517

A Victorian monteith, James Aitchison, 1897, of lobed circular section with a scrolling rim and two applied lion drop ring handles, raised on a conforming foot, 12¼in., 97oz. (Christie's) $5,075

A Continental silver-mounted wood bowl, maker's mark IL, 19th century, cylindrical and on domed base chased with scaly dolphins, shells and with shell and gadrooned border, 12¼in. high. (Christie's) $3,167

A large modern silver bowl, London 1977, maker's mark of A.E. Jones, of plain circular form, stylized beaded borders, on a raised pierced floral foot, approximate weight 52oz., diameter of bowl 32cm.
(Bonhams & Brooks) $928

Russian champlevé enamel bowl and scoop, late 19th century, enamelled all over with stylized lappets and floral motifs, diameter 5¹/₈in.; the latter with scoop-form bowl similarly enamelled, 5¼in. long, approximately 8 troy oz. total.
(Skinner) $1,495

An American silver-gilt punch bowl, Gorham Mfg. Co., Providence, RI, circa 1905, the bombé bowl with pierced rim of flowers, scrolls, and seed pods, matching pedestal foot, 68oz., diameter at rim 15in.
(Sotheby's) $3,900

An American silver rose bowl Meridan Britannia Co, Meriden, circa 1890, deep tapering cylindrical with stiff leaf and ribbon bound reeded borders, pedestal support, 11¼in. high, 3259gm.
(Sotheby's) $9,298

A rare pair of Queen Anne silver bleeding bowls, Humphrey Payne, London, 1703, Britannia standard, bulbous, with openwork strap cartouche shaped handles, 5½in. diameter, 418gm.
(Sotheby's) $9,834

An American pedestal bowl, Dominick and Haff, New York, 1870, the circular section bowl with an elaborate pierced chrysanthemum and lattice motif border, diameter 37.6cm., 50oz.
(Christie's) $2,13

An Ottoman silver bath bowl of circular form, with raised center, chased with spiral fluting, the sides chased with stylised foliage, possibly early 19th century, 20cm.
(Christie's) $690

A fine Victorian covered sugar, the domed cover with flowerhead finial and chased double scroll and shell ornament, London 1864. Maker George Adams, 13oz, 26cm.
(Thomson Roddick & Medcalf) $870

A George I silver punch bowl, Louis Laroche, London, 1726, plain circular and on spreading circular foot, the bombé shaped body with molded rim, 11in. diameter, 53oz.
(Christie's) $56,095

n early Victorian sponge box, ondon 1852, maker's mark of harles and George Fox, pull off erced domed cover with a knop nial, approximate weight 4oz., 1cm. high. (Bonhams) $441

A Polish sugar box, maker's mark of Malcz, Warsaw, 1857, the hinged lid and escutcheon with engraved foliate scroll motifs, length 15cm., 20.5oz. (Christie's) $658

A late Victorian silver playing card box, London 1899, maker's mark of William Gibson & John Langman, upright rectangular form, the hinged lid inscribed, 9cm. high. (Bonhams & Brooks) $315

Queen Anne silver mounted rtoise shell box, unmarked, circa 700, the oval box with a silver ounted rim and an applied portrait edallion, 10.4cm. :hristie's) $691

A late-Victorian silver match box cover/chamberstick, Birmingham 1897, maker's mark of George Unite, mounted with a circular capital and scrolled carrying handle, approximate weight 83g, 10.5cm. wide.   (Bonhams) $220

An Edwardian silver vesta case / stamp box, Birmingham 1906, maker's mark of WL, the front set with a smaller rectangular stamp compartment, the whole engraved with floral and foliate scrolls, approximate weight 25g., 5cm. high. (Bonhams) $470

Continental sugar box, marked ith illegible maker's name, ossibly Polish or Hungarian, ngraved overall with chinoiserie cenes and exotic animals in ndscapes, 5½in. :hristie's) $950

A silver mounted tortoiseshell bridge box, Birmingham 1921, maker's mark of Levi & Salaman, the tortoiseshell lid with piqué work playing card suits in each corner surrounding the word Bridge, 12cm. wide. (Bonhams) $1,029

An Austrian 19th century gilt-lind sugar box, of lobed oblong form and standing on four vine feet, the cover with fruit finial. (Christie's) $682

A George III silver gilt caddy shovel, with a fiddle handle engraved with initials, 8.6cm. long, Samuel Pemberton, Birmingham, 1807. (Woolley & Wallis) $191

A William IV caddy spoon, the square bowl with alternate fluting and pricked leafage, 11.1cm. long. Taylor & Perry, Birmingham, 1831. (Woolley & Wallis) $191

A George III caddy spoon, the leaf shaped bowl to a thread edge handle, 10.5cm. long, probably Thomas Wallis II, London 1799. (Woolley & Wallis) $265

A Victorian caddy spoon, the shaped shell bowl to a scroll lug handle engraved later with initials, 7.9cm. long, Martin, Hall & Co., Sheffield, 1854. (Woolley & Wallis) $118

A late Victorian caddy spoon, with hammered drop-shaped bowl and an openwork handle, inset with three orange hardstones, by Omar Ramsden, 1894, 9cm. long. (Christie's) $2,073

A George III caddy spoon, of octagonal form, with fluted sides and with a plain loop handle, by Samuel Pemberton, Birmingham 1804, 4.75cm. long. (Christie's) $259

A George III caddy spoon, the heart shape bowl pricked with a band of leafage to embossed scrolls, 2¾in., Birmingham, 1812. (Woolley & Wallis) $220

A George III fiddle pattern Scottish Provincial caddy spoon, maker's mark of *I. & G.H.*, two anchors, unidentified maker, Paisley, 1790-1820, 7.75cm. long, 0.5oz. (Christie's) $1,467

A George III jockey cap caddy spoon, with bright cut decoration the peak engraved with initials within a shield, J Thornton, Birmingham, 1798. (Woolley & Wallis) $61

A George III caddy spoon, the shell bowl to a molded bifurcated scroll handle, 8cm. long, probably George Smith III & William Fearn, London, 1795. (Woolley & Wallis) $294

A Victorian caddy spoon, the circular shaped gilt bowl embossed fruit and leaves to a fruiting branch scroll handle, 7.9cm. long,. Hilliard & Thomason, Birmingham 1853. (Woolley & Wallis) $382

A late Victorian caddy spoon, the stem and bowl pierced with flower and scrolling foliage, maker's mark *H.B.*, Birmingham, 1894, 10.25cm long. (Christie's) $20

A massive pair of French silver candelabra, A Leroy, Paris, dated 1909, the stepped circular bases molded with stiff leaves and pendant husk panels below knopped reeded stems, 70¾in. high, approximate weight 55600gm. (Sotheby's) $53,640

A pair of Edwardian silver two-light candelabra, Sheffield 1901, Hawksworth, Eyre and Co., Ltd., of knopped square form, with canted corners, scroll branches, 29cm. high. (Bonhams) $2,002

A George II style silver three light candelabrum, the three turned sconces set on hexagonal drip pans and attached to the knopped central column by scrolled arms, London 1959, Mappin & Webb, 28cm. high, approximate weight 39oz. (Bonhams) $529

A Victorian silver six-light candelabrum-cum-centerpiece, Andrew Macrae, London, 1860, stem formed as twisting fruiting grape vine with three putti, 31in. high, 9010gm. (Sotheby's) $31,588

A pair of French silver-gilt candlesticks and a pair of Victorian silver-gilt three-light branches, Eloi Guèrin, Paris, 1747, the branches John Chapple & John Mantell, London, 1883, the nozzles 1908, the candlesticks: with branches: 108oz. (Bonhams) $7,238

An impressive Sheffield plated Regency candelabrum with four leaf embossed curving branches, each holding an embossed nozzle above an acanthus leaf drip pan, two of 27¼in. high. (David Lay) $1,570

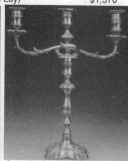

A George III silver four-light candelabrum, Benjamin Smith, London, 1815, on spreading circular partly-fluted base, cast and chased with berried acanthus foliage border, 23½in. high, 152oz. (Christie's) $10,857

Pair of Edwardian silver-gilt two-light candelabra, Lionel Alfred Crichton, 1910, each in the 18th century rococo-style with a detachable 2 light arm, height 36cm., 117oz. (Christie's) $6,580

One of a pair of early Victorian electroplated candelabra, 1846, maker's mark of Elkington & Co., of shaped square form, shell shoulders, foliated scroll branches, spool capitals, 42cm. high. (Bonhams & Brooks) (Two) $1,015

A pair of silver candlesticks, maker's mark rubbed, London, probably 1690, octagonal bases with matted decoration and engraved monogram, 16cm., 584gm.
(Sotheby's) $7,510

A pair of silver mounted tsuiki-jippo candlesticks, Meiji Period (late 19th century), each of cylindrical section and decorated in various colored enamels and silver wire, with sprays of bellflowers and foliage, 9in. high. (Christie's) $3,572

A pair of French Provincial silver candlesticks, Brest, 1770-71, maker's mark *PGR*, each on shaped hexagonal spreading base, rising to a hexagonal baluster stem and socket, 9¼in. high, 31oz.
(Bonhams) $5,429

A pair of Victorian silver candlesticks, Henry Wilkinson & Co, Sheffield, 1841, each shaped circular base chased with flutes, foliage and scrolls, 11¼in. high, gross 64oz.
(Christie's) $2,608

A pair of large Charles II style silver candlesticks, L A Crichton for Crishton Brothers, London, 1909, the quatrefoil bases molded as shells, one engraved with a crest, 11in. high, 83oz. 12dwt.
(Sotheby's) $5,006

A pair of French Provincial silver candlesticks, Paul-David Bazille, Montpellier, probably 1769, each on spreading shaped circular base and with baluster stem, 10¾in. high, 53oz. (Christie's) $5,589

A pair of German silver candlesticks, one stem formed as a naked putto astride a dolphin, the other as a putto blowing a conch shell astride a dolphin, 14½in. high, 44oz. (Christie's) $2,713

Five Victorian candlesticks, Rupert Favell, 1883 & 1891, each with a loaded square base supporting the column form stem with a classical sconce and a detachable beaded nozzle, 30.5cm.
(Christie's) (Five) $2,940

A rare pair of American silver table candlesticks, Gale & Hayden, New York, 1846, after an 18th century English model, cast and chased in full Rococo taste, 62oz., height 11in. (Sotheby's) $10,800

A pair of Victorian candlesticks modelled as Corinthian columns with waisted and beaded nozzle, raised on stepped square base with beaded edging, 9½in. high, Birmingham 1899, maker's mark *A & JC*.(Andrew Hartley) $1,078

A pair of George III travelling candlesticks, Rebecca and William Emes, London, 1808, each on spreading circular foot and with detachable plain cylindrical stems, 7.3cm. high, 309gm. (Christie's) $4,099

A pair of Belgian candlesticks, Joseph Jacquemart, Bruges, 1785, each on shaped square spreading base, chased at the corners with matted shells and scrolling acanthus, 22cm. high, 663g. (Christie's) $6,707

A pair of William III silver candlesticks, Benjamin Bathurst, London, circa 1695, the stem formed as a kneeling blackamoor with turban by his side. 9in. and 9¼in. high, 46oz. (Christie's) $24,219

A matched pair of late Victorian tortoiseshell and silver mounted dwarf candlesticks, raised on a spreading domed foot having gadroon and petal mounts, 11.2cm. and 11.4cm. high, William Comyns, London, 1890. (Woolley & Wallis) $955

A pair of George II candlesticks John Cafe, 1753, each with a six sided shell motif base and a knopped stem, with a shell decorated detachable nozzle, engraved with a crest, 23.5cm, 41oz. (Christie's) $4,836

A pair of Victorian candlesticks in the form of an ivory tusk supporting a waisted square sconce with beaded edging and issuing from a scrolling foliate bracket, 14½in. high, Sheffield 1895, by John Round. (Andrew Hartley) $1,335

A pair of George V silver short candlesticks, Sheffield 1931, in the form of Corinthian columns, the beaded sconces above a stylized capital, 6¼in. high. (Bonhams) $554

TOP TIP
18th century candlesticks are very sought after, but must be in pairs. They are made from a hollow stem cast in two halves and show two faint vertical seams where the halves are joined. Also, in the 18th century, the under-sides of candlesticks were given great attention, and are finely turned and chiselled. A rough, pitted finish is a late sign.

(Michael Bowman)

A pair of Victorian casters, Thomas Bradbury & Sons, 1887, each of baluster-form with spiral fluting, heightened by foliate, scroll and leaf motifs, 22cm. high, 20oz.
(Christie's) $1,122

An Edward VII muffineer of baluster form with spiral fluting, and flame finial, 8½in. London 1901.
(Brightwells) $270

A matched pair of sugar casters, in George III classical style, foot, the vase shaped body repoussé decorated, 9¼in. high, the Goldsmiths and Silversmiths Co. Ltd., London, 1898/1902, 33oz.
(Woolley & Wallis) $1,764

A late Victorian sugar caster, of lighthouse style, the swirl molded cylindrical body with a girdle molding, 6½in. high, William Gibson & John Langman, London 1891, 6.5oz.
(Woolley & Wallis) $485

A matched suite of three George III casters, London 1808, various makers, bun form, pull-off pierced covers, on raised circular bases on a square foot, initialled, in a later fitted case, approximate weight 7oz., height of larger caster 10cm.
(Bonhams) $617

A late Victorian sugar caster, with foliage engraving to the swirl fluted inverted elongated pear shape body, 8in., Atkin Brothers, Sheffield 1890, 8oz.
(Woolley & Wallis) $382

A rare set of three James II silver casters, Anthony Nelme, London, 1686, of lighthouse form in two sizes, engraved with armorials above crossed plumage and applied girdle, 8in., and 6in. high, 890gm.
(Sotheby's) $35,015

A German silver sugar-caster, Bernard Heinrich Weye, Augsburg, 1765/7, the pierced cover chased and with leaf and root vegetable finial, converted to a cream jug, 7½in., 10oz.
(Christie's) $2,895

A set of three George I silver casters, the larger unmarked, the pair maker's mark only of William Fleming, circa 1725, the octagonal crest and motto above applied strapwork and matting, 9½in. and 7¼in. high, 2600gm.
(Sotheby's) $72,712

An American silver centerpiece bowl, Black, Starr & Frost, New York, early 20th century, with shaped interior and everted lappet rim, on a base of four dolphins separated by shells, 1,889gm 12½in.
(Sotheby's) $3,600

A silver centerpiece bowl, Tiffany & Co., New York, 1901-1902, the broad everted wavy rim repoussé and chased with flowers, scrolls and foliage, marked under base, 22in. diameter; 182oz.
(Christie's) $14,950

A 19th century figural centerpiece by Elkington, depicting an Arab seated under a palm tree, a camel standing nearby, on rustic base, 15½in. high.
(Andrew Hartley) $616

A pair of Victorian plated centerpieces, Elkington & Co., circa 1850, each base supports a figural group, one of two boys playing a ball and stick game, the other depicting a boy and a girl with bows and arrows, height 46.3cm.
(Christie's) $4,112

Pair of German centerpiece bowls, bearing pseudomarks, late 19th century, each oval section bowl robustly decorated with cupids riding dolphins, raised on two openwork wheels, each being pulled by a winged cupid, 19.5cm., 24oz. (Christie's) $863

Large Victorian silver plated table centerpiece in Rococo taste, (lacking glass bowl to top) and standing on a circular mirrored center base, 20in. tall, circa 1860/80. (G.A. Key) $942

An American silver centerpiece bowl, Eoff & Shepherd, retailed by Ball, Black & Co, New York, 1850-70, on a domed base chased as swirling waves, with three cast dolphins supporting a simulated basketwork bowl, 54oz., height ¾in. (Sotheby's) $9,600

A silver centerpiece bowl, Whiting Mfg. Co., New York, circa 1880, on four scroll feet with stylised flame joins, the body with matted surface and dandelion and tendril cartouches, 11in. diameter, 38oz.
(Christie's) $7,475

A Chinese novelty silver condiment, maker's mark of Wang Hing, modelled as a Chinaman holding a yoke with two hanging baskets, his straw hat pulls off to reveal a condiment spoon, plus two Chinese silver condiments, modelled as rickshaws, Chinaman 4oz., 10cm. high. (Bonhams) $412

An early-Victorian miniature silver chamberstick, Charles Reiley and George Storer, the base with stylized acanthus leaves, with a side handle modelled as a leafy branch, 3oz., width 11.5cm. (Bonhams) $308

A small late Victorian bedroom candlestick, in a Regency style, the foliage capped side handle with a plain conical extinguisher, S W Smith & Co, London 1896, 4oz. (Woolley & Wallis) $368

A George III chamberstick, with urn shaped sconce, scroll handle, circular base with beaded edging, 6½in. wide, London 1781, with matched snuffer by John Schofield, 8oz 14dwt. (Andrew Hartley) $924

Good quality hallmarked silver chamberstick of circular tray form, with gadrooned edge and sconce, complete with snuffer, the base 5½in. diameter, London 1915 by The Goldsmiths & Silversmiths Company, 12oz. (G.A. Key) $565

A pair of George III bedroom candlesticks, reeded raised edges, the vase shape candleholders with snuffers slots and detachable nozzles, William Abdy II, London, 1797, 18oz. (Woolley & Wallis) $2,425

A William IV chamberstick, Thomas, James & Nathaniel Creswick, Sheffield, 1834, the shaped circular base with a piecrust rim, the scrolling handle supports the detachable conical extinguisher, height 10.5cm., 9.5oz. (Christie's) $822

A George III chamber candlestick, Paul Storr, 1809, the rectangular base with a gadroon rim, the corners heightened with shells, 16.2cm, 16oz. (Christie's) $3,290

A George II silver chamberstick, Paul de Lamerie, London, 1733, bear's claw crested below a baron's coronet within molded border strap-bound sconce, 5in. diameter, 252gm. (Sotheby's) $13,410

A George III silver chamberstick, William Stroud, London, 1804, circular and with vase-shaped socket, detachable circular nozzle, detachable snuffer and leaf-capped bracket handle, 9cm. high, 403gm. (Christie's) $1,490

Queen Anne silver chocolate-pot, William Charnelhouse, London, 1706, plain tapering cylindrical on a molded foot, the faceted scroll spout with hinged cover, 10½in. high, gross 25oz.
(Christie's) $5,609

Viennese Art Nouveau coffee and chocolate pots, of tapering cylindrical form, with floral relief decoration, 18cm. high, 765gm. total gross weight.
(Dorotheum) $1,800

John Emes, a George III chocolate biggin, of cylindrical form, raised on a spreading molded edge foot, the hinged domed cover with a detachable acorn finial, 8¾in. high, London 1806, 21.5oz. all in.
(Woolley & Wallis) $882

CHRISTENING MUGS

Victorian christening mug, Messrs Barnard, 1848, the centrally waisted mug decorated on one side with a robust farm yard scene of chickens in a field. (Christie's) $350

A William IV christening mug with deeply embossed acanthus leaves, foliate scroll handle, lobed foot, and gilt interior, 4½in. high, London 1831, 4oz 11dwt, in case.
(Andrew Hartley) $377

A William IV christening mug, Messrs Barnard, 1836, the circular section mug of lobed form, each lobe decorated with a leaf motif, 11cm., 6oz.
(Christie's) $461

CIGARETTE CASES

19th century Russian silver cigarette case / vesta case, maker's mark of G. Grachev, the whole embossed with a sunburst design, the top fitted with a hinged compartment for matches, 9.8cm.
(Bonhams) $441

A Continental silver and enamel cigarette case, probably Austrian, import marks for London 1920, the hinged lid with an enamel scene illustrating the dangers of excess, 9cm. high.(Bonhams) $2,646

A late Victorian silver and enamel cigarette case, Birmingham 1887, maker's mark possibly that of J Walker, the hinged lid depicting a woman wearing décolleté black dress, two red flowers at her corsage, 8.5cm. high.
(Bonhams) $588

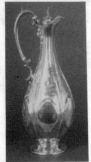

A Victorian claret jug, Martin & Hall, Sheffield, 1889, the bellied jug of faceted form, each facet with a medallion motif, overall engraved with foliate scroll motifs, 33.5cm. 23oz. gross. (Christie's) $1,277

A late Victorian cut glass claret jug, the knopped neck ovoid body with cut linked design and stars of David, on a panelled and star cut foot. (Woolley & Wallis) $191

A William IV silver claret jug, D C Rait, London, 1834, chased with bacchanalian processions on a matted vine-strewn ground below acanthus girdle, 12¾in. high, 1220gm. (Sotheby's) $6,07

A late Victorian glass claret jug, the swirl molded body with a pierced repoussé silver mounted flange and neck decorated with flowers and rocaille scrolls to a trellis ground, 9in., Gibson and Langman, London, 1896.
(Woolley & Wallis) $1,617

A pair of French silver-gilt mounted cut-glass claret jugs, maker's mark AL with cockerel between, Paris, circa 1890, the spout formed as an eagle's mask, 12in. high. (Bonhams) $6,332

A Victorian claret jug, Martin & Hall Sheffield, 1888, the pear shaped body with raised tear motifs on a graduated ground, raised on a pedestal foot with a beaded rim, 29.4cm., 23oz. gross. (Christie's) $851

A mid-Victorian silver mounted claret jug, London 1858, John Figg, the replacement later glass body of circular tapering form with bulbous base, height 27cm.
(Bonhams) $368

An early Victorian silver claret jug, London 1841, John Mortimer and John Samuel Hunt, of askos form, leaf capped bifurcated scroll handle terminating in an angel motif, 34oz, 22cm. high.
(Bonhams) $3,003

A Victorian silver-mounted cut glass claret jug, Charles Edwards, 1887, the oval body engraved with bird and exotic flower motifs, above cut diamond motifs, 33.3cm.
(Christie's) $5,452

Continental enamelled and gilt-metal-mounted ewer and hinged cover, Bohemian or South German, e spirally-molded globular body ainted and gilt with sprays of wild owers and grasses, late 19th entury, 29.5cm. high. Christie's) **$894**

Mid Victorian silver plated claret jug of circular baluster form, well engraved with foliate designs, circa 1870 by Elkington and Co, 10in. high. (G.A. Key) **$169**

An Austro-Hungarian parcel-gilt silver novelty claret jug, maker's mark *A* over *BA*, Pest, 1872-1922, modelled as a griffin, the gilt head set with red glass eyes, 8¾in. high, 28oz. (Sotheby's) **$1,848**

German silver-mounted cut glass aret jug, mid 19th century, the obular body cut with diamond otifs, raised on a short pedestal ot with four grotesque mask motif et, 33.5cm. hristie's) **$1,873**

Pair of French silver-mounted cut glass claret jugs, late 19th century, each spiral lobed tear drop form glass body with a leaf and flower motif neck, height 28.5cm. (Christie's) **$4,112**

A Victorian Scottish presentation claret jug, maker's mark *JM*, Glasgow, 1849, the pear shaped jug of lobed form, engraved with foliate scroll and lattice motifs, the hinged lid with a squirrel finial, 11½in., 28oz. gross. (Christie's) **$2,555**

19th century Chinese claret jug, ker's mark of *T. H.* unidentified, body part chased with bamboo coration on a matted ckground, approximate weight oz., 35cm. high. onhams) **$1,396**

A late 19th century Continental glass claret jug, the ribbed molded body with rococo chased silver colored metal mounts, 11¼in., 800 standard. (Woolley & Wallis) **$794**

A Victorian silver-mounted claret jug, maker's mark *CF*, Sheffield, 1870, the tapering glass body engraved with a central bird in flight motif, further decorated with fern and flower motifs, 28.6cm. (Christie's) **$1,363**

A set of four William IV silver wine coasters, Benjamin Smith, London, 1831, the openwork sides silver cast with fruiting vines, the center engraved with a regimental badge with Royal crown above, 16cm. diameter, gross 112oz.
(Christie's) $26,082

A pair of Victorian silver decanter wagons, Edward Barnard & Sons, London, 1844, four vine decorated coasters with turnover rims, turned wood bases, 18½in. long.
(Sotheby's) $29,875

Two Irish coasters, the deep sides pierced and chased with fruiting grape vines, a gadroon rim, one late 18th century Dublin, the other Dublin, 1822, maker E Power.
(Woolley & Wallis) $3,08

A pair of Victorian silver wine-coasters, Edward and James Barnard, London, 1838, with cast sides formed as openwork grapevines and with grapevine border, 6in. diameter.
(Christie's) $6,876

A pair of George III parcel-gilt wine coasters, Sheffield 1809, maker's mark of John Poyton and Co., fluted decoration, with shaped circular borders, gadroon borders, fluted silver-gilt centers, crested, wooden bases, 15.6cm. diameter.
(Bonhams) $3,381

A pair of George III wine coasters London, marks rubbed, probably 1814, circular fluted bellied from, gadroon borders, wooden bases with central initialled buttons, 15.4cm. diameter.
(Bonhams) $1,470

A pair of George III silver wine-coasters, Rebecca Emes and Edward Barnard, London, 1808, each circular and with pierced gallery sides, 13cm. diameter.
(Christie's) $3,075

Four William IV silver coasters, Henry Wilkinson & Co, Sheffield, 1833, circular, pierced with bacchanalian masks and urns between fruiting grape vines, 6in. diameter.(Sotheby's) $6,794

A pair of George III silver wind-coasters, William Plummer, London, 1781, each circular, the sides pierced with scrolls and bright-cut engraved with a band of husks, 4¾in. diameter.
(Christie's) $4,343

A George III Irish vase shape coffee-pot, raised on a domed spreading foot chased with a band of foliage, 11½in., James Graham, Dublin circa 1770, 32oz. all in. (Woolley & Wallis) $10,588

Attractive large Victorian silver pot of circular baluster form, chased with foliate scrolls, heavily embossed spout and handle in Rococo style, 10in. tall, London 1853, maker R P, 27oz. (G.A. Key) $711

An American silver large coffee pot, Joseph and Nathaniel Richardson, Philadelphia, circa 1780, the domed foot with embossed beaded border, 1,166gm, height 32.7cm. (Sotheby's) $30,650

A George II coffee pot, maker's mark rubbed, 1750, the tapering body with a carved wood handle, raised on a spreading foot, 22.8cm., 21.5oz. (Christie's) $1,415

A Baltic silver coffee-pot, Kiel, circa 1800, plain cylindrical with reeded foot, plain tapering spout, turned wooden handle and stepped domed upper section, 7½in., gross 24oz. (Bonhams) $4,343

Continental coffee pot, 19th century, baluster-form with spiral reeding, flattened handle with ivory heat stops, 7¼in. high, approximately 13 troy oz. (Skinner) $288

George II coffee pot of tapering orm, turned finial on domed lid, oliate spout, ebony scrolled handle nd molded base, 7½in. high. ondon 1738, 15oz. 2dwt. Andrew Hartley) $1,884

A Continental silver coffee pot, probably Belgian, circa 1750, pear-shaped on four bifurcated scroll feet, the broadly fluted body with scroll spout, 15cm. high, 347gm. (Christie's) $4,705

An important George II silver coffee-pot, Paul de Lamerie, London, 1742, flat chased around the lid, spout, upper and lower body with rocaille and scrolls, 9¾in. high, 1090gm. (Sotheby's) $41,869

A George III coffee biggin on stand, William Burwash & Richard Sibley, 1811, with a gadrooned rim and a carved wood handle, raised on a conforming stand, 30.5cm., 39oz. (Christie's) $1,727

A George III coffee pot, London 1760, maker's mark worn, scroll handle, domed hinged cover with a fluted finial, approximate weight 32oz., 27.5cm. high. (Bonhams) $2,205

A George IV coffee pot on stand, baluster with ivory scroll handle and cover finial, with burner, London 1829 by Robert Garrard II, 45.5oz. 29.2cm. (Bristol) $1,088

A George II coffee pot, Fuller White, circa 1750, the tapering coffee-pot with flat chased foliate scroll motifs, centering and engraved coat-of-arms, 21.4cm. 16.5oz. (Christie's) $950

A William IV Scottish coffee pot, Elder & Co., Edinburgh, 1832, the tapering coffee pot with foliate scroll and floral motifs, with an ivory insulated leaf capped handle, 27cm., 28oz. gross. (Christie's) $2,175

A George III coffee pot, London 1783, maker's mark of Hester Bateman, scroll handle, domed hinged cover with an urn finial, leaf capped spout, approximate weight 24oz., 29.8cm. high. (Bonhams) $5,880

A George III silver coffee-jug on stand with burner, Paul Storr, London, 1818, on tripod stand with claw feet on incurved base, headed by pendant rings 11in. high, gross 57oz. (Christie's) $9,951

A George II Irish silver coffee-pot, William Williamson, Dublin, 1734, plain tapering and on spreading rim foot, with curved spout, 8¼in. high, 28oz. (Christie's) $18,630

A Belgian silver coffee-pot, Mons, 1784, maker's mark a pear, fluted pear-shaped and on three bracket feet headed by flower clusters, 34.5cm. high, 1,012gm. (Bonhams) $4,720

A George II cream jug, Ayme Videau, 1740, the inverted pear shape jug with chased foliate scroll and flute motifs, raised on a conforming foot, 15cm., 6oz. (Christie's) $2,935

Fine George III silver cream jug of slightly compressed oval design, having raised body bands, bright cut decoration, well marked for London 1802 by Godbehere, Wigan and Bult. (G.A. Key) $290

Russian cream jug, 1829, ovoid form on low foot, with reeded lobing to lower section of body, with applied floral band at girdle, 4¾in. approximately 6 troy oz. (Skinner) $374

Charles Fox II, a George IV cream jug, of bellied form, on a cast and matted foot, with a beaded scroll handle, London, 1824, 7oz. (Woolley & Wallis) $500

Edwardian silver cream jug in George I style, helmet shaped, chased and embossed with foliate designs, having leaf capped scrolled handle, supported on three hoof feet, 4in. tall overall, Birmingham 1905. (G.A. Key) $94

A George III cream jug, the inverted pear shape body raised on a gadroon edge circular spreading foot, London 1774, 4.25oz. (Woolley & Wallis) $176

A George II 'Sparrow Beak' cream jug, London 1734, maker's mark of Thomas Rush, baluster form, scroll handle, plain spout, the whole on a raised circular foot, approximate weight 3oz., 9cm. high. (Bonhams) $1,470

A George II silver-gilt cream jug, circa 1750, attributed to Nicholas Sprimont, formed as a fluted shell and on shaped shell foot encrusted with seaweed and smaller shells, 5½in. long, 9oz. (Christie's) $27,945

A George IV cream jug, Robert Hennell, 1825, of inverted pear form with foliate scroll and flute motifs raised on a conforming foot, with a leaf capped handle, 12.5cm., 7oz. (Christie's) $725

A pair of late-Victorian silver novelty cruets, London 1882, Thomas Johnson, realistically modelled as a pair of chicks, with pull-off heads, height 4cm. (Bonhams) $462

A Dutch silver egg-cruet with four George III silver egg-cups, Henry Chawner, London, 1789, the cruet formed as an oval basket on four ball-and-claw feet, 6¾in. long, 24oz. (Bonhams) $7,600

An unusual George II four-bottle silver cruet, Arthur Annesley, London, 1757, armorial engraved triangular frame of trailing fruiting grape vines applied with flies and snails also forming the handle, 10in long, 945gm. (Sotheby's) $8,58:

A silver plated cruet stand with beaded borders, surmounted by an over handle, fitted with six assorted yellow glass bottles, one bottle stamped for Walker & Hall, 17cm. wide. (Bonhams) $162

A 19th century Chinese egg cruet frame, marked with pseudo English marks, maker's mark of Sunshing, central column with four spoon holders, with four circular egg cups with reeded borders, crested, approximate weight 18oz., 20.5cm. high. (Bonhams) $809

A George III silver egg-cruet, William Burwash and Richard Sibley, London, 1809, the square stand with cut corners and on four detachable winged sphinx caryatic and lion's paw feet, 11½in. high, 95oz. (Christie's) $4,84.

A George III cruet stand of rounded oblong form with reeded loop handle and splayed feet, 7in. wide, and containing five original cut glass cruets, London 1810. (Andrew Hartley) $700

A George III silver egg-cruet, William Bateman, London, 1817, fitted with twelve plain vase-shaped egg-cups with molded borders, with twelve spoon holders, 9in. high, 41oz. (Christie's) $5,216

A George III silver cruet, Robert and David Hennell, London, 1799 also with mustard-spoon, George Smith, London, 1799 and sugar spoon, London, 1798, 10in. high. (Christie's) $4,705

A George III Irish two handled cup, Matthew West, Dublin, 1777, also struck with another maker's mark, possibly *RT*, of campana form with a central reeded band, 13.9cm., 12oz. (Christie's) $851

A late 17th century / early 18th century Belgian invalid feeding cup, Ypres, maker's mark possibly that of Joannes Bapt de Somes, with two plain scroll handles, the feeding spout supported by a plain bar, approximate weight 4oz., 6.3cm. high. (Bonhams) $10,290

An American silver three-handled loving cup, Tiffany & Co., New York, circa 1885, the three scroll handles extending to form tightly-scrolled feet, 1,392gm. 22.9cm. (Sotheby's) $4,200

An important German silver-gilt cup formed as a squirrel and set with natural beryl crystal, Augsburg, 1580-1585, maker's mark a clover leaf in circular punch, holding in his front paws a natural opaque green and white hexagonal beryl crystal, 7in. high, gross 15oz.
(Christie's) $171,720

An American silver and mixed metals "American Indian style" three-handled loving cup, Tiffany & Co., New York, circa 1885, the slightly bombé bowl raised on three feet formed as hairy buffalo heads above hoofs, 2,504gm., 25.4cm. (Sotheby's) $61,125

A Chinese silver two-handled cup and cover, maker's mark of A.Lock, embossed with figural scenes in landscapes below engraved foliate decoration, approximate weight 41oz., 29.5cm. high.
(Bonhams) $1,323

Bigelow, Kennard & Co. horn mounted presentation cup, late 19th century, raised on reticulated domed foot, with diapering, rocaille scrolls and roses, 11½in. high, approximately 60 troy oz.
(Skinner) $3,105

A George III silver cup and cover, Thomas Pitts, London, 1767, the detachable domed cover with flame finial, with gadrooned borders, 15¼in., 77oz.
(Christie's) $6,332

A William and Mary Scottish thistle Cup, Andrew Law II, Edinburgh, 1694, Assay Master John Borthwick, the tapering circular section mug with a flaring rim, 7oz.
(Christie's) $8,519

Good quality late Victorian silver plated bacon dish, oval shaped with three quarter fluted decoration, supported on four fluted legs terminating in claw feet, 12 x 9in. (G.A. Key) $174

Good quality Edwardian silver plated fruit comport, embossed and pierced with shells and fruit etc, 10½in. diameter. (G.A. Key) $102

A late Victorian silver swing-handled bon-bon dish, Birmingham 1898, maker's mark of *WT*, of navette form, ovolo borders, with shell and scroll motifs, part reeded swing handle, approximate weight 7.5oz. (Bonhams) $262

A late Victorian silver gilt swing-handled dish, London 1878, Walter and John Barnard, the body with engraved and vari-colored gold floral decoration, approximate weight 6.5cm., 17.5cm. long. (Bonhams) $618

Samuel Herbert & Co., a pair of George II butter shells, engraved with a hound's head crest, scallop shell lifts, on cast scroll legs with stepped hoof feet, London, 1751, 5oz. (Woolley & Wallis) $1,764

A George III entree dish and cover, London 1810, maker's mark of Paul Storr, shell and gadroon border, the domed pull-off cover with fluted and gadrooned borders, approximate weight 62oz., 28cm. diameter.(Bonhams) $9,849

An Arts and Crafts silver and enamel dish, London 1925, maker's mark of Omar Ramsden, spot hammered surface, the center set with a silver and red enamelled medallion, approximate weight 2oz., 11in. diameter.(Bonhams) $470

An Edwardian silver comport, with a gadrooned rim, fretwork border and set on a knopped stem, Sheffield 1911, John Dixon and Sons, 20cm. diameter, approximately 15oz. (Bonhams) $279

A George I silver strawberry dish, Paul de Lamerie, London, 1715, of fluted square form on rim foot and engraved with rococo armorials, 7in. square, 308gm. (Sotheby's) $6,794

A late 18th century French vegetable dish and cover, of circular form with two leaf-capped handles, the rising cover surmounted by an artichoke finial, Paris, 1788, 28cm. wide. (Christie's) $1,029

A George III venison dish and matching Old Sheffield Plate cover and stand, Paul Storr, London, 1809, the cover by Matthew Boulton, circa 1809, dish 25¾in. long, 194oz. (Christie's) $17,697

An American silver-gilt terrapin dish and spoon, Gorham Mfg. Co., Providence, RI, retailed by Bailey, Banks, and Biddle, Philadelphia, 1898, of bombé rectangular form, 39oz., length of bowl over handles 11½in. (Sotheby's) $8,400

A pair of modern dishes, Omar Ramsden, 1936, each circular dish with a crenulated rim and a central red enamelled Tudor rose motif boss, 11.3cm., 5.5oz. (Christie's) $1,294

A pair of George IV butter shells, the shaped lifts decorated with applied shells and leafage, on three cast whelk feet, Samuel Dutton, London 1826, 10oz. (Woolley & Wallis) $1,544

Elkington & Co, a Victorian cast grape dish of naturalistic vine leaves and a tendril handle, suspended a pair of cast grape vine handle scissors. (Woolley & Wallis) $235

A pair of French covered entree dishes on stands, maker's mark *TH* in a lozenge with a clover between, 20th century, each of circular section with a shaped reed and leaf decorated border, diameter of stand 31.5cm., 141oz. (Christie's) $3,125

A Baltic silver dish, Jürgen Linden, Riga, dated *1680*, the center chased with the mythological scene of a dragon slain by arrows, the hero standing with a bow, 20¾in. long, 36oz. (Christie's) $64,800

A pair of silver-gilt strawberry dishes, unmarked, circa 1720, circular with fluted sixteen panel scalloped sides, the centers armorial engraved within baroque cartouches, 23.5cm., 1008gm. (Sotheby's) $13,946

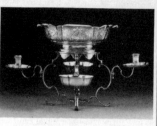

A 19th century Irish épergne, comprising a cut glass bowl with crenellated rim on baluster turned support with scroll, shell and leaf edging, 22½in. hígh.
(Andrew Hartley) $2,826

An Austrian silver épergne, Johannes Michel Laing or Johannes Martin Lobmayr, Vienna, 1737, the openwork frame with four scroll supports and with two detachable branches, 8¾in. high, 31oz.
(Christie's) $12,666

Early 20th century silver plated épergne centerpiece, having a central large trumpet shaped vase with fluted foot and foliate pierced top, 14in. tall.
(G.A. Key) $220

EWERS

An Italian ewer, the circular serpentine edge molded spreading foot to a knopped stem to a pear shaped panelled body, 11¼in. high.
(Woolley & Wallis) $1,470

A 19th century Belgian silver ewer, marks for 1831-1869, also marked with a W below a hammer, rosette mounted ivory scroll handle terminating in a mask, approximate weight 14oz., 24.2cm. high.
(Bonhams) $882

An Italian silver ewer, Naples, late 17th century, with leaf-capped and beaded winged demi-figure handle with grotesque mask terminal, 9in. high, 24oz.
(Christie's) $18,630

FLAGONS

A George IV silver flagon, Charles Price, London, 1824, the lower part of the body, the underside of the spout and the cover chased with acanthus foliage, 11in. high, 70oz.
(Christie's) $4,860

A pair of German silver-gilt flagons, unmarked, late 19th century, each with scroll handle with grotesque goat mask terminal and demi-female hippocamp and ball finial, 13½in. high, 85oz.
(Bonhams) $7,700

A George III flagon, London 1771, maker's mark probably that of Charles Wright, scroll handle, domed hinged cover with a pierced shell thumbpiece, approximate weight 42oz., 31cm. high.
(Bonhams) $2,058

A Charles II 'notched' trefid spoon, with plain rat tail, pricked *W.D. jan.6. 1673*, by Lawrence Coles, 1673, 19.5cm. long, 1.5oz. (Christie's) $976

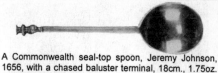

A Commonwealth seal-top spoon, Jeremy Johnson, 1656, with a chased baluster terminal, 18cm., 1.75oz. (Christie's) $2,138

A Queen Anne wavy-end or dog-nose tablespoon, with a plain rat-tail scratched *C.A.M.* on the back of the terminal, Samuel Lee, circa 1705, 20.25cm. long, 2oz. (Christie's) $135

A silver tablespoon, Paul Revere, Boston, circa 1770, with downturned handle engraved with script monogram *AJH*, 8⁷/₈in. long: 2oz. (Christie's) $9,200

A Continental silver basting spoon, probably Scandinavian, circa 1800, maker's mark *MW*, shaped handle, the reverse engraved with monogram *JJ* within oval cartouche and with wreath above, 15¾in. ong, 301g. (Christie's) $559

A James II/William & Mary Provincial trefid spoon, the stem with a line border, the reverse pricked with the initials *T.D. M.C.*, and the date *1699*, John Peard, Barnstaple, circa 1699, 19.75cm. long, 13oz., in a fitted case. (Christie's) $3,110

A George III Irish fish slice, George Nagle, Dublin, 810, Old English pattern, engraved with initials, the lade pierced with fish motifs, 11¼in., 4oz. Christie's) $766

A Danish silver basting spoon, Johan August Rettig Bang, Copenhagen, 1785, shaped handle, the reverse of bowl and handle chased with rocaille and scrolls, 15in. long, 5oz. (Christie's) $708

A George III Irish straining spoon, John Sheils, Dublin, 790, bright cut pointed Old English pattern, engraved with initials, 12in. (Christie's) $1,056

An Irish Provincial soup ladle, Joseph Johns, Limerick, circa 1770, Hook End pattern, engraved with a crest, 39cm., 8oz. (Christie's) $4,259

A George III Irish hook end soup ladle, Dublin 1760, maker's mark of Isaac D'Olier, shell shaped bowl, with a shell heel, the terminal modelled as a bird's head, rested and with a motto, approximate weight 8oz., 4cm. long. (Bonhams) $5,586

A Charles I Apostle spoon, St. Peter, Richard Crosse, 1641, the gilded figure of the saint with large nimbus, later engraved with initials, holding the Key of Heaven in his left hand, 19cm., 2oz. (Christie's) $2,632

A Continental silver soup ladle with oak leaf and acorn decorated stem, engraved initials. (Brightwells) $74

A Victorian gravy spoon, reeded Old English pattern engraved with a crest, London 1842, maker: W.E. (Brightwells) $250

A Victorian E.P. Stilton scoop with carved ivory andle. (Brightwells) $100

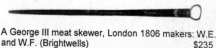

A George III meat skewer, London 1806 makers: W.E. and W.F. (Brightwells) $235

Nine Tiffany & Co. "Chrysanthemum" pattern tablespoons, late 19th century, 8½in. long., approximately 30 troy oz. total.
(Skinner) $1,265

An assembled silver flatware service, maker's mark of Tiffany & Co., New York, 20th century, Chrysanthemum pattern, variously monogramed, comprising 322 pieces, 513oz. 10dwt. weighable silver. (Christie's) $29,900

A silver canteen for twelve, Sheffield 1934 and 1935, maker's mark of *SSP & Cco*, rat-tail pattern, including, 12 table forks, 11 dessert forks, 10 dessert spoons, 12 soup spoons, 4 table spoons, 12 soup spoons, 4 table spoons, 8 teaspoons, 12 fish forks, 12 fish knives, approximate total weighable 182oz.
(Bonhams) $3,542

A Continental mahogany cased campaign flatware set, unmarked, possibly first half 18th century, the hinged octagonal mahogany case with a velvet lined, fitted interior holding three pistol grip handles, a silver spoon, three tined fork and a knife blade, a marrow scoop/spoon, a folding corkscrew and a two compartment spice box, height of box 15.3cm.
(Christie's) $4,200

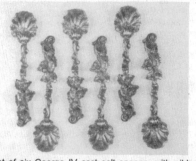

A set of six George IV cast salt spoons, with gilded shell bowls and rocaille stems of tendrils, leaves and flowers, by Charles Rawlings, 1824, 11cm. long, 6.5oz. (Christie's) $1,382

Two late 16th/early 17th century seal top spoons, York hallmarked, maker's mark indistinct.
(Brightwells) $2,145

586

A 19th century Maltese goblet, maker's mark of *E.C.,* with an engraved foliate cartouche, and inscribed, approximate weight 8oz., 13cm. high. (Bonhams) $412

A pair of George III Irish goblets, Richard Sawyer, Dublin, 1814, each of typical form raised on a pedestal foot with a reeded rim, 6in., 17.5oz. (Christie's) $2,214

A George III goblet, Solomon Hougham, 1816, the straight sided goblet with a flaring rim and a band of engraved grape, vine and leaf motifs, 6in., 10oz. (Christie's) $851

A pair of George III silver-gilt wine goblets, London 1804, maker's mark of John Emes, part fluted decoration below a chased border of raspberries, on a matted background, approximate weight 25oz., 18cm. high. (Bonhams) $3,822

A mid Victorian goblet, London 1869, maker's mark of Stephen Smith, circular tapering bowl supported by an ivy leaf and branch stem, the whole on a raised circular base with beaded border, approximate weight 10.5oz., 20.3cm. high.(Bonhams) $853

Charles Wright, a pair of George III wine goblets, the bowls engraved with a crest of a wolf's head, gilded inside, each on a cast stem foot with a fine gadroon knop, 6½in. high, London, 1771, 17oz. (Woolley & Wallis) $2,499

A Charles II goblet, maker's mark *CP,* 1661, the bowl of circular section with later chased foliate scroll and cartouche motifs, centering a shield with an engraved date, 18.6cm., 13oz. (Christie's) $3,972

A pair of George III Irish goblets, Matthew West, Dublin, 1794, each of baluster form, decorated with spiral fluting, raised on a slightly domed foot, 5¾in., 19.5oz. (Christie's) $2,896

A George III goblet, London 1781, maker's mark of William Brockwell, plain urn shaped bowl, on a raised circular foot with a beaded border, crested approximate weight 7oz., 14.2cm. high. (Bonhams) $853

A Spanish silver inkstand, Camino, Madrid, 1798, fitted with two vase-shaped inkspots, and similar pen-holder and sander, the center with a bell with baluster handle, 8¼in. square, 61oz.
(Christie's) $14,114

An Edwardian silver inkstand, set on four compressed bun feet, surmounted by two cut glass and hinged silver topped inkwells, Chester 1912, George Nathan and Ridley Hayes.
(Bonhams) $441

A William IV silver inkstand with Victorian fittings, Joseph and John Angell, London, 1834, the fittings John Newton Mappin, London, 1892, in the Gothic Revival style, 12in. long, 64oz.
(Christie's) $4,523

A 19th century Spanish ink stand, Barcelona, assay master P. Mas, with two urns of campana form, one with a sander, the other with an inkwell, and with a central winged mythical beast supporting a table bell, approximate weight 30oz., 26.5cm. long.
(Bonhams) $617

An Edwardian inkwell modelled in the form of a fox's head with hinged lid revealing glass liner, raised on molded square base with pen rests, on bun feet, 5½in. wide, London 1909.
(Andrew Hartley) $502

A George III silver inkstand, William Vincent, London, 1775, the bottle covers by Harry Wright Atkin, Sheffield, 1921, fitted with combination bell and tapestick, with spool-shaped socket and detachable openwork flame finial, 13¼in. long, 50oz.
(Christie's) $4,704

A Spanish silver inkstand, Francisco de Paula Martos, Cordoba, 1831, fitted with three detachable vase-shaped ink and sand holders with bead and scroll borders, one fitted with glass liner, 7½in. long, gross 24oz.
(Christie's) $1,677

A Victorian inkwell, Samuel Watton Smith, 1898, of circular form with a shell and leaf heightened foot, the hinged lid with a similar edge, with a glass liner.
(Christie's) $410

A William IV silver-gilt inkstand, Joseph Willmore, Birmingham, 1834, the rectangular stand with thistle, clover, leaf and flower motif sides, gilt lid, length 13.6cm., 5.5oz.
(Christie's) $739

An Edwardian hot water jug, of lobular form with a ribbed neck, on wavy apron foot, by Mappin & Vebb, 1902, 16cm., 15.5oz. Christie's) $588

Victorian previously silver plated hot water jug in the style of a watering can. (G.A. Key) $408

George III silver milk jug of slightly compressed oval design, having raised reeded body band, gadrooned rim and supported on four ball feet, 5½in. long, London 1808 by the Batemans. (G.A. Key) $251

George III silver beer-jug, William Grundy, London, 1768, plain baluster-form and on a circular foot, with leaf-capped scroll handle, 4.5cm. high, 1,289g. Christie's) $6,152

A late Victorian silver cream jug and sugar bowl, Chester 1898, maker's mark of *GNRH*, the bodies embossed and chased with rabbits and pheasants in a foliate landscape, approximate weight 9oz., height of cream jug 10cm. (Bonhams) $339

A Chinese silver milk jug, maker's mark of Khecheong, simulated bamboo scroll handle and border, with panels of bamboo decoration on matted backgrounds, approximate weight 16oz., 17.3cm. high. (Bonhams) $662

A modern bellied wine jug, with a stylized loop handle, 8½in. high. Makers Turner & Simpson Ltd, Birmingham, 1971, 19oz. Woolley & Wallis) $544

Large Victorian silver milk jug, shell and scroll engraved, on cast four footed base, 6in. tall, London 1847. (G.A. Key) $239

A Spanish silver shaving-jug, Salamanca, circa 1750, the scroll handle with ivory insulators, the short curved spout with hinged cover, 8in. high, 23oz. (Christie's) $3,240

Attractive George III silver milk jug, oval shaped with ovolo rim, reeded angular handle, later embossed with a continuous rural landscape with cattle, 4in. x 2½in., London 1810. (G.A. Key) $165

A 19th century French silver hot milk jug, Paris, domed hinged cover with a knop finial, ebonized baluster side handle, approximate weight 8oz., 15cm. high. (Bonhams) $382

A German hot water pot, maker's mark J.KA?, possibly Heilbronn, mid 18th century, of asymmetrically lobed pear form engraved with a coat-of-arms, raised on a conforming foot, 20cm., 13oz. (Christie's) $1,480

An octagonal pear shape hot milk jug, raised on a stepped foot, the short spout to a hinged domed cover with girdled globe finial, 9¼in., high, Thomas Bradbury & Sons Ltd., London 1925, 17oz. all in. (Woolley & Wallis) $147

A modern cream jug and sugar caster, in the Neo Classical style with urn shaped bodies, the upper bodies, with a frieze of medallions and garlands, maker's mark A.I. Birmingham 1911, jug 6¼in. high. (Woolley & Wallis) $338

A George I silver covered jug, John Edwards, London, 1719, Britannia standard, baluster with reeded girdle above engraved armorials and spreading support, 10in. high, 1015gm. (Sotheby's) $15,198

A George II hot water jug, William Shaw & William Priest, 1753, of pear shape with a raffia covered handle and a beaded beak form spout, 24.7cm., 20oz. (Christie's) $1,467

A George II silver cow-creamer, John Schuppe, London, 1756, fashioned with a curled tail and horns, the spine tooled with hair, the hinged cover chased with a garland of flowers and applied with a fly, 5¾in. long, 4oz. (Christie's) $9,951

A George III beer jug, plain baluster form, raised on a spreading circular foot with a large leaf capped 'S' scroll handle, 9¾in. high, probably William Cripps, London, 1764, 35oz. (Woolley & Wallis) $5,292

An Edwardian silver ring stand, Birmingham 1907, maker's mark of Deakin & Francis Ltd., the circular base mounted with a pair of silver antlers.
(Bonhams & Brooks) $140

An Edwardian silver card case, Birmingham 1904, Matthews, hinged lid, the front embossed with angels' heads amongst clouds in a raised cartouche, height 10.3cm.
(Bonhams) $308

A late Victorian or Edwardian silver plated spirit dispenser, in the form of a barrel mounted on a cart, the framework stamped to the underside with registration lozenge, 15½in. long overall.
(Christie's) $1,974

A George III lemon strainer, London 1774, maker's mark of William Vincent, circular form, scroll handle, with a clip, approximate weight 2oz., 8.8cm. diameter.
(Bonhams) $323

A pair of Art Nouveau silver Valentine napkin rings, London 1910, maker's mark for Omar Ramsden and Alwyn Carr, each with a coloured red or blue enamel heart cartouche, 5½cm. long.
(Bonhams) $1,115

An Edwardian silver cased mantel clock, London 1901, maker's mark of William Comyns, the sides and back embossed with courting couples in 18th century dress within scroll cartouches, 19.5cm. high.
(Bonhams) $1,397

A Belgian silver-gilt argyle, 1831-68, with wood loop handle, fluted spout and hinged hot-water spout, 6in. high, 22oz.
(Bonhams) $4,343

A German plaque, maker's mark ?F in a heart shaped shield, first half 18th century, with a slightly crimped and foliate scroll motif rim, 29.5cm., 8.25oz. (Christie's) $776

An Edwardian silver ink brush of circular moded form with loaded base, 6.5cm. (Thomson Roddick & Medcalf) $123

A Queen Anne mug, maker's mark *R.S, E.L*, 1702, of straight sided form with part fluting, centering a cartouche, 9cm., 5oz. (Christie's) $829

English late Victorian shaving mug, London, 1898, maker's mark *Gy & Co.*, domed lid with small trefoil thumbpiece opening to soap receptacle and folding brush bracket, 4in. high, approximately 8 troy oz. (Skinner) $431

A Queen Anne silver mug, Alice Sheene, London, 1708, the body chased with reeded bands and with scroll handle, 10.5cm. high, 234gm. (Christie's) $5,589

J.E. Caldwell & Co. coin mug, Philadelphia, mid-19th century, octagonal form, chased and embossed with floral sprays and C-scrolls, 3½in. high, approximately 5 troy oz. (Skinner) $230

A pair of Queen Anne silver mugs, Humphrey Payne, London, 1704, Britannia standard, tapering cylindrical, lion crested within baroque cartouche on the fluted sides, 4in. high, 14oz. (Sotheby's) $11,622

A George II Irish mug, maker's mark rubbed, *W?*, Dublin, circa 1740, the baluster mug raised on a slightly domed foot, with a leaf capped scroll handle, 12cm., 10oz. (Christie's) $1,192

A Victorian silver baluster mug, the body with chased floral decoration, with a scrolled side handle, London 1861, 12cm. high, approximately 10oz. (Bonhams) $250

A George II mug, Thomas Farren, 1735, of slightly tapering circular section with later chased portrait medallion of King William, 14.6cm, 18oz. (Christie's) $1,727

A George III baluster pint mug with leafage scroll handle, London 1773, Maker: FK. (Brightwells) $742

A Victorian mustard pot, William Gough, Birmingham, 1854, of circular form with pierced sides, the hinged lid with a pierced thumbpiece, 6.9cm. high. (Christie's) $344

A Victorian oval mustard pot, the part ribbed tapering body to a reeded edge and gilt interior with a clear glass liner, J A H & T Savory, London 1880, 7oz. (Woolley & Wallis) $426

A George III silver mustard pot, London 1810, Robert Metham, reeded border and reeded girdle, domed hinged lid with ball finial, approximate weight 3.5oz., width 7.5cm. (Bonhams) $265

An important early pair of George I silver mustard pots, Jacob Margos, London, 1724, barrel form, engraved with the Royal arms of George I above reeded girdle strap, 4in. high, 672gm. (Sotheby's) $116,667

A Victorian novelty mustard pot, the hinged lid with a monkey sitting on a barrel, a blue glass liner and a scroll handle, Henry Holland, London, 1871, 3.25oz. (Woolley & Wallis) $1,147

Hester Bateman, a George III cylindrical mustard pot, with bands of pierced leaves and oval florets and engraved with floral swags, a blue glass liner, London, 1787. (Woolley & Wallis) $1,205

An early Victorian silver mustard pot, London 1853, John Figg, the body pierced with scroll decoration, blue glass liner, approximate weighable 4.5cm., height 7.5cm. (Bonhams) $431

A novelty Victorian silver mustard pot, Robert Hennell, London, 1868, cast in the form of Mr Punch, 4in. high, 242gm. (Sotheby's) $16,092

A George III silver mustard pot and matching mustard spoon, London 1780, Hester Bateman, the spoon, London 1788, the body pierced with urns and stylized bands, blue glass liner, weighable 4oz., height 7.5cm. (Bonhams) $1,078

A 19th century Chinese silver pepper pot, marked with pseudo English marks, maker's mark of Yatshing, part fluted girdle, gadroon border, screw off cover with a cone finial, approximate weight 3oz., 9.8cm. high.(Bonhams) $162

Heavy pair of silver peppers of ovium form, having gadrooned rims and supported on shell and hoof feet, 2½in. tall, Chester 1922. (G.A. Key) $80

A Victorian silver novelty pepper pot, London 1873, maker's mark of Edward Charles Brown, modelled as an owl, the pull-off lid pierced and set with two glass eyes, the body realistically engraved with feathers, 7.5cm. high. (Bonhams) $617

PHOTO FRAMES

A late-Victorian silver photograph frame, London 1899, maker's mark of William Comyns, of shaped upright rectangular form, pierced with scroll and foliate decoration, easel back, 21cm. high. (Bonhams & Brooks) $276

A silver travelling photograph frame, London 1922, maker's mark of the Goldsmiths & Silversmiths Co. Ltd., with a push-button clasp opening to reveal a central hinged frame with an oval aperture, 8cm. high. (Bonhams) $441

An Art Nouveau silver photograph frame, Birmingham 1904, maker's mark of JA & S., embossed with symmetrical floral decoration and inscribed *There's Rosemary Thats For Remembrance*. (Bonhams & Brooks) $182

PIN CUSHIONS

Attractive small hallmarked silver pin cushion in the form of a chick, 1½in. long, Sheffield 1905 by Sampson Morden and Co. (G.A. Key) $277

Unusual silver encased pin cusion in the form of a duck, 'jeweled' eyes, 3½in. long, Birmingham 1908, makers C & N. (G.A. Key) $246

An Edwardian novelty silver pin cushion, Birmingham 1908, H Matthews, modelled as a swimming swan, length of swan 8cm. (Christie's) $339

Tiffany & Co. pitcher, 1875-91, squat baluster form, the foot chased and embossed with shells and seaweed, the body partially fluted, 10¾in. high, approximately 55 total oz. (Skinner) $4,025

A silver and mixed-metal pitcher, Tiffany & Co., New York, circa 1878, the hand-hammered surface applied with copper and silver carp, grasses, snail and dragonfly, 7⅞in. high; gross weight 27oz. 10dwt. (Christie's) $23,000

Towle Silversmiths pitcher, 20th century, vasiform, on trumpet foot, with wide spout and gadrooning to foot, girdle, and rim, ear handle with acanthus terminals, monogramed to one side, 10in. high, 34 troy oz. (Skinner) $920

A silver-mounted copper pitcher set with arrowheads, attributed to Joseph Heinrich, New York, 1900-1915, baluster, the circular base applied with riveted silver straps supporting the hammered body, in. high. (Christie's) $50,600

A silver pitcher, maker's mark of R. & W. Wilson, Philadelphia, circa 1850, the body chased to simulate bark and applied with scrolling grapevines, a lizard and small bird, 11¾in. high; 38oz. 10dwt. (Christie's) $5,520

An American parcel-gilt silver "Japanese style" water pitcher, Tiffany & Co., New York, circa 1880, the spot-hammered body applied with a dragonfly with gilt wings, 28oz., height 18.1cm. (Sotheby's) $11,400

American silver "Japanese style" water pitcher, Tiffany & Co., New York, circa 1885, the front etched with a seaweed and pearl monogram on spot-hammered ground, 31oz. height 8¾in. (Sotheby's) $11,400

An American water pitcher, Tiffany & Co., New York, 1891-1902, the globular body with a band of foliate scroll motifs, the neck of straight sided form with a similar band, with a C handle, 17.5cm., 21.5oz. (Christie's) $2,205

An American silver water pitcher, Gorham Mfg. Co., Providence, RI, 1869, of urn form with spiralled gadroons below chased strapwork and rosettes, palmette and bolt handle, 1,104g., height 27cm. (Sotheby's) $3,600

A set of twelve George III silver soup-plates, John Wakelin and William Taylor, London, 1786, each shaped circular and with gadrooned rim, 9¾in. diameter. (Christie's) $8,100

A Portuguese silver-gilt circular charger, maker's mark *ENDC*, Lisbon, lst quarter of the 18th century, emobossed at the center by a large sailing vessel enclosed by a lion, leopard and a fox, 17½in. diameter, 1004gm. (Sotheby's) $10,728

Eight modern dinner plates, maker's mark *WHW*, 1973, each of shaped circular form with a gadroon rim, 26.3cm., 147oz. (Christie's) $1,645

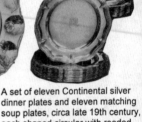

A set of twelve French silver dinner-plates, A. Aucoc, Paris, circa 1890, the border chased with wings, mistletoe, and with the inscription *Nuit porte conseil*, 10in. diameter, 172oz. (Christie's) $8,942

A set of twelve American silver place plates, Gorham Mfg. Co., Providence, RI, Martelé, .9584 standard, 1910, 280oz., 11½in. diameter. (Sotheby's) $64,000

A set of eleven Continental silver dinner plates and eleven matching soup plates, circa late 19th century, each shaped circular with a reeded border, the centers engraved with a coat-of-arms, the dinner plates 10in. diameter, the soup plates 10¼in. diameter, 353oz. (Christie's) $5,429

Thirteen Regency silver-gilt dinner plates William Burwash, London, 1812, shaped circular with shell-gadroon borders, twice armorial engraved, 10¾in. diameter, 354oz., 12dwt.(Sotheby's) $23,021

Reginald Ernest Arnold, an early 20th century massive classical charger in silver on copper embossed with Perseus et Andromeda, 26in. diameter. Signed. (Brightwells) $478

A rare and unusual set of thirty Regency silver-gilt dessert or side plates by John Craddock & William Ker Reid, London, 1812, 8¼in. diameter, 442oz. (Sotheby's) $77,853

American porringer, mid-18th century, Henrick Boelen, maker, New York, of typical form, single pierced handle, 7in. long to handle, approximately 5 troy oz. (Skinner) $1,035

A Queen Anne porringer, Nathaniel Lock, 1711, of circular section with a part spiral fluted foot, the rim with a twist motif band, one side with a leaf and scale motif cartouche, 10.7cm, 10oz. (Christie's) $1,382

A Queen Anne porringer, Humphrey Payne, 1709, of part spiral fluted form with a vacant cartouche, with two beaded handles, 7.9cm., 5oz. (Christie's) $1,554

A George I two-handled porringer, on a spreading circular foot, with two c-scroll handles, engraved with a coat of arms, by Bowles Nash, London, 1723, 16.5cm. high, 28oz. (Christie's) $4,145

A rare Commonwealth silver porringer, maker's mark *IH* in monogram, London 1657, slightly bulbous, armorial engraved between crossed plumes above lobe and acanthus leaf chased base, 6in. high, 22oz. (Sotheby's) $29,875

A large William and Mary silver porringer and cover, Ralph Leeke, London, 1692, cylindrical, armorial engraved within foliate cartouche above spiral alternative lobes and flutes between scroll handles, 9in. high, 1656gm. (Sotheby's) $18,737

A George I porringer, of plain lightly tapering cylindrical form with two c-scroll handles, maker's mark possibly that of John Barnard, 1719, 10.5cm. diameter, 8oz. (Christie's) $829

A silver porringer, Jonathan Clarke, Newport, Rhode Island, circa 1740, the keyhole handle engraved with monogram *E* over *I * M*, 7½in. long over handle; 7oz. 10dwt. (Christie's) $3,220

A Charles II silver porringer, maker's mark *IH* above a fleur-de-lys, London, 1680, cylindrical, the base chased with overlapping acanthus leaves, 11cm. high, 615gm. (Sotheby's) $5,006

A pair of George III Irish salt-cellars, marked with Hibernia & Crowned Harp only, Dublin, circa 1770, each of boat form raised on a domed part fluted pedestal foot, each with a conforming blue glass liner, 5in., 6.5oz. (Christie's) $1,447

A pair of Queen Anne salts, marks rubbed, possibly James Goodwin, circa 1710, each of oval form with a gilded bowl, engraved with a crest, 8.1cm., 3oz. (Christie's) $1,480

A pair of George III Scottish salts, Robert Clark, Edinburgh, 1761 and 1770, each of cauldron form with a crimped border, raised on three scroll capped hoof feet, 6.4cm., 4.25oz. (Christie's) $341

Set of four English George III open salts, London, 1765, Robert and David Hennell, scroll legs topped by shells, with spiral fluting and small cartouche, 3½in. wide, approximately 11 troy oz. total. (Skinner) $488

A set of four George III salts, boat shaped with reeded rim and loop handles, raised on oval base, 5in. wide, London 1784, maker's mark R H, 11oz 5dwt. (Andrew Hartley) $739

A pair of mid Victorian novelty salt cellars, London 1866, maker's mark of James Edington, modelled as grain sacks, textured surface, approximate weight 10oz., 5.8cm. high. (Bonhams) $1,176

A pair of French salt cellars, after 1838, with floral borders, 8.8cm. diameter; with a pair of silver-gilt sugar spoons, 18.8cm. long, 6.25oz. weighable silver. (Christie's) $750

A pair of Victorian silver salts, Robert Hennell, 1847, each of cauldron form with foliate scroll motifs centering cartouches, one engraved with a crest, with cobalt glass liners. (Christie's) $493

A pair of George III silver salt cellars, Paul Storr, London, 1793, the bodies applied with chased leaves, 3½in. diameter, 16oz. (Christie's) $4,471

A George III sauceboat, Joseph Craddock & William Reid, 1814, of typical form with a gadroon rim, raised on three shell capped feet, with a leaf capped handle, length 20.4cm., 15.5oz. (Christie's) $987

A parcel-gilt silver sauce boat, Tiffany & Co., New York, 1881-1891, in the Japanese taste, shaped oval, the spot-hammered surface applied with parcel-gilt flowering sumach branch, 7½in. long; 13oz. (Christie's) $4,370

A George II sauce boat, on three shell and scroll feet with a wavy rim and a double C-scroll handle by Robert Albin Cox, 1754, 16cm. long. (Christie's) $352

A pair of Regency silver sauceboats, Robert Garrard, London, 1811, oval and armorial engraved below gadroon borders, on mask and claw supports, 8¾in. long, 1446gm. (Sotheby's) $11,622

Four unusual George IV silver sauceboats, James Charles Eddington, London, 1829 and 1830, formed as shells on rocaille bases and with leaf capped flying scroll handles, 9½in. long, 2661gm. (Sotheby's) $33,302

A pair of modern silver sauce boats, Sheffield 1978, maker's mark of Mappin and Webb, of oval form, gadroon borders, leaf capped flying scroll handles, approximate weight 18oz., 16cm. long. (Bonhams & Brooks) $348

A pair of George III Irish sauceboats, John Irish, Cork, circa 1760, shaped-oval and on three shell, scroll and female's mask feet, ¾in., long, 27oz. (Christie's) $11,178

A pair of late Victorian sauce boats, in the form of sleighs, with rocaille bodies, shaped rims and lantern finials, by William Comyns, 1898, 21cm. long, 28oz. (Christie's) $3,281

A pair of George IV silver sauceboats, William Eaton, London, 1824, fluted bodies each with leaf-capped scroll handle, 19cm., 1,096gm. (Christie's) $4,844

A pearl, gold and enamel snuff box, illegible French prestige marks, Geneva, circa 1790, the lid with a central shield shaped panel painted en plein with figures seated in a garden, width 3in., in original leather case.
(Sotheby's) $11,622

An early 19th century novelty silver snuff box, circa 1827, modelled as an anvil and hammer, hinged lid, crested, the reverse inscribed *John Denvar Morrison BOILER SMITH NEWCASTLE 1827*, approximate weight 41g., 4cm. high.
(Bonhams) $2,205

A silver-gilt and Florentine pietra dura vinaigrette, Edward Edwards II, London, 1843, the lid inset with a pietra dura panel inlaid with a trophy of lovebirds and a helmet on a black Belgian marble ground, width 2¾in.
(Sotheby's) $4,112

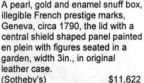

An enamel snuff box, South Staffordshire, circa 1765, of shaped rectangular form, the lid painted with the Tea Party(2), the sides with subjects from the Ladies' Amusement, width 8cm.
(Sotheby's) $9,834

A George IV Scottish silver gilt snuff box, Edinburgh 1827, maker's mark possibly that of Richard Haxton Jr., the hinged lid set with a chased and embossed panel depicting Venus within rocaille borders, approximate weight 93g., 6.7cm. wide.
(Bonhams) $1,397

A 19th century Scottish Provincial silver and agate snuff box, Perth, maker's mark of *WR*, possibly William Robertson, the hinged lid set with an oval agate panel, the sides and base engraved, 7cm. wide. (Bonhams) $1,102

A 19th century Chinese silver snuff box, with pseudo English marks, the hinged cover, sides and base chased with figural scenes in landscapes, monogramed and dated *1828*, approximate weight 98g., 6.7cm. long.
(Bonhams) $382

An Imperial presentation gold and enamel portrait snuff box Friedrich Köchli, St Petersburg, circa 1880, the miniature by Alois Gustav Rockstuhl, signed, circa 1870, width 8.7cm. (Sotheby's) $29,875

A 19th century Chinese silver snuff box, maker's mark worn, possibly that of Leeching, cushion sides, base with foliate decoration, the hinged cover with a figural scene and central vacant cartouche, gilded interior, approximate weight 113g., 8.5cm. long.
(Bonhams) $617

A Victorian parcel-gilt cagework tankard, Frederick Elkington, Birmingham, 1868, body with an elaborate pierced silver foliate scroll and exotic bird motif overlay, 17.5cm., 52oz.
(Christie's) $1,467

A Swedish parcel-gilt silver tankard, Friedrich Richter, Stockholm, circa 1680, the body, handle and hinged cover finely engraved with biblical scenes and inscriptions, 15cm. high, 644gm.
(Christie's) $26,082

A Baltic parcel-gilt silver tankard, Carl-Gustav Kretzner, Riga, circa 1720, chasing later, on three ball feet cast and chased with female busts, 22cm. high, 959g.
(Christie's) $7,452

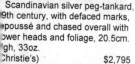

Scandinavian silver peg-tankard, 9th century, with defaced marks, repoussé and chased overall with flower heads and foliage, 20.5cm. high, 33oz.
(Christie's) $2,795

A German parcel-gilt silver tankard, Paul Solanier, Augsburg, 1680-1685, the body chased with lobes and stylized fruit and foliage, 6¾in. high, 22oz.
(Christie's) $10,246

An Edward VII large silver tankard, George Lambert, London, 1901, hinged cover chased and repoussé with flowerheads and inset with a coin, lion and ball thumpiece, 11¼in. high, 93oz.
(Christie's) $3,240

German parcel-gilt silver tankard, Friedrich I Schwestermüller, Augsburg, circa 1685, repoussé and chased with two scenes from the History of Troy, 8¼in. high, 8oz. (Christie's) $6,707

A George II quart tankard , straight sided with domed lid having scroll thumb-piece, London 1730, Maker: George Wickes.
(Brightwells) $1,288

An American silver tankard, George Hanners, Boston, circa 1740, of tapered cylindrical form, engraved with mid-19th century arms and initial P, 731gm. 22.2cm.
(Sotheby's) $3,600

A Continental tankard, marked with pseudo-marks, late 19th century, in the Swedish 17th century style, of circular section, raised on three ball feet, the handle modelled as a female, 16.3cm., 26oz.
(Christie's) $1,260

A William and Mary silver tankard, London, 1694, maker's mark IA in script monogram, the lower part of the body chased with spiral flutes, 20.5cm. high, 1,056g.
(Christie's) $7,238

A George III tankard, London 1782, maker's mark of John Lambe, domed hinged cover with a pierced thumbpiece, scroll handle, approximate weight 22oz., 19.8cm. high. (Bonhams) $1,690

A German parcel-gilt silver tankard, Johann Paul Schmidt, Leipzig, circa 1685, the sleeve pierced and chased with three oval scenes of figures and buildings with scrolling foliage between, 7½in. high, 28oz.
(Christie's) $5,962

A George III Scottish tankard, marks rubbed, apparently Edinburgh, 1810, the slightly tapering circular tankard with two horizontally reeded bands, 4½in., 18.25oz. (Christie's) $510

A James II silver tankard, London, 1688, maker's mark indistinct, with scroll handle, bifurcated thumbpiece and hinged slightly domed cover, 6¾in. high, 22oz.
(Christie's) $7,079

A George III creamware tankard with Norwegian silver mounts, the creamware body English, circa 1800, the silver cover with maker's mark of Christian Appelgren, Drammen, 1827, 7¼in. high.
(Christie's) $1,863

A German parcel-gilt silver tankard, Paul Solanier, Augsburg, probably 1710, the detachable applied sleeve pierced, repoussé and chased with an angel and biblical figures, 8in. high, 42oz.
(Christie's) $7,452

A George III silver-gilt mounted ivory tankard, Thomas Phipps and Edward Robinson, London, 1810, plain silver mounts with carved ivory body with figure scene, 6½in. high. (Christie's) $7,452

George IV four piece tea and coffee service, the circular everted melon panel bodies raised on a spreading foot, with either chased or engraved differing foliage decoration, William Eley, London 1823, 85oz. (Woolley & Wallis) $1,147

Walter & John Barnard, a Victorian oval three piece tea service, Queen Anne pattern, the partly ribbed bodies with a molded rim foot, the teapot with a scroll spout, London, 1887, 26.5oz. all in. (Woolley & Wallis) $573

American silver six-piece tea and coffee set, Dominick & Haff, New York, 1896, comprising: teapot, coffee-pot, creamer, waste bowl, covered sugar bowl, and kettle on lampstand, the bombé bodies with elaborate openwork collars and feet of flowers, leaves and scrolls, 249oz., 15¼in. (Sotheby's) $10,800

A late Victorian four piece tea and coffee service, the oval part ribbed bodies raised on a molded foot to engraved foliage sprays and chevron bands, Charles Boyton, London, 1897/98, 57.5oz. all in. (Woolley & Wallis) $1,000

A four-piece Victorian tea and coffee service, Henry Holland, 1854, each piece of pear form with elaborate foliate scroll and lattice motifs, raised on four leaf capped scroll feet, comprising: a coffee pot, a teapot, each with ivory insulated handles, a cream jug and a sugar bowl, 27cm., 91.5oz. (Christie's) $2,205

Gorham five-piece tea and coffee service, 1941-43, comprising tea and coffee pots, creamer, covered sugar, and open sugar, baluster-form, on domed foot, with gadrooning to upper rim, electroplated tray, 28½in. long, pair of Royal Danish sugar tongs, approximately 83 troy oz. total weighable silver. (Skinner) $1,150

A George IV three-piece tea service, Charles Fox, 1829, each piece of tapering lobed form, with four robust applied flowers, each terminating in a branch motif foot, the spout and handles with leaf motifs, length of teapot 29cm., 49oz.(Christie's) $1,680

A French silver tea, coffee and chocolate servic Odiot, Paris, circa 1920, comprising; chocolate-p coffee jug, teapot, sugar-bowl and cover, cream-j and biscuit-bowl, each fluted and with gadroone rims, chocolate pot: 9in. high, gross 91oz.
(Christie's) $2,2?

A three-piece George III Scottish tea service, W&P Cunningham, Edinburgh, 1802, comprising: a teapot with an ebonized handle and silver-mounted finial, a cream jug and a sugar bowl, each with gilded interiors, 29.2cm., 29.5oz gross.
(Christie's) $2,045

A six-piece modern tea and coffee service with tra Mappin & Webb, Sheffield, 1915-1917, comprising: kettle on stand, teapot, hot water pot, each w ebonized handles, a cream jug, covered sugar bow waste bowl and a two handled tray, length of tr 74cm., 261oz. (Christie's) $4,83

Victorian four piece E P B M tea and coffee set of compressed circular form, heavily chased and embossed with floral and foliate designs, comprising coffee pot, teapot, two handled sugar basin and milk jug. (G.A. Key) $196

An oval boat shape three piece tea service, with molded bodies, raised on an ovoid molded foot, the teapot with a spout incorporated in the shape of the body, the milk jug and sugar basin, with bracket shape handles, London 1925, 28oz. all in.
(Woolley & Wallis) $412

An oval four piece tea service, raised on ca anthemion appliqué scroll legs with knurled feet, on side engraved a crest of a prancing hind, Th Goldsmiths & Silversmiths Co. Ltd., Sheffield, 192 39oz. all in. (Woolley & Wallis) $77

A George I Britannia standard tea caddy, London 1715, maker's mark of John Farnell, slide off cover and pull off domed cover with a knop finial, approximate weight 6oz., 12.8cm. high.
(Bonhams) $1,250

A George III silver tea-caddy, Robert Hennell, London, 1781, fluted oval, the body and cover bright-cut engraved with bands of stylized foliage, 4in. high, gross 12oz. (Christie's) $2,713

Interesting hallmarked solid silver tea caddy in the shape of a Georgian knife box, having shaped hinged lid, 3¼in. tall, Birmingham 1913. (G.A. Key) $348

A German silver tea-caddy, Andreas Fries (e), Aurich, circa 1740, plain shaped oblong and with incurved angles, 4½in. high, 5oz. (Christie's) $3,540

Two George II silver tea-caddies, Eliza Godfrey, London, 1752, chased overall with scrolls, shells, flowers and foliage, 13cm. and 12.5cm. high, 17oz.
(Christie's) $3,632

A George II silver tea caddy, Christian Hillan, London, 1738, chased overall with scrolls, flutes, rocailles, eagles and flowers on a matted ground, 6¾in. high. 11oz.
(Christie's) $12,109

A George III tea caddy, Daniel Smith & Robert Sharp, 1772, the bombé caddy with a gadroon rim, the body decorated with swag motifs below medallions, height 12.5cm, 9.5oz.
(Christie's) $1,316

A pair of George II silver tea-caddies, Philips Garden, London, 1756, each of bombé form and on four foliate scroll feet, the lower part of the bodies chased with matted rocaille, 6in. high, 32oz.
(Christie's) $14,904

A Dutch rectangular tea caddy with domed top, four cupid figures, embossed figures and dogs in landscape, on peg feet, sliding bottom, London 1887.
(Brightwells) $400

Austrian kettle on stand, circa 1880s, Vienna, with French import marks, the tap ending in dog's head spout, the stand with shaped triangular base on three ball feet, with further foliate banding at edge, 15in. high, approximately 69 troy oz. total. (Skinner) $1,093

BUYER BEWARE

On articles of silver where there should be a space for a crest or initials within a cartouche, for example on a George III teapot, and where the space is vacant, check whether it is very thin from having had an erasure. This can affect the value.

Check for repairs around spouts and bases. Some Georgian silver has later repoussé or chasing work.

(Woolley & Wallis)

A George II kettle-on-stand, William Cripps, 1750, the globular kettle with foliate scroll and cartouche motifs, with a leaf capped reeded spout, 37cm, 62oz. (Christie's) $2,41●

Attractive Victorian silver plated spirit kettle and stand of compressed circular form, engraved with foliate designs and crests Rococo style handle and stand, circa 1870.
(G.A. Key) $145

A silver-plated kettle on stand, circa 1900, by Philip Ashberry & Sons, Sheffield, lid surmounted by a lady tennis player, the stand modelled as two pairs of crossed fishtail rackets with burner on central stretchers, 11½in. total height. (Sotheby's) $2,700

Elkington and Co silver plated spir● kettle, rectangular shaped with fluted canted corners, the stand with four scrolled legs to a central circular holder, 11in. tall, circa 1900. (G.A. Key) $19●

An Edwardian silver kettle on stand, Chester 1908, maker's mark of Nathan & Hayes, of rounded rectangular form, gadroon and shell borders, central carrying handle, fluted girdle, weight 46oz., 34cm. high.(Bonhams & Brooks) $754

A George II kettle on stand, London 1733, maker's mark of John Swift, engraved foliate, scroll, shell and fish scale decoration, the stand pierced with a scroll apron, approximate weight 68oz., 34cm. high. (Bonhams) $4,410

A Queen Anne silver teakettle on stand and burner, Richard Green, 1706, burner William Fawdery, 1709, both London, Britannia standard, 26cm. on stand, 1595gm. all in. (Sotheby's) $15,19●

eorge III silver teapot of slightly ompressed oval design, boldly uted and having an ovolo rim, crolled hollow handle and upported on four ball feet, London 813, 19oz.(G.A. Key) $408

A Chinese silver teapot, marked with Chinese characters, maker's mark of *HT* unidentified, embossed bamboo decoration on a matted background, approximate weight 10oz. (Bonhams) $470

A George III teapot, the straight sides chased with scrolling foliage and festoons centered by a blind cartouche, 10½in. wide, London 1783, maker's mark *G.S.*, 13oz. 16dwt.(Andrew Hartley) $708

George III silver teapot, London 818, maker's mark of Thomas allis II and Jonathan Hayne, oval rm, part fluted decoration, leaf pped scroll handle, approximate ight 26oz. onhams & Brooks) $348

A William IV silver teapot, London 1833, maker's mark of Joseph and John Angell, of lobed circular form, embossed with floral and foliate decoration, two cartouches, one crested, approximate weight 24oz., 15.5cm. high. (Bonhams & Brooks) $696

A George IV Scottish teapot, maker's mark *JsH*, Edinburgh, 1824, the shoulder of the squat circular teapot with a band of floral and scroll motifs on a granulated ground, 28cm., 21oz. gross. (Christie's) $508

eorge III oval teapot, Joseph ammell, 1793 , bright-cut raved around lid, top and tom of body, one side engraved n crest, 14oz. ristie's) $690

A George I silver teapot, Abraham Buteux, London, 1724, plain bullet-shaped and on a circular molded foot, straight spout, 4¾in. gross 14oz. (Christie's) $8,384

An early Victorian silver tea pot, London 1836, maker's mark of *I.W,* embossed foliate scroll decoration, leaf capped scroll handle, approximate weight 16oz. (Bonhams) $585

torian teapot, Sheffield, 1869, s. Dixon & Sons, shaped ovoid m, engraved with plain foliate ndel to sides, top with a band of al vine, height 6in., roximately 22 troy oz. inner) $575

A George III Scottish teapot, John McKay, Edinburgh, 1818, the bellied rectangular teapot with a central reeded band, the high shoulder with a thistle motif band, 27.5cm., 23oz. gross. (Christie's) $725

A George III Irish silver teapot, Dublin 1805, Richard Sawyer, flush hinged domed cover, engraved with a girdle of bright cut decoration, approximate weight 22oz., length handle to spout 33cm. (Bonhams) $924

An early Victorian silver teapot, London 1854, William Hunter, embossed with acanthus and scroll decoration, floral borders, 25oz., height 18.25cm.
(Bonhams) $493

John & Henry Lias, an early Victorian circular teapot, everted melon panelled body, domed panelled cover with flower finial, London 1844, 20oz. all in.
(Woolley & Wallis) $294

A Dutch silver teapot, Obbe Ydema, Sneek, 1755, the body chased with strapwork, the domed cover attached by two chains to the spout and handle, 6in. high, 10oz.
(Christie's) $2,895

A Scottish Provincial silver teapot, Robert Luke, Glasgow, 1725-1735, spherical and on spreading circular foot, with tapering straight spout, 6¼in. high, gross 19oz.
(Christie's) $4,620

A Queen Anne silver teapot on stand and burner, Jonathan Madden, 1710, stand Francis Garthorne, 1708, both London, Britannia standard baluster pot with faceted curved spout, 10in. high overall, 925gm.
(Sotheby's) $17,880

A Swiss silver teapot and stand, J. Wjdmer, Berne, on the tray, WB on the teapot, teapot plain oval with bright-cut borders, wooden handle and baluster finial, 4¾in. high, the stand 8in. long, 21oz.
(Bonhams) $1,990

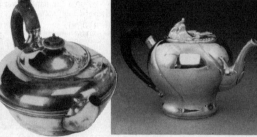

English William IV teapot, London, 1832, J.E. Terrey & Co, with cartouche to either side, one engraved with mottoed crest, chased and embossed with rocaille scrolls and foliate sprays, 7in. high, approximately 23 troy oz.
(Skinner) $1,265

A George IV teapot, of squat circular form, with a reeded body band, with wood c-scroll handle and finial, by Robert Garrard, 1824, 11.5cm. high, 22oz. gross.
(Christie's) $656

A Dutch silver teapot, Dirk Blom, Amsterdam, 1762, the body with spiral flutes, scoll spout and wood handle, the hinged cover cast with stylized scrolls and finial, 4¼in., gross 12oz.
(Christie's) $5,067

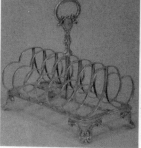

A novelty toastrack, in the form of a vintage car, the spoked wheels to a molded rectangular frame, the shaped front with an applied carriage lamp to a steering wheel, 8in. long.
(Woolley & Wallis) $470

An early Victorian six division toast rack, raised on shell and leaf edge panel feet to a molded edge base, Henry Wilkinson & Co, Sheffield 1841, 9¼oz.
(Woolley & Wallis) $338

Attractive late Victorian silver toast rack of scroll design, the openwork base having five bars, pierced and engraved and spelling the word *Toast*, 5 x 2½in., London 1901 by C C Pilling. (G.A. Key) $487

TRAYS & SALVERS

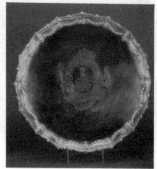

A circular silver salver, with piecrust edge on triple scrolled feet, unengraved, approximate weight 27oz, 11¾in. diameter.
(Bonhams) $370

A George III silver tray, Paul Storr, London, 1815, shaped oval and on four foliage and rosette feet, with gadrooned border chased at intervals with acanthus foliage, 28in. long, 151oz.
(Christie's) $37,260

A Victorian presentation salver, Maxfield and Sons, 1895, the circular salver with a leaf heightened blossom border, above a band of husk motif swags, diameter 36.5cm, 42oz.
(Christie's) $880

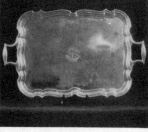

A Victorian salver, scroll engraved with shaped beaded rim, on ball and claw feet, London 1866, Maker's J.B. & E.B., 12in. diameter.
(Brightwells) $546

A large silver rectangular two handled tray with shaped edge and central *BS* monogram, maker HEB and FEB, Chester 1915, 71cm. wide, approximate weight 8.15lbs.
(Bonhams) $1,235

A George II silver salver, William Peaston, London, 1753, shaped circular and on four leaf-capped scroll feet, 15¼in. diameter, 50oz.
(Christie's) $4,844

An Adam style tureen, of half fluted oval urn shape with reeded loop handles, domed detachable lid and molded oval base, 14in. wide. (Andrew Hartley) $323

A George III silver soup-tureen and cover, Sebastian and James Crespell, London, 1764, shaped oval and on four scroll and foliage feet, with two shell and foliate scroll bracket handles, 14½in. long, 64oz. (Christie's) $12,666

A French silver soup tureen, Edmé Catherine Vanestienword, Paris, 1798-1809, the domed cover with corded rim and acanthus bud finial, 28cm. high, 90oz. (Christie's) $6,521

A George III silver two handled sauce tureen and cover, London 1813, Paul Storr, lion mask mounted shell capped reeded handles, part fluted decoration, approximate weight 41oz., length handle to handle 24cm. (Bonhams) $3,850

Interesting Scottish silver plated small soup punch tureen of circular baluster form, having deer head handles and supported on four hoof feet, the detachable lid with recumbent deer finial, 8½in. 10in. tall overall. (G.A. Key) $172

A George II silver tureen and cover, James Schruder, London, 1744, on four boldly modelled ram's mask, hoof and shell feet, the body with two leaf-capped shell and scroll handles, tureen 19in. wide, stand 27½in. long, tureen 267oz., stand 189oz. (Christie's) $177,066

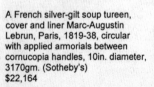

A French silver-gilt soup tureen, cover and liner Marc-Augustin Lebrun, Paris, 1819-38, circular with applied armorials between cornucopia handles, 10in. diameter, 3170gm. (Sotheby's) $22,164

A French silver soup-tureen and cover, maker's marks of Tetard Frères, Paris, circa 1890, plain shaped oval and on spreading foot, the fluted body with two scroll bracket handles, 16½in. long., 118oz. (Christie's) $3,726

Sheffield plate, a late Regency tureen, the rectangular body raised on four paw feet and reeded scroll legs, the cover with later shield and crest and a detachable open leaf scroll handle, 12½in. (Woolley & Wallis) $441

An electro-plated tea urn, of bellied circular form, on quatrefoil base and claw feet, 41cm. high.
(Bonhams) $1,029

A late Georgian silver plated tea urn with reeded handles, the cover with flower finial on square base with ball feet, 14in.
(Brightwells) $210

A Victorian electro-plated tea urn, of lobed form, on four scroll feet, with open-work foliate handles and flower finial, 49cm. high.
(Christie's) $862

A Victorian tea urn, Hawksworth, Eyre and Co., Sheffield, 1859, the openwork base conceals the burner, with two pairs of turned ivory handles and a detachable lid and a tubular spout, 44cm., 94.5oz.
(Christie's) $4,491

A pair of Regency copper and gilt-metal samovars, almost certainly made for the Russian market, each with a domed lid surmounted by an 'Adler' finial above a circular waisted body with ivory carrying handles to the sides and a tap, 17¾in. high, the other 13⅝in.
(Christie's) $13,348

A George III silver tea urn, Francis Butty and Nicholas Dumee, London, 1767, the detachable ovoid body chased with scrolls and foliage, 22in. high, 85oz.
(Christie's) $4,844

An early 19th century two-handled Old Sheffield plated tea urn, unmarked, circa 1820, leaf capped handles, pull-off cover with a flower finial, pierced shell and scroll tap, 42cm. high.
(Bonhams) $617

A George III silver tea-urn, Paul Storr, London, 1809, chased beneath the rim with a band of arcading, palmettes and anthemion on a matted ground, 11¾in. high, gross 150oz.
(Christie's) $26,082

An unusual English silver coffee urn, George Wickes, London, date letter indistinct, circa 1740, armorial engraved and crested within elaborate chasing of rococo flowers, scrolls and rocaille, 12in. high, 1479gm.
(Sotheby's) $4,649

A German silver vase, circa 1890, flared cylindrical, elaborately pierced and chased in rococo taste with putti, floral swags, and rocaille, later glass liner, 14in. high. (Sotheby's) $3,864

A pair of Art Nouveau silver vases, Birmingham 1904, H. Matthews, the bowl modelled as a flower head, spot hammered decoration, height 18cm. (Bonhams) $554

An Edwardian vase, Walker & Hall, Sheffield, 1905, modelled after the Warwick vase and supported on a square plinth foot, 27.2cm. (Christie's) $4,112

Large footed vase, Lebkuecher & Co., Newark, late 19th century, on four scrolled feet, embossed with horizontal band at girdle with paterae within cartouches, 22in. high, approximately 80 troy oz. total. (Skinner) $4,600

A set of three George III silver condiment vases, Daniel Smith and Robert Sharp, London, 1773, In the neo-classical style, each of vase form and on square base with four ball feet, 9¼in. high and two 8in., 40oz.(Christie's) $22,356

Tall Tiffany & Co. presentation vase, 1907-38, on low round foot with flat leaf band, the tapered body engraved to one side with presentation inscription, 15¼in. high, approximately 65 troy oz. total. (Skinner) $3,450

A silver vase, maker's mark of Lebkuecher & Co., Newark, circa 1900, in the Chinese taste, the lower body embossed with lotus leaves, with stylized taotie mask mid-band, 12½in. high; 81oz. 10dwt. (Christie's) $5,750

A pair of Chinese silver vases, one marked only with maker's mark of *LW*, tapering circular form, embossed with cherry blossom on a matted background, approximate weight 7oz., 12.2cm. high. (Bonhams) $353

A Victorian Scottish two-handled vase, Marshall & Sons, Edinburgh, 1877, modelled as the Warwick vase decorated with Bacchanalian masks on a lion's pelt, 10¼in., 112.5oz. (Christie's) $7,838

A late Victorian vesta case, in the form of brazil nut, John Marshall Spink, London 1896, 5.3cm. (Christie's) $872

A 20th century vesta case, in the form of a standing pig, H.C.D., Birmingham 1930, 5.5cm. (Christie's) $329

A gold combination cigarette and vesta case, black enamelled overall and with rose diamond borders, cartouche and thumbpiece, unmarked, probably Continental, 9.3cm. (Christie's) $1,562

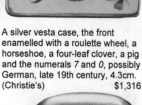

A Victorian"Trick" vesta case, operational by depressing the opposite end to the striker, Brownett & Jones, London 1879, 6.1cm. (Christie's) $2,303

A brass vesta case, in the form of a boot, a cat in the top of the boot, a mouse at the toe, stamped with registration number 218947, 6.5cm. (Christie's) $493

A silver vesta case, the front enamelled with a roulette wheel, a horseshoe, a four-leaf clover, a pig and the numerals 7 and 0, possibly German, late 19th century, 4.3cm. (Christie's) $1,316

A Victorian vesta case, of rectangular form, the front with applied gold mounted oval enamelled plaque depicting a golfer in mid swing hallmarked, Birmingham 1893, 5cm. (Christie's) $1,151

A Victorian combination vesta case and wick holder, in the form of a horseshoe, both sides part engine-turned, maker's mark indistinct, Birmingham 1887, 5.5cm. (Christie's) $410

A silver vesta case, the front enamelled with a stabled horse and four hunting dogs, the reverse engraved with initials, German, late 19th century, 5.1cm. (Christie's) $987

A Victorian vesta case, the front with an enamelled hunting scene, Sampson Mordan, London 1892, 5.7cm. (Christie's) $2,138

A Victorian novelty combination vesta case and cigar cutter, in the form of a gun, the barrel hinged to house the matches, the trigger activating the cigar cutter, Wright and Davis, London 1888, 13cm. overall. (Christie's) $1,398

A silver vesta case, the front and reverse with applied flowers, foliage and a butterfly, all part enamelled, probably Japanese, late 19th century, 5.8cm. (Christie's) $821

A Victorian vesta case, the front enamelled with a study of a lap dog, Sampson Mordan, London 1897, 5.7cm. (Christie's) $3,125

A brass novelty vesta case, in the form of a gun, the handle incorporating cigar cutter, 6cm. (Christie's) $904

A gold vesta case, the front engraved with a maiden standing on a balcony, a diamond set in her cleavage, late nineteenth century, 5.7cm. (Christie's) $2,138

A silver-gilt combination vesta case and wick holder, one side enamelled with a scene of a troika within enamelled geometric bands, Russian, late 19th century, 5.9cm. (Christie's) $1,480

An unusual novelty caricature vesta case, London 1917, maker's mark of Alfred William Hardiman, modelled as the profile of a gentleman in a peak cap, approximate weight 37g., 7.8cm. wide. (Bonhams) $1,764

A silver vesta case, the cover applied with the H.M.V. company symbol, the interior with presentation inscription, Sampson Mordan, Chester 1907, 4.5cm. (Christie's) $1,068

A Victorian vesta case, the front enamelled in monochrome with a lady fisher adjusting her stocking, Lawrence Emanuel, London 1868, 4cm. (Christie's) $904

A Victorian vesta case, in the form of a combination lock, M.W., Birmingham 1880, 3.2cm. (Christie's) $1,151

A silver vesta case, the front stamped in relief with a vignette of a lady smoking, French, late 19th century, 4.8cm. (Christie's) $592

A gold vesta case, both sides engraved with scrollwork enclosing a cartouche, American, late 19th century, 5.4cm. (Christie's) $658

A Victorian vesta case, the front enamelled with a scene of the "The Changing of the Guard", Sampson Mordan and Co, London 1890, 5.6cm. (Christie's) $4,277

A gold vesta case, the front engraved with a basket of flowers within a strapwork cartouche, American, late 19th century, 5.8cm. (Christie's) $658

A Victorian Scottish thistle-shaped vinaigrette, on matted stem with naturalistically chased flower, Edinburgh, 1881, maker's mark *A F*, 1⅞in. long.
(Christie's) $1,400

A Victorian silver gilt mounted red glass scent bottle/vinaigrette, of shouldered oblong form, the grille engraved and pierced with a symmetrical pattern of scrolls, 4in. Sampson Mordan & Co., London, 1861. (Woolley & Wallis) $456

A Victorian electroplated and parcel gilt vinaigrette cum scent bottle in the form of a curved horn, with applied gothic style borders, initialled, 4in. Sampson Mordan & Co, London. (Woolley & Wallis)
                                $220

Continental heart-shaped vinaigrette, 18th/19th century, marked *AK*, the lid with foliate and scroll reticulation with engraved detailing, 2in. long, approximately 1 troy oz. (Skinner) $575

A Victorian vinaigrette, of rectangular form, formed as a book, the lid and base forming the 'covers', by Edward Smith, Birmingham 1846, 1½in.
(Christie's) $1,050

English Victorian vinaigrette, Birmingham, 1858, Edward Smith, engraved allover with leafy scrolls, approximately 1 troy oz.
(Skinner) $201

An early Victorian vinaigrette, oblong, the grille pierced with a floral spray, initialled by E Edwards, London, 1836, 1½in. long.
(Woolley & Wallis) $368

A William IV vinaigrette, of rounded oblong form with engine turning, a cast foliate thumbpiece, reeded sides and a vacant circular cartouche on the cover, by E Edwards, London, 1832, 1½in. long. (Woolley & Wallis) $441

A George IV vinaigrette, the grille pierced and engraved with a flowering plant within an oval, by William Edwards, London, 1825, 1½in. long.
(Woolley & Wallis) $441

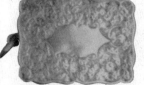

A George IV silver-gilt rectangular vinaigrette, the lid applied with a cast model of a Papillon dog, its back applied with a blister pearl, James Beebe, Birmingham 1824, 1½in. (Christie's) $4,200

A late-Victorian silver vinaigrette, Birmingham 1896, maker's mark of Cornelius Sauders & Frank Shepherd, the grille pierced with floral and foliate decoration, approximate weight 33gm. length 4.5cm. (Bonhams) $132

An oblong silver castletop vinaigrette chased with a view of Windsor Castle, by Nathaniel Mills, Birmingham, 1837.
(Christie's) $1,400

A pair of modern wine coolers, maker's mark *RWB*, Birmingham, 1961, retailed by Harrods, each of campana form, with a gadrooned rim and two applied branch motif handles, 23.2cm., 105oz. (Christie's) $1,363

A German silver wine-cooler, 19th century, struck with pseudo marks, after a design by Meissonnier, campana shaped on spreading circular base with guilloche border, with two mermaid and sea-monster handles with bifurcated tails, 10in. high, 68oz.(Christie's) $4,471

A pair of Italian silver wine-coolers and liners, Pietro Paulo Spagna, Rome, mid 19th century, with shell and foliate scroll border and with two detachable foliate scroll bracket handles, 8¾in. high, 221oz. (Christie's) $33,534

A late Victorian electrogilt wine cooler, 1898, Elkington & Co., the belly with applied vine leaves, grape trendrils and vines, height 32cm. (Bonhams) $847

WMF, a campana shape wine cooler, two cast open scroll handles to the body with lobing interspersed with flowers on stems, 9½in. (Woolley & Wallis) $206

Gorham silver plate wine cooler, late 19th century, with Greek key base, the upper portion of body with two further Greek key bands and two realistically modelled stag's heads handles, 12in. wide to handles 12in. (Skinner) $3,738

A pair of George III silver wine coolers, William Pitts & Joseph Preedy, London, 1797, barrel form with applied bands and engraved staves, armorial engraved below dove displayed crest, numbered 1 and 2, 8¾in. high, 2914gm. (Sotheby's) $41,869

A Continental silver wine-cooler, probably German, late 19th century, with pseudo French marks, the bulbous lower body cast and chased with rocaille and panels depicting Neptune and Pluto in chariots, 24.5cm. high. 70oz. (Bonhams) $3,619

A pair of George IV silver wine coolers, T. and J. Settle, Sheffield, circa 1820, chased overall with scrolls, shells, flowers and foliage, 9in. high, 82oz. (Christie's) $9,315

A combination wine funnel & tasting cup, maker's mark *ID* with star between, also marked with lion passant, circa 1775, the bowl engraved with ribbons and swags, the straight spigot with cap attached by chain, 10cm., 2.5oz. (Christie's) $2,336

An Irish Provincial wine funnel stand, maker's mark of John Nicolson, Cork, circa 1790, and a George III Irish silver wine funnel, circa 1780, 4½in. high. (Christie's) $1,540

George III two part silver wine funnel of usual design with reeded detail, 4½in. tall, London 1795 by Peter and Anne Bateman. (G.A. Key) $580

A George III wine funnel, with reeded borders and curved spigot, by William Hall, 1811, 13cm. high, 3oz. (Christie's) $735

Rebecca Emes & Edward Barnard, a Regency wine funnel and stand, the body having a reeded band to a molded rim. London 1819, 10oz. (Woolley & Wallis) $1,985

A George III wine funnel, Thomas James, 1810, of typical from with a shell heightened border and a lobed knop, the interior gilded, 14.3cm., 8oz. (Christie's) $1,618

A good George III silver wine funnel, the rounded bowl with a part fluted and curved spout, London 1805, maker William Allen III, 6¼oz. (Phillips) $1,015

George III silver two part wine funnel of usual design, having beaded rim, plain clip, 4½in. tall, London 1787, maker W A. (G.A. Key) $551

A George III silver wine funnel, London 1810, maker's Peter and William Bateman, 4½oz. (Phillips) $735

Brandy, Charles & James Fox, 1855, the name engraved on the side of a standing bull, 6cm. (Christie's) $3,003

Sherry, London, 1845, applied name on a cast fern label 8.8cm. (Christie's) $500

Claret and Whisky, unmarked, the names applied to the outstretched wings of a bat, 10.8cm. (Christie's) $3,169

Claret, William Summers, 1878, pierced name, *Lady Bountiful* above, a wide border of vine leaves and berries incorporating a lion's mask, 7cm. (Christie's) $700

S, M and P, Rawlings & Summers, 1846, the cast and pierced scrolled letters featuring Mr. Punch and Toby in various poses, 5.5cm. (Christie's) $6,674

Sherry, John Bridge, 1828, engraved name, cast in the form of a four-leaf clover, 5.5cm. (Christie's) $467

W. Wine, William Lestourgeon, circa 1771, engraved name, an elaborate crescent form with swags below and above an oval cartouche surmount, 5.4cm. (Christie's) $584

Claret and Madeira, Edward Farrell, 1815, in the form of an elephant, the names engraved on the caparison, 7.8cm. (Christie's) $11,680

Hock, Thomas Watson, Newcastle, 1827, engraved name, escutcheon type Arms of Newcastle surmount, 7cm. (Christie's) $3,169

WINE TASTERS _____ SILVER _____

A George III wine taster, maker's mark possibly *WI*, 1774, of bowl form with raised center and part embossed with faceted lobes, 10cm., 3oz.
(Christie's) $2,670

A Louis XVI silver wine-taster, Mathieu-Pierre Lamoureux, Rouen, 1774, the shaped bracket engraved with the figure of a man, his arms raised, holding a wine-bottle, 4½in. wide, 4oz.
(Christie's) $4,099

A George II wine taster, probably by Richard Bayley, 1754, of bowl form with raised center, inscribed on the side, 4in., 3oz.
(Christie's) $7,675

A French wine taster, Blaise-Simon Trottin, Paris, circa 1790, with lobed and punch beaded bowl and reeded loop handle, 8.2cm., 2.75oz.
(Christie's) $667

A very rare French interlocking double wine taster, maker's mark *VR*, Macon, circa 1785, a nest of two plain bowls and double serpent's head handles, 8cm., 3.5oz. (Christie's) $11,346

A French wine taster, Jean Baptiste-Vincent Yons, Paris, 1738, the shaped thumbpiece engraved with a dancing dog standing up on his rear legs, 19cm., 3.75oz.
(Christie's) $3,169

A Portuguese wine taster, maker's mark probably *AFR*, Oporto, 1843-1853, of bowl form with raised and dished center engraved with an armorial, 4.5in., 3oz.
(Christie's) $7,008

A German parcel-gilt wine-taster, probably Bavarian, circa 1680, lobed octafoil, the center chased with a scene of a hunter shooting a wolf amongst trees, 13cm. long, 82gm. (Christie's) $2,713

A French wine taster, Bordeaux, 1726-1730, the plain bowl and raised center, inscribed on the side with two initials and single bunch of grapes between, 4in., 3.75oz.
(Christie's) $2,168

619

An Art Deco spelter figure, cast from a model by H. Uher of a male skier. 6in. (Christie's) $531

A green patinated bronze figure cast from a model by G. Lavrof, modelled as a highly stylized downhill skier on a rectangular black onyx base, 8in. (Christie's) $2,125

A pair of snow shoes, circa 1850 with wooden frames and original woven hide, 40in. long. (Christie's) $1,594

A silvered metal figural table lamp, the domed shade on arched stem, the stem cast in relief with highly stylized figure of a skier with red enamel scarf, 16in. (Christie's) $2,656

P M Dupuy, skiing scene, offset lithograph in colors, 1934, backed on linen, 10 x 14in. (Christie's) $673

A pair of ladies skis, circa 1910, with original leather bindings and spruce poles, 65in. (Christie's) $531

A patinated bronze figure modelled as a reclining female skier, 11in. (Christie's) $1,540

A silvered metal figure, modelled as a stylized cross country skier on a black patinated wooden base, 5in. (Christie's) $744

A plaster figure, modelled as a female downhill skier, base incised 730, 21in.(Christie's) $1,062

A late 19th century sleigh, green and yellow wood and iron painted sleigh with waisted padded seat, antler handles with scrolled metal supports, 54in. long, 34in. wide. (Christie's) $3,365

A Royal Dux pottery figure, modelled as a downhill skier with gilt metal skis, applied pink triangular factory mark and printed factory mark, 8in. (Christie's) $619

A green patinated bronze figure cast from a model by Fred C. Focht, modelled as a young female skier dramatically posed downhill on a rectangular black onyx base, signed, 23½in. (Christie's) $3,542

An alabaster figure, carved from a model by Guisto Viti modelled as a young female skier kneeling adjusting her skis on a shaped rectangular base, 15½in. (Christie's) $4,428

A pair of skis, circa 1920, stamped *225, 686*, with original leather and metal bindings and silver birch poles, 88½in.(Christie's) $973

A green patinated spelter figure cast as a model by H. Fugere, modelled as a downhill male skier on a shaped rectangular black onyx base, signed, 16½in. (Christie's) $1,948

A silvered metal figure, cast from a model by Louslaud modelled as a highly stylized skier signed in the metal *Louslaud*, 11½in. (Christie's) $5,313

A wooden ski bicycle painted in black with adjustable seat and blades, 32in. high. (Christie's) $1,150

A green patinated bronze figure group, cast from a model by G.Maxim modelled as four young skiers on a sloping marble mottled cream base with incised signature, 33in. (Christie's) $3,365

A de luxe Symphonion No. 25A music box for 30cm. tin disks, with two 42-tone double combs, in walnut case, unrestored, circa 1900.
(Auction Team Köln) $2,711

A German Symphonion No 30 ST longcase clock music box for 34.5cm. diameter disks, 100-tone double comb, clockwork by Lenzkirch, Black Forest, oak case, 89in. high.   (Auction Team Köln) $12,425

A 7½in. Symphonion Disk musical box, the hinged walnut case with monochrome print, winder and eleven disks, 11in. wide.
(Christie's) $597

A 14½in. Fortuna disk musical box, with two combs, glazed motor cover, front wind and walnut case, 22in. wide, with thirty-five disks.
(Christie's) $2,418

A fine 15¾in. Symphonion table disk musical box with side-by-side combs on long bedplate of Art Nouveau design, in walnut case, on an oak pedestal cupboard, 55in. high overall, circa 1900-1910.
(Christie's) $7,254

An unusual Troubadour 56 musical box for 30cm. tin disks by B. Grosz & Co. Leipzig, 56-tone comb and side crank handle, walnut case, in working order.
(Auction Team Köln) $678

A German grandfather clock Symphonion for 34.5cm. diameter tin disks, with 100 tone double comb, walnut case with Black Forest clock mechanism, circa 1900.
(Auction Team Köln) $13,555

A 9¼in. table disk musical box, the hinged walnut case with monochrome print, winder and mandolin attachment, with nineteen disks, 11½in. wide.
(Christie's) $722

A French Aubusson tapestry of hunting scene, in the Renaissance style, circa 1890, depicting horse riders, footmen and hounds in a woodscape, with a floral border, 75¼in. high, 103in. wide.
(Christie's) $4,145

A French pastoral tapestry, circa 1900, woven in vivid colors depicting a shepherd and family resting at water's edge, within a neo-classical border and a royal-blue outer border, 80in. x 61¼in.
(Christie's) $11,600

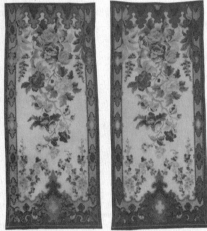

A pair of Napoleon III entre-fenêtre tapestries, circa 1860, each woven in silks, wools and metal-threads, with spring flowers on a cream-colored background, 112in. high, 50in. wide. (Christie's) $8,280

An 18th century Aubusson tapestry: woodland scene with girl on a swing, two youths and another girl, a mountain beyond, 7ft. x 7ft.6in.
(Brightwells) $2,942

A large tapestry panel woven in colored wools with a Flemish tapestry style scene with two birds in a verdant landscape, 96 x 76in., recent.
(Christie's) $2,708

A French pastoral tapestry, circa 1900, after Boucher, depicting two women and a suitor in a landscape, with foliate inner and blue outer border, 83in. x 73½in.
(Christie's) $19,660

TEDDY BEARS

A fine Farnell teddy bear with blond mohair, pronounced clipped muzzle, black stitched nose, swivel head, jointed limbs with felt pads and hump, 19in. high, 1920s. (Christie's) $2,335

A rare Farnell bear on all fours, with golden mohair, pronounced muzzle, tail and felt wood lined pads, wearing striped woollen jumper, 26¼in. long, 1930s. (Christie's) $1,835

An early British teddy bear with golden mohair, pronounced clipped muzzle, black horizontally stitched nose and black stitched mouth, 13¾in. high, circa 1920. (Christie's) $300

'George', a fine Steiff teddy bear with blond mohair, pronounced clipped muzzle, black stitched nose, mouth and claws, button in ear with remains of white label, 20in. high, circa 1908. (Christie's) $11,680

A very rare Bing clockwork crawling teddy bear, with reddish brown mohair, metal ring through nose with leather lead and clockwork mechanism operating front legs in a crawling action, original key, 10in. high, circa 1910. (Christie's) $2,168

A Steiff teddy bear, with golden mohair, pronounced clipped muzzle, brown and black glass eyes, swivel head, jointed elongated limbs with felt pads and hump, 19½in. high, 1920s. (Christie's) $2,335

A Steiff teddy bear with golden mohair, pronounced clipped muzzle, black stitched nose, mouth and claws, boot button eyes, 9¾in. high, circa 1910. (Christie's) $667

A Steiff teddy bear with white mohair, pronounced clipped muzzle, brown stitched nose, mouth and claws, brown and black glass eyes, 19½in. high, circa 1920. (Christie's) $2,502

A Chiltern musical teddy bear with golden mohair, jointed limbs with velvet pads and a pressure operated musical mechanism in body, 19in. high, 1930s. (Christie's) $584

An Alpha Farnell teddy bear with golden mohair, pronounced clipped muzzle, swivel head and jointed limbs with painted cloth pads, 26½in. high, 1930s. (Christie's) $834

A Bing somersaulting teddy bear, with reddish brown mohair, clockwork mechanism operated by winding arm back causing the bear to somersault, 11½in. high, circa 1910. (Christie's) $1,417

A rare Steiff muzzle teddy bear with blond mohair, pronounced clipped muzzle, hump and original leather muzzle and collar, button in ear, 10in. high, circa 1908. (Christie's) $2,168

A British sailor teddy bear with golden mohair, pronounced clipped muzzle, black stitched nose, mouth and claws, orange and black glass eyes, swivel head and jointed limbs, wearing sailor shirt and hat, *HMS Jupiter* hat band, 28½in. high, 1920s. (Christie's) $584

A rare Steiff record teddy bear with blond mohair, pronounced clipped muzzle, black stitched nose, mouth and claws, on metal frame with four wooden wheels stamped *Steiff*, 10½in. high, circa 1913. (Christie's) $3,169

A Steiff teddy bear with blond mohair, pronounced clipped muzzle, black stitched nose, mouth and claws, jointed elongated limbs with felt pads and hump, 15¾in. high, circa 1910. (Christie's) $2,168

An early American teddy bear with cinnamon mohair, pronounced clipped muzzle, black stitched nose and mouth, boot button eyes, 14in. high, circa 1910. (Christie's) $834

A rare Merrythought 'Punkinhead', with brown mohair, velvet muzzle, long white mohair on scalp, swivel neck, jointed limbs, yellow felt shorts, 19in. high, circa 1951. (Christie's) $4,004

A Schuco Yes/No teddy bear, with golden mohair, pronounced muzzle. tail operated head mechanism and jointed limbs with cloth pads, 18½in. high. circa 1921. (Christie's) $2.002

A Steiff teddy bear with white mohair, pronounced clipped muzzle, light brown stitched nose, mouth and claws, 12¾in. high, circa 1910. (Christie's) $1,417

A fine early Steiff teddy bear with golden apricot mohair, soft filled, pronounced muzzle, with black stitched nose, mouth and claws, boot button eyes, 28in. high, circa 1905. (Christie's) $8,343

An early British teddy bear with golden mohair, slight pronounced muzzle, jointed limbs with cloth pads and hump, 20½in. high, circa 1920. (Christie's) $500

A Steiff teddy bear with cream mohair, pronounced inset short mohair muzzle, brown stitched nose and claws, open cream felt mouth, jointed limbs with down turned hand, blue studded collar with bell, 11¾in. high, circa 1930. (Christie's) $1,501

Twin English teddy bears, a teddy bear with blond mohair, clipped muzzle, swivel head with blue cardigan, possibly Farnell, 14¼in. high, circa 1910, another identical with a pink cardigan, both in wooden chairs. (Christie's) $700

An exceptionally fine and rare Steiff black teddy bear, one of only 50 dozen black Steiff bears ordered for England after the Titanic disaster on the 14th April, 1912 when the whole country was in mourning, 19½in. high, circa 1912. (Christie's) $130,285

A Steiff teddy bear with blond mohair, pronounced clipped muzzle, black stitched nose, mouth and claws, boot button eyes, swivel head, jointed elongated limbs and hump, button in ear, 17¾in. high, circa 1910.(Christie's) $1,417

A rare red British teddy bear with red mohair, pronounced clipped muzzle, black stitched nose, mouth and claws, swivel head, jointed limbs with felt pads, possibly Farnell, 14in. high, 1920s. (Christie's) $3,169

A Steiff teddy bear with golden mohair, pronounced clipped muzzle, black stitched nose and claws, boot button eyes, swivel head, jointed elongated limbs and hump, 13¾in. high, circa 1908. (Christie's) $700

Steiff teddy bear with white ohair, pronounced clipped uzzle, pink stitched nose, mouth d claws, 17¼in. circa 1910. hristie's) $3,337

A Steiff teddy bear with golden mohair, pronounced clipped muzzle, black stitched nose, mouth and claws, boot button eyes, 12¼in., high, circa 1910. (Christie's) $1,835

A Steiff teddy bear, with cinnamon mohair, pronounced clipped muzzle, black stitched nose, mouth and claws, 23in. high, circa 1910. (Christie's) $5,339

rare Steiff 'Rod' teddy bear with ond mohair, pronounced muzzle, tched mouth, boot button eyes, rizontal seam from ear to ear, ack stitched claws, rod jointing, vivel head, jointed elongated nbs and hump, 15½in. high, circa 05. (Christie's) $8,342

'The Twins', unusual Chad Valley bear cubs, with blond mohair heads, hands and feet, red velvet muzzles, integral red and white striped baby grows, not jointed, 12in. high, 1950s. (Christie's) $500

'Willie', a fine Steiff teddy bear, with blond curly mohair, pronounced clipped muzzle, black stitched nose, mouth and claws, boot button eyes, swivel head, jointed elongated limbs, with felt pads and hump, 19in. high, circa 1910. (Christie's) $6,340

u-bear', a white Steiff center eam teddy bear, with creamy white ohair, pronounced clipped uzzle, swivel neck, elongated inted limbs and hump, button in ar, 20in. high, circa 1910. hristie's) $4,338

A British teddy bear, with golden mohair, pronounced clipped muzzle, black stitched nose, mouth and feet, jingle in body, possibly Farnell, wearing sailor's jacket, 16in. high, circa 1920. (Christie's) $633

'Brun', a fine Steiff teddy bear, with bright golden mohair, pronounced clipped muzzle, black stitched nose, mouth and claws, swivel head, jointed elongated limbs, 28in. high, circa 1906. (Christie's) $25,028

A Siemens & Halske Bj 08/54 desk telephone with drum dial, with signal key.
(Auction Team Köln) $216

A Danish extension desk telephone, wooden case, with two buttons, handset with speech key, lacking mouthpiece.
(Auction Team Köln) $339

A 'cow foot' telephone by Merck, Munich, bell, earpiece and dial restored.
(Auction Team Köln) $248

A Naglo Brothers, Berlin, M89 wall telephone, wooden case with carbon microphone, push button, with Siemens & Halske earpiece, circa 1890.
(Auction Team Köln) $1,919

A stucco Hide a Phone telephone globe, candlestick telephone cover, which opens to reveal the phone, 1910.
(Auction Team Köln) $4,235

An L M Ericsson Swedish wall desk telephone, with adjustable microphone, lightning conductor, Bell earpiece, lacking mechanism.
(Auction Team Köln) $564

A 25 piece Siemens & Halske desk exchange, the dial with bar, circa 1935.
(Auction Team Köln) $1,412

An OB O5 desk telephone by Groos & Graf, Berlin, with eagle stamps, two cranks, the receiver with horn, lacking speech key.
(Auction Team Köln) $452

An Ericsson skeleton local battery desk telephone, the handset with hygienic mouthpiece, with second bell.
(Auction Team Köln) $705

A French telephone by Grammont, Paris, wooden column with second earpiece.
(Auction Team Köln) $248

An Ericsson Swedish field telephone, wooden housing in leather case, with call key and flex, with detachable original handset.
(Auction Team Köln) $254

A Danish Ericsson skeleton desk telephone with push button, handset with speech key.
(Auction Team Köln) $1,355

A wooden wall line-dial telephone by Sterling Telephone & Electric Co., London, with alarm, and push button, handset with horn and speech key.
(Auction Team Köln) $186

A metal-cased ZB SA 24 desk telephone by KTD Nürnberg, lacking dial bar, circa 1933.
(Auction Team Köln) $310

A Danish Horsens local battery wall telephone, with wooden desk with paper clamp, metal cover, call button and complete Ericsson handset with speech key.
(Auction Team Köln) $226

An OB 05 desk telephone by Lorenz, Berlin, metal case with crank, handset with horn mouthpiece.
(Auction Team Köln) $102

A Reipos telephone by Siemens & Halske, Berlin, exchange set with 10 line levers, metal casing, 1934.
(Auction Team Köln) $169

An Ericsson skeleton telephone, handset with speech key, wooden receiver bracket, Swedish.
(Auction Team Köln) $367

A terracotta head of Zeus, late 19th/ early 20th century, probably French, 20in. high. (Christie's) $3,000

A Goldscheider terracotta figure group modelled as Europa and the Bull, stamped factory marks, 71.5cm. high. (Christie's) $1,137

A terracotta bust of an Art Nouveau maiden, with long flowing hair, embellished with large trailing poppies in a green patination, 42cm. high. (Phillips) $980

A polychrome glazed terracotta model of a lurcher, early 20th century, modelled seated on a cushion, with inset glass eyes, 43in. high. (Christie's) $4,023

A pair of 19th century terracotta urns of semi-lobed shallow form, egg and dart molded rim, on leaf molded rising foot with square base, 22in. wide, 21½in. high. (Andrew Hartley) $707

A terracotta colored plaster bust of Jean-Baptiste Poquelin Molière, after an 18th century model by Caffieri, 27in. high. (Christie's) $1,190

A French terracotta bust, entitled 'La Rieuse aux Roses' by Jean-Baptiste Carpeaux, circa 1874, inscribed *J Bt Capreaux*, with Propriété Carpeaux stamp, dated 1874, 21½in. high. (Christie's) $3,290

A pair of terracotta urns, of recent manufacture, each of splayed form with reeded ribbon and acanthus twist edge above a basket woven body, 41in. diameter. (Christie's) $2,049

A 19th century Continental Art Nouveau terracotta bust of Aurelia, her black hair tied back and applied with a flower head, and flowing down behind to form a swirling base, stamped *Cologne*, 22¾in. high. (Andrew Hartley) $308

A chinoiserie decorated terracotta jardinière, early 20th century, with stylized lion masks to the sides, with birds amidst foliage, 19½in. wide. (Christie's) $1,316

A Goldscheider terracotta wall mask, modelled as a stylized female head with orange curls and holding an apple, 13¼in. high. (Andrew Hartley) $1,005

A pair of terracotta pedestals, Doulton, Lambeth, circa 1870, of stepped rectangular form, modelled to the sides with laurel wreaths, 21in. high. (Christie's) $1,010

A French terracotta group of two cherubs, probably 18th century, the cherubs shown seated on a rocky outcrop pouring water from a jar, on an integral oval plinth, 15.5cm. high. (Christie's) $1,555

A French terracotta group, in the manner of Clodion, circa 1880, depicting three music-making Bacchic putti, one with a tambourine, the second with a shaker and the third with a flower chain, 27in. high. (Christie's) $7,050

A French terracotta figure, entitled 'Flore Accroupie' by Jean-Baptiste Carpeaux, circa 1875, inscribed *J.B. Carpeaux 1875*, with Propriété Carpeaux foundry stamp, 19½in. high. (Christie's) $6,463

A French terracotta group of a bacchante and putto in the manner of Clodion, circa 1880, inscribed *Clodion*, 15⁷/₈in. high. (Christie's) $1,880

A terracotta group figure, from a model by I. Rochard, incised signature, *Editions Recegralis Paris*, 71cm. diameter. (Christie's) $612

A Regency terracotta figure of a gentleman, early 19th century, Delaville (died 1846), shown standing with one hand inside his waistcoat, 16in. high. (Christie's) $1,006

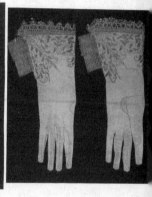

Twenty star American flag, early 19th century, handsewn cotton with double-faced stars, reinforced with machine stitching, four cotton double-faced grommets, 38½ x 53½in. (Skinner) $4,313

A pair of child's slippers, of burnished pink silk woven in metal thread with a Turkish design, edged with pink silk ruching, Turkish material for European use, 1840s. (Christie's) $1,295

Thirteen-star American flag, mid-19th century, handsewn wool with double appliquéd cotton stars, canvas hoist with pierced holes, 60 x 100in. (Skinner) $2,185

A Regency feltwork and embroidered picture of a basket of strawberries, within a comtemporary giltwood and gesso oval and later glazed frame, 19 x 16½in. (Christie's) $4,388

An Amish pieced wool quilted coverlet, Lancaster County, Pennsylvania, circa 1910, the rectangular form worked in green, crimson, turquoise, black and blue wool twill centering a Bars and Nine-Patch combined pattern with a dark green border, 76 x 75⅜in. (Christie's) $14,950

A pair of gentleman's gauntlets, of doeskin, the cuffs embroidered in gold thread with scrolling leaves and trimmed with sequins, English, circa 1640. (Christie's) $2,936

Royal 1st Devon Yeomanry Officer's sabretache, circa 1893, the dark blue cloth face bears heavily embroidered VR cypher surmounted by a bullion Crown. (Bosleys) $462

A pair of Aubusson tapestry cushions, circa 1890, each woven in wools and silks depicting spring flowers on an ivory ground within a cream outer border, with cream tassles, 23in. square. (Christie's) $2,760

Royal Bucks Hussars Officer's sabretache, pre 1901, green velvet face mounted with bullion embroidered entwined VR cypher surmounted by a Crown. (Bosleys) $493

A Regency embroidered feltwork semi-relief picture of a basket of flowers, in a giltwood and gesso shadow box, later glazed, re-gilt, 17½ x 18½in. (Christie's) $1,829

English gentleman's waistcoat, 18th century, embroidered to front with feather and boat motif, with floral and dotted border, the buttons embroidered with floral sprigs. (Skinner) $546

Victorian East Lothian Yeomanry Cavalry sabretache, 1846-1888, dark blue velvet ground, richly embroidered with a gold bullion entwined cypher surmounted by a Crown. (Bosleys) $693

One of a set of four cushions of crimson velvet, each applied with golden yellow silk satin and ivory twisted silk cord, with a leafy strapwork design, 21 x 15in., Italian, 16/17th century. (Christie's) (Four) $2,073

An Amish pieced wool and cotton quilted coverlet, Lancaster County, Pennsylvania, 1910-1920, worked in light and dark blue, burgundy and green in the Diamond-in-the-Square pattern, the central diamond with star, 72 x 71¼in. (Christie's) $7,475

A drawstring purse, of gold metal thread, woven in colored silks with pots of flowers, including lilies, carnations and roses, 17th century. (Christie's) $2,397

A drawstring purse, of gold silk, woven in colored silks and silver metal thread, with a putto at a well and figures chasing peacocks, 17th century. (Christie's) $1,476

A pair of Aubusson tapestry cushions, circa 1890, each woven in wools and silks, depicting spring flowers on a cream ground, within a garland border and green outer border, 24½in. square. (Christie's) $2,760

Quilted chintz pocket, America, circa 1825, block printed plum tree and pheasant pattern in madder, blue and drab, 14in. long. (Skinner) $1,050

A National No. 510 cast bronze cash register on mahogany base, with receipt printer and cash drawer, bears original label.
(Auction Team Köln) $734

A late 19th century pre-decimalisation till, having neo-classical boxwood stringing, in working order, 20in.
(Auction Team Köln) $630

A rare Berlin National Model 442X cash register with florid Art Nouveau decoration on the bronze casing, 1911.
(Auction Team Köln) $2,100

A National No. 78 press button cash register, highly decorative silver bronze housing, with hand crank, 1900.
(Auction Team Köln) $452

A National Model 647C cast bronze cash register with mahogany base, circa 1913.
(Auction Team Köln) $734

A National Model 7157 lever operated till, with pop-up price indicators for German currency, circa 1930.
(Auction Team Köln) $329

An Anker classic German waiter's cash register for 9 different bills, nickelled metal casing on wooden base, with drawer, circa 1920.
(Auction Team Köln) $791

A Brandt Automatic Cashier, mechanical coin changer, on pressing the keys the exact coin amounts are paid out, 1916.
(Auction Team Köln) $706

An early National Model 8 cash register for dutch currency, *N. J. Creyghton* inscribed on the ornate casing, circa 1900.
(Auction Team Köln) $1,400

Paint-decorated tôle tray, American, 19th century, rectangular with cut-out hand holds executed in red, green and gold bronzes centering a hand-painted tiger in an exotic landscape, 15¾ x 22in. (Christie's) $3,290

Polychrome decorated tin box, America, 19th century, with hinged domed lid and bail handle decorated with a band of green and leaves and red fruit on a white ground, 8⅞ in. long. (Skinner) $800

A George III tôle peinte oval tray, early 19th century, the green ground decorated with a painted roundel depicting a lady and a gentleman, 30¼in. wide. (Christie's) $3,657

A painted tin display sign, 19th century, modelled as a sailor holding a Union Jack flag, 25in. high. (Christie's) $1,217

A painted and decorated tôleware lidded box, Pennsylvania, 19th century, the rectangular domed lid with applied wire handle and scrolled strap clasp above a conforming case, 8¼in. wide. (Christie's) $1,998

A French wrought iron and tôle ware washstand, 19th century, painted pale yellow and brown, with a circular mirror supported by scrolling iron work and with a similar gallery, 28in. wide. (Christie's) $686

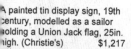

A good wrigglework tôleware coffee-pot, John B. Ketterer, Pennsylvania, mid-19th century, decorated on both sides with flowers protruding from a two-handled pot, height 11½in. x 12in. wide. (Sotheby's) $3,300

Painted tin canister, probably Connecticut, early 19th century, the round cylindrical form with attached cover and bail handle decorated with yellow brush strokes, 6½in. high. (Skinner) $1,000

A painted and decorated tôleware coffeepot, Pennsylvania, 19th century, the domed and hinged lid above a flaring cylindrical body with applied strap handle and arched spout, 10½in. high. (Christie's) $4,465

TOOLS

An early 19th century herb chopper.
(Tool Shop Auctions) $25

A four iron ⁵/₈in. Gothic sash molding plane by Wilson, Glasgow.
(Tool Shop Auctions) $378

A Cooper's side ax, 5in. edge, dupont le pertre.
(Tool Shop Auctions) $364

A massive 19th century bridgebuilders' plumb bob with steel top and tip, 8in. tall.
(Tool Shop Auctions) $112

A beautiful 18th century oak router, 7in. wide with rosewood wedge carved in the form of three turrets.
(Tool Shop Auctions) $672

A beautiful primitive French stake anvil, probably 17th century, 12in. wide.
(Tool Shop Auctions) $385

The Loch Ness Plane, A 13½in. solid lignum vitae smoothing plane, carved into the wooden body *1834*. In fact this unusual plane was made in the 1930s by a Scottish carpenter with a sense of humor.
(Tool Shop Auctions) $203

An extremely rare Holtzapffel lapping machine with three horizontal lapping disks, 2 goneostats for hand tools.
(Tool Shop Auctions) $3,640

A very high quality iron Scottish smoothing plane with beautifully finished overstuffed mahogany handle and wave formed tote.
(Tool Shop Auctions) $616

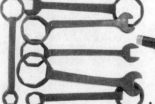

A set of six coachbuilders' hub wrenches.
(Tool Shop Auctions) $45

A fine quality rosewood plough plane by Mathieson with rosewood stem wedges and brass fittings, skate front.
(Tool Shop Auctions) $826

An unusual handled, 4in. twin iron cornice plane by Stewart.
(Tool Shop Auctions) $308

An early masting ax by G. Dowson, 17in. x 5½in.
(Tool Shop Auctions) $126

A tiny pair of 3in. 18th century dividers. Delightful.
(Tool Shop Auctions) $35

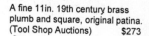

A fine 11in. 19th century brass plumb and square, original patina.
(Tool Shop Auctions) $273

An important screwstem plough by Green, one of only five ploughs of his style found to date.
(Tool Shop Auctions) $280

A lovely Austrian compassed fluting plane dated 1834, elegantly shaped mouth.
(Tool Shop Auctions) $182

An early ax head, possibly 16/17th century, pitted, excavated from the footings of a building in Amsterdam. Good for age.
(Tool Shop Auctions) $63

A 14½in. dovetailed and rosewood infilled panel plane with Norris type adjuster and original Norris iron. Handmade by Master Craftsman Bob Funnell from Coventry England.
(Tool Shop Auctions) $1,120

A most unusual 13½in. beech handled molding plane by Nelson. The profile suggests creating fluting for columns, or possibly the corners of chests. Round topped iron by Moseley.
(Tool Shop Auctions) $364

A magnificent French stake anvil, 17in. high and 20in. wide, decorated on both sides with a series of Smiths' punch marks in the form of a cross.
(Tool Shop Auctions) $1,750

A rosewood and beech 1in. screwbox and tap.
(Tool Shop Auctions) $105

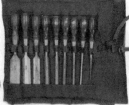

A set of 9 Stanley Everlasting chisels in the original, worn roll, chisels in superb condition.
(Tool Shop Auctions) $1,288

A rare half gallon steel oil 'kettle' by Kayes, probable early replaced lid.
(Tool Shop Auctions) $77

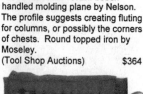

Set 68 Second Bombay Native Infantry, first version, oval bases with officer and pioneer, in original printer's type box, 1900, and Set 36 Sussex Regiment at the slope, 1898. (Christie's) $691

Extremely rare set 1397 model fort, with garrison of soldiers in khaki, the cardboard fort assembled from flat lithographed card parts provided in an envelope laid flat across the top of a standard size two-row illustrated display box, 1937.
(Christie's) $2,940

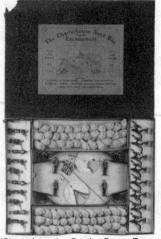

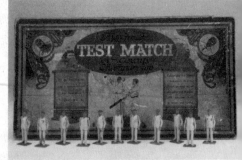

The 'Charterhouse' Sand Bag Encampment, comprising ten Gordon Highlanders firing as in Britains Set 156, eight Zulus as in Britains Set 147, four Royal Lancaster Regiment gunners with ramrods as from Britains Set 148, four Simon and Rivollet toy cannons with ammunition.
(Christie's) $7,772

The Great Test match or County Championship, extremely rare Pealland Series 115 contained eleven Britains cricketers, a cricket ball and board, in original color illustrated box with label.
(Christie's) $4,317

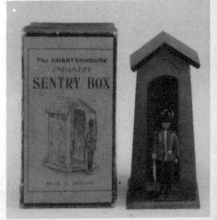

British Camel Corps, only available in Britains largest Set 131, two non-matching examples, 1912 and 1915. (Christie's) $1,899

The 'Charterhouse' Infantry sentry box, comprising wooden sentry box with Britains Grenadier Guard at attention, in original box, 1909.
(Christie's) $517

Display Set 73, comprising General Officer with binoculars, Royal Horse Artillery at the walk with officer, Life Guards, Royal Scots Greys, 17th Lancers, Band of the Line, the Black Watch at the slope, Norfolk Regiment, in original two-tier box with interior fittings, 1960. (Christie's) $3,972

Paris Office Production Matelots, running at the trail with petty officer, 1920. (Christie's) $604

Set 1871 Historical Collector's Series, rare un-cataloged set, containing Buffs, Grenadier Guards, Royal Sussex Regiment, Royal Welsh Fusilier, Scots Guards, Royal Warwickshire Regiment, Royal Marine, Royal Navy Blue Jackets, Whitejacket, Petty Officer, Midshipman and Admiral, in original box, 1940. (Christie's) $2,073

The Texas Rangers, set 1508, non-cataloged set with character merchandise box label, in original box, end label Texas Rangers No. 150 – Made in England, 1937. (Christie's) $5,182

Set 91 United States infantry, extremely rare first version in white spiked helmets, valise packs, at the slope with 'bemedalled' officer, box, 1898. (Christie's) $4,836

Set 38 South African mounted infantry, two on black horses and two on brown horses, officer with pistol on brown horse, 1912. (Christie's) $724

Set 12 11th Hussars, in original Whisstock box, 1935. (Christie's) $328

City Imperial Volunteers on guard, Set 104 with officer with sword and pistol, in original early illustrated box, 1905, three similar soldiers in red jackets, 1903 and four U.S. Infantry on guard figures in red jackets, 1908. (Christie's) $517

A Linemar clockwork Mickey Mouse xylophone player, lithographed tinplate, with playing action, 1950s, 17cm. high. (Christie's) $624

A rare Steiff polar bear, with white mohair, elongated head, black stitched nose and claws, rotating head joint and jointed limbs with felt pads, 14in. long, circa 1910. (Christie's) $1,167

Painted and carved rocking horse, J.A. Yost, Philadelphia, 1860-90, the fully carved red-brown horse with leather saddle rocks on a black painted platform, 73in. long. (Skinner) $1,72

A rare Steiff camel on wheels, with brown felt body, beige mohair head, neck, humps, tops of front legs and tip of tail, leather bridle and red felt saddle cloth, 9in. circa 1908. (Christie's) $917

A Roullet & Decamps skin covered clockwork pig, with brown glass eyes, and serrated wheels on the feet, when wound, he walks forward, moves his head from side to side, squeaks and grunts, 11in. long. (Christie's) $1,068

A Bing Trippel-Trappel dog, with white felt with black patch over one eye, ear and tail, boot button eyes, black stitched nose, jointed legs with pull-along walking mechanism 5½in. high, 1920s. (Christie's) $300

Louis Marx clockwork 'Let The Drummer Boy Play While You Swing and Sway', parade bass drummer beating with right hand and pushing drum on trolley 1930s, 19cm. (Christie's) $624

Donald Duck, a Japanese clockwork celluloid and tinplate toy by Kuramochi for Masudaya, distributed in the U.K. by Paradise, circa 1935, 6in. high, in original cardboard box. (Christie's) $1,295

A Wyandotte Clockwork 'Humphreymobile' tricycle, lithographed tinplate, portly character riding tricycle with outhouse on back, 1940s, 18cm. high. (Christie's) $410

A large Steiff rabbit, with brown and cream mohair, brown and black plastic eyes, red stitched nose and mouth, black stitched claws, felt lined ears, 1950s.
(Christie's) $433

Lehmann 725 Echo cycle, blue machine with rider dressed in brown suit.
(Christie's) $1,562

A Dean's rag book Mickey Mouse, with black velvet body, white velvet face with printed features, blue integral velvet shorts, yellow felt hands, wire limbs, rare metal button to back, 6¼in. high, circa 1932.
(Christie's) $633

Rare Steiff cat skittles, a pre-button part set comprising of white felt cat Kingpin, 9in. high, seven similar cats with gray felt, red ribbon with bell around necks, 8in. high and a green and pink felt ball, in a contemporary red box, 1890s.
(Christie's) $8,009

A Unique Art clockwork Howdy Doody piano, lithographed tinplate, with dancing Howdy Doody and Bob Smith at the piano, 1940s, 16.5cm. wide.
(Christie's) $822

A Steiff elephant on wheels, with gray mohair, boot button eyes backed with red felt, white felt tusks, embroidered red felt saddle cloth, pull-cord voice to back, 16in. long, circa 1920.
(Christie's) $1,251

A pair of Steiff Boston bull-terriers, both with brown rough plush, large boot button eyes, black wrinkle lines to face, white mohair chests and front paws, squeakers, 15in. long, circa 1912.
(Christie's) $834

A Carette clockwork two-seat open tourer, lithographed in cream, with red black and gold detailing, coal-scuttle bonnet, two lamps, rubber tyres and driver, painted in blue with brown gaiters, circa 1907, 26cm. long.
(Christie's) $4,935

A rare large Chiltern rabbit skater, with short white mohair, blue wool jacket with white high collar, pink artificial silk toggles and rexine belt, original orange card swing tag, 24in., 1930s.
(Christie's) $500

An large Alps police motorcyclist, lithographed tinplate toy with push-and-go action, with electric headlamps and rear light, circa 1965, 31.5cm. long.
(Auction Team Köln) $2,937

An early child's tricycle with rubber tyres, pedal drive to the two rear wheels, upholstered seat and back rest, American, by Kirk-Latty Mfg., Cleveland, circa 1900.
(Auction Team Köln) $479

A battery-operated lithographed tinplate 'Friendship' space capsule by T.M. Modern Toys, Japan, circa 1960.
(Auction Team Köln) $16

A children's wooden cart, English, early 20th century, painted bottle green with yellow chassis and brown wheels with two seats one behind the other, 53in. long.
(Christie's) $451

An Indian polychrome carved wood cart, possibly late 19th/early 20th century, modelled with the standing figures of two horses, shown richly caparisoned on a shaped platform with a twin axle, 32in long.
(Christie's) $209

A painted wood doll house, American, 19th century, the peaked roof with chimney and keystone above two floors each with two rooms, on straight feet, 30¾in. wide. (Christie's) $4,46

A Lehmann 'Mars' lithographed tinplate balloon, the balloon rises when the lower part of the string is pulled, after 1896.
(Auction Team Köln) $2,823

A Günthermann clockwork Vis-a-Vis motor car, lithographed in blue, driver painted in gray with black cap, with bellows action driven from rear wheels, 1890s, 25cm. long.
(Christie's) $2,961

A battery-operated lithographed tinplate Apollo – United States space capsule, by S. Horikawa, plastic underside and nose, circa 1968, 24cm. long.
(Auction Team Köln) $18

A mid 19th century carved and painted wooden rocking horse, on sharply bowed rockers with turned stretchers, glass eyes, distressed saddle, hair mane and tail and leather straps, 215cm. long. (Bristol) $1,805

A carved and painted rocking horse, American, 19th century, the black-painted, carved head with brass eyes above a rectangular saddleboard, 41in. long. (Christie's) $1,528

A Continental hobby horse, 19th century, with horsehair applied mane and leather upholstered seat supported on two wooden spoked and wrought-iron bound wheels, restorations, 75in. long. (Christie's) $9,564

Mickey Mouse Doll, circa 1930s-1940s with replaced applied pie eyes, mother of pearl buttons, with the Walt Disney stamp on the bottom of each foot, bottom right foot signed by Walt Disney, 18in. high. (Christie's) $2,350

A row of two Irish town houses, of ten bays and two storeys, the doors and windows on the ground floor set back under arches, 28in. wide, circa 1830. (Christie's) $2,306

A rare Steiff 'Jack Rabbit' with white and golden mohair head, ears, hand and tail, swivel head, jointed arms wearing purple velvet jacket, pink velvet knickerbockers, 8¾in. high, 1930s.(Christie's) $1,001

A very rare Tipp & Co. lithographed tinplate motorcycle and sidecar, clockwork,with steerable front wheel, circa 1935, 31cm. long. (Auction Team Köln) $13,555

Meier penny toy sailing boat, lithographed yellow and pale blue. (Christie's) $575

Baron von Drais's Draisine, a model of the Drais bicycle of 1817, dated *1884*, mainly wood, with balancing shelf, mudguards and leather saddle, propelled by running. (Auction Team Köln) $6,777

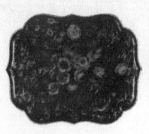

A papier-mâché tray of shaped rectangular form decorated with urn of flowers and gilt, 31in. (Brightwells) $1,788

A George III brass-bound mahogany oval tray, with scrolled carrying-handles, 24 x 16in. (Christie's) $2,502

A 19th century English tôle peinte tray with gilt decoration. (Bonhams & Brooks) $450

Mahogany butler's table, the tray top with hinged sides and raised on an earlier ring turned X framed support, 18th/19th century, 29in. (G.A. Key) $2,198

A 19th century rectangular black papier mâché tray, having serpentine edges and a raised border, polychrome decorated wild strawberries and other foliage, with gilt highlights, 31½in. (Woolley & Wallis) $1,540

A 19th century mahogany butler's tray, with raised sides incorporating loop handles, the stand with baluster turned folding legs joined by turned stretchers, 28½in. high. (Andrew Hartley) $493

An early Victorian papier mâché tray, second quarter 19th century, B.Walton & Co., the shaped rectangular ground painted with a coastal scene within a redecorated border, 27½in. wide. (Christie's) $3,474

A Regency papier mâché tray, early 19th century, of rectangular outline with raised borders, decorated with an Oriental style landscape of pavilions in a woodland, 30¾in. wide. (Christie's) $2,726

Two Regency graduated papier mâché trays, early 19th century, of cartouche outline, the green grounds decorated with flowers, foliage and exotic birds heightened with gilt scrolls, 60.6cm. and 38in. wide. (Christie's) $1,829

An Edwardian mahogany, inlaid and penwork kidney shaped tray, 70cm. wide.
(Bonhams & Brooks) $585

A Victorian papier mâché rectangular tray, mid 19th century, the black ground decorated with flowers, foliage and some insects, heightened with gilt, 76cm. wide.
(Christie's) $1,097

A 19th century marquetry and satinwood tray of oval form with pierced brass gallery and loop handles, central foliate patera with initials, 26¾in. wide.
(Andrew Hartley) $1,000

A Regency black and gilt-japanned papier mâché tray, by Dyson and Benson, on a later stand, the canted rectangular tray with pierced handles, and Greek-key gallery, with central cartouche of a farmhouse on a river, 29½in. wide.
(Christie's) $5,589

A Regency polychrome and gilt-japanned tôle tray of rounded rectangular form with flared rim, the sealing-wax red ground decorated with flowers and panels of fruit, the center with a scene of two figures in a landscape, 21¼ x 28¾in.
(Christie's) $4,171

A mahogany and teak butler's tray-on-stand, early 19th century, the oval tray with hinged sides and pierced handles, carved throughout with rosettes, lozenges and geometric devices, 33in.
(Christie's) $872

A Victorian japanned metal tray, mid 19th century, of rectangular outline with raised border, the black ground decorated overall with flowers and foliage heightened with gilt, 77cm. wide.
(Christie's) $1,189

A Victorian painted papier mâché tray, mid 19th century, B. Walton & Co., of cartouche outline with molded shaped borders, the center decorated with a mountainous landscape, 25½in. wide. (Christie's) $3,619

A Regency tôle peinte rectangular tray, early 19th century, decorated with figures in classical dress, possibly Josephine, shown seated under a portico with a landscape beyond, 22 x 30½in.
(Christie's) $2,743

A Luba stool, D.R. Congo, the circular seat supported by a pair of caryatid male and female figures, the former holding a lance, 48cm. high. (Bonhams) $1,029

A Yoruba Opon Ifa circular cover, Nigeria, divided into four panels, carved in relief with self-dompting figures, a figure in horseback flanked by attendants, 47.5cm. diameter. (Bonhams) $588

An unusual Awka figural stool, Nigeria, the support carved with a standing figure, the upraised arms holding the slightly concave circular seat, 57cm. high. (Bonhams) $1,029

A bronze bell, Benin, Nigeria, 19th century, of quadrangular form, cast on one side with a face, with raised edges and ball corners, 17cm. high. (Bonhams) $441

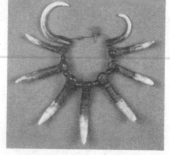

A fine Toraja necklace, Sulawesi, composed of seven crocodile teeth pendants and two boar's tusk pendants, bound with plaited rattan to the wood sockets, 33cm. wide. (Bonhams) $1,029

A pair of paddles, Noa or Nee, Santa Cruz, the leaf-shaped blades carved in shallow relief on one side with pair of anthropomorphic legs and arms, 180cm. long. (Bonhams) $8,085

BUYER BEWARE

Cracks in wooden tribal art have a detrimental effect not just on its appearance but also on its value - but it can depend on where the damage is to be found.

An obvious crack in, say, a fetish figure could halve the amount it would be worth in perfect condition. If the damage is hidden on the back, however, the value could fall by just a third.

A war canoe prow figurehead, Toto Isu, New Georgia, Western District, Solomon Islands, carved with a head with prognathous jaw and long nose, open mouth bearing clenched teeth, 21cm. high. (Bonhams) $2,205

An Ngeende mask, Ishende-Mala-Dia-Masheke, D.R. Congo, the shield-shaped face below a large pair of curving horns suspended from a conical forehead, circular protruding eyes, 37cm. high. (Bonhams) $588

A Bamun prestige stool, Cameroon, the circular seat and base supported by two registers of leopards, scorched detail, 37cm. high. (Bonhams) $882

An unusual whale tooth currency necklace, Fiji, composed of twenty-two carved pump sections of sperm whale tooth, a large central pendant of semicircular form in the middle, 32cm. long. (Bonhams) $1,764

A Dan mask, Liberia, carved with pierced slit eyes, incised brows and forehead ridges, 34cm. tall. (Bonhams) $441

A Jima chair, Ethiopia, the three C-shaped legs supporting a circular seat, with solid curved stepped back, 86cm. high. (Bonhams) $441

A Mbunda mask, Samahongo, Zambia, the large round face with slit pierced almond eyes beneath arched brows and furrowed forehead, 49cm. diameter. (Bonhams) $1,470

A dogan mask, Ireli, Mali, of rectangular form with pierced triangular eyes, tapering horns and pointed ears, 49cm. high. (Bonhams) $441

A Lovale mask, Western Zambia, with slit pierced almond eyes, straight nose and open pierced oval mouth with carved teeth, 26cm. high. (Bonhams) $662

A Chimu figural boulder, Peru, the flat face carved with a standing priest wearing elaborate head-dress, the hands held to the chest, 12cm. high. (Bonhams) $294

FASCINATING FACT

The Yoruba area of Nigeria has an unusual number of twin births. If one of the twins died, however, the village carver would fashion a pair of wooden statues to honour the dead child, and help the family cope with their loss.

These figures are very popular with collectors of tribal art.

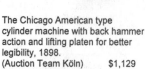

A white Mignon Model 4 export model of the German pointer typewriter for the French market, with wooden cover, 1923.
(Auction Team Köln) $847

The Chicago American type cylinder machine with back hammer action and lifting platen for better legibility, 1898.
(Auction Team Köln) $1,129

A Japanese 'Nippon –Type' single type machine with flat bed for 2,205 symbols and characters, circa 1958.
(Auction Team Köln) $903

An unusual Lambert decorative American typewriter by Frank Lambert. 1896.
(Auction Team Köln) $875

A Liliput Typewriter Model A export version of the German index typewriter by Justin Bamberger, 1907.
(Auction Team Köln) $3,671

A Tip-Tip typewriter, a Czech version of the Mignon type, with cover and original box, circa 1936
(Auction Team Köln) $310

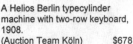

An American Hall index typewriter, perhaps the first practical portable typewriter, with original wooden case, 1881.
(Auction Team Köln) $903

A Helios Berlin typecylinder machine with two-row keyboard, 1908.
(Auction Team Köln) $678

A rare National No. 2 3-row American portable typewriter, 1920
(Auction Team Köln) $282

An unusual Burnett American typewriter with oblique typebasket, only 7 models known worldwide, 1907.
(Auction Team Köln) $6,495

An American Crown pointer typewriter by Byron Brooks, New York, with round front and three-row typebar, 1894.
(Auction Team Köln) $7,625

A red Mignon Model 2 example from an early production run of the first German pointer typewriter by AEG, 1904.
(Auction Team Köln) $1,468

An early American pointer typewriter, World No. 2, with semi-circular index, in original wooden case, 1886.
(Auction Team Köln) $1,017

A Lambert decorative typewriter of unusual design by Frank Lambert, 1896.
(Auction Team Köln) $1,129

The Keaton Music Typewriter, American notation typewriter, 1947.
(Auction Team Köln) $1,977

A bronze Rem-Sho American understrike machine with attractive copper casing, lacking carriage, 1896.
(Auction Team Köln) $339

A Liliput Model A typewriter, second model of the German index machine by Justin Bamberger, Munich, with tin cover, 1907.
(Auction Team Köln) $3,783

An American The Postal typewheel machine of classic design, 1902.
(Auction Team Köln) $791

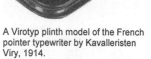

Kanzler No. 4 robust German typebar machine, with two shift keys, lacking bell, 1912
(Auction Team Köln) $1,242

A Virotyp plinth model of the French pointer typewriter by Kavalleristen Viry, 1914.
(Auction Team Köln) $621

A Hammond No. 2 typewriter with unusual wide carriage, missing two keys, 1893.
(Auction Team Köln) $197

French Mignon Model 2 version of the popular German pointer typewriter, with metal cover, 1905.
(Auction Team Köln) $508

An Aluminum Featherweight Blickensderfer, lightweight model of the popular Blick No. 5, folding color ribbon holder for easy transportation, 1893.
(Auction Team Köln) $259

A New American Typewriter No. 5 index typewriter with carriage at right angles to the type direction, 1890.
(Auction Team Köln) $988

A Toshiba Model BW 1113
Japanese typewriter with 36
typestrips each of 39 symbols, with
three further wooden type boxes,
circa 1955.
(Auction Team Köln) $1,016

A German Frister & Rossmann
understrike machine with so-called
Berlin sleeping board, 1900.
(Auction Team Köln) $734

An early German post-war Olympia
Orbis typewriter with unusual
Arabic keyboard, 1949.
(Auction Team Köln) $147

North's Typewriter, one of the rare
four models of typewriter history,
with the type bar behind the
carriage for visible typing, 1892 .
(Auction Team Köln) $7,907

A New American Typewriter No. 5
index typewriter with carriage at
right angles to type direction, 1890.
(Auction Team Köln) $1,694

An early American Remington
Standard Typewriter No. 2
understrike machine, with original
wooden platen, 1879.
(Auction Team Köln) $310

A Salter Standard No. 6 British
typebar machine with two
decorated typebasket pillars, 1900.
(Auction Team Köln) $903

A Jewett No. 10 American
understrike machine with full
keyboard, forerunner of the
German Urania, 1898.
(Auction Team Köln) $1,129

A Culema Model 3 early version of
the elegant type-bar machine from
Lehmann Brothers, Erfurt, 1919.
(Auction Team Köln) $847

A Germania No 5 German understrike machine by H. & A. Scheffer, under licence from The Jewett Typewriter Co., circa 1900. (Auction Team Köln) $931

A Fitch typewriter, American version, No. 338, the front paper 'basket' with spring-loaded wire retainer and curved sheet steel back with patent dates including 1886, 10in. (Christie's) $7,254

A Caligraph No. 3 early American understrike machine with full keyboard and two shift keys, 1883. (Auction Team Köln) $791

A Williams No 4 four row model of the popular American Grasshopper typebar machine, 1900. (Auction Team Köln) $1,129

A Hammond No. 2 American type shuttle machine with round Ideal keyboard and back hammer action, 1893. (Auction Team Köln) $339

A Rossmannia prototype four-row front strike machine by Frister & Rossmann, similar to the Royal Model 10, circa 1910. (Auction Team Köln) $2,485

A Pittsburgh Visible No. 10 American typebar machine, keyboard and typebars can be removed by two levers, 1902. (Auction Team Köln) $847

A Fitch typewriter, by The Fitch Typewriter Company Ltd, London, England, with open sheet-metal front 'basket' with rule, adjustable left-hand margin device, 11¼in. (Christie's) $10,018

A very rare round Williams No.1 typewriter with curved three-row keyboard and Grasshopper mechanism, 1891. (Auction Team Köln) $5,648

A mahogany walking stick with gold plated ferrule, the box wood handle carved as a dog's head with glass eyes, 35¼in. long, late 19th/early 20th century. (Andrew Hartley) $439

A 19th century ebony walking stick with white metal mount modelled as a head of a military gentleman, 35¾in. long. (Andrew Hartley) $447

A carved wood mounted walking stick, circa 1850, the crook handle carved as a face of a moustached gentleman emerging from a crustacean like form, 38in.(Christie's) $362

An ivory gadget walking stick, second quarter 20th century, the knob handle inset with a watch, on an ebony shaft, 34½in. (Christie's) $995

An ivory mounted gadget walking stick, circa 1890, with a bulbous knob opening to reveal a compass and a marine etching to the interior, 35¼in. (Christie's) $906

An ivory mounted walking stick, late 19th century, the knob handle carved as the 'Man in the Moon', with a silver collar on a knarled coromandel shaft, 34¾in. (Christie's) $995

A flask or "Tippling" walking stick, early 20th century, the root wood crock handle with a brass collar unscrewing to reveal a glass spirit phial, 35in. (Christie's) $634

A Victorian bamboo walking stick, the tiger's eye finial applied with gold plated mounts embossed with scrolling foliage, 33¼in. long. (Andrew Hartley) $477

A Victorian fruitwood walking stick, the ivory handle of baluster form carved with a figure of a soldier over an inscription and stiff leaf banding, 34¼in. long. (Andrew Hartley) $616

A George III stained and carved wood walking stick, 18th century, the handle modelled as a male head, with ribbon tied wig, the tapering shaft with knopped tip, 33in. long. (Christie's) $1,391

An ivory mounted walking stick, second quarter 20th century, the bulbous knob handle carved as the head of Janus, with two skull faces between the faces of a bearded man and a woman, 39¾in. (Christie's) $1,991

An ebony walking stick the silver covered handle in the form of a golf club, leafage scroll engraved, Birmingham 1925. (Brightwells) $1,036

A late Victorian malacca cane with ivory grip, the grip modelled as a dog's head, 36¼in. long. (Christie's) $1,490

A 19th century bamboo walking stick, the white metal handle modelled as a vixen on a branch with a cub, 36in. long. (Andrew Hartley) $646

A 19th century ebony walking stick with white metal finial, modelled as a bust of Punch, 36½in. long. (Andrew Hartley) $431

An antler horn mounted walking stick with an L-shaped handle and metal collar on a bamboo shaft, late 19th century, 33¾in. (Christie's) $145

A white metal mounted walking stick, early 20th century, the crock handle cast as a racing horse, with inset glass eyes, 36½in. (Christie's) $1,086

A Victorian bamboo walking stick with gold ferrule, agate ball finial, the shaft embellished with poker work, 34½in. long. (Andrew Hartley) $200

A 19th century thorn walking stick, the white metal handle modelled as a dog's head, 35in. long. (Andrew Hartley) $447

A late Victorian malacca cane with ivory grip, the grip modelled as a boxer dog's head, inset with glass eyes, 36½in. long. (Christie's) $782

An ivory handled walking stick, late 19th century, carved as a head, possibly Mephistopheles, with silver collar, hallmarks indistinct, on a knotted ebonized shaft, 36in. (Christie's) $2,194

A gadget walking stick, early 20th century, the plated metal and leather bound flared knob handle, swivelling open to reveal an adjustable telescope, 33¾in. (Christie's) $815

An ivory mounted walking stick, the knob handle carved as a bust of a Chinaman, with a metal collar on a plain ebony shaft, the handle late 19th century, 40¼in. (Christie's) $579

A 19th century malacca walking stick, the white metal handle modelled as a dog's head, similar ferrule with waved banding, and tapering shaft, 33in. (Andrew Hartley) $385

A molded copper horse and sulky weathervane, attributed to J.W. Fiske and Company, New York City, the full bodied form with rider in helmet and habit seated in a two-wheel sulky holding the reins to a running horse, 37in. long. (Christie's) $12,925

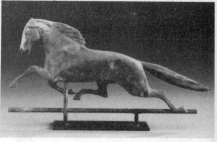

A molded copper and zinc Dexter weathervane, Cushing and White, Waltham, Massachusetts, late 19th century, with cast head above a molded mane, articulated body and tail, 26in. long. (Christie's) $3,525

A molded copper Dexter weathervane, J.W. Fiske and Company, New York City, the cast zinc head with cast applied ears above a molded body of a running horse with applied molded tail, on a rod support with modern base, 31in. long. (Christie's) $2,938

A molded and gilded copper steeplechase horse weathervane, A.L. Jewell (active 1852-1867), Waltham, Massachusetts, molded in two parts, leaping with forelegs tucked underneath and rear legs extended over a stamped sheet metal fence, 37in. long. (Christie's) $94,000

A molded and gilded copper hackney horse weathervane, attributed to Cushing and White, Waltham, Massachusetts, late 19th century, the molded body with crimped and cut sheet copper ears, mane and cropped tail, on a modern base, 26½in. wide. (Christie's) $10,575

A molded copper and zinc horse and sulky weathervane, Cushing and White, Waltham, Massachusetts, late 19th century, the full bodied form with rider in helmet and habit seated in a two-wheel sulky holding the reins to a running horse, 26½in. long. (Christie's) $17,625

Colonel Patchen molded copper horse weather vane, America, late 19th century, full-bodied figure of a running horse, zinc head, verdigris surface with traces of ocher paint, with wall brackets, no stand, 18½in. high x 41in. long.
(Skinner) $6,900

Cushing & White full bodied copper running horse and jockey weathervane, Waltham, Massachusetts, 19th century, old ocher paint, traces of gilt, impressed maker's tag on rod, 26¾in. long.
(Skinner) $13,800

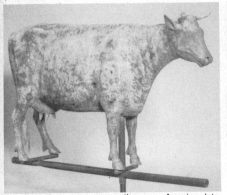

Gilt molded copper cow weathervane, America, late 19th century, full-bodied figure with weathered gilt surface, 33in. wide.(Skinner) $13,800

A molded copper and zinc yellow-painted steer weathervane, probably Cushing and White, Waltham, Massachusetts, late 19th century, the cast head with applied horns, ears, and tail above a yellow-painted molded body, 25¼in. long. (Christie's) $9,400

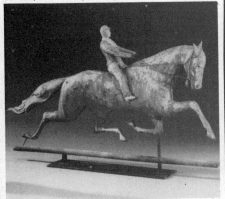

A molded copper and zinc horse and rider weathervane, attributed to J.W. Fiske and Company, New York City, the full-bodied form with separate jockey in helmet and habit astride a galloping horse, 33in. long. (Christie's) $18,800

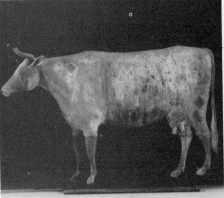

A cast zinc and copper cow weathervane, J. Howard and Company, West Bridgewater, Massachusetts, the cast applied horns above a molded head and shoulders with molded copper body, legs, udder and tail, 28¾in. long. (Christie's) $18,800

A cast iron and copper arrow weathervane, possibly by Deacon Shem Drowne Boston, the pierced arow with lyre shaped banner continuing to a fluttering tail, 3in. wide. (Christie's) $12,925

A gilded and molded zinc and sheet copper bannerette weathervane, attributed to J. Howard and Company, West Bridgewater, Massachusetts, 82in. high. (Christie's) $9,400

A small cast zinc and molded copper weathervane, J. Howard and Company, West Bridgewater, Massachusetts, the molded head and body with shaped comb and feathers above a groove and punch decorated arched tail, 12½in. long. (Christie's) $8,225

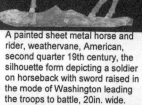

A molded copper leaping horse weathervane, A.L. Jewell (active 1852-1867), Waltham, Massachusetts, the abstracted form depicted with hole eyes, notched mouth, applied ears and flowing stamped and serrated tail, 36in. long. (Christie's) $127,000

A molded copper and zinc rooster weathervane, attributed to J.W. Fiske and Company, New York City, the molded body with applied grooved comb above an applied molded and punched tail, 23in. high. (Christie's) $4,113

A painted sheet metal horse and rider, weathervane, American, second quarter 19th century, the silhouette form depicting a soldier on horseback with sword raised in the mode of Washington leading the troops to battle, 20in. wide. (Christie's) $4,113

A painted and cast zinc and copper rooster weathervane, attributed to J. Howard and Company, West Bridgewater, Massachusetts, with abstracted comb, wattle, beak and eyes and articulated breast and wing feathers, 25½in. long. (Christie's) $12,925

A zinc and sheet copper Indian weathervane, attributed to A.L. Jewell, Waltham, Massachusetts, depicting an Indian with zinc left arm holding a drawn bow and arrow, 26in. high. (Christie's) $11,750

Gilt molded copper rooster weather vane, America, late 19th century, full-bodied figure perched on an arrow, (minor gilt loss), 39½in. high. (Skinner) $12,650

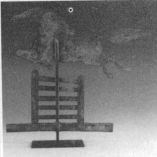

A cast zinc and copper bannerette church weathervane, attributed to J. Howard and Company, Bridgewater, Massachusetts, with paddlewheel tail, all surmounted by a sphere and prong terminus, 25½in.wide. (Christie's) $2,115

Large cast iron rooster weather vane, America, 19th century, attributed to Rochester Iron Works, gilt sheet iron tail, traces of gilt on the body. (Skinner) $4,313

A molded copper and zinc steeplechase horse weathervane, A.L. Jewell, Waltham, Massachusetts, with zinc head with hole-eyes, 28in. long. (Christie's) $28,200

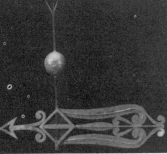

A molded and painted copper rooster weathervane, stamped by J.W. Fiske and Company, New York City, the molded body with applied comb, wattle and feather-molded tail above spurred feet, 33in. high. (Christie's) $32,900

A gilded copper and zinc bannerette weathervane, attributed to J. Howard and Company, West Bridgewater, Massachusetts, the gilt iron lightning rod with gilt ball above a gilt cast-zinc diamond terminating in a scrolled tail with cast-zinc arrow, 54in. long. (Christie's) $5,640

A cast zinc and copper weathervane, J. Howard and Company (active 1850-1868), West Bridgewater, Massachusetts, the cast and molded zinc head with applied ears and crinkle cut mane and tail, 48in.high. (Christie's) $35,250

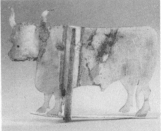

A molded copper and zinc prancing horse weathervane, A. L. Jewell and Co, Waltham, Massachusetts, the head with sharply cut applied mane above a molded body, 28in. high. (Christie's) $11,750

Gilt-copper and iron sailing ship weathervane, America, late 19th century, from Gloucester, Massachusetts area, with three directionals (no west), 32in. high. (Skinner) $2,300

A copper and zinc bull weathervane, possibly J. Howard and Company, West Bridgewater, or Tuckerman, Boston, Massachusetts, mid 19th century, 18in. wide. (Christie's) $1,645

A carved, gessoed and gilded pine American eagle wall plaque, American, late 19th/20th century, perched atop a medallion carved in deep relief with several sailing ships, 42½in. long.
(Sotheby's) $8,050

A fine and well patinated wood kogo, signed *Itsumin*, Edo Period (19th century), modelled as a group of blind men climbing on an elephant, 3½in. long.
(Christie's) $9,378

A large polychrome relief carved wood Royal coat-of-arms, circa 1820, the shield flanked by lion and unicorn, the shaped backplate with raised foliage, 40in. wide.
(Christie's) $10,971

A Black Forest carved and stained walnut figure of a hunter, 19th century, with a stag tied over his shoulders and with his dog by his side, signed *J. Huggler*, 39in. high.
(Bonhams) $5,181

One of a pair of Continental carved limewood and wrought iron three light wall appliques, 19th century, the scroll branches with later nozzles and drip pans issuing from cartouche shaped backplates, 28in. high.(Christie's)(Two) $4,023

A pair of Black Forest carved wood bears, each hollowed out to form a lidded container, one standing, and one seated, 16in. and 13in.
(Brightwells) $2,280

Painted wood mansion model, America, late 19th century, the brick painted Italianate-style building with central octagonal tower, an 'S' banner weathervane, 28in. wide.
(Skinner) $4,025

A pair of polychrome figures of kings, German, late 18th or early 19th century, each shown standing in formal costume, re-decorated, 30in. high.
(Christie's) $5,120

A set of six giltwood altar candlesticks, 20th century, the knopped and waisted foliate clasped stems on triform bases and raised on scroll feet, 31in. high.
(Christie's) $1,463

WOOD

A carved oak ceiling boss, possibly 16th century, the circular panel carved in relief with seven faces, 10¼in. wide.
(Christie's) $1,097

Carved and painted swan figure, America, 19th century, flattened full-bodied figure painted white with black and yellow features, mounted on a carved oblong base, 16¾in. long. (Skinner) $14,950

A large carved and stained wood relief panel of The Virgin and a cherub on a nimbus, 19th century, the figure shown with arms outstretched above a painted scroll supported by a cherub with nimbus below, losses, 59in. high.
(Christie's) $4,388

A Malines polychrome carved wood figure of Christ, early 16th century, with right hand raised, His left hand holding a copper orb and cross, on a stepped square section plinth, 13½in. high.
(Christie's) $4,023

A pair of Ceylonese carved ebony models of lions, 18th century, each shown seated on their haunches, inset with bone eyes, teeth and claws, with tails looping over their backs, 13in. and 13½in. high.
(Christie's) $5,486

A carved wood polychrome figure of a Saint depicted standing, his green and red robes with gilt embellishment, on circular base, 19th century or possibly earlier, 19¼in. high.
(Andrew Hartley) $363

A Continental carved tobacco jar of owl form, early 20th century, set with glass eyes, on a circular base, some damage, 28cm. high.
(Bonhams) $1,750

A carved and painted pine 'Tramp Art' bird cage, American, 20th century, in the form of a three-storied rustic turreted house with shuttered windows and a central clock tower, 31in. long.
(Sotheby's) $1,035

A carved pine library bust of Charles Darwin, late 19th century, with carved inscription *Charles Darwin* to the base, with traces of paint overall, mounted on a painted wood socle, 26½in. high.
(Christie's) $5,851

A Spanish silvered and giltwood reliquary bust of The Virgin, 18th century, her cloak with a circular glazed aperture, the integral base with colored bosses to the border, 17½in. high.(Christie's) $1,477

A carved and stained wood figure of a cow and calf, American, late 19th century, full-bodied group depicting a cow and her calf suckling on an oval base, 6¼in. high. (Christie's) $1,998

A carved wood head of an apostle, Spanish, 17th century, with traces of polychrome, 11in. high. (Christie's) $690

A Northern European treen standing cup, the bowl carved in relief with flowerheads and foliage, on a waisted stem and circular foot with gadrooned border, 8in. high. (Christie's) $869

A pair of Colonial polychrome wood models of lions, 19th century, shown contra posto, with black penwork decoration to the heads, lacking tails, 14¼in. high. (Christie's) $1,739

A South German carved pine figure of Hercules and the Nemean lion, 18th century, shown standing prising apart the lion's jaws, on an integral base, 10½in. high. (Christie's) $822

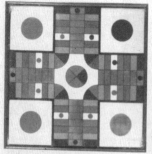

A paint-decorated double-sided gameboard, American, probably 19th century, the square form painted on one side for parchesi; and on verso with a central field of alternating black and gold squares, 19½in.square. (Christie's) $5,288

A carved and polychrome painted Royal Appointment cresting, early 20th century, with inscription below the Royal Arms *By Royal Appointment*, 29½in. wide. (Christie's) $2,049

A carved and painted double-sided gameboard, signed *John A. Rich, Ware, Massachusetts,* dated *1877*, paint-decorated on one side with a ludo board, the reverse side carved and decorated for Chinese checkers, 14½ x 14¼in. (Christie's) $4,700

A polychrome carved wood figure of a saint, 18th century, his drapery decorated with flowers and foliage, lacking his right hand, 25½in. high. (Christie's) $1,912

A carved and painted wood figure of an eagle, attributed to Wilhelm Schimmel, Carlisle County, Cumberland Valley, Pennsylvania, late 19th century, 12in. wide. (Christie's) $5,875

A polychrome carved wood group 'The Charity of St. Martin', North German, probably 16th century, the Saint shown seated on a horse turning to cut off a section of his cloak for the traveller, 8½in. high. (Christie's) $1,817

A polychrome carved wood group of Saint George and the Dragon, German, 19th century, in the 15th century style, the figure in suit of armor standing over the dragon, 23½in. high. (Christie's) $1,817

A pair of polychrome carved wood models of eagles, 20th century, each shown standing on a naturalistic plinth holding down a serpent with a talon, 49in. high. (Christie's) $822

A painted wooden two-sided gameboard, American, late 19th century, executed in red, black, yellow, blue and white on softwood, a checkerboard on one side, a parchese board on the reverse, 20 x 28in. (Christie's) $19,975

A large polychrome carved wood group of St George and the Dragon, probably South German, early 19th century, the helmeted figure with billowing drapery and shown holding a lance, the group 32½in. high. (Christie's) $13,912

A pair of carved and stained wood reliquary busts, 18th century, each shown with drapery over one shoulder, later gilded, restorations, 22½in. high. (Christie's) $4,174

A carved wood bust store display, American, late 19th century, the laminated carved pine figure with strongly articulated nose, eyes and mouth, 17in. high. (Christie's) $1,880

A Regency mahogany brass bound stickstand, with a molded rim and three brass bands, with later lion mask ring handles, 12½in. diameter. (Christie's) $1,974

A carved and painted spreadwing eagle, John Halley Bellamy (1836-1914), Kittery Point, Maine, late 19th century, with articulated gold and black-painted facial features clutching a red, white and blue-painted banner, 25½in. wide. (Christie's) $28,200

An oak coopered stickstand, with six brass bands, circa 1900, 55cm. (Bristol) $133

A wooden bust, of a Roman emperor, carved from a model by Prof. Poertzel, signed, 41cm. high. (Christie's) $454

A carved pine putto figure, late 19th century, shown standing on a shellwork base holding a shell to his lips, with hair and waist entwined with trailing vines, 55in. high. (Christie's) $2,726

A painted composition ceremonial fireman's parade hat, probably Philadelphia, mid 19th century, painted with a spread-winged American eagle grasping a banner in its talons, inscribed in gilded lettering *Colombia Hose Co.*, height 8in. (Sotheby's) $6,000

A fine carved and stained pine and mahogany American elk , anonymous, Northeastern Seaboard, late 19th century, with wide spread antlers, 20¼in. high. (Sotheby's) $8,400

A carved wood and horn mounted butcher's or dairy sign, probably early 20th century, modelled as a bull mask, 14in. high, 22in. wide. (Christie's) $1,463

An Art Nouveau bust, of a female amidst foliate mound, 18cm. high. (Christie's) $447

INDEX

INDEX